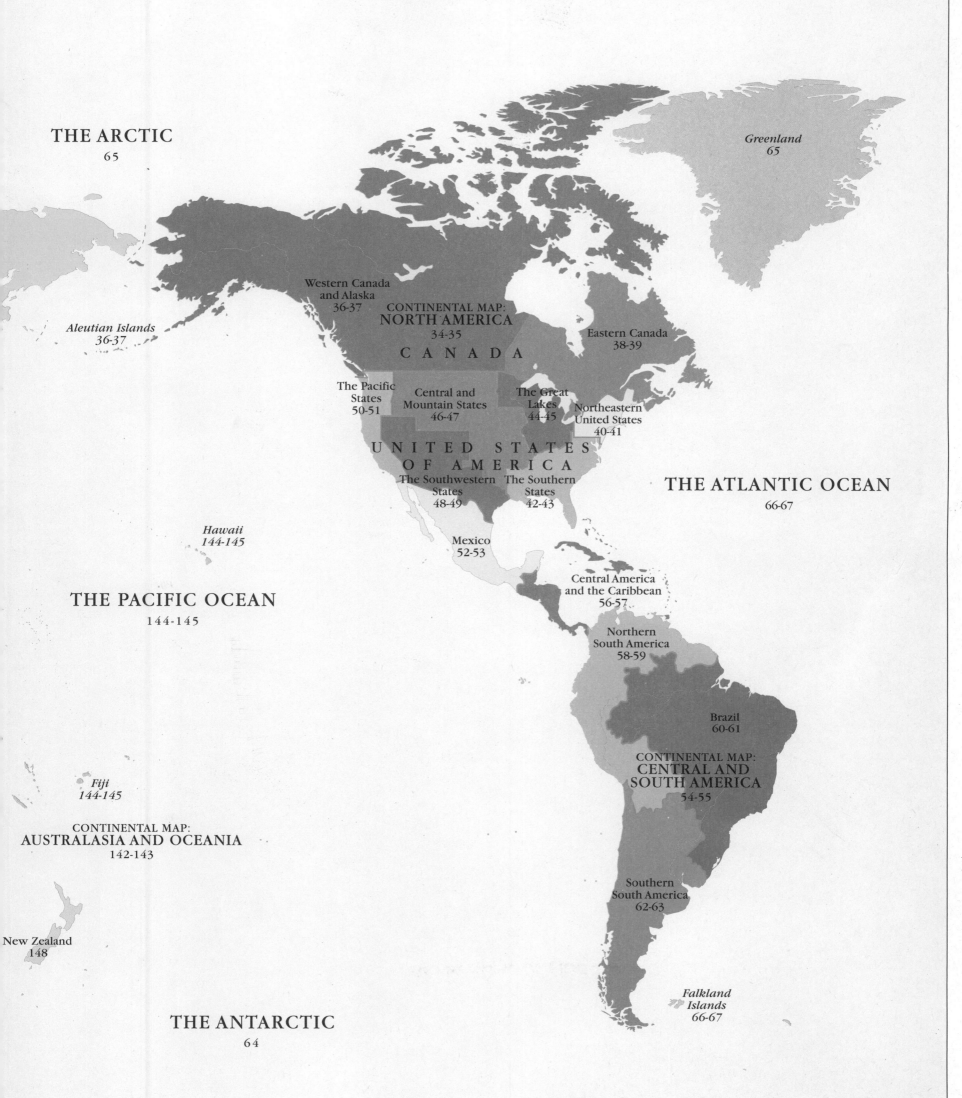

THE ARCTIC
65

Greenland
65

Aleutian Islands
36-37

Western Canada
and Alaska
36-37

CONTINENTAL MAP:
NORTH AMERICA
34-35

C A N A D A

Eastern Canada
38-39

The Pacific
States
50-51

Central and
Mountain States
46-47

The Great
Lakes
44-45

Northeastern
United States
40-41

U N I T E D   S T A T E S
O F   A M E R I C A

THE ATLANTIC OCEAN
66-67

The Southwestern
States
48-49

The Southern
States
42-43

Hawaii
144-145

Mexico
52-53

Central America
and the Caribbean
56-57

THE PACIFIC OCEAN
144-145

Northern
South America
58-59

Brazil
60-61

Fiji
144-145

CONTINENTAL MAP:
CENTRAL AND
SOUTH AMERICA
54-55

CONTINENTAL MAP:
AUSTRALASIA AND OCEANIA
142-143

Southern
South America
62-63

New Zealand
148

*Falkland
Islands*
66-67

THE ANTARCTIC
64

Dorling Kindersley

Children's ATLAS

A DORLING KINDERSLEY BOOK

DORLING KINDERSLEY

LONDON • NEW YORK • SYDNEY •
DELHI • PARIS • MUNICH • JOHANNESBURG

NEW EDITION

Project Editor
Elizabeth Wyse

Editorial Assistance
Sam Atkinson

US Editor
Gary Werner

Index Gazetteer
Julia Lynch

Systems Coordinator
Phil Rowles

Cartographic Publisher
Andrew Heritage

Project Cartographers
James Anderson • Martin Darlison

Cartography
Ruth Hall • Christine Johnston
John Plumer • Jane Voss • Peter Winfield

Digital Maps Created in DK Cartopia by
Rob Stokes

Senior Cartographic Editor
Roger Bullen

Senior Managing Cartographer
David Roberts

Project Art Editors
Nicola Liddiard
Carol Ann Davis

Senior Managing Art Editor
Philip Lord

Picture Research
Deborah Pownall

Production
Shivani Pandey

FIRST EDITION

Project Editor
Elizabeth Wyse
Caroline Lucas

Editors
Jayne Parsons • Phillip Boys
Chris Whitwell • Donna Rispoli
Margaret Hynes • Ailsa Heritage
Sue Peach • Laura Porter

Project Cartographer
Julia Lunn

Cartography
Roger Bullen • Michael Martin
James Mills-Hicks • James Anderson
Yahya El-Droubie • Tony Chambers
Simon Lewis • Caroline Simpson

Project Art Editor
Nicola Liddiard

Design
Lesley Betts • Rhonda Fisher
Paul Blackburn • Jay Young

Illustrations
John Woodcock • Kathleen McDougall
Mick Gillah • David Wright

Photography
Andy Crawford • Tim Ridley • Steve Gorton

Picture Research
Clive Webster • Charlotte Bush • Frances Vargo
Sharon Southren • Caroline Brook

Art Director
Chez Picthall

Production
Susannah Straughan

US Editor
Chuck Wills

CONSULTANTS

Consultant editor
Dr. David R. Green,
Department of Geography, King's College

Contributors
Peter Clark, Former Keeper,
Royal Geographical Society, London
Martin McCauley, Senior Lecturer in Politics,
School of Slavonic and East European Studies, University of London

Dorling Kindersley would also like to thank

Dr. Andrew Tatham, Keeper, and the Staff of the Royal Geographical Society,
London, for their help and advice in preparing this atlas

Professor Jan-Peter A. L. Muller,
Professor of Image Understanding and Remote Sensing,
Department of Photogrammetry and Surveying, University College London

Department of Photogrammetry and Surveying, University College London:
Philip Eales (Producer) • Kevin Tildsley • David Rees
James Pearson • Peter Booth • Tim Day • Planetary Visions Ltd

Published in the United States by Dorling Kindersley Publishing, Inc.
95 Madison Avenue, New York, New York, 10016

*Dorling Kindersley books are available at special discounts for bulk purchases for sales promotions or premiums. Special editions, including personalized covers, excerpts of existing
guides, and corporate imprints can be created in large quantities for specific needs. For more information, contact Special Markets Dept./Dorling Kindersley Publishing, Inc./95
Madison Ave./New York, NY 10016/Fax: 800-600-9098.*

ISBN 0-7894-5845-4

*Color reproduction by Colourscan, Singapore
Printed and bound in Spain by Artes Gráficas Toledo, S.A.U.
D.L. TO: 656 - 2000*

This atlas was first published in 1994 as the DK Eyewitness Atlas of the World

See our complete catalog at www.dk.com

CONTENTS

THE EARTH IN SPACE

THE EARTH IS ONE OF NINE PLANETS that orbit a large star – the Sun. Together they form the solar system. All life on Earth – plant, animal, and human – depends on the Sun. Its energy warms our planet's surface, powers the wind and waves, drives the ocean currents and weather systems, and recycles water. Sunlight also gives plants the power to photosynthesize – to make the foods and oxygen on which organisms rely. The fact that the Earth is habitable at all is due to its precise position in the solar system, its daily spin, and its annual journey around the Sun at a constant tilt. Without these, and the breathable atmosphere that cloaks and protects the Earth, it would be as barren as our near-neighbors Venus and Mars.

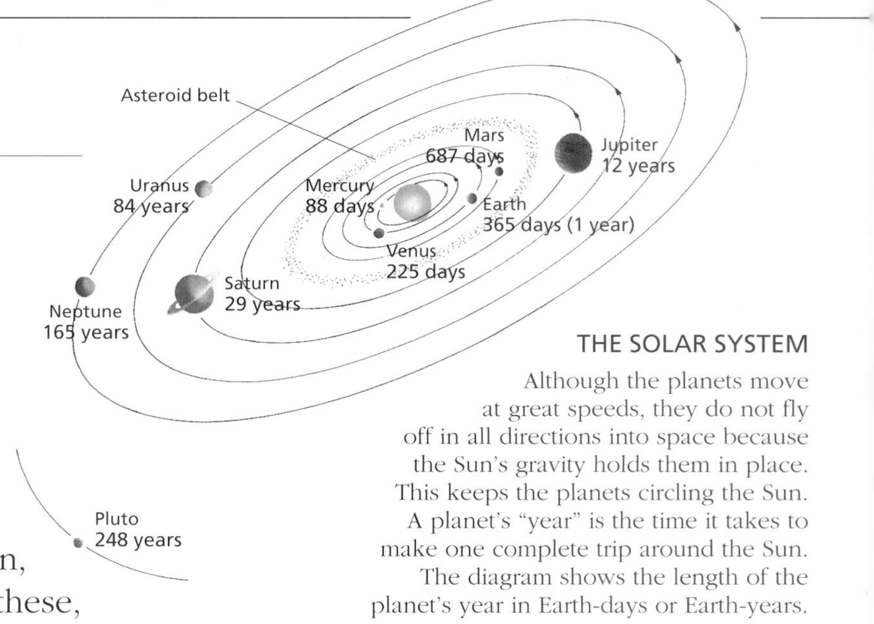

Asteroid belt
Mars
687 days
Jupiter
12 years
Uranus
84 years
Mercury
88 days
Earth
365 days (1 year)
Venus
225 days
Neptune
165 years
Saturn
29 years
Pluto
248 years

THE SOLAR SYSTEM

Although the planets move at great speeds, they do not fly off in all directions into space because the Sun's gravity holds them in place. This keeps the planets circling the Sun. A planet's "year" is the time it takes to make one complete trip around the Sun. The diagram shows the length of the planet's year in Earth-days or Earth-years.

THE SUN

The Sun is 865,000 miles (1,392,000 km) across. It has a core temperature of 25 million°F (14 million°C).

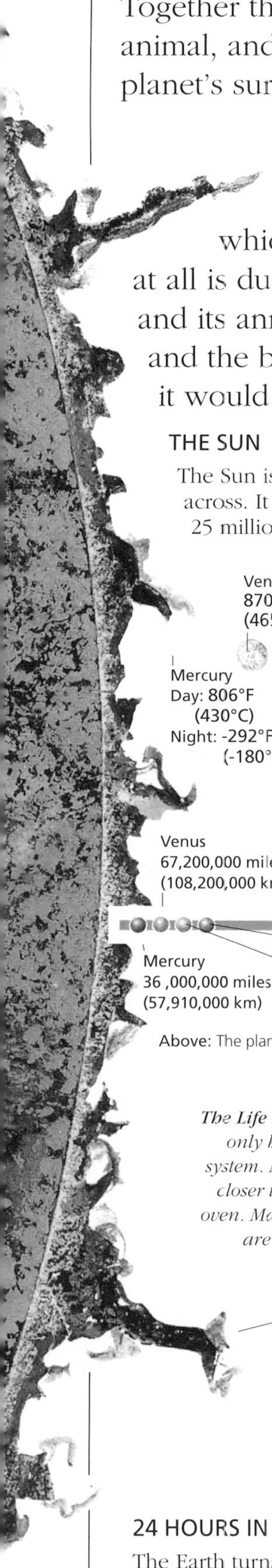

Saturn
-292°F
(-180°C)

Jupiter
-238°F
(-150°C)

Venus
870°F
(465°C)

Mars
-9.5°F
(-23°C)

Mercury
Day: 806°F
(430°C)
Night: -292°F
(-180°C)

Earth
60°F
(15°C)

You can use this sentence to remember the sequence of planets: Many Very Eager Mountaineers Jog Swiftly Up New Peaks.

Pluto
-382°F
(-230°C)

Uranus
-346°F
(-210°C)

Neptune
-364°F
(-220°C)

Above: The relative sizes of the Sun and planets, with their average temperature.

Venus
67,200,000 miles
(108,200,000 km)

Jupiter
483,000,000 miles
(778,330,000 km)

Mercury
36,000,000 miles
(57,910,000 km)

Earth
92,900,000 miles
(149,500,000 km)

Mars
141,600,000 miles
(227,940,000 km)

Saturn
886,700,000 miles
(1,426,980,000 km)

Uranus
1,783,000,000 miles
(2,870,990,000 km)

Neptune
2,800,000,000 miles
(4,497,070,000 km)

Pluto
3,670,000,000 miles
(5,913,520,000 km)

Above: The planets and their distances from the Sun.

The Life Zone: The Earth seems to be the only habitable planet in our solar system. Mercury and Venus, which are closer to the Sun, are hotter than an oven. Mars, and planets still farther out, are colder than a deep freeze.

Huge solar flares, up to 125,000 miles (200,000 km) long, lick out into space

THE FOUR SEASONS

The Earth always tilts in the same direction on its 590 million-mile (950 million-km) journey around the Sun. This means that each hemisphere in turn leans toward the Sun, then leans away from it. This is what causes summer and winter.

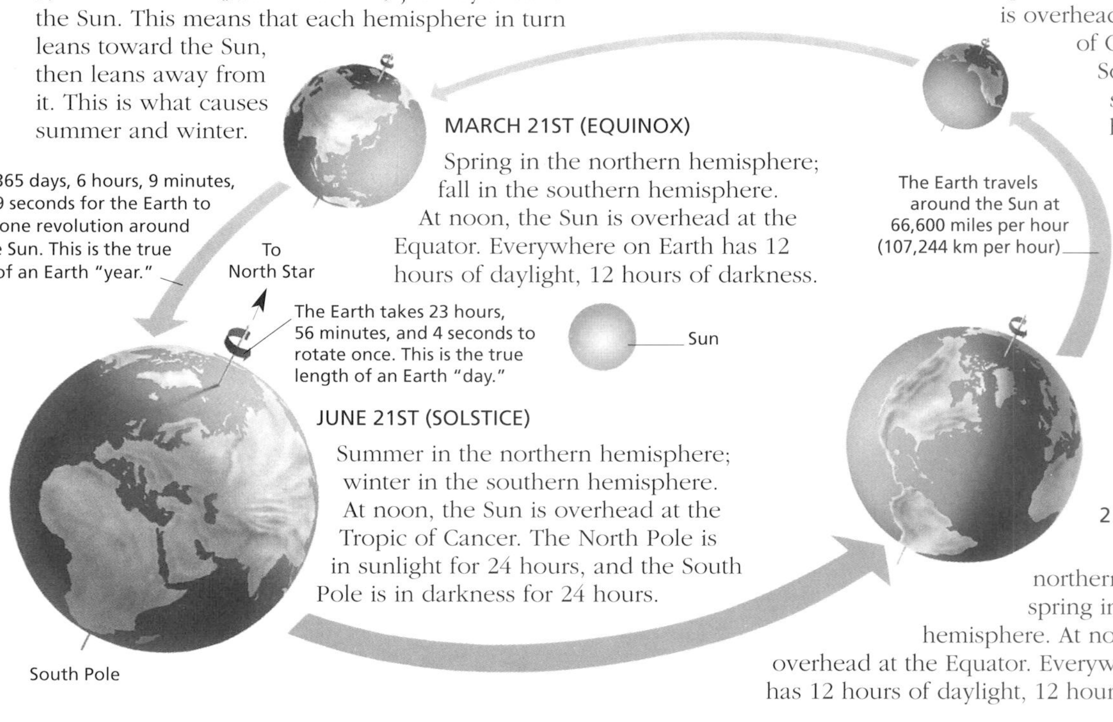

DECEMBER 21ST (SOLSTICE)

Summer in the southern hemisphere; winter in the northern hemisphere. At noon, the Sun is overhead at the Tropic of Capricorn. The South Pole is in sunlight for 24 hours, and the North Pole is in darkness for 24 hours.

MARCH 21ST (EQUINOX)

Spring in the northern hemisphere; fall in the southern hemisphere. At noon, the Sun is overhead at the Equator. Everywhere on Earth has 12 hours of daylight, 12 hours of darkness.

The Earth travels around the Sun at 66,600 miles per hour (107,244 km per hour)

It takes 365 days, 6 hours, 9 minutes, and 9 seconds for the Earth to make one revolution around the Sun. This is the true length of an Earth "year."

To North Star

The Earth takes 23 hours, 56 minutes, and 4 seconds to rotate once. This is the true length of an Earth "day."

Sun

JUNE 21ST (SOLSTICE)

Summer in the northern hemisphere; winter in the southern hemisphere. At noon, the Sun is overhead at the Tropic of Cancer. The North Pole is in sunlight for 24 hours, and the South Pole is in darkness for 24 hours.

South Pole

SEPTEMBER 21ST (EQUINOX)

Fall in the northern hemisphere; spring in the southern hemisphere. At noon, the Sun is overhead at the Equator. Everywhere on Earth has 12 hours of daylight, 12 hours of darkness.

24 HOURS IN THE LIFE OF PLANET EARTH

The Earth turns a complete circle (360°) in 24 hours, or 15° in one hour. Countries on a similar line of longitude (or "meridian") usually share the same time. They set their clocks in relation to "Greenwich Mean Time" (GMT). This is the time at Greenwich (London, UK), on longitude 0°. Countries east of Greenwich are ahead of GMT. Countries to the west are behind GMT.

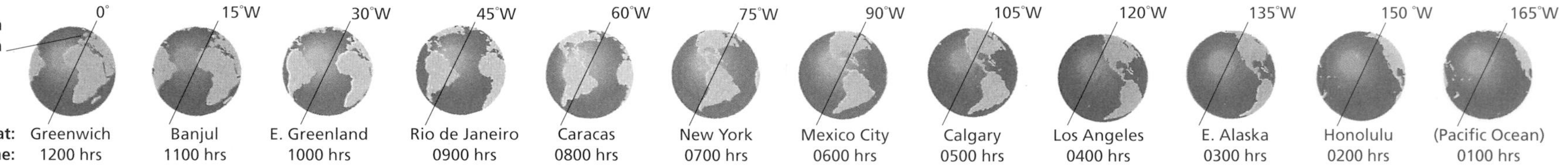

Noon on this meridian

	0°	15°W	30°W	45°W	60°W	75°W	90°W	105°W	120°W	135°W	150°W	165°W
Noon at:	Greenwich	Banjul	E. Greenland	Rio de Janeiro	Caracas	New York	Mexico City	Calgary	Los Angeles	E. Alaska	Honolulu	(Pacific Ocean)
Greenwich time:	1200 hrs	1100 hrs	1000 hrs	0900 hrs	0800 hrs	0700 hrs	0600 hrs	0500 hrs	0400 hrs	0300 hrs	0200 hrs	0100 hrs

MOON AND EARTH

Craters made by collision with meteors

The Moon is a ball of barren rock 2,156 miles (3,476 km) across. It orbits the Earth every 27.3 days at an average distance of 238,700 miles (384,400 km). The Moon's gravity is only one-sixth that of Earth's – too small to keep an atmosphere around itself, but strong enough to exert a powerful pull on the Earth. The Moon and Sun together create tides in the Earth's oceans. The period between successive high tides is 12 hours, 25 minutes. The highest (or "spring") tides occur twice a month, when the Moon, Sun, and Earth are in line.

The Moon's surface temperature falls from 220°F (105°C) in sunlight to -247°F (-155°C) when it turns away from the Sun

MAGNET EARTH

The Earth acts like a gigantic bar magnet. As the Earth spins in space, swirling currents are set up within its molten core. These movements generate a powerful magnetic field.

Magnetic North Pole, close to the true North Pole

The geographical North and South Poles are the two ends of the Earth's axis – the line around which the Earth spins.

The magnetic field spreads out into space

Magnetic South Pole

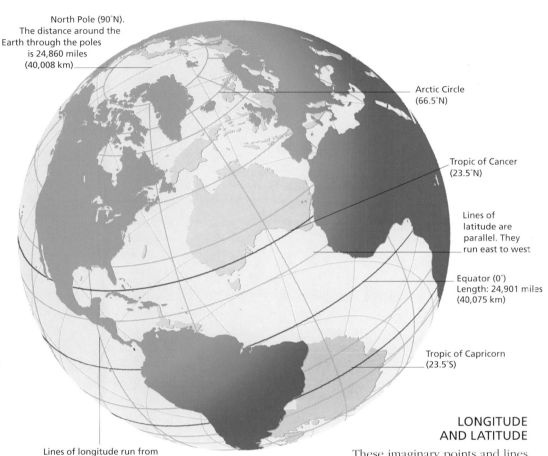

North Pole (90°N). The distance around the Earth through the poles is 24,860 miles (40,008 km)

Arctic Circle (66.5°N)

Tropic of Cancer (23.5°N)

Lines of latitude are parallel. They run east to west

Equator (0°) Length: 24,901 miles (40,075 km)

Tropic of Capricorn (23.5°S)

Lines of longitude run from north to south. They meet at the North and South Poles. They are farthest apart at the Equator

THE ATMOSPHERE

An envelope of gases such as nitrogen and oxygen surrounds our planet. It provides us with breathable air, filters the Sun's rays, and retains heat at night.

Height in miles (km)

INTERPLANETARY SPACE

EXOSPHERE 300–1,240 miles (500–2,000 km) Outer limit of atmosphere

COMMUNICATIONS AND SOME ASTRONOMICAL SATELLITES 300–1,240 miles (35,880 km)

25,000 (40,000)

SPACE STATION 86 miles (300 km)

THERMOSPHERE 50–300 miles (80–500 km)

SPACE SHUTTLE 186–372 miles (300–600 km)

300 (500)

MESOSPHERE 31–50 miles (50–80 km)

WEATHER BALLOON *up to* 31 miles (50 km)

50 (80)

STRATOSPHERE 9–31 miles (15–50 km)

31 (50)

OZONE LAYER 9–18 miles (15–30 km)

PASSENGER AIRCRAFT 5–10 miles (8–16 km)

CLOUDS *Usually below* 6 miles (10 km)

SKYDIVING *Typical leap:* 2.5 miles (4 km)

HELICOPTER *Usually below* 1.5 miles (2.5 km)

TROPOSPHERE 0–9 miles (0–15 km)

KITE *Usually below* 0.06 miles (0.1 km)

Sea level

LONGITUDE AND LATITUDE

These imaginary points and lines drawn on the Earth's surface help locate places on a map or globe. The Earth spins around an axis drawn between the North and South poles through the center of the planet. Lines of longitude are vertical lines running through the poles. Lines of latitude are horizontal lines drawn parallel to the Equator, the line around the middle of the Earth.

Diameter of Earth at equator: 7,927 miles (12,756 km). Diameter from pole to pole: 7,900 miles (12,714 km). Mass: 5,988 million, million million tons (tonnes).

WINDS AND CURRENTS

Cold air descends from the poles toward the Equator

Warm air and water travel to the poles from the Equator

Air circulates between the poles and the Equator in stages called "cells"

Winds and currents do not move in straight lines because the Earth spins

The world's winds and ocean currents are caused by the way the Sun heats the Earth's surface. More heat energy arrives at the Equator than at the poles because the Earth is curved and tilted. Warm air and warm water carry much of this energy toward the poles, heating up the higher latitudes. Meanwhile, cool air and water moves back toward the Equator, lowering its temperature.

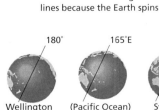

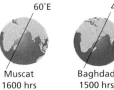

180°	165°E	150°E	135°E	120°E	105°E	90°E	75°E	60°E	45°E	30°E	15°E	0°
Wellington 2400 hrs	(Pacific Ocean) 2300 hrs	Sydney 2200 hrs	Tokyo 2100 hrs	Manila 2000 hrs	Jakarta 1900 hrs	Dhaka 1800 hrs	Karachi 1700 hrs	Muscat 1600 hrs	Baghdad 1500 hrs	Cairo 1400 hrs	Berlin 1300 hrs	Greenwich 1200 hrs

THE EARTH'S STRUCTURE

IN SOME WAYS, the Earth is like an egg, with a thin shell around a soft interior. Its hard, rocky outer layer – the crust – is up to 45 miles (70 km) thick under the continents, but less than 5 miles (8 km) thick under the oceans. This crust is broken into gigantic slabs called "plates," in which the continents are embedded. Below the hard crust is the mantle, a layer of rocks so hot that some melt and flow in huge swirling currents. The Earth's plates do not stay in the same place. Instead, they move, carried along like rafts on the currents in the mantle. This motion is very slow – usually less than 2 in (5 cm) a year – but enormously powerful. Plate movement makes the Earth quake and volcanoes erupt, causes immense mountain ranges such as the Himalayas to grow where plates collide, and explains how, over millions of years, whole continents have drifted across the face of the planet.

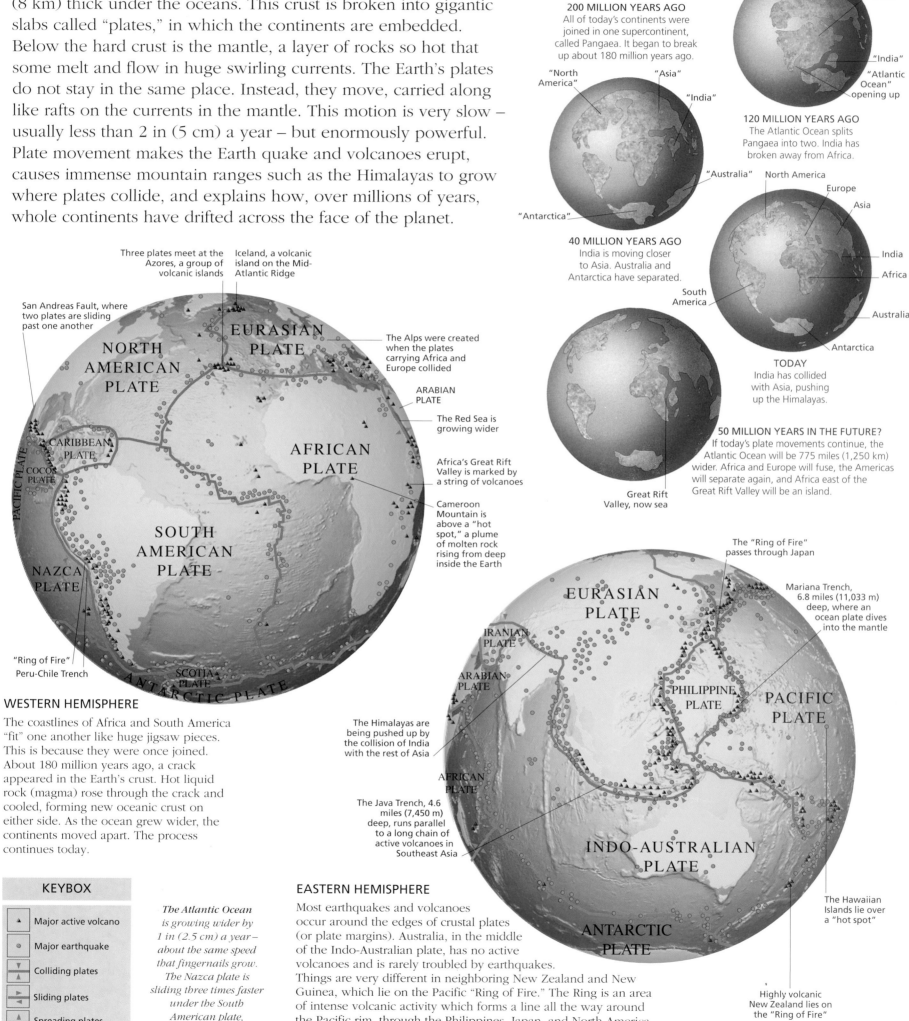

DRIFTING CONTINENTS
Currents of molten rock deep within the mantle slowly move the continents. Over time, they appear to "drift" across the Earth's surface.

Pangaea

200 MILLION YEARS AGO
All of today's continents were joined in one supercontinent, called Pangaea. It began to break up about 180 million years ago.

"Africa"

"India"

"Atlantic Ocean" opening up

120 MILLION YEARS AGO
The Atlantic Ocean splits Pangaea into two. India has broken away from Africa.

"North America"   "Asia"

"India"

"Australia"   North America

"Antarctica"   Europe

Asia

India

South America

Africa

Australia

Antarctica

40 MILLION YEARS AGO
India is moving closer to Asia. Australia and Antarctica have separated.

TODAY
India has collided with Asia, pushing up the Himalayas.

50 MILLION YEARS IN THE FUTURE?
If today's plate movements continue, the Atlantic Ocean will be 775 miles (1,250 km) wider. Africa and Europe will fuse, the Americas will separate again, and Africa east of the Great Rift Valley will be an island.

Great Rift Valley, now sea

Three plates meet at the Azores, a group of volcanic islands

Iceland, a volcanic island on the Mid-Atlantic Ridge

San Andreas Fault, where two plates are sliding past one another

EURASIAN PLATE

NORTH AMERICAN PLATE

The Alps were created when the plates carrying Africa and Europe collided

ARABIAN PLATE

The Red Sea is growing wider

CARIBBEAN PLATE

COCOS PLATE

AFRICAN PLATE

Africa's Great Rift Valley is marked by a string of volcanoes

Cameroon Mountain is above a "hot spot," a plume of molten rock rising from deep inside the Earth

PACIFIC PLATE

SOUTH AMERICAN PLATE

NAZCA PLATE

"Ring of Fire" Peru-Chile Trench

SCOTIA PLATE

ANTARCTIC PLATE

WESTERN HEMISPHERE
The coastlines of Africa and South America "fit" one another like huge jigsaw pieces. This is because they were once joined. About 180 million years ago, a crack appeared in the Earth's crust. Hot liquid rock (magma) rose through the crack and cooled, forming new oceanic crust on either side. As the ocean grew wider, the continents moved apart. The process continues today.

KEYBOX

▲	Major active volcano
○	Major earthquake
▽ ▲	Colliding plates
▷ ◁	Sliding plates
▽ ▲	Spreading plates

The Atlantic Ocean is growing wider by 1 in (2.5 cm) a year – about the same speed that fingernails grow. The Nazca plate is sliding three times faster under the South American plate, pushing up the Andes.

The "Ring of Fire" passes through Japan

Mariana Trench, 6.8 miles (11,033 m) deep, where an ocean plate dives into the mantle

EURASIAN PLATE

IRANIAN PLATE

ARABIAN PLATE

PHILIPPINE PLATE

PACIFIC PLATE

AFRICAN PLATE

The Himalayas are being pushed up by the collision of India with the rest of Asia

The Java Trench, 4.6 miles (7,450 m) deep, runs parallel to a long chain of active volcanoes in Southeast Asia

INDO-AUSTRALIAN PLATE

ANTARCTIC PLATE

The Hawaiian Islands lie over a "hot spot"

Highly volcanic New Zealand lies on the "Ring of Fire"

EASTERN HEMISPHERE
Most earthquakes and volcanoes occur around the edges of crustal plates (or plate margins). Australia, in the middle of the Indo-Australian plate, has no active volcanoes and is rarely troubled by earthquakes. Things are very different in neighboring New Zealand and New Guinea, which lie on the Pacific "Ring of Fire." The Ring is an area of intense volcanic activity which forms a line all the way around the Pacific rim, through the Philippines, Japan, and North America, and down the coast of South America to New Zealand.

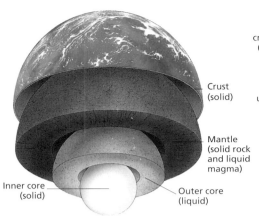

Crust (solid)

Mantle (solid rock and liquid magma)

Inner core (solid)

Outer core (liquid)

THE LAYERED EARTH

The Earth has layers, like an egg. The core is made of metals such as iron and nickel. This is surrounded by a rocky mantle and a thin crust.

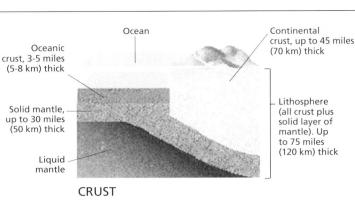

Ocean

Oceanic crust, 3-5 miles (5-8 km) thick

Solid mantle, up to 30 miles (50 km) thick

Liquid mantle

Continental crust, up to 45 miles (70 km) thick

Lithosphere (all crust plus solid layer of mantle). Up to 75 miles (120 km) thick

CRUST

Crust is of two kinds: continental and oceanic. Continental crust is older, thicker, and less dense. Beneath the crust is a solid layer of mantle. Together, these form the lithosphere, which is broken into several plates. These float on the liquid mantle layer.

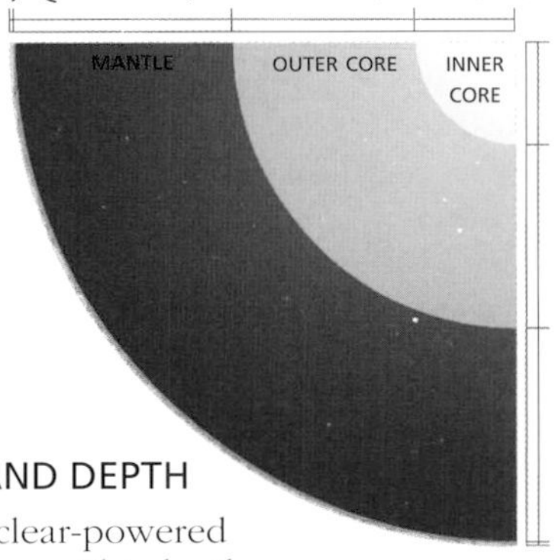

59°F (15°C)   5,400°F (3,000°C)   7,200°F (4,000°C)   8,100°F (4,500°C)

CRUST   MANTLE   OUTER CORE   INNER CORE

3,955 miles (6,370 km)

3,100 miles (5,000 km)

1,850 miles (3,000 km)

Sea level

TEMPERATURE AND DEPTH

Our planet is a nuclear-powered furnace, heated from within by the breakdown of radioactive minerals such as uranium. Temperature increases with depth: 60 miles (100 km) down it is 2,460°F (1,350°C), hot enough for rocks to melt.

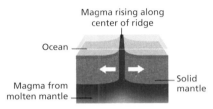

Magma rising along center of ridge

Ocean

Magma from molten mantle

Solid mantle

SPREADING PLATES

When two plates move apart, molten rock (magma) rises from the mantle and cools, forming new crust. This is called a constructive margin. Most are found in oceans.

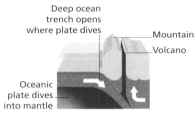

Deep ocean trench opens where plate dives

Mountain

Volcano

Oceanic plate dives into mantle

COLLIDING PLATES THAT DIVE

When two ocean plates or an ocean plate and a continent plate collide, the denser plate is forced under the other, diving down into the mantle. These are destructive margins.

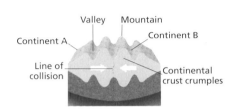

Valley   Mountain

Continent A   Continent B

Line of collision

Continental crust crumples

COLLIDING PLATES THAT BUCKLE

When two continents collide, their plates fuse, crumple, and push upward. Mountain ranges like the Himalayas and the Urals have been formed in this way.

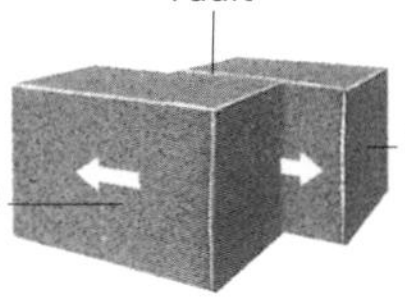

Fault

Plate

Plate

SLIDING PLATES

When two plates slide past one another, intense friction is created along the "fault line" between them, causing earthquakes. These are called conservative margins.

ICELAND, MID-ATLANTIC RIDGE

Most constructive margins are found beneath oceans, but here in volcanic Iceland one comes to the surface.

VOLCANO, JAVA

Diving plates often build volcanic islands and mountain chains. Deep ocean trenches form offshore.

FOLDING STRATA, ENGLAND

The clash of continental plates may cause the Earth to buckle and twist far from the collision zone.

SAN ANDREAS FAULT

A huge earthquake is expected soon somewhere along California's San Andreas Fault, seen here.

EXPLOSIVE VOLCANO

About 50 of the world's 600 or so active volcanoes erupt each year. Explosive pressure is created by the buildup of magma, gases, or superheated steam.

Crater

Cloud of ash, gases, and steam

Lava flows

Main vent (opening)

Cone of ash and lava from old eruptions

SOME MAJOR QUAKES AND ERUPTIONS

This map shows some of the worst natural disasters in recorded history. Over one million earthquakes and about 50 volcanic eruptions are detected every year. Most are minor or occur where there are few people, so there is no loss of human life or great damage to property. But crowded cities and poorly-constructed buildings are putting ever-greater numbers at risk.

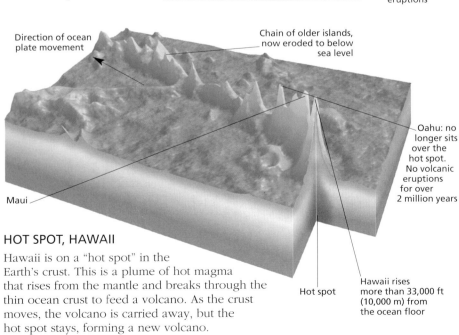

Direction of ocean plate movement

Chain of older islands, now eroded to below sea level

Maui

Oahu: no longer sits over the hot spot. No volcanic eruptions for over 2 million years

Hot spot

Hawaii rises more than 33,000 ft (10,000 m) from the ocean floor

HOT SPOT, HAWAII

Hawaii is on a "hot spot" in the Earth's crust. This is a plume of hot magma that rises from the mantle and breaks through the thin ocean crust to feed a volcano. As the crust moves, the volcano is carried away, but the hot spot stays, forming a new volcano.

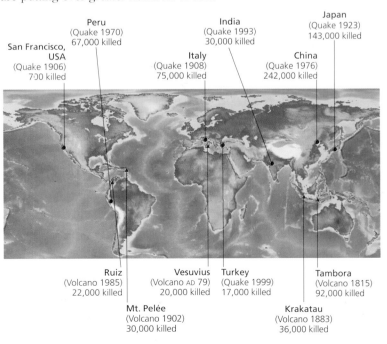

Peru (Quake 1970) 67,000 killed

India (Quake 1993) 30,000 killed

Japan (Quake 1923) 143,000 killed

San Francisco, USA (Quake 1906) 700 killed

Italy (Quake 1908) 75,000 killed

China (Quake 1976) 242,000 killed

Ruiz (Volcano 1985) 22,000 killed

Vesuvius (Volcano AD 79) 20,000 killed

Turkey (Quake 1999) 17,000 killed

Tambora (Volcano 1815) 92,000 killed

Mt. Pelée (Volcano 1902) 30,000 killed

Krakatau (Volcano 1883) 36,000 killed

SHAPING THE LANDSCAPE

LANDSCAPES ARE CREATED AND CHANGED – even destroyed – in a continuous cycle. Over millions of years, constant movements of the Earth's plates have built up continents, islands, and mountains. But as soon as new land is formed, it is shaped (or "eroded") by the forces of wind, water, ice, and heat. Sometimes change is quick, as when a river floods and cuts a new channel, or a landslide cascades down a mountain slope. Usually, however, change is so slow that it is invisible to the human eye. Extremes of heat and cold crack open rocks and expose them to attack by wind and water. Rivers and glaciers scour out valleys, the wind piles up sand dunes, and the sea attacks shorelines and cliffs. Eroded materials are blown away or carried along by rivers, piling up as sediments on valley floors or the seabed. Over millions of years, these may be compressed into rock and pushed up to form new land. As soon as the land is exposed to the elements, the cycle of erosion begins again.

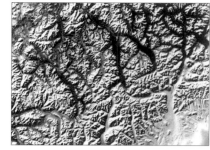

□ ICE ACTION, ALASKA

Areas close to the North Pole are permanently covered in snow and ice. Glaciers are rivers of ice that flow toward the sea, scouring the landscape as they cross it. Some glaciers are over 40 miles (60 km) long.

MAP FEATURES

Area covered in ice today	Area drained by major river
Ice and snow 18,000 years ago	Protected coastline
Desert	Coast affected by tidal swell
Wind direction (simplified)	Coast affected by storm waves

THE "ROOF OF NORTH AMERICA"

Steeply-sloping Mount McKinley (also called Denali), Alaska, is North America's highest mountain at 20,320 ft (6,194 m). It is a fairly "young" mountain, less than 70 million years old. The gently sloping Appalachians in the east of the continent are very much older. Once, they were probably higher than Mount McKinley is today. But more than 300 million years of ice, rain, and wind have ground them down.

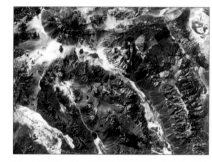

■ SEA ACTION, CAPE COD

Cape Cod, a sandy peninsula 65 miles (105 km) long, juts out like a beckoning finger into the Atlantic Ocean. Its strangely curved coastline has been shaped by wave action.

This section of the globe shows North America and the different forces working on its landscape. The landscape in every part of the world is changed by the action of ice, running water, sea waves, and wind.

□ WIND ACTION, DEATH VALLEY

Death Valley is the hottest, driest place in North America. Its floor is covered in sand and salt. Winds sweeping across the valley endlessly reshape the loose surface.

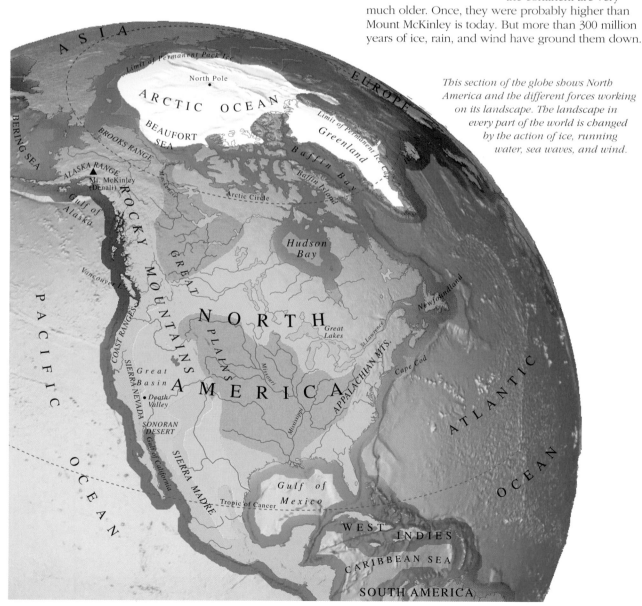

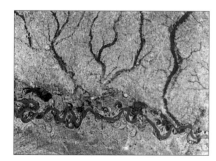

■ WATER ACTION, MISSISSIPPI

The Mississippi River and its many tributaries frequently change course. Where two loops are close together, the river may cut a new path between them, leaving an "oxbow lake."

ICE COVER

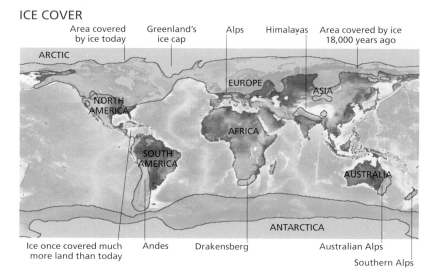

Area covered by ice today
Greenland's ice cap
Alps
Himalayas
Area covered by ice 18,000 years ago
ARCTIC
EUROPE
NORTH AMERICA
ASIA
AFRICA
SOUTH AMERICA
AUSTRALIA
ANTARCTICA
Ice once covered much more land than today
Andes
Drakensberg
Australian Alps
Southern Alps

Ice floats because it is less dense than seawater
Only one-ninth of an iceberg shows above sea level

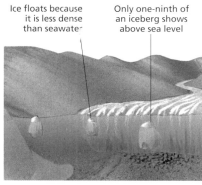

A GLACIER REACHES THE SEA

When a glacier enters the sea, its front edge, or "snout," breaks up and forms icebergs – a process called calving. These "ice mountains" are then carried away by ocean currents.

NORDFJORD, NORWAY

One sign of glacial action on the landscape is the fjord. These long, narrow, steep-sided inlets are found along the coasts of Norway, Alaska, Chile, and New Zealand. They mark the points where glaciers once entered the sea.

COASTAL EROSION

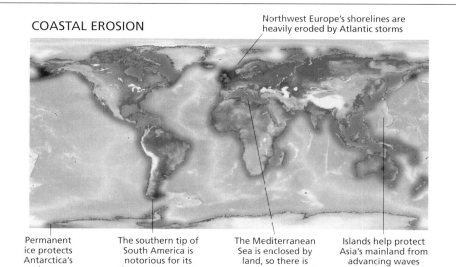

Northwest Europe's shorelines are heavily eroded by Atlantic storms

Permanent ice protects Antarctica's shores
The southern tip of South America is notorious for its devastating storms
The Mediterranean Sea is enclosed by land, so there is little coastal erosion
Islands help protect Asia's mainland from advancing waves

Rock eroded here
Rock fragments and sand deposited here
Hard rock headland broken into small sections
Bay
Headland
Advancing sea waves

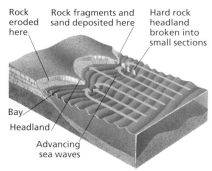

COASTAL ATTACK

The ceaseless push and pull of waves on a shore can destroy even the hardest rocks. The softest rocks are eroded first, leaving headlands of hard rock that survive a little longer.

WAVE POWER

The powerful action of waves on an exposed coast can erode a coastline by several feet a year.

THE GREAT DESERTS

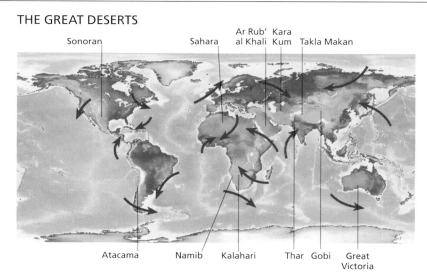

Sonoran
Sahara
Ar Rub' al Khali
Kara Kum
Takla Makan
Atacama
Namib
Kalahari
Thar
Gobi
Great Victoria

The sheltered slope is steeper than the slope facing the wind
Dunes advance when sand particles are blown over the top of the dune
Wind direction

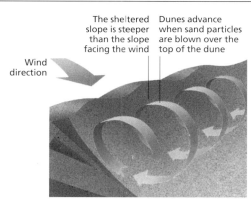

DESERT DUNE

Dunes are slow-moving mounds or ridges of sand found in deserts and along some coastlines. They only form when the wind's direction and speed is fairly constant.

NAMIB DESERT, SOUTHERN AFRICA

The sand dunes seen in the center of the picture are about 160 ft (50 m) high. Winds are driving them slowly but relentlessly toward the right. Not all deserts are sandy. Wind may blow away all the loose sand and gravel, leaving bare rock.

THE GREAT RIVER BASINS

Mackenzie
Mississippi
Ob'
Yenisey
Lena
Amur
Amazon
Paraná
Niger
Congo
Nile
Ganges
Yangtze

This crescent-shaped oxbow lake was once a meander
Old river channel, now filled with sand and gravel
New river channel
Sand and gravel deposited here so bank grows
Direction of flow
Swift currents on outer bends cut steep banks

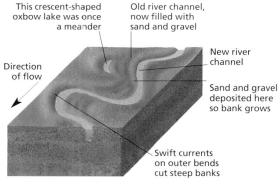

MEANDERS

River banks are worn away most on the outside of bends, where water flows fastest. Eroded sand and gravel are built up into banks on the inside of bends in slower-moving water.

WINDING RIVER, ALASKA

The more a river meanders across a plain, the longer it becomes and the more slowly it flows.

CLIMATE AND VEGETATION

THE EARTH IS the only planet in our solar system which supports life. Most of our planet has a breathable atmosphere and sufficient light, heat, and water to support a wide range of plants and animals. The main influences on an area's climate are the amount of sunshine it receives (which varies with latitude and season), how close it is to the influence of ocean currents, and its height above sea level. Since there is more sunlight at the Equator than elsewhere, and rainfall is highest here too, this is where we find the habitats which have more species of plants and animals than anywhere else: rain forests, coral reefs, and mangrove swamps. Where rainfall is very low, and where it is either too hot, such as in deserts, or too cold, few plants and animals can survive. Only the icy North and South Poles and the frozen tops of high mountains are practically without life of any sort.

WEATHER EXTREMES

Weather is a powerful influence on how we feel, the clothes we wear, the buildings we live in, the plants that grow around us, and what we eat and drink. Extreme weather events – heat waves, hurricanes, blizzards, tornadoes, sandstorms, droughts, and floods, can be terrifyingly destructive.

TORNADO

Tornadoes are whirlwinds of cold air that develop when thunderclouds cross warm land. They are extremely violent and unpredictable. Wind speeds often exceed 180 miles (300 km) per hour.

TROPICAL STORMS

These devastating winds develop when air spirals upward above warm seas. More air is sucked in and the storm begins to move. They bring torrential rain, thunder, lightning, and destruction.

DROUGHT

Long periods without water kill plants. Stripped of its protective covering of vegetation, the soil is easily blown away.

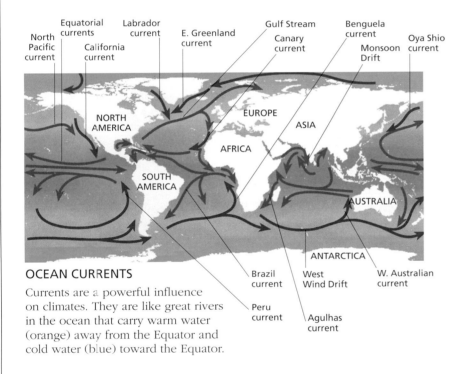

OCEAN CURRENTS

Currents are a powerful influence on climates. They are like great rivers in the ocean that carry warm water (orange) away from the Equator and cold water (blue) toward the Equator.

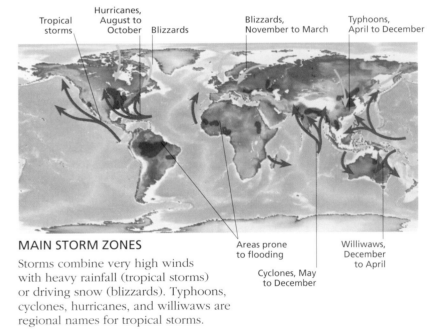

MAIN STORM ZONES

Storms combine very high winds with heavy rainfall (tropical storms) or driving snow (blizzards). Typhoons, cyclones, hurricanes, and williwaws are regional names for tropical storms.

TEMPERATURE

Average temperatures vary widely around the world. Areas close to the Equator are usually hot (orange on the map); those close to the Poles usually cold (deep blue). The hottest areas move during the year from the southern to the northern hemispheres.

AVERAGE JANUARY TEMPERATURE

AVERAGE JULY TEMPERATURE

Highest: 136°F (58°C), Saharan Libya

Lowest: -129°F (-89°C), Antarctica

RAINFALL

The wettest areas (gray) lie near the Equator. The driest are found close to the tropics, in the center of continents, or at the poles. Elsewhere, rainfall varies with the season, but it is usually highest in summer. Asia's wet season is known as the monsoon.

AVERAGE JANUARY RAINFALL

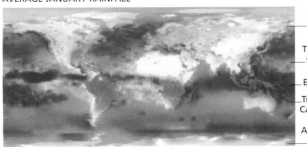

AVERAGE JULY RAINFALL

Highest in 1 year: 460 in (11.68 m), Hawaii

Lowest: No rain in more than 14 years, Atacama

■ BROADLEAF FOREST

Temperate climates have no great extremes of temperature, and drought is unusual. Forests usually contain deciduous (broadleaf) trees, such as beeches or oaks, that shed their leaves in fall.

Traveling southward from the North Pole, a number of distinct life zones or "biomes" can be seen. Plant and animal life is closely adapted to local climate.

☐ TUNDRA

As long as frozen soil melts for at least two months of the year, some mosses, lichens, and ground-hugging shrubs can survive. They are found around the Arctic Circle and on mountains.

■ NEEDLELEAF FOREST

Forests of coniferous (needleleaf) trees, such as pines and firs, cover much of northern North America, Europe, and Asia. They are evergreen and can survive long frozen winters. Most have tall, straight trunks and down-pointing branches. This reduces the amount of snow that can settle on them. The forest floor is dark because leaves absorb most of the incoming sunlight.

☐ MEDITERRANEAN

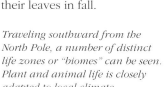

The hot dry summers and warm wet winters typical of the Mediterranean region are also found in small areas of southern Africa, the Americas, and Australia. Mediterranean-type vegetation can vary from dense forest to thinly spread evergreen shrubs like these.

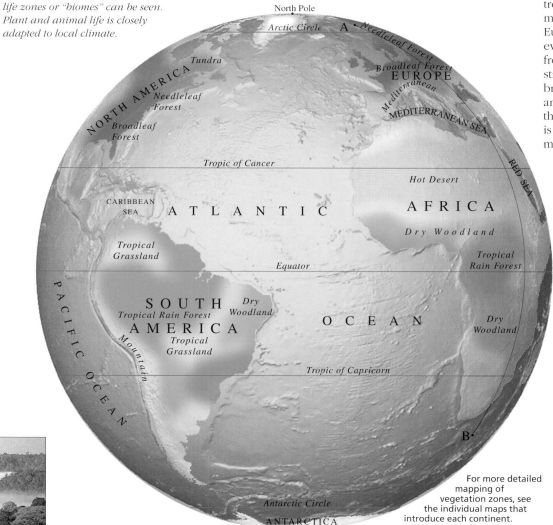

North Pole

Arctic Circle · A · Needleleaf Forest

Tundra

NORTH AMERICA

Needleleaf Forest

Broadleaf Forest

Broadleaf Forest

EUROPE

Mediterranean

MEDITERRANEAN SEA

RED SEA

Tropic of Cancer

CARIBBEAN SEA

ATLANTIC

AFRICA

Hot Desert

Dry Woodland

Tropical Grassland

Equator

SOUTH AMERICA

Dry Woodland

OCEAN

Tropical Rain Forest

Mountain

Tropical Rain Forest

Dry Woodland

Tropical Grassland

Tropic of Capricorn

B ·

Antarctic Circle

ANTARCTICA

South Pole

For more detailed mapping of vegetation zones, see the individual maps that introduce each continent.

☐ MOUNTAIN

Vegetation changes with height because the temperature drops and wind increases. Even on the Equator, mountain peaks can be covered in snow. Although trees may cloak the lower slopes, at higher altitudes they give way to sparser vegetation. Near the top, only tundra-type plants can survive.

■ TROPICAL RAIN FOREST

The lush forests found near the Equator depend on year-round high temperatures and heavy rainfall. Worldwide, they may contain 50,000 different kinds of trees, and support several million other plant and animal species. Trees are often festooned with climbing plants, or covered with ferns and orchids that have rooted in pockets of water and soil on trunks and branches.

☐ DRY WOODLAND

Plants in many parts of the tropics have to cope with high temperatures and long periods without rain. Some store water in enlarged stems or trunks, or limit water losses by having small, spiny leaves. In dry (but not desert) conditions, trees are widely spaced, with expanses of grassland between, called savannah.

☐ HOT DESERT

Very few plants and animals can survive in hot deserts. Rainfall is low – under 4 in (10 cm) a year. Temperatures often rise above 104 °F (40°C) during the day, but drop to the freezing point at night. High winds and shifting sands can be a further hazard to life. Only specially adapted plants, such as cacti, can survive.

NORTH-SOUTH CROSS-SECTION THROUGH EUROPE AND AFRICA

The line running between points "A" and "B" on the map is the line of the cross-section

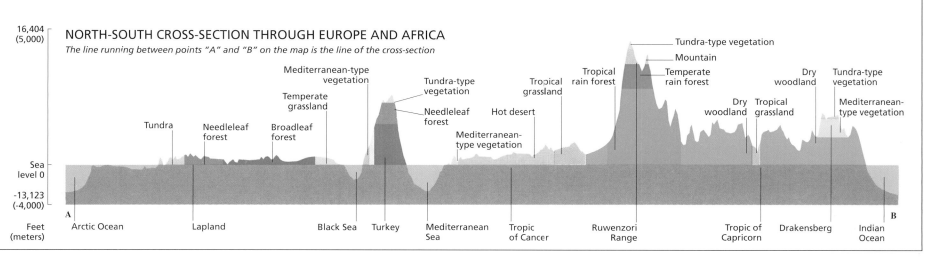

16,404 (5,000)

Tundra-type vegetation

Mountain

Mediterranean-type vegetation

Temperate grassland

Tropical rain forest

Tundra-type vegetation

Temperate rain forest

Dry woodland

Dry woodland

Tundra-type vegetation

Tropical grassland

Needleleaf forest

Tropical grassland

Hot desert

Mediterranean-type vegetation

Mediterranean-type vegetation

Tundra

Needleleaf forest

Broadleaf forest

Sea level 0

-13,123 (-4,000)

Feet (meters)

A Arctic Ocean   Lapland   Black Sea   Turkey   Mediterranean Sea   Tropic of Cancer   Ruwenzori Range   Tropic of Capricorn   Drakensberg   Indian Ocean B

PEOPLE AND PLANET

THE EARTH'S POPULATION IS OVER 6 billion and numbers are rising at the rate of about 1 million every week. The Earth's population is not distributed evenly. Some areas, such as parts of Europe, India, and China, are very densely populated. Other areas – particularly deserts, polar regions, and mountains – can support very few people. Over half of the world's people now live in towns or cities. Until 1800, most people lived in small villages in the countryside and worked on the land. But since then, more and more people have lived and worked in much larger communities. A century ago, most of the world's largest cities were in Europe and North America, where new industries and businesses were flourishing. Today, the most rapidly growing cities are in Asia, South America, and Africa. People who move to these cities are usually young adults, so the birth rate among these new populations is very high.

A CROWDED PLANET?

JAMAICA

0   100   KM

0   100   MILES

If the 6 billion people alive today stood close together, they could all fit into an area no larger than the small Caribbean island of Jamaica. Of course, so many people could not live in such a small place. Areas with few people are usually very cold, such as land near the poles and in mountains, or very dry, such as deserts. Areas with large populations often have fertile land and a good climate for crops. Cities can support huge populations because they are wealthy enough to import everything they need.

KEYBOX

- Towns and cities with more than 50,000 people
- City with more than 1 million people
- City with more than 5 million people

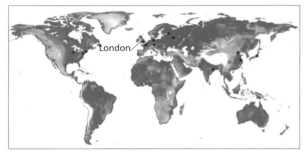

MILLIONAIRE CITIES 1900

Less than a century ago there were only 13 cities with more than 1 million people living in them. All the cities were in the Northern Hemisphere. The largest was **London**, with 7 million people.

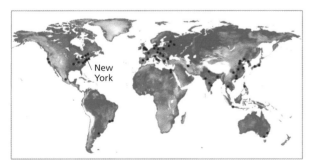

MILLIONAIRE CITIES 1950

By 1950, there were nearly 70 cities with more than 1 million inhabitants. The largest was **New York City**.

WORLD POPULATION GROWTH 1500–2020

Each figure on the graph represents 500 million people. *Note: 1 billion is 1,000 million.*

*There are just over 560 million people in **North America**. About 7 in 10 live in a city.*

SAHARA, AFRICA

The Sahara, like all deserts, is thinly populated. The Tuareg of the northern Sahara are nomads. They travel in small groups because food sources are scarce. Their homes have to be portable.

MONGOLIA, ASIA

Traditionally, Mongolia's nomadic people lived by herding their animals across the steppe. Today, their felt tents, or *gers*, are often set up next to more permanent houses.

AMAZONIA, SOUTH AMERICA

The Yanomami people gather plants in the rain forest and hunt game, but they also grow crops in small forest gardens. Several families live together in a "village" under one huge roof.

MALI, AFRICA

The Dogon people of Mali use mud to construct their elaborate villages. Every family has its own huts and walled areas in which their animals are penned for the night.

NORTH AMERICA

New York 7.4 million

Mexico City 16.7 million

Jamaica

Bogotá 6 million

SOUTH AMERICA

Lima 6.5 million

Santiago 5.1 million

Rio de Janeiro 10.2 million

Sao Paulo 16.6 million

Buenos Aires 11.7 million

*There are about 330 million people in **South America**. More than 7 in 10 live in a city.*

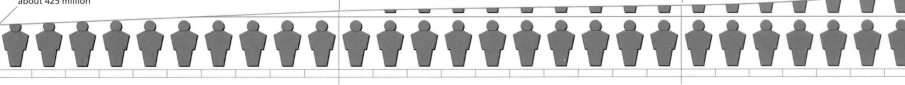

The world's population in 1500 was about 425 million

The world's population in 1600 was about 545 million

The world's population in 1700 was about 610 million.

1500   1600   1700

POOR SUBURB

Densely populated "shantytowns" have grown on the fringes of many cities in the developing world. Houses are usually built from discarded materials.

RICH SUBURB

Cities are often surrounded by areas where the richest people live. Population densities are low, and the houses may be luxurious, with large gardens or swimming pools. People in these suburbs rely on their cars for transportation. This allows them to live a great distance from places of work and leisure in the city center.

CULTIVATION

Only a small portion of the Earth's surface can grow crops. It may be possible to bring more land – such as deserts – into production, but yields may be costly.

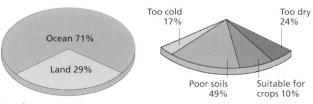

Too cold 17%
Too dry 24%
Ocean 71%
Land 29%
Poor soils 49%
Suitable for crops 10%

Land covers less than a third of the Earth's surface.

Only one-tenth of the total land area can grow crops.

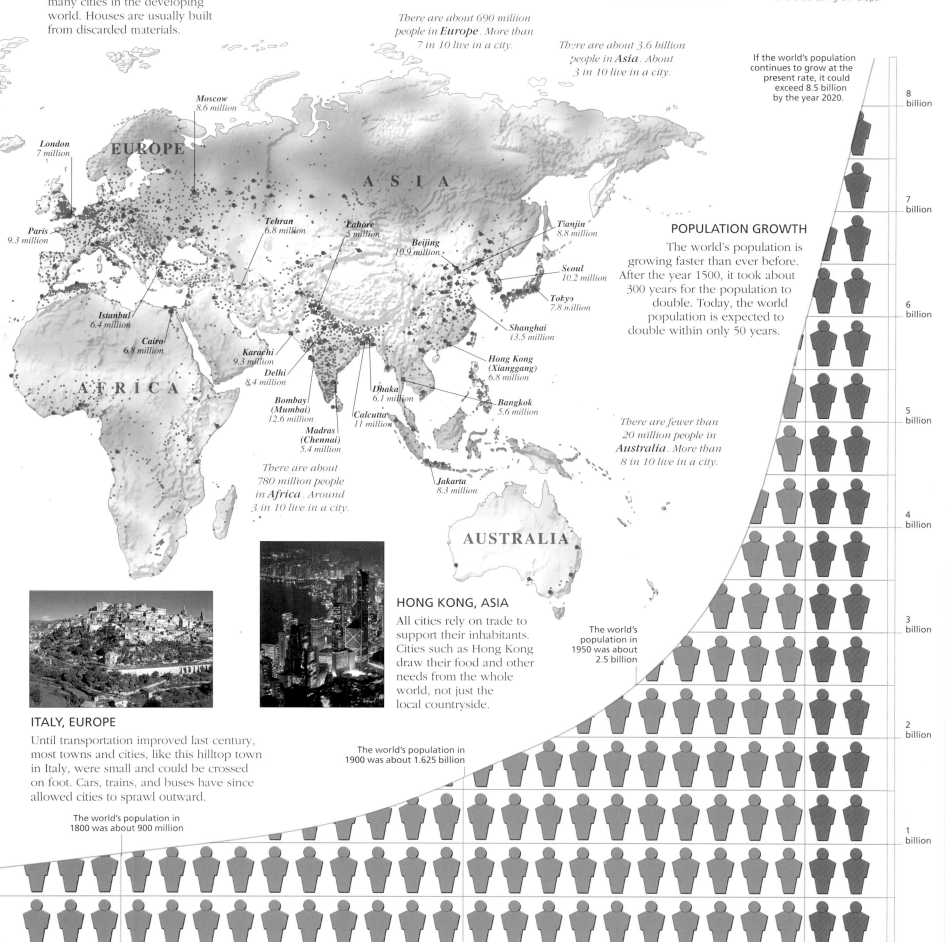

*There are about 690 million people in **Europe**. More than 7 in 10 live in a city.*

*There are about 3.6 billion people in **Asia**. About 3 in 10 live in a city.*

Moscow 8.6 million

London 7 million

EUROPE

ASIA

Paris 9.3 million

Tehran 6.8 million

Lahore 5 million

Beijing 10.9 million

Tianjin 8.8 million

Seoul 10.2 million

Tokyo 7.8 million

Istanbul 6.4 million

Cairo 6.8 million

AFRICA

Karachi 9.3 million

Delhi 8.4 million

Shanghai 13.5 million

Hong Kong (Xianggang) 6.8 million

Bombay (Mumbai) 12.6 million

Dhaka 6.1 million

Calcutta 11 million

Bangkok 5.6 million

Madras (Chennai) 5.4 million

Jakarta 8.3 million

*There are about 780 million people in **Africa**. Around 3 in 10 live in a city.*

AUSTRALIA

If the world's population continues to grow at the present rate, it could exceed 8.5 billion by the year 2020.

8 billion
7 billion
6 billion

POPULATION GROWTH

The world's population is growing faster than ever before. After the year 1500, it took about 300 years for the population to double. Today, the world population is expected to double within only 50 years.

*There are fewer than 20 million people in **Australia**. More than 8 in 10 live in a city.*

5 billion
4 billion

HONG KONG, ASIA

All cities rely on trade to support their inhabitants. Cities such as Hong Kong draw their food and other needs from the whole world, not just the local countryside.

The world's population in 1950 was about 2.5 billion

3 billion

ITALY, EUROPE

Until transportation improved last century, most towns and cities, like this hilltop town in Italy, were small and could be crossed on foot. Cars, trains, and buses have since allowed cities to sprawl outward.

The world's population in 1900 was about 1.625 billion

2 billion

The world's population in 1800 was about 900 million

1 billion

1800

1900

2000

THE WORLD TODAY

THERE ARE **192** INDEPENDENT countries in the world today. With the exception of Antarctica, every land area of the Earth's surface belongs to, or is claimed by, one country or another. In 1950, there were only 82 countries. Since then, many former colonies of the European countries have gained independence. The final stage in this process was the breakup of the Soviet Union after 1990. The world's nations vary enormously in size and shape. The largest country in the world is the Russian Federation; the smallest is Vatican City.

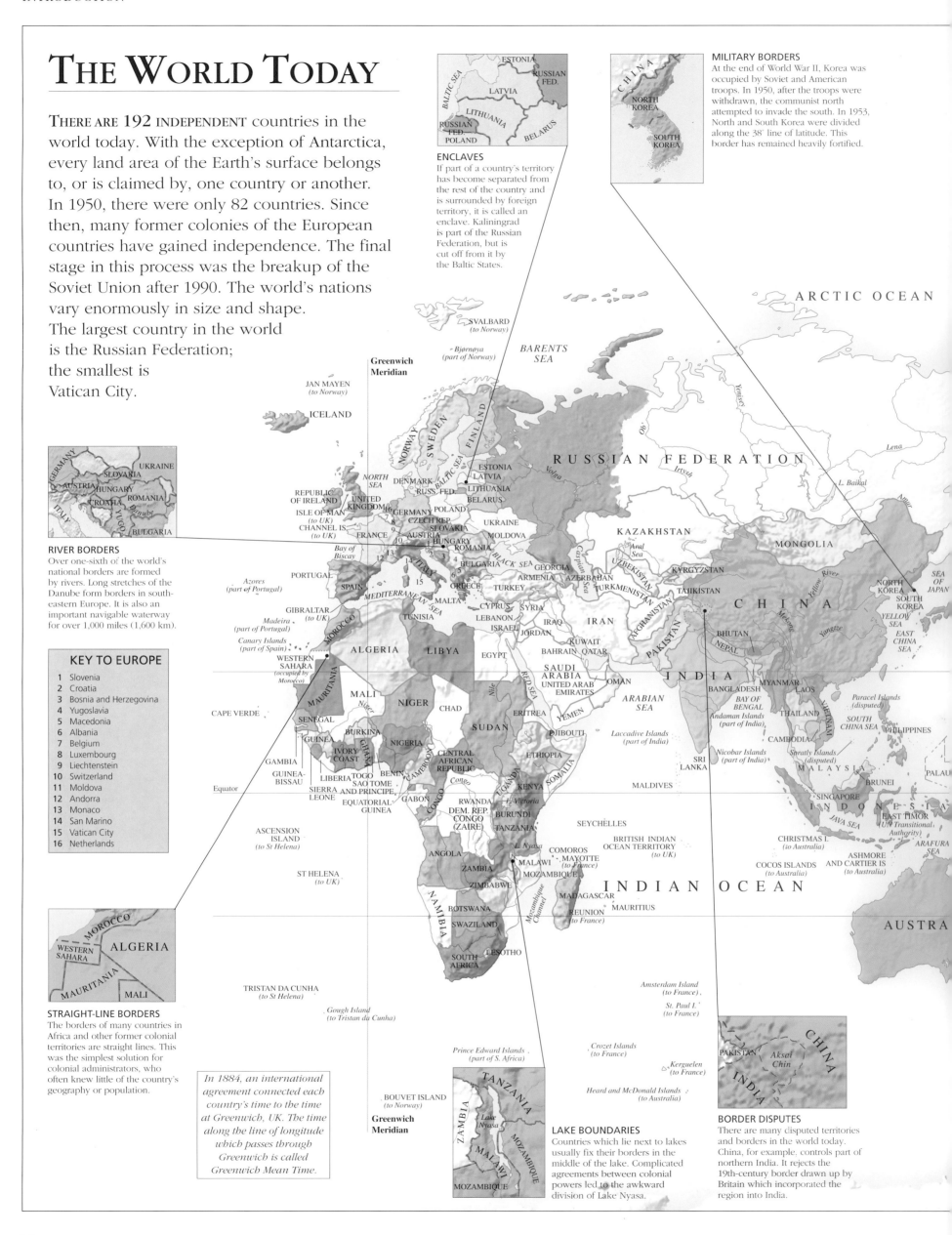

ENCLAVES
If part of a country's territory has become separated from the rest of the country and is surrounded by foreign territory, it is called an enclave. Kaliningrad is part of the Russian Federation, but is cut off from it by the Baltic States.

MILITARY BORDERS
At the end of World War II, Korea was occupied by Soviet and American troops. In 1950, after the troops were withdrawn, the communist north attempted to invade the south. In 1953, North and South Korea were divided along the 38° line of latitude. This border has remained heavily fortified.

RIVER BORDERS
Over one-sixth of the world's national borders are formed by rivers. Long stretches of the Danube form borders in south-eastern Europe. It is also an important navigable waterway for over 1,000 miles (1,600 km).

KEY TO EUROPE

1 Slovenia
2 Croatia
3 Bosnia and Herzegovina
4 Yugoslavia
5 Macedonia
6 Albania
7 Belgium
8 Luxembourg
9 Liechtenstein
10 Switzerland
11 Moldova
12 Andorra
13 Monaco
14 San Marino
15 Vatican City
16 Netherlands

STRAIGHT-LINE BORDERS
The borders of many countries in Africa and other former colonial territories are straight lines. This was the simplest solution for colonial administrators, who often knew little of the country's geography or population.

In 1884, an international agreement connected each country's time to the time at Greenwich, UK. The time along the line of longitude which passes through Greenwich is called Greenwich Mean Time.

LAKE BOUNDARIES
Countries which lie next to lakes usually fix their borders in the middle of the lake. Complicated agreements between colonial powers led to the awkward division of Lake Nyasa.

BORDER DISPUTES
There are many disputed territories and borders in the world today. China, for example, controls part of northern India. It rejects the 19th-century border drawn up by Britain which incorporated the region into India.

THE CHANGING MAP

Borders between nations can change dramatically during their history. In 1634, Poland was Europe's largest nation; between 1772 and 1795 it was absorbed into Prussia, Russia, and Austria. After World War I, it again became an independent country, but its borders changed again in 1945 following German and Russian invasions.

1. 1634

In 1634, Poland was Europe's biggest nation.

2. 1772

From 1772, Poland was part of Austria, Russia, and Prussia.

3. 1918

After World War I, Poland became a nation again.

4. 1945

After World War II, the Polish borders were again redrawn.

The world is divided into 24 time zones. The 180° line of longitude is called the International Date Line. Places just west of this line are 24 hours ahead of places to the east, so by traveling east across the Date Line you can go back a whole day.

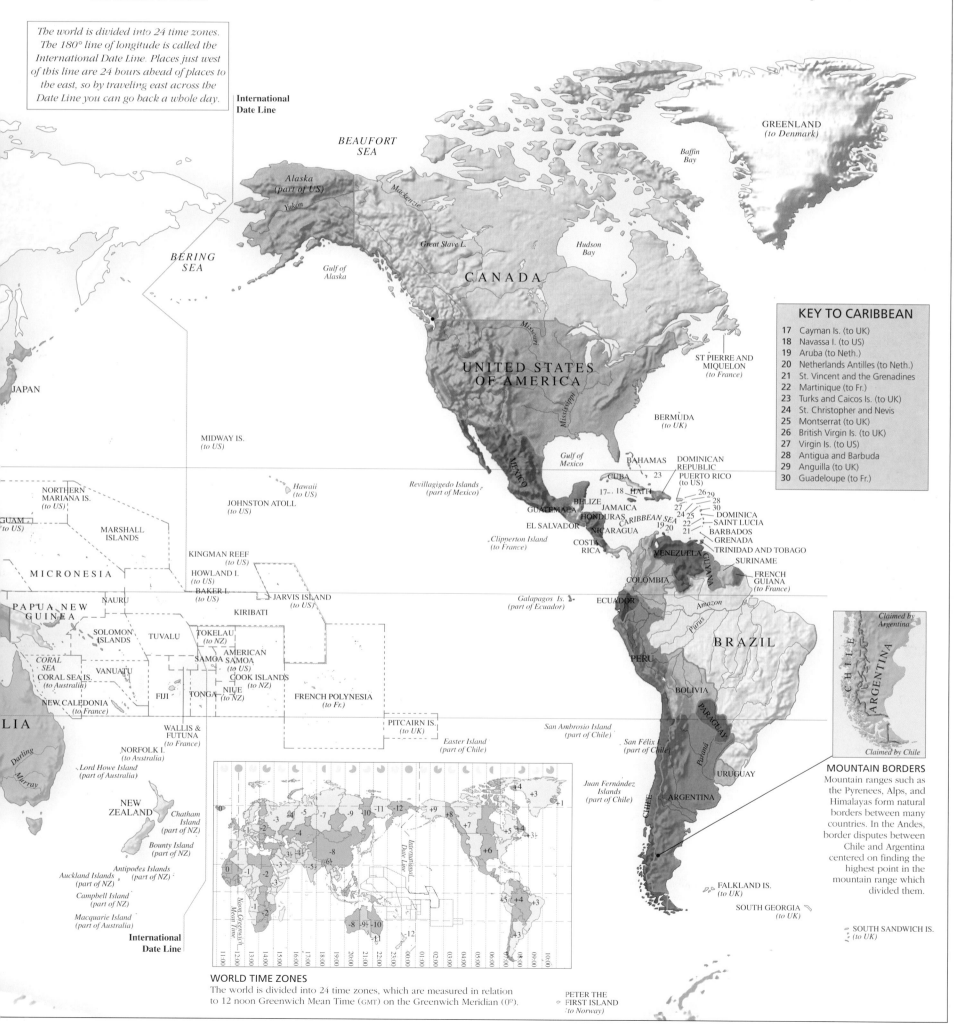

KEY TO CARIBBEAN

17 Cayman Is. (to UK)
18 Navassa I. (to US)
19 Aruba (to Neth.)
20 Netherlands Antilles (to Neth.)
21 St. Vincent and the Grenadines
22 Martinique (to Fr.)
23 Turks and Caicos Is. (to UK)
24 St. Christopher and Nevis
25 Montserrat (to UK)
26 British Virgin Is. (to UK)
27 Virgin Is. (to US)
28 Antigua and Barbuda
29 Anguilla (to UK)
30 Guadeloupe (to Fr.)

MOUNTAIN BORDERS

Mountain ranges such as the Pyrenees, Alps, and Himalayas form natural borders between many countries. In the Andes, border disputes between Chile and Argentina centered on finding the highest point in the mountain range which divided them.

WORLD TIME ZONES

The world is divided into 24 time zones, which are measured in relation to 12 noon Greenwich Mean Time (GMT) on the Greenwich Meridian (0°).

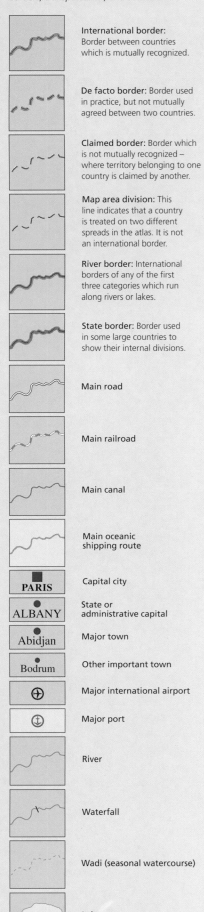

KEY TO MAPS

Certain symbols will appear on every spread, and are listed below. These symbols represent physical features, or the country's infrastructure: borders, transportation, and settlement.

	International border: Border between countries which is mutually recognized.
	De facto border: Border used in practice, but not mutually agreed between two countries.
	Claimed border: Border which is not mutually recognized – where territory belonging to one country is claimed by another.
	Map area division: This line indicates that a country is treated on two different spreads in the atlas. It is not an international border.
	River border: International borders of any of the first three categories which run along rivers or lakes.
	State border: Border used in some large countries to show their internal divisions.
	Main road
	Main railroad
	Main canal
	Main oceanic shipping route
PARIS	Capital city
ALBANY	State or administrative capital
Abidjan	Major town
Bodrum	Other important town
⊕	Major international airport
⚓	Major port
	River
	Waterfall
	Wadi (seasonal watercourse)
	Lake
	Seasonal lake
▲800m	Spot height of mountains
▼-800m	Spot depth of oceans

ABBREVIATIONS

The following abbreviations are used on maps:

Arch. = Archipelago	Pen. = Peninsula
C. = Cape	R. = River
Fr. = France	Res. = Reservoir
L. = Lake	Fed. = Federation
I. = Island	W. = Wadi
Is. = Islands	UK = United Kingdom
Mts. = Mountains	US = United States
Neth. = Netherlands	of America
NZ = New Zealand	

HOW TO USE THIS ATLAS

THE MAPS IN THIS ATLAS are organized by continent: North America; Central and South America; Europe; Africa; North and West Asia; South and East Asia; Australasia and Oceania. Each section of the book opens with a large double-page spread introducing you to the physical geography – landscapes, climate, animals, and vegetation – of the continent. On the following pages, the continent is divided by country or group of countries. These pages deal with the human geography; each detailed map is supplemented by photographs, illustrations, and landscape models. Finally, a glossary defines unfamiliar terms used in the text, and the index provides a list of all place names in the atlas and facts about each country.

CONTINENT SPREAD

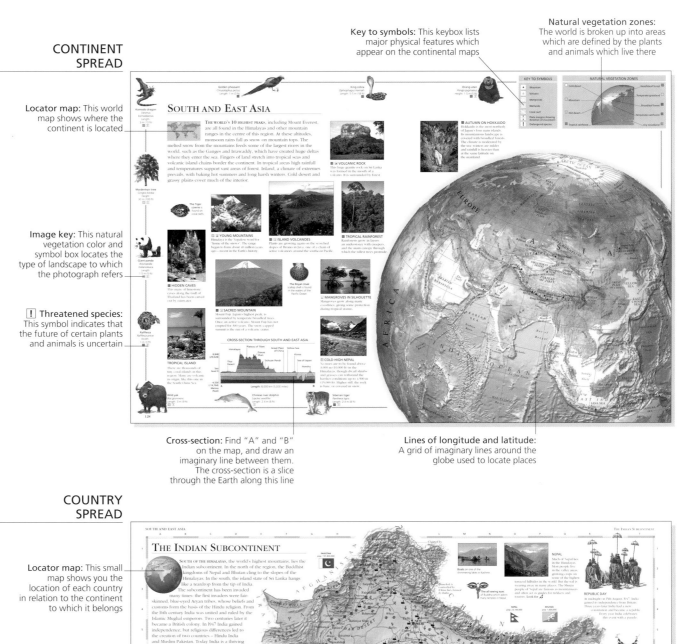

Locator map: This world map shows where the continent is located

Image key: This natural vegetation color and symbol box locates the type of landscape to which the photograph refers

⚠ Threatened species: This symbol indicates that the future of certain plants and animals is uncertain

Key to symbols: This keybox lists major physical features which appear on the continental maps

Natural vegetation zones: The world is broken up into areas which are defined by the plants and animals which live there

Cross-section: Find "A" and "B" on the map, and draw an imaginary line between them. The cross-section is a slice through the Earth along this line

Lines of longitude and latitude: A grid of imaginary lines around the globe used to locate places

COUNTRY SPREAD

Locator map: This small map shows you the location of each country in relation to the continent to which it belongs

Reference grid: The letters and numbers around this grid help you to locate places listed in the index. For an explanation on how to use the grid, see the opening page of the Index

Keybox: A keybox on each spread lists the symbols which appear on the map. These symbols have been chosen to illustrate particularly important or interesting aspects of the country

Compass point: This will show you the direction of North

Scale bar: This shows you how distance on the map relates to miles and kilometers

Flags: The flag of each nation is positioned next to the country. Population figures are also given

Raccoon

American Bald Eagle

Moose

THE GEOGRAPHY OF
NORTH
AMERICA

Vancouver, British Columbia,
see p.36

Toronto, Ontario, *see p.38*

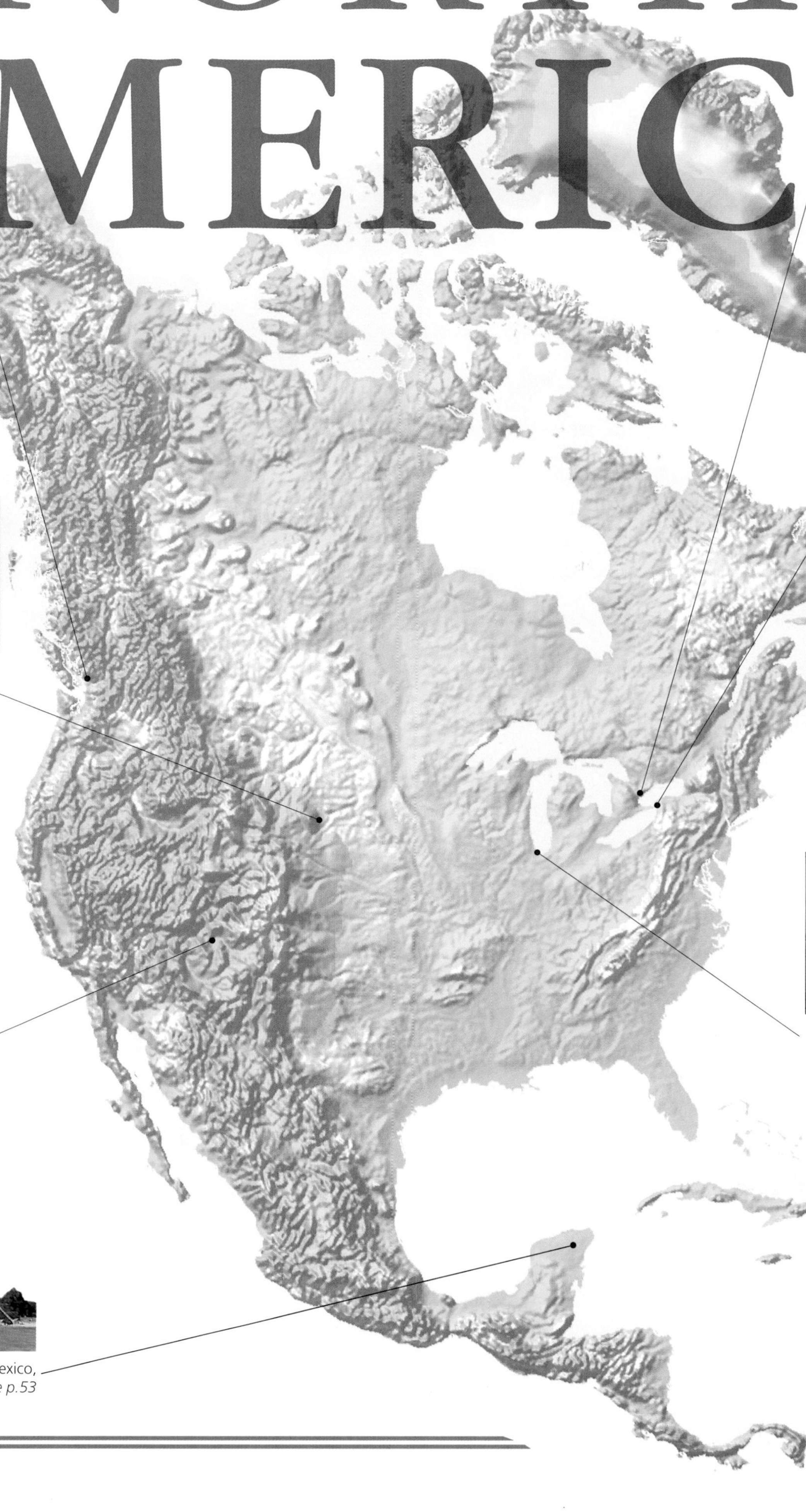

Niagara Falls, near Buffalo,
New York State, *see p.40*

Mount Rushmore, South Dakota,
see p.47

Monument Valley, Arizona,
see p.48

Chicago, at the southern tip of
Lake Michigan, *see p.44*

Maya Pyramid, Chichén-Itzá, Mexico,
see p.53

PHYSICAL NORTH AMERICA

THE CANADIAN SHIELD IS THE ANCIENT HEART of the North American continent. This vast plain, which contains rocks over two billion years old, has been subjected to repeated ice ages and the processes of weathering and erosion. Thousands of lakes, gouged out by glaciers at the end of the last Ice Age, lie scattered across its surface. Glacial activity also created the Great Lakes, which contain 20 percent of the world's fresh water. Deposits left by melting glaciers have made the Great Plains and Central Lowlands exceptionally fertile. Farther south, the huge Missouri/Mississippi river system has deposited sediment and silt over hundreds of years, leaving fertile floodplains and deltas. The mountains of the Western Cordillera were created by the collision of the Pacific and North American plates some 80 million years ago. These young mountains are still being formed; the eroded Appalachians are some of the oldest mountains in the world.

FROZEN TUNDRA

The cold, treeless landscapes of the north, where temperatures rarely rise above freezing, can only support tundra – shrubs, mosses, and lichens. Tundra blankets much of the plain that stretches across northern Canada, as well as Alaska.

MACKENZIE RIVER

The Mackenzie River issues from the Great Slave Lake, and flows northward across the Canadian Shield to the Beaufort Sea. It forms the largest river basin in Canada, only exceeded in North America by the Missouri/Mississippi basin. Its lake-strewn delta is 50 miles wide.

Mount St. Helens last erupted in May 1980.

California's San Andreas Fault is an area of earthquake activity.

SHAPING THE CONTINENT

The North American landscape is still being shaped by many processes. In the north, glaciers scour the frozen land. In the west, the movement of continental plates leads to earthquakes and volcanoes. Huge rivers, with their power to erode and deposit sediment, are constantly changing the plains of the interior.

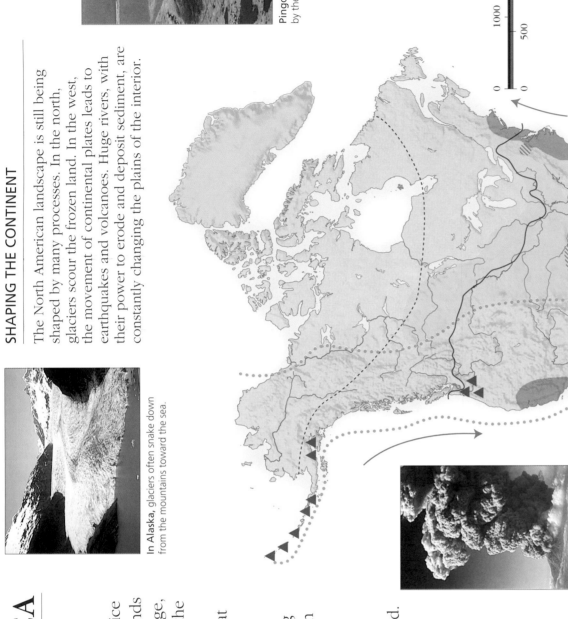

Pingos in Canada are formed by the freeze-thaw cycle.

In Alaska, glaciers often snake down from the mountains toward the sea.

MAP FEATURES

▨ Limestone region	◀ Active volcano
▦ Sinking land	⋯ Area of tectonic activity
▦ Stable land	---- Limit of permafrost
▦ Uplifting land	— Maximum limit of glaciation
	→ Ocean current

2000 KM
1000 MILES
1000 500 0
1000 500 0

GREENLAND

ARCTIC OCEAN

BEAUFORT

Bering Strait

500 1000 KM
250 500 MILES

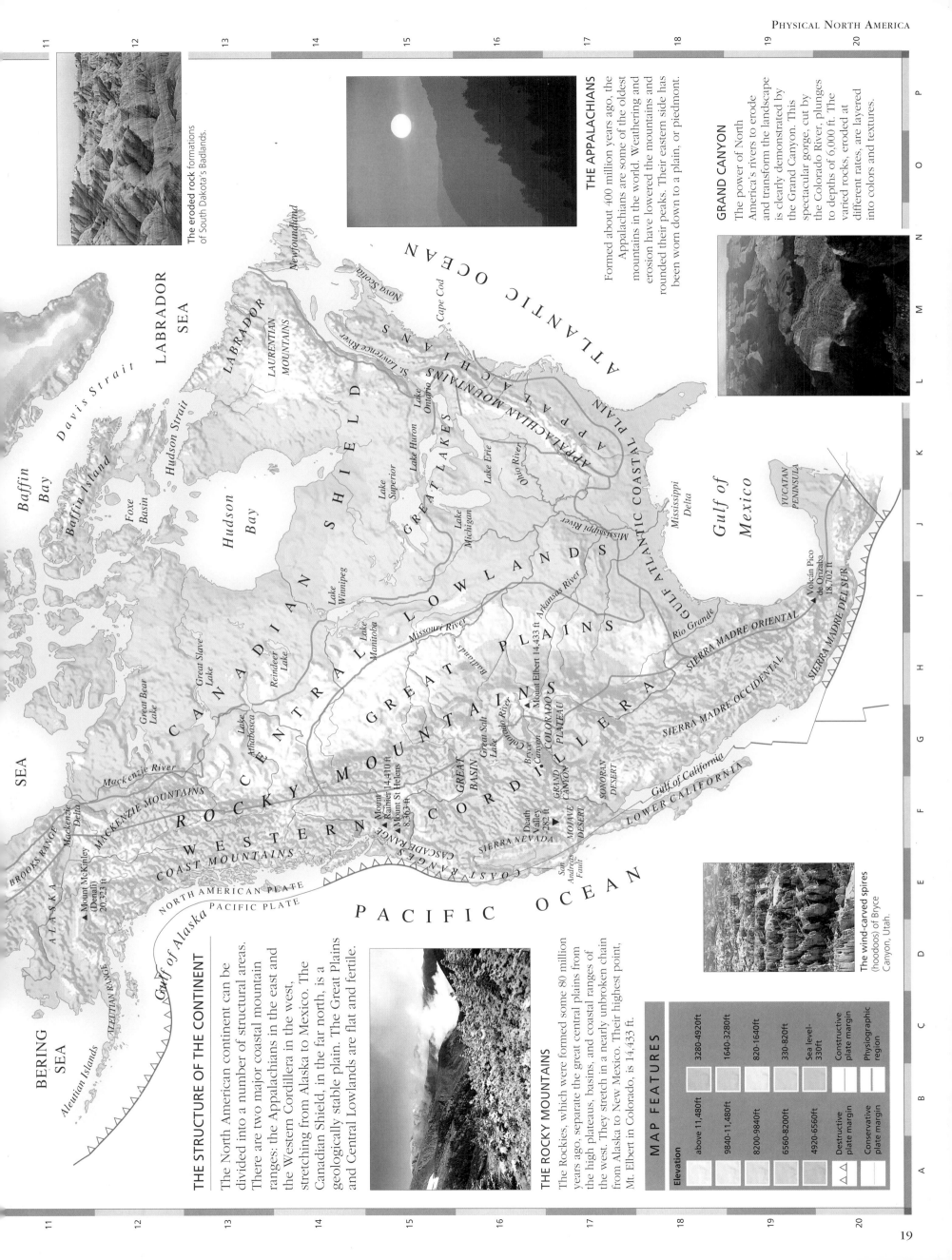

The eroded rock formations of South Dakota's Badlands.

THE APPALACHIANS

Formed about 400 million years ago, the Appalachians are some of the oldest mountains in the world. Weathering and erosion have lowered the mountains and rounded their peaks. Their eastern side has been worn down to a plain, or piedmont.

GRAND CANYON

The power of North America's rivers to erode and transform the landscape is clearly demonstrated by the Grand Canyon. This spectacular gorge, cut by the Colorado River, plunges to depths of 6,000 ft. The varied rocks, eroded at different rates, are layered into colors and textures.

The wind-carved spires (hoodoos) of Bryce Canyon, Utah.

THE STRUCTURE OF THE CONTINENT

The North American continent can be divided into a number of structural areas. There are two major coastal mountain ranges: the Appalachians in the east and the Western Cordillera in the west, stretching from Alaska to Mexico. The Canadian Shield, in the far north, is a geologically stable plain. The Great Plains and Central Lowlands are flat and fertile.

THE ROCKY MOUNTAINS

The Rockies, which were formed some 80 million years ago, separate the great central plains from the high plateaus, basins, and coastal ranges of the west. They stretch in a nearly unbroken chain from Alaska to New Mexico. Their highest point, Mt. Elbert in Colorado, is 14,433 ft.

MAP FEATURES

Elevation		
above 11,480ft	3280-4920ft	
9840-11,480ft	1640-3280ft	
8200-9840ft	820-1640ft	
6560-8200ft	330-820ft	
4920-6560ft	Sea level-330ft	

Destructive plate margin
Constructive plate margin
Conservative plate margin
Physiographic region

Map labels

BERING SEA
LABRADOR SEA
SEA
Baffin Bay
Davis Strait
Baffin Island
Foxe Basin
Hudson Strait
Hudson Bay
LABRADOR
LAURENTIAN MOUNTAINS
Newfoundland
Nova Scotia
Cape Cod
ATLANTIC OCEAN
CANADIAN SHIELD
GREAT LAKES
Lake Superior
Lake Michigan
Lake Huron
Lake Ontario
Lake Erie
Ohio River
APPALACHIAN MOUNTAINS
APPALACHIANS
GULF ATLANTIC COASTAL PLAIN
CENTRAL LOWLANDS
Lake Winnipeg
Lake Manitoba
Reindeer Lake
Great Slave Lake
Great Bear Lake
Lake Athabasca
Missouri River
GREAT PLAINS
Badlands
Mississippi River
Mississippi Delta
Gulf of Mexico
YUCATAN PENINSULA
Rio Grande
Arkansas River
Mount Elbert 14,433 ft
Colorado River
Great Salt Lake
COLORADO PLATEAU
GRAND CANYON
Bryce Canyon
GREAT BASIN
SIERRA MADRE ORIENTAL
SIERRA MADRE OCCIDENTAL
SIERRA MADRE DEL SUR
Volcán Pico de Orizaba 18,702 ft
Mackenzie River
Mackenzie Delta
MACKENZIE MOUNTAINS
ROCKY MOUNTAINS
WESTERN CORDILLERA
BROOKS RANGE
ALASKA
Mount McKinley (Denali) 20,321 ft
Gulf of Alaska
Aleutian Islands
ALEUTIAN RANGE
COAST MOUNTAINS
COAST RANGES
CASCADE RANGE
Mount Rainier 14,410 ft
Mount St Helens 8,363 ft
SIERRA NEVADA
Death Valley -282 ft
MOJAVE DESERT
San Andreas Fault
SONORAN DESERT
Gulf of California
LOWER CALIFORNIA
NORTH AMERICAN PLATE
PACIFIC PLATE
PACIFIC OCEAN

THE NORTH AMERICAN CLIMATE

THE PHYSICAL GEOGRAPHY OF NORTH AMERICA influences its climate; the great width of the continent in the north extends the Arctic and cool climates, which predominate overall. The tapering shape of the land in the south accounts for the comparatively small area of the continent that is subject to tropical conditions. The wettest parts of the continent are the Pacific slopes of the Rocky Mountains and the humid zones to the southeast. In the center and east, rain- and snow-laden westerly winds bring moderate annual rainfall, ranging from 20-45 inches (500-1,100 mm) a year. The driest parts of the continent are the deserts of the southwest, where rainfall is less than 10 inches (254 mm) per year (and sometimes nonexistent), and the Arctic, where water is frozen for six to nine months a year. A strong continental airflow, called the jetstream, moves storms from west to east. Hurricanes and tornadoes are frequent occurrences in the south and east, and the vast Mississippi/Missouri river system is prone to severe flooding.

CLIMATIC ZONES

North America contains a range of climatic zones. In the extreme north, much of the land is frozen for most of the year. Subarctic and cool continental zones are distinguished by long, severe winters and low rainfall. In the humid zones of the Southeast, influenced by tropical air from the Gulf, winters are mild, summers long, and rainfall high. The west of the continent is more arid than the east; the Southwestern deserts are the driest places. Mexico has a mainly tropical climate.

CANADIAN ICE STORM

Canada's winters are notoriously hard, with average temperatures in January dropping below 0°F (-18°C). In 1998, clashing weather fronts caused ice storms. Huge lumps of ice fell from the sky, crushing power lines and leaving 3 million people without electricity.

DAKOTA SKIES

Cool, temperate weather extends over much of Canada and the northern US. While summers can be very hot, winters are hard, with heavy snowfall and severe frosts. Frozen lakes and seas chill surrounding air, further lowering winter temperatures.

THE FLORIDA WETLANDS

Warm, moist air from the Gulf of Mexico influences the humid southeast, where winters are short and mild. Southern Florida has heavy rainfall in summer; the cycle of dry winters and wet summers is the life force behind the unique ecosystem of the Everglades wetlands.

MAP FEATURES

Ice cap

Tundra

Subarctic

Cool continental

Semiarid

Arid

Humid equatorial

Tropical

Warm humid

Daily hours of sunshine, January

Daily hours of sunshine, July

Temperature

below -22°F
-22 to -4°F
-4 to 14°F
14 to 32°F
32 to 50°F
50 to 68°F
68 to 86°F
above 86°F

Rainfall

0 to 1 in
1 to 2 in
2 to 4 in
4 to 8 in
8 to 12 in
12 to 16 in
16 to 20 in
more than 20 in

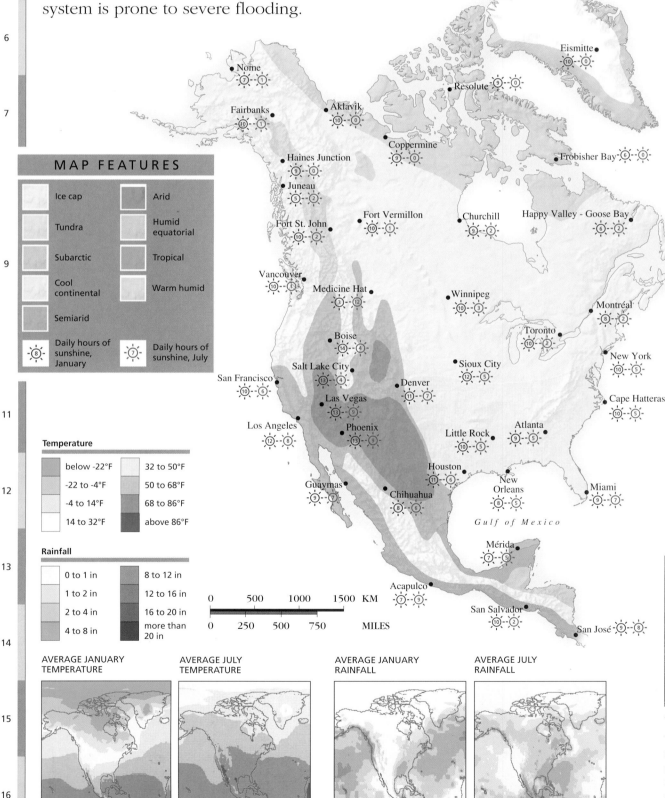

0   500   1000   1500 KM

0   250   500   750   MILES

Gulf of Mexico

AVERAGE JANUARY TEMPERATURE

AVERAGE JULY TEMPERATURE

AVERAGE JANUARY RAINFALL

AVERAGE JULY RAINFALL

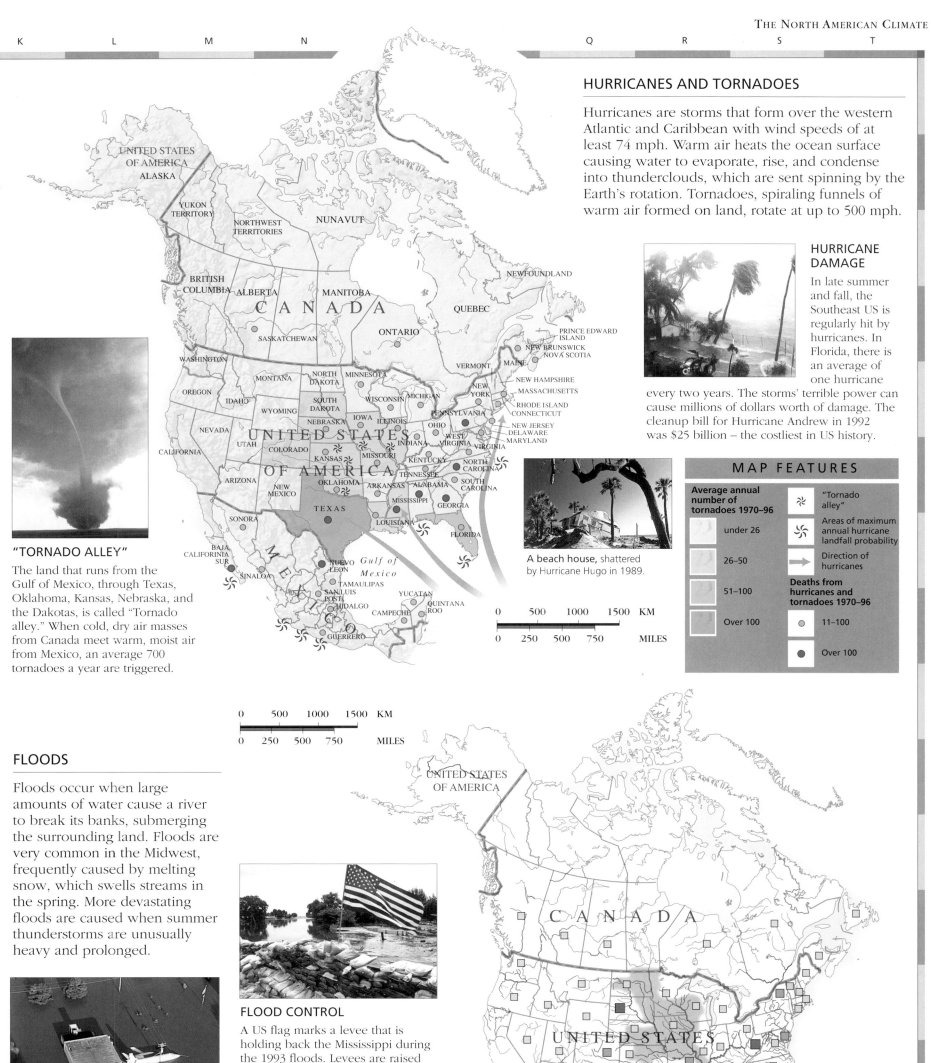

HURRICANES AND TORNADOES

Hurricanes are storms that form over the western Atlantic and Caribbean with wind speeds of at least 74 mph. Warm air heats the ocean surface causing water to evaporate, rise, and condense into thunderclouds, which are sent spinning by the Earth's rotation. Tornadoes, spiraling funnels of warm air formed on land, rotate at up to 500 mph.

HURRICANE DAMAGE

In late summer and fall, the Southeast US is regularly hit by hurricanes. In Florida, there is an average of one hurricane every two years. The storms' terrible power can cause millions of dollars worth of damage. The cleanup bill for Hurricane Andrew in 1992 was $25 billion – the costliest in US history.

A beach house, shattered by Hurricane Hugo in 1989.

"TORNADO ALLEY"

The land that runs from the Gulf of Mexico, through Texas, Oklahoma, Kansas, Nebraska, and the Dakotas, is called "Tornado alley." When cold, dry air masses from Canada meet warm, moist air from Mexico, an average 700 tornadoes a year are triggered.

MAP FEATURES

Average annual number of tornadoes 1970–96	"Tornado alley"
under 26	Areas of maximum annual hurricane landfall probability
26–50	Direction of hurricanes
51–100	**Deaths from hurricanes and tornadoes 1970–96**
Over 100	11–100
	Over 100

0	500	1000	1500	KM
0	250	500	750	MILES

FLOODS

Floods occur when large amounts of water cause a river to break its banks, submerging the surrounding land. Floods are very common in the Midwest, frequently caused by melting snow, which swells streams in the spring. More devastating floods are caused when summer thunderstorms are unusually heavy and prolonged.

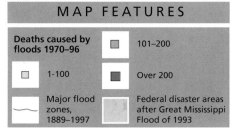

FLOOD CONTROL

A US flag marks a levee that is holding back the Mississippi during the 1993 floods. Levees are raised riverbanks; they can be formed by natural silt deposits or man-made embankments to prevent flooding.

MISSISSIPPI FLOODS

In 1993, record-breaking rainfall deluged the Midwest. Rain and floodwater from the Mississippi River swamped Illinois, Iowa, and Missouri, causing damages estimated at over $10 billion. Farmland was submerged and whole towns were flooded.

MAP FEATURES

Deaths caused by floods 1970–96	101–200
1–100	Over 200
Major flood zones, 1889–1997	Federal disaster areas after Great Mississippi Flood of 1993

0	500	1000	1500	KM
0	250	500	750	MILES

THE NORTH AMERICAN ENVIRONMENT

DENSELY POPULATED CITIES, high concentrations of industry, intensive farming, and millions of cars all pose a threat to North America's fragile ecosystems. Air pollution levels are very high in some cities – the most notorious are Los Angeles and Mexico City, where pollution generated by cars and factories is trapped by surrounding mountains. The centers of heavy industry in the northeast US, in particular the area around the Great Lakes, are still discharging pollution into the air and rivers and emitting acid rain. In addition, areas of great natural beauty are under threat – the temperate rain forest of Canada's northwest, the cypresses in Florida's Everglades, and tropical rain forest in the Yucatan have all suffered from commercial logging. The US and Canada both have an impressive network of national parks, preserves, and wildlife refuges and sanctuaries. Parks protect vast areas of wilderness, but they are increasingly under threat from visitors, cars, and surrounding air pollution.

NATIONAL PARKS

At the end of the 19th century, a growing conservation movement, alarmed by further urbanization, called on the government to set aside and protect vast areas of wilderness. President Woodrow Wilson established the National Park Service in 1916. Today, there are a total of 51 national parks, as well as numerous seashores, lakeshores, rivers, parkways, trails, preserves, and recreation areas. In the early 1990s over 270 million people visited the national parks annually, stretching resources to the limit.

Mountains and fall tundra in Denali National Park, Alaska.

SALT SPRINGS, YELLOWSTONE

Yellowstone is the largest and oldest national park in the US, established in 1872, and stretching across Wyoming, Montana, and Idaho. It is a volcanic landscape, and the park's main attractions are its 10,000 hot springs, geysers, hot pools, and mud cauldrons.

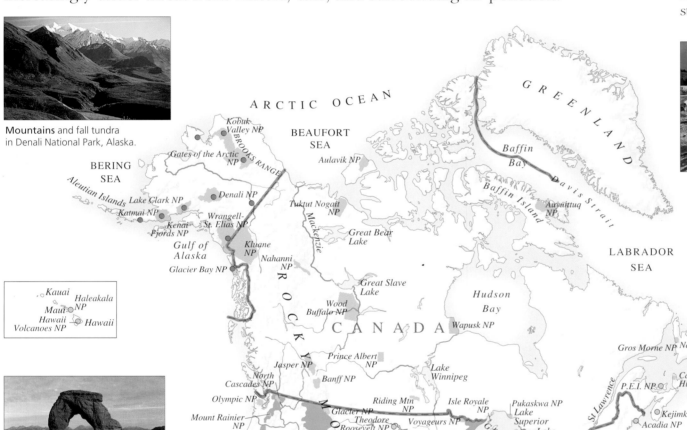

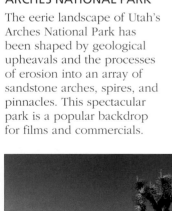

ARCHES NATIONAL PARK

The eerie landscape of Utah's Arches National Park has been shaped by geological upheavals and the processes of erosion into an array of sandstone arches, spires, and pinnacles. This spectacular park is a popular backdrop for films and commercials.

JOSHUA TREE

The Joshua Tree National Park in California's southern deserts was established in 1936 to preserve groves of these unusual trees. They can grow to 30 ft and live for up to 1,000 years.

SMOKY MOUNTAINS

The Great Smoky Mountains National Park straddles the Appalachian backbone of North Carolina and Tennessee. It is accessible to densely populated regions, and is the most visited national park in the US. Its diverse forest includes five distinct habitats, from pine and oak to spruce and fir.

Big Cypress National Preserve, a part of Florida's Everglades.

MAP FEATURES

- National park
- National preserve
- National forest

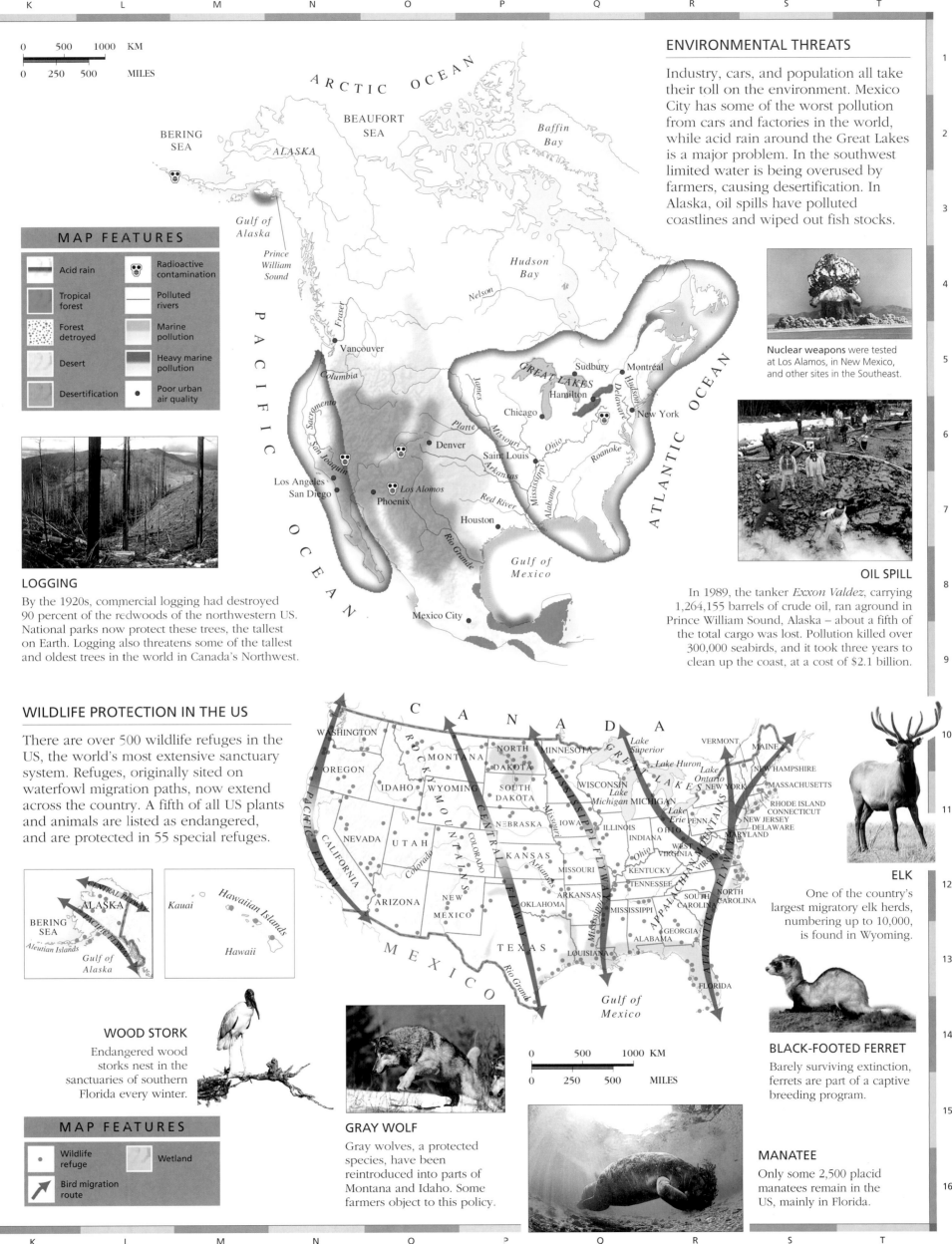

MAP FEATURES

- Acid rain
- Tropical forest
- Forest destroyed
- Desert
- Desertification
- Radioactive contamination
- Polluted rivers
- Marine pollution
- Heavy marine pollution
- Poor urban air quality

ENVIRONMENTAL THREATS

Industry, cars, and population all take their toll on the environment. Mexico City has some of the worst pollution from cars and factories in the world, while acid rain around the Great Lakes is a major problem. In the southwest limited water is being overused by farmers, causing desertification. In Alaska, oil spills have polluted coastlines and wiped out fish stocks.

Nuclear weapons were tested at Los Alamos, in New Mexico, and other sites in the Southeast.

OIL SPILL

In 1989, the tanker *Exxon Valdez*, carrying 1,264,155 barrels of crude oil, ran aground in Prince William Sound, Alaska – about a fifth of the total cargo was lost. Pollution killed over 300,000 seabirds, and it took three years to clean up the coast, at a cost of $2.1 billion.

LOGGING

By the 1920s, commercial logging had destroyed 90 percent of the redwoods of the northwestern US. National parks now protect these trees, the tallest on Earth. Logging also threatens some of the tallest and oldest trees in the world in Canada's Northwest.

WILDLIFE PROTECTION IN THE US

There are over 500 wildlife refuges in the US, the world's most extensive sanctuary system. Refuges, originally sited on waterfowl migration paths, now extend across the country. A fifth of all US plants and animals are listed as endangered, and are protected in 55 special refuges.

ELK

One of the country's largest migratory elk herds, numbering up to 10,000, is found in Wyoming.

BLACK-FOOTED FERRET

Barely surviving extinction, ferrets are part of a captive breeding program.

MAP FEATURES

- Wildlife refuge
- Bird migration route
- Wetland

WOOD STORK

Endangered wood storks nest in the sanctuaries of southern Florida every winter.

GRAY WOLF

Gray wolves, a protected species, have been reintroduced into parts of Montana and Idaho. Some farmers object to this policy.

MANATEE

Only some 2,500 placid manatees remain in the US, mainly in Florida.

Pre-Columbian History

NORTH AMERICA, before the arrival of the Europeans, was a land of great cultural diversity. The tropical lowlands on the Gulf of Mexico, with their productive soils, were able to support rapidly growing populations. From the 1st millennium BC, this region was occupied by increasingly sophisticated urban societies. By contrast, the harsh landscapes of the Arctic and sub-Arctic regions were very sparsely populated by resourceful hunters, such as the Inuit and Algonquin, who were able to trade furs, copper, and animal oils with the rest of the continent. Further to the south, more fertile land and temperate climates were suited to settled agriculture. Staple crops, such as beans and corn, were imported from Mexico, and supported large farming villages and towns in both the southwest and southeast. The entire continent remained largely untouched by contact with other regions. This was to change dramatically in the 16th century, when the Europeans arrived.

MAYA AND AZTEC CULTURES

The city-states of the Maya civilization, which emerged in the 3rd century AD, are found throughout the jungles of the Yucatan Peninsula and modern Guatemala. The Maya used a hieroglyphic writing system and are thought to be the first literate civilization in the Americas. The Aztecs established their empire in the Valley of Mexico c.1200. By 1519, most of the city-states of central Mexico paid tribute to the highly militarized Aztecs.

TIKAL

The Maya city of Tikal had a population of 50,000 in the 8th century AD. A series of five ceremonial complexes, dominated by pyramid temples and palaces, were linked by broad causeways.

MAP FEATURES

Maya cultural area	Maximum extent of Aztec Empire, 1520
Classic Maya site c.AD 290–790	Provincial tribute centre
Maya trade route	Important Aztec site

AZTEC MASK

A mask, made of turquoise, shell, and wood, represents Quetzacoatl, the feathered serpent god. In about AD 987, followers of the god had been exiled from Mexico. The Aztecs feared his return.

AZTEC SACRIFICE

The bloodthirsty nature of much Aztec art reflects a religion which demanded sacrifice. The Aztecs believed that the sun god needed to be fed with human hearts and blood each day.

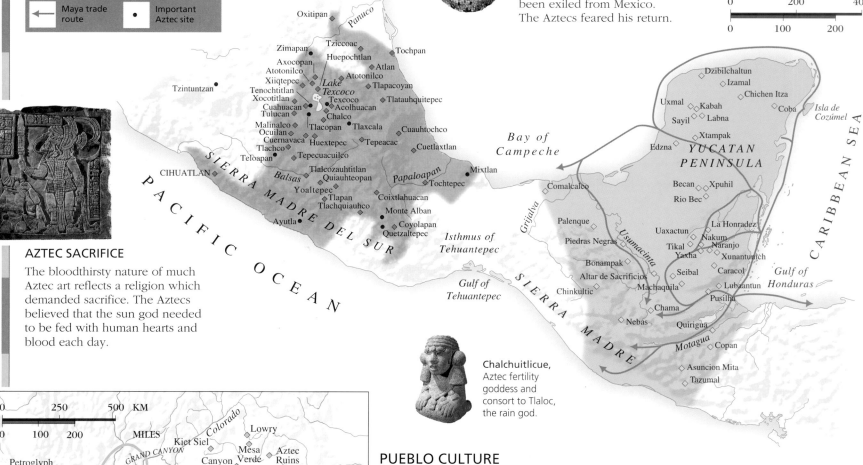

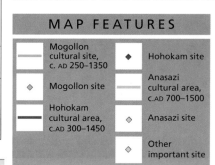
Chalchuitlicue, Aztec fertility goddess and consort to Tlaloc, the rain god.

PUEBLO CULTURE

The peoples of southwestern North America lived in small villages, or pueblos, during the 1st millennium AD, where they cultivated corn, squash, and beans. Hohokam farmers located their villages near rivers, where they could divert and channel water into their fields, while the Mogollon and Anasazi relied on rainfall and flash floods.

Mimbres pottery bowl, c.AD 950. These burial offerings were broken, so the owner's spirit could escape.

MAP FEATURES

Mogollon cultural site, c. AD 250–1350	Hohokam site
Mogollon site	Anasazi cultural area, c.AD 700–1500
Hohokam cultural area, c.AD 300–1450	Anasazi site
	Other important site

Mesa Verde, a defended village carved high into the canyon wall.

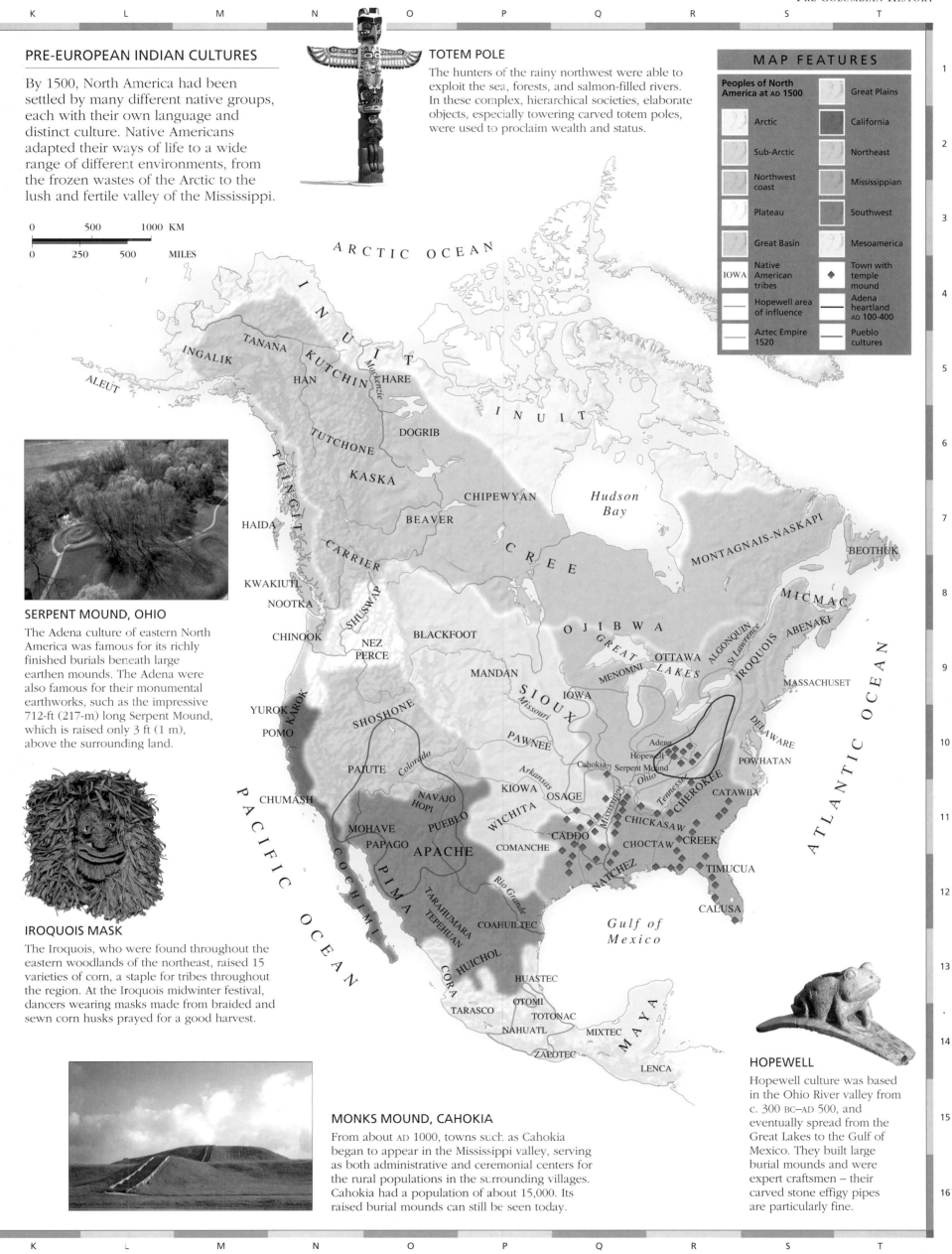

PRE-EUROPEAN INDIAN CULTURES

By 1500, North America had been settled by many different native groups, each with their own language and distinct culture. Native Americans adapted their ways of life to a wide range of different environments, from the frozen wastes of the Arctic to the lush and fertile valley of the Mississippi.

TOTEM POLE

The hunters of the rainy northwest were able to exploit the sea, forests, and salmon-filled rivers. In these complex, hierarchical societies, elaborate objects, especially towering carved totem poles, were used to proclaim wealth and status.

MAP FEATURES

Peoples of North America at AD 1500

Arctic	Great Plains
Sub-Arctic	California
Northwest coast	Northeast
Plateau	Mississippian
Great Basin	Southwest
	Mesoamerica

IOWA — Native American tribes

◆ — Town with temple mound

Hopewell area of influence

Adena heartland AD 100-400

Aztec Empire 1520

Pueblo cultures

SERPENT MOUND, OHIO

The Adena culture of eastern North America was famous for its richly finished burials beneath large earthen mounds. The Adena were also famous for their monumental earthworks, such as the impressive 712-ft (217-m) long Serpent Mound, which is raised only 3 ft (1 m), above the surrounding land.

IROQUOIS MASK

The Iroquois, who were found throughout the eastern woodlands of the northeast, raised 15 varieties of corn, a staple for tribes throughout the region. At the Iroquois midwinter festival, dancers wearing masks made from braided and sewn corn husks prayed for a good harvest.

MONKS MOUND, CAHOKIA

From about AD 1000, towns such as Cahokia began to appear in the Mississippi valley, serving as both administrative and ceremonial centers for the rural populations in the surrounding villages. Cahokia had a population of about 15,000. Its raised burial mounds can still be seen today.

HOPEWELL

Hopewell culture was based in the Ohio River valley from c. 300 BC–AD 500, and eventually spread from the Great Lakes to the Gulf of Mexico. They built large burial mounds and were expert craftsmen – their carved stone effigy pipes are particularly fine.

25

COLONIZATION AND CONFLICT

IN 1521, A SMALL SPANISH ARMY defeated the mighty Aztec Empire and transformed Mexico into a Spanish colony until 1821, when it gained its independence. English, Dutch, and French settlers soon followed, and by the end of the 17th century, a string of colonies along the Atlantic coast were trading with Native Americans and exporting tobacco, furs, and cotton to Europe. Slaves were brought from Africa to work on the cotton plantations of the south. European diseases ravaged native populations; by the mid-18th century those that remained had retreated westward. In the 18th century, rivalries between Britain and France culminated in a British victory. In 1763, Britain gained control of Canada and dominance of North America. In 1776, American colonists demanded their independence from the British. The Revolutionary War led to the foundation of a new nation, with a federal system of government, a constitution, and a bill of rights guaranteeing the liberties of every citizen of the United States.

THE COLONIAL ERA

The Spanish embarked on their conquest of Central and South America in the 16th century – the Aztec capital, Tenochtitlan, was captured in 1521. The Spanish then began to penetrate northward into North America. In the 17th century, the Dutch, and then the British, set up colonies along the Atlantic coast, trading in tobacco, timber, and food. The French gained a foothold in Canada, where they traded in fur.

Québec in 1886, when it was a British colony.

COLONIAL QUÉBEC

Québec was established in 1608 as a base for trade in furs with the Huron and Algonquin tribes. In 1663, it became the capital of the colony of New France, the thinly settled land that extended along the St. Lawrence River valley. In 1759, Québec fell to the British, bringing to an end the French presence in Canada.

New Amsterdam (New York), a Dutch colony 1625–64.

A British colonial farm in 18th-century Williamsburg, Va.

ENGLISH ARRIVALS

Between 1580 and 1590, the English made two attempts to set up a colony on Roanoke Island in Virginia. The colonies failed because of arduous conditions and conflict with the natives, but the colonists soon returned.

THE SPANISH CONQUEST

Tenochtitlan was the capital of the Aztec Empire from 1428. At its height, it was a city of over 300,000 people. Yet a Spanish army of only 450 men was able to forge alliances with Aztec foes, and take the city in 1521, devastating the empire.

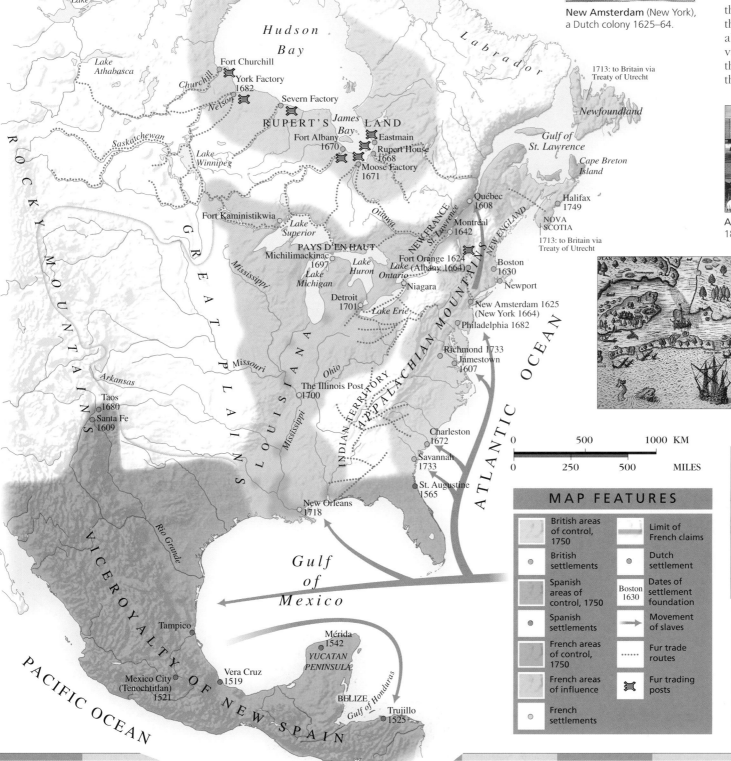

MAP FEATURES

- British areas of control, 1750
- British settlements
- Spanish areas of control, 1750
- Spanish settlements
- French areas of control, 1750
- French areas of influence
- French settlements
- Limit of French claims
- Dutch settlement
- Boston 1630 Dates of settlement foundation
- Movement of slaves
- Fur trade routes
- Fur trading posts

Great Slave Lake

Lake Athabasca

Churchill

Fort Churchill

York Factory 1682

Nelson

Severn Factory

Hudson Bay

RUPERT'S LAND

James Bay

Fort Albany 1670

Eastmain

Rupert House 1668

Moose Factory 1671

Labrador

1713: to Britain via Treaty of Utrecht

Newfoundland

Gulf of St. Lawrence

Cape Breton Island

Saskatchewan

Lake Winnipeg

Fort Kaministikwia

Lake Superior

PAYS D'EN HAUT

Michilimackinac 1697

Lake Michigan

Lake Huron

Ottawa

NEW FRANCE

Québec 1608

Montreal 1642

St. Lawrence

NEW ENGLAND

Halifax 1749

NOVA SCOTIA

1713: to Britain via Treaty of Utrecht

ROCKY MOUNTAINS

GREAT PLAINS

Mississippi

Detroit 1701

Lake Erie

Lake Ontario

Niagara

Fort Orange 1624 (Albany 1664)

Boston 1630

Newport

New Amsterdam 1625 (New York 1664)

Philadelphia 1682

Missouri

Ohio

INDIAN TERRITORY

APPALACHIAN MOUNTAINS

The Illinois Post 1700

Richmond 1733

Jamestown 1607

Arkansas

Taos 1680

Santa Fe 1609

LOUISIANA

Mississippi

Charleston 1672

Savannah 1733

St. Augustine 1565

ATLANTIC OCEAN

New Orleans 1718

Gulf of Mexico

VICEROYALTY OF NEW SPAIN

Rio Grande

Tampico

Mérida 1542

YUCATAN PENINSULA

Mexico City (Tenochtitlan) 1521

Vera Cruz 1519

BELIZE

Gulf of Honduras

Trujillo 1525

PACIFIC OCEAN

500 1000 KM
250 500 MILES

THE REVOLUTIONARY WAR

In the 1760s Britain's American subjects were becoming resentful of colonial control, particularly taxation. The Revolutionary War began in Boston in 1775. British forces were well-equipped, but as the war progressed the Americans gained support, and were eventually joined by the French, Dutch, and Spanish. The surrender of Yorktown in 1781 brought the war to an end, and a new nation was born.

BATTLE OF BUNKER HILL

On June 17, 1775, British troops struggled to break the American encirclement of Boston. The battle reinforced the Americans' belief in their ability to stand united under fire.

DECLARATION OF INDEPENDENCE

This radical document, drafted by Thomas Jefferson, was adopted by all 13 of Britain's colonies on July 4, 1776, after the British government had rejected several attempts by the colonists to reach a compromise.

The 13 British colonies signing the Declaration of Independence

Map labels (Revolutionary War):
0 250 500 KM
0 100 200 MILES

CANADA

Lake Superior
Lake Huron
Lake Michigan
Lake Ontario
Lake Erie

Québec Dec 30–31, 1775
DISTRICT OF MAINE
Montréal
Fort Chambly
Fort St. John's
NEW HAMPSHIRE
Crown Point
Concord Apr 19, 1775
Lexington Apr 19, 1775
Bennington
Saratoga
Boston
Fort Stanwix
Fort Oswego
Cambridge
Bunker Hill, Jun 16, 1775
Fort Niagara
Albany
NEW YORK MASS.
Providence
Bemis Heights Sep 19 & Oct 7, 1777
Hartford
Newport
RHODE ISLAND CONNECTICUT
New Haven
West Point
New London
Fort Detroit
Wilkes Barre
White Plains
New York
Fort Malden
Princeton
Monmouth
PENNSYLVANIA
Trenton
NEW JERSEY
Fort Pitt
Brandywine Sep 11, 1777
Philadelphia
Redstone Fort
Wilmington
DELAWARE
Fort Henry
MARYLAND
Charlottesville
Richmond
Petersburg
Jamestown Jul 6, 1781
INDIAN
Williamsburg
VIRGINIA
Saint Louis
Vincennes
Bedford
Yorktown Oct 19, 1781
Norfolk
Cahokia
Kaskaskia
Harrodsburg
RESERVE
Roanoke
Boonesborough
Guilford
NORTH CAROLINA
Ramsay's Mill
Charlotte
Cape Fear
Cheraw
Wilmington
Fort Ninety Six
Camden
SOUTH CAROLINA
GEORGIA
Charleston Jun 28, 1776
Augusta
Savannah
Ohio
Tennessee
Mississippi
LOUISIANA
Illinois
Alabama
FLORIDA
New Orleans
Gulf of Mexico
ATLANTIC OCEAN
St. Lawrence

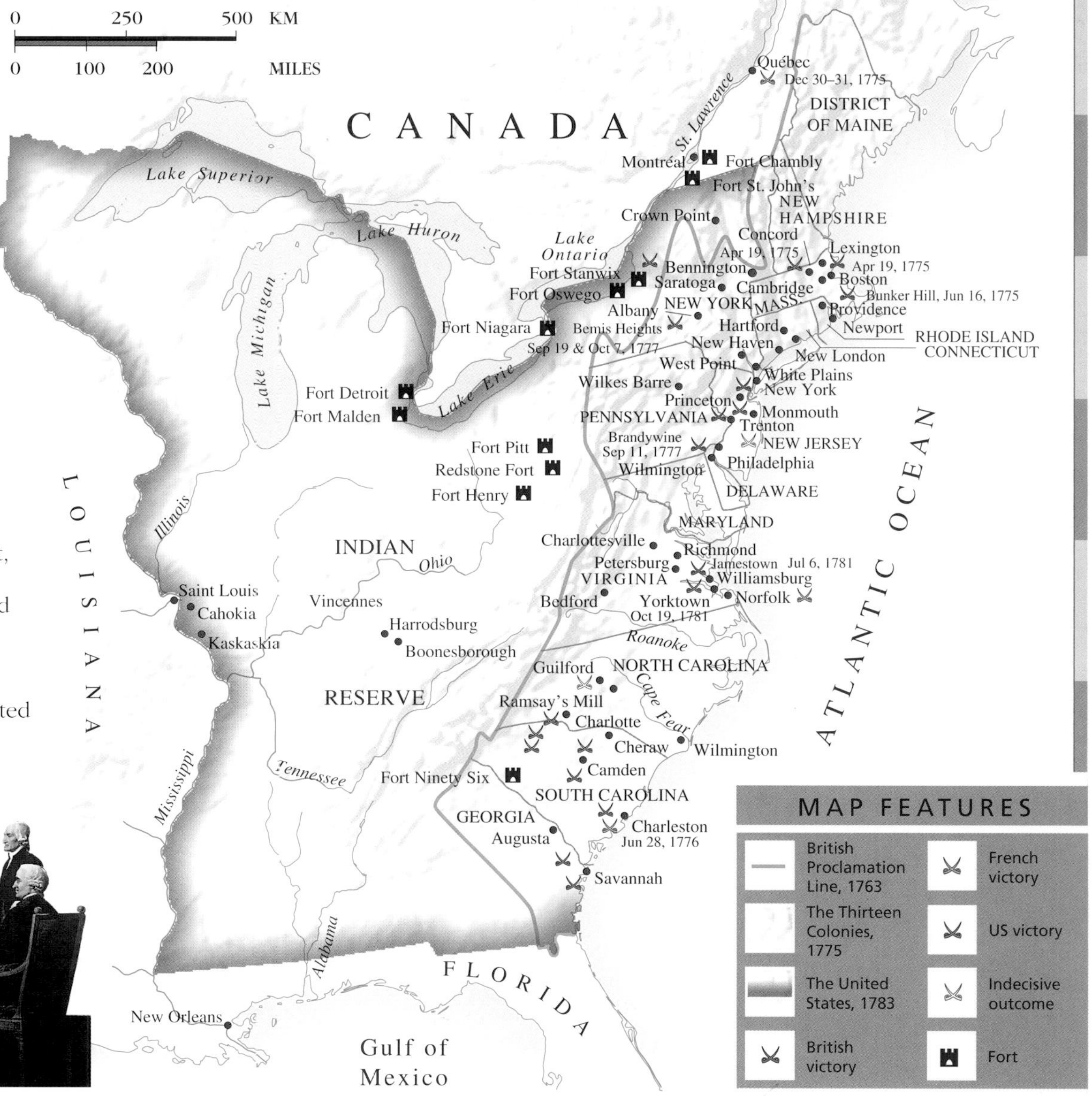

MAP FEATURES

—	British Proclamation Line, 1763	⚔	French victory
	The Thirteen Colonies, 1775	⚔	US victory
	The United States, 1783	⚔	Indecisive outcome
⚔	British victory	🏰	Fort

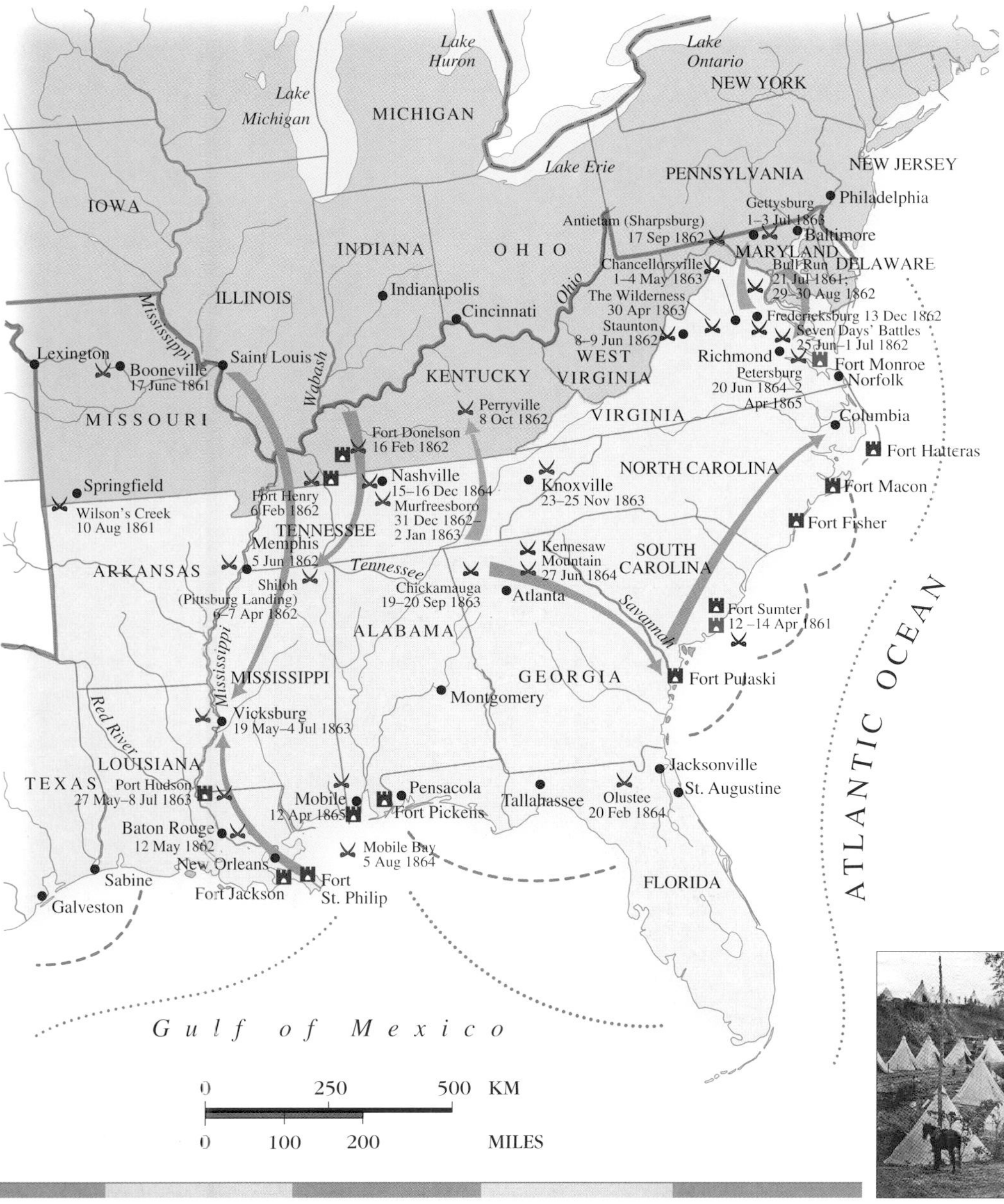

THE CIVIL WAR, 1861–65

Slavery was opposed in the industrialized North, but supported in the agricultural South. In 1860 the issue came to a head when 7 southern states formed the Confederacy. The civil war started in 1861 when Confederate troops fired on Fort Sumter. Union forces, with more men and equipment, eventually wore down the Confederate troops, who surrendered in 1865. Over half a million lives had been lost.

Map labels (Civil War):
Lake Huron
Lake Ontario
Lake Michigan
Lake Erie
NEW YORK
MICHIGAN
PENNSYLVANIA
NEW JERSEY
IOWA
Gettysburg 1–3 Jul 1863
Philadelphia
INDIANA
OHIO
Antietam (Sharpsburg) 17 Sep 1862
Baltimore
ILLINOIS
Indianapolis
Chancellorsville 1–4 May 1863
MARYLAND
DELAWARE
Cincinnati
Bull Run 21 Jul 1861; 29–30 Aug 1862
Ohio
The Wilderness 30 May 1863
Staunton
Fredericksburg 13 Dec 1862
Lexington
Booneville 17 June 1861
Saint Louis
Wabash
Seven Days' Battles 25 Jun–1 Jul 1862
Richmond
Fort Monroe
Norfolk
WEST VIRGINIA
Petersburg 20 Jun 1864–2 Apr 1865
MISSOURI
KENTUCKY
VIRGINIA
Columbia
Springfield
Perryville 8 Oct 1862
Fort Donelson 16 Feb 1862
Fort Hatteras
Wilson's Creek 10 Aug 1861
Fort Henry 6 Feb 1862
Nashville 15–16 Dec 1864
NORTH CAROLINA
Fort Macon
Knoxville 23–25 Nov 1863
Murfreesboro 31 Dec 1862–2 Jan 1863
TENNESSEE
Memphis 5 Jun 1862
Fort Fisher
ARKANSAS
Tennessee
Kennesaw Mountain 27 Jun 1864
SOUTH CAROLINA
Shiloh (Pittsburg Landing) 6–7 Apr 1862
Chickamauga 19–20 Sep 1863
Atlanta
Fort Sumter 12–14 Apr 1861
ALABAMA
MISSISSIPPI
GEORGIA
Savannah
Fort Pulaski
Red River
Vicksburg 19 May–4 Jul 1863
Montgomery
LOUISIANA
Jacksonville
St. Augustine
TEXAS
Port Hudson 27 May–8 Jul 1863
Mobile 12 Apr 1865
Pensacola
Tallahassee
Olustee 20 Feb 1864
Baton Rouge 12 May 1862
Fort Pickens
Sabine
New Orleans
Mobile Bay 5 Aug 1864
FLORIDA
Fort Jackson
Fort St. Philip
Galveston
ATLANTIC OCEAN
Gulf of Mexico
0 250 500 KM
0 100 200 MILES

MAP FEATURES

	Confederate states, 1861	····	Union sea blockades, 1861–62
	Union states, 1861	– – –	Union sea blockades, 1863–65
🏰	Union fort	→	Confederate campaign
🏰	Confederate fort	→	Union campaign
⚔	Union victory	—	Northern limit of slave states
⚔	Confederate victory		

RUINS OF RICHMOND

In 1862 Union forces, defeated by the South's superior military skills, were repulsed when they attempted to take Richmond, the Confederate capital. It eventually fell to Union troops in 1865, and most of the city was torched.

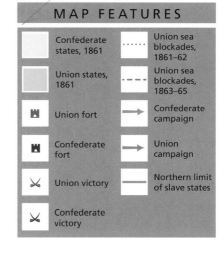

A MODERN WAR

Many aspects of 20th-century conflict first appeared during the Civil War. Railroads were used to transport troops, messages were sent by telegraph, and news photographers recorded the devastation of war for their readers.

A NEW NATION

THE MASSIVE EXPANSION, by conquest and purchase, of US territory in the 19th century opened up the West to farmers, cattle ranchers, and gold prospectors. Covered wagon trains rolled across the Great Plains, and huge areas of new land were brought under the plow by pioneer farmers. The first American steam railroad opened in 1830; by 1880 a network of rail lines crossed the continent, carrying freight and passengers over vast distances and opening up new land for settlement. Immigrants from Europe and Asia poured into both the US and Canada, in search of wealth and opportunity. This influx of people brought the settlers into bloody conflict with the Native American population. Their lands were seized and whole tribes were forcibly relocated to remote reservations.

SETTLING THE CONTINENT

In 1803, France sold all its claims to the area between the Mississippi and the Rocky Mountains for $15 million (the Louisiana Purchase), doubling the size of the US. Settlers poured across the Great Plains in search of better lands and wealth, and railroads, canals, and waterways soon crossed the continent.

AMERICAN PIONEERS

Pioneers crossed the Great Plains in covered wagons, enduring great hardships to reach new lands. The Homestead Act of 1862 gave farmers 160 acres (65 hectares) of land after they had cultivated it for five years.

LAND OF OPPORTUNITY

During the 19th century, nearly 50 million immigrants arrived in Canada and the US. Initially, most of the immigrants came from Britain and northern Europe. After 1880, however, the bulk of the immigrants came from eastern and southern Europe.

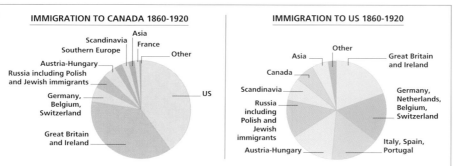

IMMIGRATION TO CANADA 1860-1920

- Asia
- France
- Scandinavia
- Southern Europe
- Other
- Austria-Hungary
- Russia including Polish and Jewish immigrants
- Germany, Belgium, Switzerland
- US
- Great Britain and Ireland

IMMIGRATION TO US 1860-1920

- Asia
- Other
- Great Britain and Ireland
- Canada
- Scandinavia
- Germany, Netherlands, Belgium, Switzerland
- Russia including Polish and Jewish immigrants
- Italy, Spain, Portugal
- Austria-Hungary

Cowboys drove cattle to rail junctions so they could be sent to the East.

CANADA

PACIFIC OCEAN

ROCKY MOUNTAINS

GREAT PLAINS

UNITED STATES OF AMERICA

APPALACHIAN MOUNTAINS

ATLANTIC OCEAN

MEXICO

Gulf of Mexico

Olympia · Portland · Salem · Virginia City · Helena · Bozeman Pass · Boise · Donner Pass · Sacramento · San Francisco · Carson Pass · Carson City · Jenny Lind · Bear Valley · South Pass · Salt Lake City · Cheyenne · Denver · Los Angeles · San Diego · Phoenix · Santa Fe · El Paso · Rio Grande · Red River · Fort Worth · Austin · San Antonio · San Antonio · Bismarck · St. Paul · Pierre · Madison · Des Moines · Chicago · Ogallala · Lincoln · Junction City · Abilene · Topeka · Dodge City · Kansas City · Jefferson City · Springfield · Saint Louis · Indianapolis · Little Rock · Nashville · Jackson · Montgomery · Baton Rouge · New Orleans · Lansing · Cleveland · Columbus · Charleston · Frankfort · Atlanta · Columbia · Raleigh · Richmond · WASHINGTON (DC from 1878) · Dover · Annapolis · Harrisburg · Philadelphia · Trenton · New York · Hartford · Albany · Providence · Boston · Concord · Montpelier · Augusta · Tallahassee

Missouri · Colorado · Mississippi · Ohio · Tennessee

Lake Superior · Lake Michigan · Lake Huron · Lake Erie · Lake Ontario

Immigration from Southeast Asia, China, and Japan

Immigration to US from Europe, total 1860-1920: 28,200,000

New arrivals in the West virtually wiped out the American buffalo.

0 200 400 KM
0 100 200 MILES

MAP FEATURES

- ⬛ European settlement by c.1860
- → Immigration
- ---- Cattle trails
- Railroads
- ── Pony Express route
- ✳ Gold Rush towns 1848–60
- • City

Wagon trails
- ····· Oregon Trail
- ····· Mormon Trail
- ····· Central Overland Trail
- ····· Santa Fe Trail
- ····· Old Spanish Trail
- ····· California Trail
- ····· Bozeman Trail

NEW YORK CITY

New York was the main port of entry for many immigrants arriving from Europe. Many settled there; the notorious slum districts of the Lower East Side provided a home for many new arrivals. The city developed into a lively patchwork of ethnic districts.

Gold brought many settlers to the West. In 1849 a gold-rush hit California.

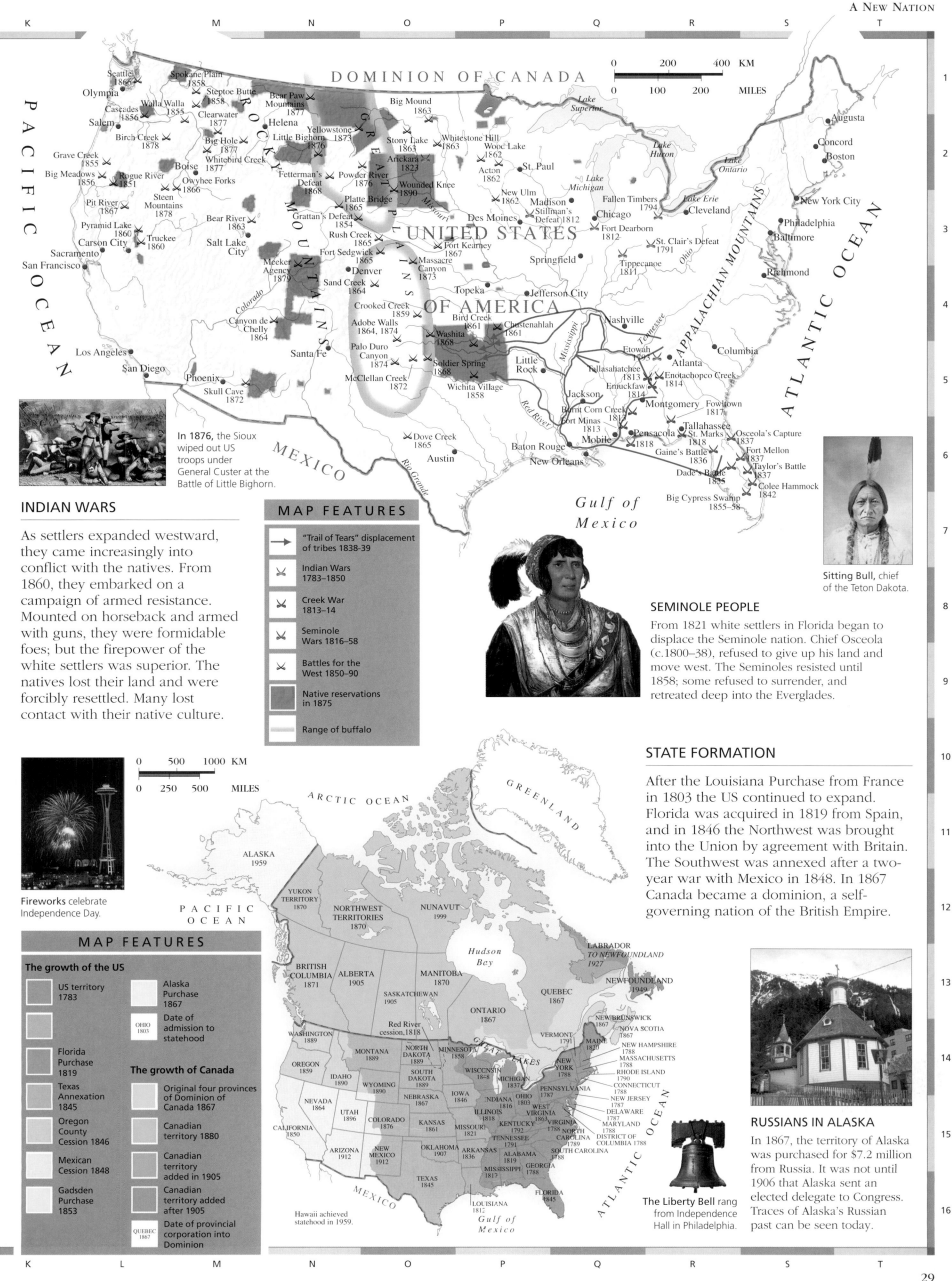

INDIAN WARS

As settlers expanded westward, they came increasingly into conflict with the natives. From 1860, they embarked on a campaign of armed resistance. Mounted on horseback and armed with guns, they were formidable foes; but the firepower of the white settlers was superior. The natives lost their land and were forcibly resettled. Many lost contact with their native culture.

In 1876, the Sioux wiped out US troops under General Custer at the Battle of Little Bighorn.

MAP FEATURES

"Trail of Tears" displacement of tribes 1838-39

Indian Wars 1783–1850

Creek War 1813–14

Seminole Wars 1816–58

Battles for the West 1850–90

Native reservations in 1875

Range of buffalo

Sitting Bull, chief of the Teton Dakota.

SEMINOLE PEOPLE

From 1821 white settlers in Florida began to displace the Seminole nation. Chief Osceola (c.1800–38), refused to give up his land and move west. The Seminoles resisted until 1858; some refused to surrender, and retreated deep into the Everglades.

STATE FORMATION

After the Louisiana Purchase from France in 1803 the US continued to expand. Florida was acquired in 1819 from Spain, and in 1846 the Northwest was brought into the Union by agreement with Britain. The Southwest was annexed after a two-year war with Mexico in 1848. In 1867 Canada became a dominion, a self-governing nation of the British Empire.

Fireworks celebrate Independence Day.

MAP FEATURES

The growth of the US

US territory 1783

Alaska Purchase 1867

OHIO 1803 Date of admission to statehood

Florida Purchase 1819

Texas Annexation 1845

Oregon County Cession 1846

Mexican Cession 1848

Gadsden Purchase 1853

The growth of Canada

Original four provinces of Dominion of Canada 1867

Canadian territory 1880

Canadian territory added in 1905

Canadian territory added after 1905

QUEBEC 1867 Date of provincial corporation into Dominion

Hawaii achieved statehood in 1959.

RUSSIANS IN ALASKA

In 1867, the territory of Alaska was purchased for $7.2 million from Russia. It was not until 1906 that Alaska sent an elected delegate to Congress. Traces of Alaska's Russian past can be seen today.

The Liberty Bell rang from Independence Hall in Philadelphia.

THE PEOPLES OF NORTH AMERICA

NORTH AMERICA TODAY is a diverse ethnic patchwork. In the 19th and early 20th centuries, most immigration to the continent was from Europe. But after World War II, and especially during the more liberal 1960s, this situation changed, and increasing numbers of immigrants from Asia, South and Central America, and Africa were admitted to both the US and Canada. The 1960s also brought an end to laws that discriminated against the black population of the US, following nonviolent protest campaigns in the 1950s led by the influential Martin Luther King, Jr. Since the 1960s, North America has become a haven for many political refugees: the Cubans of Miami, who have fled from the communist regime of Fidel Castro, are the largest group. Illegal immigration from Mexico to the US is a continuing problem – each year the immigration service sends back over a million illegal Mexican immigrants.

NATIVE AMERICANS

In the 1950s and 1960s many Native Americans were encouraged to move from reservations to urban areas. They were offered tickets and financial assistance; the goal was to end reservations. Today, over half the US and Canada's 2.5 million natives now live outside reservations. The American Indian Movement was founded in 1968 to promote natives' rights.

POW WOW

Blackfoot and other Plains nations celebrate at a pow wow in Edmonton, Canada. At least 2,000 annual pow wows are held across the US and Canada. They celebrate and preserve the culture of America's first settlers. Visitors can also learn about native ways of life.

MAP FEATURES

Native reservations 1970	Urban relocation destinations 1970

Native American population by state or province

Under 10,000	50,000-100,000
10,000-50,000	100,000-200,000

• Selected pow wow sites 1995

0   500   1000 KM

0   250   500   MILES

NAVAJO CRAFTS

Over 200,000 Navajo live on the largest reservation in the US, which sprawls across Arizona and New Mexico. Traditional Navajo art, such as weaving and silverwork, is an important source of income. Weaving skills are passed down from mother to daughter.

CASINOS

Native Americans' rights to their own lands, confirmed by an Act of Congress in 1988, have enabled them to open casinos in 33 states. Profits are used to pay for health care, schools, and houses. But there are worries about the impact of gambling on traditional societies.

ASIAN POPULATION

Asian immigration to North America has increased over the past 20 years. Most immigrants from Asia settle in states bordering the Pacific Ocean. There are also Vietnamese enclaves in Minnesota and Wisconsin and a large Korean population in New York. South Asians have mostly settled in Canada, especially British Columbia.

CHINATOWN

The Chinese first arrived in New York in the late 19th century. Chinatown in San Francisco is the largest US Chinese enclave.

CANADIAN SIKHS

South Asians have settled throughout Canada. Sikhs from the Punjab are concentrated in the Vancouver region, where their numbers exceed 40,000.

MAP FEATURES

Asian population by state

- over 100,000
- 50,000-99,999
- 25,000-49,999
- 10,000-24,999
- Less than 10,000

HISPANICS IN THE US

Mexicans have been migrating to the US since the 19th century. They provided labor for mines, farms, and railroad construction. In the 20th century, they dispersed from the border regions of Texas and California to the rest of the US. In the 1970s, immigrants from Central America also began to move north, driven by civil wars and economic hardship.

ALASKA

HAWAII

WASHINGTON, MONTANA, NORTH DAKOTA, VERMONT, MAINE, OREGON, IDAHO, WYOMING, SOUTH DAKOTA, MINNESOTA, WISCONSIN, NEW YORK, NEW HAMPSHIRE, MASSACHUSETTS, RHODE ISLAND, CONNECTICUT, MICHIGAN, NEVADA, NEBRASKA, IOWA, ILLINOIS, INDIANA, OHIO, PENNSYLVANIA, NEW JERSEY, DELAWARE, MARYLAND, WEST VIRGINIA, VIRGINIA, CALIFORNIA, UTAH, COLORADO, KANSAS, MISSOURI, KENTUCKY, NORTH CAROLINA, ARIZONA, NEW MEXICO, OKLAHOMA, ARKANSAS, TENNESSEE, SOUTH CAROLINA, GEORGIA, MISSISSIPPI, ALABAMA, TEXAS, LOUISIANA, FLORIDA

MAP FEATURES

Hispanics as a percentage of total population

- 7.9–38.2
- 4.0–7.8
- 2.0–3.9
- 1.0–1.9
- 0.5–0.9

BORDER PATROL

The US-Mexican border is heavily patrolled in order to prevent illegal immigration. Many would-be immigrants are sent back, then try again.

LANGUAGES

Several hundred native tongues – ranging from Sioux to Mayan and Inuit – were spoken before the Europeans arrived in the Americas. Today, the colonial languages – English, Spanish and French predominate. Most Native American languages have now been lost, though languages such as Navajo and Mohawk are still spoken on some reservations.

Inuit is still spoken in the far north.

MAP FEATURES

Language groups

- Native American
- English
- Romance
- Eskimo-Aleut
- Uninhabited

ARCTIC OCEAN

PACIFIC OCEAN

Hudson Bay

Edmonton, Saskatoon, Vancouver, Calgary, Winnipeg, Seattle, Portland, Québec, Montréal, OTTAWA, Toronto, Boston, Milwaukee, Detroit, New York, Chicago, Cleveland, Philadelphia, Baltimore, San Francisco, Indianapolis, Columbus, WASHINGTON DC, Kansas City, Memphis, Los Angeles, Phoenix, El Paso, Dallas, Jacksonville, Houston, New Orleans, Miami

Gulf of Mexico

ATLANTIC OCEAN

ESKIMO–ALEUT, ATHABASCAN, ALGONQUIN, FRENCH, ENGLISH, ENGLISH/SPANISH, UTO-AZTECAN, FRENCH/ENGLISH, ENGLISH/SPANISH, MAYAN

0   500   1000 KM
0   250   500   MILES

0   500   1000 KM
0   250   500   MILES

0   1000   2000 KM
0   500   1000   MILES

POLITICAL NORTH AMERICA

THE US, CANADA, AND MEXICO are all federal democracies. Political power is shared between national and state governments. Issues of national and international interest, such as income tax, defense, and trade policy, are dealt with by the national government, while more local issues, such as health and education, are handled by the state. Both the US and Canada, two of the world's wealthiest countries, are politically stable, but Mexico has had a troubled history of dictatorship and revolt – as recently as 1994, there was a rebellion by landless peasants in the south. In Canada, two political issues dominate: the rights of native Canadians to their own lands and culture, and the desire of the French-speaking minority in Quebec to separate from the rest of Canada. In the US, pockets of severe urban poverty and rising crime figures are both hotly debated issues.

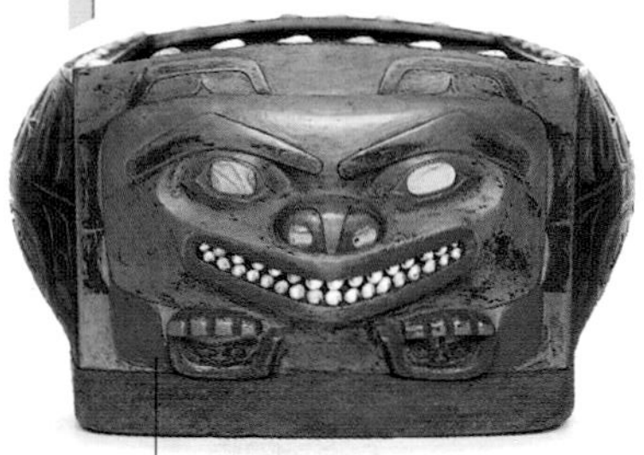

GUN LAWS

The Bill of Rights is a series of 10 amendments to the US Constitution (1788), guaranteeing certain personal liberties, such as freedom of speech and the right to bear arms. Many people now question liberal gun laws, arguing that easy access to weapons is fueling the rising crime figures in the US.

INUIT PARLIAMENT

There are some 38,000 Inuit living in northern Canada. The Inuit have long laid claim to their northern lands, and in 1992 an agreement was reached with the government. In 1999, the Inuit Nunavut area became a territory with its own parliament, the first part of Canada to be governed by indigenous people in modern history.

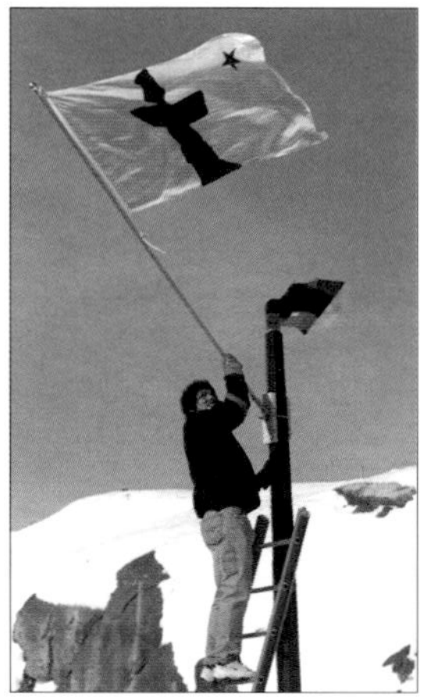

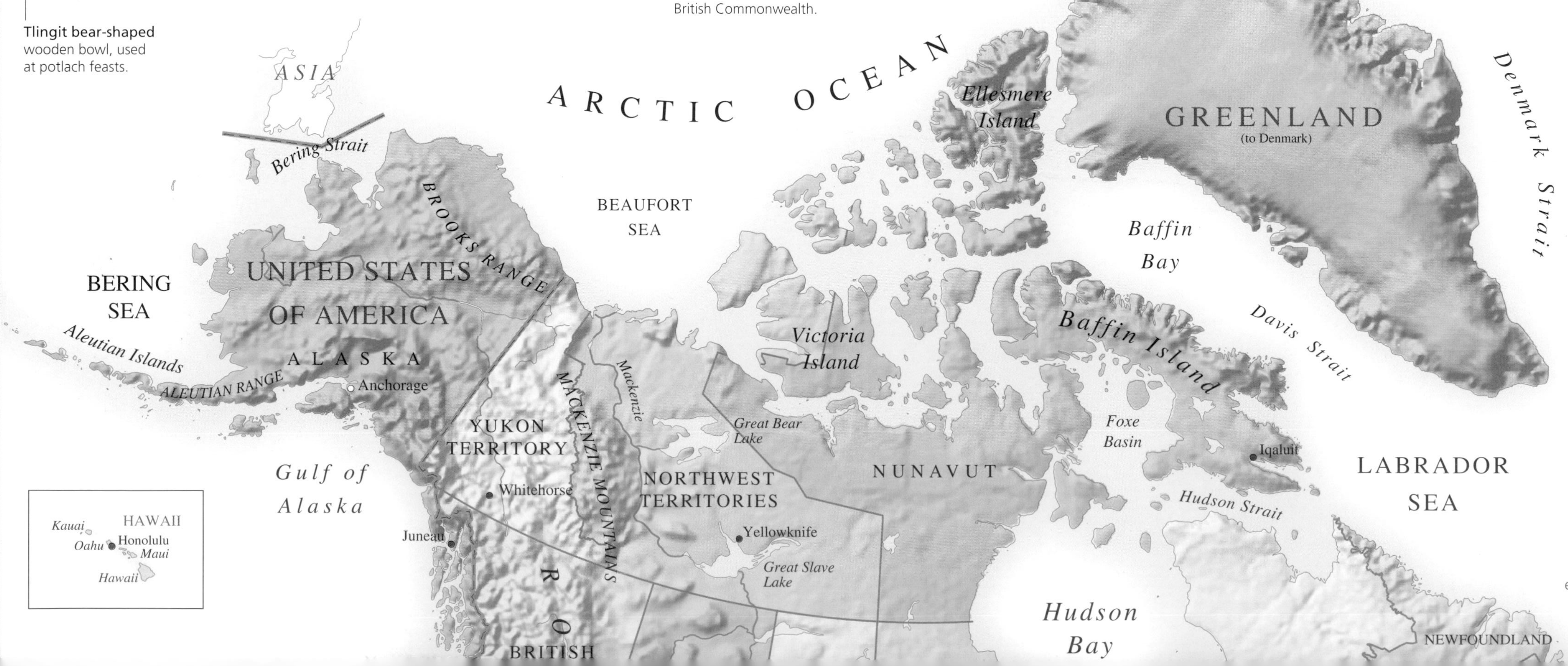

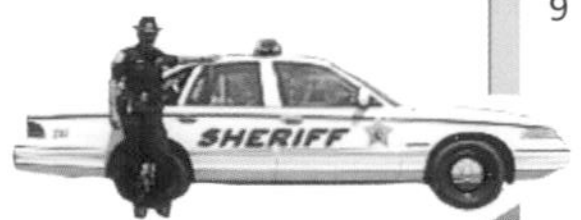

POTLACH REVIVAL

There are some 630,000 Canadians of indigenous descent living in the north. Government attempts to suppress native culture are now being overturned. The Tlingit potlach ceremony, a lavish ritual of feasting and gift-giving, was banned from 1884 to 1951, but is now being revived.

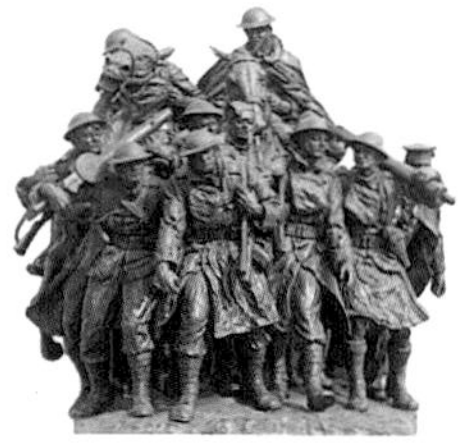

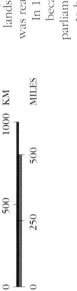

Tlingit bear-shaped wooden bowl, used at potlach feasts.

Canadian troops have fought in both world wars as part of the British Commonwealth.

Sheriffs are US law enforcement officers elected by popular vote.

MILES / KM 0 250 500 0 500 1000

Denmark Strait

GREENLAND (to Denmark)

LABRADOR SEA

NEWFOUNDLAND

Baffin Bay

Davis Strait

Hudson Strait

Iqaluit

Baffin Island

Foxe Basin

Ellesmere Island

NUNAVUT

Hudson Bay

ARCTIC OCEAN

Victoria Island

Great Bear Lake

NORTHWEST TERRITORIES

Yellowknife

Great Slave Lake

BEAUFORT SEA

Mackenzie

MACKENZIE MOUNTAINS

BROOKS RANGE

YUKON TERRITORY

Whitehorse

BRITISH

ASIA

Bering Strait

UNITED STATES OF AMERICA

ALASKA

Anchorage

Juneau

Gulf of Alaska

BERING SEA

Aleutian Islands

ALEUTIAN RANGE

HAWAII

Honolulu

Oahu

Kauai

Maui

Hawaii

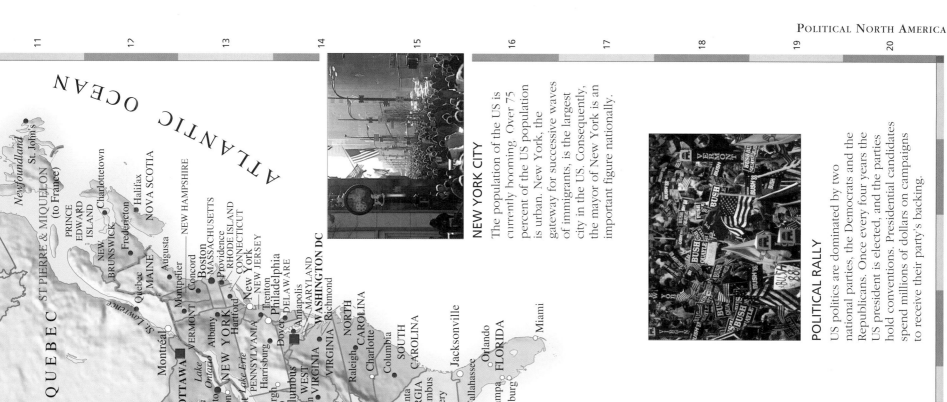

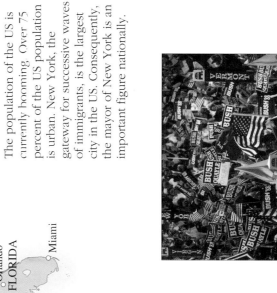

NEW YORK CITY

The population of the US is currently booming. Over 75 percent of the US population is urban. New York, the gateway for successive waves of immigrants, is the largest city in the US. Consequently, the mayor of New York is an important figure nationally.

POLITICAL RALLY

US politics are dominated by two national parties, the Democrats and the Republicans. Once every four years the US president is elected, and the parties hold conventions. Presidential candidates spend millions of dollars on campaigns to receive their party's backing.

MEXICO CITY

Over 70% of the Mexican population lives in cities; and people living in extreme poverty in rural areas continue to move to cities. With a population of over 16.7 million, Mexico City is sprawling, unplanned, and heavily polluted. Yet it is Mexico's most economically developed region.

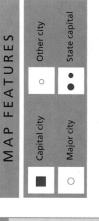

Benito Juarez (1806–72), founder of the Democratic Republic of Mexico.

THE LONGEST BORDER

The US and Canada share the longest undefended border in the world, and access between the two countries is easy. Recently, problems have been caused by US border industries which are responsible for much of the acid rain that is damaging Canada's forests.

CALIFORNIA STATE CAPITOL

The state governments of the US mirror the federal government in Washington, DC. Each state has its own constitution, and is headed by an elected governor. Representatives (the state legislature) are responsible for lawmaking. States run their own health, education, and penal systems.

MAP FEATURES

■ Capital city	●	Other city
○ Major city	●	State capital

33

NORTH AMERICA

NORTH AMERICA LOOKS LIKE a gigantic downward-pointing triangle out of which two bites have been taken – Hudson Bay and the Gulf of Mexico. Huge parallel mountain chains run down the eastern and western sides. The oldest are the Appalachians to the east, which have been worn away by wind and rain for so long that they are now considerably lower than the younger Rockies to the west. The vast landscape between the mountain chains is mostly flat. There are large forests in the north, while the central Great Plains are covered by grasslands on which huge herds of buffalo once roamed. North America is a continent of climatic extremes. In the farthest north, temperatures drop to a freezing -87°F (-66°C), and a dome of ice up to 2 miles (3 km) thick covers Greenland. In the hot deserts of the southwest, temperatures can soar to 134°F (57°C).

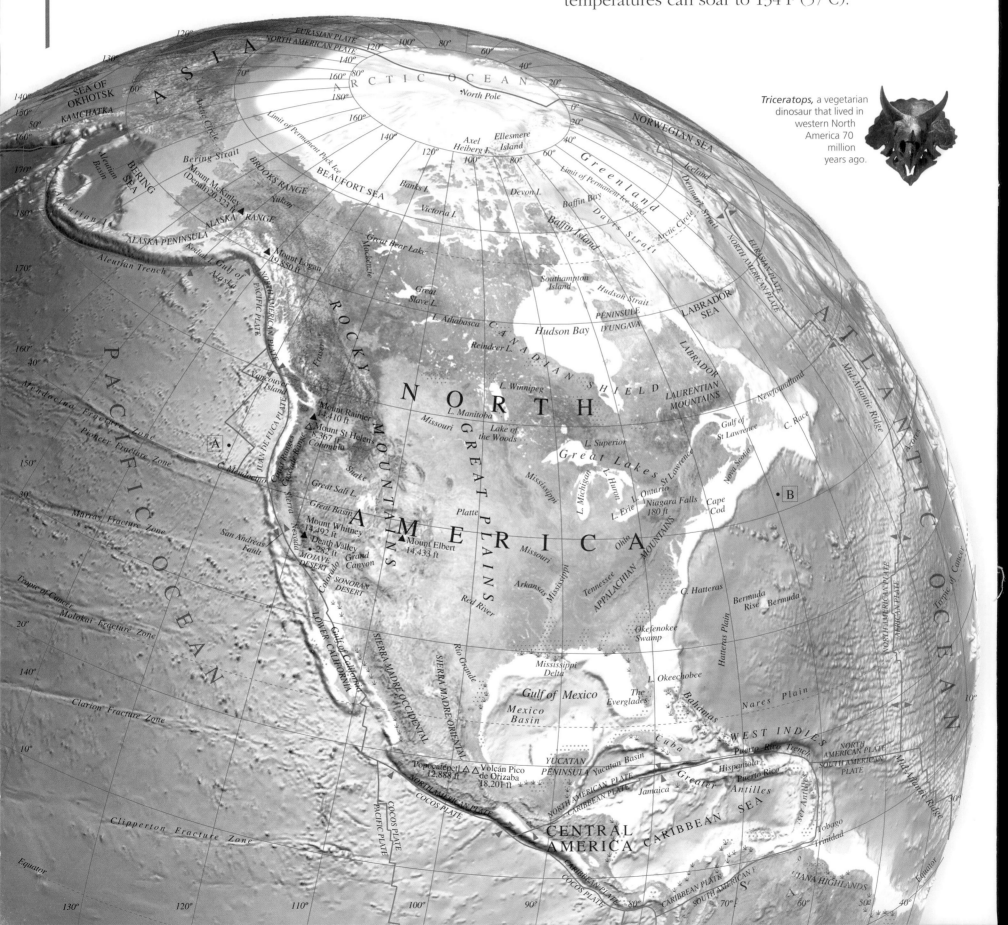

Triceratops, a vegetarian dinosaur that lived in western North America 70 million years ago.

Douglas fir cone
Pseudotsuga menziesii
Length: 3 in (8 cm)

Road runner
Geococcyx californianus
Length: 2 ft (60 cm)

Loggerhead
turtle
Caretta caretta
Length: 4 ft (1.2 m)

FALL IN ALASKA

Only short grasses, low shrubs, and small trees can survive the climate of the northern tundra. In the brief Alaskan summer, plants burst into bloom, changing color in fall.

▲ THE ROOF OF AMERICA

When water-laden ocean air rises over the Alaska Range, moisture freezes and falls as snow. It is so cold that mountain slopes as low as 3,000 ft (900 m) are always snow-covered.

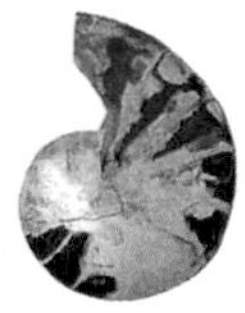

Eutrephoceras, which lived in North America 100 million years ago. It swam by squirting water out of its body cavity.

▲ VOLCANIC ACTIVITY

The volcanic island of Iceland lies above the Mid-Atlantic Ridge. Intense heat generated deep underground creates bubbling hot mud pools and hot springs.

Priscacara, a perch that swam in North America's lakes and rivers 50 million years ago.

RAIN FORESTS

Temperate rain forests thrive between the Pacific and the Coast Ranges. Heavy rainfall carried inland by moist ocean winds makes their lush growth possible.

▲ RIVERS, TREES, AND GRASSLAND

For millions of years, rivers flowing east from the Rockies have deposited silt on the Great Plains. This has helped to create a deep and very fertile soil which supports huge areas of grassland.

NORTHERN FORESTS

Forests grow across most of the northern region and on cold mountain slopes. These contain mostly coniferous trees which are well suited to growing in cold conditions.

Coast redwood
Sequoia sempervirens
Height: 330 ft (100 m)

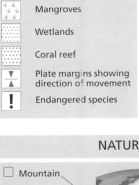

DRY WINDS AND SAND DUNES

Dry winds blowing from the center of the continent, combined with the lack of rain, are responsible for the extensive deserts in the southwest. Because the climate is so dry, vegetation is sparse.

DESERT RIVER

The brown silt-laden waters of the Colorado River have cut a spectacular gorge through solid rock – the Grand Canyon – nearly 6,135 ft (2,000 m) deep.

OKEFENOKEE SWAMP

The Okefenokee Swamp is part of the complex river system of the southeast. This large wetland area has a warm climate, providing a haven for reptiles such as alligators and snakes. It is also an important resting place for many migratory birds.

Bald eagle
Haliaeetus leucocephalus
Wingspan: 7 ft (2.2 m)

KEY TO SYMBOLS

▲	Mountain
△	Volcano
	Mangroves
	Wetlands
	Coral reef
▼ ▲	Plate margins showing direction of movement
!	Endangered species

DESERT TREES

With searing temperatures and low rainfall, deserts are home to plants which are adapted to conserve water, like cacti and the Joshua trees shown here.

American beaver
Castor canadensis
Length: 5 ft (1.6 m)

NATURAL VEGETATION ZONES

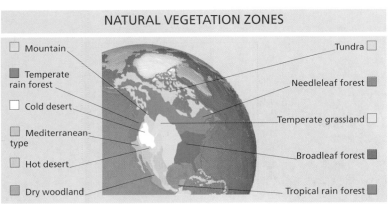

	Mountain	Tundra	
	Temperate rain forest	Needleleaf forest	
	Cold desert	Temperate grassland	
	Mediterranean-type		
	Hot desert	Broadleaf forest	
	Dry woodland	Tropical rain forest	

CROSS-SECTION THROUGH NORTH AMERICA

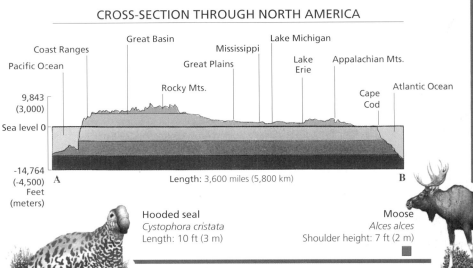

Great Basin
Lake Michigan
Mississippi
Coast Ranges
Great Plains
Lake Erie
Appalachian Mts.
Pacific Ocean
Rocky Mts.
Cape Cod
Atlantic Ocean

9,843 (3,000)
Sea level 0
-14,764 (-4,500)
Feet (meters)

A

Length: 3,600 miles (5,800 km)

B

Hooded seal
Cystophora cristata
Length: 10 ft (3 m)

Moose
Alces alces
Shoulder height: 7 ft (2 m)

WESTERN CANADA AND ALASKA

THOUSANDS OF YEARS AGO, the first people to settle in North America crossed the Bering Strait and arrived in present-day Alaska. Their descendants – peoples such as the Inuit (Eskimos) – still inhabit this region. European immigrants began to arrive in large numbers in the 19th century. Alaska was bought by the US from Russia for $7.2 million in 1867. Many Americans thought this was a waste of money until gold was discovered there in 1896 and then oil in 1968. Canada is a huge country with a small population, most of which lives in cities within about 100 miles (160 km) of the Canada-US border. The fertile plains and dense forest in the south give way to tundra and icefields farther north.

ALASKAN OIL

The largest oilfield in the US is at Prudhoe Bay in Alaska. But drilling is made difficult by temperatures as low as -110° F (-79° C), ground that is frozen for most of the year, and long periods of darkness in winter. Look for ⚒

LOGGING

About 40 percent of Canada is covered by forests. Until recently, there were no controls on logging, and huge areas of forest were cut down. Trees like this one are used to make lumber or plywood. Look for 🌲

UNITED STATES
pop: 268,739,000
(ALASKA)
pop: 609,000

PIPELINE

When the 795-mile (1,270-km) long Trans-Alaskan pipeline from Prudhoe Bay to the ice-free port of Valdez was constructed, it was feared it would harm the environment and wildlife of this remote and beautiful region. To prevent disruption to the moose and caribou migration routes, and to stop the pipeline from freezing, it was raised on stilts above ground. The pipeline crosses plains, mountain ranges, and several rivers on its journey south.

MAP FEATURES

Oil: Alberta is rich in oil, but new sources are being sought, such as the tar sands near Athabasca where the oil has to be separated from sand. Look for ⚒	
Border: The world's longest undefended border runs between Canada and the US. People and goods can cross it with few restrictions. Look for ⬇	
Radar: The joint Canada-US Distant Early Warning system has been a key component in the defense of the North American continent since 1957. Look for ◡	

🐂 Cattle		⛏ Mining	
🌾 Cereals		✳ Coal	
🪓 Timber		🛢 Gas	
🐟 Fishing		🏭 Industrial center	

CALGARY STAMPEDE

The city of Calgary in Alberta started life as a center for the cattle trade. Although today it is an oil center, its cowboy traditions are continued in the Stampede, a huge rodeo held every July. For 10 days, spectators watch events that include bronco-busting, bull-riding, and chuck-wagon racing.

VANCOUVER

This city began as a small settlement for loggers and is now a major port. Grain from Canada's prairies and timber from its forests are shipped from Vancouver's ice-free harbor to countries across the Pacific. The city has attracted many immigrants; at first from Europe, then more recently from Asia.

Brilliant fall colors
in British Columbia.

Map labels

ARCTIC OCEAN
Attu I.
Agattu I.
Kiska I.
Adak I.
Atka I.
Amlia I.
Aleutian Islands
BERING SEA
Umnak I.
Dutch Harbor
Unalaska I.
Unimak I.
Bering Strait
Kotzebue Sound
St. Lawrence I.
St. Matthew I.
Nunivak I.
Gold
Nome
Norton Sound
Bethel
Bristol Bay
Shelikof Strait
Kodiak
Kodiak I.
Colville River
Barrow
BROOKS RANGE
Prudhoe Bay
BEAUFORT
Mackenzie Bay
Tuktoyaktuk
Yukon River
ALASKA (part of US)
ALASKA RANGE
Fairbanks
Porcupine River
Old Crow
Gold
Inuvik
Ft. McPherson
Tanana River
Yukon River
Iliamna L.
Dairy
Palmer
Anchorage
Kenai
Homer
Valdez
Seward
Cordova
Dawson
YUKON TERRITORY
Norman Wells
Gulf of Alaska
Kluane L.
Pelly River
Lead
Silver
Faro
Zinc
Haines Junction
WHITEHORSE
Teslin L.
Skagway
Haines
Watson Lake
JUNEAU
Sitka
Alexander Archipelago
Petersburg
Wrangell
Ketchikan
PACIFIC OCEAN
Fort Nelson
Queen Charlotte Is.
Prince Rupert
Kitimat
Silver
Copper
Nechako
Prince George
Queen Charlotte Sound
BRITISH COLUMBIA
ROCKY MOUNTAINS
MACKENZIE MTS
Port Hardy
Campbell River
Vancouver I.
Trans-Canada Highway
Squamish
Dairy
Vancouver
VICTORIA

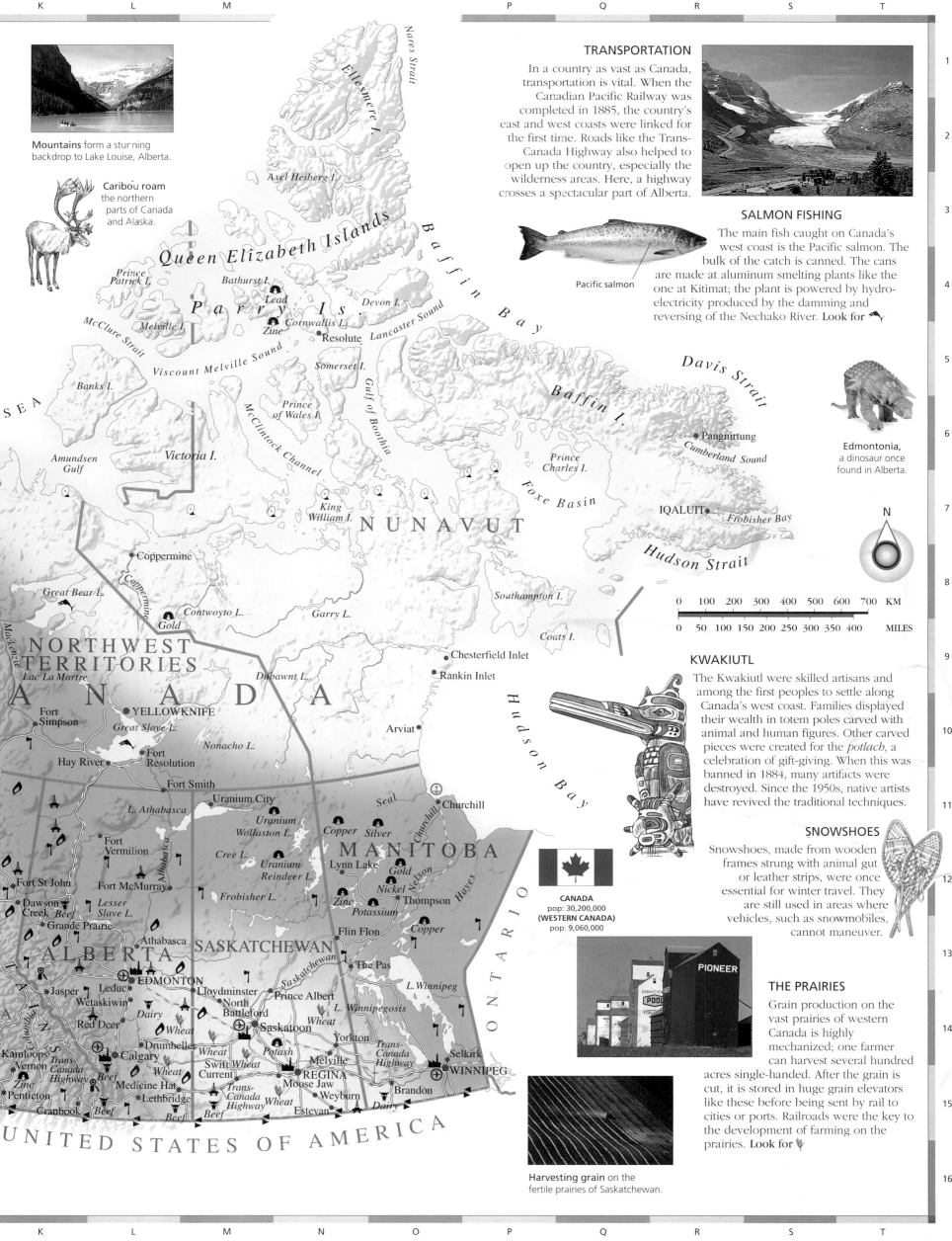

Mountains form a stunning backdrop to Lake Louise, Alberta.

Caribou roam the northern parts of Canada and Alaska.

TRANSPORTATION

In a country as vast as Canada, transportation is vital. When the Canadian Pacific Railway was completed in 1885, the country's east and west coasts were linked for the first time. Roads like the Trans-Canada Highway also helped to open up the country, especially the wilderness areas. Here, a highway crosses a spectacular part of Alberta.

SALMON FISHING

The main fish caught on Canada's west coast is the Pacific salmon. The bulk of the catch is canned. The cans are made at aluminum smelting plants like the one at Kitimat; the plant is powered by hydro-electricity produced by the damming and reversing of the Nechako River. Look for

Pacific salmon

Edmontonia, a dinosaur once found in Alberta.

KWAKIUTL

The Kwakiutl were skilled artisans and among the first peoples to settle along Canada's west coast. Families displayed their wealth in totem poles carved with animal and human figures. Other carved pieces were created for the *potlach*, a celebration of gift-giving. When this was banned in 1884, many artifacts were destroyed. Since the 1950s, native artists have revived the traditional techniques.

SNOWSHOES

Snowshoes, made from wooden frames strung with animal gut or leather strips, were once essential for winter travel. They are still used in areas where vehicles, such as snowmobiles, cannot maneuver.

CANADA
pop: 30,200,000
(WESTERN CANADA)
pop: 9,060,000

THE PRAIRIES

Grain production on the vast prairies of western Canada is highly mechanized; one farmer can harvest several hundred acres single-handed. After the grain is cut, it is stored in huge grain elevators like these before being sent by rail to cities or ports. Railroads were the key to the development of farming on the prairies. Look for

Harvesting grain on the fertile prairies of Saskatchewan.

CANADA

NORTHWEST TERRITORIES

NUNAVUT

ALBERTA

SASKATCHEWAN

MANITOBA

ONTARIO

UNITED STATES OF AMERICA

Nares Strait
Ellesmere I.
Axel Heiberg I.
Queen Elizabeth Islands
Baffin Bay
Prince Patrick I.
Bathurst I.
Lead
Devon I.
Melville I.
Cornwallis I.
Zinc
Resolute
Lancaster Sound
McClure Strait
Parry Is.
Somerset I.
Davis Strait
Banks I.
Prince of Wales I.
Baffin I.
SEA
Amundsen Gulf
Victoria I.
McClintock Channel
Gulf of Boothia
Pangnirtung
Cumberland Sound
Prince Charles I.
Foxe Basin
King William I.
IQALUIT
Frobisher Bay
Coppermine
Hudson Strait
Great Bear L.
Coppermine
Contwoyto L.
Gold
Garry L.
Coats I.
Lac La Martre
Dubawnt L.
Chesterfield Inlet
Rankin Inlet
Fort Simpson
YELLOWKNIFE
Great Slave L.
Hudson Bay
Hay River
Nonacho L.
Fort Resolution
Arviat
Fort Smith
Seal
Uranium City
Churchill
L. Athabasca
Uranium
Wollaston L.
Copper
Silver
Fort Vermilion
Cree L.
Nelson
Athabasca
Uranium
Reindeer L.
Lynn Lake
MANITOBA
Fort McMurray
Frobisher L.
Gold
Fort St John
Lesser
Slave L.
Zinc
Nickel
Thompson
Dawson Creek
Beef
Potassium
Hayes
Grande Prairie
Flin Flon
Copper
Athabasca
Jasper
Leduc
EDMONTON
Lloydminster
The Pas
L. Winnipeg
Wetaskiwin
North Battleford
Prince Albert
L. Winnipegosis
Red Deer
Dairy
Saskatchewan
Wheat
Kamloops
Drumheller
Saskatoon
Yorkton
Vernon
Wheat
Wheat
Trans-Canada Highway
Selkirk
Zinc
Calgary
Swift Current
Wheat
Melville
WINNIPEG
Penticton
Wheat
REGINA
Moose Jaw
Brandon
Cranbrook
Medicine Hat
Trans-Canada Highway
Weyburn
Dairy
Lethbridge
Wheat
Estevan
Beef
Beef
ALASKA
Columbia
Mackenzie
SASKATCHEWAN
ONTARIO

EASTERN CANADA

The Toronto Sky Dome, a huge stadium which seats 50,000.

THE VIKINGS WERE THE FIRST Europeans to visit eastern Canada in about AD 986. Then, in the 15th and 16th centuries, two expeditions, one from England and one from France, reached Canada and each claimed it. Traders and fur trappers from the two countries followed, setting up rival trading posts and settlements. The struggle for territory led to war between Britain and France. The French were forced to give up their Canadian territories to Britain in 1763, but the French language is still spoken in the province of Quebec today. Canada eventually achieved effective independence from Britain in 1867. Today, southern Quebec and Ontario form eastern Canada's main industrial region, containing most of its population and two of its largest cities – Montréal and Toronto. The Hudson Bay area, while rich in minerals, is a wilderness of forests, rivers, and lakes. Snowbound for much of the year, it is sparsely inhabited except by Inuit in the far north.

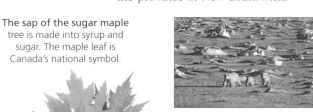

FRENCH / ENGLISH
Most Canadians speak English, but the country is officially bilingual – as can be seen from the use of both French and English on this stamp which commemorates the province of New Brunswick.

The sap of the sugar maple tree is made into syrup and sugar. The maple leaf is Canada's national symbol.

A polar bear mother and cubs on the ice in Hudson Bay.

Evergreen and silver birch forests in southern Quebec.

Thousand Island salad dressing

Salad dressing, named after the islands in the St. Lawrence River.

INDUSTRY

Ontario is Canada's most important industrial province and produces about 55 percent of the country's manufactured goods. Electronics, steel, and food processing are among the major industries, but cars are Ontario's main manufacturing industry and largest export. Many of the factories are owned by US multinational companies.
Look for 🏭

HOCKEY
In winter, Canadians play or watch their favorite sport: hockey. The country produces some of the best players in the world.

TORONTO

The CN tower – the world's tallest free-standing structure – dominates the skyline of Toronto, seen here across the waters of Lake Ontario. Toronto is Canada's biggest city, the main commercial and industrial center, and an important port. Toronto and its surrounding area produce over half Canada's manufactured goods. Its wealthy, multicultural population includes Italians, Chinese, Greeks, and Poles.

MAP FEATURES
Potatoes: The Atlantic provinces, especially Prince Edward Island, grow some of North America's finest potatoes – seed-potatoes in particular. Look for ⚘

Mining: Canada is rich in iron ore, nickel, gold, silver, and other minerals and is a major uranium exporter – mainly from Ontario. Look for ⛑

High-tech industry: Ottawa has most of the electronics and computer companies in Canada, centered on an area known as Silicon Valley North. Look for 💻

🦐 Mixed fruit		🐟 Shellfishing	
🪓 Timber		⚡ Hydro-electricity	
🎣 Fishing		🏭 Industrial center	

THE MOUNTIES

The Royal Canadian Mounted Police – the Mounties – were established in 1873 during the opening up of the vast areas in the west to trade and industry. Today, they are one of the world's most efficient and sophisticated police forces, with their headquarters in Ottawa.

The Canadian or Horseshoe Falls at Niagara.

OTTAWA

These Parliament buildings in Ottawa, Canada's capital city, were inspired by the British Houses of Parliament. Many older buildings reflect the city's British origins. Others, such as the National Gallery, are thoroughly modern.

Hudson Bay

MANITOBA

C A N A D A

ONTARIO

James Bay

Severn
Winisk
Attawapiskat
Attawapiskat
Albany
Moosonee

Gold
L. Seul
Kenora
Lake of the Woods
L. Nipigon
Iron
Platinum
Thunder Bay
Gold

UNITED STATES OF AMERICA

Lake Superior

Copper
Zinc
Nickel
Gold
Cochrane
Timmins
Wawa
Uranium

Sault Sainte Marie
Nickel
Cobalt
Uranium
Sudbury
Copper
Platinum

Lake Michigan
Lake Huron
Owen Sound
Kitchener
Sarnia
London
Windsor
L. Erie

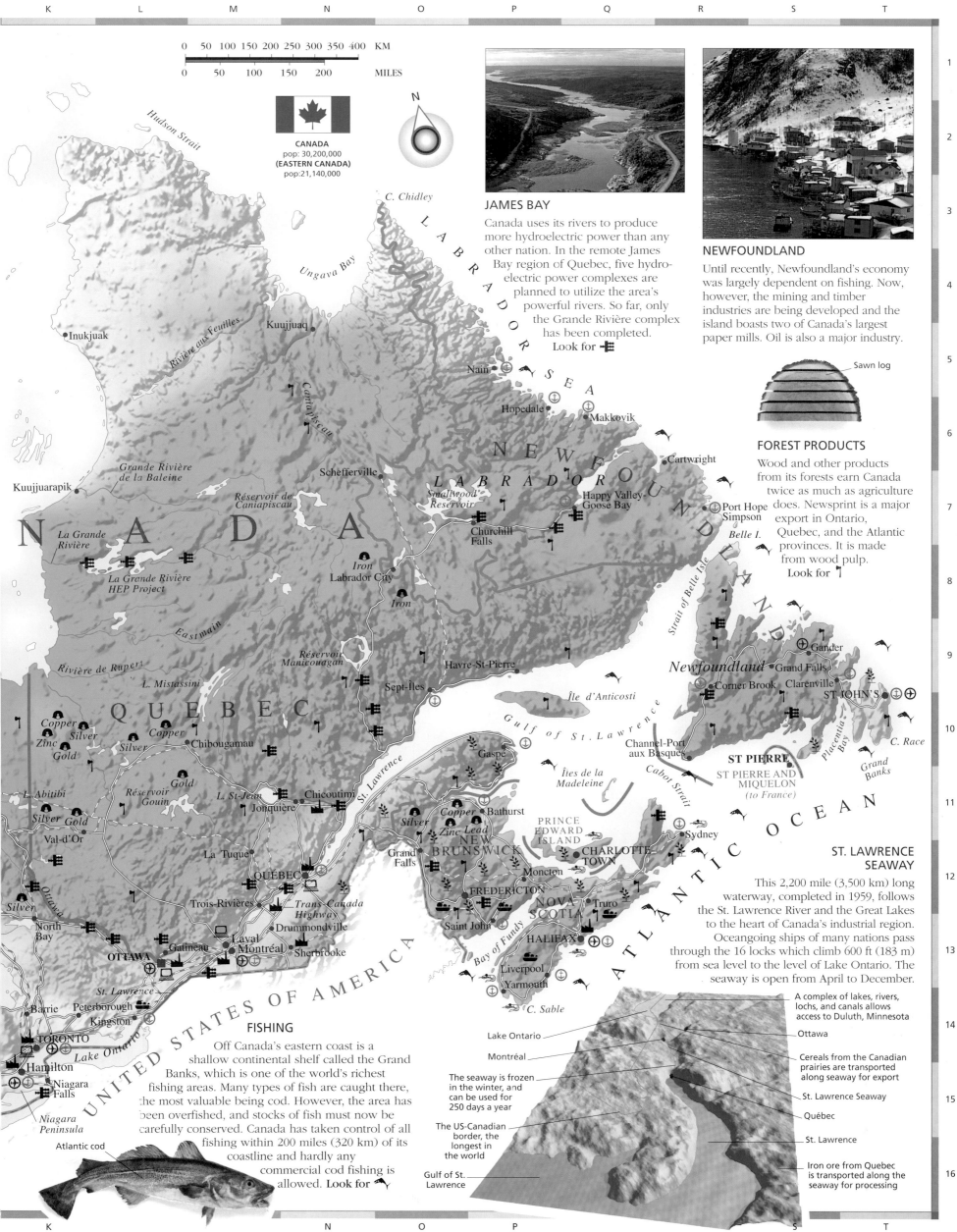

K L M N O P Q R S T

0 50 100 150 200 250 300 350 400 KM

0 50 100 150 200 MILES

N

CANADA
pop: 30,200,000
(EASTERN CANADA)
pop:21,140,000

JAMES BAY

Canada uses its rivers to produce more hydroelectric power than any other nation. In the remote James Bay region of Quebec, five hydro-electric power complexes are planned to utilize the area's powerful rivers. So far, only the Grande Rivière complex has been completed.
Look for

NEWFOUNDLAND

Until recently, Newfoundland's economy was largely dependent on fishing. Now, however, the mining and timber industries are being developed and the island boasts two of Canada's largest paper mills. Oil is also a major industry.

Sawn log

FOREST PRODUCTS

Wood and other products from its forests earn Canada twice as much as agriculture does. Newsprint is a major export in Ontario, Quebec, and the Atlantic provinces. It is made from wood pulp.
Look for

Hudson Strait

C. Chidley

Ungava Bay

Rivière aux Feuilles

L A B R A D O R   S E A

Inukjuak

Kuujjuaq

Caniapiscau

N A D A

Kuujjuarapik

Grande Rivière de la Baleine

Réservoir de Caniapiscau

Schefferville

N E W F O U N D L A N D

Smallwood Reservoir

Happy Valley-Goose Bay

Nain

Hopedale

Makkovik

Cartwright

Port Hope Simpson

Belle I.

La Grande Rivière

La Grande Rivière HEP Project

Eastmain

Iron
Labrador City

Iron

Churchill Falls

L A B R A D O R

Strait of Belle Isle

Gander

Grand Falls

Clarenville

ST. JOHN'S

Newfoundland

Corner Brook

Rivière de Rupert

L. Mistassini

Q U E B E C

Réservoir Manicouagan

Havre-St-Pierre

Sept-Îles

Île d'Anticosti

Gulf of St. Lawrence

Placentia Bay

C. Race

Grand Banks

Copper
Silver
Zinc
Gold

Copper

Silver

Chibougamau

Gold

Réservoir Gouin

L. Abitibi

Silver Gold

Val-d'Or

L. St-Jean

Jonquière

Chicoutimi

Gaspé

Îles de la Madeleine

Cabot Strait

Channel-Port aux Basques

ST PIERRE

ST PIERRE AND MIQUELON
(to France)

A T L A N T I C   O C E A N

La Tuque

Silver

QUÉBEC

Copper
Zinc Lead

Bathurst

PRINCE EDWARD ISLAND

Sydney

Trois-Rivières

Trans-Canada Highway

Grand Falls

N E W B R U N S W I C K

CHARLOTTE-TOWN

Silver

Drummondville

FREDERICTON

Moncton

North Bay

OTTAWA

Gatineau

Laval

Montréal

Sherbrooke

NOVA SCOTIA

Truro

Ottawa

St. Lawrence

Saint John

HALIFAX

Barrie

Peterborough

Kingston

Bay of Fundy

Liverpool

Yarmouth

TORONTO

Hamilton

Niagara Falls

Niagara Peninsula

Lake Ontario

U N I T E D   S T A T E S   O F   A M E R I C A

St. Lawrence

C. Sable

FISHING

Off Canada's eastern coast is a shallow continental shelf called the Grand Banks, which is one of the world's richest fishing areas. Many types of fish are caught there, the most valuable being cod. However, the area has been overfished, and stocks of fish must now be carefully conserved. Canada has taken control of all fishing within 200 miles (320 km) of its coastline and hardly any commercial cod fishing is allowed. Look for

Atlantic cod

ST. LAWRENCE SEAWAY

This 2,200 mile (3,500 km) long waterway, completed in 1959, follows the St. Lawrence River and the Great Lakes to the heart of Canada's industrial region. Oceangoing ships of many nations pass through the 16 locks which climb 600 ft (183 m) from sea level to the level of Lake Ontario. The seaway is open from April to December.

A complex of lakes, rivers, lochs, and canals allows access to Duluth, Minnesota

Lake Ontario

Montréal

The seaway is frozen in the winter, and can be used for 250 days a year

The US-Canadian border, the longest in the world

Gulf of St. Lawrence

Ottawa

Cereals from the Canadian prairies are transported along seaway for export

St. Lawrence Seaway

Québec

St. Lawrence

Iron ore from Quebec is transported along the seaway for processing

K L M N O P S T

NORTHEASTERN UNITED STATES

THE MOST DENSELY populated, heavily industrialized, and ethnically diverse region of the US, the Northeast can be divided into New England – Maine, New Hampshire, Vermont, Massachusetts, Rhode Island, and Connecticut – and the Mid-Atlantic states – New York, New Jersey, Pennsylvania, and Delaware. The terrain of the region ranges from the near-wilderness of New York's Adirondack Mountains to the rocky coastline of northern New England and the rolling hills of Pennsylvania; climate is temperate, with cold winters and warm summers. First settled in the early 1600s, the region's good harbors, mineral resources, fast-flowing rivers, and rich coastal fishing grounds contributed to its early economic development; by the American Revolution, New York City, Boston, and Philadelphia were leading cities. Rapid industrialization after about 1800 brought millions of immigrants from Europe and elsewhere. In recent decades, a decline in manufacturing and a population shift toward the "Sun Belt" states of the South and West has weakened the Northeast's economy, but high-tech and service industries have taken up some of the slack. Today, New York is the nation's largest city and a financial, communications, and artistic center for the world.

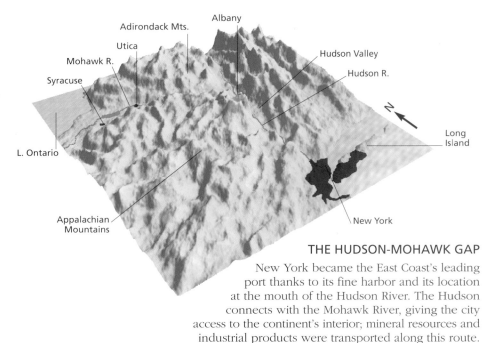

THE HUDSON-MOHAWK GAP

New York became the East Coast's leading port thanks to its fine harbor and its location at the mouth of the Hudson River. The Hudson connects with the Mohawk River, giving the city access to the continent's interior; mineral resources and industrial products were transported along this route.

THE AMISH

This isolated Amish farm near Lancaster, Pennsylvania, is run without any modern technology. The Amish are a Protestant sect who came to America from Switzerland in the 18th century. They live by farming, make all their own clothes, and use horses for transportation.

The spectacular Niagara Falls near Buffalo, New York.

PUMPKINS

Pumpkins are grown all over New England, and pumpkin pie is a favorite American dish. Pumpkins are also hollowed out to make Jack-O'-Lanterns for Halloween.

TOMATO SOUP

Many of the fruits and vegetables used in the region's big cities, especially New York, are grown on farms called market gardens in New Jersey (known as "the Garden State"). Tomatoes are grown in huge quantities, and made locally into canned tomato soup. Look for 🐂

MAP FEATURES

Sailing: Yachting is a popular pastime on New England's Atlantic coast. The Bermuda Race starts from Rhode Island. Look for ⛵

Universities: There are more centers of further education and research and development in New England than in any other part of the US. Look for 🎓

Maple syrup: Both sugar and syrup are obtained from the sap of maple trees. Vermont is the main producer in the US. Look for ❀

🐂 Cattle		🚢 Fishing port	
🦃 Poultry		⛏ Coal	
Market gardening		🏭 Industrial center	
Fishing		💻 High tech industry	

Severe winter weather is common in New England.

Blueberries

Cranberries

NEW ENGLAND BERRIES

Cranberries and blueberries both came from New England and large quantities are grown there. Cranberries are used in sauces, especially to go with roast turkey at Thanksgiving. Blueberries are sweeter and are often used in pies.

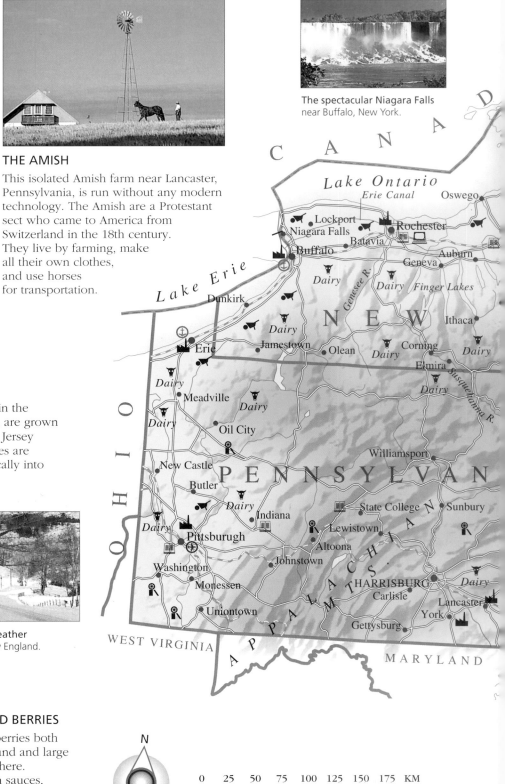

N

0	25	50	75	100	125	150	175	KM

0	25	50	75	100	MILES

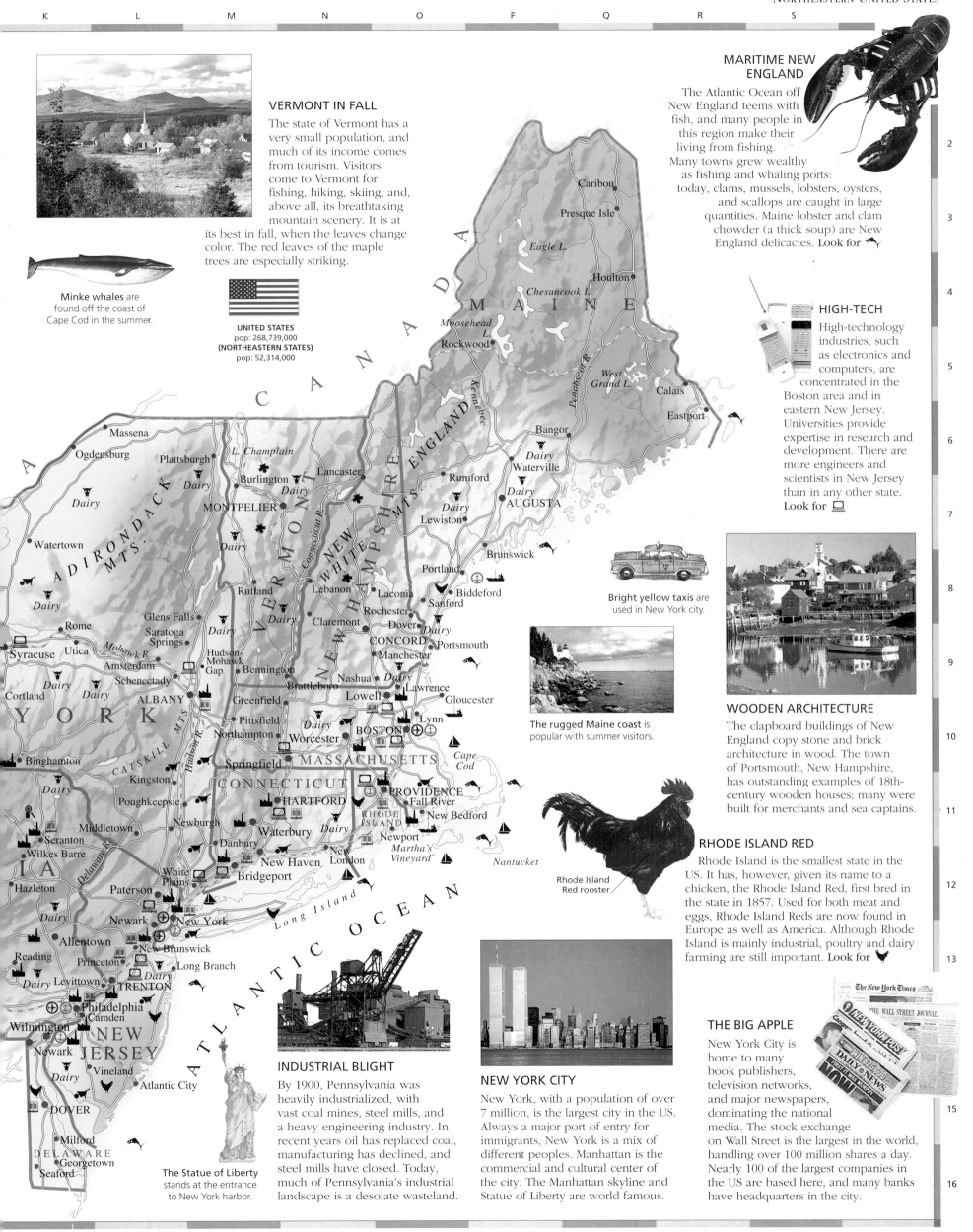

VERMONT IN FALL

The state of Vermont has a very small population, and much of its income comes from tourism. Visitors come to Vermont for fishing, hiking, skiing, and, above all, its breathtaking mountain scenery. It is at its best in fall, when the leaves change color. The red leaves of the maple trees are especially striking.

Minke whales are found off the coast of Cape Cod in the summer.

UNITED STATES
pop: 268,739,000
(NORTHEASTERN STATES)
pop: 52,314,000

MARITIME NEW ENGLAND

The Atlantic Ocean off New England teems with fish, and many people in this region make their living from fishing. Many towns grew wealthy as fishing and whaling ports: today, clams, mussels, lobsters, oysters, and scallops are caught in large quantities. Maine lobster and clam chowder (a thick soup) are New England delicacies. **Look for**

HIGH-TECH

High-technology industries, such as electronics and computers, are concentrated in the Boston area and in eastern New Jersey. Universities provide expertise in research and development. There are more engineers and scientists in New Jersey than in any other state. Look for

Bright yellow taxis are used in New York city.

The rugged Maine coast is popular with summer visitors.

WOODEN ARCHITECTURE

The clapboard buildings of New England copy stone and brick architecture in wood. The town of Portsmouth, New Hampshire, has outstanding examples of 18th-century wooden houses; many were built for merchants and sea captains.

RHODE ISLAND RED

Rhode Island is the smallest state in the US. It has, however, given its name to a chicken, the Rhode Island Red, first bred in the state in 1857. Used for both meat and eggs, Rhode Island Reds are now found in Europe as well as America. Although Rhode Island is mainly industrial, poultry and dairy farming are still important. **Look for**

Rhode Island Red rooster

INDUSTRIAL BLIGHT

By 1900, Pennsylvania was heavily industrialized, with vast coal mines, steel mills, and a heavy engineering industry. In recent years oil has replaced coal, manufacturing has declined, and steel mills have closed. Today, much of Pennsylvania's industrial landscape is a desolate wasteland.

The Statue of Liberty stands at the entrance to New York harbor.

NEW YORK CITY

New York, with a population of over 7 million, is the largest city in the US. Always a major port of entry for immigrants, New York is a mix of different peoples. Manhattan is the commercial and cultural center of the city. The Manhattan skyline and Statue of Liberty are world famous.

THE BIG APPLE

New York City is home to many book publishers, television networks, and major newspapers, dominating the national media. The stock exchange on Wall Street is the largest in the world, handling over 100 million shares a day. Nearly 100 of the largest companies in the US are based here, and many banks have headquarters in the city.

THE SOUTHERN STATES

THE SOUTH'S GEOGRAPHY includes the Tidewater along the Atlantic coast, the Piedmont extending to the coal-rich Appalachian Mountains, the Mississippi River Valley, and the subtropical coastal belt along the Gulf of Mexico. The region was settled mostly by British colonists, beginning with the founding of Jamestown, Virginia, in 1607. The South soon developed an agricultural economy based on tobacco, rice, indigo, and especially cotton, grown by African-American slaves. The American Civil War (1861-65) left the region devastated. The war ended slavery, but a system of legal segregation (separation by race) lasted into the 1960s in much of the South. Today, the South's economy is more varied, thanks to the discovery of oil reserves in the Gulf region and the development of industry. Florida has experienced great growth in recent years, becoming the fourth-largest state in the 1980s. Its population includes retirees from other states and refugees from Cuba, the Caribbean, and Latin America.

Horses graze on a Kentucky farm, in the Bluegrass country.

ATLANTA

The commercial center of the region is Atlanta, which is the hub of the South's transportation network, and has one of the world's busiest airports. Raw materials flood into Atlanta and manufactured goods pour out: clothes, books, iron and steel products, and Coca-Cola are all made here.

DERBY DAY

Kentucky is called the "Bluegrass State" after the grasslands around the city of Lexington, which provide superb grazing for livestock. This area has the world's greatest concentration of stud farms for breeding thoroughbred horses. The Kentucky Derby, held at Louisville, is one of the world's most famous horse races.

Orange

Lemon

Grapefruit

Lime

Florida produces three-quarters of the oranges and grapefruits in the US.

MAP FEATURES

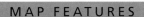

Soybeans: The main crop in the South is the soybean. Used for oil, margarine, and livestock feed, it has found both domestic and export markets. Look for

Coal: Coal, mined from the rich reserves of the Appalachian Mountains, is being overtaken by oil and gas. Look for

High-tech industry: The South, with its skilled labor force and good communications, is attracting many high-tech industries. Look for

Space center: The Space Shuttle is launched from the Kennedy Space Center, the launch site of the US space program. Look for

	Cereals		Fishing
	Citrus fruits		Oil
	Peanuts		Mining
	Cotton		Industrial center
	Tobacco		Tourism

Jazz saxophone

JAZZ

Jazz developed in New Orleans in the early 1900s. Originally it was the music of the bands who marched through the streets, playing at funerals and weddings. Jazz combined many influences – blues and spirituals (sung by slaves) and popular songs. Wind instruments are accompanied by drums, piano, and double bass.

MISSISSIPPI

Steamboats carry tourists on scenic trips along the Mississippi, one of the world's busiest waterways. Barges transport heavy cargoes from the industrial and agricultural regions near the Great Lakes to the Gulf coast.

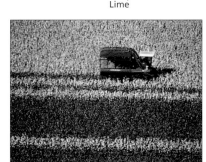

KING COTTON

Cotton, grown on large plantations using slave labor, was once the basis of the southern economy. Today, it is still grown on farms in some parts of the South. Look for

Okra

Shrimp

Gumbo is a spicy seafood and vegetable stew from Louisiana.

BOURBON

Corn is one of Kentucky's major crops. It is used for making Bourbon whisky, which is a worldwide export.

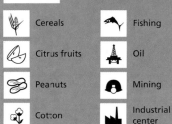

RETIREMENT STATE

Nearly 30 percent of Florida's inhabitants are over 55 years old. Large numbers of people retire to Florida, lured by its climate and sports facilities. Many settle in retirement developments or in the coastal cities.

Map labels

MISSOURI
OKLAHOMA
Fayetteville
BOSTON MTS.
White R.
Black R.
Fort Smith
ARKANSAS
L. Ouachita
Hot Springs
North Little Rock
LITTLE ROCK
Memphis
Aluminum
Pine Bluff
Arkansas R.
Mississippi R.
TEXAS
Ouachita R.
Corn
Greenville
Shreveport
Red R.
Yazoo R.
Corn
Monroe
LOUISIANA
JACKSON
Meridian
Alexandria
Mississippi R.
MISSISSIPPI
Corn
Hattiesburg
Lake Charles
Lafayette
BATON ROUGE
Pearl R.
Marsh I.
L. Pontchartrain
Gulfport
New Orleans
Biloxi
Sulfur
Sulfur
Breton Sound
Mississippi R. Delta

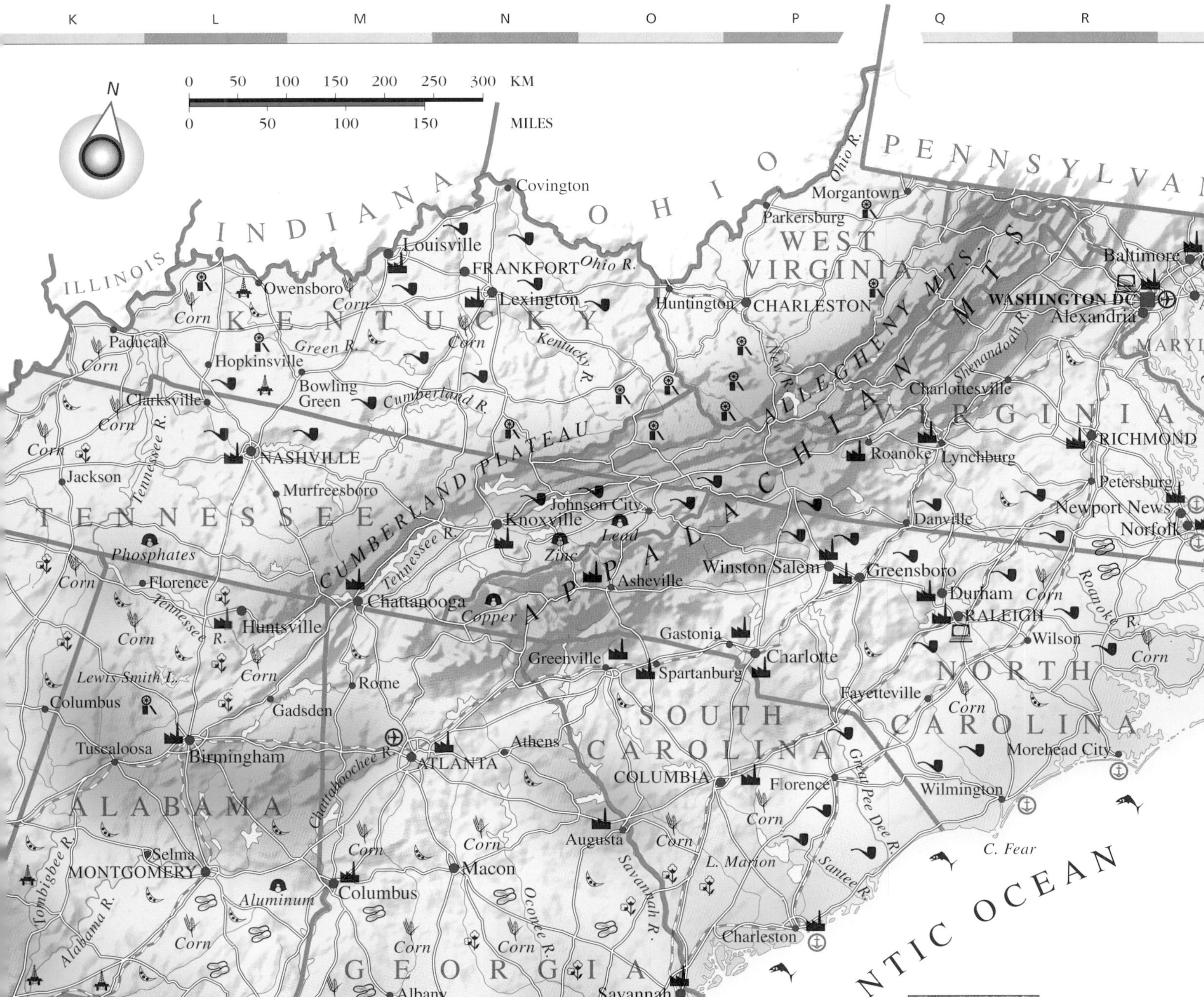

N

0	50	100	150	200	250	300	KM

0	50	100	150	MILES

ILLINOIS
INDIANA
OHIO
PENNSYLVANIA

Covington
Morgantown
Parkersburg
WEST VIRGINIA
Baltimore
Louisville
FRANKFORT
Ohio R.
Lexington
Huntington
CHARLESTON
WASHINGTON DC
ANNAPOLIS
Owensboro
Corn
Alexandria
MARYLAND
DELAWARE
Paducah
KENTUCKY
Corn
Green R.
Corn
Kentucky R.
ALLEGHENY MTS.
Shenandoah R.
Chesapeake Bay
Corn
Hopkinsville
Bowling Green
Charlottesville
VIRGINIA
Clarksville
Cumberland R.
CUMBERLAND PLATEAU
RICHMOND
Corn
NASHVILLE
Roanoke
Lynchburg
Petersburg
Jackson
Murfreesboro
Johnson City
Danville
Newport News
C. Charles
TENNESSEE
Knoxville
Lead
Norfolk
Tennessee R.
Zinc
Winston Salem
Asheville
Greensboro
Phosphates
Chattanooga
Copper
APPALACHIAN MTS.
Durham
Corn
Florence
Tennessee R.
RALEIGH
Corn
Huntsville
Corn
Greenville
Gastonia
NORTH CAROLINA
Wilson
Lewis Smith L.
Rome
Spartanburg
Charlotte
Corn
Columbus
Gadsden
SOUTH
Fayetteville
C. Hatteras
Tuscaloosa
Athens
CAROLINA
Corn
Birmingham
ATLANTA
COLUMBIA
Morehead City
ALABAMA
Chattahoochee R.
Florence
Wilmington
Tombigbee R.
SELMA
Corn
Corn
Augusta
Corn
L. Marion
C. Fear
MONTGOMERY
Macon
Savannah R.
Santee R.
ATLANTIC OCEAN
Aluminum
Columbus
Great Pee Dee R.
Alabama R.
Corn
GEORGIA
Charleston
Corn
Ocmulgee R.
Corn
Mobile
Dothan
Albany
Savannah
Flint R.
Alapaha R.
Pensacola
Okefenokee Swamp
Brunswick
Panama City
TALLAHASSEE
Valdosta
Gulf of Mexico
Phosphates
Suwannee R.
Jacksonville
Gainesville
FLORIDA
Daytona Beach
Phosphates
Kennedy Space Center
Orlando
Disney World
C. Canaveral
Clearwater
Tampa
Melbourne
Saint Petersburg
Phosphates
Fort Myers
L. Okeechobee
West Palm Beach
The Everglades
Fort Lauderdale
Hollywood
Hialeah
Miami
Key West
Florida Keys
Straits of Florida

UNITED STATES
pop: 268 739,000
(SOUTHERN STATES)
pop: 70,532,000

Fields of ripening tobacco in North Carolina.

The Everglades – a vast tropical marsh in southern Florida.

The elegant mansions of cotton plantation owners can still be seen in the South.

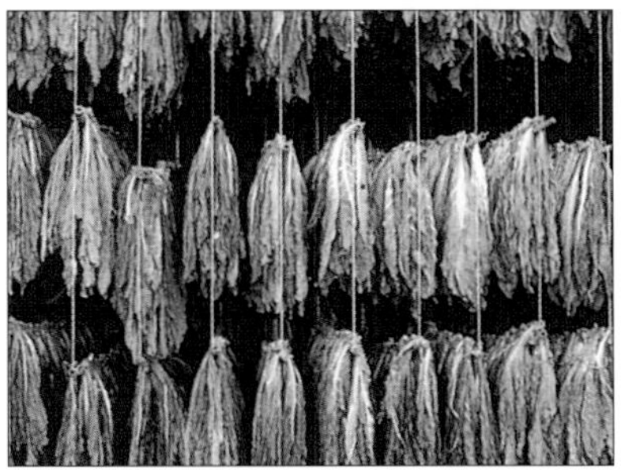

AMERICAN CAPITAL

The city of Washington, also known as the District of Columbia, became the US capital and seat of the federal government in 1800. This picture shows the lighted dome of the Capitol building.

DISNEY WORLD

In 1971, Disney World was opened near Orlando, Florida. Millions of visitors come each year to this vast fantasy land. It occupies a huge area of reclaimed swamp, lake, and forest. Tourists also come to Florida to visit the Epcot Center – a trip through a vision of the future – and the Kennedy Space Center.

TOBACCO

The southern states grow high-quality Virginia tobacco. The leaves are cured for 4-6 days in controlled temperatures before being moistened and sorted. Tobacco factories can produce up to 450 million cigarettes a day. Look for ⌇

Peanut butter

Peanut

PEANUTS

Georgia grows nearly half the total US crop of peanuts. Half the crop is used for making peanut butter, the rest for edible oil and animal feed. Look for ◌

THE GREAT LAKES

THE FIVE GREAT LAKES of North America – Erie, Ontario, Huron, Michigan, and Superior – together form the largest area of fresh water in the world. The states of Indiana, Illinois, Michigan, Ohio, Wisconsin, and Minnesota, all of which border on one or more of the lakes, are often called the industrial and agricultural heartland of the United States. This region is rich in natural resources, including coal, iron, copper, and timber, and there are large areas of fertile farmland on the flat plains of the prairies. First explored by French traders, fur trappers, and missionaries in the 17th century, the region began to attract large numbers of settlers in the early 1800s. Trading links were improved by the opening of the Erie Canal in 1825, which connected the region to the Atlantic coast, while the Mississippi and other rivers gave access to the Gulf of Mexico and the rest of the continent. When railways reached the region in the 1840s, cities such as Chicago grew and prospered as freight-handling centers. Steel production and the car industry later became the main industries in the region. In recent years, a decline in these traditional industries has led to high unemployment in some areas.

Walleyes live in the Great Lakes, but their numbers are falling due to pollution.

HOGS

In the 19th century, huge numbers of animals from all over this region were sent to the stockyards in Chicago for slaughter and processing. Rearing livestock is still important in Illinois. Corn and soybeans, both grown locally, are used as animal feed. **Look for** 🐖

HAMBURGERS

Hamburgers are America's own fast food, first produced on a massive scale in Illinois in the 1950s. It has been calculated that in every second of the day, 200 Americans are eating a hamburger. American-style hamburgers and fast food can now be found all over the world.

MAP FEATURES

Cherries: One-third of the world cherry crop is grown along the shores of Lake Michigan. **Look for** 🍒	
Iron ore: Iron ore deposits are found around the shores of Lake Superior. It is mined, processed, then shipped to industrial centers in pellet form. **Look for** ⛏	
🐂 Cattle	🌙 Soybeans
🐖 Hogs	⚙ Coal
🌾 Cereals	⛏ Oil
🍠 Sugar beet	🏭 Industrial center
🛒 Market gardening	🚗 Vehicle manufacture

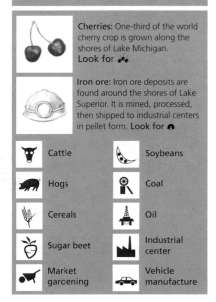

COLD WINTERS

The Great Lakes region has severe winters, and Minnesota, in particular, suffers from heavy snowstorms. Parts of the Great Lakes themselves can freeze over in winter, and lakeside harbors can be frozen from December to early April.

Baseball and fielder's glove. Baseball is the US national game.

MILWAUKEE BEER

The Great Lakes region has attracted many immigrants, especially from Germany, the Netherlands, and the Scandinavian countries. Milwaukee, where many Germans settled, is home to several of the largest breweries in the US.

THE WINDY CITY

Chicago is situated at the southern tip of Lake Michigan. It gets its nickname – the Windy City – from the weather conditions in this area. Chicago was ideally positioned for trading with the Midwest region and quickly became a wealthy modern city. By 1900 it had vast complexes of lumber mills, meat processing factories, railroad yards, and steel mills.

PRAIRIE LANDS

The fertile soil and hot, humid summers make the flat expanses of the Midwestern prairies ideal for farming. Nearly half of the world's corn crop is grown on the huge farms in this region.

An isolated farm on the open prairies of Illinois.

CORNFLAKES

Food processing is a major industry throughout this agricultural region. Wisconsin, for example, is the major producer of canned peas and sweet corn in the US. Corn- and wheat-based breakfast cereals are exported all over the world from Battle Creek, Michigan. **Look for** 🌾

K L M N O P Q R S T

1

UNITED STATES
pop: 268,739,000
(GREAT LAKES STATES)
pop: 48,642,000

A wooded island
in Minnesota.

Over 10,000 loons,
the state bird of
Minnesota, spend the
summer on its lakes.

LAKESIDE VACATIONS

The lakes attract millions of visitors
a year. Summer vacation homes line
accessible parts of the shores, and
huge marinas have been built for the
pleasure craft that sail on the lakes.

2

Parts of the shores have
been eroded by water,
endangering buildings

3

LAKES UNDER THREAT

Heavy industry around the shores
of the Great Lakes has caused
disastrous water pollution. In
some regions, fish are now unsafe
to eat and swimming is dangerous.
In addition, changes to the weather, such as
heavy rainfall and cooler temperatures, have
led to much higher water levels. Lakeside resort
towns are often flooded, threatening tourism.
Many houses, perched precariously on the
lakes' crumbling shores, are under threat.

4

5

6

Model of a 1956
Ford Fairlane

7

THE MOTOR CITY

In the early 20th century
Detroit became the center of
a revolution in transportation
when two engineers, Henry
Ford and Ransom Olds, began
mass-producing cars there.
Today, Detroit is still the center
of the US car industry, with
several of America's biggest car
manufacturers based in the city.
Look for

8

9

10

TAMLA MOTOWN

In 1961 Berry Gordy,
a worker from the Ford
factory in Detroit, launched the
Tamla Motown record label to promote
local black talent. Motown artists, such
as Smokey Robinson, the Supremes,
and Stevie Wonder, perfected the
unique style of soul music.

11

12

13

14

OPEN HIGHWAYS

The Great Lakes states have benefited
from their central location and well-
developed rail and water transportation
systems. The region is also well served
by roads – Indianapolis has more major
highways than any other American city.

15

16

Isle Royale

Lake Superior

Keweenaw Bay

Copper

Marquette

Sault Sainte Marie

M I C H I G A N

Iron

Iron

Dairy

Escanaba

Beaver I.

Straits of Mackinac

Cheboygan

C A N A D A

Lake Huron

S I N

Wolf R.

Marinette

Stevens Point

Wausau

Green Bay

Appleton

Manitowoc

Oshkosh

L. Winnebago

Fond du Lac

Sheboygan

Corn

Dairy

Wauwatosa

MADISON

Milwaukee

Dairy

Janesville

Racine

Beloit

Kenosha

Freeport

Rockford

Waukegan

Beef

Beef

Chicago

Evanston

De Kalb

Aurora

Sterling

Joliet

Gary

La Salle

Ottawa

Kankakee

Corn

Peoria

Bloomington

Rantoul

Danville

N O I S

Decatur

Champaign

SPRINGFIELD

Corn

Terre Haute

Corn

Mattoon

Kaskaskia R.

White R.

Carlyle L.

Corn

Centralia

Mount Vernon

Lead

Carbondale

Zinc

Rend L.

Corn

Mississippi R.

K E N T U C K Y

Robie House, Chicago (built 1910),
was designed by the world famous
US architect, Frank Lloyd Wright.

N

0 50 100 150 200 250 KM

0 25 50 75 100 125 150 MILES

A farmhouse and barn in
the rich farm country of Indiana.

Traverse City

Manistee R.

Manistee

Muskegon R.

Alpena

Saginaw Bay

Midland

Dairy

Mount Pleasant

Bay City

Dairy

Muskegon

Saginaw

Dairy

Flint

Owosso

Grand Rapids

Pontiac

Holland

LANSING

Sterling Heights

Saint Clair Shores

Dairy

Battle Creek

Ann Arbor

Detroit

Kalamazoo

Jackson

Lake Erie

Benton Harbor

Adrian

Monroe

Niles

Corn

South Bend

Toledo

Huron

Ashtabula

P E N N S Y L V A N I A

Elyria

Cleveland

Warren

Youngstown

Michigan City

Maumee R.

Dairy

Akron

East Liverpool

I N D I A N A

Corn

Fort Wayne

Findlay

Canton

Massillon

Steubenville

Corn

Logansport

Marion

Lima

Scioto R.

Marion

Mansfield

Kokomo

Muncie

Piqua

Corn

Newark

Zanesville

Beef

Frankfort

Anderson

Springfield

COLUMBUS

Lancaster

Ohio R.

Decatur

Champaign

Richmond

Dayton

O H I O

Corn

Chillicothe

INDIANAPOLIS

Corn

Columbus

Cincinnati

Bloomington

Portsmouth

Bedford

Ohio R.

W E S T V I R G I N I A

New Albany

Vincennes

Wabash R.

Evansville

Lake Michigan

Lake Ontario

CENTRAL AND MOUNTAIN STATES

THIS REGION INCLUDES the lowlands on the west bank of the Mississippi River, the vast expanses of the Great Plains, and the majestic Rocky Mountains. In climate, it is a region of extremes: hot summers alternate with cold winters, and hailstorms, blizzards, and tornadoes are frequent events. Once home to large numbers of Native Americans and great herds of buffalo, the plains were settled in the 19th century; the Native Americans were pushed onto reservations and the buffalo slaughtered. Originally dismissed as a desert because of low rainfall and lack of trees, the Great Plains proved to be one of the world's great agricultural regions; today, vast amounts of cereals are grown on mechanized farms, and cattle are grazed on huge ranches. The Rockies are rich in minerals, and reserves of coal, oil, and natural gas are being exploited.

The foothills of the snow-covered Rockies in Montana.

AGRICULTURAL INDUSTRIES

Shredded wheat

A great range of cereals are grown in the Midwest and transported to local cities for processing. Iowa has the largest cereal processing factory in the world, and it is in the cities of this region that many cereals are prepared for the world's breakfast tables. Cities also provide storage facilities for grain and cereals, as well as markets for grain, livestock, and farm machinery.

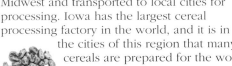
Corn flakes   Oats   Toasted rice

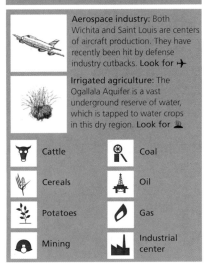

COWBOYS

Cattle are raised on the Great Plains and foothills of the Rocky Mountains. Ranches often have thousands of cattle. In summer, mounted cowboys herd cattle to upland pastures and drive them back to the ranch for the winter. Cattle are then taken to markets in nearby towns for cattle auctions. Look for 🐄

WYOMING COAL

Wyoming now leads the US in coal production. Coal from the West is in demand because it has a lower sulfur content than coal mined in the East and causes less pollution when burned. Shallow coal reserves are extracted from open-pit mines, like this one, which spoil the landscape. Look for ⛏

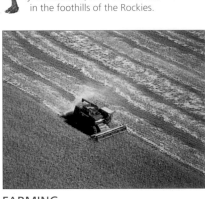
Fossils of dinosaurs, such as *Tyrannosaurus*, have been found in the foothills of the Rockies.

MAP FEATURES

Aerospace industry: Both Wichita and Saint Louis are centers of aircraft production. They have recently been hit by defense industry cutbacks. Look for ✈

Irrigated agriculture: The Ogallala Aquifer is a vast underground reserve of water, which is tapped to water crops in this dry region. Look for 🌾

🐄 Cattle		⛏ Coal	
🌾 Cereals		🛢 Oil	
🌱 Potatoes		Gas	
⛏ Mining		🏭 Industrial center	

Railroad towns are now surrounded by agricultural land
A central route over the Rockies links mining towns
Main east-west railroad route
To Minnesota and Chicago
N
Snake River valley: potato farming on fertile floodplain

THE ROCKY MOUNTAINS

The Rocky Mountains divide the North American continent in two; rivers to the west of the range flow toward the Pacific, while those to the east drain into the Arctic and Atlantic oceans and the Gulf of Mexico. First explored by fur trappers and traders in the 19th century, the mountain passes were used by settlers on their way west. Miners followed the settlers, and the mining towns of Montana were established. By 1869, the Transcontinental railroad had crossed the Rockies, linking the Pacific coast with the rest of the country.

FARMING

Corn is the main crop in Iowa, while wheat is more important in the center of this region. Nearer the Rockies, the rainfall decreases and wheat farming gives way to cattle ranching. Farming in the Midwest is large-scale and mechanized. These vast wheat fields in Nebraska stretch to the far horizon. Farmers often produce more than they can sell. Look for 🌾

Map labels

CANADA
WASHINGTON
OREGON
NEVADA
UTAH
MONTANA
IDAHO
WYOMING
ROCKY MOUNTAIN RANGE
BITTERROOT RANGE
WIND RIVER RANGE
BIGHORN MTS.

Zinc
Lead
Coeur d'Alene
Silver
Silver
Lewiston
Missoula
Kalispell
Flathead L.
Barley
Wheat
Shelby
Barley
L. Elwell
Havre
Beef
Wheat
Missouri R.
Fort Peck L.
Great Falls
HELENA
Canyon Ferry L.
Beef
Anaconda
Copper Butte
Beef
Beef
Yellowstone R.
Salmon R.
Bozeman
Dillon
Billings
Beef
Beef
Bighorn R.
Beef
Sheridan
Beef
Beef
Cody
Nampa
BOISE
Yellowstone L.
Jackson L.
Grand Teton Mts.
Worland
Idaho Falls
Wheat
Snake R.
Phosphate
Pocatello
Wind R.
Uranium
Twin Falls
Beef
Iron
Beef
Wheat
Pathfinder Res.
Snake R.
Green R.
Rock Springs
Rawlins
Flaming Gorge Res.

TOURISM

Huge carvings of the heads of four great American presidents – Washington, Lincoln, Jefferson, and Theodore Roosevelt – can be seen at Mount Rushmore in South Dakota. Millions of people have visited the monument since its completion in 1927. The mountainous scenery and wildlife of this region attract tourists from all over the world.

Fewer than 1,000 grizzly bears are left in the US; many live in the mountains of Wyoming and Idaho.

BISON

Millions of bison (American buffalo) used to roam the Great Plains. Native Americans hunted them for food and used their hides to make clothing and shelter. Settlers and railroad workers virtually wiped out the bison herds in the late 19th century, killing them for food and profit. Today, the bison population is protected, and there are now about 50,000 bison living on reserves.

UNITED STATES
pop: 268,739,000
(CENTRAL & MOUNTAIN STATES)
pop: 19,803,000

The Badlands of South Dakota have been eroded into hills and gullies.

ON THE ROAD

An extensive road network holds this vast, sparsely inhabited region together. Highways often run through long stretches of nearly empty land, fringed by gas stations, motels, and roadside restaurants. Cars are a necessity in much of the West; in Wyoming, children age 14 can drive to school.

Popcorn is a midwestern export.

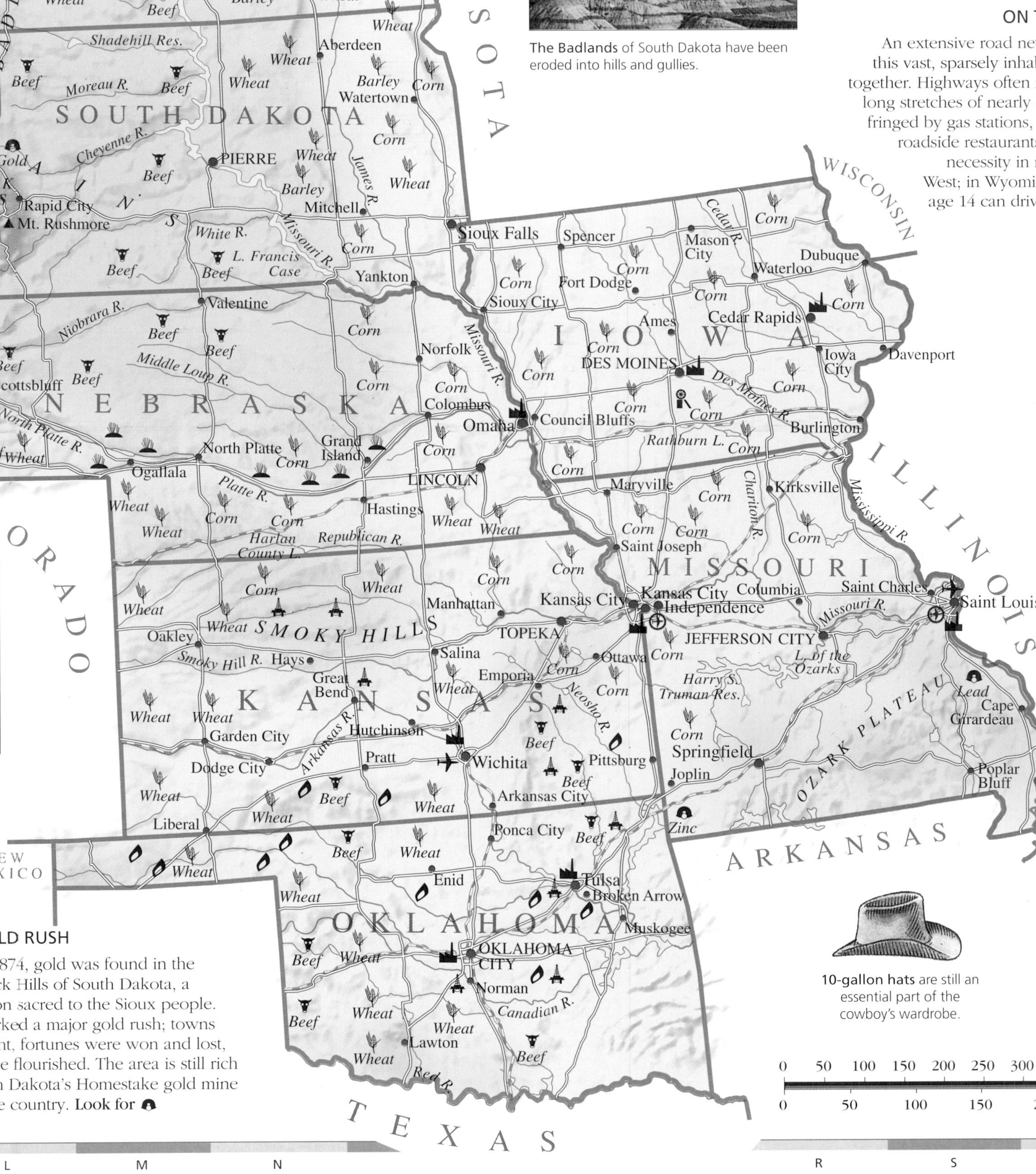

The Grand Teton Mountains, northern Wyoming.

GOLD RUSH

In 1874, gold was found in the Black Hills of South Dakota, a region sacred to the Sioux people. The discovery sparked a major gold rush; towns sprang up overnight, fortunes were won and lost, gambling and crime flourished. The area is still rich in minerals – South Dakota's Homestake gold mine is the biggest in the country. **Look for**

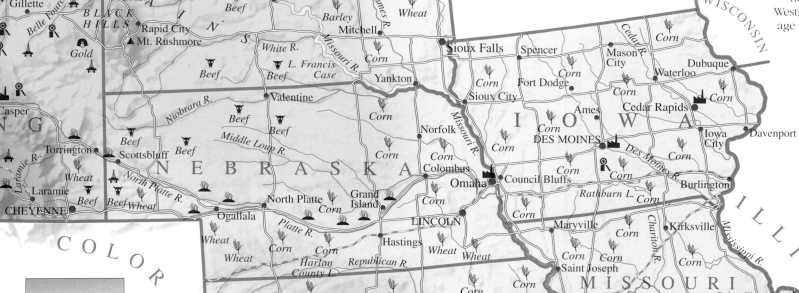

10-gallon hats are still an essential part of the cowboy's wardrobe.

N

| 0 | 50 | 100 | 150 | 200 | 250 | 300 | 350 KM |

| 0 | 50 | 100 | 150 | 200 MILES |

47

A B C D E F G H I J

THE SOUTHWESTERN STATES

THE SOUTHWESTERN USA is a region of deserts and high tablelands, broken by the ridges of the southern Rocky Mountains. Many different Native American peoples lived in the Southwest. The region still has the country's largest concentration of Native Americans. The first Europeans to settle in this region were the Spanish who came north from Mexico. This mixed Spanish and Native American heritage is reflected in the region's folk art, architecture, and foods. American settlers in Texas rebelled against Mexican rule in 1836, and Texas was annexed to the USA a decade later. The rest of the region became part of the USA after the Mexican War of 1846-48. Gold and silver mining and cattle ranching attracted settlers to the region in the late 19th century, and oil became a major part of Texas's economy in the 20th century. The region's natural beauty draws tourists from all over the world.

The Saguaro cactus thrives in the deserts of Arizona.

Jordan Mormon Temple, Utah

MORMON CITY

Salt Lake City in Utah is the headquarters of the Latter-day Saints, or Mormons. They settled in Utah in the 1840s, after fleeing from the eastern states, where they had been persecuted for their beliefs. There are now more than six million Mormons worldwide.

NAVAJO RUGS

Many Navajo people live on a vast reservation in Arizona and New Mexico. They still practise weaving, pottery, silver-working, and other traditional crafts. Navajo rugs are woven into geometric patterns, and colored with natural dyes such as juniper and blackberry.

An 11th-century pottery bowl, made by the Mogollon people.

THE GREAT OUTDOORS

Riding, hiking, canoeing, skiing, and fishing are just some of the outdoor activities which draw tourists to the Southwest. But the region's main attraction is the Grand Canyon. About 10,000 visitors each year navigate the Canyon's dangerous waters on rubber rafts, and many others explore it on foot or by donkey.

These strangely shaped rocks in Monument Valley, Arizona, have been carved by the wind.

UNITED STATES
pop: 268,739,000
(SOUTHWESTERN STATES)
pop: 35,552,000

MAP FEATURES

High-tech industry: The space program has attracted high technology industries to the area. Look for 💻

Irrigated agriculture: Sprinklers fixed on central pivots create circular oases of green fields in the arid landscape. Look for 🌾

Dams: Acute water shortages are being remedied by the construction of dams on the region's rivers. Look for 🗼

Military bases: The first nuclear bombs were tested in New Mexico and Nevada. Military installations are common in the region. Look for ⫼

🐂	Cattle	🛢	Oil
🌾	Cereals	🔻	Gas
⚓	Cotton	🏭	Industrial center
⛏	Mining	⛷	Skiing

TAOS

The *pueblo*, or village, of Taos in New Mexico is built of unbaked clay brick, called adobe. This style of building dates back to the Pueblo people, who lived in the region a thousand years ago, farming corn, cotton, beans, and squash.

THE GRAND CANYON

Over the last million years, the Colorado River has cut its way through the rocky plateaus of northern Arizona. At the same time, the plateaus have risen. This combined action has formed the largest land gorge in the world – the Grand Canyon. It is more than 1 mile (1.6 km) deep, and 220 miles (350 km) long. Some of the oldest rocks in North America have been found at the base of the canyon.

Grand Canyon
Bright Angel Point
Colorado River
From Lake Powell
Eroded sediment carried down rivers creates fertile plains
To Lake Mead
N

Map labels

OREGON
IDAHO
BLACK ROCK DESERT
Mercury
Beef
Winnemucca
Beef
Bear L.
Rye Patch Res.
Gold
Elko
Humboldt R.
GREAT BASIN
Brigham City
Logan
Pyramid L.
Great Salt L.
Ogden
Reno
Sparks
NEVADA
Bountiful
SALT LAKE CITY
Tooele
CARSON CITY
L. Tahoe
Zinc
L. Utah
Orem
Provo
Copper
Walker L.
Ely
Beef
Silver
UTAH
Sevier L.
Salina
Nellis Air Force Range
Iron
Bryce Canyon
Uranium
L. Powell
Nevada Test Site
Glen Canyon Dam
Uranium
North Las Vegas
Las Vegas
Henderson
L. Mead
Grand Canyon
Bright Angel Point
Monument Valley
PAINTED DESERT
Hoover Dam
COLORADO PLATEAU
CALIFORNIA
Davis Dam
Flagstaff
Beef
ARIZONA
Parker Dam
Prescott
Colorado R.
Theodore Roosevelt L.
Glendale
Scottsdale
Copper
Copper
PHOENIX
Mesa
SONORAN
Central Arizona Project
Salt R.
Imperial Dam
Yuma
Colorado Project
Casa Grande
Luke Air Force Range
Copper
Silver
DESERT
Copper
Tucson
Santa Cruz R.
Beef
Copper
Douglas

A B C D E F

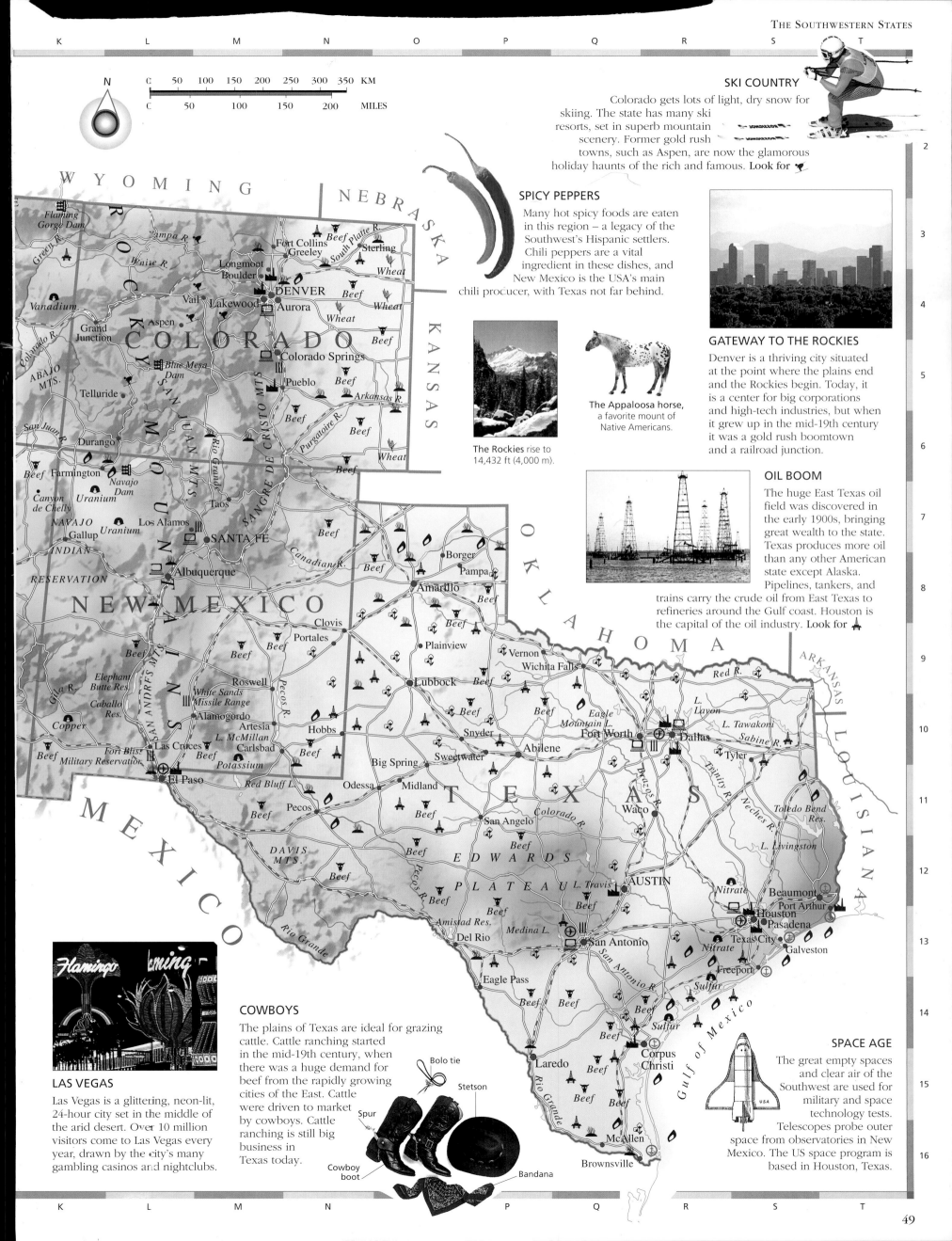

SKI COUNTRY

Colorado gets lots of light, dry snow for skiing. The state has many ski resorts, set in superb mountain scenery. Former gold rush towns, such as Aspen, are now the glamorous holiday haunts of the rich and famous. **Look for** ⛷

SPICY PEPPERS

Many hot spicy foods are eaten in this region – a legacy of the Southwest's Hispanic settlers. Chili peppers are a vital ingredient in these dishes, and New Mexico is the USA's main chili producer, with Texas not far behind.

The Rockies rise to 14,432 ft (4,000 m).

The Appaloosa horse, a favorite mount of Native Americans.

GATEWAY TO THE ROCKIES

Denver is a thriving city situated at the point where the plains end and the Rockies begin. Today, it is a center for big corporations and high-tech industries, but when it grew up in the mid-19th century it was a gold rush boomtown and a railroad junction.

OIL BOOM

The huge East Texas oil field was discovered in the early 1900s, bringing great wealth to the state. Texas produces more oil than any other American state except Alaska. Pipelines, tankers, and trains carry the crude oil from East Texas to refineries around the Gulf coast. Houston is the capital of the oil industry. **Look for** ⚒

LAS VEGAS

Las Vegas is a glittering, neon-lit, 24-hour city set in the middle of the arid desert. Over 10 million visitors come to Las Vegas every year, drawn by the city's many gambling casinos and nightclubs.

COWBOYS

The plains of Texas are ideal for grazing cattle. Cattle ranching started in the mid-19th century, when there was a huge demand for beef from the rapidly growing cities of the East. Cattle were driven to market by cowboys. Cattle ranching is still big business in Texas today.

Bolo tie
Stetson
Spur
Cowboy boot
Bandana

SPACE AGE

The great empty spaces and clear air of the Southwest are used for military and space technology tests. Telescopes probe outer space from observatories in New Mexico. The US space program is based in Houston, Texas.

49

The Pacific States

THE PACIFIC COAST STATES boast some of the most varied scenery in the US. California, for example, contains the snow-capped peaks of the Sierra Nevada mountains and the lowest point in North America – Death Valley. Much of California is arid, with farming dependent on irrigation, while vast forests and well-watered fertile valleys are characteristic of Washington and Oregon. American settlers began to cross the Rockies to the Pacific coast in the 1840s. California became part of the US as a result of the Mexican-American War (1846-48), and the discovery of gold in 1848 led to its rapid settlement. All three states are now major agricultural producers and centers of high-technology industry. In the early 1960s, California became the most highly populated state in the US. Despite recent problems, the state's economy rivals those of many wealthy nations.

SILICON VALLEY

Santa Clara Valley south of San Francisco has one of the largest concentrations of high-technology industry in the world. More than 3,000 companies there specialize in micro-electronics and computer hardware and software, but US manufacturers face increasing competition from Asia. Look for 🖳

Computer discs capable of storing vast amounts of information

SAN FRANCISCO

San Francisco is located on one of the world's finest natural harbors and is the West Coast's trade and shipping center. The city is built on a hilly peninsula, with some of the steepest streets in the world. San Francisco suffers from frequent earthquakes because it is situated right on the San Andreas Fault. The city's large skyscrapers are specially designed to withstand earthquakes.

Waves batter the rugged Pacific coast of Oregon.

TIMBER

Oregon and Washington are America's major timber producers. The region's cedar and fir forests supply one-third of the country's softwood timber. The trees are cut into logs at one of the thousands of sawmills in the forests and then floated down rivers on rafts to the large coastal cities. Some of the wood is made into paper at pulp mills like the one pictured here. Much of the region's timber is exported to Japan. Logging has reduced the region's stocks of mature trees; efforts are now being made to plant more trees. Look for 🌲

AGRICULTURE

California alone produces half of the fruits and vegetables in the US. Fertile soils and a warm climate have contributed to the state's success, but dry conditions mean that much of the state's farmland has to be irrigated. California's main crops are cotton and grapes. Look for 🍇

Almond

Avocado

Peach

Plum

AEROSPACE

The Boeing Corporation, the world's largest aircraft manufacturer, is based in Seattle. Boeing is the city's main employer, and any decline in orders can result in unemployment. California is a major producer of military aircraft; but cuts in US defense spending have badly affected this industry. Look for ✈

Boeing 767 aircraft

Washington's Mount Rainier is permanently snow-covered.

California redwoods are evergreen trees which can reach 330 ft (100 m).

Fortune cookie served in San Francisco's Chinese restaurants

IMMIGRATION

California attracts many immigrants from Asia and South America. Many Chinese immigrants have settled in San Francisco's Chinatown. This area of the city is a magnet for the Chinese community and is famous for its exotic shops and restaurants. Immigrants from Latin America, especially Mexico, make up a growing part of the state's population.

[Map of the Pacific States showing Washington, Oregon, and parts of Canada and Idaho, with cities including Spokane, Seattle, OLYMPIA, Tacoma, Bellevue, Everett, Bellingham, Port Angeles, Aberdeen, Astoria, SALEM, Portland, Vancouver, Eugene, Springfield, Corvallis, Newport, Coos Bay, Bandon, Roseburg, Bend, Pendleton, Walla Walla, Richland, Kennewick, Yakima, Ellensburg, Moses Lake, La Grande, Baker, Burns, and geographic features such as Columbia R., Snake R., Blue Mountains, Cascade Range, Mt. Rainier, Ross L., L. Chelan, Banks L., Yakima R., John Day R., Malheur L., Harney L., Summer L., Owyhee R., Strait of Juan de Fuca, Olympic National Park, C. Blanco]

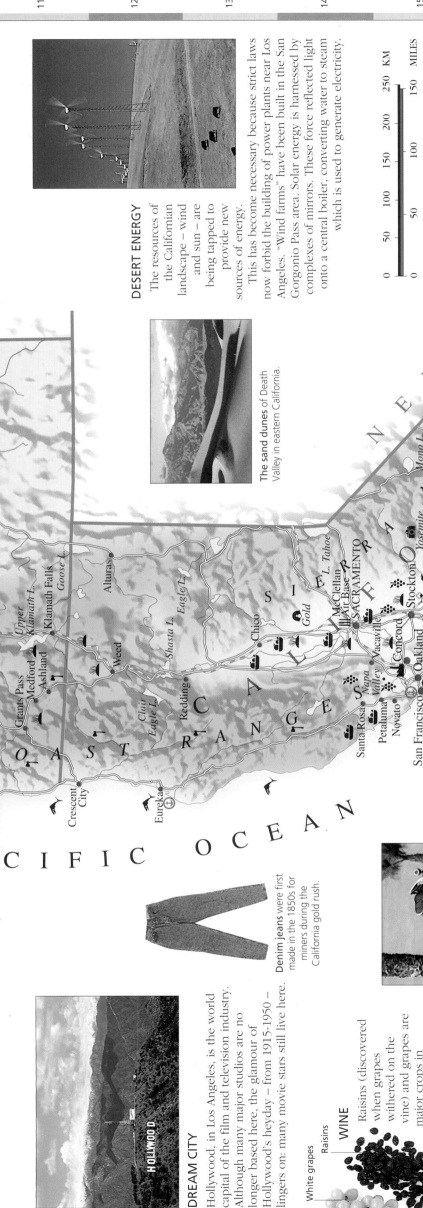

DESERT ENERGY

The resources of the Californian landscape – wind and sun – are being tapped to provide new sources of energy.

This has become necessary because strict laws now forbid the building of power plants near Los Angeles. "Wind farms" have been built in the San Gorgonio Pass area. Solar energy is harnessed by complexes of mirrors. These force reflected light onto a central boiler, converting water to steam which is used to generate electricity.

The sand dunes of Death Valley in eastern California.

N

250 KM   MILES
200   150
150
100   100
50   50
0   0

UNITED STATES:
pop: 268,739,000
(PACIFIC STATES)
pop: 42,102,000

LOS ANGELES

Los Angeles is a vast, sprawling city, stretching for 60 miles (100 km) along the Pacific coast. The city has grown rapidly over the last 100 years and is a focus for immigrants from the rest of the US. Today, it consists of many separate residential centers, linked by an extensive road system built in the 1930s. Most residents are dependent on cars for transportation. The city suffers from pollution as it is surrounded by mountains which trap exhaust fumes.

Green abalone shells found off the California coasts are used to make jewelry.

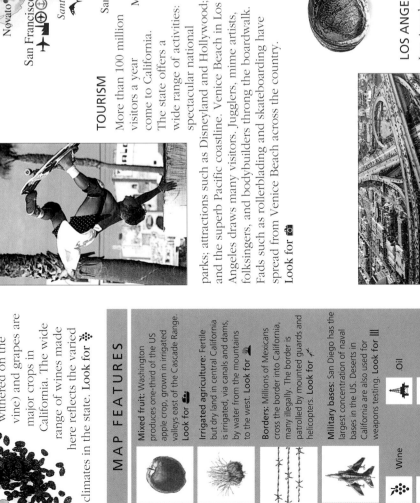

TOURISM

More than 100 million visitors a year come to California. The state offers a wide range of activities: spectacular national parks; attractions such as Disneyland and Hollywood; and the superb Pacific coastline. Venice Beach in Los Angeles draws many visitors. Jugglers, mime artists, folksingers, and bodybuilders throng the boardwalk. Fads such as rollerblading and skateboarding have spread from Venice Beach across the country.
Look for 📷

Denim jeans were first made in the 1850s for miners during the California gold rush.

DREAM CITY

Hollywood, in Los Angeles, is the world capital of the film and television industry. Although many major studios are no longer based here, the glamour of Hollywood's heyday – from 1915-1950 – lingers on: many movie stars still live here.

HOLLYWOOD

WINE

Raisins (discovered when grapes withered on the vine) and grapes are major crops in California. The wide range of wines made here reflects the varied climates in the state. Look for 🍇

White grapes
Raisins

MAP FEATURES

Mixed fruit: Washington produces one-third of the US apple crop, grown in irrigated valleys east of the Cascade Range. Look for 🍎

Irrigated agriculture: Fertile but dry land in central California is irrigated, via canals and dams, by water from the mountains to the west. Look for 🌵

Borders: Millions of Mexicans cross the border into California, many illegally. The border is patrolled by mounted guards and helicopters. Look for ✈

Military bases: San Diego has the largest concentration of naval bases in the US. Deserts in California are also used for weapons testing. Look for ✈

Oil	
Industrial center	
Aerospace industry	
High-tech industry	
Tourism	
Wine	
Cotton	
Timber	
Fishing	
Mining	

51

MEXICO

THE LAND OF MEXICO consists of a dry plateau crossed by broad valleys and enclosed to the west and east by mountains, some of which are volcanic. Lower California, the Yucatan Peninsula, and along the country's coasts are the main low-lying areas. Mexico was once home to civilizations such as the Maya and Aztec, who built magnificent cities containing plazas, palaces, and pyramids. Lured by legends of fabulous hoards of gold and silver, Spanish *conquistadores* invaded Mexico in 1519 and destroyed the Aztec Empire. For 300 years the Spanish ruled the country, unifying it with their language and the Roman Catholic religion. Mexico succeeded in winning its independence from Spain by 1821. Today, most Mexicans are *mestizo* – which means they are descendants of the native peoples and the Spanish settlers. Although half the population lives in towns, many people still inhabit areas only accessible on horseback, but rail and air transportation are improving. So much of the country is mountainous or dry that only 12 percent of the land can be used for farming. Mexico has vast oil reserves and mineral riches, but suffers from overpopulation and huge foreign debts. However, closer links with the US are strengthening Mexico's economy.

MEXICO
pop: 95,800,000

Isla Cedros, off the northwest coast of Mexico.

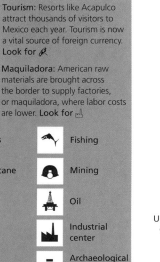

THE DAY OF THE DEAD

Mexicans believe that life is like a flower; it slowly opens and then closes again. During the annual festival of the Day of the Dead, the streets are decorated with flowers, and ghoulish skeletons are everywhere.

Skeleton made of papier-mâché

TEXTILES

Although many fabrics are machine-made now, some Mexicans still practice their traditional art of handweaving colorful textiles. This *sarape*, part of the traditional Mexican dress for men, is worn over the shoulder.

Teeth made of shell

Aztec mask, inlaid with turquoise, depicting a god.

AGRICULTURE

Although Mexico is rapidly industrializing, over half the working population still makes its living from farming. They grow crops like corn, beans, and vegetables, and raise cattle, sheep, pigs, and chickens.

Cacti growing on Mexico's dry central plateau.

SPIKED DRINKS

The desert and dry regions of Mexico are home to many varieties of the spiny-leaved *agave* plant. Juice from two varieties is used to make the alcoholic drinks *tequila* and *mezcal*. The *agave* plant is grown on plantations, then cooked, crushed, and fermented. The drink is exported worldwide.

MAP FEATURES

Tourism: Resorts like Acapulco attract thousands of visitors to Mexico each year. Tourism is now a vital source of foreign currency. Look for ⚓

Maquiladora: American raw materials are brought across the border to supply factories, or maquiladora, where labor costs are lower. Look for 🏭

Cereals		Fishing	
Sugar cane		Mining	
Coffee		Oil	
Cotton		Industrial center	
Forest products		Archaeological site	

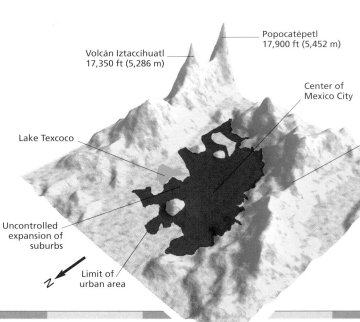

Popocatépetl 17,900 ft (5,452 m)

Volcán Iztaccihuatl 17,350 ft (5,286 m)

Center of Mexico City

Lake Texcoco

Mountains prevent pollution from escaping

Uncontrolled expansion of suburbs

Limit of urban area

MEXICO CITY

The Aztec capital, Tenochtitlán, was built on islands in Lake Texcoco. The city was destroyed by the Spanish, but modern-day Mexico City is built on the ruins. With a population of over 16 million, it is the world's largest city. Mexico City is very polluted because it is surrounded by a ring of mountains which trap polluted air from cars and factories.

Map labels

Tijuana
Mexicali
Ensenada
Colorado
UNITED STATES
Nogales
Ciudad Juárez
Millet
Copper
Isla Ángel de la Guarda
LOWER CALIFORNIA
Isla Tiburón
Hermosillo
Isla Cedros
Millet
Guaymas
Lead
Zinc
Millet Conchos
Gulf of California
Santa Rosalia
Ciudad Obregón
Zinc Silver
SIERRA MADRE
SIERRA DE LA GIGANTA
Manganese
Isla Carmen
Isla Santa Catalina
Los Mochis
Isla San José
Isla del Espíritu Santo
Culiacán
Isla Cerralvo
La Paz
Corn
Islas Tres Marías
Millet
Mazatlán

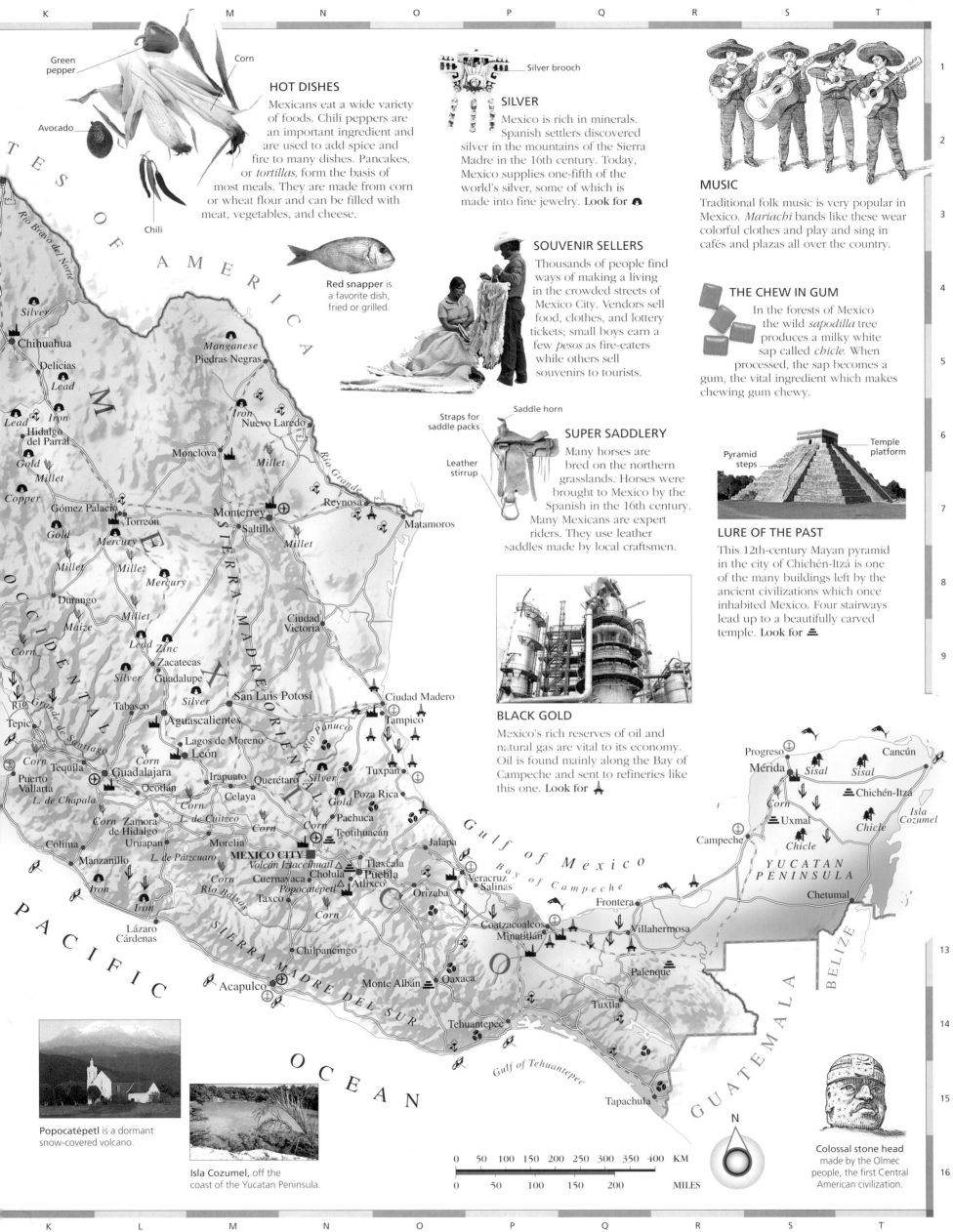

Green pepper

Corn

Avocado

Chili

HOT DISHES
Mexicans eat a wide variety of foods. Chili peppers are an important ingredient and are used to add spice and fire to many dishes. Pancakes, or *tortillas*, form the basis of most meals. They are made from corn or wheat flour and can be filled with meat, vegetables, and cheese.

Red snapper is a favorite dish, fried or grilled.

Silver brooch

SILVER
Mexico is rich in minerals. Spanish settlers discovered silver in the mountains of the Sierra Madre in the 16th century. Today, Mexico supplies one-fifth of the world's silver, some of which is made into fine jewelry. Look for 🔗

SOUVENIR SELLERS
Thousands of people find ways of making a living in the crowded streets of Mexico City. Vendors sell food, clothes, and lottery tickets; small boys earn a few *pesos* as fire-eaters while others sell souvenirs to tourists.

Straps for saddle packs

Saddle horn

Leather stirrup

SUPER SADDLERY
Many horses are bred on the northern grasslands. Horses were brought to Mexico by the Spanish in the 16th century. Many Mexicans are expert riders. They use leather saddles made by local craftsmen.

MUSIC
Traditional folk music is very popular in Mexico. *Mariachi* bands like these wear colorful clothes and play and sing in cafés and plazas all over the country.

THE CHEW IN GUM
In the forests of Mexico the wild *sapodilla* tree produces a milky white sap called *chicle*. When processed, the sap becomes a gum, the vital ingredient which makes chewing gum chewy.

Pyramid steps

Temple platform

LURE OF THE PAST
This 12th-century Mayan pyramid in the city of Chichén-Itzá is one of the many buildings left by the ancient civilizations which once inhabited Mexico. Four stairways lead up to a beautifully carved temple. Look for ☰

BLACK GOLD
Mexico's rich reserves of oil and natural gas are vital to its economy. Oil is found mainly along the Bay of Campeche and sent to refineries like this one. Look for ⛽

Popocatépetl is a dormant snow-covered volcano.

Isla Cozumel, off the coast of the Yucatan Peninsula.

Colossal stone head made by the Olmec people, the first Central American civilization.

UNITED STATES OF AMERICA

PACIFIC OCEAN

GULF OF MEXICO

Bay of Campeche

Gulf of Tehuantepec

YUCATAN PENINSULA

SIERRA MADRE OCCIDENTAL

SIERRA MADRE ORIENTAL

SIERRA MADRE DEL SUR

GUATEMALA

BELIZE

Río Bravo del Norte

Río Grande

Río Pánuco

Río Grande de Santiago

Río Balsas

Chihuahua, Delicias, Hidalgo del Parral, Gómez Palacio, Torreón, Durango, Monclova, Nuevo Laredo, Monterrey, Saltillo, Reynosa, Matamoros, Ciudad Victoria, Ciudad Madero, Tampico, Tuxpán, Poza Rica, Pachuca, Teotihuacán, Zacatecas, Guadalupe, San Luis Potosí, Aguascalientes, Lagos de Moreno, León, Tepic, Puerto Vallarta, Guadalajara, Ocotlán, Irapuato, Querétaro, Celaya, Zamora de Hidalgo, Uruapan, Morelia, Colima, Manzanillo, MEXICO CITY, Volcán Iztaccíhuatl, Cuernavaca, Popocatépetl, Taxco, Tlaxcala, Cholula, Puebla, Atlixco, Jalapa, Veracruz, Orizaba, Salinas, Chilpancingo, Acapulco, Lázaro Cárdenas, Monte Albán, Oaxaca, Tehuantepec, Coatzacoalcos, Minatitlán, Frontera, Villahermosa, Palenque, Tuxtla, Tapachula, Chetumal, Campeche, Uxmal, Mérida, Progreso, Cancún, Chichén-Itzá

Manganese, Piedras Negras, Silver, Lead, Iron, Gold, Copper, Mercury, Millet, Maize, Corn, Zinc, Tabasco, Tequila, Sisal, Chicle, Isla Cozumel

L. de Chapala, L. de Cuitzeo, L. de Pátzcuaro

0 50 100 150 200 250 300 350 400 KM

0 50 100 150 200 MILES

N

Toco toucan
Ramphastos toco
Length: 24 in (60 cm)

Emerald tree boa
Corallus caninus
Length: 6 ft (1.8 m)

Lower California

CENTRAL AND SOUTH AMERICA

SOUTH AMERICA is shaped like a giant triangle that tapers southward from the Equator to Cape Horn. A huge wall of mountains, the Andes, stretches for 4,500 miles (7,250 km) along the entire Pacific coast. Until 3 million years ago South America was not connected to North America, so life there evolved in isolation. Several extraordinary animal groups developed, including sloths and anteaters. Many unique plant species originated here, too, such as the potato and tomato. South America has the world's largest area of tropical rain forest, through which run the Amazon River and its many tributaries. Central America is mountainous and forested.

Geoffroy's spider monkey
Ateles geoffroyi
Length: 5 ft (1.5 m)

Mahogany
Swietenia macrophylla
Height: 82 ft (25 m)

Alpaca
Lama pacos
Height: 5 ft (1.5 m)

Passionflower
Passiflora caerulea
Across flower: 6 in (15 cm)

■ TROPICAL TOBAGO

Coconut palms grow along the shores of many Caribbean islands. Palms have flexible trunks that enable them to withstand tropical storms.

▲ VOLCANIC ISLANDS

One of the extinct volcanic craters of the Galapagos Island group breaks the surface of the Pacific Ocean. Like other isolated regions of the world, many unique species have evolved here, such as the giant tortoise, 4 ft (1.2 m) long.

☑ SEA-DWELLING TREES

Mangroves grow along tropical coastlines. The tangled roots of Pinuelo mangroves create ideal homes for tiny aquatic species.

□ PAMPAS

Giant grasses up to 10 ft (3 m) high grow on Argentina's dry southern Pampas. Here, further north, more plentiful rainfall supports a few scattered trees.

Archaeogeryon, a crab that lived in this region 20 million years ago.

■ THE FOREST FLOOR

Tropical rain forest trees form such a dense canopy that little sunlight or rain can reach the ground 200 ft (70 m) below. Rain forest soils are easily washed away when the trees and plants are removed.

□ THE BLEAK SOUTH

Patagonia's cold desert environment contrasts starkly with the lush hot forests of the Amazon Basin. Plants take root in the cracks of bare rock and grow close to the ground to survive icy winds.

△ VOLCANIC ANDES

Steam and smoke rises from Villarrica, an active volcano. Many peaks in the Andes are active or former volcanoes. Despite the intense heat within these lava-filled mountains, the highest are permanently covered in snow – even those on the Equator.

□ ▲ BIRTH OF A RIVER

The snow-capped peaks of the Andes are the source of the Amazon, the world's second longest river. It is 4,080 miles (6,570 km) long.

CROSS-SECTION THROUGH SOUTH AMERICA

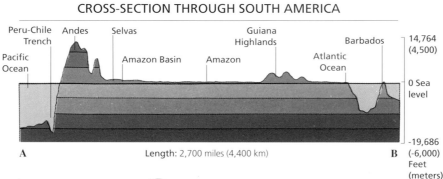

Peru-Chile Trench — Andes — Selvas — Guiana Highlands — Barbados

Pacific Ocean — Amazon Basin — Amazon — Atlantic Ocean

14,764 (4,500)

0 Sea level

-19,686 (-6,000) Feet (meters)

A — Length: 2,700 miles (4,400 km) — B

□ ▲ DRY ATACAMA DESERT

The Atacama Desert is the world's driest place outside Antarctica. Rain has not fallen in some areas for hundreds of years. Winds that pass over cold coastline currents absorb no moisture.

Giant anteater
Myrmecophaga tridactyla
Length: 7 ft (2 m)

Galapagos fur seal
Arctocephalus galapagoensis
Length: 6 ft (1.8 m)

Ocelot
Felis pardalis
Length: 6 ft (1.7 m)

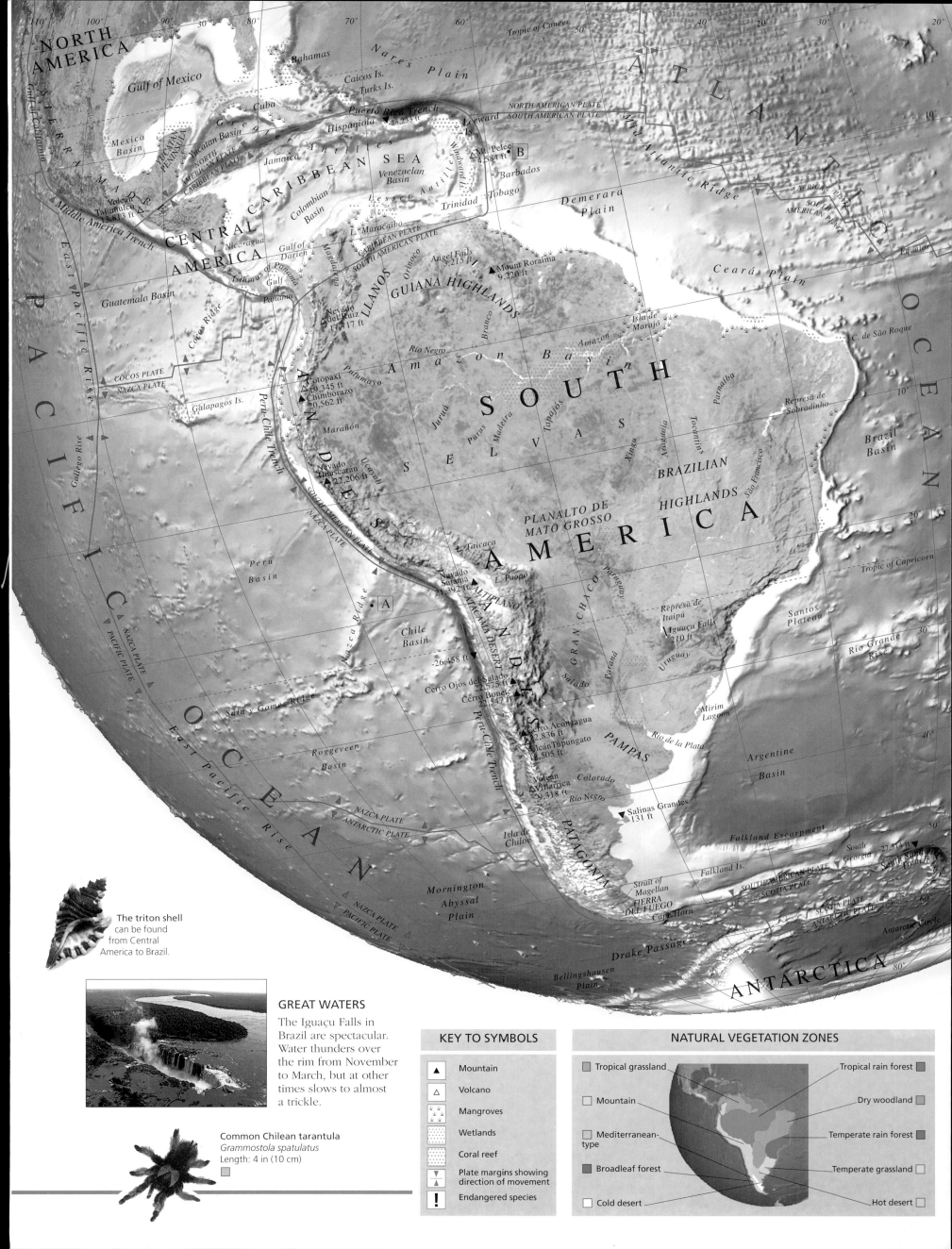

The triton shell can be found from Central America to Brazil.

GREAT WATERS

The Iguaçu Falls in Brazil are spectacular. Water thunders over the rim from November to March, but at other times slows to almost a trickle.

Common Chilean tarantula
Grammostola spatulatus
Length: 4 in (10 cm)

KEY TO SYMBOLS

- ▲ Mountain
- △ Volcano
- Mangroves
- Wetlands
- Coral reef
- ▼▲ Plate margins showing direction of movement
- ! Endangered species

NATURAL VEGETATION ZONES

- Tropical grassland
- Mountain
- Mediterranean-type
- Broadleaf forest
- Cold desert
- Tropical rain forest
- Dry woodland
- Temperate rain forest
- Temperate grassland
- Hot desert

CENTRAL AMERICA AND THE CARIBBEAN

THE TROPICAL REGION OF Central America and the Caribbean was settled by hunters and farmers many thousands of years ago. By 300 BC the Maya had established a sophisticated civilization on the mainland – ruins of their pyramids and temples can still be seen deep in the forests of Guatemala. The Maya, as well as the native peoples who lived on the Caribbean islands, were almost wiped out by European explorers who arrived in the 15th century. From this time, European nations, in particular the British, French, Spanish, and Dutch, competed for control of the region, and some countries did not gain independence until recently. Europeans brought slaves from Africa to work on vast sugar plantations. In the last few decades, tourism has enriched the Caribbean, but in Central America, poverty is still a major problem.

A Jamaican beach devastated by a hurricane.

GUATEMALA
pop: 11,600,000

CUBA
pop: 11,100,000

BELIZE
pop: 200,000

Conches from the shallow waters of the Caribbean are edible.

HONDURAS
pop: 6,100,000

Jamaican Blue Mountain coffee is prized by experts.

JAMAICA
pop: 2,500,000

EL SALVADOR
pop: 6,100,000

The ancient Maya temple of Altun Ha is hidden deep in the rain forest of Belize.

NICARAGUA
pop: 4,500,000

NICARAGUA

Since Nicaragua became independent in 1838 it has been devastated by civil war and foreign interference. During the 1980s, a desperate conflict took place between the socialist government and the right-wing *Contras*, supported by the US. Although democracy has now been restored, little progress has been made in fighting the huge problems of poverty, ill-health, and homelessness.

RURAL MARKETS

Many Guatemalans live in small villages, growing corn and beans and making brightly colored cloth, baskets, pottery, and wood carvings. These goods, as well as fruit and tobacco, are sold at local markets.

Hot pepper sauce, made with spicy chilis, is used all over the region.

COSTA RICA
pop: 3,700,000

PANAMA
pop: 2,800,000

MAP FEATURES

Archaeological sites: Great civilizations, such as the Maya, flourished in Central America from 300 BC. They built temples, palaces, and cities. Look for ▲

Shellfishing: Shrimp and lobster thrive in the mangrove swamps on the coasts of Central America, which provide rich feeding grounds. Look for 🦐

Shipping registry: Ships from all over the world fly Panama's flag. They register there because of low fees and limited controls on the labor force. Look for ⚑

Sugarcane		Tobacco	
Bananas		Timber	
Coffee		Mining	
Cocoa		Industrial center	
Cotton		Tourism	

Swamps near the Honduran coast.

N

0 50 100 150 200 250 300 350 400 KM

0 50 100 150 200 MILES

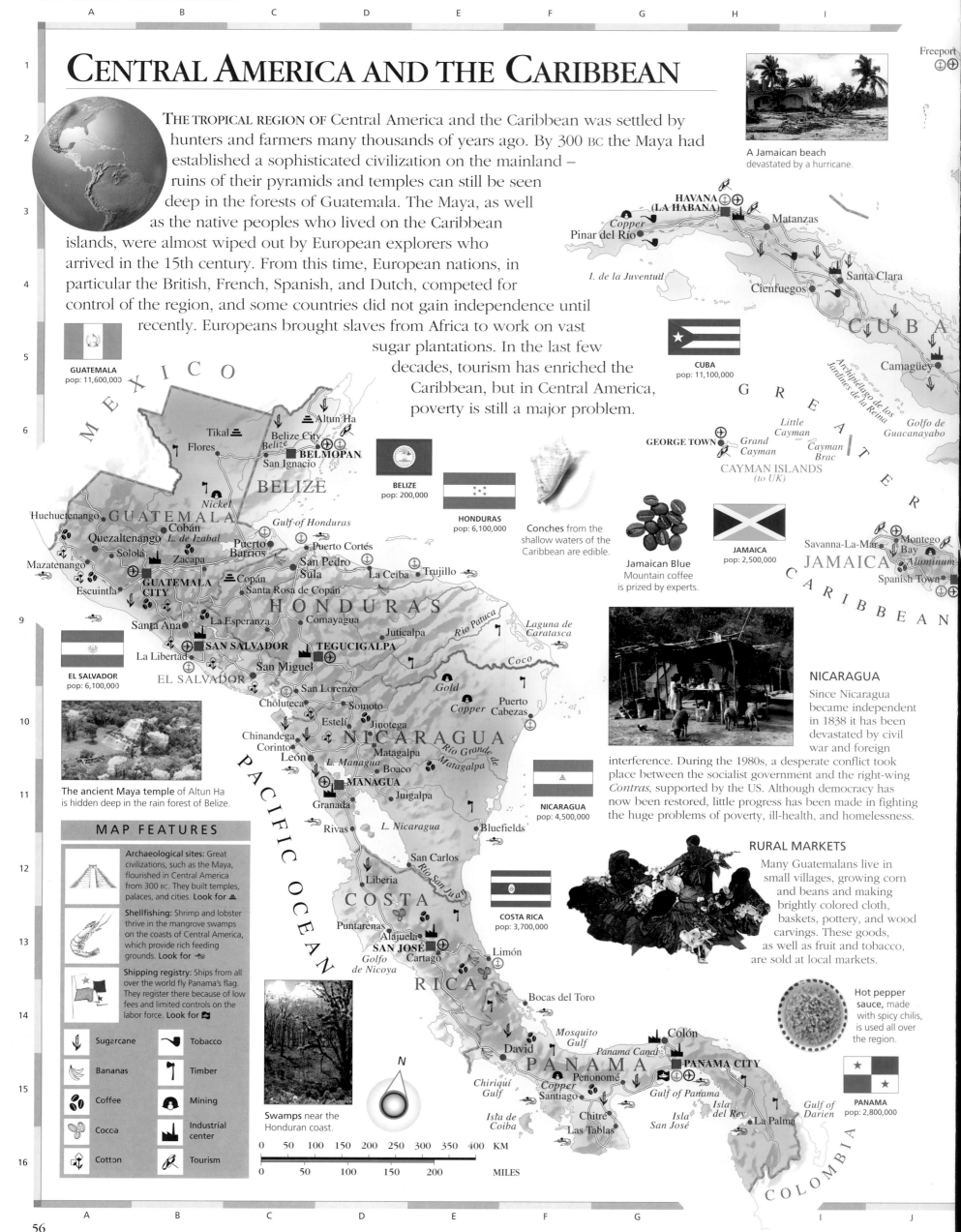

56

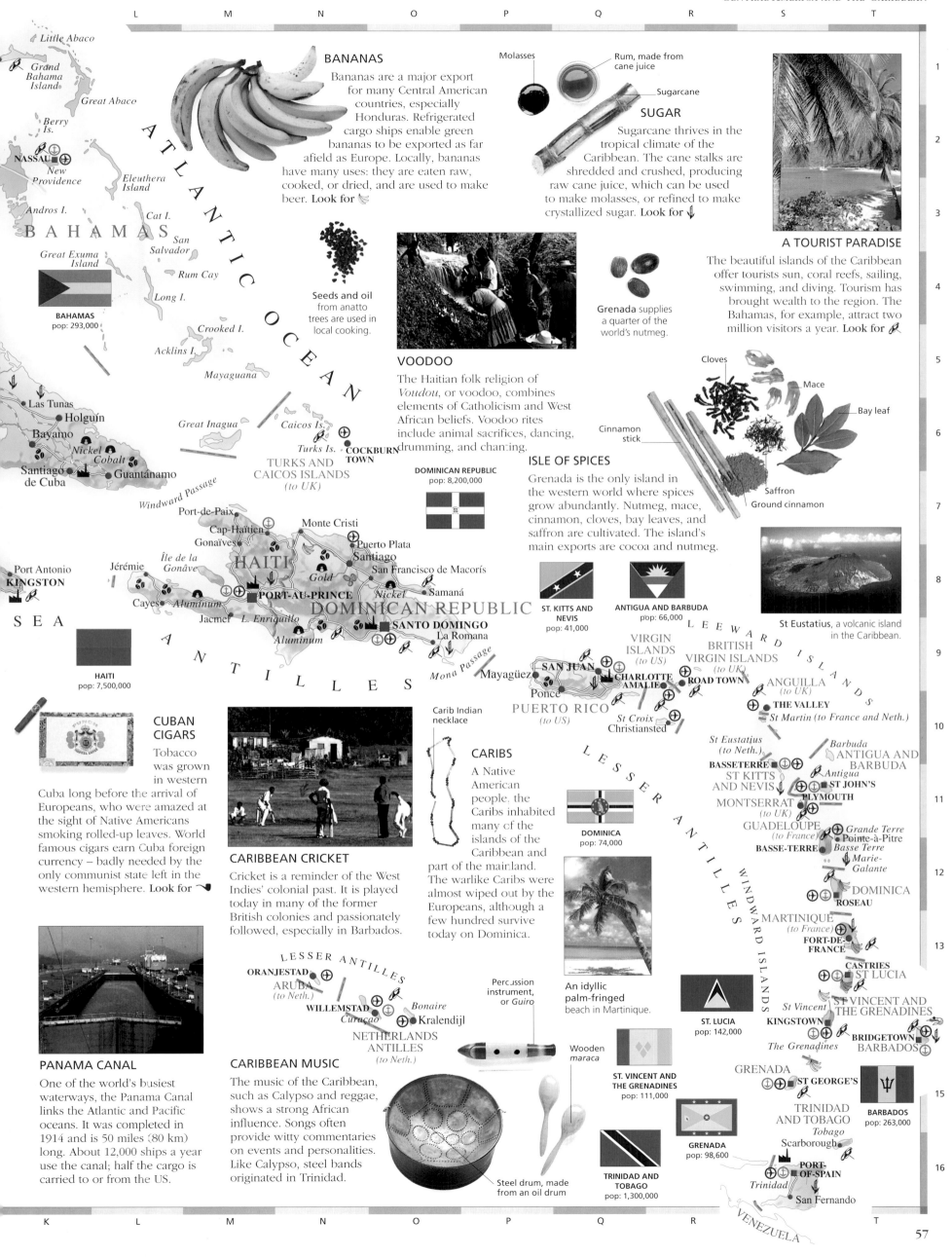

BANANAS

Bananas are a major export for many Central American countries, especially Honduras. Refrigerated cargo ships enable green bananas to be exported as far afield as Europe. Locally, bananas have many uses: they are eaten raw, cooked, or dried, and are used to make beer. Look for

Molasses

Rum, made from cane juice

Sugarcane

SUGAR

Sugarcane thrives in the tropical climate of the Caribbean. The cane stalks are shredded and crushed, producing raw cane juice, which can be used to make molasses, or refined to make crystallized sugar. Look for ⇓

A TOURIST PARADISE

The beautiful islands of the Caribbean offer tourists sun, coral reefs, sailing, swimming, and diving. Tourism has brought wealth to the region. The Bahamas, for example, attract two million visitors a year. Look for

Seeds and oil from anatto trees are used in local cooking.

Grenada supplies a quarter of the world's nutmeg.

VOODOO

The Haitian folk religion of *Voudou*, or voodoo, combines elements of Catholicism and West African beliefs. Voodoo rites include animal sacrifices, dancing, drumming, and chanting.

Cloves

Mace

Bay leaf

Cinnamon stick

Saffron

Ground cinnamon

ISLE OF SPICES

Grenada is the only island in the western world where spices grow abundantly. Nutmeg, mace, cinnamon, cloves, bay leaves, and saffron are cultivated. The island's main exports are cocoa and nutmeg.

St Eustatius, a volcanic island in the Caribbean.

BAHAMAS
pop: 293,000

DOMINICAN REPUBLIC
pop: 8,200,000

ST. KITTS AND NEVIS
pop: 41,000

ANTIGUA AND BARBUDA
pop: 66,000

HAITI
pop: 7,500,000

CUBAN CIGARS

Tobacco was grown in western Cuba long before the arrival of Europeans, who were amazed at the sight of Native Americans smoking rolled-up leaves. World famous cigars earn Cuba foreign currency – badly needed by the only communist state left in the western hemisphere. Look for

CARIBBEAN CRICKET

Cricket is a reminder of the West Indies' colonial past. It is played today in many of the former British colonies and passionately followed, especially in Barbados.

Carib Indian necklace

CARIBS

A Native American people, the Caribs inhabited many of the islands of the Caribbean and part of the mainland. The warlike Caribs were almost wiped out by the Europeans, although a few hundred survive today on Dominica.

DOMINICA
pop: 74,000

An idyllic palm-fringed beach in Martinique.

PANAMA CANAL

One of the world's busiest waterways, the Panama Canal links the Atlantic and Pacific oceans. It was completed in 1914 and is 50 miles (80 km) long. About 12,000 ships a year use the canal; half the cargo is carried to or from the US.

CARIBBEAN MUSIC

The music of the Caribbean, such as Calypso and reggae, shows a strong African influence. Songs often provide witty commentaries on events and personalities. Like Calypso, steel bands originated in Trinidad.

Percussion instrument, or Guiro

Wooden maraca

Steel drum, made from an oil drum

ST. LUCIA
pop: 142,000

ST. VINCENT AND THE GRENADINES
pop: 111,000

GRENADA
pop: 98,600

TRINIDAD AND TOBAGO
pop: 1,300,000

BARBADOS
pop: 263,000

Map labels

Little Abaco
Grand Bahama Island
Great Abaco
Berry Is.
NASSAU
New Providence
Eleuthera Island
Andros I.
Cat I.
San Salvador
BAHAMAS
Great Exuma Island
Rum Cay
Long I.
Crooked I.
Acklins I.
Mayaguana
ATLANTIC OCEAN
Great Inagua
Caicos Is.
Turks Is.
COCKBURN TOWN
TURKS AND CAICOS ISLANDS (to UK)
Las Tunas
Holguín
Bayamo
Nickel
Cobalt
Santiago de Cuba
Guantánamo
Windward Passage
Port-de-Paix
Monte Cristi
Cap-Haïtien
Gonaïves
Puerto Plata
Santiago
HAITI
Île de la Gonâve
Gold
San Francisco de Macorís
Jérémie
Port Antonio
KINGSTON
PORT-AU-PRINCE
Nickel
Samaná
Cayes
Aluminum
DOMINICAN REPUBLIC
Jacmel
L. Enriquillo
SANTO DOMINGO
La Romana
SEA
Aluminum
Mona Passage
Mayagüez
SAN JUAN
Ponce
CHARLOTTE AMALIE
PUERTO RICO (to US)
VIRGIN ISLANDS (to US)
ROAD TOWN
BRITISH VIRGIN ISLANDS (to UK)
St Croix
Christiansted
ANTILLES
LEEWARD ISLANDS
ANGUILLA (to UK)
THE VALLEY
St Martin (to France and Neth.)
St Eustatius (to Neth.)
Barbuda
ANTIGUA AND BARBUDA
BASSETERRE
ST KITTS AND NEVIS
Antigua
ST JOHN'S
MONTSERRAT (to UK)
PLYMOUTH
GUADELOUPE (to France)
Grande Terre
Pointe-à-Pitre
BASSE-TERRE
Basse Terre
Marie-Galante
LESSER ANTILLES
DOMINICA
ROSEAU
MARTINIQUE (to France)
FORT-DE-FRANCE
WINDWARD ISLANDS
CASTRIES
ST LUCIA
St Vincent
ST VINCENT AND THE GRENADINES
KINGSTOWN
The Grenadines
BRIDGETOWN
BARBADOS
GRENADA
ST GEORGE'S
TRINIDAD AND TOBAGO
Tobago
Scarborough
PORT-OF-SPAIN
Trinidad
San Fernando
VENEZUELA
ORANJESTAD
ARUBA (to Neth.)
Bonaire
WILLEMSTAD
Curaçao
Kralendijk
NETHERLANDS ANTILLES (to Neth.)

NORTHERN SOUTH AMERICA

THIS REGION IS DOMINATED BY the volcanic peaks and mountain ranges of the Andes. The powerful Incas ruled much of this area in the 15th century, and large numbers of their descendants still live in Peru, Bolivia, and Ecuador today. In the 16th century, Spanish *conquistadores* reached South America, swept the Incas and other native peoples aside, and colonized the region from Venezuela to Bolivia. Areas to the east were later settled by the French, Dutch, and British. Although all the countries except French Guiana are now independent republics, independence has brought many problems, such as military dictatorships, high inflation, organized crime, the illegal drug trade, and huge foreign debts. Many of the cities are overcrowded, but large numbers of people still flock there from the countryside, looking for jobs.

SHRIMP

Shrimp living in the muddy waters of Ecuador's mangrove swamps have become the country's second most important source of foreign currency, after oil. But as the industry expands, it is destroying the mangroves – the shrimps' natural habitat. Look for 🦐

ECUADOR
pop: 12,200,000

MARKET DAY

Brightly dressed in their traditional Andean clothes and hats, local people display their wares in the market of the Peruvian town of Pisac. They sell fruit and vegetables, together with pottery and clothes produced for the tourist trade.

CARACAS

The discovery of oil in 1917 made Venezuela the richest country in the region. Its capital, Caracas, was built with oil money. Modern highways and skyscrapers dominate the city, but many people live in shantytowns on the surrounding hillsides.

Hammered gold

A figure made by ancient Colombian craftsmen.

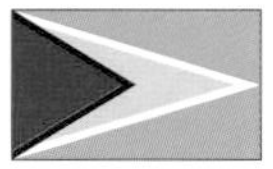

SURINAME
pop: 442,000

GUYANA
pop: 856,000

The lush Caribbean coastline of northern Venezuela.

EMERALDS
Some of the world's finest emeralds are mined near Bogotá, the capital of Colombia. Long before the Spanish invaded the country in search of gold, native peoples mined the emeralds for their gold jewelry and ceremonial objects. Look for 🟢

Emerald

VENEZUELA
pop: 23,200,000

COLOMBIA
pop: 37,700,000

Quinine from the bark of the Peruvian *cinchona* tree is used to treat malaria.

Cinchona leaves

The ancient Inca city of Machupicchu in the Peruvian Andes.

PANAMA HATS

Panama hats are made of fiber from a palm tree that grows in the coastal forests of Ecuador. One hat can take up to three months to make.

LIMA

Pizarro, a leader of the Spanish *conquistadores*, founded Peru's capital city in the 16th century, and his bones are buried in the cathedral on the Plaza de Armas, the main square, in the city's center.

Lima Cathedral

COCAINE

The steep slopes of the Andes are ideally suited to growing the coca bush. The native peoples have always chewed coca leaves to protect themselves against cold and altitude sickness. But the drug cocaine, made from the leaves, is now a major world problem. Today, Colombia's economy is virtually dependent on the illegal export of cocaine.

Coca leaves

HIGHEST RAILROAD

Peru's railroads are the highest in the world. The single-track railroad from Lima to Huancayo in the Andes zigzags through tunnels and over wooden bridges, reaching an altitude of 15,885 ft (4,843 m) where it crosses through one of the passes.

Rug decorated with llamas, the traditional Andean pack animals

OTAVALO PEOPLE

Woolen rugs woven by the Otavalo people from Ecuador are sold all over the Americas and Europe. The Otavalo have developed new techniques, such as replacing traditional natural dyes with synthetic ones.

Clay body

Strap handle

Water jar, found at the ancient Inca city of Cusco in Peru.

Permanent snow and ice

Inland river valleys: sugar, coffee

9,850 ft (3,000 m)

6,550 ft (2,000 m)

3,280 ft (1,000 m)

Altiplano: high plateaus between mountains used for grazing animals

Highland areas: barley, potatoes, wheat

Temperate zone: coffee, tobacco, corn

Coastal lowland: sugar, cacao, bananas, rice

Sea level

N

Peru-Chile Trench: c.19,686 ft (6,000 m) below sea level

Pacific Ocean floor

ANDEAN CULTIVATION

On the steep hillsides of the Andes, every scrap of soil must be made to work efficiently. Like their Inca ancestors, Andean farmers suit the crop to the temperature, which gets lower higher up the mountains. This region is the original home of the potato, which can be grown successfully at high altitudes.

Llamas grazing on the high plains of the Andes in Bolivia.

PERU
pop: 24,800,000

BOLIVIA
pop: 8,000,000

BOLIVIA'S TWO CAPITALS

LA PAZ – legislative and administrative capital

SUCRE – legal capital

The Andes are the world's longest chain of mountains.

The native peoples of the Andes were the first to grow potatoes.

LAKE TITICACA

Stretching across the border between Bolivia and Peru is the world's highest lake, Lake Titicaca, 13,000 ft (4,000 m) above sea level. The Uru people sail on the lake in boats of woven reeds.

CORPUS CHRISTI

Every town commemorates its patron saint with a festival. Events such as this colorful procession on Corpus Christi Day in Cusco, Peru, combine the religious beliefs of the native peoples with Christian ceremonies.

MAP FEATURES

Bananas: Bananas are grown as a cash crop in Ecuador's tropical lowlands. Ecuador is now the world's main exporter. Look for

Oil: Oil is vital to Venezuela's economy; today the country's oil revenues account for 80 percent of its export earnings. Look for

Archaeological sites: The remains of many magnificent ancient cities and temples can still be seen in the Andes. Look for

Space center: The European Space Agency launches its rocket, Ariane, from its rocket base at Kourou, French Guiana. Look for

Cattle

Rice

Sugarcane

Coffee

Timber

Shellfishing

Mining

Industrial center

Map labels

PACIFIC OCEAN

Río Ucayali

P E R U

A N D E S

C H I L E

B O L I V I A

B R A Z I L

PARAGUAY

ARGENTINA

Chiclayo
Cajamarca
Trujillo
Chimbote
Pucallpa
Huánuco
Yungay
Cerro de Pasco
La Oroya
LIMA
Callao
Ica
Nazca
San Juan
Ayacucho
Huancayo
Cusco
Machupicchu
Ollantaytambo
Pisac
Arequipa
Juliaca
Puno
Mollendo
Tacna
Copiaó
L. Titicaca
LA PAZ
Oruro
Cochabamba
SUCRE
Potosí
Tarija
Uyuni
L. Poopó
Trinidad
Santa Cruz
Río Mamoré
Río Beni
Río Madre de Dios
Río San Miguel

Beef, Iron, Silver, Copper, Lead, Zinc, Tin, Tungsten

BRAZIL

OCCUPYING NEARLY HALF of South America, Brazil possesses the greatest river basin in the world. The Amazonian rain forest, which covers some two-thirds of the country, is a vast storehouse of natural riches, still largely untapped. But land is needed for agriculture, ranching, and new roads, and each year vast tracts of forest are cleared. The Portuguese colonized the country in the 16th century, intermarrying with the local population. They planted sugar in the northeast, working the plantations with slaves brought from Africa. With a further influx of Europeans, Brazil is now one of the world's most populous and ethnically diverse democracies. A land of opportunity for some – like those in the industrial region around São Paulo – it is one of poverty and deprivation for many, especially in the northeast. In spite of improved industrial output, Brazil still has high unemployment and huge foreign debts.

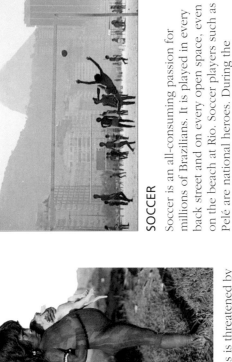

SOCCER

Soccer is an all-consuming passion for millions of Brazilians. It is played in every back street and on every open space, even on the beach at Rio. Soccer players such as Pelé are national heroes. During the World Cup, Brazil comes to a standstill.

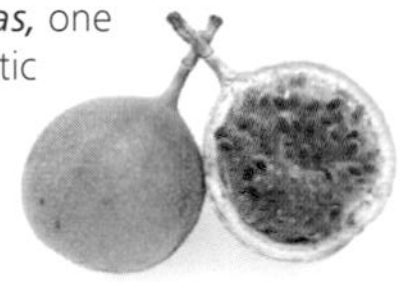

DANCE MUSIC

Transported to the north-eastern region of Brazil to work on the sugar plantations, African slaves brought their musical rhythms of their homelands with them. Their music has blended with other musical influences to produce the music for dances, such as the *samba* and the *lambada*. The instruments include this drum, called a *conga*.

A stretch of coast near Salvador in the northeast.

NATIVE PEOPLES

There were once some two million native people in the Amazon Basin. Today only about 240,000 survive. This Xingu girl is fortunate: she was born into a tribe which lives in a protected area of the Amazon rain forest. The well-being of many peoples is threatened by the ever-shrinking rain forest and by disease, logging, farming, and gold prospecting.

Grandillas, one of the many exotic fruits found in Brazil.

A huge tree trunk deep in the Brazilian rain forest.

The wings of the *Morpho* butterfly are often used to decorate jewelry.

BRAZIL
pop: 165,200,000

N

0 100 200 300 400 500 600 KM
MILES
0   100   200   300

ATLANTIC OCEAN

VENEZUELA
GUYANA
SURINAME
FRENCH GUIANA (to France)
COLOMBIA
PERU

B R A Z I L
AMAZON BASIN
PLANALTO DE MATO GROSSO
CHAPADA

Macapá
Belém
São Luís
Parnaíba
Teresina
Fortaleza
C. de São Roque
Natal
João Pessoa
Recife
Maceió
Aracaju
Mossoró
Campina Grande
Juazeiro
Picos
Carolina
Palmas do Tocantins
Santarém
Manaus
Boa Vista
Porto Velho
Cruzeiro do Sul
Salvador

Rio Negro
Rio Branco
Rio Jari
Rio Xingu
Rio Tapajós
Rio São Manuel
Rio Madeira
Rio Purus
Rio Juruá
Amazon
Rio Tocantins
Rio Araguaia
Rio Paranaíba

Represa de Tucuruí
Represa Balbina
Represa de Sobradinho

Beef
Aluminum
Sisal
Tungsten
Sisal
Gold
Chromium
Iron
Manganese
Tin
Rubber
Brazil Nuts

COLONIAL LEGACY

When the Portuguese arrived in Brazil in the 16th century, they brought their distinctive style of architecture. At the heart of many towns and cities in modern Brazil lie cobbled streets, squares, and churches. The historic town of Ouro Prêto – center of the 18th-century gold rush – remains today as a perfect example of a 16th-century town.

CARNIVAL

Every year, just before Lent, Rio de Janeiro erupts into carnival. Often called "The Biggest Party on Earth," carnival involves five days of music and dance. The main event is the competition to find the most outrageous costumes and best decorated floats as they parade through the city to the sound of *samba* music.

The huge statue of Christ the Redeemer which towers over Rio de Janeiro.

From Rio, good road and rail routes lead inland

Guanabara Bay provides access to the sea

Rio-Niterói Bridge

Rio de Janeiro

Suburbs have grown rapidly

Favelas lacking sanitation and other amenities

Favelas on steep slopes vulnerable to heavy rain

N

RIO DE JANEIRO

Once the capital of Brazil, the beautiful city of Rio de Janeiro sprawls among the bays, islands, and hills around Guanabara Bay. The city acts like a magnet, drawing people from poor rural areas who come in search of work. A severe lack of housing has given birth to endless shantytowns, called *favelas*, which creep up the hillsides and crowd every piece of land unfit for other development.

Brazilian-made Fiat sedan

STEEL

Attracted by Brazil's steel industry, cheap labor, and plentiful electricity, several multinational companies have invested money in the country. US and European car manufacturers have established successful factories around São Paulo. Look for 🚗

BRASÍLIA

In the mid-1950s the government of Brazil decided to build a new capital city in the sparsely inhabited central plateau region. Built in the shape of an airplane, the futuristic city of Brasília became the country's official capital in 1960. The wide boulevards and open spaces contain spectacular buildings like this cathedral.

ORANGE JUICE

Oranges are grown in the region around São Paulo, where the climate is frost-free. Over a million tons are picked each year. Most of it is processed into orange juice concentrate. Brazil now supplies 85 percent of the world's orange juice, exporting it mainly to the US and Europe. Look for 🍊

The Iguaçu River as it drops over the Iguaçu Falls.

COFFEE

Coffee originated in Africa, but Brazil is now the world's largest producer. When the trees have shed their white blossoms, the green berries ripen into red "cherries." Each cherry contains two seeds, or coffee beans, which are washed, dried, and roasted. Look for ☕

BRAZIL NUTS

Sometimes known as the *inferno verde*, or green hell, Brazil's vast rain forest is home to an astonishing variety of animals and plants from which products such as chemicals, drugs, and rubber can be made. Scattered through the forest are Brazil nut trees. Their nuts can be eaten or crushed to make an oil used in cosmetics. Look for 🌰

Shelled nut

Nuts fit into a shell, like segments of an orange

GOLD MINING

Brazil has vast mineral reserves. This huge human anthill is the result of a gold rush which began in the 1980s near the Serra Pelada. Thousands of prospectors – called *garimpeiros* – burrow into the hillsides hoping to find gold. Look for 🔶

MAP FEATURES

Cattle: Vast areas of Brazilian rain forest have been destroyed to clear the land for cattle ranching. Look for 🐂

Sugarcane: In the 1970s Brazil began to make an alternative to gasoline out of sugarcane, but now falling oil prices have made this uneconomic. Look for 🌾

Aerospace industry: In recent years Brazil has been successful in developing an aerospace industry, designing planes that are sold worldwide. Look for ✈️

🍂	Tobacco
🪓	Timber
🌲	Forest products
🐟	Mining
🏭	Industrial center
🚗	Vehicle manufacture

🍌	Bananas
🍊	Citrus fruits
☕	Coffee
🍫	Cocoa
🫘	Soybeans
🌱	Cotton

ATLANTIC OCEAN

BRAZILIAN HIGHLANDS

SERRA DO RONCADOR

DOS PARECIS

BOLIVIA

PARAGUAY

ARGENTINA

URUGUAY

PANTANAL

Rio São Francisco

Salvador

Feira de Santana

Ibotirama

Barreiras

Cuiabá

Corumbá

Goiânia

BRASÍLIA

Campo Grande

Uberlândia

Uberaba

Belo Horizonte

Ouro Prêto

Vitória

C. de São Tomé

Rio de Janeiro

Juiz de Fora

São José dos Campos

São Paulo

Santos

Campinas

Ribeirão Prêto

Curitiba

Joinville

Londrina

Florianópolis

Porto Alegre

Passo Fundo

Santa Maria

Uruguai

Pelotas

Rio Grande

Lagoa dos Patos

Mirim Lagoon

Represa de Furnas

Represa de Itaipú

Iguaçu Falls

Rio Iguaçu

Paraná

Paraguay

Beef, Gold, Iron, Zinc, Lead, Diamonds, Gold, Manganese, Iron, Nickel, Manganese, Uranium, Copper

SOUTHERN SOUTH AMERICA

ALL FOUR COUNTRIES in this region were colonized in the 16th century by Spain. With the exception of Argentina, their populations are almost entirely *mestizo* – people of mixed Spanish and native descent. In Argentina, 98 percent of the population is descended from European settlers, as the native peoples were killed or driven out by the immigrants. Argentina falls into three regions: the hot, damp lands of the Gran Chaco in the north, the grasslands of the Pampas in the center, and the barren plateau of Patagonia in the south. Argentina gets its wealth from the rich soil of the Pampas, where cereals are grown and vast herds of sheep and cattle graze. The Pampas spills into neighboring Uruguay, where sheep provide the country with its main export, wool. Paraguay's economy is mainly dependent on agriculture. Chile is a long, narrow country, stretching along the western side of the Andes from the mineral-rich Atacama desert to the icy wastes of the south. Both Chile and Argentina, despite a troubled history, are now relatively stable and prosperous.

ASUNCIÓN

Plaza Constitución is just one of many squares where beautiful Spanish buildings still stand in Asunción, Paraguay's capital and only large city.

MAINLY MEAT

In the late 19th century, processing and packing meat became an important industry in Uruguay. Today, canned meats, such as corned beef, are still a major export. Look for ▼

THE PEOPLES OF THE CHACO

Only five percent of Paraguay's population lives in the grasslands and swamps of the Gran Chaco. The main people still living there are the Guaranís, the first inhabitants of Paraguay. A smaller group, the Macá, make money by selling colorful hand-woven cloth and goods, like this bag, to tourists.

PARAGUAY
pop: 5,200,000

URUGUAY
pop: 3,200,000

Tomatoes were first grown in South America.

ITAIPÚ DAM

On the mighty Paraná River is one of the world's largest hydroelectric projects, the Itaipú Dam. This joint venture between Brazil and Paraguay boosted Paraguay's economy, creating jobs for thousands of people. Look for ▦

The Atacama Desert in Chile is the driest place on Earth.

CHILE
pop: 13,800,000

COPPER

Near Calama, Chile, shining orange metal is extracted from the largest open-pit copper mine in the world. Giant trucks remove thousands of tons of ore a day. However, the world price of copper is now falling, causing severe economic problems in Chile. Look for ⊙

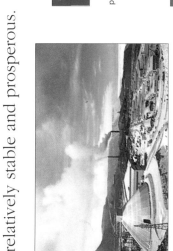

BRAZIL

PARAGUAY

BOLIVIA

PERU

ARGENTINA

URUGUAY

CHILE

ANDES

GRAN CHACO

ATACAMA DESERT

PACIFIC OCEAN

Itaipú Dam
Ciudad del Este
Salto del Guairá
Concepción
Pedro Juan Caballero
San Pedro
Fuerte Olimpo
Capitán Pablo Lagerenza
General Eugenio A. Garay
Filadelfia
Doctor Pedro P. Peña
Pozo Colorado
Paraguarí
ASUNCIÓN
Villarrica
Caazapá
San Juan Bautista
Encarnación
Posadas
Corrientes
Resistencia
Formosa
Pilar
Concordia
Paysandú
Artigas
Rivera
Melo
Treinta y Tres
Rocha
Tacuarembó
Durazno
Florida
Salto
Mercedes
Fray Bentos
Colón
Paraná
Colonia del Sacramento
MONTEVIDEO
La Plata
BUENOS AIRES
Santa Fe
Rosario
San Nicolás de los Arroyos
Junín
Villa María
Río Cuarto
San Luis
Mendoza
Córdoba
La Rioja
Santiago del Estero
San Fernando del Valle de Catamarca
San Miguel de Tucumán
Salta
San Salvador de Jujuy
L. Mar Chiquita
Godoy Cruz
San Juan
San Felipe
Quillota
SANTIAGO
San Bernardo
Valparaíso
Viña del Mar
La Ligua
Illapel
Ovalle
Coquimbo
La Serena
Vallenar
Copiapó
Chañaral
Antofagasta
Tocopilla
Iquique
Arica

Río Bermejo
Río Salado
Pilcomayo
Paraná
Paraguay
Negro
L. Mar Chiquita
Mirim Lagoon

Silver, Lead, Zinc, Copper, Iron

Beef, Wheat, Corn, Dairy

Pan-American Highway

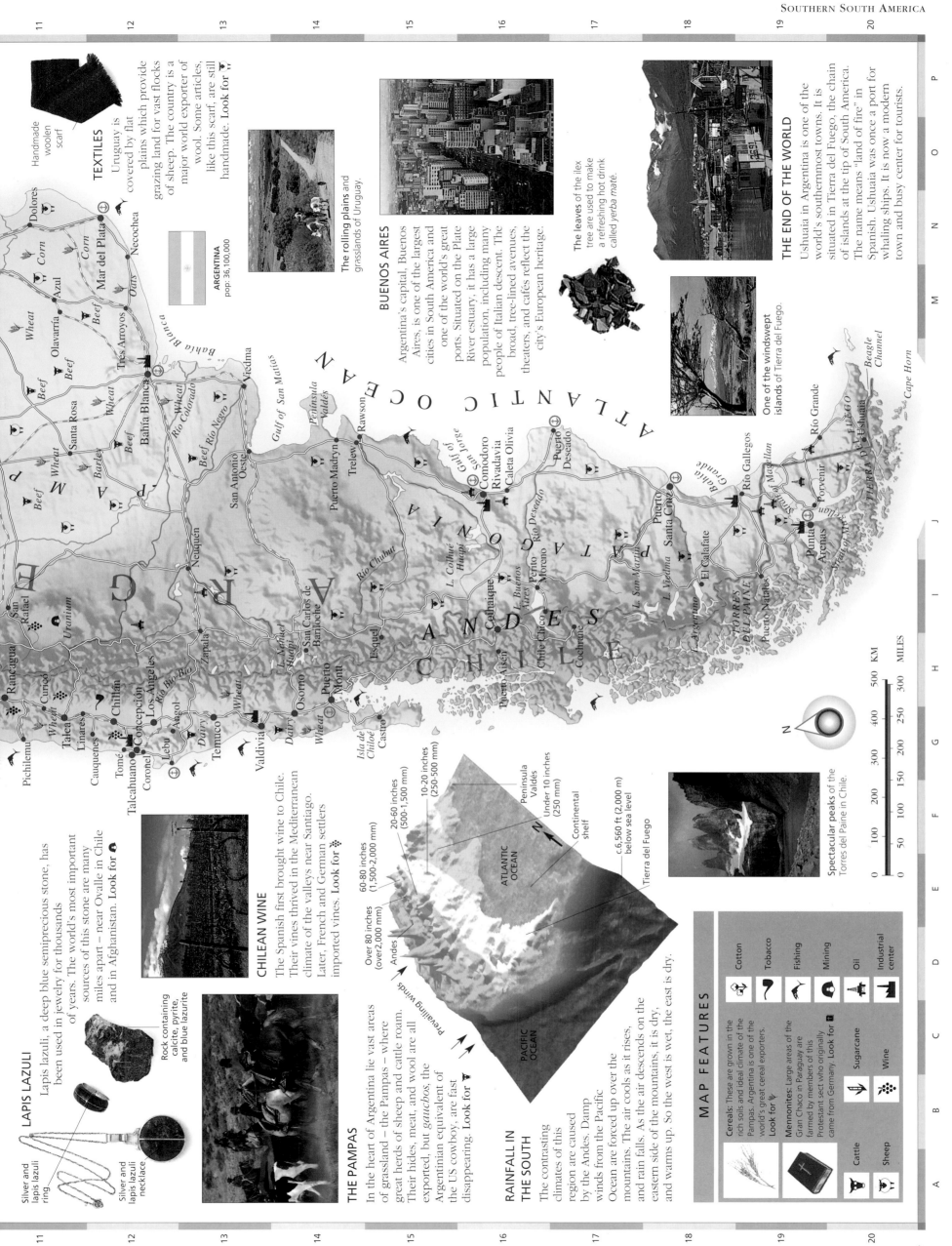

TEXTILES

Handmade woolen scarf

Uruguay is covered by flat plains which provide grazing land for vast flocks of sheep. The country is a major world exporter of wool. Some articles, like this scarf, are still handmade. Look for ⚑

The rolling plains and grasslands of Uruguay.

ARGENTINA
pop: 36,100,000

BUENOS AIRES

Argentina's capital, Buenos Aires, is one of the largest cities in South America and one of the world's great ports. Situated on the Plate River estuary, it has a large population, including many people of Italian descent. The broad, tree-lined avenues, theaters, and cafés reflect the city's European heritage.

The leaves of the ilex tree are used to make a refreshing hot drink called *yerba maté.*

THE END OF THE WORLD

Ushuaia in Argentina is one of the world's southernmost towns. It is situated in Tierra del Fuego, the chain of islands at the tip of South America. The name means "land of fire" in Spanish. Ushuaia was once a port for whaling ships. It is now a modern town and busy center for tourists.

One of the windswept islands of Tierra del Fuego.

ATLANTIC OCEAN

LAPIS LAZULI

Lapis lazuli, a deep blue semiprecious stone, has been used in jewelry for thousands of years. The world's most important sources of this stone are many miles apart – near Ovalle in Chile and in Afghanistan. Look for ◈

Silver and lapis lazuli ring

Silver and lapis lazuli necklace

Rock containing calcite, pyrite, and blue lazurite

THE PAMPAS

In the heart of Argentina lie vast areas of grassland – the Pampas – where great herds of sheep and cattle roam. Their hides, meat, and wool are all exported, but *gauchos*, the Argentinian equivalent of the US cowboy, are fast disappearing. Look for ⚑

CHILEAN WINE

The Spanish first brought wine to Chile. Their vines thrived in the Mediterranean climate of the valleys near Santiago. Later, French and German settlers imported vines. Look for ✿

RAINFALL IN THE SOUTH

The contrasting climates of this region are caused by the Andes. Damp winds from the Pacific Ocean are forced up over the mountains. The air cools as it rises, and rain falls. As the air descends on the eastern side of the mountains, it is dry, and warms up. So the west is wet, the east is dry.

prevailing winds

Over 80 inches (over 2,000 mm)
Andes
60-80 inches (1,500-2,000 mm)
20-60 inches (500-1,500 mm)
10-20 inches (250-500 mm)
Under 10 inches (250 mm)
Peninsula Valdés
Continental shelf
c.6,560 ft (2,000 m) below sea level
Tierra del Fuego
ATLANTIC OCEAN
PACIFIC OCEAN

Spectacular peaks of the Torres del Paine in Chile.

MAP FEATURES

Cereals: These are grown in the rich soils and ideal climate of the Pampas. Argentina is one of the world's great cereal exporters. Look for ⬡

Mennonites: Large areas of the Gran Chaco in Paraguay are farmed by members of this Protestant sect who originally came from Germany. Look for ▣

Cattle
Sheep
Cotton
Tobacco
Fishing
Mining
Oil
Industrial center
Sugarcane
Wine

N

KM
MILES
0 100 200 300 400 500
0 50 100 150 200 250 300

Map place names

Dolores
Corn
Corn
Necochea
Mar del Plata
Azul
Ouse
Olavarría
Wheat
Tres Arroyos
Beef
Beef
Santa Rosa
Beef
Wheat
Wheat
Bahía Blanca
Beef
Barley
Wheat
Bahía Blanca
Beef
Viedma
Gulf of San Matías
Wheat
Río Colorado
Río Negro
Beef
San Antonio Oeste
Peninsula Valdés
Rawson
Puerto Madryn
Trelew
Neuquén
Gulf of San Jorge
Comodoro Rivadavia
Caleta Olivia
Puerto Deseado
Río Deseado
San Rafael
Uranium
Río Chubut
L. Colhué Huapí
L. Buenos Aires
Coihaique
Perito Moreno
Chile Chico
Cochrane
Puerto San Martín
L. San Martín
L. Viedma
Puerto Deseado
Puerto Santa Cruz
El Calafate
Río Gallegos
Bahía Grande
Zapala
San Carlos de Bariloche
Esquel
Puerto Aisén
L. Argentino
Strait of Magellan
Punta Arenas
Porvenir
Río Grande
Ushuaia
Puerto Natales
TORRES DEL PAINE
TIERRA DEL FUEGO
Beagle Channel
Cape Horn
Rancagua
Curicó
Talca
Linares
Chillán
Los Angeles
Concepción
Angol
Cauquenes
Tomé
Lebu
Coronel
Talcahuano
Temuco
Valdivia
Osorno
Puerto Montt
Castro
Isla de Chiloé
Pichilemu
Wheat
Wheat
Wheat
Dairy
Río Bío-Bío
L. Llanquihue
L. Ranco
San Rafael
ATLANTIC OCEAN
PATAGONIA
ANDES
CHILE

THE ANTARCTIC

THE CONTINENT OF ANTARCTICA has such a cold, harsh climate that no people live there permanently. The land is covered by a huge sheet of ice up to 1.2 miles (2 km) thick, and seas around Antarctica are frozen over. Even during the short summers the temperature barely climbs above freezing, and the sea ice only partly melts; in winter, temperatures can plummet to -112° F (-80° C). Few animals and plants can survive on land, but the seas around Antarctica teem with fish and mammals. The only people on the continent are scientists working in the Antarctic research stations and tourists who come to see the dramatic landscape and the unique creatures that live here. But even these few people have brought waste and pollution to the region.

KRILL

Krill are the main food of the baleen whale. Japanese and Russian ships catch about 400,000 tons of krill each year, threatening the whales' food supply. Mainly used for animal feed, krill are also considered a delicacy in Japan. Krill gather in such huge numbers that they are visible from airplanes or even satellites.

Adélie penguins live in huge colonies on rocks or Antarctic pack ice.

Crozet Is. (to France)

Various nations claimed territory in Antarctica when it was first discovered in the 19th century. These claims have been suspended under the 1959 Antarctic Treaty (signed by 39 nations). Stations can be set up for scientific research, but military bases are forbidden.

Icebergs are huge blocks of ice which float in the sea.

ATLANTIC OCEAN

SCOTIA SEA

South Orkney Is.

Elephant I.

South Shetland Is.

Marambio (to Argentina)

Faraday (to UK)

Larsen Ice Shelf

Adelaide I.

San Martín (to Argentina)

Antarctic fishing fleets are reducing stocks of the Antarctic cod.

Drake Passage

Peter I Island (to Norway)

BELLINGSHAUSEN SEA

PALMER LAND

ELLSWORTH LAND

LESSER ANTARCTICA

MARIE BYRD LAND

AMUNDSEN SEA

Getz Ice Shelf

These mountains are on Anvers Island, which lies off the Antarctic Peninsula.

PACIFIC OCEAN

ROSS SEA

C. Adare

Riiser-Larsen Ice Shelf

Fimbul Ice Shelf

Georg von Neumayer (to Germany)

Novolazarevskaya (to Russian Fed.)

DRONNING MAUD LAND

Halley (to UK)

Belgrano II (to Argentina)

Filchner Ice Shelf

Ronne Ice Shelf

WEDDELL SEA

TRANSANTARCTIC MTS.

South Pole

Amundsen-Scott (to US)

Ross Ice Shelf

Scott Base (to NZ)

VICTORIA LAND

Lutzow-Holm Bay

Syowa (to Japan)

Molodezhnaya (to Russian Fed.)

ENDERBY LAND

Mawson (to Australia)

C. Darnley

Amery Ice Shelf

Lambert Glacier

Mackenzie Bay

Prydz Bay

Zhongshan (to China)

GREATER ANTARCTICA

Mirny (to Russian Fed.)

Vostok (to Russian Fed.)

West Ice Shelf

DAVIS SEA

Shackleton Ice Shelf

WILKES LAND

Vincennes Bay

Casey (to Australia)

Cape Poinsett

Porpoise Bay

Leningradskaya (to Russian Fed.)

Dumont d'Urville (to France)

Balleny Is.

INDIAN OCEAN

Kerguelen (to France)

Heard I. (to Australia)

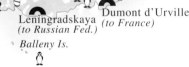

ANTARCTIC TOURISM

Cruise liners have been bringing tourists to the Antarctic region since the 1950s. Several thousand visitors each year observe the harsh beauty of the landscape and its extraordinary wildlife from the comfort of cruise ships. Look for 📷

0   250   500   750   1000 1250 1500   KM

0   250   500   750   1000   MILES

WHALES

Whales thrive in the seas around the Antarctic, which are rich in plankton and krill, their main food sources. Large-scale whale hunting started in the 20th century, and the numbers of whales soon fell. In 1948 the International Whaling Commission was set up to regulate the numbers and species of whales killed, and to create protected areas. Look for ⤙

Blue whale

POLLUTION

The Antarctic research stations have yet to find effective ways of disposing of their waste. Although some of it is burned, cans, bottles, machine parts, and chemicals are often simply dumped near the bases, spoiling the area's natural beauty. The only solution to the problem is to take the garbage out of Antarctica. Look for ☠

RESEARCH

The scientific base in this picture is the US Amundsen-Scott station, which is built underground at the South Pole. Scientists at the Antarctic research stations are monitoring changes to the weather and environment. Look for ⌒

MAP FEATURES

Oil: Much of the Arctic region is rich in oil, but the difficulty of drilling and moving oil, as well as environmental concerns, have slowed exploitation. Look for 🛢

Penguin grounds: Penguin breeding grounds are found near Antarctic coasts. Some are being disturbed by tourists, airstrips, and construction. Look for 🐧

🐟 Fishing   ⌒ Polar research center

⛏ Coal   ☠ Pollution

📷 Tourism   ⤙ Whales

THE ARCTIC

THE ARCTIC OCEAN is covered by drifting ice up to 98 feet (30 m) thick, which partially melts and disperses in the summer. Much of the surrounding land is tundra – plains and moorlands that are carpeted with moss and lichens, but permanently frozen beneath the surface. People have lived around the Arctic for thousands of years, hunting the mammals and fish that live in the ocean. This region has large deposits of oil, but the harsh climate makes it difficult to extract from the ground.

FISH STICKS

Large numbers of cod, haddock, halibut, and other fish live in the Arctic Ocean. Cod and haddock are taken to fish-processing factories in Greenland. Here they are frozen, canned, or – in the case of cod – made into fish sticks and exported to the markets of the US and Europe. **Look for** 🐟

ARCTIC PEOPLES

Traditionally, the people of the Arctic survived by hunting animals. They used sealskin for boats and clothing and seal fat (blubber) for fuel. Today, tools, clothes, and buildings are made from modern materials. Rifles now replace harpoons and snowmobiles are used for transportation.

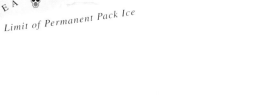

The northern lights can be seen over the Arctic at night.

Polar bears spend summers on the Arctic ice. They move farther south in winter.

ICEBREAKER

About half the Arctic Ocean is covered with ice in winter, but special ships called icebreakers can still sail across it. In 1969, a large tanker, the *S.S. Manhattan*, penetrated the pack ice of the Northwest Passage from eastern Canada to Alaska for the first time.

GREENLAND

The first Europeans to explore and settle Greenland were Vikings, who arrived in about AD 986. Greenland later came under Danish rule and is now a self-governing part of Denmark.

The Arctic tern migrates every year between the Arctic and Antarctica.

Map labels

ALASKA *(part of US)*   CHUKCHI SEA   Pevek   Ambarchik   EAST SIBERIAN SEA   RUSSIAN FEDERATION
Barrow   Prudhoe Bay   Wrangel I. *(part of Russian Fed.)*
BEAUFORT SEA   Limit of Permanent Pack Ice
New Siberian Is. *(part of Russian Fed.)*   LAPTEV SEA   Tiksi
Banks I. *(part of Canada)*
CANADA   Mould Bay   Prince Patrick I. *(part of Canada)*   Melville I. *(part of Canada)*
ARCTIC OCEAN
POLUOSTROV TAYMYR
Queen Elizabeth Is. *(part of Canada)*   Resolute   Axel Heiberg I. *(part of Canada)*   Limit of Permanent Pack Ice
Severnaya Zemlya *(part of Russian Fed.)*   Limit of Permanent Pack Ice   KARA SEA   Dikson
Devon I. *(part of Canada)*   Ellesmere I. *(part of Canada)*   Alert
• North Pole
Qaanaaq
Franz Josef Land *(part of Russian Fed.)*
Baffin I. *(part of Canada)*   KNUD RASMUSSEN LAND
Nord   SVALBARD *(to Norway)*   BARENTS SEA
Pangnirtung   Baffin Bay   Upernavik   GREENLAND *(to Denmark)*
Danmarkshavn   LONGYEARBYEN   Spitsbergen
Davis Strait   Qeqertarsuaq   GREENLAND SEA
Søndre Strømfjord
NUUK
Paamiut   Illoqqortoormiut   JAN MAYEN *(to Norway)*
Narsarsuaq   Tasiilaq   Denmark Strait
Qaqortoq
ATLANTIC OCEAN
Nunap Isua
ICELAND

Mountains on Svalbard reflected in a melted ice pond.

ARCTIC COAL

The island of Spitsbergen has rich deposits of minerals, especially coal. It is part of Norway, but other countries are allowed to mine there. The Norwegian coal town of Longyearbyen is 620 miles (1,000 km) from the mainland. It can be reached by sea for only eight months a year, making it difficult and expensive to ship coal out. Coal screes and long, severe winters make this a desolate place. **Look for** ⛏

Scale bar

0   250   500   750   1000   KM

0   100   200   300   400   500   MILES

THE ATLANTIC OCEAN

THE WORLD'S OCEANS cover almost three-quarters of the Earth's surface. Beneath the surface of the Atlantic Ocean lie vast, featureless plains and long chains of mountains called ridges. The Mid-Atlantic Ridge is one of the world's longest mountain chains; some of its peaks are so high that they pierce the surface as volcanic islands, such as the Azores. A huge rift valley 15-30 miles (24-48 km) wide runs down the ridge's center. The deepest part of the Atlantic is 5 miles (8 km) below the surface. On average, the Atlantic has the warmest and saltiest waters of any ocean. Before regular shipping routes were established, the Atlantic isolated the Americas from the prosperous countries of Europe, but today it is crossed by some of the world's most important trade routes. The North Atlantic has always been one of the world's richest fishing grounds, but it has been overfished, and fish stocks are now dangerously low.

NATO

The North Atlantic Treaty Organization (NATO) is an association of North American and European countries established in 1949 to defend its members – principally against the former Soviet Union. Look for ▥

SARGASSO SEA

At the center of three great North Atlantic currents lies the Sargasso Sea – an area of calm water, covered with sargassum weed. Sailors once believed their ships would be trapped by the weeds.

Puffins breed on rocky islands, like the Faeroes.

FISHING

Catches of cod, herring, and haddock in the North Atlantic have been severely reduced by overfishing. Fishing fleets must now travel long distances and remain at sea for months at a time. The fish are processed on the fleet's factory ship to keep them fresh. Look for ▱

WHALING

Whaling has been going on in the world's oceans for hundreds of years. But with the invention of the explosive-tipped harpoon, catches increased rapidly. Today some species of whales are threatened with extinction. Attempts are being made to ban whaling worldwide until numbers recover. Look for ▱

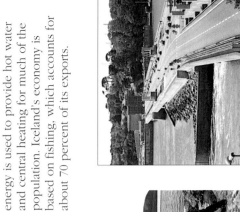

LAND OF ICE AND FIRE

There are more than 100 volcanoes on Iceland. Many of them are still active. Beneath the island's harsh, rocky surface lie vast natural heat reserves. This energy is used to provide hot water and central heating for much of the population. Iceland's economy is based on fishing, which accounts for about 70 percent of its exports.

TIDAL ENERGY

Electricity can be generated from the sea in areas where there is a big difference between high and low tide levels. A barrage, like this one at La Rance in France, has to be built across the estuary. Water passing backward and forward through the barrage drives the turbines. Look for ⚡

ICELAND pop: 277,000

CAPE VERDE pop: 417,000

Tomatoes and other fruit are grown in the warm climate of the Canary Islands.

Map labels

ARCTIC OCEAN

ATLANTIC OCEAN

EUROPE

AFRICA

NORTH AMERICA

Greenland

Baffin Bay
Davis Strait
Hudson Bay
Labrador Sea
Denmark Strait
Greenland Sea
NORTH SEA
BLACK SEA
MEDITERRANEAN SEA
SARGASSO SEA
CARIBBEAN SEA
Gulf of Mexico
Bay of Fundy
Grand Banks
Newfoundland
Mid-Atlantic Ridge

ICELAND
Reykjavik
FAEROE ISLANDS (to Denmark)
Rockall (part of UK)

Murmansk
Kristiansund
Ålesund
Bergen
Stavanger
Haugesund
Skagen
Esbjerg
Bremerhaven
Rotterdam
Boulogne-sur-Mer
La Rance
Lorient
A Coruña
Oporto
Gibraltar
Casablanca
Safi
Aberdeen
Grimsby
Tallinn
Liepāja
Marseille
Livorno
Ancona
Naples
Algiers
Sfax
Madeira (part of Portugal)
Canary Islands (part of Spain)
Azores (part of Portugal)
CAPE VERDE
PRAIA
Port Said
Nile

St. John's
Halifax
St. Lawrence
Saint John
Portland
Gloucester
New York
Baltimore
New Orleans
Mississippi
Bermuda (to UK)

Fish like these live among the sargassum weed.

TOURISM

A number of islands in the Atlantic, including the Canaries and Madeira, are great tourist attractions, especially during winter in the Northern Hemisphere. The Canaries are a chain of seven mountainous islands; some areas are green and lush, others volcanic. The volcanic lava produces dramatic black landscapes. Look for 🏖

SAILING

Areas of the Atlantic have become pleasure grounds. Sailing is one of the main activities, much of it in the warm seas of the Caribbean. Long-distance races are increasingly popular, some of them transatlantic. Boats range from yachts sailed single-handed to ships like this tea clipper, sailed by large crews.

CABLES

Cables snake across the ocean floor carrying many forms of modern communication, such as telephone calls and fax messages. The first transatlantic cable was laid in 1866. The cables are laid by special ships, like this one in the North Atlantic.

Massive icebergs drift among the pack ice, a threat to shipping in the Atlantic.

An isolated settlement on the island of West Falkland in the South Atlantic.

Lobsters are caught in lobster pots baited with dead fish.

SALMON

The early years of an Atlantic salmon are spent in the river where it was born. Then it swims downriver to the ocean. It rapidly gains weight in the rich feeding grounds of the North Atlantic. When it is ready to breed, the salmon's amazing homing ability enables it to return to its native river. Here, on their long, hard journey upriver, salmon negotiate a waterfall. Few salmon survive this endurance test to breed a second time.

An extinct volcano on an island in the West Indies.

ATLANTIC OCEAN

The Atlantic Ocean floor is spreading at a rate of 1 in (2.5 cm) a year. As the South American and African plates move apart, molten rock spills onto the ocean floor, cools, and forms solid rock. This is the Mid-Atlantic ridge, the world's longest mountain range. Although most of the ridge lies beneath the sea, some of its peaks emerge as volcanic islands.

Ocean basins descend to 18,000 ft (5,000 m) below sea level

Mid-Atlantic Ridge. At its center is a rift valley up to 10 miles (48 km) wide

Abyssal plains: the deep ocean bed, occasionally interrupted by volcanic hills and mountains

Brazil Basin
Angola Basin
St. Helena
Walvis Ridge
Tristan da Cunha

MAP FEATURES

Underwater wrecks: Marine archaeology and location of wrecks was greatly advanced by the development of deep-sea diving equipment. Look for ⚓

Pollution: Oil rig blowouts and spills from oil tankers along the coastlines and around the Gulf of Mexico are a major problem in the Atlantic. Look for ▲

Hurricane: The warm Atlantic waters off the north coast of Brazil are the gathering grounds for hurricanes, which then sweep northwestward. Look for 🌀

Fishing	Alternative power
Fishing ports	Tourism
Oil	Military bases
Gas	Whales

Map labels

Niger
Lagos
Libreville
Congo
Gulf of Guinea
São Tomé
Príncipe
Guinea Basin
Angola Basin
Walvis Bay
Lüderitz
Port Nolloth
Cape Town
Cape of Good Hope
Cape Basin
Walvis Ridge
Atlantic-Indian Ridge
Atlantic-Indian Basin
Mid-Atlantic Ridge
SAINT HELENA (to Saint Helena)
ASCENSION ISLAND (to Saint Helena)
TRISTAN DA CUNHA (to Saint Helena)
Gough Island
BOUVET ISLAND (to Norway)
C Verde
Cape Verde Basin
Atlantic Ridge
Fernando de Noronha (part of Brazil)
Brazil Basin
Ilha da Trindade (part of Brazil)
ATLANTIC OCEAN
SOUTH GEORGIA (to UK)
SOUTH SANDWICH ISLANDS (to UK)
WEDDELL SEA
ANTARCTICA
Recife
Fortaleza
Salvador
Rio de Janeiro
Argentine Basin
FALKLAND ISLANDS (to UK)
South Orkney Is.
SCOTIA SEA
South Shetland Is.
Cayenne
Georgetown
La Guaira
Cartagena
Panama City
Amazon
SOUTH AMERICA
Buenos Aires
Mar del Plata
Bahía Blanca
C. Horn

0 500 1000 1500 2000 KM
0 500 1000 MILES

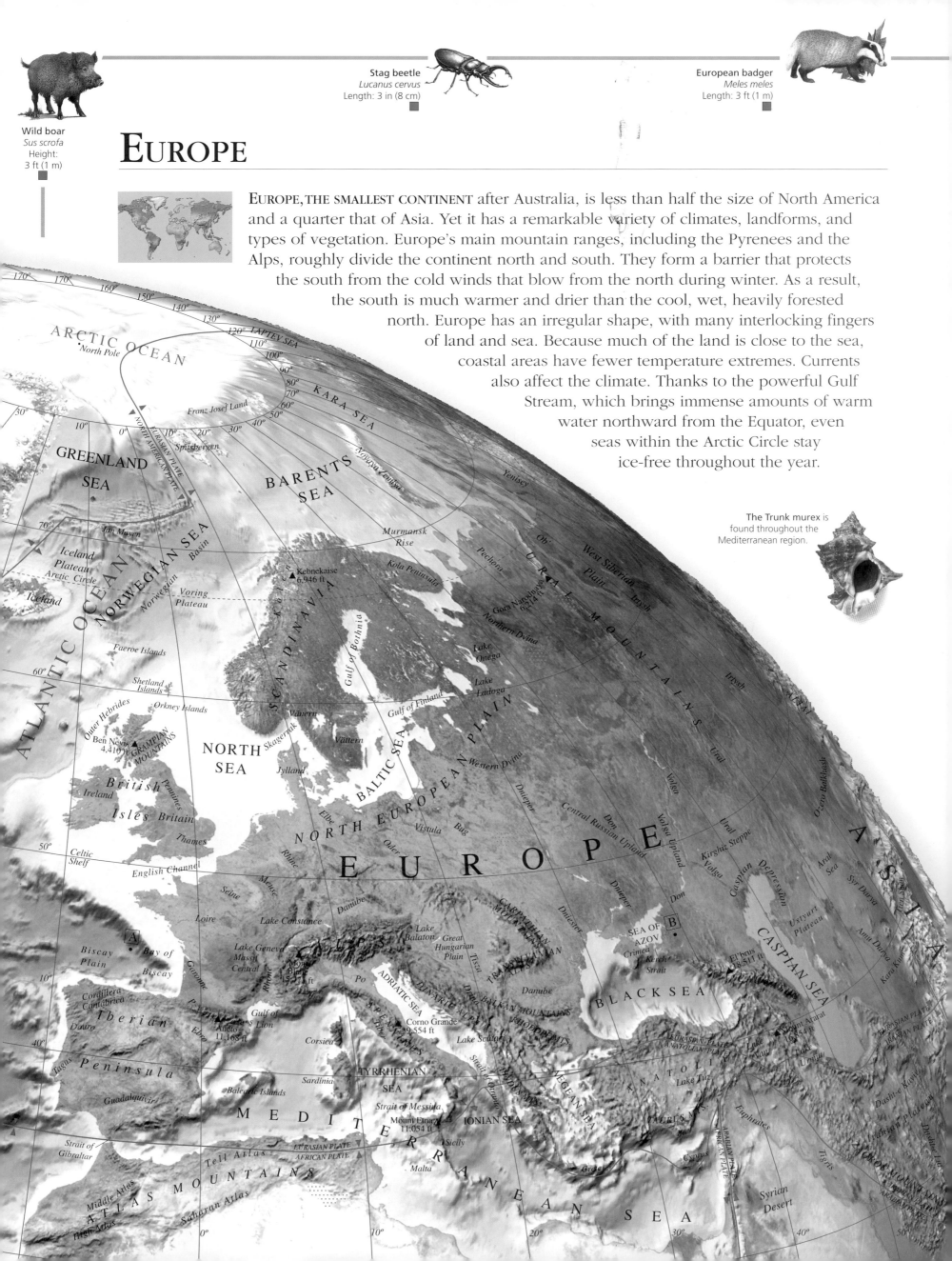

Wild boar
Sus scrofa
Height:
3 ft (1 m)

Stag beetle
Lucanus cervus
Length: 3 in (8 cm)

European badger
Meles meles
Length: 3 ft (1 m)

EUROPE

EUROPE, THE SMALLEST CONTINENT after Australia, is less than half the size of North America and a quarter that of Asia. Yet it has a remarkable variety of climates, landforms, and types of vegetation. Europe's main mountain ranges, including the Pyrenees and the Alps, roughly divide the continent north and south. They form a barrier that protects the south from the cold winds that blow from the north during winter. As a result, the south is much warmer and drier than the cool, wet, heavily forested north. Europe has an irregular shape, with many interlocking fingers of land and sea. Because much of the land is close to the sea, coastal areas have fewer temperature extremes. Currents also affect the climate. Thanks to the powerful Gulf Stream, which brings immense amounts of warm water northward from the Equator, even seas within the Arctic Circle stay ice-free throughout the year.

The Trunk murex is found throughout the Mediterranean region.

Siberian tit
Parus cinctus
Length: 5 in (13 cm)

Green toad
Bufo viridis
Length: 4 in (10 cm)

Osprey
Pandion haliaetus
Wingspan: 5 ft (1.6 m)

BOGLANDS

Bogs cover many of northern Europe's wettest areas. Mosses and reeds are among the few plants that grow in waterlogged soils. Wetlands take thousands of years to develop, because plants grow so slowly there.

WAVE POWER

Waves can wear away the shore, creating odd land-forms. This seastack off the Orkneys in the British Isles is 450 ft (135 m) high.

Ammonites, fossil relatives of today's octopus, were once found in Europe. They died out 65 million years ago.

PIONEERING BIRCH

Light-loving birches are often the first trees to appear on open land. Although quick to grow, they are short-lived. After a few years, birches are replaced by trees that can survive shade, such as oaks.

BARE MOUNTAIN

Ice, rain, wind, and gravity strip steep slopes of all soil. Rocks pile up at the foot of peaks, where plants can take root.

NEEDLELEAF FOREST

Cone-bearing trees such as pines, larches, and firs cover Scandinavia. Most are evergreen: they keep their needlelike leaves even when covered in snow for many months of the year.

English oak
Quercus robur
Height: 130 ft (40 m)

FJORDS

Glaciers have cut hundreds of narrow inlets, or fjords, into Scandinavia's Atlantic coastline. The water in the inlet is calmer than in the open sea.

This fossil of *Stauranderaster*, a starfish once found in this region, dates from around 70 million years ago.

TREELESS TUNDRA

Arctic summers are so cool that only the topmost layer of frozen soil thaws. Only shallow-rooted plants can survive in the tundra.

Pine marten
Martes martes
Length: 20 in (52 cm)

ANCIENT WOODLANDS

Relics of Europe's ancient forests, such as these oaks stunted by the rain and wind, are found only in a few valleys in southwest Britain.

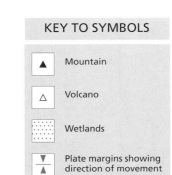

DRY SOUTH

Crete is a mountainous Mediterranean island with hot dry summers. Many plants survive the summer as underground bulbs, blooming briefly in the wet spring.

▢ ▲ YOUNG MOUNTAINS

The Alps are some of western Europe's highest mountains. They are part of an almost continuous belt that stretches from the Pyrenees in the west to the Himalayas in Asia. The Alps are still rising because of plate movements in the Mediterranean region.

Sweetbriar
Rosa rubiginosa
Height: 10 ft (3 m)

CROSS-SECTION THROUGH EUROPE

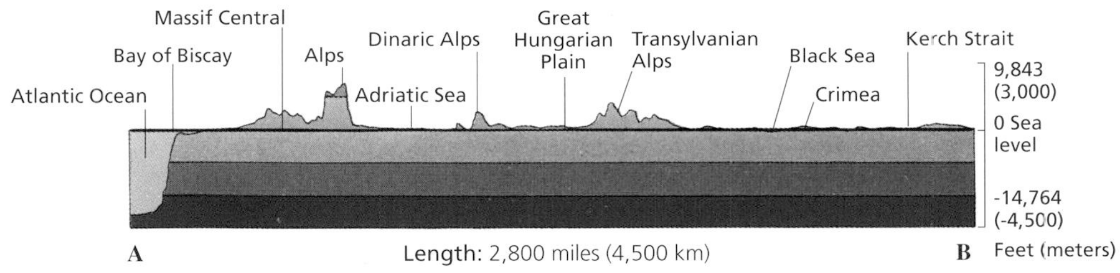

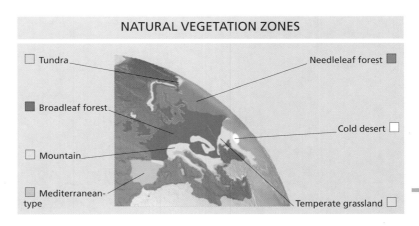

Massif Central
Bay of Biscay   Alps   Dinaric Alps   Great Hungarian Plain   Transylvanian Alps   Black Sea   Kerch Strait
Atlantic Ocean   Adriatic Sea   Crimea

9,843 (3,000)
0 Sea level
-14,764 (-4,500)

A   Length: 2,800 miles (4,500 km)   B   Feet (meters)

KEY TO SYMBOLS

▲ Mountain

△ Volcano

▒ Wetlands

▼ ▲ Plate margins showing direction of movement

! Endangered species

NATURAL VEGETATION ZONES

▢ Tundra

▢ Broadleaf forest

▢ Mountain

▢ Mediterranean-type

Needleleaf forest ▢

Cold desert ▢

Temperate grassland ▢

Spanish lynx
Felis lynx
Length: 4 ft (1.3 m)

SCANDINAVIA AND FINLAND

THE SCANDINAVIAN COUNTRIES of Norway, Sweden, and Denmark and neighboring Finland are situated around the Baltic Sea in northern Europe. During past ice ages, glaciers gouged and scoured the land, leaving deep fjords, lakes, and valleys in their wake. Much of Norway and Sweden, and nearly two-thirds of Finland, is covered by dense forests of pine, spruce, and birch trees. In the far north, winters are long and dark, and snow falls for about eight months of the year. Most Swedish people live in the central lowlands. Norway's economy depends on its shipbuilding, fishing, and merchant fleets. Denmark is flat and low-lying, with abundant rainfall and excellent farmland. The Finnish people originally came from the east, via Russia, and consequently differ from the Scandinavians both in language and culture. All four countries have small populations, are highly industrialized and enjoy some of the highest standards of living in the world.

FISHING

As Norway has so little farmland, fishing has always been a vital source of food. Today, about 95 percent of the total catch is processed, about half of which is made into fishmeal and oil. Fish farming is on the increase, especially of salmon in the fjords. Look for 🐟

Vast schools of herring gather in the seas around Scandinavia

STAVE CHURCHES

Fantoft Church, Bergen

The wooden stave churches of Norway were built between AD 1000 and 1300. There were once 600 of them, but today only 25 are still standing. A stave church has a stone foundation with a wooden frame on top. The four wooden corner posts are called staves. Further wooden extensions can be added to the basic framework.

SMÖRGÅSBORD

Scrambled eggs
Prawn
Caviar
Asparagus
Smoked salmon

Smörgåsbord means "sandwich table" in Swedish. Other countries in this region have their own versions, but the idea is the same: a great spread of local delicacies, served cold on bread, which can include ingredients such as reindeer, fish, cheese, and salad.

MAP FEATURES

Hydroelectric power: The region's mountainous terrain enables the majority of its electricity to be supplied by HEP. Look for ⊬	
Bridges: Tunnels and bridges now link the Danish islands of Fyn and Zealand. Linking Denmark and Sweden is under construction. Look for ⌒	
🐄 Cattle	🐬 Fishing
🐖 Pigs	⚓ Fishing port
🌾 Cereals	⛏ Mining
Timber	Industrial center

COPENHAGEN

Copenhagen's fine natural harbor and its position at the main entrance to the Baltic Sea helped it to become a major port and Denmark's capital city. The city's tiny shops, cobbled streets, museums, and cafés attract more than a million tourists each year.

Meadow crops grown for livestock
Rough upland grazing for sheep and goats
Deep water enables ships to reach far inland
Coastal fishing communities are declining
Cultivation limited to warm, south-facing slopes
Fish farming of salmon in sheltered waters
Coastal islands form natural breakwaters
N

A NORWEGIAN FJORD

Norway is so mountainous that only 3 percent of the land can be cultivated. Long inlets of sea, called fjords, cut into Norway's west coast. The best farmland is found around the head of the fjords and in the lowland areas around them. Over 70 percent of Norway's population lives in cities, many in towns situated along the sheltered fjords.

The still waters of a Norwegian fjord.

NORWAY
pop: 4,400,000

LAPLAND

Lapland is a land of tundra, forests, and lakes. Here the *Samer*, or Lapps, still herd reindeer for their meat and milk. Development in the north now threatens their way of life.

Lego building blocks were invented in Denmark.

SKIING

For thousands of years skiing has been the most efficient way of crossing deep snow on foot. This region is often thought to be the original home of skiing – in fact, "ski" is the Norwegian word for a strip of wood. Long-distance cross-country skiing, or *langlaufen*, is a popular sport in Norway, Finland, and Sweden.

Danish bacon for export

DENMARK
pop: 5,300,000

DANISH AGRICULTURE

Two-thirds of the total area of Denmark is used for farming. Denmark exports agricultural products all over the world. The main exports are bacon, dairy products, cereals, and beef. Cereals are widely grown, but mainly as fodder for pigs. Look for 🐖

Map labels:
Iron, Steinkjer, Hitra, Smøla, Vanadium, Trondheim, Molde, Ålesund, Iron, Copper, Copper, Røros, L. Femunden, Nordfjord, Sognefjord, Hermansvert, Lillehammer, Gjøvik, Hamar, Mjøsa, Oats, Bergen, Honefoss, Hardangerfjord, Haugesund, Kongsberg, Drammen, OSLO, Boknafjorden, Stavanger, Porsgrunn, Moss, Fredrikstad, Sandnes, Halden, Titanium, Dairy, Iron, Dairy, Arendal, Oslofjorden, Kristiansand, Dairy, Vikna, Skagerrak, Uddevalla, Trollhättan, DENMARK, Gothenburg, Hjørring, Frederikshavn, Borås, Ålborg, Oats, Varberg, Holstebro, Dairy, Rye, Randers, Halmstad, Barley, Ringkøbing, JUTLAND, Wheat, Århus, Kattegat, Horsens, Helsingborg, Barle, Vejle, Helsingør, Esbjerg, COPENHAGEN, Malmö, Ribe, Odense, Skagelse, Abenrå, Fyn, Naesteved, Ystad, Sønderborg, Nakskov, Barle, Zealand, GERMANY, Nykøbing

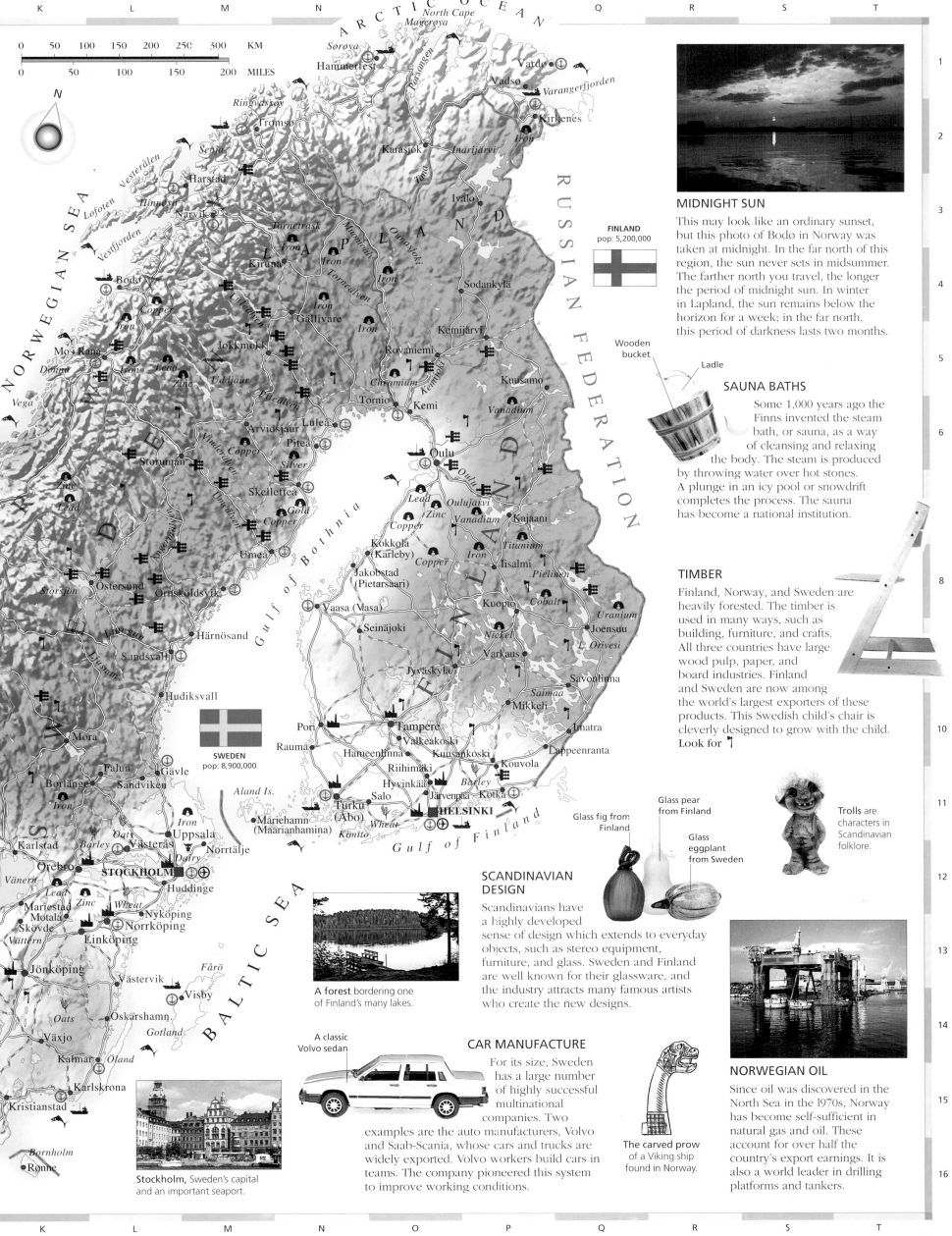

Map labels and geographic features:

ARCTIC OCEAN

North Cape
Magerøya

NORWEGIAN SEA

RUSSIAN FEDERATION

Sørøya
Hammerfest
Vardø
Vadsø
Varangerfjorden
Kirkenes
Ringvassøy
Tromsø
Senja
Harstad
Karasjok
Inarijärvi
Ivalo
Vesterålen
Lofoten
Hinnøy
Narvik
Vestfjorden
Torneträsk
Iron
Kiruna
Sodankylä
Iron
Ornasjoki
Muonio
Muonio
Iron
Bodø
Copper
Iron
Gällivare
Iron
Kemijärvi
Mo i Rana
Torneälven
Iron
Jokkmokk
Rovaniemi
Kemiljoki
Donna
Iron
Lead
Chromium
Kuusamo
Zinc
Uddjaur
Piteälven
Tornio
Kemi
Vega
Arvidsjaur
Luleå
Vanadium
Storuman
Copper
Piteå
Oulu
Zinc
Silver
Skellefteå
Lead
Oulujärvi
Lead
Gold
Zinc
Vanadium
Copper
Umeå
Kajaani
Östersund
Ångermanälven
Örnsköldsvik
Kokkola (Karleby)
Iron
Titanium
Iisalmi
Storsjön
Copper
Pielinen
Jakobstad (Pietarsaari)
Cobalt
Härnösand
Ljusnan
Vaasa (Vasa)
Kuopio
Uranium
Sandvall
Vänern
Seinäjoki
Nickel
Joensuu
L. Orivesi
Narkaus
Hudiksvall
Jyväskylä
Savonlinna
Saimaa
Mora
Mikkeli
Pori
Tampere
Imatra
Falun
Rauma
Valkeakoski
Lappeenranta
Borlänge
Hämeenlinna
Kuusankoski
Gävle
Riihimäki
Kouvola
Iron
Barley
Hyvinkää
Kotka
Karlstad
Oats
Järvenpää
Örebro
Barley
Uppsala
Salo
Västerås
Turku (Åbo)
HELSINKI
Dairy
Norrtälje
Wheat
STOCKHOLM
Huddinge
Åland Is.
Gulf of Finland
Vänern
Lead
Mariehamn (Maarianhamina)
Kimito
Mariestad
Zinc
Wheat
Motala
Nyköping
Skövde
Vättern
Norrköping
Linköping
Färö
Jönköping
Västervik
Visby
Gotland
Oats
Oskarshamn
Växjö
Öland
Kalmar
Karlskrona
Kristianstad
Bornholm
Rønne

Gulf of Bothnia

LAPLAND

SWEDEN
FINLAND
BALTIC SEA

FINLAND
pop: 5,200,000

SWEDEN
pop: 8,900,000

MIDNIGHT SUN

This may look like an ordinary sunset, but this photo of Bodø in Norway was taken at midnight. In the far north of this region, the sun never sets in midsummer. The farther north you travel, the longer the period of midnight sun. In winter in Lapland, the sun remains below the horizon for a week; in the far north, this period of darkness lasts two months.

SAUNA BATHS

Wooden bucket
Ladle

Some 1,000 years ago the Finns invented the steam bath, or sauna, as a way of cleansing and relaxing the body. The steam is produced by throwing water over hot stones. A plunge in an icy pool or snowdrift completes the process. The sauna has become a national institution.

TIMBER

Finland, Norway, and Sweden are heavily forested. The timber is used in many ways, such as building, furniture, and crafts. All three countries have large wood pulp, paper, and board industries. Finland and Sweden are now among the world's largest exporters of these products. This Swedish child's chair is cleverly designed to grow with the child. Look for ⌐

SCANDINAVIAN DESIGN

Scandinavians have a highly developed sense of design which extends to everyday objects, such as stereo equipment, furniture, and glass. Sweden and Finland are well known for their glassware, and the industry attracts many famous artists who create the new designs.

A forest bordering one of Finland's many lakes.

Glass fig from Finland
Glass pear from Finland
Glass eggplant from Sweden

Trolls are characters in Scandinavian folklore.

CAR MANUFACTURE

A classic Volvo sedan

For its size, Sweden has a large number of highly successful multinational companies. Two examples are the auto manufacturers, Volvo and Saab-Scania, whose cars and trucks are widely exported. Volvo workers build cars in teams. The company pioneered this system to improve working conditions.

Stockholm, Sweden's capital and an important seaport.

The carved prow of a Viking ship found in Norway.

NORWEGIAN OIL

Since oil was discovered in the North Sea in the 1970s, Norway has become self-sufficient in natural gas and oil. These account for over half the country's export earnings. It is also a world leader in drilling platforms and tankers.

THE BRITISH ISLES

THE BRITISH ISLES CONSIST OF two large islands – Britain and Ireland – surrounded by many smaller ones. They are divided into two countries: the United Kingdom (UK), and the Republic of Ireland. At the end of the 18th century, the UK became the first country in the world to undergo an industrial revolution. It became the world's leading manufacturing and trading nation and built up an empire that covered more than a quarter of the world. The UK's traditional industries, including coal mining, textiles, and car manufacturing, have declined in recent years, but service industries such as banking and insurance have been extremely successful. The Republic of Ireland, which became independent from the UK in 1921, is still a mainly rural country, and many Irish people make their living from farming. However, tourism and high-tech industries like computers and pharmaceuticals are increasingly important. The UK and Ireland still have close trading links, and many Irish people go to the UK to find work.

"THE TROUBLES"

British Protestants, who settled in Ireland in the 17th century, celebrate their history with parades and marching bands. In 1922, when the Protestants in the north refused to join the newly independent Catholic south, Catholics were discriminated against and violence erupted. In the 1960s, British troops were sent to police the province. The peace process of the 1990s was disrupted by sporadic violence.

AGRICULTURE AND INDUSTRY

Farming has always been Ireland's principal source of income. Dairy products, beef, and potatoes are still important, but recently the number of high-tech industries has increased.

Irish butter

OIL

Rich reserves of both oil and natural gas were found under the North Sea in the 1960s. By the late 1970s, natural gas was being piped to most homes, factories and businesses in the UK. Massive oil rigs were moored in the North Sea, and wells were dug by drilling into the ocean bed below the platforms. Oil rigs and onshore refineries brought employment to many areas, especially in eastern Scotland. But oil reserves are being steadily used up, and oil production is now in decline. Look for ⬛

TARTAN

TOURISM

Tourism is an important source of income for Scotland. People come to enjoy the beautiful highland scenery and visit the ancient castles. For centuries, Scotland was dominated by struggles between rival families, known as clans. Today one of the most popular tourist souvenirs is tartan – textiles woven in the colors of the clans.

Tartan scarf

Scottish shortbread

Bright red mailboxes are a common sight on British streets.

FISHING

The waters of the northeast Atlantic are among the world's richest fishing grounds, well stocked with mackerel, herring, cod, haddock, and shellfish. The British Isles has many fishing ports, like this one in the northeast of England. But EU regulations – designed to reduce catches and conserve fish stocks – are causing widespread discontent among fishermen. Look for ⬛

INDUSTRY

Many Japanese companies, car and electronics manufacturers in particular, are now based in the UK, attracted by a skilled labor force and access to European markets. Britain's traditional industries – such as textiles, steel, and pottery – have been joined by newer, high-tech industries. Look for ⬛

MEDIA CENTER

The British media is highly influential around the English-speaking world. There are several high-quality national newspapers, including *The Times*, *The Guardian*, and *The Observer*. The state-owned British Broadcasting Corporation (BBC) has an international reputation and sells its television programs all over the world. London is a major center of publishing, advertising, and video production.

A deep inlet of water – or *loch* – in the north of Scotland.

NORTH SEA

Shetland Islands
Lerwick

Orkney Islands
Kirkwall
Stromness

ATLANTIC OCEAN

Outer Hebrides

Isle of Lewis
Stornoway
Beef
Harris
Isle of Skye
North Uist
Beef
South Uist
Barra
The Little Minch
The Minch
Canna
Rhum
Eigg
Muck
Coll
Tiree
Colonsay
Jura
Islay
Kintyre

C. Wrath
Thurso
Beef
Loch Shin
Ullapool
Oats
Loch Ness
Inverness
Moray Firth
Elgin
Spey
Barley
Beef
Dee
Oats
Fraserburgh
Peterhead
Aberdeen
Beef

GRAMPIAN MTS.
SCOTLAND
Beef
Loch Lomond
Oban
Mallaig
Fort William
Perth
Forth
Dundee
Firth of Forth
Stirling
Oats
Edinburgh
Firth of Clyde
Glasgow
Greenock
Dairy
Beef
Ayr
Clyde
Tweed
SOUTHERN UPLANDS
Beef
Grangemouth

UNITED KINGDOM

Lough Foyle
Londonderry

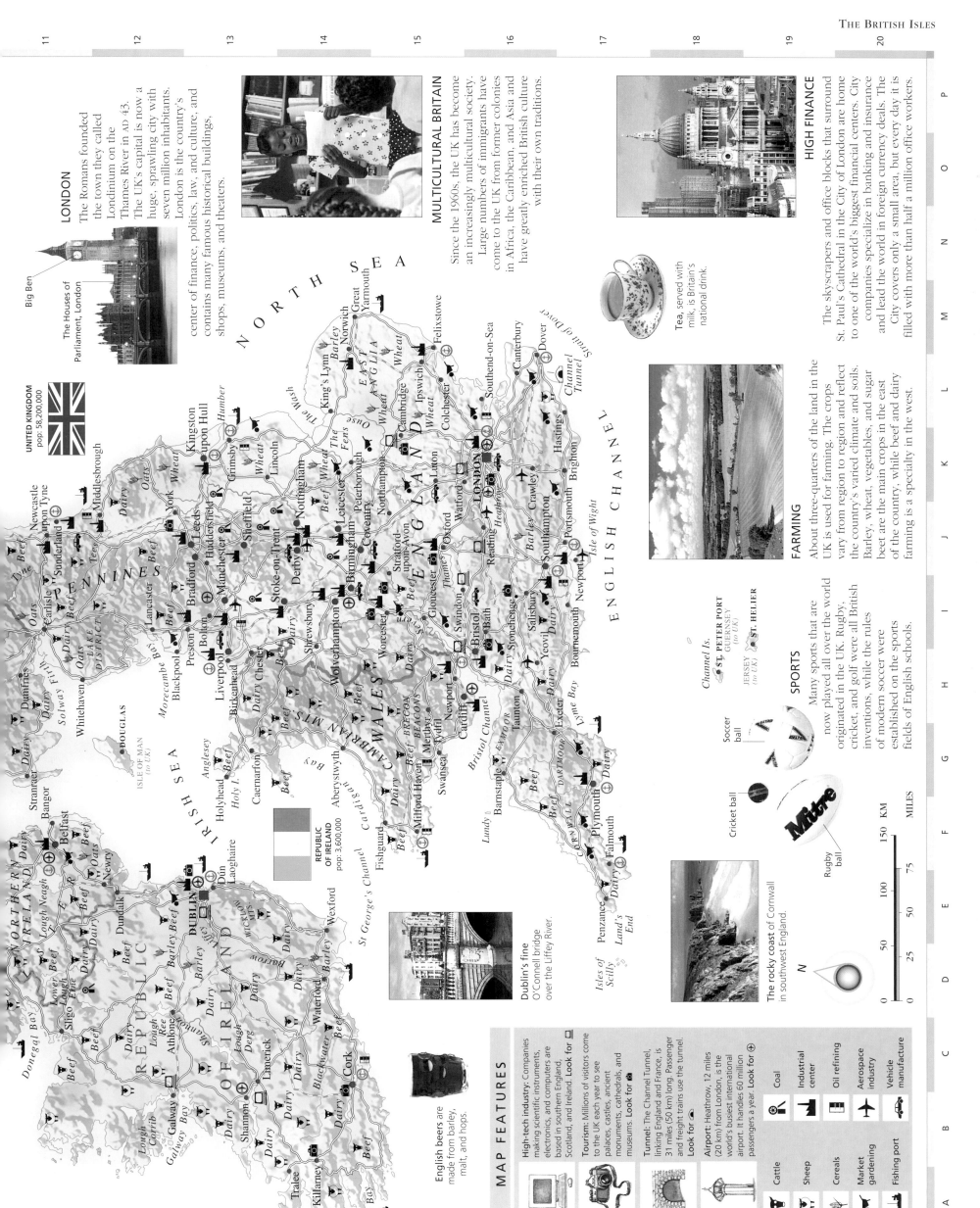

LONDON

The Romans founded the town they called Londinium on the Thames River in AD 43. The UK's capital is now a huge, sprawling city with seven million inhabitants. London is the country's center of finance, politics, law, and culture, and contains many famous historical buildings, shops, museums, and theaters.

Big Ben

The Houses of Parliament, London

MULTICULTURAL BRITAIN

Since the 1960s, the UK has become an increasingly multicultural society. Large numbers of immigrants have come to the UK from former colonies in Africa, the Caribbean, and Asia and have greatly enriched British culture with their own traditions.

HIGH FINANCE

The skyscrapers and office blocks that surround St. Paul's Cathedral in the City of London are home to one of the world's biggest financial centers. City companies specialize in banking and insurance and lead the world in foreign currency deals. The City covers only a small area, but every day it is filled with more than half a million office workers.

Tea, served with milk, is Britain's national drink.

UNITED KINGDOM
pop: 58,200,000

REPUBLIC
OF IRELAND
pop: 3,600,000

FARMING

About three-quarters of the land in the UK is used for farming. The crops vary from region to region and reflect the country's varied climate and soils. Barley, wheat, vegetables, and sugar beet are the main crops in the east of the country, while beef and dairy farming is a specialty in the west.

SPORTS

Many sports that are now played all over the world originated in the UK. Rugby, cricket, and golf were all British inventions, while the rules of modern soccer were established on the sports fields of English schools.

Soccer ball

Cricket ball

Rugby ball

The rocky coast of Cornwall in southwest England.

Dublin's fine O'Connell bridge over the Liffey River.

English beers are made from barley, malt, and hops.

MAP FEATURES

High-tech industry: Companies making scientific instruments, electronics, and computers are based in southern England, Scotland, and Ireland. Look for 🖥

Tourism: Millions of visitors come to the UK each year to see palaces, castles, ancient monuments, cathedrals, and museums. Look for 🏛

Tunnel: The Channel Tunnel, linking England and France, is 31 miles (50 km) long. Passenger and freight trains use the tunnel. Look for 🚇

Airport: Heathrow, 12 miles (20 km) from London, is the world's busiest international airport. It handles 60 million passengers a year. Look for ✈

Cattle	Coal
Sheep	Industrial center
Cereals	Oil refining
Market gardening	Aerospace industry
Fishing port	Vehicle manufacture

N

0 25 50 75 100 150 KM
0 25 50 75 100 150 MILES

73

SPAIN AND PORTUGAL

SPAIN AND PORTUGAL are located on the Iberian Peninsula, which is cut off from the rest of Europe by the Pyrenees. This isolation, combined with the region's closeness to Africa and the Atlantic Ocean, has shaped the history of the two countries. The Moors, an Islamic people from North Africa, occupied the peninsula in the 8th century AD, leaving an Islamic legacy that is still evident today. In 1492 the Moors were finally expelled from Catholic Spain. The oceangoing Spanish and Portuguese took the lead in exploring and colonizing the New World, and both nations acquired substantial overseas empires. During this era, Portugal was ruled by Spain from about 1580 to 1640. Eventually, both nations lost most of their colonies, and their once-great wealth and power declined. Spain was torn apart by a vicious civil war from 1936-39, and right-wing dictators ruled both Spain and Portugal for much of the 20th century. In the 1970s, both countries emerged as modern democracies and have since experienced rapid economic growth, benefiting from their membership of the European Union. Today, their economies are dominated by tourism and agriculture, although Spanish industry is expanding rapidly.

Portugal exports large numbers of oysters from the Atlantic.

The Cordillera Cantábrica in northwestern Spain.

PORTUGAL
pop: 9,800,000

ORANGES

Oranges were introduced to Spain by the Moors in about the 9th century AD. They are grown along the Mediterranean coast and are an important export. The best Spanish oranges come from Valencia. Oranges from Seville are used for making fine marmalade. **Look for** 🍊

GROWING CORKS

Spain and Portugal produce two-thirds of the world's cork. It is made from the outer bark of these evergreen oak trees. The bark is stripped off, seasoned, flattened, and laid out in sheets.

Sherry   Port

FORTIFIED WINES

This region is famous for its fortified wines. They are made by adding extra alcohol to the wine during the fermentation process. Sherry is named after Jeréz de la Frontera, while port comes from Oporto. **Look for** 🍷

MAP FEATURES

Forest products: Spain and Portugal are Europe's only source of eucalyptus, which is grown for its gum, resin, oil, and wood. **Look for** 🌲

Fishing: Spanish fishing fleets are among the largest in Europe, concentrated around the northwest Atlantic coast. **Look for** 🐟

Vehicle manufacture: Spain ranks sixth in world car exports, specializing in small cars. **Look for** 🚗

🐑	Sheep	🚢	Fishing ports
🍃	Citrus fruits	⛏	Mining
🍇	Wine	🏭	Industrial center
🏺	Vegetable oil	✍	Tourism

LISBON

Portugal's great navigators and explorers set sail from Lisbon, on the mouth of the Tagus River. The city, which grew rich on global trade, was completely rebuilt after an earthquake destroyed two thirds of it in 1755.

A castle is visible on the wooded hills north of Lisbon.

Spain is one of the world's leading olive producers.

ATLANTIC OCEAN

Ferrol
A Coruña
Eucalyptus
GALICIA
Santiago
Lugo
Iron
Eucalyptus
Avilés
Gijón
Oviedo
CORDILLERA CANTÁBRICA
Eucalyptus
Zinc
Lead
Pontevedra
Eucalyptus
Tin
Iron
León
Vigo
Ourense
Tungsten
Minho
Viana do Castelo
Bragança
Embalse de Ricobayo
Palencia
Braga
Tin
Zamora
Valladolid
Eucalyptus
Iron
Douro
Oporto (Porto)
Espinho
S
Salamanca
Eucalyptus
Tin
Aveiro
Viseu
Guarda
Uranium
Ávila
Eucalyptus
Tungsten
SIERRA DE GREDOS
Figueira da Foz
Coimbra
Covilhã
Tungsten
Tagus
Leiria
Castelo Branco
Embalse de Alcántara
Olives
Tagus
Caldas da Rainha
Cáceres
Eucalyptus
Santarém
Eucalyptus
Portalegre
Uranium
Olives
Embalse de Orellana
Eucalyptus
Olives
Guadiana
Mercury
LISBON (LISBOA)
Eucalyptus
Barragem do Maranhão
Cork
Olives
Mérida
Barreiro
Cork
Badajoz
PORTUGAL
Setúbal
Eucalyptus
Évora
Olives
Guadiana
Eucalyptus
Cork
Cork
Eucalyptus
Copper
Beja
Cork
SIERRA MORENA
Lead
Sines
Cork
Eucalyptus
Cork
Zinc
Olives
Córdoba
Cork
Copper
Olives
Olives
Copper
Olives
Guadalquivir
Olives
Lagos
Portimão
Eucalyptus
Seville (Sevilla)
Olives
Cabo de São Vicente
Faro
Huelva
Eucalyptus
Olives
Cork
Gulf of Cádiz (Golfo de Cádiz)
Jeréz de la Frontera
Iron
Málaga
Torremolinos
Marbella
Cádiz
San Fernando
Cork
Costa
Algeciras
Gibraltar
GIBRALTAR (to UK)
Strait of Gibraltar

FISH DISHES

Paella is a classic Spanish dish from the Valencia region, where rice is grown. It consists of a variety of meat, fish, fresh vegetables, and saffron-flavored rice, simmered in a stock. The Spanish eat a lot of fish, and fish stew is another popular dish. Spain is also famous for its cured meats, especially ham, or *jamón serrano*.

The Spanish-French border runs through the center of the Pyrenean mountain chain

Skiing resorts attract tourists to the central Pyrenees

ANDORRA

The Basque Country

Pamplona

Fertile valley of Ebro R.

Vines, vegetables, and fruit are grown in the eastern Pyrenees

Lleida (Lérida)

Southeastern slopes of the Pyrenees are humid; *levantor* winds carry damp air from the Mediterranean

THE PYRENEES

Traditionally, the peoples of the Pyrenees lived by agriculture and livestock raising. Sheep and cattle were moved seasonally up and down the mountains, grazing the high snow-free pastures in summer. Fast-flowing rivers have great potential for hydroelectric power and in the 19th century steel and paper mills were built in the Pyrenean foothills. Today, the region is in decline, as young people abandon traditional mountain communities for cities. The area's abundant natural beauty is, however, attracting increasing numbers of tourists.

Bay of Biscay

Many tourists visit the beautiful Balearic Islands.

Islands (Islas Baleares)

Minorca (Menorca)

Mahón

Majorca (Mallorca)

Palma de Mallorca

Balearic

Ibiza (Eivissa)

Ibiza (Eivissa)

Formentera

TOURISM

Fifty million visitors a year visit Spain's Mediterranean coast alone, and tourism accounts for 10 percent of Spain's income. But large numbers of high-rise hotels have spoiled some stretches of the coastline, and popular beaches are often overcrowded. Look for

Castanets

FLAMENCO

Flamenco music and dance, developed by the Andalusian gypsies, are the major folk arts of Spain. Flamenco songs deal with the entire range of human emotion, from despair to ecstasy, and are performed with a passionate intensity. Dancers dress in traditional costume and accompany themselves on castanets and guitars.

Flamenco dancer's fan and comb

SPAIN
pop: 39,800,000

THE ALHAMBRA

The Alhambra, at Granada in southern Spain, is a Moorish palace and fortress built during the 13th and 14th centuries. It was the Moors' last stronghold in Spain. It is a beautiful example of Moorish architecture, famous for its delicately carved stone, brilliantly patterned mosaics and tiles, and alabaster fountains.

Gibraltar has been a British colony since the 18th century.

BULLFIGHTING

In Spain, bullfighting is a national sport. During a bullfight, brightly colored capes are fluttered to tempt the bull to charge. When it charges, the matador sticks long, pointed barbs into the bull's shoulders. Once it is exhausted, the matador uses his sword to kill the bull, exposing himself to mortal danger.

CATHOLICISM

Like the Portuguese, the Spanish blend Roman Catholicism with customs and traditions dating back to pre-Christian times. Their *fiestas* combine religious ceremonies with wine and dancing.

A   B   C   D   E   F   G   H   I   J

FRANCE

FOR CENTURIES FRANCE has played a central role in European civilization. Reminders of its long history can be found throughout the land; prehistoric cave dwellings, Roman amphitheaters, medieval cathedrals and castles, and the 17th- and 18th-century palaces of the powerful French monarchs. The French Revolution of 1789 swept away the monarchy and changed the face of France forever. The country survived the Napoleonic Wars and occupation during World Wars I and II, and now has a thriving economy based on farming and industry. France is a land of varied scenery and strong regional traditions – the only country which belongs to both northern and southern Europe. Farming is still important, but many people have moved from the country to the cities. France still administers a number of overseas territories, all that remain of its once widespread empire. Today, France's population includes immigrants from its former colonies, especially Muslims from North Africa. France is one of the most enthusiastic members of the European Union.

PARIS

Paris, the capital of France, is the largest and most important city in the country. It lies on both banks of the Seine River. One of the world's great cities, Paris contains magnificent buildings, art treasures, and elegant shops. The wrought-iron Eiffel Tower, the symbol of Paris, looms above the city.

A cyclist in the *Tour de France*, the world's most famous bicycle race.

FRANCE
pop: 58,700,000

AGRICULTURE

France is a mainly rural country producing a wide range of farm products. Some farms still use traditional methods, but modern technology has transformed regions like the Paris Basin, where cereals are grown on a large scale. Look for 🌾

THE AIRBUS

Developing new aircraft is so costly that sometimes several countries form a company together to share the costs. One example is Airbus Industrie: the main factory is at Toulouse, but costs are shared by France, Germany, the UK, and Spain. With successful aircraft already flying, Airbus Industrie is planning a jumbo jet. Look for ✈

MAP FEATURES

Market gardening: In the northwest, the mild climate and sheltered conditions are ideal for growing early vegetables, called *primeurs*. Look for 🛒

Nuclear power: Lacking its own energy sources, France has developed its nuclear power industry. It now produces 70% of its electricity. Look for 🏭

Tourism: In the underdeveloped Mediterranean region, tourism has been encouraged by the construction of attractive vacation resorts. Look for ⛱

Rail routes: France has Europe's largest rail network. Intercity trains (TGVs) travel at speeds of up to 186 miles (300 km) per hour. Look for 🚄

⬡	Cheese	⛏	Coal
🌾	Cereals	🏭	Industrial center
🌱	Sugar beet	✈	Aerospace industry
🍇	Wine	🚗	Vehicle manufacture
⚫	Mining	⛷	Skiing

CHATEAUS

France has many beautiful historic buildings. Along the banks of the Loire River and its tributaries are royal palaces, or chateaus, built by the royalty of France from the 15th-17th centuries. Chambord, once a hunting lodge, has 440 rooms and 85 staircases. Fairy-tale palaces like these attract thousands of visitors each year.

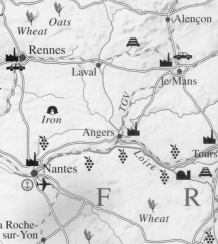

Fields of sunflowers can be seen in many areas of France.

Head of garlic

Snail

Clove of garlic

Snails, served with butter and garlic, are a great French delicacy.

Camembert

CHEESE

France is famous for its cheese. Over 300 different varieties are made. Many, like Camembert, Roquefort, and Brie, are world famous and copied in many other countries. Each region has its traditional way of making and packaging its cheeses. Goat's and sheep's milk are used as well as cow's. Look for ⬡

Brie

The principality of Andorra is situated in the Pyrenees.

ANDORRA
pop: 65,000

Map labels

ENGLISH CHANNEL
Cherbourg
le Havre
Wheat
Channel Islands (to UK)
Caen
St-Lô
NORMANDY (NORMANDIE)
Camembert
Iron
St-Malo
Wheat
Île d'Ouessant
St-Brieuc
Oats
Brest
Wheat
BRITTANY (BRETAGNE)
Barley
Oats
Wheat
Rennes
Alençon
Quimper
Barley
Laval
le Mans
Lorient
Vannes
Barley
Iron
Angers
Tours
Belle Île
St-Nazaire
Nantes
Loire
F   R
la Roche-sur-Yon
Wheat
Wheat
Poitiers
les Sables-d'Olonne
Wheat
la Rochelle
Charente
Wheat
Saintes
Angoulême
Barley
Dordogne
Bordeaux
Arcachon
Garonne
ATLANTIC OCEAN
Mont-de-Marsan
Corn
Bayonne
Corn
Pau
Tarbes
PYRENEES

A   B   C   D   E   F   G   H   I   J

K L M N O P Q R S T

WINE

Bottle of Champagne

When the Romans occupied France 2,000 years ago, they planted vines. From these early beginnings, France became the center of world wine making. The wine's quality depends on the region, soil, and climate, and on the producer's skillful blending and fermentation. Champagne is produced in the area around Reims. **Look for** ✿

A circular poster display, a common sight in Paris.

CAFE LIFE

In the late 17th century, when cafés first became fashionable in Paris, they were used as places to meet for a snack and to exchange news and gossip. The word café means "coffee" in French. Two centuries later, cafés have become popular throughout the world.

FRENCH STYLE

Perfume spray

The 14th-century French kings and their courts established a tradition of elegance and style which the French have maintained ever since. Paris is still the world's capital of "haute couture" – high fashion. French clothes designs, perfumes, and cosmetics have a major influence on the world's fashion industry.

FRENCH FOOD

The French place enormous importance on food and wine. Food can be just as delicious in small provincial restaurants as in Parisian ones. French cooks have created many great dishes which are widely imitated.

Fillet de Boeuf

French sedan

MOTOR VEHICLES

France has the second-largest vehicle industry in western Europe, producing about 3 million a year. Paris is the center of production, although companies are encouraged to open factories in other cities. **Look for** 🚗

An Alpine peak in southeastern France.

MONACO

Monaco is a tiny country situated on the Mediterranean coast. Its orchestra is larger than its army. Many people have settled in Monaco because of its lenient tax laws and extensive gambling facilities.

MONACO
pop: 32,000

The rugged landscape of the French island of Corsica.

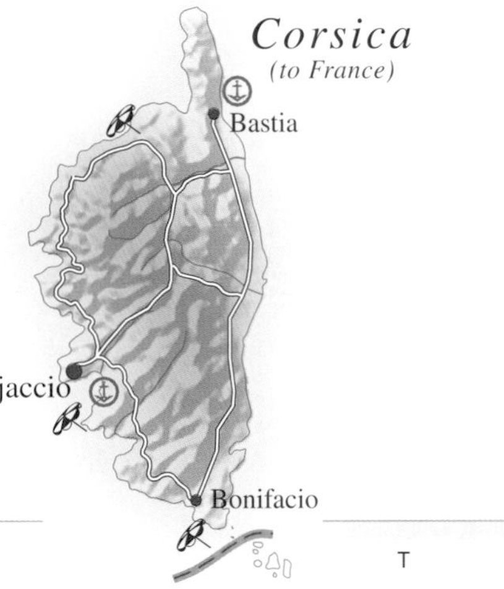

Corsica
(to France)

Map labels

Strait of Dover
Dunkirk
Calais
Boulogne-sur-Mer
Channel Tunnel
BELGIUM
Arras
Valenciennes
Lille
Wheat
Somme
Oats
Dieppe
Amiens
St-Quentin
Charleville-Mézières
LUXEMBOURG
GERMANY
Beauvais
Laon
Wheat
Thionville
Iron
Rouen
Seine
Reims
Verdun
Metz
Iron
Evreux
Marne
Châlons-en-Champagne
Nancy
Boursin
Bar-le-Duc
Strasbourg
PARIS
Wheat
Moselle
Versailles
Seine
Chartres
Brie
Melun
Oats
Troyes
Chaumont
Épinal
Colmar
VOSGES
Wheat
Wheat
Mulhouse
Orléans
Barley
Potassium
Auxerre
Oats
Belfort
Blois
TGV
Vesoul
Wheat
Chambord
BURGUNDY (BOURGOGNE)
Dijon
Besançon
Bourges
Saône
Nevers
Doubs
Wheat
Rye
JURA
Châteauroux
Wheat
Moulins
L. Geneva
Uranium
Wheat
Mâcon
SWITZERLAND
Uranium
Loire
Bourg-en-Bresse
Vichy
Annecy
Barley
Wheat
Limoges
Clermont-Ferrand
Lyon
Chambéry
MASSIF CENTRAL
St-Etienne
Grenoble
Rye
le Puy
Valence
ALPS
Périgueux
Corn
Aurillac
Allier
Gap
ITALY
Rhône
Mende
CEVENNES
Cahors
Tungsten
Rodez
Digne
Lot
Corn
PROVENCE
Durance
Corn
Agen
Corn
MONACO
Montauban
Albi
Roquefort
Avignon
Nice
MONACO
Yarn
Lead
Nîmes
Corn
Grasse
Wheat
Zinc
Arles
Aix-en-Provence
Aluminum
Cannes
Barley
Corn
Gold
Silver
Montpellier
Marseille
Côte d'Azur
Auch
Toulouse
Barley
Wheat
Carcassonne
Toulon
Îles d'Hyères
Wheat
Foix
Corn
Perpignan
MEDITERRANEAN SEA
ANDORRA
ANDORRA LA VELLA
Bastia
Ajaccio
Bonifacio

N

0 25 50 75 100 125 150 KM
0   25   50   75   100 MILES

THE LOW COUNTRIES

BELGIUM, THE NETHERLANDS, and Luxembourg are the most densely populated countries in Europe. They are known as the "Low Countries" because much of the land is flat and low-lying. In the Netherlands, much of the land lies below sea level, and has been reclaimed from the sea over the centuries by ingenious technology. The marshy, drained soils are extremely fertile. All three countries enjoy high living standards, with well-developed industries and excellent rail, road, and waterway communications with the rest of Europe. During the course of their history, the Low Countries have often been the battleground between warring nations, and both Belgium and Luxembourg only achieved independence in the 19th century. Belgium is still divided by language – Dutch is spoken in the north, while the Walloons in the south speak French.

The northern Netherlands are mainly Protestant; the rest of the region is basically Roman Catholic. Today, the Low Countries are unswerving supporters of the European Union. The cities of Brussels, The Hague, and Luxembourg are all headquarters of important European institutions.

DELFT TILE

Delft pottery has been made in the Netherlands since the 17th century. The technique of glazing pottery with tin, used in Delft, came to the Netherlands from the Middle East via Spain and Italy. This Delft tile is decorated with a windmill, a familiar sight in the Netherlands. There are about 1,000 windmills still standing today, dating mainly from the 18th and 19th centuries.

ROTTERDAM

Rotterdam is one of the world's largest ports, lying within a massive built-up and industrialized area called Randstad Holland. Rotterdam is situated near the mouth of the Rhine River, an important trade route. Imported oil is refined locally. The port also handles minerals, grain, timber, and coal.

DELTA PROJECT

Much of the Netherlands lies below sea level, and is at risk from flooding. Over the centuries, barriers called dikes have been built to keep the sea out and water has been drained and pumped into canals. The Delta Project, completed in 1986, used dikes to close off the Rhine, Maas, and Scheldt estuaries from the North Sea, creating freshwater lakes. The region had long been exposed to the destructive power of the North Sea; in 1953 floods killed 1,835 people.

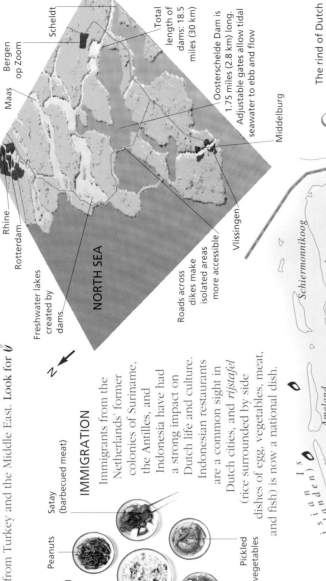

Scheldt

Bergen op Zoom

Maas

Rhine

Rotterdam

Freshwater lakes created by dams

NORTH SEA

Total length of dams: 18.5 miles (30 km)

Oosterschelde Dam is 1.75 miles (2.8 km) long. Adjustable gates allow tidal seawater to ebb and flow

Middelburg

Vlissingen

Roads across dikes make isolated areas more accessible

FLOWERS

The Netherlands are Europe's largest producers of flowers, and spectacular fields of spring flowers in full bloom are a major tourist attraction. Cut flowers are flown daily from the Netherlands to cities all over the world. Cultivation of bulbs such as crocuses, hyacinths, daffodils, and tulips is a specialty. They have been grown here since about 1600, when they were introduced from Turkey and the Middle East. Look for

Tulip

IMMIGRATION

Immigrants from the Netherlands' former colonies of Suriname, the Antilles, and Indonesia have had a strong impact on Dutch life and culture. Indonesian restaurants are a common sight in Dutch cities, and *rijstafel* (rice surrounded by side dishes of egg, vegetables, meat, and fish) is now a national dish.

Satay (barbecued meat)

Peanuts

Beef Rendang

Egg-fried rice

Prawns and garlic

Pickled vegetables

Salad in peanut sauce

The rind of Dutch Edam cheese is colored with anatto dye.

Both Belgium and the Netherlands are major beer exporters.

CITY OF CANALS

The Dutch capital, Amsterdam, is a city of islands built on swampy land. It is crisscrossed by 160 canals. Many of the city's finest gabled houses date from the 16th–18th centuries, when merchants grew rich from trade and exploration. Amsterdam is not only the country's historic center, it is also its second-largest port.

NETHERLANDS
pop: 15,700,000

GERMANY

Delfzijl

Winschoten

Beef

Wheat

Wheat

Wheat

Beef

Emmen

Almelo

Hengelo

Enschede

Schiermonnikoog

Groningen

Assen

Dairy

Wheat

Hoogeveen

Wheat

Dairy

Wheat

Deventer

Zutphen

Beef

Leeuwarden

Dairy

Drachten

Heerenveen

Dairy

Meppel

Zwolle

Beef

Ameland

Beef

IJssel

Hardewijk

Dairy

Apeldoorn

Terschelling

Dairy

Harlingen

Dairy

Wheat

Elevoland

Wheat

Amersfoort

Vieland

Dairy

Lelystad

Hilversum

Utrecht

IJSSELMEER

Hoorn

Dairy

Alphen aan den Rijn

Texel

Den Helder

Wheat

Alkmaar

Purmerend

Zaanstad

Dairy

AMSTERDAM

Amstelveen

Dairy

Velsen-Noord

IJmuiden

Wheat

Haarlem

Leiden

Zoetermeer

THE HAGUE
('S-GRAVENHAGE)

WADDEN ZEE

W e s t F r i s i a n I s (W a d d e n e i l a n d e n)

N O O R D H O L L A N D

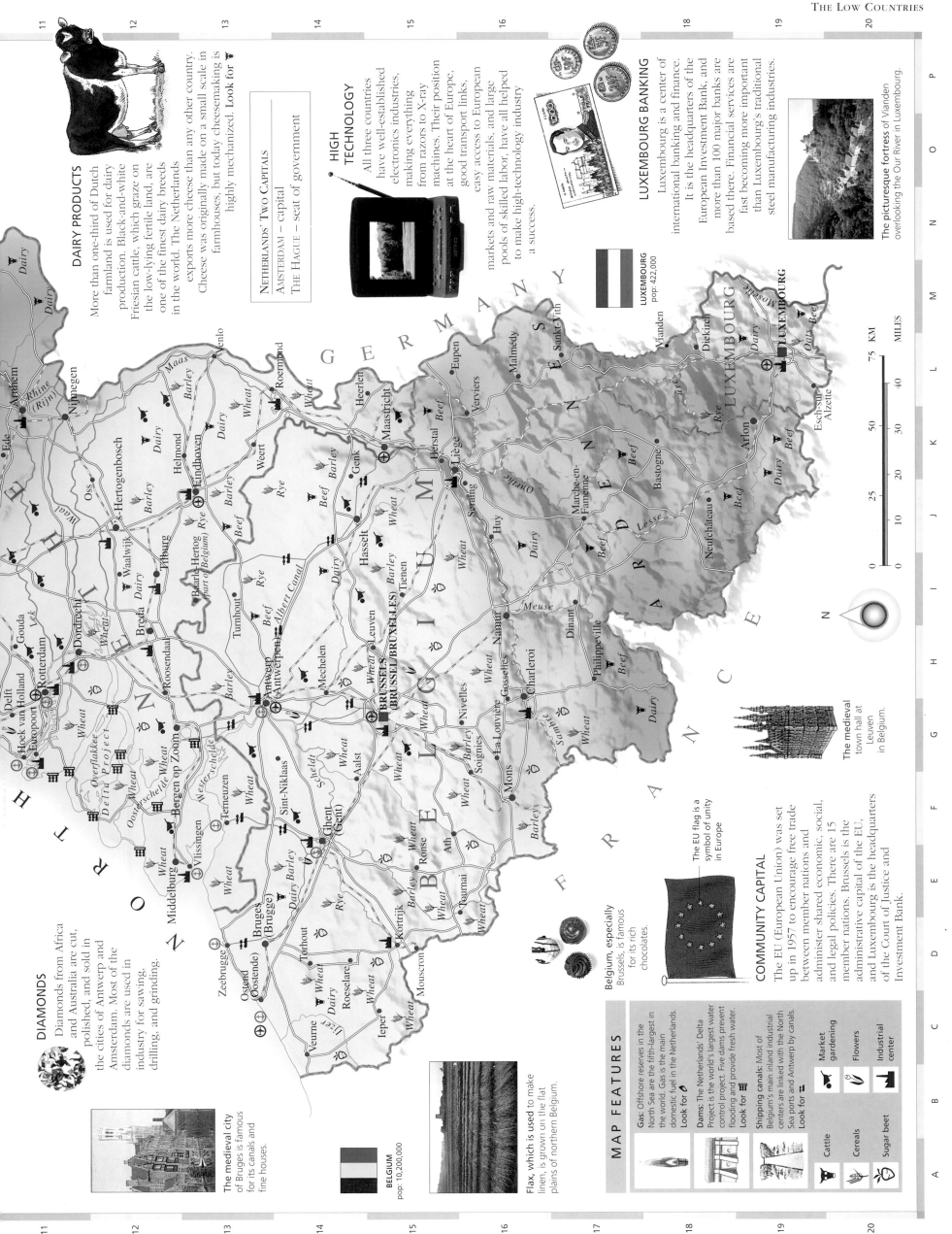

DAIRY PRODUCTS

More than one-third of Dutch farmland is used for dairy production. Black-and-white Friesian cattle, which graze on the low-lying fertile land, are one of the finest dairy breeds in the world. The Netherlands exports more cheese than any other country. Cheese was originally made on a small scale in farmhouses, but today cheesemaking is highly mechanized. Look for ⚊

NETHERLANDS' TWO CAPITALS

AMSTERDAM – capital
THE HAGUE – seat of government

HIGH TECHNOLOGY

All three countries have well-established electronics industries, making everything from razors to X-ray machines. Their position at the heart of Europe, good transport links, easy access to European markets and raw materials, and large pools of skilled labor, have all helped to make high-technology industry a success.

LUXEMBOURG
pop: 422,000

LUXEMBOURG BANKING

Luxembourg is a center of international banking and finance. It is the headquarters of the European Investment Bank, and more than 100 major banks are based there. Financial services are fast becoming more important than Luxembourg's traditional steel manufacturing industries.

The picturesque fortress of Vianden overlooking the Our River in Luxembourg.

DIAMONDS

Diamonds from Africa and Australia are cut, polished, and sold in the cities of Antwerp and Amsterdam. Most of the diamonds are used in industry for sawing, drilling, and grinding.

The medieval city of Bruges is famous for its canals and fine houses.

Flax, which is used to make linen, is grown on the flat plains of northern Belgium.

BELGIUM
pop: 10,200,000

MAP FEATURES

Gas: Offshore reserves in the North Sea are the fifth-largest in the world. Gas is the main domestic fuel in the Netherlands. Look for ♢

Dams: The Netherlands' Delta Project is the world's largest water control project. Five dams prevent flooding and provide fresh water. Look for ⊞

Shipping canals: Most of Belgium's main inland industrial centers are linked with the North Sea ports and Antwerp by canals. Look for ≣

Cattle	Market gardening
Cereals	Flowers
Sugar beet	Industrial center

Belgium, especially Brussels, is famous for its rich chocolates.

The EU flag is a symbol of unity in Europe

COMMUNITY CAPITAL

The EU (European Union) was set up in 1957 to encourage free trade between member nations and administer shared economic, social, and legal policies. There are 15 member nations. Brussels is the administrative capital of the EU, and Luxembourg is the headquarters of the Court of Justice and Investment Bank.

The medieval town hall at Leuven in Belgium.

KM
MILES
0   10   20   30   40
0   25   50   75

N

GERMANY

SITUATED IN THE CENTER OF EUROPE, Germany is now the continent's leading economic power. In the past it has been an area of great conflict; it was not until 1871 that a patchwork of independent states, which had fought bitterly for centuries, were united under Prussian leadership to form Germany. Last century, Germany was defeated in two world wars. By 1945 the economy was shattered and the country divided between a Soviet-dominated communist East and a democratic West. The postwar years saw an amazing recovery in West Germany's economy. Natural advantages – a central position in Europe, large reserves of coal and iron, along with the construction of an efficient transportation system and the determination to succeed – have all helped to create a dynamic economy. The East, on the other hand, lagged behind. In 1989, the Soviet Union began to disintegrate, and communism collapsed throughout Eastern Europe. The two halves of Germany were reunified in 1990, but problems soon became apparent. West Germans resented the huge amounts of money invested in the East to bring it up to their standards. East Germans became impatient with the slow pace of change. These resentments have led to violence against refugees, immigrants, and "guest workers," many of whom have lived in Germany for most of their lives.

CARS

Germany is Europe's largest vehicle producer, specializing in high-quality cars. American and Japanese car companies are based here, too, attracted by the skilled workforce. Look for 🚗

BERLIN

At the end of World War II, Berlin, Germany's capital city, was divided between the four victorious Allies. In 1961, the Berlin Wall was built to separate the Russian sector from the other three. In 1989, the wall came down: East Germans streamed through this gate into West Berlin.

Brandenburg Gate

AGRICULTURE

Germany produces all its own food and is one of the world's main growers of sugar beet, barley, and rye. Oats, rye, and barley thrive in the mild, wet north, while wheat is grown in the warmer south. Look for 🌾

This decorated *stein*, or mug, is used for beer.

Green pastures and woodland on the flat Baltic coast.

DRESDEN

Once Dresden was a beautiful old city, with many 18th-century buildings. But in World War II it was devastated by Allied bombing. After extensive reconstruction, the city's historic buildings have now been restored to their former state.

SAUSAGES

Peppered salami

Salami

Sausages are Germany's favorite snack. There are many regional variations; Frankfurt has even given its name to the Frankfurter sausage. Germany also has over 200 varieties of bread.

A windmill in the fertile farmland of the northeast.

Many German towns have half-timbered buildings dating back to the Middle Ages.

Map labels

POLAND

NETHERLANDS

DENMARK

BALTIC SEA

NORTH SEA

GERMANY

SACHSEN (SAXONY)

North Frisian Is. (Nordfriesische Inseln)
East Frisian Is. (Ostfriesische Inseln)

Sylt
Föhr
Nordstrand
Helgoland
Helgoländer Bucht
Rügen
Fehmarn

Rhine
Ems
Elbe
Saale
Weser
Oder
Müritz
Schweriner See
Mittelland Canal
Kiel Canal
Dortmund-Ems Canal

Flensburg
Schleswig
Husum
Kiel
Neumünster
Lübeck
Wismar
Rostock
Stralsund
Greifswald
Neubrandenburg
Schwerin
Hamburg
Bremerhaven
Cuxhaven
Wilhelmshaven
Emden
Oldenburg
Bremen
Lüneburg
Celle
Hannover (Hanover)
Braunschweig
Salzgitter
Wolfsburg
Hildesheim
Magdeburg
Stendal
Potsdam
BERLIN
Frankfurt an der Oder
Cottbus
Wittenberg
Dessau
Halle
Minden
Osnabrück
Bielefeld
Paderborn
Münster
Hamm
Recklinghausen
Gelsenkirchen
Oberhausen
Duisburg
Essen
Bochum
Dortmund
Nordhausen
Göttingen

Oats, Rye, Wheat, Beef, Dairy, Barley, Potassium, Lead, Zinc

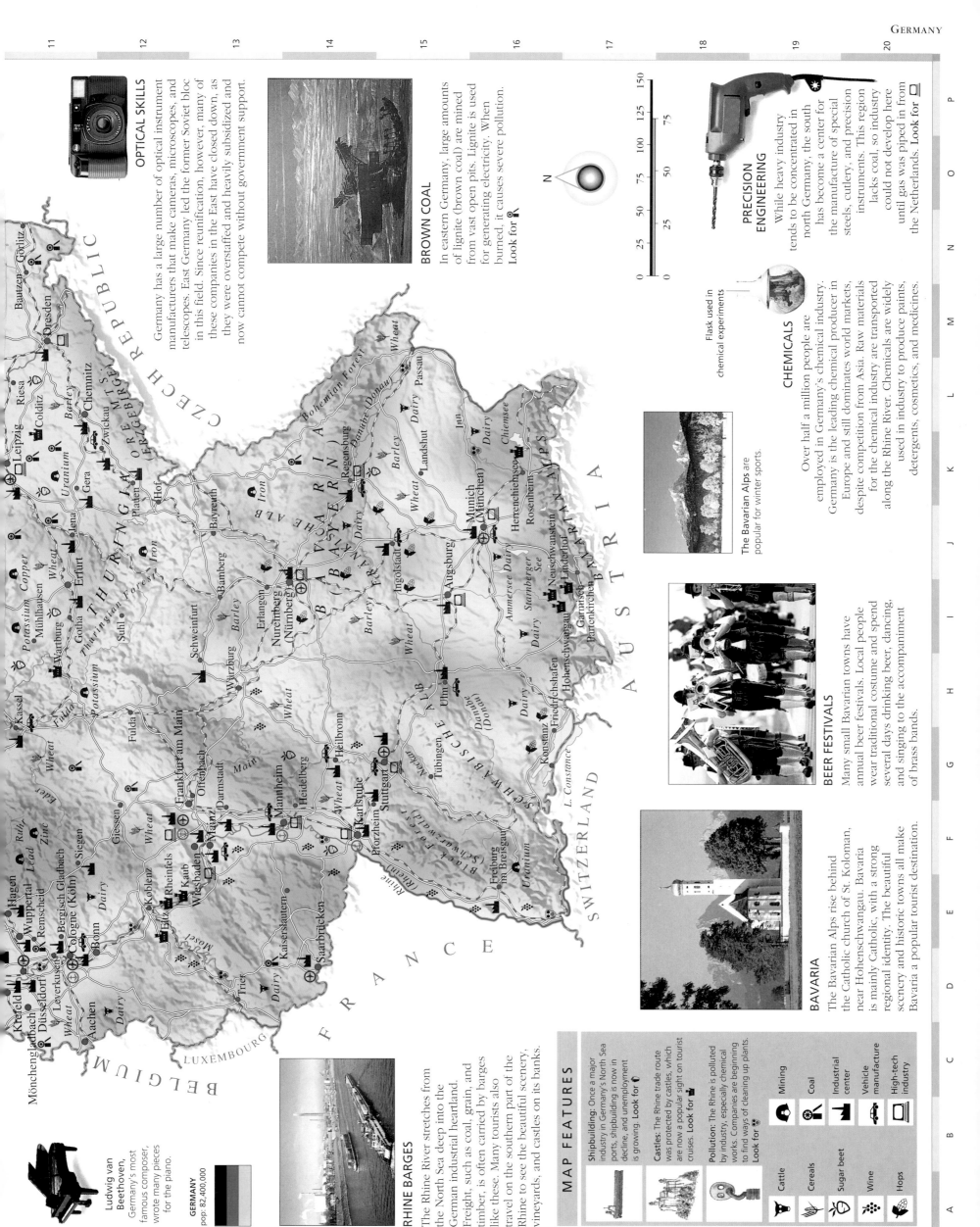

OPTICAL SKILLS

Germany has a large number of optical instrument manufacturers that make cameras, microscopes, and telescopes. East Germany led the former Soviet bloc in this field. Since reunification, however, many of these companies in the East have closed down, as they were overstaffed and heavily subsidized and now cannot compete without government support.

BROWN COAL

In eastern Germany, large amounts of lignite (brown coal) are mined from vast open pits. Lignite is used for generating electricity. When burned, it causes severe pollution. Look for ⛏

PRECISION ENGINEERING

While heavy industry tends to be concentrated in north Germany, the south has become a center for the manufacture of special steels, cutlery, and precision instruments. This region lacks coal, so industry could not develop here until gas was piped in from the Netherlands. Look for ▢

CHEMICALS

Over half a million people are employed in Germany's chemical industry. Germany is the leading chemical producer in Europe and still dominates world markets, despite competition from Asia. Raw materials for the chemical industry are transported along the Rhine River. Chemicals are widely used in industry to produce paints, detergents, cosmetics, and medicines.

Flask used in chemical experiments

The Bavarian Alps are popular for winter sports.

BEER FESTIVALS

Many small Bavarian towns have annual beer festivals. Local people wear traditional costume and spend several days drinking beer, dancing, and singing to the accompaniment of brass bands.

BAVARIA

The Bavarian Alps rise behind the Catholic church of St. Koloman, near Hohenschwangau. Bavaria is mainly Catholic, with a strong regional identity. The beautiful scenery and historic towns all make Bavaria a popular tourist destination.

RHINE BARGES

The Rhine River stretches from the North Sea deep into the German industrial heartland. Freight, such as coal, grain, and timber, is often carried by barges like these. Many tourists also travel on the Rhine to see the beautiful scenery, vineyards, and castles on its banks.

Ludwig van Beethoven, Germany's most famous composer, wrote many pieces for the piano.

GERMANY pop: 82,400,000

MAP FEATURES

Shipbuilding: Once a major industry in Germany's North Sea ports, shipbuilding is now in decline, and unemployment is growing. Look for ⛴

Castles: The Rhine trade route was protected by castles, which are now a popular sight on tourist cruises. Look for 🏰

Pollution: The Rhine is polluted by industry, especially chemical works. Companies are beginning to find ways of cleaning up plants. Look for ☠

⛏	Mining
❋	Coal
⚒	Industrial center
🚗	Vehicle manufacture
▢	High-tech industry
🐄	Cattle
🌾	Cereals
🌱	Sugar beet
🍇	Wine
🌾	Hops

N

| 0 | 25 | 50 | 75 | 100 | 125 | 150 |

| 0 | 25 | 50 | 75 |

THE ALPINE STATES

RUNNING THROUGH the middle of Austria and Switzerland are the Alps, the highest mountains in Europe. Both countries lie on Europe's main north-south trading routes, with access to the heart of Europe via the great Danube and Rhine waterways. Switzerland was formed in the Middle Ages when a number of Alpine communities united in defensive leagues against their more powerful neighbors. Modern Switzerland is a confederation of 26 separate provinces, called cantons. The country has three main languages – German, French, and Italian. In contrast, Austria was once the center of the mighty Habsburg Empire. When the empire collapsed in 1918, Austria became an independent country. Both Austria and Slovenia, which became independent from communist Yugoslavia in 1991, have mineral resources and thriving industries. With few natural resources, Switzerland has concentrated instead on skilled, high-technology manufacturing.

Gold bar

BANKING

Switzerland is one of the world's main financial centers. People from all over the world put their money into Swiss bank accounts as the country is well known for its political stability. Liechtenstein is also a major banking center. Look for 🏦

DAIRY FARMING

Swiss dairy cattle spend the winter in the Alpine valleys and in summer are taken up to the Alpine pastures for grazing. The milk is used to make many varieties of cheese, such as Gruyère. Look for 🐄

Porcelain teeth

FALSE TEETH

Liechtenstein is the headquarters of world dental manufacturing. False teeth, filling materials, and plastic for crown and bridge dental work are exported to more than 100 countries.

Mount Eiger can be glimpsed through clouds.

St. Bernard dogs were trained to rescue travelers lost in the Alps.

Liechtenstein is famous for its beautiful stamps.

The castle at Vaduz, the capital of Liechtenstein.

LIECHTENSTEIN
pop: 31,000

GENEVA

Switzerland has not been at war for 150 years and is therefore seen as a neutral meeting place. Many international organizations have their headquarters in the city of Geneva.

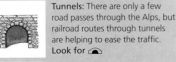
The Swiss consume more chocolate than any other nationality in the world.

SWITZERLAND
pop: 7,300,000

MAP FEATURES

Hydroelectric power: The Swiss pioneered hydroelectricity. Today, Austria is an important producer, tapping the potential of the Danube. Look for ⬛

Climbing: Mountaineers first started climbing the Alps in the 19th century. Some of the peaks are still thought to be the world's toughest climbs. Look for ⛏

Tunnels: There are only a few road passes through the Alps, but railroad routes through tunnels are helping to ease the traffic. Look for 🚇

Pollution: Tourism in the Alps, especially the heavy use of roads, is causing environmental problems. Look for ☠

🌾 Cereals	🕐 Watchmaking
🐂 Cattle	💉 Pharmaceuticals
🍇 Wine	💰 Financial center
🏭 Industrial center	⛷ Skiing

GERMANY

Schaffhausen
L. Constance
Dairy
Frauenfeld
Bregenz
Basel
Rhine (Rhein)
Rye
Winterthur
Herisau
Sankt Gallen
Dornbirn
Dairy
Liestal
Aare
Zürich
Appenzell
Feldkirch
Delémont
Olten
Aarau
Dairy
L. Zurich (Zürichsee)
VADUZ
Landeck
St. Anton
Solothurn
Dairy
Beef
Zug
Linth
Walensee
LIECHTENSTEIN
Arlberg Tunnel
La Chaux-de-Fonds
Biel
Rye
Luzern
Schwyz
Glarus
Dairy
Bieler See
Beef
Vierwaldstätter See
Rhine (Rhein)
Chur
Neuchâtel
BERN
Sarnen
Stans
Altdorf
SWITZERLAND
L. de Neuchâtel
Dairy
Thun
Beef
Yverdon
Fribourg
Brienzer See
P Beef
San Bernardino Tunnel
St. Moritz
Dairy
Wheat
Dairy
Thuner See
Interlaken
A L
RHAETIAN ALPS
Dairy
Lötschberg Tunnel
Eiger
Jungfrau
St. Gotthard Tunnel
LEPONTINE ALPS
Beef
Lausanne
Gstaad
BERNER ALPEN
Brig
Simplon Tunnel
Montreux
Sierre
Simplon Pass
Locarno
Bellinzona
L. Geneva
Sion
Rhône
Dairy
PENNINE ALPS
L. Maggiore
Lugano
Geneva (Genève)
Martigny
Matterhorn
L. di Lugano
Great St. Bernard Tunnel
ITALY
FRANCE
JURA

N

| 0 | 25 | 50 | 75 | 100 KM |
| 0 | | 25 | | 50 MILES |

ALPINE PASSES

Although the Alps are a formidable obstacle to communications, mountain passes have been used since prehistoric times. Since the 19th century, major engineering feats have made the Alps more accessible: bridges cross gorges and deep valleys, and tunnels pass under the mountains.

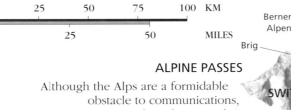

Rhône valley offers a route into the heart of the Alps

Simplon rail tunnel, built in 1906

SWITZERLAND

Berner Alpen

Brig

ITALY

N

The spectacular scenery of northern Slovenia.

Simplon Pass, built 1801-06, open to cars all year round

Heavily used trans-Alpine routes are congested and difficult to cross in winter

VIENNA

For many centuries, Austria was ruled by the Habsburg family. Their empire included Hungary; their capital was Vienna. The city contained many grand buildings and elegant palaces such as this one, the Schönbrunn Palace, which was the Habsburg family's summer residence. The Habsburg empire finally collapsed in 1918.

AUSTRIAN INDUSTRY

Iron ore

Hydroelectric power from the Austrian Alps is a major source of energy for heavy industry. Iron ore deposits around Linz and Donawitz fuel the Austrian steel industry, but some Austrian steel plants have been forced to close by lower world steel prices. Look for

PHARMACEUTICALS

One of Switzerland's main industries is pharmaceuticals (making drugs and medicines). The industry has benefited from the Swiss emphasis on the importance of research and product development, the latest technology, and a highly skilled workforce. Perfumes, cosmetics, and drugs are all made in the Basel area. Look for

AUSTRIA
pop: 8,200,000

Edelweiss is a rare Alpine flower.

Cowbells help farmers to locate animals in remote Alpine pastures.

SLOVENIA
pop: 1,900,000

WATCHMAKING

Watches and clocks have been made in Switzerland since the 16th century. Recently, however, Swiss companies have been under pressure from the Japanese and Americans, who developed quartz technology. The Swiss have saved their industry by making certain of their more famous watches cheaper. Look for

Nugget of mercury ore

Slovenia is a major producer of mercury, used in thermometers.

The Abbey at Melk in Austria was built in the 18th century.

SKI CENTER

The Alps are visited by over 100 million people each year. But ski runs, improved roads, and expanding resorts are all having a harmful effect on the environment. Huge numbers of trees have been cut down to make way for ski runs, but these can provide routes for avalanches. Look for

AUSTRIAN TOURISM

Austria's tourist industry is booming due to the attractions of its beautiful scenery, historical towns, picturesque villages, and winter sports facilities. Tourism is now one of Austria's most profitable industries. A quarter of Austria's tourists visit during the winter; many of the visitors come from nearby Germany.

Sachertorte

COFFEE AND CAKES

The Ottoman Turks, who besieged Vienna in 1529 and 1683, first brought coffee to the city. It was in Vienna that the first coffee shop in Western Europe was opened. There are still many cafés in Vienna, where people drink coffee and eat Austria's famous chocolate cakes. *Sachertorte* is named after the Viennese pastry shop where it is made.

LJUBLJANA

The Slovenian capital, Ljubljana, is a major center of manufacturing, textiles, electronics, and chemical industries. One in seven Slovenes live in the capital. The recent conflict to the south has hit Slovenia's tourist industry, which is now slowly recovering. Visitors are attracted by its historic towns and villages, mountains, and beaches.

Map labels

CZECH REPUBLIC
SLOVAKIA
GERMANY
ITALY
HUNGARY
CROATIA
AUSTRIA
SLOVENIA

Gmünd, Dairy, Wheat, Stockerau, Klosterneuburg, VIENNA (WIEN), Hainburg, Mödling, Baden, Eisenstadt, Wiener Neustadt, Neunkirchen, Neusiedler See
Freistadt, Krems an der Donau, Melk, Sankt Pölten, Amstetten
Schärding, Linz, Danube (Donau), Wheat, Traun, Wels, Steyr
Braunau am Inn, Vöcklabruck, Gmunden, Attersee, L. Traun
Salzburg, Hallein, Bad Ischl, Liezen
Kufstein, Kitzbühel, Zell am See, Radstadt
Jenbach, Mittersill, NIEDERE TAUERN, Donawitz, Leoben, Kapfenberg
Innsbruck, HOHE TAUERN, Felbertauern Tunnel, Badgastein, Katsbergtunnel, Tauern Tunnel, Knittelfeld, Judenburg, Graz
ZILLERTALER ALPEN, Millstätter See, Wolfsberg
ÖTZTALER ALPEN, Brenner Pass, Lienz, Spittal, Sankt Veit an der Glan, Wörther See, Klagenfurt, Villach, Drau, Drava, Maribor, Ptuj
Enns, Mur, Inn
Mercury, Tolmin, LJUBLJANA, Velenje, Celje, Trbovlje, Krško, Sava
Jesenice, Kranj, Nova Gorica, Novo Mesto
SLOVENIA, Maize, Postojna, Kočevje, Kozina, Koper
Murska Sobota, Rye, Mura

CENTRAL EUROPE

IN 1989 THE COMMUNIST governments of Central Europe collapsed and the region entered a period of momentous change. All four countries of Central Europe only became independent states early in the last century. After World War II, they were incorporated into the Soviet bloc and ruled by communist governments. These states started to industrialize rapidly, but they were heavily dependent on the former Soviet Union for their raw materials and markets. When communism collapsed in 1989, the new, democratically elected governments were faced with many problems: modernizing industry, huge foreign debts, soaring inflation, rising unemployment, and terrible pollution. In 1993 the former state of Czechoslovakia was split into two countries, the Czech Republic and Slovakia.

Grudziądz, a medieval Polish town on the Vistula River.

POLAND
pop: 38,700,000

POLLUTION

Central European industry has blighted the forests of the Czech Republic. Acid rain, caused by emission of various pollutants into the air, is killing the forests. Lakes and streams are also becoming acidified, creating impossible living conditions for many organisms. The poisoned and scarred landscape will take decades to recover. **Look for** 💀

PUPPETS

Puppet shows are popular throughout Central Europe, but the former Czechoslovakia is acknowledged as the original home of European puppetry. Today, over a thousand Czech Republic and Slovak puppet companies perform plays.

Wooden puppet

GLASS

The Czech Republic's glass industry is centuries old. Glassware, such as this decanter and glasses, is often intricate and brightly colored. The industry uses local supplies of sand to make the glass. Bohemian crystal is manufactured principally in the northwest around Karlovy Vary and is also popular with the ever-increasing number of tourists.

PRAGUE

The Czech Republic's capital, Prague, has some of the most beautiful and well-preserved architecture in Europe. Since 1989, when the country was opened to tourists, thousands of people have flocked to the city. **Look for** 📷

CZECH REPUBLIC
pop: 10,200,000

MAP FEATURES

 Mining: Poland is one of the world's largest coal producers, but recently the industry has been affected by competition from abroad. **Look for** ⛏

 Financial center: In Hungary, the Budapest stock exchange opened in 1990, and many new banks have now opened in the city. **Look for** 💰

 **Dam:** The dam built by the Slovaks on the Danube at Gabčíkovo has caused a major dispute between Hungary and Slovakia. **Look for** ▦

🌾	Cereals	🏭	Industrial center
🌱	Sugar beet	🍶	Shipbuilding
🍤	Mixed fruits	📷	Tourism
⚓	Timber	🌿	Spas
⛏	Mining	💀	Pollution

HUNGARIAN INDUSTRY

Since the end of World War II, Hungary has industrialized rapidly. It manufactures products such as aluminum, steel, electronic goods, and vehicles, especially buses. But when the Soviet Union disintegrated, Hungarian manufacturers lost many of the traditional markets for their products – especially in heavy industry – and now face many problems. **Look for** ⬛

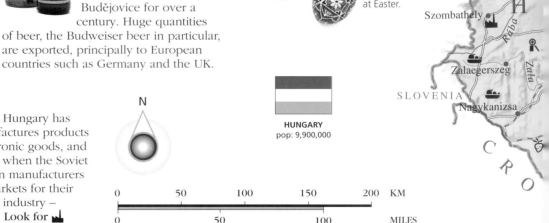

BEER

Some of Europe's finest beers and lagers are brewed in the Czech Republic. Pilsener lager originated in the town of Plzeň; Budweiser beer has been brewed at České Budějovice for over a century. Huge quantities of beer, the Budweiser beer in particular, are exported, principally to European countries such as Germany and the UK.

Beautifully painted eggs are sold in the Czech Republic and Slovakia at Easter.

N

HUNGARY
pop: 9,900,000

0   50   100   150   200   KM

0   50   100   MILES

A   B   C   D   E   F   G   H   I   J

SEA

RUSSIAN
FEDERATION
(KALININGRAD OBLAST)

LITHUANIA

Gulf of
Danzig

Gdynia
Gdansk
Elbląg

Słupia
Wheat
Wda

Suwałki

Jezioro Mamry

Chojnice
Wheat
Rye

Jezioro
Jeziorak

Olsztyn

Ełk

Jezioro
Śniardwy

Grudziądz

Narew
Rye

Rye
Rye
Rye

Ostrołęka

Białystok

Rye

Bydgoszcz
Barley
Toruń

K U J A W Y

Notec

Wheat
Wheat
Wheat

Włocławek
Płońsk

Rye

Bug

PODLASIE

BELARUS

P O L A N D

Jezioro
Włocławskie

Płock

Rye
Wheat

WARSAW
(WARSZAWA)

Rye

Prosna

Rye
Rye
Kalisz

Łódź

Wheat

Visula (Wisła)

Rye

Rye

Piotrków
Trybunalski

Rye

Radom

Lublin

Chełm

Rye

Warta

Rye

Barley

Barley

Oder

Częstochowa

Kielce

Sulfur

Wheat

Wheat

Opole
Iron
Wheat

Zinc
Bytom

Barley
Wheat

Vistula (Wisła)
Wheat

San

Wheat

UKRAINE

Gliwice
Katowice
Rybnik
Sosnowiec

Wheat

Kraków

Tarnów

Wisłoka

Rzeszów

Wheat

Ostrava

Bielsko-Biała

Wheat

M A Ł O P O L S K A

Wheat

Jezioro
Solińskie

C A R P A T H I A N   M O U N T A I N S

Žilina

Martin

Poprad

Prešov

Ondava

Morava

Vah

Trenčín

S L O V A K I A

Nitra

Košice

Laborec

Banská
Bystrica
Magnesite

Magnesite
Lučenec
Nitra
Trnava

Hron

Iron

Vah

Ipel

Miskolc

Tisza

SLOVAKIA
pop: 5,400,000

Gabčíkovo
Corn

Győr
Danube (Duna)

Nyíregyháza

Aluminum
Corn

BUDAPEST

H U N G A R Y

Wheat

Wheat

Debrecen

Wheat

Székesfehérvár
Veszprém

Szolnok

Beretiyó

Wheat

L. Balaton
Corn

Kecskemét

Körös

Danube (Duna)

Corn

Corn

Corn

Wheat

Szekszárd

Szeged

Tisza

Corn

Pécs
Uranium

Baja

Corn

Aluminum
Wheat

G R E A T   H U N G A R I A N   P L A I N

Y U G O S L A V I A

R O M A N I A

...A T I A

SOLIDARITY

Many Polish people work in heavy industries, like coal mining and shipbuilding. In 1980, discontent over poor working conditions led to a strike at this shipyard in Gdansk and to the birth of Solidarity, the Soviet bloc's first independent trade union. Solidarity has significantly influenced Polish politics.

TIMBER

Beechwood
toy

Apart from the lowland area around the Danube River, the landscape of the Czech Republic and Slovakia is mountainous. Both countries have relatively small populations and much of the land is still covered with forest. Both countries have large timber industries. Some timber – mainly pine – is used to make furniture. Beech is often used for the manufacture of toys. **Look for**

RELIGION

For a thousand years, through invasions, wars, repression – and times when the country almost ceased to exist – the Polish people have found strength in their religious faith. Even during the last 40 years of communist government – which actively discouraged religion of any kind – 90 percent of the population remained devout Catholics.

1.50
POLSKA

Wild boar, shown on this Polish stamp, are still found in the region.

PAPRIKA

Hungarian
Paprika

mester

The flat plains in Hungary are among the most fertile farming areas in Europe. Cereals, sugar beet, and fruit are among the main crops. Sweet red peppers – from which paprika is made – are also grown. Paprika is a vital ingredient in many Hungarian dishes.

Morning mist rising over the western Carpathians.

BUDAPEST

Budapest, the Hungarian capital, was once two towns – Buda on the Danube's right bank, and Pest on the left. The town was very badly damaged during World War II, but many of its historic buildings have since been carefully restored. This vast, domed parliament building in Pest faces across the river to Buda.

SPA BATHS

Hot thermal springs were used for medicinal purposes in ancient Greece and Rome. The Romans were the first to develop baths – like this one in Budapest, where bathers enjoy a game of chess. Hungary now has 154 hot-spring baths which are open to the public. The Czech Republic and Slovakia have 900 mineral springs and 58 health spas, which are reserved for medicinal purposes only. It is hoped that more tourists will come to the region to use the thermal springs. **Look for**

Ernö Rubik, a Hungarian, invented this complex puzzle.

Hungary's famous horses are bred on the Great Hungarian Plain.

ITALY AND MALTA

AT VARIOUS TIMES in the past 2,000 years Italy has influenced the development of European civilization. From this narrow, boot-shaped peninsula the Romans established a vast empire throughout Europe and North Africa; Christianity was first adopted as an official religion by a Roman emperor, and Rome later became the center of the Catholic Church. In the 14th century, an extraordinary flowering of the arts and sciences, known as the Renaissance, or "rebirth," started in Italy and transformed European thought and culture. Italy at this time was divided into independent city-states and was later ruled by foreign nations, including France and Austria. But in 1870, after centuries of foreign domination, Italy became an independent and unified country. Despite a lack of natural resources and defeat in World War II, Italy has become a major industrial power. The country has long suffered from corruption and organized crime, but recent changes show promise of more political stability in the future.

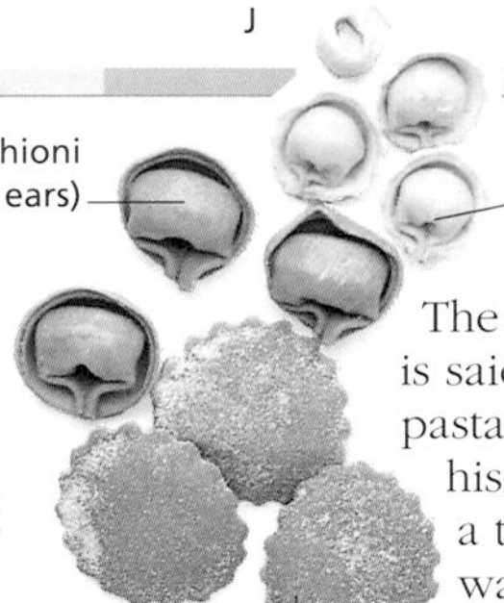

PASTA

The Italian explorer Marco Polo is said to have brought the recipe for pasta to Italy when he returned from his great journey to China. Pasta is a type of dough made by adding water to wheat flour. It has become one of the world's most popular foods. It can be made into different shapes and filled with meat or vegetables.

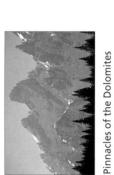

Orecchioni (large ears)

Cappelletti (little hats)

Round tortellini (small pies)

VERONA

The ancient Romans were skillful engineers, and many of their remarkable buildings are still standing today. The foundations of much of Italy's road system was also built by the Romans. Verona is based on the Roman grid street plan. The town's ancient amphitheater seats 22,000 and is still used.

DESIGN

Silk scarf

Suede shoe

Italians place great emphasis on design and produce beautiful products. This flair for design is particularly obvious in their cars and clothes. The fashion houses of Rome, Florence, Milan, and Venice rival those of Paris, and Italian shoes and clothes are widely exported.

THE PO VALLEY

Between the Alps and the Apennines lies a huge triangular plain, drained by Italy's greatest river, the Po. The majority of the country's agriculture, population, and industry is concentrated in this region. Its major cities like Milan and Turin are important industrial and commercial centers.

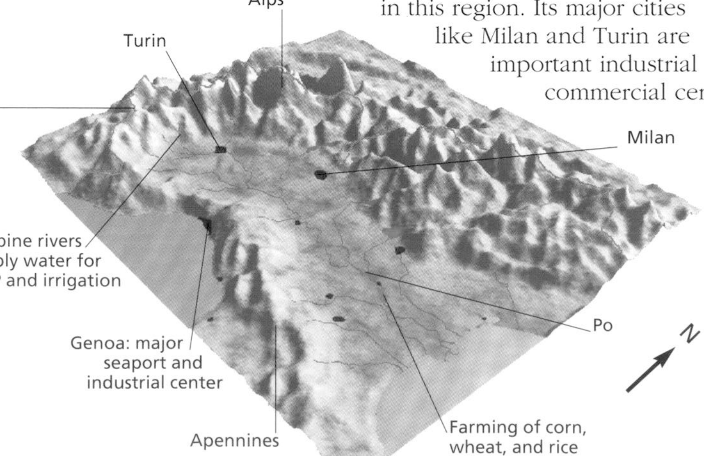

Milan

Po

N

Farming of corn, wheat, and rice

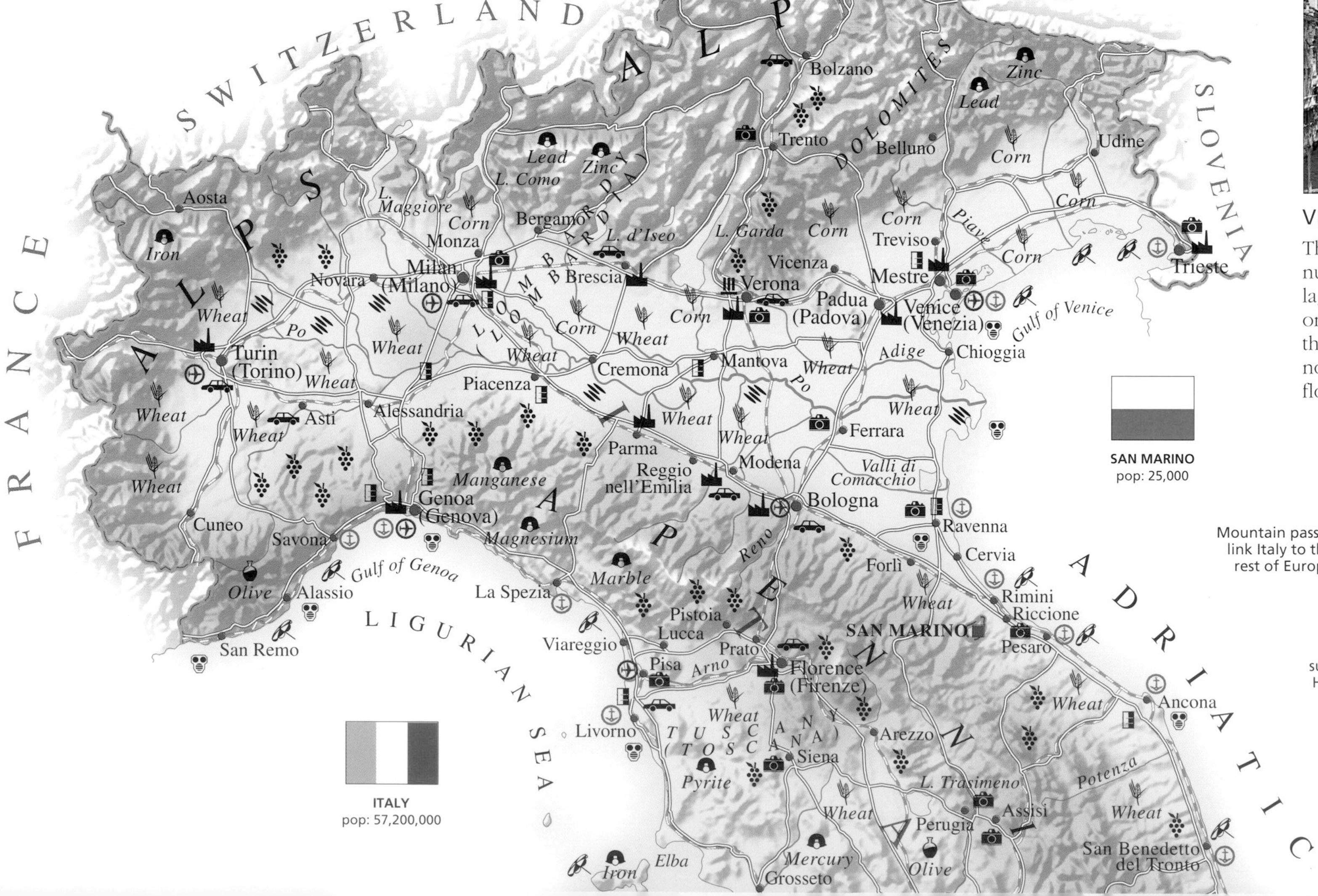

Apennines

Genoa: major seaport and industrial center

Alpine rivers supply water for HEP and irrigation

Alps

Turin

Mountain passes link Italy to the rest of Europe

Masks like these are worn during the February carnival in Venice, which includes plays, masked balls, and fireworks.

Pinnacles of the Dolomites in northeastern Italy.

VENICE

This historic city is built on a number of islands in a shallow lagoon. Many buildings stand on wooden stilts driven into the mud. Venice's future is now uncertain, threatened by flooding and pollution.

SAN MARINO
pop: 25,000

ITALY
pop: 57,200,000

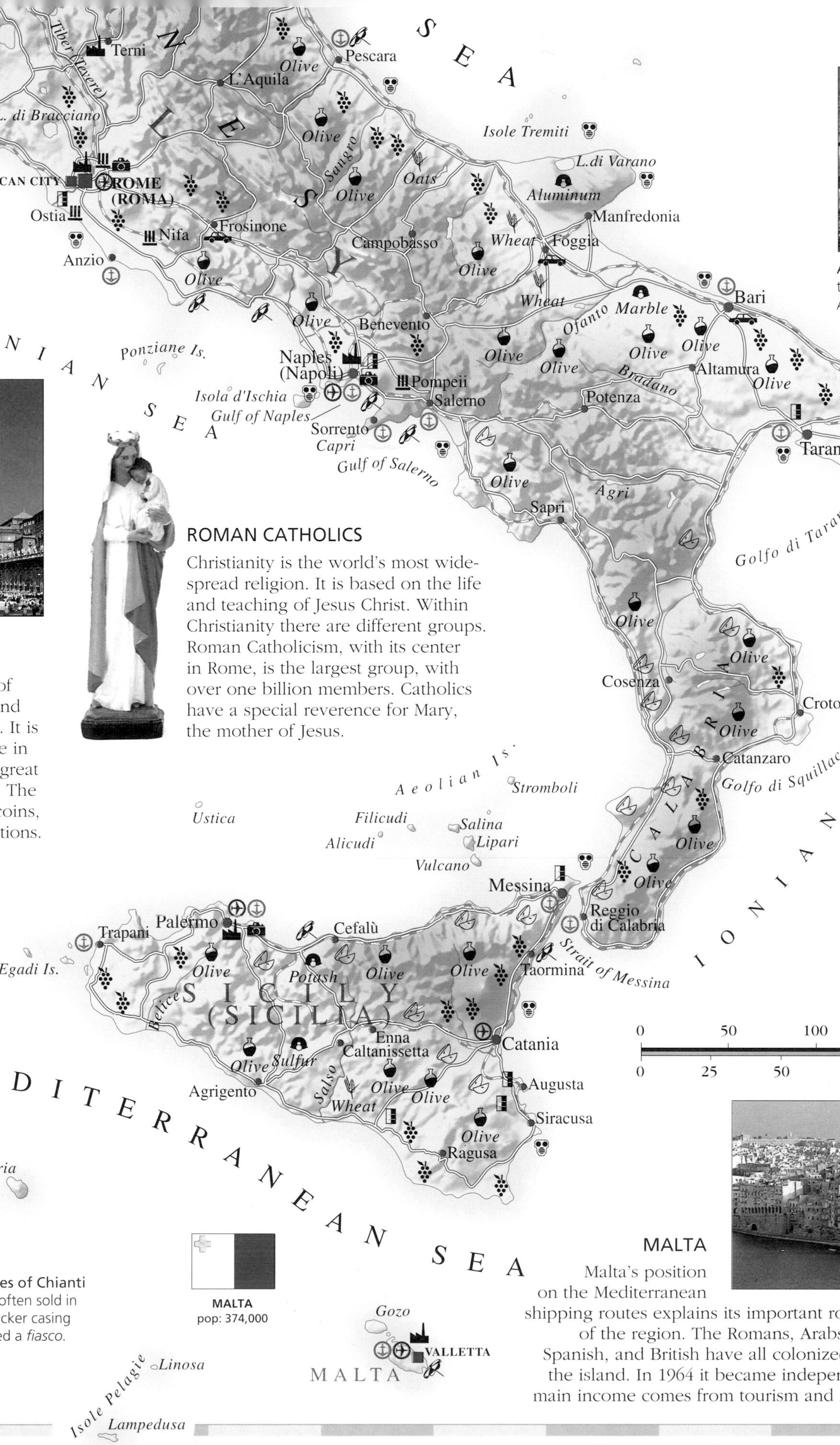

MOTOR VEHICLES

Many Italian car manufacturers are based around the cities of Milan and Turin. Italian engineers and designers have developed some of the finest vehicles in Europe, both high-performance cars and cheaper, economical models. Look for 🚗

Model of Ferrari car

Sardinia, a large island in the Mediterranean.

ROMAN CATHOLICS

Christianity is the world's most widespread religion. It is based on the life and teaching of Jesus Christ. Within Christianity there are different groups. Roman Catholicism, with its center in Rome, is the largest group, with over one billion members. Catholics have a special reverence for Mary, the mother of Jesus.

VATICAN CITY

This walled city in the center of Rome is the headquarters of the Roman Catholic Church and official residence of the Pope. It is the smallest independent state in the world, dominated by the great St. Peter's Basilica, seen here. The city has its own newspaper, coins, stamps, railroad, and radio stations.

VATICAN CITY
pop: 1,000

A distant view of the snow-capped Apennines.

Italian national team shirt

Italians are passionate soccer fans.

AGRICULTURE

Agriculture is very important to the Italian economy. The main crops are olives, citrus fruits, and wine. The best farming region is the Po Valley in the north. Southern Italy has always suffered from its hilly terrain and low rainfall, but thanks to irrigation and modern farming methods, agriculture has improved since the 1950s.

Bottles of Chianti are often sold in a wicker casing called a *fiasco*.

MALTA

Malta's position on the Mediterranean shipping routes explains its important role in the history of the region. The Romans, Arabs, French, Turks, Spanish, and British have all colonized or fought over the island. In 1964 it became independent. Today, its main income comes from tourism and its port facilities.

MALTA
pop: 374,000

MAP FEATURES

Wine: Italy is the world's largest wine producer. Recently, the wine industry has brought in rules for higher quality and better control. Look for 🍷

Oil refining: Italy is more dependent on imported fuel than any European country. Crude oil has to be imported and refined. Look for 🛢

Sightseeing: Millions of tourists visit Italy each year to see its historic towns, famous buildings, and museums. Look for 📷

- Cereals
- Rice
- Citrus fruits
- Vegetable oil
- Mining

- Industrial center
- Vehicle manufacture
- Tourism
- Archaeological sites
- Pollution

N

MILES
KM

0   25   50   75   100   150

Map labels

SEA

Isole Tremiti
L. di Varano
Manfredonia
Foggia
Aluminum
Wheat
Oats
Pescara
L'Aquila
Olive
Terni
Tiber (Tevere)
L. di Bracciano
L. di Bolsena
Vulci
Civitavecchia
Ostia
VATICAN CITY
ROME (ROMA)
Nifa
Anzio
Frosinone
Ofne
Campobasso
Benevento
Naples (Napoli)
Pompeii
Salerno
Sorrento
Capri
Gulf of Naples
Gulf of Salerno
Isola d'Ischia
Ponziane Is.
Archipelago Toscano

Bari
Altamura
Olive
Marble
Bradano
Ofanto
Potenza
Agri
Sapri
Olive
Wheat

Brindisi
Lecce
Olive
Otranto
Olive
Gallipoli
Taranto
Golfo di Taranto
Crotone
Olive
Olive
Cosenza
Catanzaro
Golfo di Squillace
Reggio di Calabria
Taormina di Messina
Strait of Messina
Messina
Stromboli
Aeolian Is.
Lipari
Salina
Vulcano
Filicudi
Alicudi
Ustica

IONIAN SEA

TYRRHENIAN SEA

MEDITERRANEAN SEA

SICILY (SICILIA)
Palermo
Trapani
Egadi Is.
Cefalù
Enna
Caltanissetta
Catania
Augusta
Siracusa
Ragusa
Agrigento
Wheat
Olive
Salso
Sulfur
Potash
Olive
Pantelleria

SARDINIA (SARDEGNA)
Strait of Bonifacio
Sassari
Alghero
Nuoro
Copper
Oristano
Tirso
Flumini
Cagliari
Golfo di Cagliari
Iglesias
Zinc
Lead
Sarroch
C. Spartivento
Isola di San Pietro
Isola di San Antioco

MALTA
VALLETTA
Gozo

Linosa
Lampedusa
Isole Pelagie

SOUTHEAST EUROPE

THIS TROUBLED REGION of southeastern Europe consists of a wide variety of landscapes, religions, peoples, and languages. The region was invaded many times, and from the 14th-19th centuries was under foreign occupation. After World War II, both Albania and Yugoslavia were ruled by communist governments. When the Yugoslav dictator, Marshal Tito, died in 1980 the Yugoslav government became less centralized, and former republics demanded their independence. Serbia, the largest and most powerful republic, resisted the breakup of Yugoslavia. In 1991, a bloody civil war broke out between Serbia and Croatia and, eventually, between Serbs and Muslims in Bosnia. In 1999, when conflict broke out between Serbia and its Albanian minority population in Kosovo, NATO bombing raids destroyed much of the Serbian infrastructure, forcing the Serbs to seek a peace agreement. Albania was isolated by its communist government from the rest of Europe and became economically backward. But the country has now shaken off its communist rulers and held democratic elections.

CROATIA
pop: 4,500,000

BOSNIA AND HERZEGOVINA
pop: 4,000,000

Walnuts flourish in the warm summers and well-drained soils of Yugoslavia.

YUGO

This car, the Yugo, is manufactured in the Serbian city of Kragujevac. It was designed for foreign export, but the economic disruption caused by the civil war and the NATO bombing of Serbia in 1999 have dealt a deathblow to this industry. International trade sanctions, combined with a lack of foreign investment, have crippled Serbia's manufacturing industry.

TOURISM

Many tourists are attracted to Croatia's Dalmatian coast, which is famous for its beautiful scenery, warm climate, and stunning coastline. The conflict of the early 1990s brought Croatia's tourist industry to a violent halt, but over the last five years visitors have gradually returned, and are helping to revitalize Croatia's economy.
Look for 🖌

UNDER FIRE

The world looked on in horror as Dubrovnik, a beautiful city with an untouched center dating back 1,000 years, came under Serbian attack in 1991. Sarajevo, the Bosnian capital, was another casualty; many of its historic mosques and churches were hit by shells. Other historic towns in Bosnia and Croatia have also suffered irreparable damage during the war.

Mixed valley farming gives way to barren mountains in central Albania.

MAP FEATURES

Mining: Albania has some of the world's largest chromium reserves. Exports are hampered by outdated mining equipment and frequent strikes. **Look for** 🜚

🌾	Cereals	⚙	Coal
🚢	Mixed fruit	⚡	Hydroelectric power
🍇	Wine	🏭	Industrial center
🚬	Tobacco	🚗	Vehicle manufacture
🐟	Fishing	🖌	Tourism

MARKETS

In peacetime, local markets in the region are packed with people and well-stocked with a wide range of produce from nearby farms. Large quantities of fruit and vegetables are grown in the mild, warm climate of the Croatian coast and in western Bosnia. **Look for** 🚢

FOLKLORE

Variations in national costume reflect the contrasting cultural traditions and the great ethnic variety of the people living in this region. The oriental influence, for example, can be seen clearly in the Turkish-style costumes of the south. The Dubrovnik region is famous for its costume of white dresses, embroidered blouses, and waistcoats. Folk music and dancing take place at religious festivals and on market-days, and are also performed for tourist groups.

0	50	100	150	KM
0		50		100 MILES

N

YUGOSLAVIA
pop: 10,400,000

ALBANIA
pop: 3,400,000

Map labels:

HUNGARY

ROMANIA

BULGARIA

GREECE

ADRIATIC SEA

BOSNIA AND HERZEGOVINA

Drava
Subotica
Kanjiža
Senta
Corn
Sombor
Bačka Topola
Wheat
Apatin
Bečej
Osijek
Corn
Đakovo
Vukovar
Danube
Zrenjanin
Corn
Slavonski Brod
Wheat
Novi Sad
Corn
Vršac
Wheat
Modriča
Sava
Wheat
Doboj
Corn
Pančevo
Gračanica
Šabac
BELGRADE (BEOGRAD)
Corn
Smederevo
Danube
Tuzla
Loznica
Wheat
Požarevac
Iron Gates
Zvornik
Corn
Velika Plana
Copper
Zenica
Manganese
Lead Zinc
Arandelovac
Corn
Iron
Valjevo
SERBIA
Visoko
Srebrenica
Lead
Zinc
Kragujevac
SARAJEVO
Čačak
Zaječar
Konjic
Kraljevo
Neretva
Foča
Lead Zinc
Priboj
Corn
Nis
Mostar
Lead Zinc
Novi Pazar
Barley
Barley
Kruševac
Aleksinac
Aluminum
Bijelo Polje
YUGOSLAVIA
KOPAONIK
Oats
MONTENEGRO
Nikšić
Ivangrad
Kosovska Mitrovica
Oats
Leskovac
Trebinje
Aluminum
Ibar
Lead
Zinc
BALKAN MTS.
Dubrovnik
Beli Drim
Lead
Lead
Pristina
Zinc
Podgorica
Peć
KOSOVO
Gnjilane
L. Scutari
Uroševac
Chromium
Lumi i Drinit
Prizren
Bar
Shkodër
Chromium
Chromium
Kumanovo
Gulf of Drin
Aluminum
Chromium
Tetovo
SKOPJE
Iron
Kičevo
Gostivar
Kočani
MACEDONIA
Veles
Stip
Strumica
Aluminum
Chromium
Iron
Kavadarci
Bregalnica
TIRANA (TIRANË)
Iron
Prilep
Crna Reka
Vardar
Durrës
Shkumbin
Ohrid
Elbasan
L. Ohrid
Bitola
Nickel
L. Prespa
Lumi i Devollit
Iron
Fier
Berat
Korçë
Wheat
ALBANIA
Vlorë
Lumi i Osumit
Lumi i Vjosës
Strait of Otranto
Wheat
Corn

IRON GATES

The Danube, the second-longest river in Europe, passes through Serbia on its journey from Germany to the Black Sea. As the river leaves the broad plains of northern Serbia, it is forced through this narrow gorge, called the Iron Gates. In 1972, Romania and Yugoslavia built a power station here to use the water to make electricity.
Look for ⚒

CIVIL WAR

When Yugoslavia broke up into independent countries in 1990, civil war broke out between the Serbs and both Croatia and Bosnia. The Serbs cleared and resettled Bosnian Muslim homes, a policy called "ethnic cleansing." In 1999, conflict erupted again, caused by discrimination against Serbia's Albanian minority, which make up 80% of the population of Kosovo. Many were forced to flee to adjacent countries.

LANGUAGE DIFFERENCES

The main language of the former Yugoslavia is Serbo-Croatian. It can be written in two different ways, reflecting both ethnic origin and religion. The Eastern Orthodox Serbs use Cyrillic, a Slavic alphabet created in the 9th century by two Greek brothers, who were Christian. Croats, on the other hand, use the Roman alphabet.

Postage stamp using Roman alphabet

Postage stamp using Cyrillic alphabet

MACEDONIA
pop: 2,200,000

ALBANIA

There is little traffic in the central square of Albania's capital, Tirana: until recently, private cars were banned. Albania is now emerging from 50 years of isolation. Under communism, free speech and religion were forbidden. Even beards were not allowed. In 1997, the catastrophic failure of private investment schemes left many people penniless and the economy collapsed. Many Albanians fled the country, which was forced to accept international aid. Although a new democratic government has been installed, the impact of these events on the economy is still being felt.

Grapes
Tomato
Watermelon
Potatoes

ALBANIAN AGRICULTURE

Although its economy is based on farming, Albania still has difficulties feeding its own population, which is the fastest-growing in Europe. The main crops are potatoes, corn, wheat, sugar beets, fruits, and vegetables. Until recently, most of the land was owned and farmed by the state, but today it is farmed by individual families.

There is very little farming in the mountains of Montenegro.

RELIGION

This beautiful church on the shores of Lake Ohrid dates back to the medieval period, when Macedonia followed the Eastern Orthodox church. Later, Bosnia, Montenegro, and Serbia were occupied by the Ottoman Turks and became largely Muslim countries.

ROMANIA AND BULGARIA

ROMANIA AND BULGARIA are located in southeastern Europe, on the shores of the Black Sea. The River Danube forms the border between the two countries, and the most fertile land in the region is found in the river's vast valley and delta. Forests of oak, pine, and fir trees grow on the slopes of the Carpathian and Balkan Mountains. Romania and Bulgaria were occupied by Romans, Bulgars, Hungarians, and Turkish Ottomans, but this troubled history ended when they became independent countries in the late 19th and early 20th centuries. After two world wars, both countries became part of the Soviet communist bloc. Although they are no longer communist, economic reform has been slow, and unemployment, high prices, and food shortages are still constant problems.

Rose petal

ROSE OIL
Used in perfume, rose oil is literally worth its weight in gold. Central Bulgaria produces most of the world's supply. The world's largest rose gardens are at Kazanlûk. Look for 🌹

THE PRESIDENTIAL PALACE
Under Romania's repressive communist leader, President Ceauşescu, food and energy supplies were rationed. Despite this, the president started a series of expensive building projects, such as this presidential palace in Bucharest. In 1989, the Romanian people rose up against communism and executed their president.

TOBACCO
Bulgaria is the world's second largest exporter of cigarettes. Tobacco is grown in the fertile valleys of the Maritsa River. This woman is sorting tobacco leaves, ready for selling. Look for ⚲

YOGURT
Yogurt, made from the milk of cows, sheep, or goats, is an important part of the Bulgarian diet. Many Bulgarians claim that eating yogurt helps them live to a ripe old age.

Small farms in the wooded valleys of central Romania.

The **Alexander Nevsky** church in Sofia celebrates liberation from Turkish rule.

MAP FEATURES

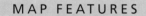

Vehicle manufacture: Romanian factories make copies of French vehicles for export to China, Russia, and many Western countries. Look for 🚚

High-tech industry: Electronics earn Bulgaria foreign currency, although the computer industry is suffering from international competition. Look for 💻

Spas: Mineral springs and health treatments are provided by many spa resorts, which are a popular tourist attraction. Look for 🏊

Shipping canal: The Danube-Black Sea Canal enables ships to avoid the slow journey through the Danube Delta. Look for ⇄

🐂	Cattle	⛏	Mining
🌾	Cereals	🛢	Oil
🍇	Wine	💧	Gas
⚲	Tobacco	🏭	Industrial center
🌹	Roses	✈	Tourism

Bulgaria is the world's fourth largest wine exporter.

RILA MONASTERY
The walls of Rila monastery are decorated with no less than 1,200 superb wall paintings. The monastery became a symbol of the Bulgarians' struggle to preserve the Christian faith during centuries of Turkish rule. The monastery was originally founded in 1335 and was rebuilt after it burned to the ground in the 19th century.

Map labels: U K R, HUNGARY, Satu Mare, Wheat, Zinc, Lead, Copper, Baia Mare, Gold, Sângeorz-Bâi, Wheat, Beef, Corn, Bistrita, Oradea, Beef, Dairy, Iron, Beef, Wheat, Aluminum, Cluj-Napoca, Corn, TRANSYLVANIA, ROM, Wheat, Corn, Arad, Alba Iulia, Copşa Mică, Mureş, Deva, Dairy, Sibiu, Wheat, Dairy, Timişoara, Iron, Iron, Beef, Wheat, Corn, Iron, Iron, Manganese, TRANSYLVANIAN, Reşiţa, Râmnicu Vâlcea, Târgu Jiu, Beef, Copper, Băile Herculane, Chromium, Drobeta-Turnu Severin, Beef, Dairy, YUGOSLAVIA, Corn, Corn, Slatina, Vidin, Wheat, Jiu, Craiova, Corn, Danube (Dunărea), Wheat, Corabia, Wheat, Wheat, Corn, Beef, Iron, Beef, Montana, Corn, Vratsa, Iskur, Copper, Beef, BU, Iron, BALKAN, Pravets, SOFIA (SOFIYA), Copper, Pernik, Dairy, Yazovir Iskur, Beef, Corn, Struma, Zinc, Lead, Rila, Pazardzhik, Velingrad, MACEDONIA, RHODOPE MTS, Sandanski, Beef, GRE

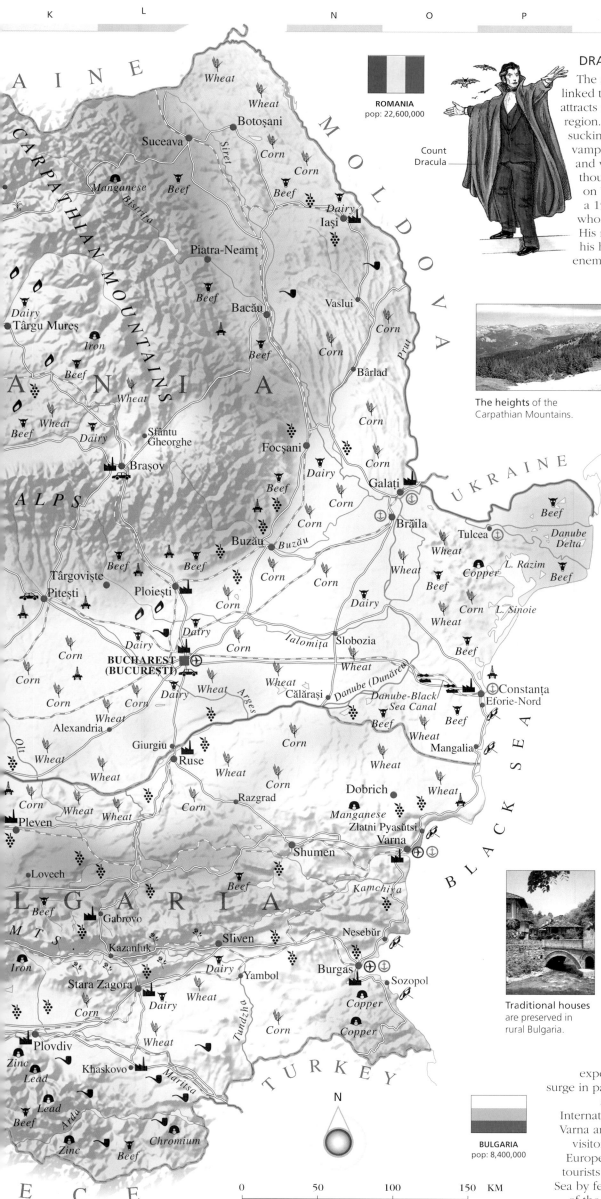

ROMANIA
pop: 22,600,000

DRACULA

Count Dracula

The story of Dracula is linked to Transylvania and attracts many tourists to the region. Tales of the blood-sucking Count, complete with vampire bats, garlic cloves, and wooden stakes, are thought to be based on Vlad the Impaler, a 15th-century prince who resisted Turkish rule. His name is explained by his habit of impaling his enemies on wooden stakes.

INDUSTRY

These chimneys at Copsa Micâ in Romania are belching out hydrocarbons, which pollute the air, water, and soil. Romania's industrialization was not subject to pollution controls.

The heights of the Carpathian Mountains.

This rare ghost orchid grows in shady parts of Bulgarian forests.

FARMING

The fertile lands of the Danube valley and the Black Sea plains are rich farming country: wheat, corn, potatoes, and fruit are the main crops. Country traditions continue, especially in Romania, where many village scenes seem unchanged since medieval times.

POSTAGE STAMPS

The lettering on these Bulgarian postage stamps is in the Cyrillic alphabet. It dates back to the 9th century AD, when Saints Cyril and Methodius devised the alphabet so that they could translate the Bible into Old Bulgarian. The Cyrillic alphabet is also used in the Russian Federation.

GYPSIES

Large numbers of gypsies (or Romanies) live in both Romania and Bulgaria. The gypsies are thought to have arrived from India, via the Middle East, in the 5th century AD. Many gypsies still wander from place to place, trading goods for a living. Gypsies are often persecuted by their host countries, who find it hard to understand their different customs and way of life.

Traditional houses are preserved in rural Bulgaria.

TOURISM

This region has experienced a great surge in package holidays since the 1980s. International airports at Varna and Burgas serve visitors from Western Europe, while Russian tourists cross the Black Sea by ferry. Many new resorts have been built, and the natural beauty of the coastline, with its sandy beaches, pine forests, and old fishing villages, is often spoiled by ugly, high-rise developments. Look for 🦢

BULGARIA
pop: 8,400,000

N

0   50   100   150   KM

0   25   50   75   MILES

GREECE

FROM THE EARLIEST TIMES, the life and economy of Greece has been shaped by its geography. It is a country of rugged mountains, isolated valleys, remote peninsulas, and more than 1,400 scattered islands. The difficulty of traveling by land has turned Greece into a seafaring nation, which owns the second-largest fleet of merchant ships in the world. 90 percent of its imports and exports are carried by sea rather than by road. Most people in Greece make their living from farming, but in recent years, tourism has become an important source of income. Tourists visit Greece not only for its warm, Mediterranean climate and beautiful landscape, but also for its ancient ruins. Many of these date from the 5th century BC, when the country was the cultural center of the western world, the birthplace of democracy, and home of great thinkers such as Socrates, Plato, and Aristotle.

THE ORTHODOX CHURCH

Greek Orthodox bishop

Most Greek Christians belong to the Orthodox Church. This was founded in Constantinople (modern Istanbul) in the 4th century AD. The Eastern Orthodox Church established there still flourishes in Greece, Eastern Europe, and Russia.

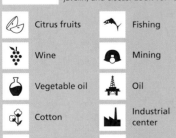

GREEK SALAD

Parsley

Many Greek farms are small, growing just enough vegetables and fruit for the farmer's family. Lettuces, cucumbers, tomatoes, olives, herbs, and cheese are the most common products.

Eggplant
Cucumber
Beef tomato

ATHENS

Athens is famous for its Acropolis ("high place"), crowned by the Parthenon temple. Smog all too often obscures the Acropolis, and cars are banned from the city on certain days to reduce pollution.

MAP FEATURES

Archaeological sites: Remains from ancient Greece are found all over the country, attracting many visitors. Look for 🏛	
Sultanas and currants: Greece is the world's largest exporter of these fruits. Small, black currants are named after the town of Corinth. Look for 🍇	
The Olympic Games: The event started in Olympia in 776 BC. Sports included running, wrestling, boxing, horse racing, javelin, and discus. Look for 🎽	

🍋 Citrus fruits	🐟 Fishing		
🍇 Wine	⛏ Mining		
🫒 Vegetable oil	🛢 Oil		
🌱 Cotton	🏭 Industrial center		
🌿 Tobacco	✈ Tourism		

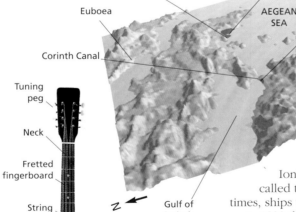

Piraeus is the largest port in Greece, linked to Athens by rail and road

Athens

Corinth is a major communication hub between north and south Greece, exporting fruit, raisins, and tobacco

Euboea

AEGEAN SEA

Corinth Canal

Peloponnese

Gulf of Corinth

CLASSICAL MUSIC

Tuning peg
Neck
Fretted fingerboard
String
Pegbox inlaid with mother-of-pearl
Soundhole
Body
Bridge

The bouzouki is a stringed instrument, similar to a lute or a guitar, which is used in traditional Greek music. Folk dances, national costumes, and music are still very popular at religious festivals such as Easter, and on special occasions such as weddings.

CORINTH CANAL

Athens is separated from the Ionian Sea by a narrow neck of land called the Isthmus of Corinth. In ancient times, ships were dragged across the isthmus. In 1893 the Greeks cut a canal through the isthmus. It is 3.9 miles (6.3 km) long, but only just wide enough for a ship to squeeze between the cliffs on either side. The canal shortened the journey from the Ionian Sea to Athens' main port, Piraeus, by 200 miles (320 km).

The Parthenon temple (built 432 BC) was the center of religious life in classical Athens.

SACRED OIL

Olives have been grown in Greece for over 2,000 years. In ancient times, the olive was sacred to Athena, the goddess of war, and olive wreaths were worn as a symbol of victory. Today, olives and olive oil are major exports. Look for 🫒

MACEDONIA

Kilkis
Lake Prespa
Florina
L. Vegoritis
Edessa
Veroia
Salonica (Thessaloniki)
Kastoria
L. Kastoria
Chromium
Kozani
Kateríni
Thermaic Gulf
Grevena
GREECE
Trikala
Larisa
Corfu (Kerkyra)
Ioannina
Olives
Volos
Igoumenitsa
Corfu (Kerkyra)
Olives
PINDUS MOUNTAINS
Karditsa
Arta
Chromium
Preveza
Lamia
Stylida
Lefkada
Loutra Aidipsou
Lefkada
Olives
Olives
Aluminum
Nickel
Astakos
L. Trichonis
Amfissa
Delphi
Olives
IONIAN SEA
Mesolongi
Itea
Lixouri
Kefalonia
Gulf of Corinth
Argostoli
Gulf of Patra
Patra
Corinth Canal
Kyllini
Andravida
Corinth (Korinthos)
Zakynthos
Marble
Zakynthos
Katakolo
Mycenae
Epidaurus
Pyrgos
Olympia
Nafplio
Olives
Tripoli
PELOPONNESE
Manganese
Olives
Olives
Sparti
Leonido
Kalamata
Olives
Pylos
Gulf of Messenia
Gytheio
Lakonikos Kolpos
Neapoli
Kythira

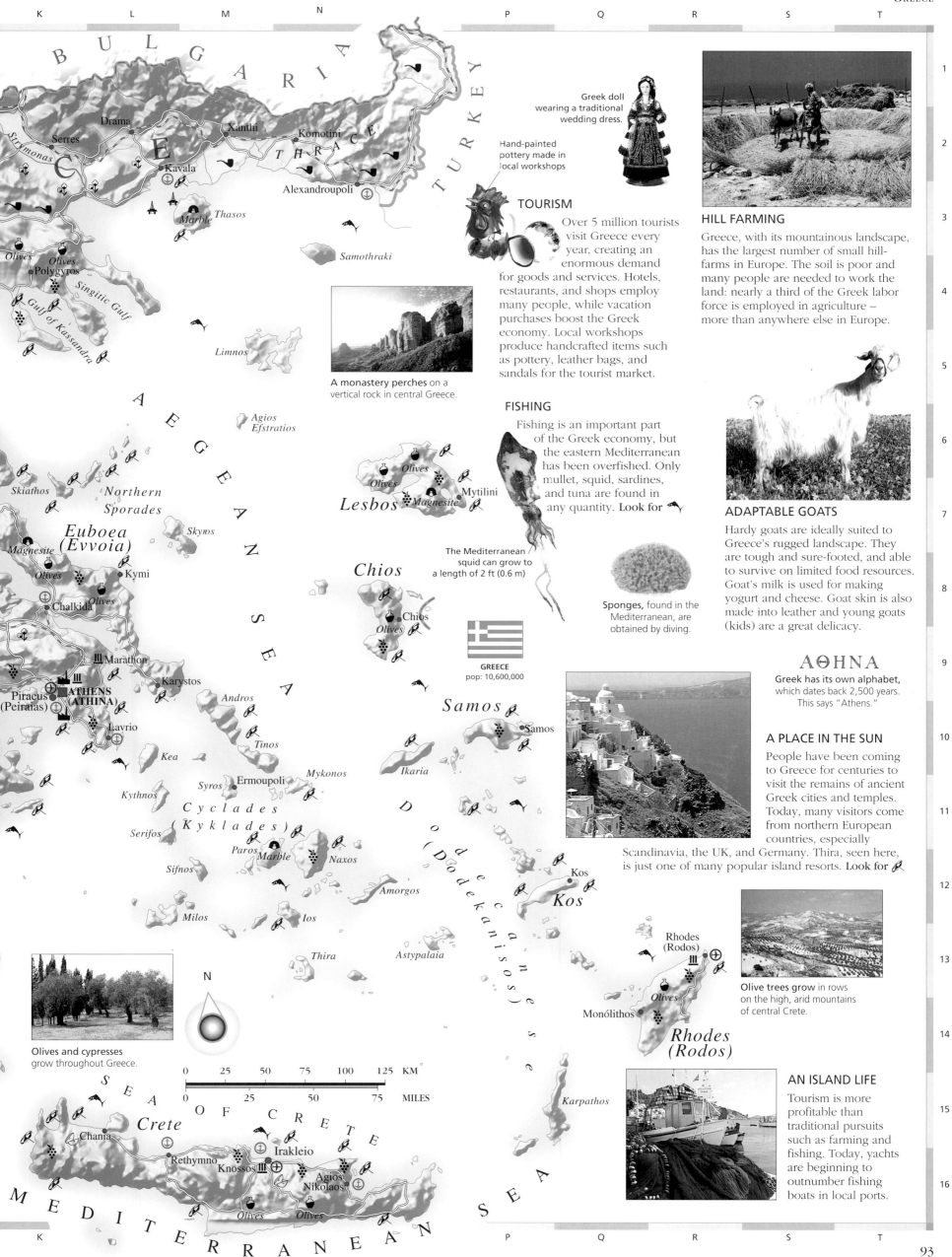

Greek doll wearing a traditional wedding dress.

Hand-painted pottery made in local workshops

TOURISM

Over 5 million tourists visit Greece every year, creating an enormous demand for goods and services. Hotels, restaurants, and shops employ many people, while vacation purchases boost the Greek economy. Local workshops produce handcrafted items such as pottery, leather bags, and sandals for the tourist market.

A monastery perches on a vertical rock in central Greece.

FISHING

Fishing is an important part of the Greek economy, but the eastern Mediterranean has been overfished. Only mullet, squid, sardines, and tuna are found in any quantity. Look for ⌐

The Mediterranean squid can grow to a length of 2 ft (0.6 m)

Sponges, found in the Mediterranean, are obtained by diving.

GREECE
pop: 10,600,000

HILL FARMING

Greece, with its mountainous landscape, has the largest number of small hill-farms in Europe. The soil is poor and many people are needed to work the land: nearly a third of the Greek labor force is employed in agriculture – more than anywhere else in Europe.

ADAPTABLE GOATS

Hardy goats are ideally suited to Greece's rugged landscape. They are tough and sure-footed, and able to survive on limited food resources. Goat's milk is used for making yogurt and cheese. Goat skin is also made into leather and young goats (kids) are a great delicacy.

ΑΘΗΝΑ

Greek has its own alphabet, which dates back 2,500 years. This says "Athens."

A PLACE IN THE SUN

People have been coming to Greece for centuries to visit the remains of ancient Greek cities and temples. Today, many visitors come from northern European countries, especially Scandinavia, the UK, and Germany. Thira, seen here, is just one of many popular island resorts. Look for ⌐

Olive trees grow in rows on the high, arid mountains of central Crete.

AN ISLAND LIFE

Tourism is more profitable than traditional pursuits such as farming and fishing. Today, yachts are beginning to outnumber fishing boats in local ports.

Olives and cypresses grow throughout Greece.

N

0   25   50   75   100   125   KM
0   25   50   75   MILES

Map labels:

BULGARIA
TURKEY
GREECE
THRACE
Drama
Xanthi
Komotini
Serres
Strymonas
Kavala
Alexandroupoli
Marble
Thasos
Samothraki
Olives
Polygyros
Singitic Gulf
Gulf of Kassandra
Limnos
Agios Efstratios
AEGEAN SEA
Skiathos
Northern Sporades
Skyros
Euboea (Evvoia)
Magnesite
Olives
Kymi
Chalkida
Marathon
Piraeus (Peiraias)
ATHENS (ATHINA)
Lavrio
Karystos
Andros
Tinos
Kea
Kythnos
Syros
Ermoupoli
Mykonos
Cyclades (Kyklades)
Serifos
Sifnos
Paros
Marble
Naxos
Amorgos
Milos
Ios
Thira
Astypalaia
Lesbos
Olives
Magnesite
Mytilini
Chios
Olives
Samos
Ikaria
Dodecanese (Dodekanisos)
Kos
Rhodes (Rodos)
Monólithos
Olives
Karpathos
SEA OF CRETE
Crete
Chania
Rethymno
Knossos
Irakleio
Agios Nikolaos
Olives
MEDITERRANEAN SEA

THE BALTIC STATES AND BELARUS

ESTONIA
pop: 1,400,000

THE THREE BALTIC STATES – Latvia, Lithuania, and Estonia – made history in 1990-91 when they became the first republics to declare their independence from the Soviet Union. This was the end of a long series of invasions and occupations by the Vikings, Germans, Danes, Poles, and Russians. A new era had begun, but many of the old problems – food shortages, pollution, weak economies – still remained. The region's flat landscape is well drained by lakes and rivers and is ideal for farming. The main crops are grains, sugar beets, and potatoes. In Belarus, heavy industry such as machine-building and metalworking is important, while the Baltic states manufacture electronics and consumer goods. Following independence, many Russians who moved to the Baltic states to work in industry were returned to their homeland. The Baltic Sea, although frozen in the winter months, gives access to the markets of northern Europe. Industrialization has left a terrible legacy. Summer resorts along the Baltic coast have been closed to visitors because of polluted seawater, and Belarus was badly hit by the nuclear accident at Chornobyl' in the Ukraine in 1986, when 70 percent of the radioactive fallout landed on its territory.

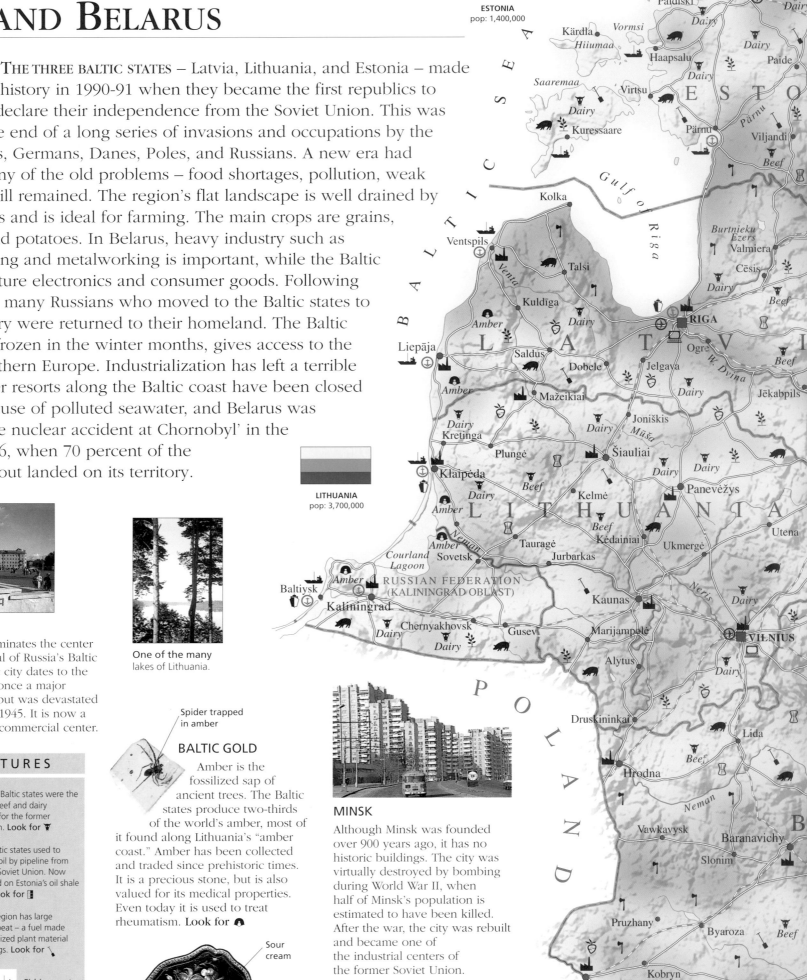

LITHUANIA
pop: 3,700,000

KALININGRAD

A statue of Lenin dominates the center of Kaliningrad, capital of Russia's Baltic enclave. This historic city dates to the 13th century. It was once a major German Baltic port, but was devastated by Russian forces in 1945. It is now a major industrial and commercial center.

One of the many lakes of Lithuania.

MAP FEATURES

Cattle: The Baltic states were the centers of beef and dairy production for the former Soviet Union. Look for ♉

Oil: The Baltic states used to obtain free oil by pipeline from the former Soviet Union. Now they depend on Estonia's oil shale deposits. Look for 🛢

Peat: This region has large supplies of peat – a fuel made from carbonized plant material found in bogs. Look for ⚒

🐖 Pigs		⚓ Fishing port	
🌱 Sugar beet		⚒ Mining	
🌿 Potatoes		🏭 Industrial center	
⚱ Flax		🚢 Shipbuilding	
🪓 Timber		💻 High-tech industry	

Spider trapped in amber

BALTIC GOLD

Amber is the fossilized sap of ancient trees. The Baltic states produce two-thirds of the world's amber, most of it found along Lithuania's "amber coast." Amber has been collected and traded since prehistoric times. It is a precious stone, but is also valued for its medical properties. Even today it is used to treat rheumatism. Look for 🟠

MINSK

Although Minsk was founded over 900 years ago, it has no historic buildings. The city was virtually destroyed by bombing during World War II, when half of Minsk's population is estimated to have been killed. After the war, the city was rebuilt and became one of the industrial centers of the former Soviet Union.

Sour cream

NATIONAL DISH

Draniki is the national dish of Belarus. It is made of grated potatoes fried in vegetable oil and served with sour cream. Potatoes are grown everywhere, and are one of Belarus's main products. Large numbers of dairy cattle are kept on its extensive pastureland.

Beets, mixed with sour cream

Draniki

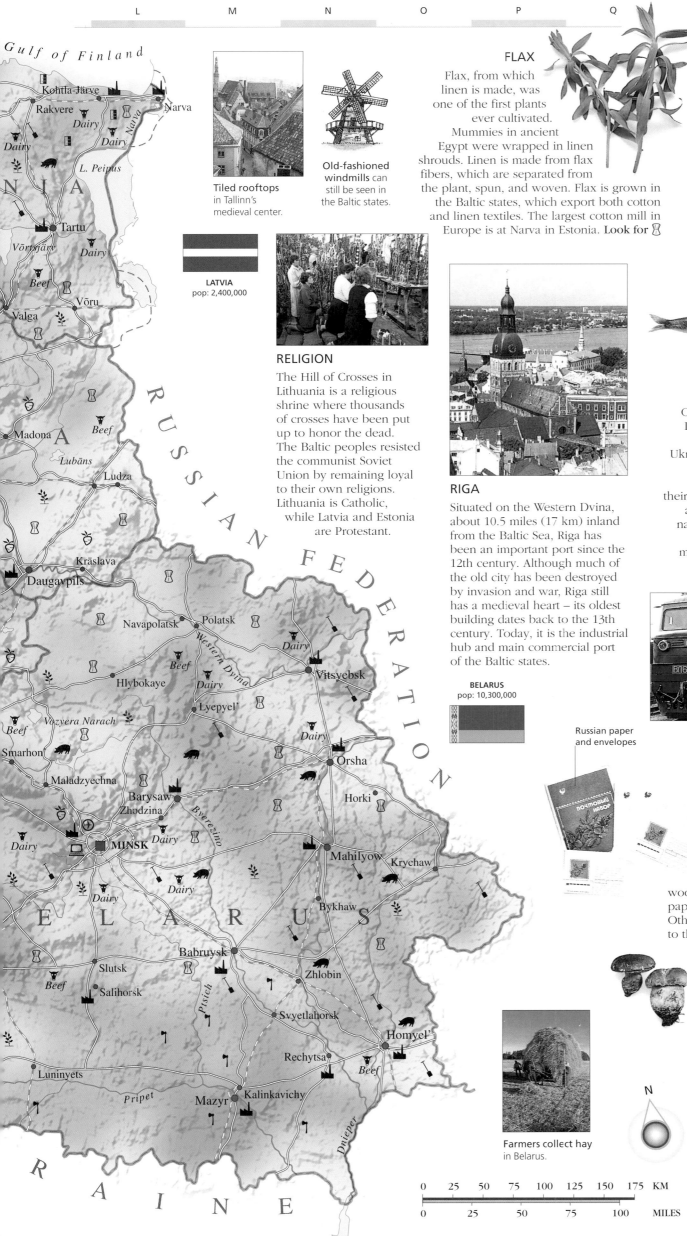

Gulf of Finland

FLAX

Flax, from which linen is made, was one of the first plants ever cultivated. Mummies in ancient Egypt were wrapped in linen shrouds. Linen is made from flax fibers, which are separated from the plant, spun, and woven. Flax is grown in the Baltic states, which export both cotton and linen textiles. The largest cotton mill in Europe is at Narva in Estonia. Look for

Tiled rooftops in Tallinn's medieval center.

Old-fashioned windmills can still be seen in the Baltic states.

TALLINN
Tallinn, Estonia's capital, is an important Baltic port, with regular ferries to Finland. In contrast to the modern port, the city center has changed little since medieval times, with cobbled streets, ancient walls, turrets, and gables.

LATVIA
pop: 2,400,000

Herring are caught in the Baltic Sea and are served with onions.

RELIGION
The Hill of Crosses in Lithuania is a religious shrine where thousands of crosses have been put up to honor the dead. The Baltic peoples resisted the communist Soviet Union by remaining loyal to their own religions. Lithuania is Catholic, while Latvia and Estonia are Protestant.

A LATVIAN IDENTITY
Only 55 percent of the people of Latvia were born in the country. Russians, Belarusians, and Ukrainians were resettled in Latvia when it was part of the Soviet Union. As a near minority in their own country, Latvians are acutely aware of their own national identity. They promote their language, national dress, dances, and music – there are more than a million known Latvian folk songs.

RIGA
Situated on the Western Dvina, about 10.5 miles (17 km) inland from the Baltic Sea, Riga has been an important port since the 12th century. Although much of the old city has been destroyed by invasion and war, Riga still has a medieval heart – its oldest building dates back to the 13th century. Today, it is the industrial hub and main commercial port of the Baltic states.

BELARUS
pop: 10,300,000

HEAVY INDUSTRY

Many of the former Soviet Union's railroad cars and locomotives were made in Latvia, the most industrialized of the Baltic states. Latvia also produces minibuses, streetcars, mopeds, washing machines, and tape recorders. Look for

Russian paper and envelopes

TIMBER
About one-third of this region is still covered with fir and pine forest, and timber is an important industry. Inland waterways are used to transport the wood, which is either made into wood pulp for paper or used to make furniture and matches. Other former Soviet states also send their timber to the Baltic region for processing. Look for

Many mushrooms grow in the Belarusian forests. Picking mushrooms is a popular summer outing.

Farmers collect hay in Belarus.

VODKA

Potatoes are one of the most important crops in Belarus. They are exported to the Russian Federation, where they are fermented and used to make the national drink, vodka. The name vodka comes from the Russian word *voda* which means "water." Cheap vodka has led to a high rate of alcoholism, which governments have tried to curb by heavily taxing alcohol.

N

| 0 | 25 | 50 | 75 | 100 | 125 | 150 | 175 | KM |
| 0 | | 25 | | 50 | | 75 | | 100 | MILES |

EUROPEAN RUSSIA

THE RUSSIAN FEDERATION is the largest country in the world. Stretching across two continents – Europe in the west and Asia in the east – it is twice the size of the US. The Ural Mountains form the division between the European and Asian parts of the country. The Russian Federation has fertile farmlands, vast mineral deposits, and abundant timber, oil, and other natural resources. Despite its size and natural wealth, Russia is currently in a state of political and economic turmoil. After centuries of rule by czars (emperors), the world's first communist government took power in Russia in 1917. The Union of Soviet Socialist Republics (USSR) included many of the territories that were formerly parts of the Russian Empire. During 74 years of communist rule, the Soviet Union became an industrial and military superpower, but at an appalling cost to its people and environment. Economic problems led to liberal reforms beginning in the mid-1980s, and ultimately to the fall of the communist regime in December 1991. By then most of the non-Russian republics had declared independence. The new Russian Federation is now governed by a democratic multiparty system, but the economy is stagnating. Conflict with ethnic and religious enclaves, such as Muslim Chechnya in the south, is an ongoing problem.

RELIGION

Moscow is the spiritual center of the Russian Orthodox church. For many decades, the church was persecuted in Russia; today, churches are reopening, and many Russian people are turning back to religion. Beautiful icons (religious images painted on wood), like this one, adorn the churches and people's homes.

САНКТ-ПЕТЕРБУРГ

The name "Saint Petersburg," written in Russia's Cyrillic alphabet, which was devised by Christian missionaries in the 10th century.

SAINT PETERSBURG

Saint Petersburg, the capital of Russia from 1712–1918, was founded by Czar Peter the Great in 1703. It is built on 12 islands linked by bridges and has many elegant 18th-century buildings.

Northern Russia is covered with coniferous forest called taiga.

MOSCOW

The city of Moscow was founded in the 12th century. At its center is a fortified citadel called the Kremlin. Its stone walls enclose the grand palace of the czars, four cathedrals, and a church. The Kremlin became – and remains – the country's seat of government.

St. Basil's, Moscow, built in the 16th century

Many wooden churches built in the 17th century still stand on small islands in Lake Onega.

NOVAYA ZEMLYA

KARA SEA (KARSKOYE MORE)

Baydaratskaya Guba

Vorkuta

Ostrov Vaygach

Kara Strait

Ostrov Kolguyev

USA

Pechora

Cheshskaya Guba

Izhma

KIYE GORY MOUNTAINS

Uranium

Kam o

Potassium

Syktyvkar

Mezen'

Kotlas

Pinega

Veluga

Kirov

Northern Dvina

Oats

BARENTS SEA

Murmansk

Iron

Copper

Nickel

Ozero Umbozero

Phosphate

KOLA PENINSULA (KOLSKIY POLUOSTROV)

Aluminum

Iron

Nickel

Iron

Ozero Imandra

Ozero Pyaozero

Ozero Topozero

Kem'

WHITE SEA

Archangel (Arkhangel'sk)

Ozero Segozero

RUSSIAN FEDERATION

Vologda

Barley

Oats

Rye

Oats

Kostroma

Barley

Ivanovo

Vladimir

L. Onega

Petrozavodsk

Cherepovets

Rybinsk Reservoir

Rye

Volga

Yaroslavl'

Uglich-Volga Canal

Gzhel'

MOSCOW (MOSKVA)

Kaluga

NORWAY

FINLAND

L. Ladoga

Oats

Rye

Novgorod

Aluminum

Rye

Oats

Barley

Rye

Tver'

Gulf of Finland

Saint Petersburg (Sankt-Peterburg)

Pskov

Rye

Rye

Smolensk

Dnieper

ESTONIA

LATVIA

Neva'

Oats

Oats

BELARUS

Historic cathedrals and monasteries line the banks of the Volga at Yaroslavl'.

STREET SELLERS

Rising unemployment and galloping inflation are major problems in post-communist Russia. In addition, many workers have to wait for months to receive their salaries. People have had to find new ways of surviving. They grow fruit and vegetables in small suburban plots of land, and sell their products on the streets of Moscow.

FAST FOOD?

With the end of communism, foreign companies are investing in Russia and many joint ventures are being encouraged. For Western companies, Russia provides a vast new market. Several western fast-food companies have opened restaurants in Moscow. They accept payment in roubles and are popular with local people, although waiting for four hours is not unknown.

MINERAL WEALTH

Mines are a common sight in Russia. There are large reserves of coal around Moscow. Nickel, copper, phosphates, and cobalt are found in the far north. Iron, sulfur, copper, gold, and nickel are mined in the south and southwest. Look for ⛏

Traditional hand-made wooden toy, in the form of a child and dancing bear.

MAP FEATURES

Reindeer: Nomads in the north herd reindeer, which are used to carry loads and for their meat, milk, and skins. Look for ✈

Hydroelectric power: Vast dams on the Dnieper and Volga rivers power electricity generators, which supply large cities and other republics. Look for ⊞

Vehicle manufacture: Cars are manufactured along the Volga. The truck plant at Naberezhnyye Chelny is the largest in the world. Look for 🚛

Pollution: Huge numbers of factories, which have grown without environmental controls, are polluting the region's rivers. Look for ⚙

Cereals 🌾
Sugar beet
Citrus fruits 🍊
Tobacco 🌿
Mining ⛏
Coal
Industrial center 🏭
Aerospace industry ✈

BALLET

A tutu, the costume worn by ballerinas

Ballet was originally developed in Western Europe, but in the late 19th century it was completely changed by Russian artists. Inspired largely by one man, Diaghilev, Russian ballet became creative and exciting. The male dancer was paid to the music and the costumes. Russia's two most famous ballet companies are the Kirov and the Bolshoi. Both are a source of national pride.

Ballet shoe

MAKING WAVES

The manufacture and sale of weapons, such as this MiG fighter plane, has been badly hit by the end of the Cold War. At Nizhniy Novgorod, where nuclear submarines used to be built, many shipyard workers are now making a semiautomatic washing machine, called the "Wave." Large numbers of unsold machines fill the former shipyard's warehouses. Look for ✈

MiG fighter plane

CHESS

Pottery from the town of Gzhel' near Moscow is collected by people all over the world. The patterns are painted by hand using brushes made from squirrel hair. Cobalt-blue patterns are then enameled on to a background of white. This chess set, made in Gzhel', reflects the popularity of the game here – Russia has produced many of the world's grand masters of chess.

Enameled chessboard

Chess piece

LADA

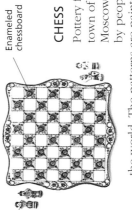

Model of a Lada hatchback

In 1965, the Russians signed a deal with Fiat, the Italian car company. A factory was built at Tol'yatti and is the largest car plant in the former Soviet Union. Ladas (based on the Fiat) are manufactured here, and some are exported to the West. Few Russians own a car, but the demand for imported Western cars is growing. Look for 🚗

Fur hats with earflaps are essential in Russia's freezing winters.

500 KM
300 MILES
0 100 200 300 400
0 50 100 150 200 250

N

Map labels

U R A L S

KAZAKHSTAN

UKRAINE

CAUCASUS

GEORGIA

AZERBAIJAN

BLACK SEA

SEA OF AZOV

CASPIAN SEA

Kerch Strait

Kamskoye Vodokhranilishche
Platinum
Vanadium
Iron
Perm
Izhevsk
Barley
Oats
Magnesium
Ufa
Copper
Wheat
Orsk
Nickel
Wheat
Copper
Copper
Orenburg
Nickel
Wheat
Nickel
Vyatka
Yoshkar-Ola
Cheboksary
Naberezhnyye Chelny
Kazan'
Tol'yatti
Samara
Ul'yanovsk
Rye
Wheat
Wheat
Wheat
Gorodets
Nizhniy Novgorod
Rye
Saransk
Penza
Balakovo
Sulfur
Wheat
Barley
Rye
Oats
Corn
Wheat
Saratov
Corn
Ryazan'
Tambov
Volga
Krasnoarmeysk
Volgograd
Volga
Astrakhan
Kuma
Rye
Barley
Tula
Orël
Lipetsk
Iron
Corn
Don
Wheat
Corn
Elista
Corn
Bryansk
Kursk
Belgorod
Iron
Voronezh
Rye
Wheat
Tsimlyanskoye Vodokhranilishche
Rostov-na-Donu
Wheat
Severskiy D.
Corn
Stavropol'
Kuban
Maykop
Sochi
Krasnodar
Cherkessk
Zinc
Lead
Nal'chik
Vladikavkaz
Groznyy
CHECHNYA
Makhachkala

UKRAINE, MOLDOVA, AND THE CAUCASUS REPUBLICS

THE CAUCASUS MOUNTAINS run between the Black and Caspian Seas. Higher in places than the Alps, they form a natural barrier between the flat steppes of the Russian Federation to the north and the plateaus of Southwest Asia. The newly independent states which lie to the south of the Russian Federation are rich in a variety of natural resources. Ukraine is dominated by a flat and fertile plain, where huge quantities of cereals are grown on large farms. Ukraine also possesses extensive coal and iron ore deposits and is heavily industrialized. Wine and fruit are produced in Moldova and Georgia, where the climate is mild and the soil fertile. Mountainous Armenia is rich in minerals, while Azerbaijan has plentiful oil.

Cereals being harvested in the fertile fields of Ukraine.

WINE

Georgian brandy

Moldovan wine

A quarter of the former Soviet Union's wine was produced in Moldova, which is well known for its champagne. Vines also thrive on the warm, sunny hills of eastern Georgia, where wine and brandy are produced. Look for 🍇

BORSCHT

Borscht, beet soup

Sour cream

Vegetable soups are the main food for many country people in cold regions throughout the world. Russia's famous beet soup, *borscht*, comes from Ukraine. There, the *borscht* also contains other root vegetables such as potatoes and carrots. *Borscht* is often served with savory turnovers called *piroshki*.

Piroshki, savory pastries

CHORNOBYL'

In 1986, a radiation leak at Chornobyl' nuclear power station caused panic all over Europe. More than 100,000 people were evacuated from the area around the plant, where towns now stand desolate and empty. More than two million people still live in fear and uncertainty in the contaminated areas. Look for ☢

MAP FEATURES

Oil: There is a large oilfield under the delta of the Kura River in Azerbaijan. Offshore wells are also being dug in the Caspian Sea. Look for ⛽

Hydroelectric power: Dams on the Dnieper River supply water for crops and for electricity. The rivers of the Caucasus also provide electricity. Look for ⊞

High-tech: Electrical and electronic equipment, such as TVs and computers, are made in the Caucasus republics. Look for 🖥

🌾	Cereals	⛏	Mining
🍇	Wine	🪨	Coal
🌿	Tea	🏭	Industrial center
🌻	Sunflowers	⚒	Tourism
🐟	Fishing	☢	Nuclear pollution

BLACK SEA TOURISM

The Crimea attracts millions of visitors who cram onto the crowded beaches to enjoy the warm sun. Many visitors come for their health, rest and a regimen of healthy eating, massage, and exercise. Look for ⚒

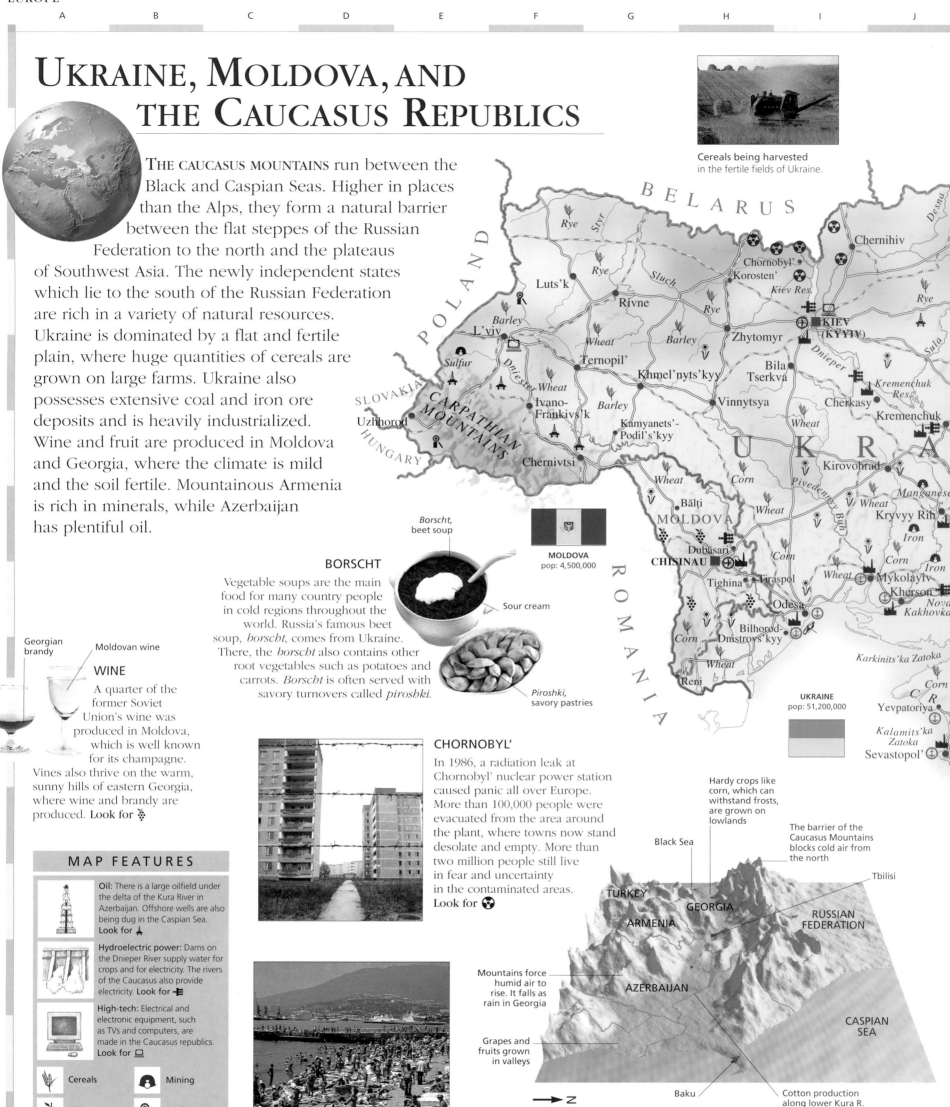

MOLDOVA
pop: 4,500,000

UKRAINE
pop: 51,200,000

Hardy crops like corn, which can withstand frosts, are grown on lowlands

The barrier of the Caucasus Mountains blocks cold air from the north

Black Sea

Tbilisi

TURKEY
GEORGIA
ARMENIA
RUSSIAN FEDERATION
AZERBAIJAN
CASPIAN SEA

Mountains force humid air to rise. It falls as rain in Georgia

Grapes and fruits grown in valleys

Baku

Cotton production along lower Kura R.

THE CAUCASUS

Armenia, Azerbaijan, and Georgia – the Caucasus republics – are isolated from the Russian Federation by the Caucasus Mountains. The warm subtropical climate of the region allows an exotic range of crops to be grown. Georgia has a humid climate, so tea and citrus fruits are cultivated. In the drier east, the rivers running down from the mountains are used to water the fields.

BLACK BREAD

Ukraine was known as the former Soviet Union's "breadbasket." Its broad, flat steppes, with their fertile black earth, are intensively cultivated: wheat, buckwheat, potatoes, rye, and flax are grown on vast farms. Much of Ukraine's countryside consists of endless fields of cereals, the view broken only by the occasional haystack.

Matrioshka dolls are hand painted. Each is made from a single piece of wood.

The Ukraine is the world's largest producer of buckwheat. Although it is ground up to make flour, buckwheat is not a true cereal.

KIEV

Kiev, founded in the 9th century, is the capital of Ukraine. St. Sophia's Cathedral, with its gilded domes, has been Kiev's most famous landmark since 1037. Kiev is situated on the banks of the Dnieper River, the republic's main waterway. It is within easy reach of the Black Sea ports, as well as being near Ukraine's industrial center.

COAL

About a third of the former Soviet Union's coal came from the area around Donets'k in Ukraine, where there are about 40 deep mines. Miners working here are reasonably well paid, but gas explosions and the frequent breakdown of equipment put them at risk. Death rates in these mines are 10 times higher than in mines in the US. Look for ⛏

INDUSTRIAL HEARTLAND

Ukraine's Donbass region, with its rich reserves of coal, iron, manganese, and other minerals, is a major industrial area. Heavy industry, such as iron- and steelworks, engineering, and chemicals, still dominate the region; but today cars, aircraft, televisions, and computers are also manufactured here. Look for 🏭

CAUCASUS CONFLICT

When the Caucasus republics were part of the Soviet Union, many different peoples were forced to live side by side. Since these countries became independent, many pent-up resentments have been unleashed. Within Muslim Azerbaijan, the Christian, mainly Armenian, region of Nagornyy-Karabakh has caused great tension and conflict. A peace agreement has now been negotiated.

TEA

Tea is a popular drink throughout the former Soviet Union, and over 90 percent of the tea consumed there is grown in Georgia. Both black and green teas are grown on large tea plantations. Tea is served black and strong, with sugar or lemon. Look for 🌿

Decorated Black Sea fiddle, from Georgia.

SUNFLOWERS

Sunflowers are an important crop in southern Ukraine. The seeds, which can be eaten, contain oil and protein. Sunflower oil is used for cooking. The seeds are also used in the manufacture of margarine and soap and are mixed with corn and peas for cattle feed. Look for 🌻

The snow-capped peaks of the Caucasus mountains.

AZERBAIJAN
pop: 7,700,000

Caviar, served on toast

CAVIAR

The Russian sturgeon is a large fish which can grow up to 23 ft (7 m) in length. Sturgeon eggs, called caviar, are an expensive delicacy. Sturgeon live in the Black and Caspian Seas and swim up rivers like the Dnieper to breed in fresh water. Hydroelectric dams on these rivers have disrupted the sturgeons' routes, and polluted water is causing concern about falling numbers of fish. Look for 🐟

GEORGIA
pop: 5,400,000

TEXTILES

Georgia is famous for its silk and textiles. Brightly colored and patterned cotton fabrics are woven with gold and silver thread. Worn by women as headscarves, these fabrics are seen throughout the Caucasus.

The Swallow's Nest Castle, high on a rock near Yalta.

ARMENIA
pop: 3,600,000

Map labels

RUSSIAN FEDERATION

Sumy
Barley
Wheat
Kharkiv
Iron
Poltava
Corn
Corn
UKRAINE
Donets
DONBASS
Wheat
Kramators'k
Dnipropetrovs'k
Horlivka
Luhans'k
Makiyivka
Aluminum
Zaporizhzhya
Donets'k
Nikopol'
Corn
Uranium
Melitopol'
Mariupol'
Corn
Kakhovka Res.
Berdyans'k
Corn
SEA OF AZOV
Wheat
Kerch Strait
Kerch
CRIMEA
Feodosiya
Simferopol'
Yalta

BLACK SEA

RUSSIAN FEDERATION

Gagra
Sokhumi
Enguri
Och'amch'ire
GEORGIA
P'ot'i
CAUCASUS
K'ut'aisi
Alazani
Bat'umi
Manganese
TBILISI
Rust'avi
Kura
Mingacevir Su Anbari
Quba
TURKEY
Copper
Vanadzor
Iron
Corn
Ganca
Sumqayit
BAKU (BAKI)
Gyumri
Sevan-Hrazdan
CASPIAN SEA
L. Sevan
AZERBAIJAN
YEREVAN
NAGORNYY
ARMENIA
Xankandi
KARABAKH
Aras
Wheat
AZERBAIJAN
Naxcivan
Lankaran
IRAN

N

| 0 | 50 | 100 | 150 | 200 | 250 | 300 KM |

| 0 | 50 | 100 | 150 | MILES |

White-backed vulture
Gyps bengalensis
Wingspan:
7 ft (2.2 m)

Cheetah
Acinonyx jubatus
Length: 7 ft (2.2 m)

Aye-aye
Daubentonia madagascariensis
Length: 18 in (45 cm)

AFRICA

AFRICA IS THE SECOND largest continent after Asia, and the only one through which the Equator and both tropics run. It is also home to the world's longest river, the Nile. The climate and vegetation roughly mirror each other on either side of the Equator. In the extreme south and along the Mediterranean coast in the north, hot dry summers are followed by mild wet winters. Similarly, the land around each tropic is hot and starved of rain, so great deserts have formed. Africa's immense tropical savannah grasslands are prone to drought, but around the Equator high rainfall has produced lush tropical rain forests. The volcanoes and strangely elongated lakes in the Great Rift Valley are evidence of cracks in the Earth's crust that threaten to split Africa apart eventually.

☐ HOT SAHARA

The inhospitable Sahara desert covers one-third of Africa. Temperatures can exceed 120°F (50°C).

Burchell's zebra
Equus burchelli
Height:
4 ft (1.2 m)

Malachite is a copper-rich ore found in many parts of eastern Africa.

☐ THUNDERING WATERFALL

The Zambezi River winds slowly through dry woodlands before reaching the Victoria Falls. Here it plummets 354 ft (108 m), creating so much noise and spray that local people call it "the smoke that thunders."

☐ GREAT RIFT VALLEY

Cracks in the Earth's crust have made a valley 3,750 miles (6,000 km) long, and up to 55 miles (90 km) wide.

☐ MISTY RAIN FOREST

Tropical rain forests only grow where temperatures are always high and rain is abundant. Here in central Africa, it rains every day – more than 7 ft (2 m) falls each year.

Umbrella thorn acacia
Acacia tortillis
Height:
60 ft (18 m)

The South African turban shell looks like a headdress made of coiled cloth.

☐ SERENGETI PLAIN

Savannah – grassland and open woodland – is home to huge herds of grazing animals, including wildebeest and zebra.

☐ SAND DUNES IN THE NAMIB

The intensely hot Namib Desert forms a narrow strip down Africa's southwest coast. Rainfall is less than 6 in (15 cm) a year, but sea mists from the cold currents along the coast provide enough moisture for some plants and animals to survive.

Shells like this black miter can be found in shallow water along the west African coast.

Gaboon viper
Bitis gabonica
Length:
7 ft (2 m)

☐ SOUTHERN AFRICA

Rainfall is so low in southern Africa that for most of the year few plants show themselves above ground. But as soon as the rains come, a barren landscape is transformed into a brilliant mass of flowers.

☐ ☐ OKAVANGO DELTA

Not all rivers run to the sea. The Okavango River ends in a huge inland swamp that attracts thousands of water loving animals, such as hippopotamuses.

CROSS-SECTION THROUGH AFRICA

L. Victoria
Great Rift Valley (western)
Serengeti Plain
Atlantic Ocean
Congo Basin
Ruwenzori Mountains
Great Rift Valley (eastern)
Indian Ocean

9,843 (3,000)
Sea level 0
-14,764 (-4,500)
Feet (meters)

A   Length: 2,800 miles (4,500 km)   B

African elephant
Loxodonta africana
Height: 13 ft (4 m)

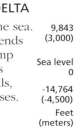

Desert scorpion
Androctonus australis
Length: 3 in (8 cm)

Mountain gorilla
Gorilla gorilla
Height: 6 ft (1.8 m)

BOTTLE TREES

Plants can resist drought by reducing their leaf size and enlarging their stems to store water. Here in Madagascar's dry woodlands, huge-trunked baobabs, or "bottle trees," grow alongside spiny Dideria.

Black rhinoceros
Diceros bicornis
Length: 12 ft (3.6 m)

KEY TO SYMBOLS

▲ Mountain

△ Volcano

Mangroves

Wetlands

Coral reef

Plate margins showing direction of movement

! Endangered species

NATURAL VEGETATION ZONES

Mediterranean-type

Temperate grassland

Hot desert

Mountain

Tropical grassland

Tropical rain forest

Dry woodland

NORTHWEST AFRICA

OVER THE CENTURIES, northwest Africa has been invaded by many peoples. The entire north coast from the Red Sea to the Atlantic was once part of the Roman Empire. While subsequent colonization by Italy, Great Britain, Turkey, Spain, and France contributed to the culture of the countries, it was the 7th-century Arab conquest which fundamentally changed the region. The conversion of the original peoples – the Berbers – to Islam, and the use of Arabic as a common language, gave these countries a sense of unity which remains today. In fact, the region is sometimes called the Maghreb, which means "west" in Arabic. In the northwest, the Atlas Mountains form a barrier between the wetter, cooler areas along the coast and the arid Sahara. This desert is the biggest on Earth and is still growing. Water shortages and lack of land for farming are problems throughout the region, especially as the population of the Maghreb is increasing rapidly. In Algeria and Libya, however, the desert has revealed hidden riches – abundant oil and natural gas.

FEZ – AN ISLAMIC CITY

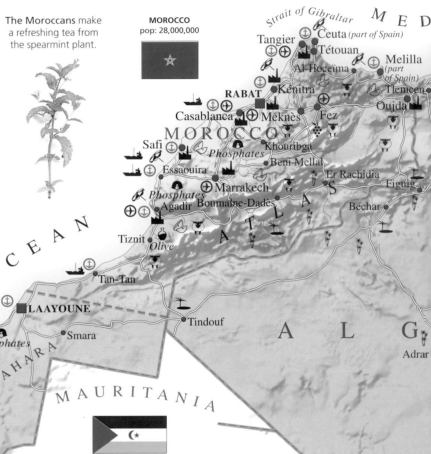

This view of the city of Fez in Morocco shows the flat-roofed houses that are traditional in this region. Seen from the narrow streets, the houses look blank and windowless, but this is because they are designed to face inward onto central courtyards which are cool and private. Islamic cities may appear to be chaotic mazes of streets, but in fact they are laid out following guidelines set in the holy book of Islam, the *Koran*.

The Moroccans make a refreshing tea from the spearmint plant.

MOROCCO
pop: 28,000,000

Map labels: Strait of Gibraltar, M E D, Tangier, Ceuta (part of Spain), Tétouan, Al-Hoceima, Melilla (part of Spain), Kénitra, Tlemcen, RABAT, Fez, Oujda, Casablanca, Meknès, MOROCCO, Safi, Khouribga, Phosphates, Beni-Mellal, Essaouira, Er Rachidia, Figuig, Phosphates, Marrakech, ATLAS, Béchar, Agadir, Boumalne-Dades, Tiznit, Olive, Tan-Tan, LAAYOUNE, Tindouf, ALG, Adrar, Phosphates, Smara, WESTERN SAHARA, MAURITANIA, ATLANTIC OCEAN, Ad Dakhla, Lagouira, MALI

Morocco occupied the whole of Western Sahara in 1979

WESTERN SAHARA
pop: 230,000

BERBERS

Berbers were the original people of northwest Africa. When the Arabs invaded, they were driven out of the fertile coastal areas. Many Berbers still live in remote villages or towns high in the Atlas Mountains – such as here at Boumalne-Dadès – where their lifestyle and language have remained unchanged for centuries.

Couscous is the basic ingredient of many North African dishes. It is made of tiny pellets of flour, called semolina.

WESTERN SAHARA

Western Sahara is a sparsely populated desert area lying between Morocco and Mauritania. It was a Spanish colony until 1976 but is now fighting for independence from Morocco, which claims the country and the phosphates found there. This photo shows young members of the liberation movement.

The Ahaggar mountains, Algeria, jut up in the middle of the Sahara.

MAP FEATURES

Mining: Huge quantities of phosphates come from the sands of Western Sahara and Morocco. They are the vital raw material for fertilizers. Look for ⛑

Gas: Algeria has vast reserves of natural gas, much of it exported to Europe – some by pipeline to Italy across the Mediterranean Sea. Look for 🔥

Archaeological sites: Early civilizations, such as the Romans, built cities in the desert and along the coast of North Africa. Look for ⚏

🐑 Sheep	⚓ Fishing port	
🍋 Citrus fruits	⚙ Oil	
🌴 Dates	🏭 Industrial center	
🍇 Wine	✈ Tourism	
🫒 Vegetable oil	🌴 Oases	

CARPETS AND RUGS

Hand-knotted carpets and rugs, with their distinctive bold patterns and deep pile, are made throughout the region. In Morocco the most important carpet factories are in Rabat and Fez. Craftworkers often work together in cooperatives to maintain high quality and to control prices.

Painted plate   Leather bag

TOURISM

Tourism is a vital source of foreign income for Morocco and Tunisia. When oil prices fell in the 1980s, tourism took the place of oil as the main source of foreign income. Modern hotels, built in traditional styles, have sprung up along the coast. Both countries produce handicrafts for tourists, such as leather and brassware. Look for ✈

THE TUAREG

The Tuareg are a nomadic tribe who inhabit a huge area of the Sahara. In the past they controlled the great camel caravans which crossed the desert to the Mediterranean, carrying slaves, ivory, gold, and salt. Today, some Tuareg still follow the traditional desert way of life, but many have become settled farmers.

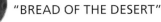

NORTH COAST AGRICULTURE

Along the Mediterranean coast and in sheltered valleys in the Atlas Mountains, the soil is rich and the climate mild. In these areas, farmers can grow crops such as grapes, olives, cereals, and citrus fruits. Sheep, goats, and cattle are kept throughout the region, especially in Tunisia.

"BREAD OF THE DESERT"

. The fruit of the date palm has been eaten for centuries. Dates are rich in protein and provide food for people and animals. They grow around desert oases, where the climate is hot and dry and there is water in the ground. Every part of a date palm has some use. **Look for**

TUNISIA
POP: 9,500,000

Ruins of the Roman port of Leptis Magna in Libya.

KAIROUAN

For Muslims, the 9th-century Great Mosque in the desert at Kairouan, Tunisia, is the holiest place in Africa. The enormous courtyard – where the people pray – is paved in marble and surrounded by a forest of columns. The interior is decorated with beautiful glazed tiles.

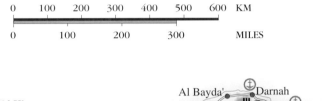

N

0 100 200 300 400 500 600 KM
0 100 200 300 MILES

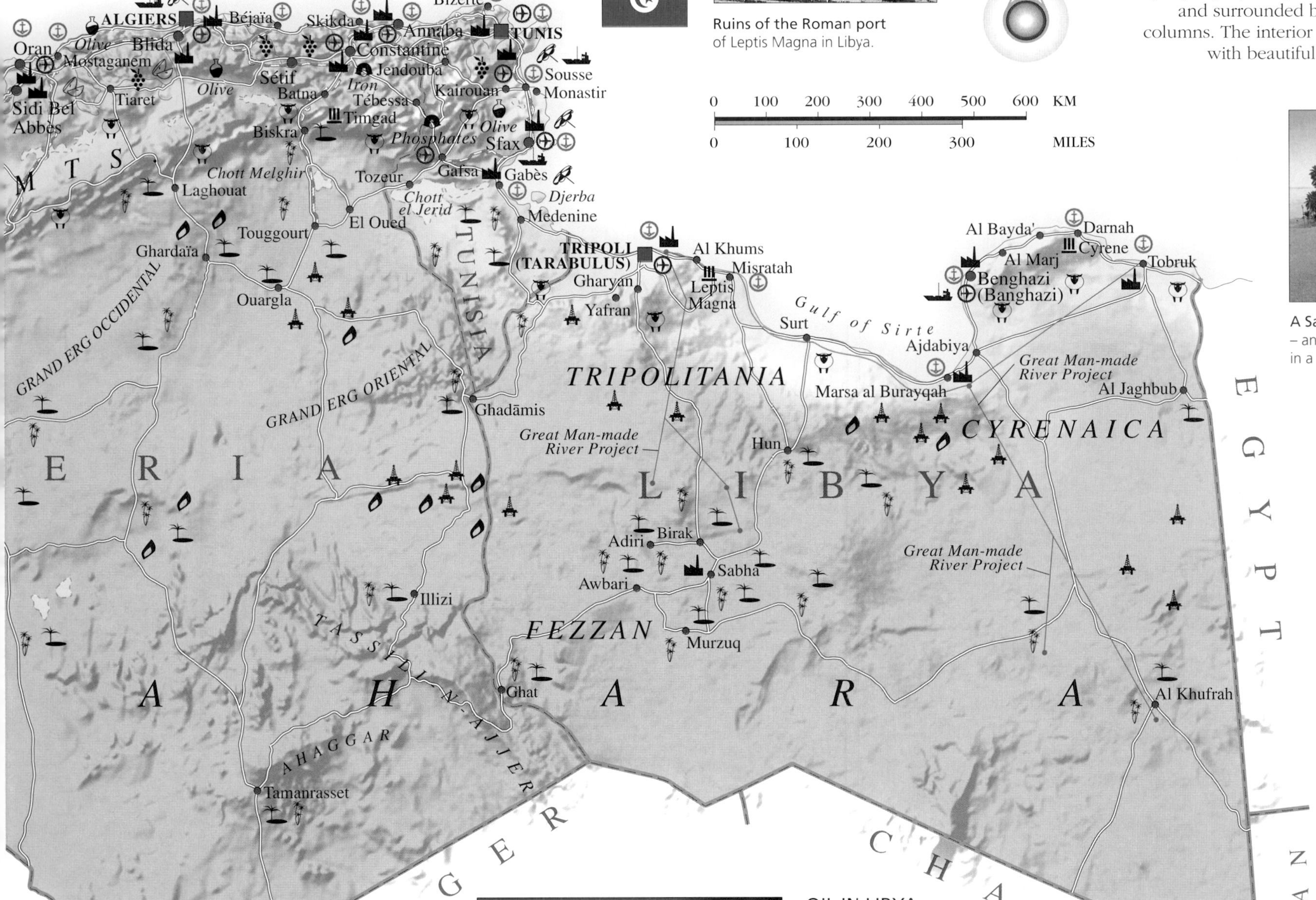

A Saharan oasis
– an island of green in a sea of sand.

LIBYA
pop: 6,000,000

Classical Arab lute from Morocco.

OIL IN LIBYA

Until the discovery of oil in l958, many people in Libya were very poor. The money from oil has enabled Libya to construct roads and railroads, improve education, and develop industry and agriculture. Libyan oil is in great demand because it has no sulfur in it. This means that when it is burned, it gives out very little pollution. **Look for**

ALGERIA
pop: 30,200,000

WOOD SHORTAGE

The main source of energy for many African people is burning wood. But tree roots help to bind the soil together, and when large numbers of trees are cut down, the soil can be blown or worn away. This allows the desert to spread. People who live in treeless areas spend hours searching for wood to burn and must then carry it long distances to their villages. Collecting wood is traditionally women's work.

An Algerian stamp showing the traditional dress for men.

WATER PIPELINE

Deep beneath the Sahara are vast underground supplies of water. The Libyans are building a series of huge pipelines like the one shown under construction here, which will carry this water across the desert to the coastal areas. It will be used to water the farmland and increase crop production. This is known as the Great Man-made River project, and two cross-desert pipelines have already been completed.

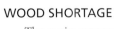

103

NORTHEAST AFRICA

WATERED AND FERTILIZED BY THE NILE, the longest river in the world, Egypt is a fertile strip running through the Sahara desert. The first people settled there about 8,000 years ago, and by the time of the pharaohs, Egypt had become one of the world's first great civilizations. Today, Egypt is a relatively stable democracy, with a growing number of industries and control of the Suez Canal, one of the world's most important waterways. To the south are the highlands of Ethiopia and Eritrea. This area is fertile and well-watered in places, but recent droughts have made life precarious for the farmers and nomads who live there. The countries of Somalia, Sudan, and Ethiopia have been beset by terrible problems, including drought, famine, religious conflicts, and civil war. Thousands of refugees from these areas depend on international aid. In 1993, Eritrea gained independence from Ethiopia, after a civil war which lasted 30 years.

TOURIST SOUVENIRS

Large numbers of "ancient Egyptian" scarabs (beetles) and other fake antiques are made locally and sold to tourists. City streets are lined with market stalls and the small workshops where these goods are made. Tourism has stimulated this informal economy.

SUEZ CANAL

Opened in 1869, the Suez Canal is one of the world's largest artificial waterways and a vital source of income for Egypt. It connects the Red Sea with the Mediterranean, offering a short cut from Europe to the Persian Gulf, India, and the Far East. On average, 21,250 ships a year use the canal.

The ancient Egyptians used this reedlike plant, called *papyrus*, to make paper.

THE COPTIC CHURCH

Although Ethiopia is surrounded by Islamic countries, about 40 percent of its population is Christian. The isolated Ethiopian church developed into a unique branch of Christianity, called the Coptic church.

Coptic cross

COTTON

Egypt produces about a third of the world's high-quality cotton. Textile industries, such as spinning, weaving, and dyeing cotton, are also important. Cotton is the coolest fabric to wear during hot summers. Egyptian men often wear a long-sleeved cotton garment, or *jelaba*. Look for 🧥

Cotton *jelaba*

The gold death mask of the Pharaoh Tutankhamun, c. 1352 BC

CAIRO AND THE DELTA

Cairo is the largest city in the Islamic world and is also one of the fastest growing. Its current population is estimated at 13 million. To the north, dams and irrigation canals have disturbed the flow of the Nile River, reducing the amount of sediment it deposits at the delta. This causes a reduction in cultivable land, forcing more farmers into the cities.

El Faiyum oasis is cultivated with vines, olives, wheat, and legumes

Site of pyramids at El Giza

Alexandria marks the western limit of the delta

WESTERN DESERT

Nile

DELTA

MEDITERRANEAN SEA

MEDITERRANEAN SEA

Gulf of Suez

Cairo, center of the rail and road network, lies at the foot of the delta

The Suez Canal is 121 miles (195 km) long, and links the Mediterranean and Red Seas

Port Said marks the eastern limit of the delta

N

The Nile Delta is extensively cultivated, but is gradually shrinking and becoming salinated

TOURISM

Visitors from all over the world go to Egypt to see the pyramids and other ancient sites. Income from tourism helps to maintain these ancient sites. The Temple of Isis at Philae would have been flooded by the Aswan Dam, so it was moved, brick by brick, to another island. Look for 🏛

AGRICULTURE

Although there is fertile land in southern Ethiopia, farming methods are inefficient. The scratch plough is widely used but, as its name implies, it is only able to turn over the surface of the soil. After a few years, the nutrients in the soil are used up, and crops will no longer grow.

The pyramids at El Giza were built as tombs for the pharaohs.

THE GIFT OF THE NILE

The Nile River floods in the summer, carrying rich mud from the highlands of Sudan and Ethiopia to the deserts of Egypt. This creates some of the most fertile land in the world. Nearly 99 percent of the Egyptian population lives along the banks of the Nile.

EGYPT
pop: 65,700,000

MEDITERRANEAN SEA

ISRAEL
Port Said
Suez Canal
Isma'iliya
Suez
Gulf of Aqaba
SINAI
Gulf of Suez
RED SEA
Tanta
El Mansura
Alexandria
Helwan
Beni Suef
Ras Gharib
Bur Safaga
CAIRO
El Giza
Saqqara
El Faiyum
El Minya
Qena
Thebes
Luxor
Asyut
Sohag
Abydos
Valley of the Kings
Idfu
Kom Ombo
Aswan
Aswan Dam
Philae
L. Nasser
Abu Simbel
Sub Temple
Wadi Halfa
(administered by Egypt)
(administered by Sudan)
NUBIAN DESERT
Matruh
Qattara Depression
E G Y P T
L I B Y A
Nile

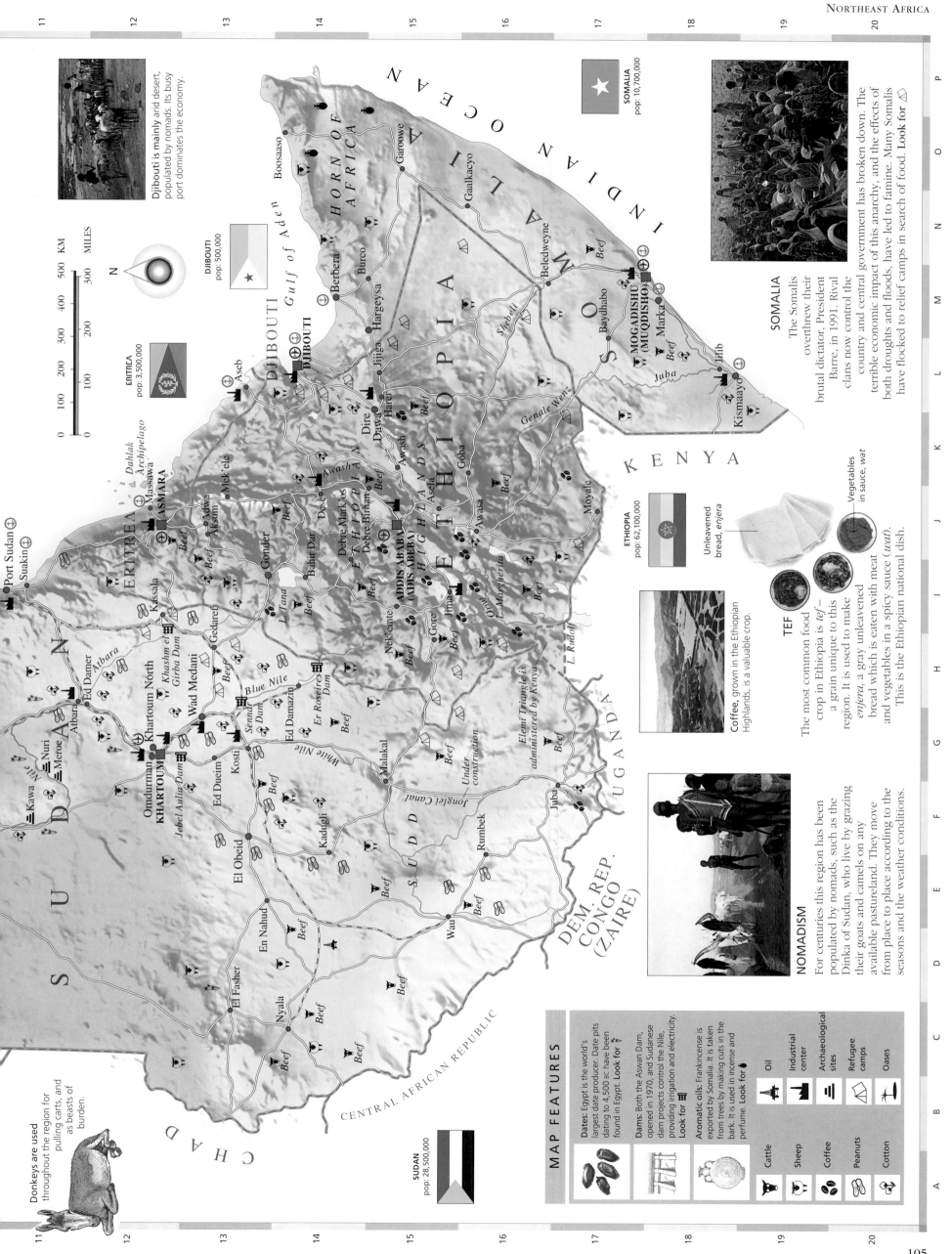

Djibouti is mainly arid desert, populated by nomads. Its busy port dominates the economy.

SOMALIA
pop: 10,700,000

DJIBOUTI
pop: 500,000

ERITREA
pop: 3,500,000

N

KM MILES
500 300
400
300 200
200
100 100
0   0

SOMALIA

The Somalis overthrew their brutal dictator, President Barre, in 1991. Rival clans now control the country and central government has broken down. The terrible economic impact of this anarchy, and the effects of both droughts and floods, have led to famine. Many Somalis have flocked to relief camps in search of food. **Look for** ⌂

ETHIOPIA
pop: 62,100,000

Unleavened bread, *enjera*

Vegetables in sauce, *wat*

TEF

The most common food crop in Ethiopia is *tef* – a grain unique to this region. It is used to make *enjera*, a gray unleavened bread which is eaten with meat and vegetables in a spicy sauce (*wat*). This is the Ethiopian national dish.

Coffee, grown in the Ethiopian Highlands, is a valuable crop.

NOMADISM

For centuries this region has been populated by nomads, such as the Dinka of Sudan, who live by grazing their goats and camels on any available pastureland. They move from place to place according to the seasons and the weather conditions.

SUDAN
pop: 28,500,000

MAP FEATURES

Dates: Egypt is the world's largest date producer. Date pits dating to 4,500 BC have been found in Egypt. **Look for** 🌴

Dams: Both the Aswan Dam, opened in 1970, and Sudanese dam projects control the Nile, providing irrigation and electricity. **Look for** 🏛

Aromatic oils: Frankincense is exported by Somalia. It is taken from trees by making cuts in the bark. It is used in incense and perfume. **Look for** 🏺

Cattle
Sheep
Coffee
Peanuts
Cotton

Oil
Industrial center
Archaeological sites
Refugee camps
Oases

Donkeys are used throughout the region for pulling carts, and as beasts of burden.

INDIAN OCEAN

HORN OF AFRICA

Gulf of Aden

SOMALIA

ETHIOPIA

ERITREA

DJIBOUTI

SUDAN

KENYA

UGANDA

DEM. REP. CONGO (ZAIRE)

CENTRAL AFRICAN REPUBLIC

CHAD

ETHIOPIAN HIGHLANDS

Boosaaso
Garoowe
Gaalkacyo
Berbera
Burco
Beledweyne
Beef
Baydhabo
MOGADISHU (MUQDISHO)
Marka
Beef
Jilib
Kismaayo
Juba
Genale Wenz
Shebeli
Hargeysa
Jijiga
Harer
Dire Dawa
Awash
Goba
Asela
Awasa
Moyale
L. Margherita
Omo
Jima
Gore
Nek'emte
L. Tana
Bahir Dar
Gonder
ADDIS ABABA (ADIS ABEBA)
Debre Mark'os
Debre Birhan
Desē
Adwa
Aksum
Mek'ele
ASMARA
Massawa
Dahlak Archipelago
Aseb
Awash
Beef
Beef
Beef
Beef
Beef
Beef
Beef
Beef
Beef
Beef
Beef
Beef
Beef

Port Sudan
Suakin
Atbara
Ed Damer
Nuri
Meroe
Kawa
Nile
Omdurman
KHARTOUM
Khartoum North
Kassala
Gedaref
Khashm el Girba Dam
Jebel Aulia Dam
Wad Medani
Sennar Dam
Blue Nile
Ed Damazin
Er Roseires Dam
Kosti
Ed Dueim
El Obeid
Kadugli
En Nahud
Nyala
El Fasher
White Nile
Malakal
Rumbek
Wau
Juba
Jonglel Canal
Under construction
Elemi Triangle is administered by Kenya
L. Rudolf
Beef
Beef
Beef
Beef
Beef
Beef
Beef
Beef
Beef
Beef
Beef
Beef
Beef
Beef
Beef
Beef
Beef
Beef

WEST AFRICA

Calabash (bowl) made from a decorated gourd.

MAURITANIA
pop: 2,500,000

THE LANDSCAPE OF WEST AFRICA ranges from the sand dunes of the Sahara through the dry grasslands of the Sahel region to the tropical rain forests in the south. There is just as much variety in the peoples of the region – more than 250 different tribes live in Nigeria alone. In the north, most people are Muslim, a legacy of the Arab traders who controlled the great caravan routes across the Sahara and brought Islam with them. It was from West Africa, particularly the coastal regions, that millions of Africans were transported to North and South America as slaves. Today many people in West Africa make their living by farming or herding animals. Crops such as coffee and cocoa are grown on large plantations. Like the logging industry, which is also a major source of earnings, these plantations are often owned by foreign multinational companies who take most of the profits out of the region. Recent discoveries of oil and minerals offer the promise of economic prosperity, but this has been prevented by falling world prices, huge foreign debts, corruption, and civil wars.

SENEGAL
pop: 9,000,000

GAMBIA
pop: 1,900,000

Kano mosque, built to serve the largely Islamic population in northern Nigeria.

GUINEA-BISSAU
pop: 1,100,000

GUINEA
pop: 7,700,000

SIERRA LEONE
pop: 4,600,000

DAKAR

Dakar, the capital of Senegal, is one of the main ports in West Africa. It lies on the Atlantic coast and has a fine natural harbor, large modern docks, and ship repair facilities. It is the country's main industrial center.

MAP FEATURES

Vegetable oil: The oil palm is widely grown throughout West Africa. Palm oil is used by people in the region and some is exported. Look for

Research center: At a center in Ibadan, Nigeria, new disease-resistant varieties of corn, cassava, and other crops have been bred. Look for

Film industry: Burkina has a large film industry, subsidized by the government, with studios in Ouagadougou and an annual film festival. Look for

Shipping registry: Many of the world's shipping countries register their ships in Liberia because of low taxes and lax employment rules. Look for

☕	Coffee	🌲	Forest products
🫘	Cocoa	⚓	Fishing
🥜	Peanuts	⛏	Mining
🌿	Cotton	🛢	Oil
🪵	Timber	■	Industrial center

TOURISM

Tourism in this region has expanded rapidly. In Gambia, the number of visitors rose from 300 in 1965 to over 100,000 a year in the 1990s. Most tourists stay along the Atlantic coast, but many also go on trips into the bush.

Cocoa pod

Cocoa beans

Pulp

COCOA

The ancient Aztec people of Mexico were the first to make a drink called *chocolatl* from the seeds of the cacao tree – brought to West Africa by European colonizers. The region now produces over half the world's supply of cocoa beans. Look for

LIBERIA
pop: 2,700,000

IVORY COAST
pop: 14,600,000

DEFORESTATION

The population of West Africa is growing rapidly. Vast areas of forest have been cut down, for wood or to clear farmland to feed these extra people. This problem is particularly bad in the Ivory Coast, where little forest is left. Look for

AFTER INDEPENDENCE

Since independence, some African countries have been plagued by many problems, such as unstable governments and foreign debts. Ivory Coast, however, is one of West Africa's most prosperous countries. Its last president built this cathedral when he had the capital moved to his family village at Yamoussoukro.

Map labels:
WESTERN SAHARA
Zouérat
Fdérik
Iron
Nouâdhibou
Râs Nouâdhibou
Gum arabic
Gum arabic
Atar
Gum arabic
Iron
Râs Timirist
S A H A R A
M A U R I T A N I A
Tidjikja
NOUAKCHOTT
Copper
Gum arabic
L. Rkiz
Aleg
Kiffa
Néma
Rosso
Saint Louis
Phosphates
Kaédi
Louga
Matam
Phosphates
Nioro
Copper
DAKAR
Diourbel
Kayes
Kaolack
SENEGAL
BANJUL
GAMBIA
Tambacounda
BAMAKO
Georgetown
Ziguinchor
Kolda
Palm
Bafata
Iron
Niger
Iron
BISSAU
Palm
Labé
Aluminum
Gold
Bougouni
GUINEA-BISSAU
Palm
Bijagós Archipelago
Palm
Aluminum
Niger
Sikasso
A T L A N T I C
Palm
Kindia
Kankan
G U I N E A
CONAKRY
Iron
Odienné
SIERRA
Makeni
Diamonds
Korhogo
Palm
FREETOWN
Diamonds
Voinjama
IVORY
LEONE
Bo
Kénema
Nzérékoré
Gold
Bouaké
Man
L. de Kossou
Rubber
Iron
Gold
Daloa
Gbanga
Gold
YAMOUSSOUKRO
Robertsport
O C E A N
MONROVIA
Rubber
L. de Buyo
Buchanan
Rubber
Palm
Zwedru
Gagnoa
L I B E R I A
Manganese
Rubber
Palm
Greenville
Harper

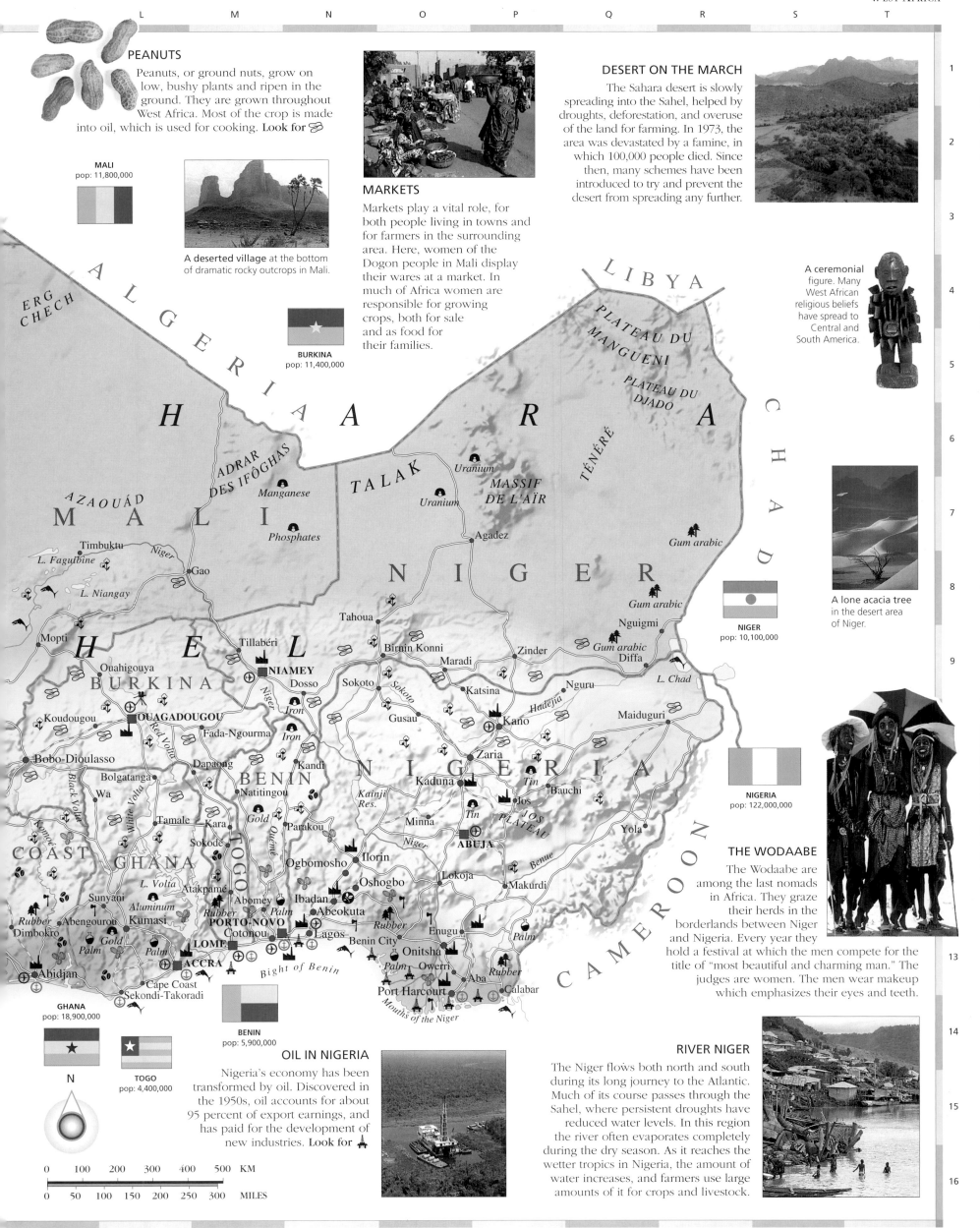

PEANUTS

Peanuts, or ground nuts, grow on low, bushy plants and ripen in the ground. They are grown throughout West Africa. Most of the crop is made into oil, which is used for cooking. **Look for**

MALI
pop: 11,800,000

A deserted village at the bottom of dramatic rocky outcrops in Mali.

MARKETS

Markets play a vital role, for both people living in towns and for farmers in the surrounding area. Here, women of the Dogon people in Mali display their wares at a market. In much of Africa women are responsible for growing crops, both for sale and as food for their families.

BURKINA
pop: 11,400,000

DESERT ON THE MARCH

The Sahara desert is slowly spreading into the Sahel, helped by droughts, deforestation, and overuse of the land for farming. In 1973, the area was devastated by a famine, in which 100,000 people died. Since then, many schemes have been introduced to try and prevent the desert from spreading any further.

A ceremonial figure. Many West African religious beliefs have spread to Central and South America.

A lone acacia tree in the desert area of Niger.

NIGER
pop: 10,100,000

NIGERIA
pop: 122,000,000

THE WODAABE

The Wodaabe are among the last nomads in Africa. They graze their herds in the borderlands between Niger and Nigeria. Every year they hold a festival at which the men compete for the title of "most beautiful and charming man." The judges are women. The men wear makeup which emphasizes their eyes and teeth.

RIVER NIGER

The Niger flows both north and south during its long journey to the Atlantic. Much of its course passes through the Sahel, where persistent droughts have reduced water levels. In this region the river often evaporates completely during the dry season. As it reaches the wetter tropics in Nigeria, the amount of water increases, and farmers use large amounts of it for crops and livestock.

OIL IN NIGERIA

Nigeria's economy has been transformed by oil. Discovered in the 1950s, oil accounts for about 95 percent of export earnings, and has paid for the development of new industries. **Look for**

GHANA
pop: 18,900,000

TOGO
pop: 4,400,000

BENIN
pop: 5,900,000

N

0   100   200   300   400   500 KM
0   50   100   150   200   250   300 MILES

Map labels

ERG CHECH
ALGERIA
LIBYA
PLATEAU DU MANGUENI
PLATEAU DU DJADO
ADRAR DES IFÔGHAS
AZAOUÁD
MALI
S A H A R A
TALAK
Manganese
Uranium
Uranium
MASSIF DE L'AÏR
TÉNÉRÉ
NIGER
Phosphates
CHAD
Timbuktu
L. Faguibine
Niger
Gao
L. Niangay
Gum arabic
Agadez
Gum arabic
Mopti
S A H E L
Tahoua
Nguigmi
Gum arabic
Diffa
Ouahigouya
Tillabéri
Birnin Konni
Maradi
Zinder
Nguru
L. Chad
BURKINA
NIAMEY
Dosso
Sokoto
Katsina
Maiduguri
Koudougou
OUAGADOUGOU
Fada-Ngourma
Iron
Sokoto
Gusau
Kano
Hadejia
Bobo-Dioulasso
Dapaong
Iron
Zaria
Red Volta
Kandi
Kaduna
Tin
Bauchi
Bolgatanga
BENIN
Kainji Res.
NIGERIA
Wa
Natitingou
Jos
Black Volta
White Volta
Tamale
Kara
Gold
Parakou
Minna
Tin
JOS PLATEAU
Yola
Sunyani
Sokodé
ABUJA
L. Volta
Ilorin
Niger
Lokoja
Makurdi
Benue
Rubber
Abengourou
Kumasi
Aluminum
Atakpamé
Abomey
Palm
Ogbomosho
Oshogbo
Dimbokro
GHANA
Gold
Palm
Rubber
Ibadan
Abeokuta
Enugu
Rubber
CAMEROON
Abidjan
Palm
PORTO-NOVO
Cotonou
Lagos
Benin City
Onitsha
Owerri
Palm
ACCRA
Bight of Benin
Palm
Aba
Rubber
Cape Coast
Sekondi-Takoradi
Port Harcourt
Calabar
Mouths of the Niger
COAST
GHANA
TOGO
LOMÉ
Comoé
Oueme
COAST

CENTRAL AFRICA

MUCH OF THIS REGION IS COVERED in dense tropical rain forest, drained by the great Congo (Zaire) River and its tributaries. The climate is hot and humid. All the countries in the area have small populations – although some are increasing rapidly. French is the official language in many of the countries – a legacy from the days when they were French colonies. The third-largest country in Africa, Dem. Rep. Congo (Zaire), has rich mineral deposits, but has declined economically since independence. Chad has been torn apart by civil wars, and the Central African Republic has suffered from corrupt governments. Both countries are desperately poor. Equatorial Guinea has suffered so much from bad government that one-third of its population now lives in exile. Abundant minerals and oil have made Gabon the richest country in the region. Oil is also of major importance in the Congo, and both countries have relatively large urban populations. Relatively prosperous, Cameroon is home to more than 200 different peoples.

A wooden figure from Cameroon, made to honor an ancestor.

HEALTH CLINIC

Traditional African medicine is still widely practiced in this region. Western medicine has also been successfully used to cure or control many diseases. Medicines are often dispensed at village clinics like this one. But there are still major problems – many babies do not survive and there is a great shortage of doctors. In Chad, for example, over 30,000 people have to share one doctor.

LAKE CHAD

Lake Chad lies at the point where Chad, Cameroon, Niger, and Nigeria meet. Due to a series of droughts, the rivers that feed the lake have shrunk to little more than streams and reduced it to a tenth of its former size. Fish from Lake Chad – such as this *tilapia* – are a major source of food for the people who live in the surrounding areas. But each year the fishermen must haul their boats farther to reach the lake's receding water.

PYGMIES

Several groups of pygmies live scattered through the rain forests of central Africa. They still survive mainly by hunting and gathering, but also trade with neighboring peoples and have learned to speak their languages. Pygmies rarely reach a height of more than 4 ft (125 cms). This pygmy hut, made of banana fronds, is in a forest clearing in the Central African Republic.

CENTRAL AFRICAN REPUBLIC
pop: 3,500,000

Forested valleys and hills around Dolisie, Congo.

CHAD
pop: 6,900,000

RELIGION

The main religion in this region is Christianity, but many Africans follow the traditional religions of their ancestors. They believe in many gods and spirits, who are often associated with natural forces or the elements, such as trees and thunder. This photo shows a ritual dance from Cameroon.

Dancer dressed as a leopard spirit

River flowing through dense rain forest in Cameroon.

CAMEROON
pop: 14,300,000

EQUATORIAL GUINEA
pop: 430,000

TRADITIONAL HOUSING

Traditional African houses vary from area to area, according to the building materials available locally. The walls of these houses in Cameroon are made of mud and the roofs of straw. Building a house is one of the regular family tasks. As the family grows, new houses are added to the group.

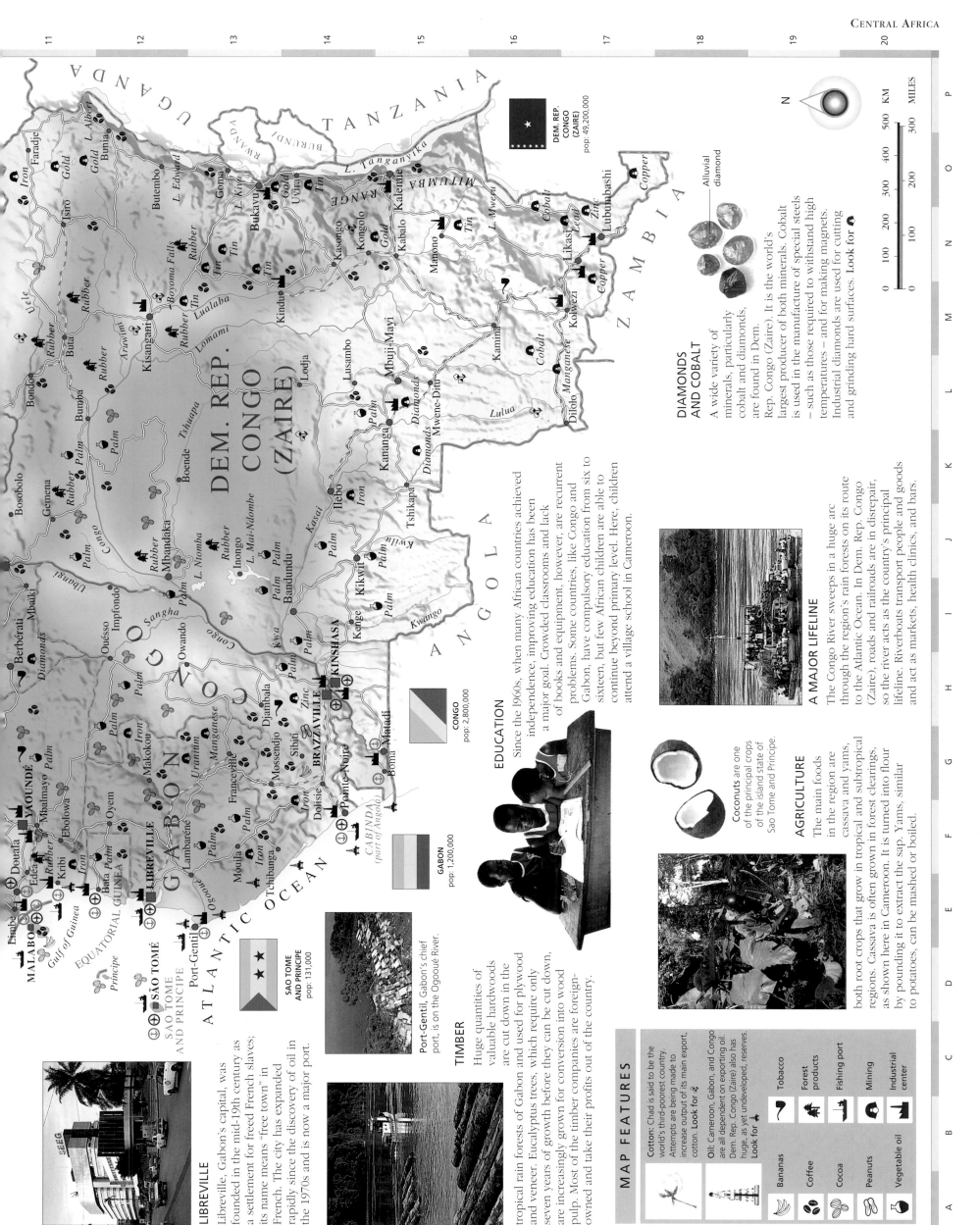

LIBREVILLE

Libreville, Gabon's capital, was founded in the mid-19th century as a settlement for freed French slaves; its name means "free town" in French. The city has expanded rapidly since the discovery of oil in the 1970s and is now a major port.

TIMBER

Huge quantities of valuable hardwoods are cut down in the tropical rain forests of Gabon and used for plywood and veneer. Eucalyptus trees, which require only seven years of growth before they can be cut down, are increasingly grown for conversion into wood pulp. Most of the timber companies are foreign-owned and take their profits out of the country.

Port-Gentil, Gabon's chief port, is on the Ogooué River.

MAP FEATURES

Cotton: Chad is said to be the world's third-poorest country. Attempts are being made to increase output of its main export, cotton. Look for 🐝

Oil: Cameroon, Gabon, and Congo are all dependent on exporting oil. Dem. Rep. Congo (Zaire) also has huge, as yet undeveloped, reserves. Look for ⛽

🍌 Bananas	🌿 Tobacco
☕ Coffee	🍁 Forest products
🫘 Cocoa	⚓ Fishing port
🥜 Peanuts	⛏ Mining
🫙 Vegetable oil	🏭 Industrial center

SAO TOME AND PRINCIPE
pop: 131,000

GABON
pop: 1,200,000

CONGO
pop: 2,800,000

DEM. REP. CONGO (ZAIRE)
pop: 49,200,000

EDUCATION

Since the 1960s, when many African countries achieved independence, improving education has been a major goal. Crowded classrooms and lack of books and equipment, however, are recurrent problems. Some countries, like Congo and Gabon, have compulsory education from six to sixteen, but few African children are able to continue beyond primary level. Here, children attend a village school in Cameroon.

Coconuts are one of the principal crops of the island state of Sao Tome and Principe.

AGRICULTURE

The main foods in the region are cassava and yams, both root crops that grow in tropical and subtropical regions. Cassava is often grown in forest clearings, as shown here in Cameroon. It is turned into flour by pounding it to extract the sap. Yams, similar to potatoes, can be mashed or boiled.

A MAJOR LIFELINE

The Congo River sweeps in a huge arc through the region's rain forests on its route to the Atlantic Ocean. In Dem. Rep. Congo (Zaire), roads and railroads are in disrepair, so the river acts as the country's principal lifeline. Riverboats transport people and goods and act as markets, health clinics, and bars.

DIAMONDS AND COBALT

A wide variety of minerals, particularly cobalt and diamonds, are found in Dem. Rep. Congo (Zaire). It is the world's largest producer of both minerals. Cobalt is used in the manufacture of special steels – such as those required to withstand high temperatures – and for making magnets. Industrial diamonds are used for cutting and grinding hard surfaces. Look for 🔶

Alluvial diamond

N

KM
MILES

A   B   C   D   E   F   G   H   I   J

CENTRAL EAST AFRICA

EAST AFRICA'S WEALTH lies in its land. Most people make their living from farming or cattle herding. Large areas covered with long grass, scrub, and scattered trees, called savannah, provide grazing for domestic and wild animals alike. Tea, coffee, and tobacco are grown as cash crops throughout the area, especially in Kenya and Malawi. The economy of Uganda, crippled by civil wars over the last 20 years, is being reformed with the help of international aid. However, Uganda's great agricultural potential is still not being exploited. Zambia, Rwanda, Burundi, and Uganda all suffer from having no seaports. Industry is poorly developed in the region, except in Kenya, and only Zambia is rich in minerals. After economic decline in the l980s, Tanzania is slowly recovering. In Rwanda, conflict between two ethnic groups, the Hutu and Tutsi, led to the slaughter of up to 500,000 Tutsis in 1994, and a mass exodus of refugees.

THE SAMBURU
In Kenya's northern plateau region, tribes like the Samburu continue to follow the traditional way of life of their ancestors. They live by grazing their herds of cattle, sheep, and goats on the savannah. This *moran*, or warrior, wears numerous strings of beads, distinctive ivory earrings, and always carries two spears and a knife.

TRAINS
Countries with no coastline are very dependent on road and rail transport to link them to industrial centers and main ports. Although the African rail network is expanding, tracks are often poorly maintained. Here, people board a train at Kampala in Uganda.

Tsetse fly carries a disease that can kill cattle and humans.

AIDS
AIDS is a worldwide problem, but it is particularly widespread in Africa. Many people on the continent already suffer from diseases and malnutrition, which makes them more vulnerable to the illnesses associated with AIDS.

WILDLIFE RESERVES
Africa's great plains contain some of the world's most spectacular species of wildlife. All the countries in the region have set aside huge areas as national parks where animals are protected. Wildlife safaris attract thousands of tourists and provide countries with much needed foreign income. Look for ▤

POACHING
Africa's wildlife parks have helped preserve the animals, but poaching remains a major problem. In an attempt to save the elephants, a worldwide ban on the sale of ivory has been imposed. But policing the parks is very costly; poachers are armed and dangerous. Here, in Tanzania, wardens are burning a poacher's hut.

PREDATORY FISH
The Nile perch was introduced into Lake Victoria to increase fish production in the 1960s. Although the lake is vast, this fish now occupies every corner and is killing off the original fish population. Look for ⌁

Vultures cluster in a lone tree on the Tanzanian grasslands.

Copper bracelets

COPPER
There are huge desposits of copper in central Africa, centered around Ndola in Zambia. This region is often called the Copperbelt. Copper accounts for 90 percent of Zambia's export earnings, but low prices in recent years and the discovery of cheaper substitutes have badly affected the industry. Supplies of copper are nearly used up, which could mean disaster for the Zambian economy. The Copperbelt now has improved transport links, such as the Tanzam Railway, which take the refined copper to various destinations. Look for ◉

MAP FEATURES

Coffee: A valuable cash crop, coffee is grown in Uganda, Kenya, Tanzania, and Rwanda. In recent years, coffee production in Kenya has increased rapidly. Look for ☘

Market gardening: Kenya has ideal conditions for growing vegetables and fruit, which are exported in large quantities, mainly to Europe. Look for ✈

Hydroelectric power: The Kariba Dam on the Zambezi River, built by Zambia and Zimbabwe, supplies both nations with electricity. Look for ⊞

Refugee camps: Warfare in neighboring countries has caused thousands of refugees to flee to temporary camps in the region. Look for ⛺

↓	Sugarcane	♠	Forest products
⚘	Coconuts	⚓	Fishing
⚘	Tea	⛏	Mining
⚘	Cotton	⬛	Industrial center
⚘	Tobacco	▤	Wildlife reserves

AFRICAN VILLAGE
East African villages usually consist of a series of huts enclosed by thorn fences. This aerial photo shows a village belonging to the Masai tribe. A Masai man may have several wives. Each wife has her own huts, enclosed by a fence. The livestock is taken out to graze by day and driven into the fenced enclosure at night.

0   100   200   300   400   500   KM

0   50   100   150   200   250   300   MILES

N

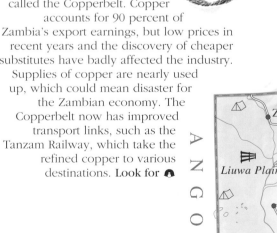

Solwezi

West Lunga

Cobalt

ANGOLA

Zambezi

ZAMBI

Liuwa Plain

Kafue

Kafue

Mongu

KAFUE FLATS

Zambezi

Choma

Senanga

Sioma

NAMIBIA

Livingstone

Victoria Falls

BOTSWANA

ZIMB

A   B   C   D   E   F   G   H

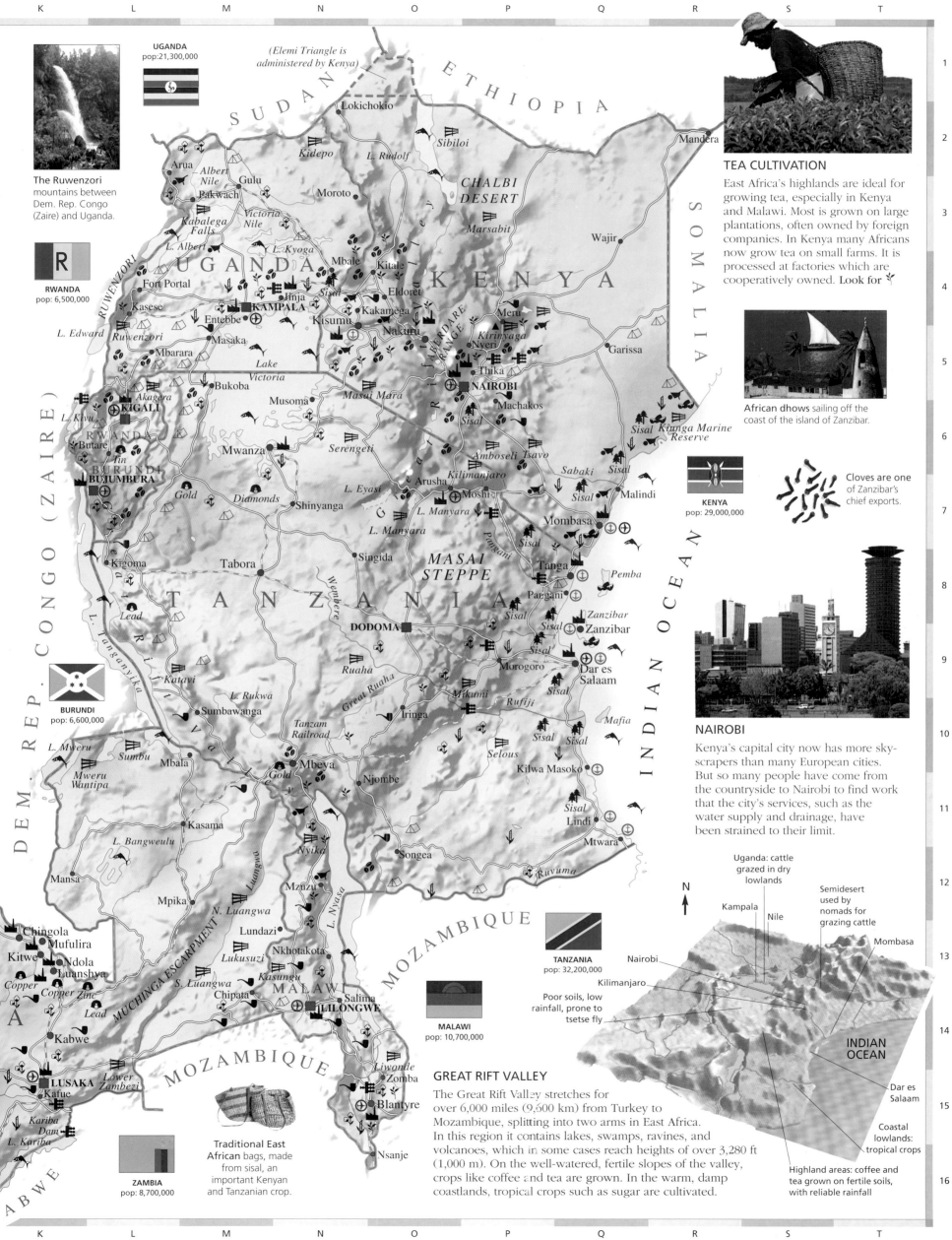

The Ruwenzori mountains between Dem. Rep. Congo (Zaire) and Uganda.

UGANDA
pop: 21,300,000

RWANDA
pop: 6,500,000

BURUNDI
pop: 6,600,000

KENYA
pop: 29,000,000

TANZANIA
pop: 32,200,000

MALAWI
pop: 10,700,000

ZAMBIA
pop: 8,700,000

(Elemi Triangle is administered by Kenya)

TEA CULTIVATION

East Africa's highlands are ideal for growing tea, especially in Kenya and Malawi. Most is grown on large plantations, often owned by foreign companies. In Kenya many Africans now grow tea on small farms. It is processed at factories which are cooperatively owned. **Look for** 🌱

African dhows sailing off the coast of the island of Zanzibar.

Cloves are one of Zanzibar's chief exports.

NAIROBI

Kenya's capital city now has more sky-scrapers than many European cities. But so many people have come from the countryside to Nairobi to find work that the city's services, such as the water supply and drainage, have been strained to their limit.

Traditional East African bags, made from sisal, an important Kenyan and Tanzanian crop.

GREAT RIFT VALLEY

The Great Rift Valley stretches for over 6,000 miles (9,600 km) from Turkey to Mozambique, splitting into two arms in East Africa. In this region it contains lakes, swamps, ravines, and volcanoes, which in some cases reach heights of over 3,280 ft (1,000 m). On the well-watered, fertile slopes of the valley, crops like coffee and tea are grown. In the warm, damp coastlands, tropical crops such as sugar are cultivated.

Uganda: cattle grazed in dry lowlands

Semidesert used by nomads for grazing cattle

Kampala

Nile

Mombasa

Nairobi

Kilimanjaro

Poor soils, low rainfall, prone to tsetse fly

INDIAN OCEAN

Dar es Salaam

Coastal lowlands: tropical crops

Highland areas: coffee and tea grown on fertile soils, with reliable rainfall

111

SOUTHERN AFRICA

THE WEALTHIEST and most dominant country in this region is South Africa. Black African lands were gradually settled in the 19th century by Dutch colonists, their descendants – the Afrikaners – and the British. When vast deposits of gold and diamonds were discovered in the late 19th century, the country became rich. In 1948 the government introduced a system of "separate development," called *apartheid*, which separated people according to their color and gave political power to whites only. This policy led to isolation and sanctions from the rest of the world's nations, which only ended after the abolition of apartheid. The first democratic elections were held in 1994. After years of conflict, South Africa has now become a more integrated society. Most of the countries around South Africa rely on its industries for trade and work. After 30 years of unrest, Namibia has won independence from South Africa. Mozambique and Angola are both struggling for survival after years of civil war. Zimbabwe has a relatively diverse economy, based on agriculture and its rich mineral resources.

SOUTH AFRICA'S THREE CAPITALS
PRETORIA – administrative capital
CAPE TOWN – legislative capital
BLOEMFONTEIN – judicial capital

The Ndebele people of South Africa often paint their houses in bright colors.

ANGOLA
pop: 12,000,000

NAMIBIA
pop: 1,700,000

The *ilimba* drum from Zimbabwe is made from the hard shell of a gourd.

SOUTH AFRICA
pop: 44,300,000

INDUSTRY

South Africa is the region's industrial leader. Johannesburg, the country's largest city, is seen here behind the huge mounds of earth excavated from the gold mines. Look for ⚒

URANIUM

Namibia is rich in copper, diamonds, tin, and other minerals. Its mining industry accounts for 90 percent of its export earnings. At Rössing, in the Namib Desert, uranium is extracted from a huge open-pit mine and exported abroad. Look for ⛏

MAP FEATURES

Fishing: Overfishing by both foreign and local fleets is a major threat to Namibia's once-rich fishing grounds. Controls are in operation. Look for 🐟

Oil: Civil war in Angola has disrupted industry, but its oil reserves – the only major ones in the region – so far have been little affected. Look for 🛢

Wildlife reserves: Most of the region's countries have set aside large areas as wildlife parks, which are popular tourist attractions. Look for 🦒

🐂 Cattle		🌿 Tea
🌾 Cereals		🚬 Tobacco
🍋 Citrus fruits		⛏ Mining
🍇 Wine		⚒ Coal
☕ Coffee		🏭 Industrial center

BUSHMEN

Bushmen – or *San* – are one of the few groups of hunter-gatherers left in Africa. These tiny people can be traced far back into African history. Today, some 1,000 bushmen still live in the harsh environment of the Kalahari Desert.

A lone thorn tree in the hot, sandy Namib Desert.

CAPE TOWN

Sprawled along the lower slopes of Table Mountain, and overlooking Table Bay, Cape Town has a spectacular setting. It is a busy port and the city where South Africa's parliament meets. Until the Suez Canal was opened, Cape Town lay on the main shipping route between Europe and Asia. Its harbor was often used by ships sheltering from the gales and stormy seas off the Cape of Good Hope.

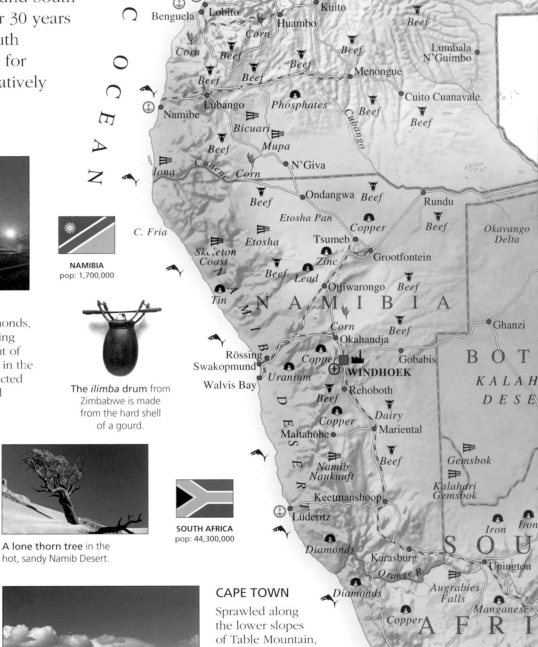

THE SANGOMA

In most African tribal societies there is a traditional healer called a *sangoma*, who cares for the sick, predicts the future, and generally looks after the well-being of the people.

CORN

Fresh corn

Corn is one of the main crops grown in this region. In the 1980s, the introduction of new kinds of seed and wider use of fertilizer greatly increased corn production. Because most men work in industry, women cultivate the crops required to feed the family. Look for 🌾

DIAMONDS

Botswana was one of the world's poorest nations when it became independent. Its economy has now been transformed by the discovery of diamonds in the Kalahari Desert, and diamonds make up 80 percent of its exports. Look for 🔷

SUN CITY

The tourist resort of Sun City lies to the west of Johannesburg. Visitors from the region, and the rest of the world, are drawn to its luxury hotels, casino, game park, and other attractions.

Acacia trees are a common sight on the savannah.

CIVIL WARS

Both the former Portuguese colonies of Mozambique and Angola were plunged into civil war following independence in 1975. Today, there is a fragile peace and both countries are beginning to rebuild their shattered economies.

Lake Kariba is a huge artificial lake.

ZIMBABWE pop: 11,900,000

BOTSWANA pop: 1,600,000

MOZAMBIQUE pop: 18,700,000

OSTRICH FARMS

Ostrich feathers were once in great demand as fashion accessories. Ostrich farmers grew rich and became known as Feather Barons. Feathers are no longer fashionable, but ostriches are still farmed for their meat around Oudtshoorn, in South Africa.

"TOWNSHIPS"

The apartheid system meant that many black people were forced to live in "townships," often some distance from their work. The largest and best known is Soweto. People from Soweto – which means "South-Western Townships" – travel daily to work in Johannesburg.

Platinum is mined in northwestern South Africa

SWAZILAND pop: 931,000

Platinum crystal

GOLD

Southern Africa has the richest deposits of valuable minerals in Africa. These miners are drilling for gold near Johannesburg, the area where gold was first discovered in 1886. This work is usually done by black Africans, but a mixed labor force will be more common in future. Gold from South Africa is often sold abroad in the form of coins called *Krugerrands*. Look for 🔶

LESOTHO pop: 2,200,000

LESOTHO'S WATER PROJECT

In contrast with surrounding areas, Lesotho's Maluti Mountains have plenty of water. Dams and tunnels are being constructed to transfer water and electricity to neighboring South Africa.

Matsoku Dam
Maluti Mts.
Lengthy tunnels transfer water between dams
Katse Dam
Mashai Dam
Mohale Dam
SOUTH AFRICA
LESOTHO
Tsoelike Dam
Ntoahae Dam
Orange R.

Map labels

TANZANIA
ZAMBIA
MALAWI
MOZAMBIQUE
ZIMBABWE
BOTSWANA
SWAZILAND
LESOTHO
SOUTH AFRICA
INDIAN OCEAN
Mozambique Channel

Ruvuma
L. Nyasa
Rio Lugenda
Mocímboa da Praia
Pemba
Nacala
Nampula
Moçambique
Tete
Zambezi
Quelimane
L. Cabora Bassa
Mana Pools
Chromium
Bindura
Chinhoyi
L. Kariba
HARARE
Chitungwiza
Victoria Falls
Hwange
Tin
Iron
Gold
Gorongosa
Mutare
Chimoio
Beira
Gweru
Gold
Corn
Chromium
Bulawayo
Masvingo
Chromium
Zinave
Rio Save
Corn
Diamonds
Orapa
Diamonds
Serowe
Selebi-Phikwe
Nickel
Beef
Banhine
Maun
Nxai Pan
Chobe
Beef
Corn
Mahalapye
Corn
Thohoyandou
Limpopo
Kruger
Inhambane
Pietersburg
Diamonds
Jwaneng
Wheat
GABORONE
Platinum
Lobatse
Platinum
Sun City
Diamonds
PRETORIA
Mmabatho
Platinum
Diamonds
Xai-Xai
Soweto
MBABANE
MAPUTO
Vryburg
Diamonds
Uranium
Johannesburg
Manzini
Klerksdorp
Vereeniging
Corn
SWAZILAND
Vaal
Gold
Corn
Beef
Gold
Beef
Diamonds
Corn
Gold
Corn
Beef
Kimberley
Wheat
LESOTHO
MASERU
Pietermaritzburg
BLOEMFONTEIN
Orange
Beef
Durban
Mafeteng
Tugela
De Aar
Corn
Corn
Umtata
Corn
Beef
Bisho
East London
Grahamstown
Beef
Port Elizabeth

N

0 100 200 300 400 500 600 KM
0 100 200 300 MILES

THE INDIAN OCEAN

SOME 5,000 ISLANDS – many of them surrounded by coral reefs – are scattered across the Indian Ocean. Beneath its surface three great mountain ranges converge toward the ocean's center – an area of strong seismic and volcanic activity. The ocean reaches its greatest depth – 24,400 ft (7,440 m) – in the Java Trench. More than one billion people – about a fifth of the world's population – live in the countries that surround the Indian Ocean, representing an immense range of cultures and religions. Heavy monsoon rain and tropical storms cause flooding along the ocean's northern coasts. The world's largest oil fields are located around the Persian Gulf.

KARACHI

In the mid-19th century a railroad was built along the Indus River valley to Karachi, which developed into a large port and industrial city. When Pakistan became an independent nation in 1947, Karachi became the country's capital. It has now been replaced by the new city of Islamabad in the north.

ISLANDS

The islands of the Indian Ocean include enormous ones like Madagascar, coral atolls like the Maldives, and volcanic islands like Réunion. All are threatened by rising sea levels, which reduce the area of land available. Coral reefs are being eroded, leaving islands increasingly exposed to ocean tides and flooding.

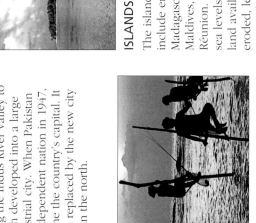

FISHING

Large-scale fishing is far less developed in the Indian Ocean than in either the Atlantic or Pacific. Fishing is difficult because there are relatively few areas of shallow sea. Small-scale fishing, however, provides a valuable source of food. Many fishermen, like these Sri Lankans, use basic and often inefficient methods. Tuna is the most important catch in the area. Look for 🐟

The loggerhead turtle is one of the Indian Ocean's many endangered species.

MONSOON

Farmers in the lands around the Indian Ocean are wholly dependent on the coming of the monsoon rains. In May or June, the western arm of the monsoon sweeps in from the Arabian Sea, bringing torrential downpours which move north through India. At the same time, the monsoon's eastern arm curves out of the Bay of Bengal, driving north as far as the Himalayan foothills. About 85 percent of India's annual rainfall occurs during the monsoon periods.

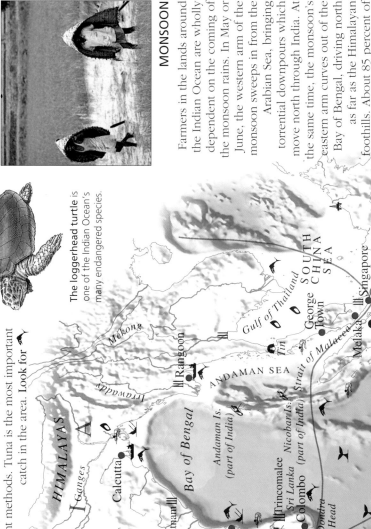

SUGAR

Sugarcane

Sugar was first brought to Mauritius by the Dutch in the 1600s. 90 percent of the island's arable farmland is covered by sugar plantations. But today sugar has been replaced in importance by textiles, which now account for nearly half the island's exports. Look for ➤

TOURISM

Hotel complex on an island in Mauritius

The Indian Ocean islands are great tourist attractions. The islands welcome the money this brings, but the sheer number of visitors threatens to destroy the islands' environment. Look for ✿

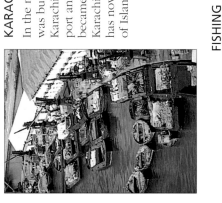

Once thought extinct, the coelacanth has been found, alive and well, off southeast Africa.

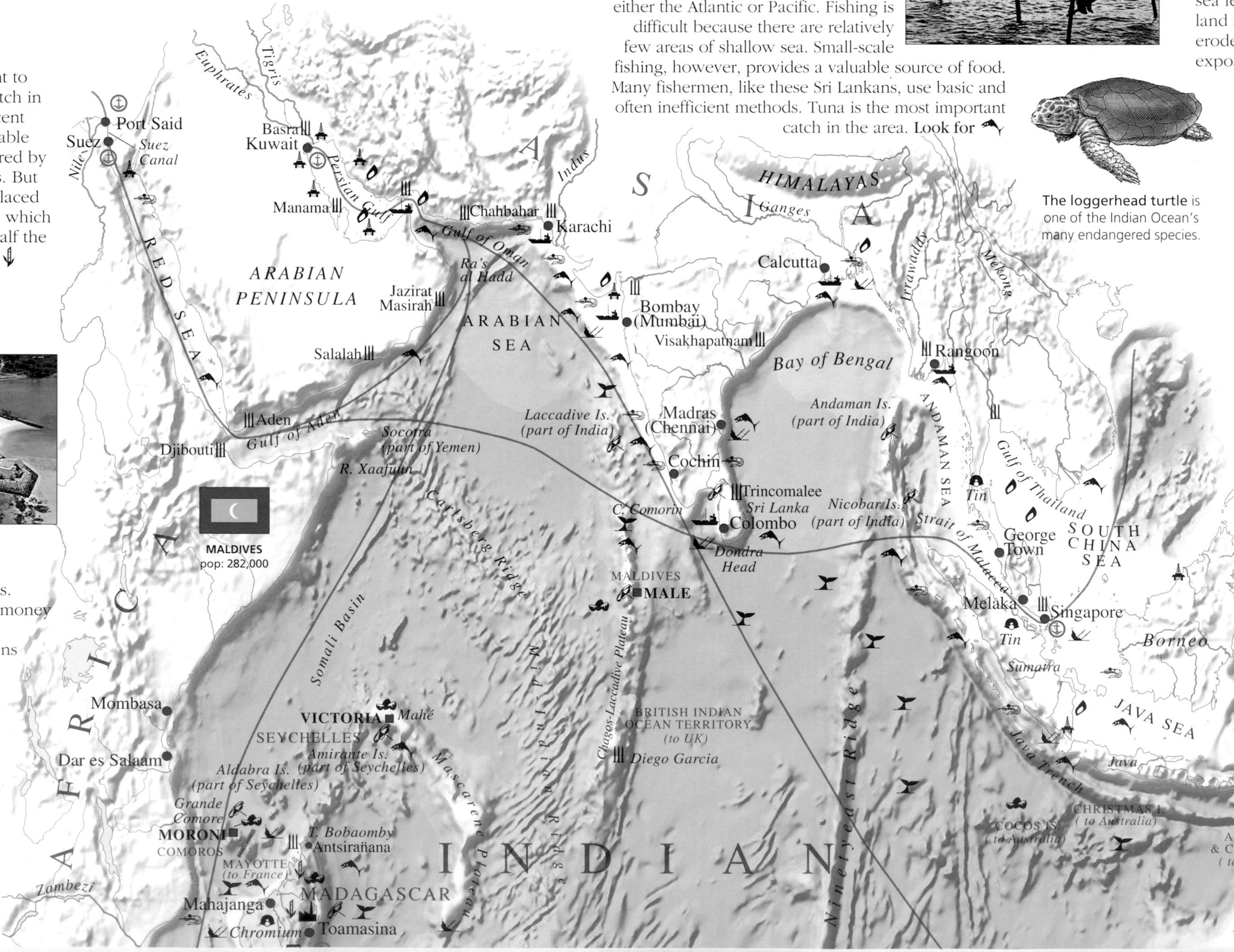

COMOROS pop: 672,000

MALDIVES pop: 282,000

SEYCHELLES
VICTORIA • Malé

COMOROS
MORONI

MADAGASCAR

ASHMORE & CARTIER IS. (to Australia)

CHRISTMAS I. (to Australia)

COCOS IS. (to Australia)

BRITISH INDIAN OCEAN TERRITORY (to UK)
Diego Garcia

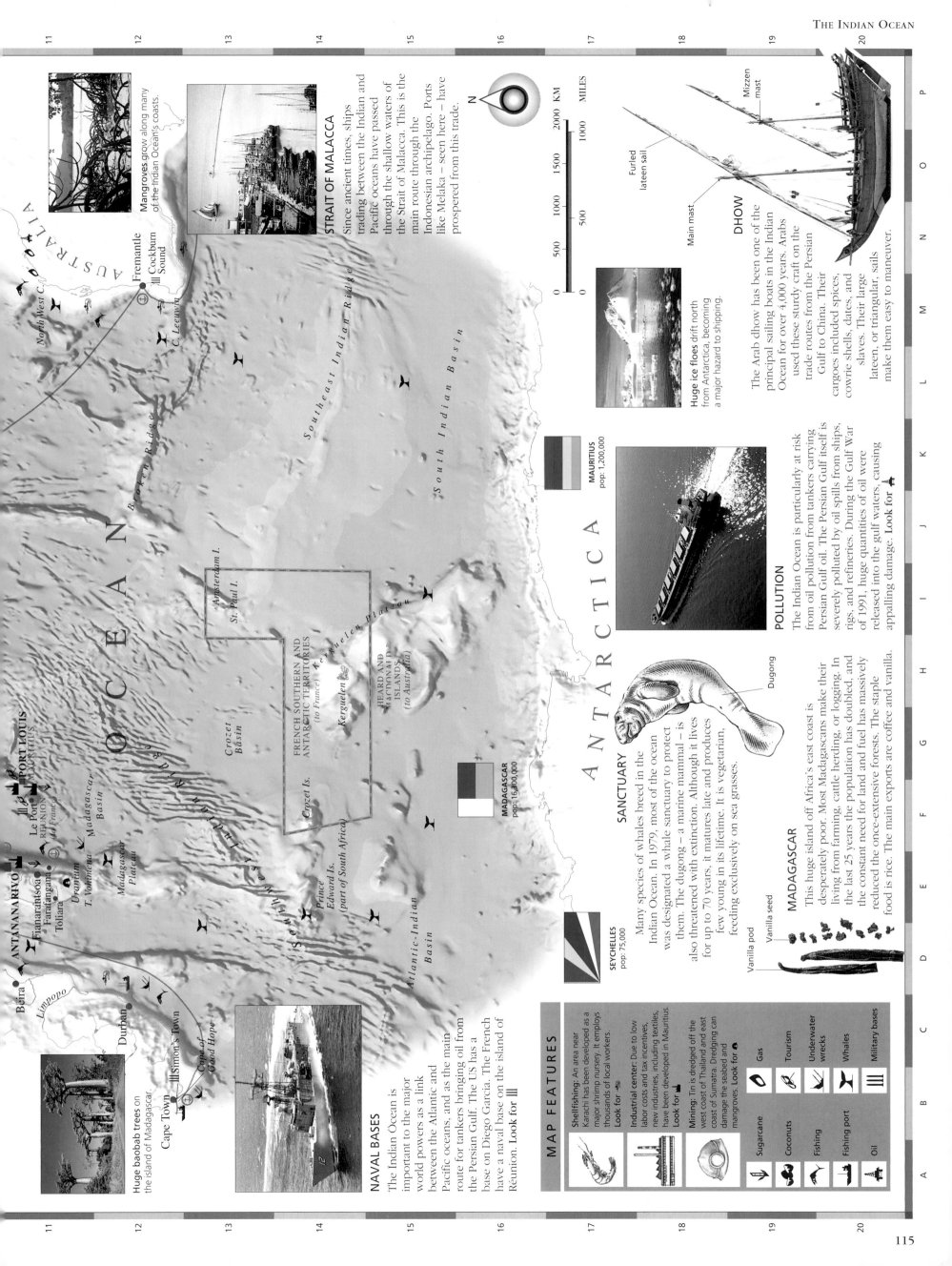

Mangroves grow along many of the Indian Ocean's coasts.

STRAIT OF MALACCA

Since ancient times, ships trading between the Indian and Pacific oceans have passed through the shallow waters of the Strait of Malacca. This is the main route through the Indonesian archipelago. Ports like Melaka – seen here – have prospered from this trade.

Huge ice floes drift north from Antarctica, becoming a major hazard to shipping.

DHOW

The Arab dhow has been one of the principal sailing boats in the Indian Ocean for over 4,000 years. Arabs used these sturdy craft on the trade routes from the Persian Gulf to China. Their cargoes included spices, cowrie shells, dates, and slaves. Their large lateen, or triangular, sails make them easy to maneuver.

Mizzen mast

Furled lateen sail

Main mast

POLLUTION

The Indian Ocean is particularly at risk from oil pollution from tankers carrying Persian Gulf oil. The Persian Gulf itself is severely polluted by oil spills from ships, rigs, and refineries. During the Gulf War of 1991, huge quantities of oil were released into the gulf waters, causing appalling damage. Look for ⚓

MAURITIUS pop: 1,200,000

MADAGASCAR pop: 16,300,000

SEYCHELLES pop: 75,000

SANCTUARY

Many species of whales breed in the Indian Ocean. In 1979, most of the ocean was designated a whale sanctuary to protect them. The dugong – a marine mammal – is also threatened with extinction. Although it lives for up to 70 years, it matures late and produces few young in its lifetime. It is vegetarian, feeding exclusively on sea grasses.

Dugong

MADAGASCAR

This huge island off Africa's east coast is desperately poor. Most Madagascans make their living from farming, cattle herding, or logging. In the last 25 years the population has doubled, and the constant need for land and fuel has massively reduced the once-extensive forests. The staple food is rice. The main exports are coffee and vanilla.

Vanilla seed

Vanilla pod

Huge baobab trees on the island of Madagascar.

NAVAL BASES

The Indian Ocean is important to the major world powers as a link between the Atlantic and Pacific oceans, and as the main route for tankers bringing oil from the Persian Gulf. The US has a base on Diego Garcia. The French have a naval base on the island of Réunion. Look for ⚓

MAP FEATURES

Shellfishing: An area near Karachi has been developed as a major shrimp nursery. It employs thousands of local workers. **Look for** ⬤

Industrial center: Due to low labor costs and tax incentives, new industries, including textiles, have been developed in Mauritius. **Look for** ⬤

Mining: Tin is dredged off the west coast of Thailand and east coast of Sumatra. Dredging can damage the seabed and mangroves. **Look for** ⬤

Sugarcane
Gas
Coconuts
Tourism
Fishing
Underwater wrecks
Fishing port
Whales
Oil
Military bases

AUSTRALIA
North West C.
Fremantle
Cockburn Sound
C. Leeuwin
Broken Ridge
Southeast Indian Ridge
South Indian Basin
OCEAN
ANTARCTICA
Amsterdam I.
St. Paul I.
Kerguelen Plateau
Kerguelen
FRENCH SOUTHERN AND ANTARCTIC TERRITORIES (to France)
HEARD AND MCDONALD ISLANDS (to Australia)
Crozet Basin
Crozet Is.
Prince Edward Is. (part of South Africa)
Atlantic-Indian Basin
Southwest Indian Ridge
Madagascar Plateau
Madagascar Basin
PORT LOUIS
MAURITIUS
Le Port
RÉUNION (to France)
ANTANANARIVO
Fianarantsoa
Farafangana
Toliara
T. Vohimena
Uranium
Beira
Durban
Limpopo
Cape Town
Simon's Town
Cape of Good Hope

Cedar of
Lebanon
Cedrus libani
Height:
130 ft (40 m)
☐ !

Arabian oryx
Oryx leucoryx
Height:
4 ft (1.2 m)
☐ !

Baikal seal
Phoca sibirica
Length:
5 ft (1.5 m)
Only found
in Lake Baikal

Darkling beetle
Sternodes species
Length:
1 in (2 cm)
☐

Reindeer
Rangifer tarandus
Body length: 7 ft (2.2 m)
☐

Common hamster
Cricetus cricetus
Length: 12 in (30 cm)
☐

Pallas's cat
Felis manul
Length: 26 in (65 cm)
☐

Waxwing
Bombycilla garrulus
Length: 8 in (18 cm)

Gray wolf
Canis lupus
Length: 5 ft (1.4 m)
☐ !

NORTH AND WEST ASIA

NORTH AND WEST ASIA contains some of the world's most inhospitable environments. In the south, the Arabian Peninsula is almost entirely a baking hot desert where no plants can grow. To the north, a belt of rugged, snow-capped mountains and high plateaus cross the continent. The climate becomes drier and more extreme towards the center of the continent. Dry hot summers contrast with bitterly cold winters. Cold deserts give way to treeless plains known as steppe, then to huge marshes, and to the world's largest needleleaf forest. In the extreme north, both land and sea are frozen for most of the year. Only in summer do the top layers of soil thaw briefly allowing plants of the tundra, such as moss and lichen, to cover the land.

■ COLD FOREST
Strong but flexible trunks and a tentlike shape help needleleaf trees to withstand the great weight of snow that covers them throughout the long winter.

HOT BATHS
These strange white terraces formed in southwestern Asia in much the same way that a kettle develops scale. Underground water heated by volcanic activity dissolves minerals in rocks. These are deposited when the water reaches the surface and cools.

Blue turquoise, a semiprecious stone mainly found in cold areas of north Asia.

■ DROUGHT-TOLERANT TREES
Plants growing near the Black Sea minimize water loss during the long hot summers. Most have wax-covered leaves through which little water can escape.

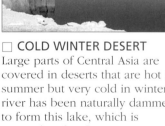

■ REGENERATING FOREST
Unlike many plants, juniper trees are able to withstand the acid soils of needleleaf forests. Here junipers cover the floor of a dense pine forest.

The fossilized head of
Gallimimus, an ostrichlike
dinosaur that once lived in Asia.

■ SINAI'S ROCK "MUSHROOMS"
In deserts, sand particles whipped along by high-speed winds create natural sculptures. Rock at the base of the "mushroom" has been more heavily eroded than rock above, leading to these unusual landforms.

■ ▲ VOLCANO
There are more than 30 active volcanoes on the Kamchatka peninsula, part of the Pacific Ocean's "Ring of Fire." Volcanic activity is due to the deep underground movements of the Eurasian plate.

■ FROZEN RIVER
The River Lena rises near Lake Baikal, the world's deepest and oldest freshwater lake. Like other Siberian rivers, it flows into the Arctic Ocean and is frozen over for eight or nine months of the year.

HOT DESERTS
The Arabian desert is one of the hottest and driest places in the world. Temperatures frequently reach 120°F (45°C) and very little rain falls.

CROSS-SECTION THROUGH NORTH AND WEST ASIA

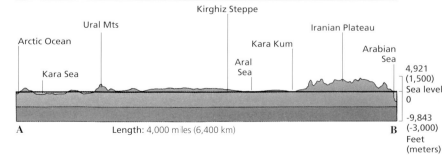

Kirghiz Steppe
Ural Mts
Iranian Plateau
Arctic Ocean
Kara Kum
Kara Sea
Aral Sea
Arabian Sea
4,921 (1,500)
Sea level 0
-9,843 (-3,000)
Feet (meters)
A
Length: 4,000 miles (6,400 km)
B

■ COLD WINTER DESERT
Large parts of Central Asia are covered in deserts that are hot in summer but very cold in winter. A river has been naturally dammed to form this lake, which is unusual in this dry region.

Siberian iris
Iris sibirica
Height: 4 ft (1.2 m)

The head of a fossilized Benthosuchus, which lived in Asia over 200 million years ago.

■ BROADLEAF DECIDUOUS FOREST

Broadleaf trees, such as oaks, have larger, wider leaves than needleleaf trees, such as pines. Broadleaf (or deciduous) trees shed all their leaves at once in fall; needleleaf (or coniferous) trees shed and replace their leaves all through the year.

ARCTIC OCEAN · North Pole
NORTH AMERICAN PLATE
EURASIAN PLATE
Bering Strait
BERING SEA
Aleutian Basin
Vulkan Klyuchevskaya Sopka 15,583 ft
KAMCHATKA
EAST SIBERIAN SEA
Arctic Circle
LAPTEV SEA
VERKHOYANSKIY KHREBET
Lena
SEA OF OKHOTSK
Sakhalin

Greenland
Franz Josef Land
Severnaya Zemlya
POLUOSTROV TAYMYR
CENTRAL SIBERIAN PLATEAU
STANOVOY KHREBET
Amur

Novaya Zemlya
KARA SEA
BARENTS SEA
POLUOSTROV YAMAL
Ob
Yenisey
Lake Baikal
Kerulen
MANCHURIAN PLAIN
Amur

NORWEGIAN SEA
Arctic Circle
Gora Narodnaya 6,214 ft
WEST SIBERIAN PLAIN
Ob
Angara
Yellow River
GREAT PLAIN OF CHINA
Yangtze

BALTIC SEA
URAL MOUNTAINS
ALTAI MOUNTAINS
ASIA
GOBI

EUROPE
KIRGHIZ STEPPE
Lake Zaysan
Ozero 'Alakol'
DZUNGARIA
TIEN SHAN
Lake Balkhash
Ili
Pik Pobedy 24,407 ft
TAKLA MAKAN DESERT
Yangtze

BLACK SEA
CAUCASUS
Caspian Sea
Aral Sea
Syr Darya
KYZYL KUM
Amu Darya
KARA KUM
Lenin Peak 23,407 ft
PAMIRS
Communism Peak 24,591 ft
HINDU KUSH
PLATEAU OF TIBET
HIMALAYAS
Tropic of Cancer

EURASIAN PLATE
ANATOLIAN PLATE
AFRICAN PLATE
ANATOLIA
EURASIAN PLATE
IRANIAN PLATE

MEDITERRANEAN SEA
Euphrates
Tigris
GREAT SALT DESERT
IRANIAN PLATEAU
DASHT-E LUT
ZAGROS MOUNTAINS
Indus
THAR DESERT
Ganges
Mouths of the Ganges
Irrawaddy
Mekong

Dead Sea -1,444 ft
SYRIAN DESERT
Sinai
AN NAFUD
Persian Gulf
Gulf of Oman
IRANIAN PLATE
DECCAN
Bay of Bengal
Gulf of Thailand

AFRICA
Tropic of Cancer
RED SEA
ARABIAN PENINSULA
AR RUB' AL KHALI (EMPTY QUARTER)
ARABIAN PLATE
INDO-AUSTRALIAN PLATE
ARABIAN SEA
Sri Lanka
EURASIAN PLATE
ANDAMAN SEA

ARABIAN PLATE
AFRICAN PLATE
Socotra
Gulf of Aden
Arabian Basin
INDO-AUSTRALIAN PLATE
Ceylon Plain
INDIAN OCEAN
Equator
Cocos Basin

TURKEY AND CYPRUS

SITUATED PARTLY IN EUROPE and partly in Asia, Turkey is also balanced between modern Europe and its Islamic past. For 600 years, the Ottoman Turks ruled over a great empire covering a quarter of Europe, but by the early 20th century their empire had disappeared. In the 1920s, Mustapha Kemal Atatürk forcibly modernized Turkish society. Today, Turkey is becoming increasingly industrialized; textile and food-processing industries dominate the economy. In the central plateau, however, farmers and herders live as they have done for centuries, adapting their lives to the harsh environment. To the north, the Black Sea is rich in fish, and the fertile areas around its shores are well suited to farming. The beautiful western and southern coasts are strewn with the remains of ancient Greek settlements, attracting 1.5 million tourists to Turkey every year.

ISTANBUL

Istanbul is divided in two by a strait of water called the Bosporus. One part of the city is in Europe, the other in Asia. Its buildings are also a mix of East and West: grand mosques, graceful minarets, and exotic bazaars rub shoulders with modern shops, offices, and restaurants.

TURKEY
pop: 63,800,000

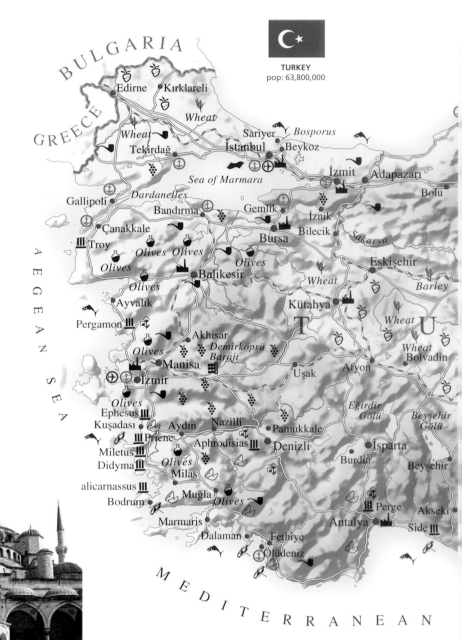

The harbor and castle of St. Peter at Bodrum.

STREET TRADERS

Large numbers of people from the countryside go to Turkey's cities to try to make a living. Many of them sell goods, food, or drink on the streets or from makeshift market stalls. Others work as shoeshiners, carrying their equipment in highly decorated brass cases.

A CLASSICAL LEGACY

The temple of Athena in Priene is one of Turkey's many ancient treasures. The Aegean coast was colonized by the ancient Greeks as early as 700 BC. Many people go to Turkey to visit the dramatic remains of Greek cities and temples.
Look for ⌗

Blue Mosque, Istanbul

MOSQUE

Modern Turkey does not have a state religion. It was once an Islamic country, but in the 20th century reforms limited the powers of the clerics and introduced civil law. Recently, however, there has been an Islamic revival, and modern Turks are going back to many customs from their rich Islamic past.

Dried apricot
Almond
Hazelnut
Peach
Fig

This strange landscape is in Cappadocia, central Turkey.

MAP FEATURES

 Tobacco: Turkey is a major producer. Dark Turkish tobacco is grown around the Black Sea and Aegean coasts. **Look for** ⌇

 Tourism: Coastal resorts are developing rapidly. Airports cater for growing numbers of visitors from northern Europe. **Look for** ✈

 Dams: Ambitious dam-building programs, especially in the southeast, are being used for hydroelectric power and for watering farmland. **Look for** ⌗

Cereals		Cotton	
Sugar beet		Fishing	
Citrus fruits		Carpet weaving	
Wine		Industrial center	
 Vegetable oil		⌗ Archaeological site	

ANKARA

Ankara has been the capital of Turkey since 1923. It is a planned modern city with boulevards, parks, and many high-rise apartments. Until recently, the city suffered from terrible pollution, caused by people burning brown coal, or lignite, for heating. Now, clean natural gas is piped into the city from the Russian Federation.

AGRICULTURE

Turkey has a varied landscape and climate. This means that many different types of crop can be grown there, and the Turks are able to produce all their own food. Cereals, sugar beet, grapes, nuts, cotton, and tobacco are all major exports. Hazelnuts are grown along the shores of the Black Sea. Figs, peaches, olives, and grapes are grown along the Mediterranean coast and in the coastal lowlands. Cereals are cultivated on the central plateau. Farms are still relatively small and only gradually being modernized, but despite this productivity is high.

TURKISH FOOD

Typical Turkish food consists of fresh fruit, vegetables, meat, and fish, flavored with spices such as cinnamon and cumin. Lamb is the most common meat. It is often grilled on a skewer to make a kebab, or minced and made into spiced meatballs, served with rice or cracked wheat (*bulgur*). Yogurt is eaten everywhere, often mixed with cucumber, garlic, or mint to make a refreshing side dish.

Bulgur wheat

Tomato

Olive

Bay leaf

Yogurt with cucumber

Lamb shish kebab

Valuable Black Sea oyster beds are being destroyed by these whelks.

Veined rapa whelk

KILIMS

Knotted-pile carpets, called *kilims*, were first made many centuries ago by the Turks' nomadic ancestors. Each region of Turkey produces carpets with slightly different patterns and colors, although today chemical dyes are often used instead of the traditional vegetable colorings. **Look for**

Anchovies are caught in the Black Sea.

Map labels

BLACK SEA

Sinop
Zonguldak
Kastamonu
Karabük
ILGAZ DAĞLARI
Altınkaya Barajı
Samsun
Ünye
Ordu
Giresun
Trabzon
Rize
Hopa
Artvin
Kars
GEORGIA
ARMENIA
IRAN

Çankırı
Amasya
Çorum
Yeşilırmak
Tokat
Kelkit Çayı
Gümüşhane
Erzincan
Erzurum
Ağrı
Barley

Wheat
ANKARA
Yozgat
Kırıkkale
Sivas
Kızıl Irmak
Divriği
Tunceli
Barley
Bingöl
Muş
Barley
L. Van
Van

Barley
Hirfanlı Barajı
Kırşehir
Wheat
TURKEY
CAPPADOCIA
Göreme
Nevşehir
Kayseri
Keban Barajı
Elazığ
Murat Nehri
Tatvan
Bitlis
Siirt
Hakkâri

L. Tuz
Barley
Aksaray
Malatya
Karakaya Barajı
Wheat
Diyarbakır
Tigris
Batman

Konya
Niğde
Adıyaman
Kahramanmaraş
Mardin
IRAQ

Wheat
Ereğli
Atatürk Barajı
Gaziantep
Şanlıurfa

TAURUS MTS.
Karaman
Seyhan
Wheat
Ceyhan
Wheat
Kilis
SYRIA
Adana
Osmaniye
Tarsus
Mersin
İskenderun
Olives
Antakya
Alanya
Silifke
Anamur

SEA
Tatlısu (Akanthou)
Dipkarpaz (Rizokárpason)
Girne (Kyrenia)
Salamis
TURKISH REPUBLIC OF NORTHERN CYPRUS
Polis
NICOSIA
Larnaca
Famagusta
Pafos
Limassol
CYPRUS

In 1983 the north of the island proclaimed itself the Turkish Republic of Northern Cyprus. It is only recognized by Turkey.

A 10th-century church on Lake Van in eastern Turkey.

N

0 50 100 150 200 KM
0 50 100 150 MILES

Mohair comes from the Angora goat, native to central Turkey.

CYPRUS pop: 766,000

Glazed tiles made in Iznik decorate many Turkish mosques.

RURAL LIFE

Life in the high plateaus of central Turkey is very hard. The winters are severe and the landscape is desolate. Most people live as nomadic herders or small-scale farmers. Many people leave these areas to live in the overcrowded cities, or go to the rich countries of northern Europe as "guest workers."

Turkish delight

Turkish coffee pot

CYPRUS

Cyprus is the largest island in the east Mediterranean. Cypriots are a mixture of Greek and Turkish speakers. After independence in 1959, conflict between the two communities resulted in the United Nations sending a peacekeeping force, which still remains. Despite their presence, there was a Turkish invasion in 1974. Since then the island has been split into two parts.

WOMEN WORKERS

Although Turkish women are equal by law, traditions of male authority still persist, especially in the countryside. It is common to see old women doing backbreaking work in the fields, while their husbands look on. On the other hand, some Turkish women have succeeded in powerful jobs as politicians, judges, or bank directors.

COFFEE

Turkey, like other Middle Eastern countries, has a long tradition of coffee drinking. Turkish coffee is made by pounding the beans to a powder and then boiling this with sugar to make a strong, dark brew. Coffee houses are favorite meeting places, where people also smoke pipes, play cards, and chat.

THE NEAR EAST

CAUGHT BETWEEN the continents of Europe and Asia, the Near East is bordered on the west by the fertile coasts of the Mediterranean Sea, and on the east by the arid deserts of Arabia. Some of the world's earliest civilizations were born here, while the history of three of the world's greatest religions – Judaism, Christianity, and Islam – is closely bound up with the region. Imperial conquerors, crusaders, and Muslim warriors battled fiercely over this territory, and by the 17th century much of the region was part of the Turkish Ottoman empire. In 1918, the region came under the control of Britain and France; a dangerous mixture of religions and passionate nationalism plunged the area into conflict. Today, Lebanon is emerging from a fierce civil war between Christians and Muslims. Israel, which became a Jewish state in 1948, has been involved in numerous wars with its neighbors and there is considerable unrest among its minority Palestinian population. Many Palestinian refugees, who have left Israel, are living in camps in Jordan and Lebanon. Despite these problems, the Near East continues to survive economically. Israel is highly industrialized and a world leader in advanced farming techniques. Syria has its own reserves of oil and is gradually becoming more industrialized.

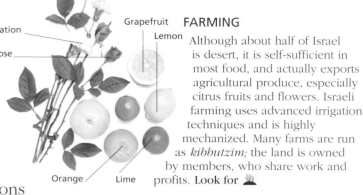

Carnation
Rose
Grapefruit
Lemon
Orange
Lime

FARMING

Although about half of Israel is desert, it is self-sufficient in most food, and actually exports agricultural produce, especially citrus fruits and flowers. Israeli farming uses advanced irrigation techniques and is highly mechanized. Many farms are run as *kibbutzim;* the land is owned by members, who share work and profits. Look for

JERUSALEM THE GOLDEN

The historic city of Jerusalem is held sacred by three major religions: Judaism, Christianity, and Islam. Throughout its history, it has been the object of pilgrimage and religious crusades. For Jews, the Wailing Wall, seen here, is the holiest site, while the Dome of the Rock is sacred to Muslims.

Skullcap, yarmulke

JUDAISM

Judaism is one of the oldest religions in the world. Jews believe in one God and follow codes of behavior based on the *Torah*. This holy book contains the first part of the Old Testament, which is written in Hebrew, plus other scriptures. Modern Hebrew is the official language of Israel.

The *Torah*

Prayer shawl

WATER WARS

Water is in very short supply throughout this region. Where water resources are shared (for example, Israel and Jordan share the Jordan River), disputes can occur. Israel leads the way in irrigation techniques. Fields are watered by drip irrigation – holes in pipes dispense exactly the right amount of water required, avoiding wastage.

UZI GUNS

Israel is a major arms producer, developing weapons for its own army, such as this Uzi gun, as well as medium-range missiles to deter Arab enemies. Military service in the Israel Defence Force (IDF) is compulsory for all Israeli citizens. Men must serve three years, unmarried women two years.

Lake Tiberias, known in the Bible as the Sea of Galilee.

Dead Sea mud is used as a skin conditioner and cure for arthritis

DEAD SEA MUD

The Dead Sea, 1,300 ft (400 m) below sea level, is an enclosed salt lake. Salt levels are six times higher than in other seas, so no fish live in these waters. The Dead Sea is rich in minerals, some of which have medical properties.

Soap made from Dead Sea mud

MAP FEATURES

Cotton: Syria's most profitable cash crop is cotton. The area of land devoted to cotton has been expanded in recent years. Look for

Tourism: People come to this region from all over the world to visit archaeological sites, ancient cities, and holy places. Look for 📷

Refugee camps: Palestinian refugees have fled from Israel to Jordan and Lebanon. Many fled to Jordan from Kuwait after the 1991 Gulf War. Look for

🌾 Cereals		⛏ Mining
🌱 Sugar beet		Oil
Citrus fruits		Industrial center
Vegetable oil		Tourism
Tobacco		Irrigated agriculture

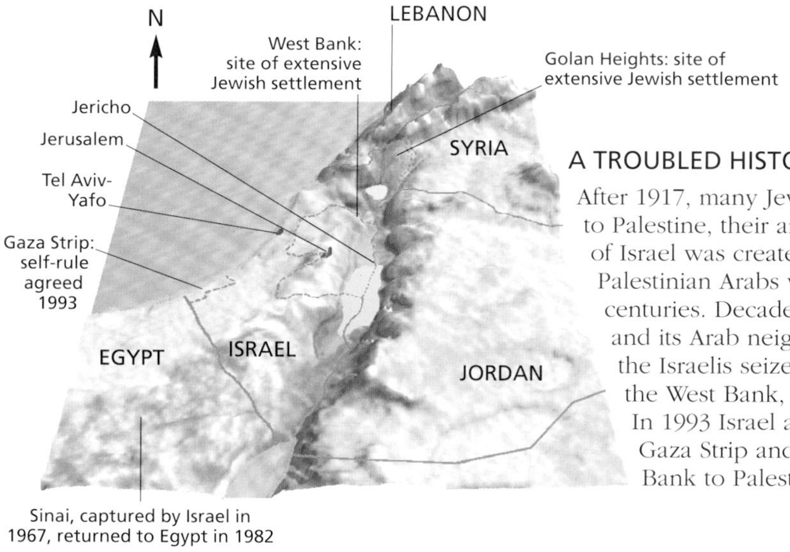

N ↑

West Bank: site of extensive Jewish settlement

LEBANON

Golan Heights: site of extensive Jewish settlement

Jericho
Jerusalem
Tel Aviv-Yafo

SYRIA

Gaza Strip: self-rule agreed 1993

EGYPT   ISRAEL   JORDAN

Sinai, captured by Israel in 1967, returned to Egypt in 1982

A TROUBLED HISTORY

After 1917, many Jews emigrated from Europe to Palestine, their ancient homeland. The State of Israel was created in 1948, driving out the Palestinian Arabs who had also lived there for centuries. Decades of conflict between Israel and its Arab neighbors followed. In 1967 the Israelis seized Sinai, the Gaza Strip, the West Bank, and the Golan Heights. In 1993 Israel agreed to restore the Gaza Strip and parts of the West Bank to Palestinian home rule.

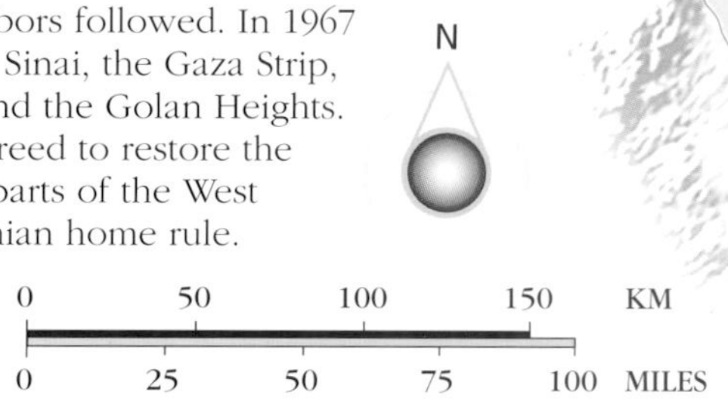

SAN

Gulf of Suez

N

0	50	100	150	KM
0	25	50	75	100 MILES

WAR-TORN LEBANON

Lebanon became independent in 1944. Christians, about 40 percent of the population, held most of the wealth and power. The Muslim majority felt discriminated against. This grievance exploded into a bitter civil war in 1975. Democracy has now been restored and the devastated streets of Beirut are gradually being rebuilt.

The pomegranate fruit is grown in Israel.

LEBANON
pop: 3,200,000

ISRAEL
pop: 5,900,000

Krak des Chevaliers is a 12th-century crusader castle in Syria.

SYRIA
pop: 15,300,000

Hubble-bubble tobacco pipe

HUBBLE-BUBBLE

Throughout the Arab world, men enjoy spending their leisure hours in cafés, drinking tea or coffee, playing cards or backgammon, and smoking. Often they smoke pipes called hubble-bubbles which draw the smoke into the mouth through water and a long tube. Tobacco is grown in Syria and exported to other countries in the region. Look for ⤵

DAMASCUS SOUK

Damascus, the capital of Syria, is one of the oldest cities in the world – its history goes back 4,000 years. At its center, next to the main mosque, is a typical Middle Eastern *souk* (marketplace). Small, winding covered streets are lined with stalls selling a wide range of produce. Behind the stalls are the workshops where craftsmen make their wares.

The Arabian *tibia*, one of the rich variety of shells found in the Red Sea.

The hills and plateaus of Israel's Negev desert.

Golan Heights: Occupied by Israel

West Bank and Gaza Strip: Occupied by Israel under Palestinian administration

JORDAN
pop: 6,000,000

Wadi Rum in Jordan, where the desert meets sandstone hills.

ROSE-RED CITY

Petra, founded in about 400 BC, was the capital city of the Nabateans, a people from the Arabian Peninsula who grew wealthy on the profits of the Arabian incense and spice trade. The city is located deep in a canyon, and its buildings are carved out of the soft pink limestone of the canyon walls. Large numbers of visitors come to Jordan to see ancient sites such as Petra, and to enjoy the resorts and scuba diving in the Red Sea.

BEDOUIN

The Bedouin are nomadic herders who live in dry regions of the Near East and Africa. They keep cattle, sheep, and goats, which provide them with milk and meat and can be sold for food such as wheat, dates, and coffee. The Bedouin move from place to place, following the wet and dry seasons, in search of grazing land for their animals.

A   B   C   D   E   F   G   H   I   J

THE MIDDLE EAST

THE WORLD'S FIRST CITIES grew up about 5,500 years ago in the area between the Tigris and Euphrates rivers. The land in this region is dry, but these early people created ingenious irrigation techniques to direct the river water on to their fields of crops. In AD 570, the Prophet Mohammed, founder of the Islamic religion, was born in Mecca in modern-day Saudi Arabia. Islam soon spread throughout the Middle East, where it is now the dominant religion, and then to the rest of the world. In recent years, the discovery of oil has brought great wealth to the region, and with it, rapid industrial and social change. Both Iran and Iraq earn huge revenues from oil, but they have been troubled by dictatorship and political unrest, as well as by a 10-year war. In 1991, the region was devastated by the Gulf War, which brought UN troops to the Middle East to fight against Iraq.

ARAB DRESS

Khimar, veil worn by women

Hirz, amulet charm case

Kufiyah, male headdress

Aqaal, used to secure headdress

In summer, when temperatures in the region reach 122°F (50°C), layers of loose robes and a headdress are worn to make the heat bearable.

MAP FEATURES

Archaeological sites: The ancient cities of the Middle East, such as Ur, date back to 3,500 BC. They are the oldest cities in the world. Look for ⛩

Dams: A series of dams and barrages have been built along the Tigris and Euphrates to provide water for the dry plains of southern Iraq. Look for ▦

Industrial center: Saudi Arabia's economy has been dominated by oil. It is seeking to widen its range of industries. Look for ⚒

Cereals		Oil
Dates		Gas
Rice		Carpet weaving
Fishing		Desalination plants

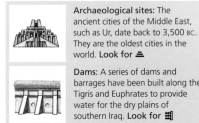

YEMEN

Unlike the rest of the Arabian Peninsula, Yemen has enough rainfall to water its crops. Most crops are grown on mountain terraces in the highlands. The country is self-sufficient in barley, lentils, sorghum, corn, and coffee. Look for 🌿

MIDDLE EASTERN FOOD

Farming in the Arabian Peninsula has been transformed by new irrigation methods. Saudi Arabia now exports wheat; the United Arab Emirates exports vegetables. Elsewhere, lentils and chickpeas are the main food crops.

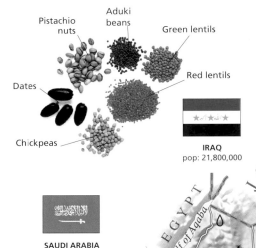

Pistachio nuts

Aduki beans

Green lentils

Dates

Red lentils

Chickpeas

KUWAIT
pop: 1,800,000

IRAQ
pop: 21,800,000

SAUDI ARABIA
pop: 20,200,000

For centuries, Marsh Arabs have lived in the swampy delta of the Tigris and Euphrates.

ISLAM

Mecca is Islam's holiest place; according to Islamic teaching, every Muslim should make a pilgrimage to the city. Believers should also pray five times a day, give alms to the poor, and fast during the month-long period of *Ramadan*.

Camels, known as "ships of the desert," can go for days without water. They are used to carry loads.

MAKING THE DESERT BLOOM

Water, scarce all over this region, is carefully managed. More than 60 percent of the world's desalination plants are on the Arabian Peninsula. They are used to extract the salt from seawater to make it drinkable. Look for ◊

YEMEN
pop: 16,900,000

The minaret of the Great Mosque at Samarra, Iraq.

Yemen's capital, Sana, dates back to the 7th century.

BAGHDAD

Baghdad, Iraq's capital since 1918, has grown dramatically over the last 20 years but was badly damaged during the Gulf War. The city has been rebuilt. Massive monuments to President Hussein once again adorn its streets.

SYRIA

Wheat
Annah
Hit
Wadi Hawran
Wadi al Ghadaf
JORDAN
SYRIAN DESERT
An Nabk
EGYPT
Gulf of Aqaba
'Ar'ar
Al Jawf   Sakakah
Tabuk
AN NAFUD
Wheat
Ha'il
HEJAZ
Wheat
Buraydah
Wheat
NEJD
Yanbu al Bahr   Medina
RED SEA
Jedda
Mecca
Ta'if
SAU
ARA
Wheat
ASIR
Al Bahah
Wheat
Barley
AR RUB
Abha   Khamis Mushayt
Najran
Sa'dah
RAMLAT
Barley
Kamaran   Barley
Jizan   Mar'ib
Hajjah   SANA
Hodeida   YE
Millet
Dhamar   HA
Millet
Ibb   Al Bayda
Ta'izz
Al Mukha   Lahij   Zinjibar
Bab el Mandeb   Aden

K L M N O P Q R S T

KURDS

There are 25 million Kurds. They are one of the largest groups of stateless people in the world. Their homeland, Kurdistan, straddles three countries: Turkey, Iraq, and Iran. Many Kurds were forced into refugee camps by the Gulf War. Kurdish separatists are in open conflict with the Turkish government.

Shahyad Monument

TEHRAN

The last shah (king) of Iran used his great wealth to modernize the country by building dams, power stations, factories, and roads. He ruled as a dictator, and the cities of Iran were filled with monuments in his name. Islamic fundamentalists overthrew the shah in 1979.

IRAN
pop: 73,100,000

TEXTILES

Iran is famous for its superb handmade carpets. They are produced by a combination of weaving and knotting the wool, often using patterns which are several hundred years old. They are colored with vegetable dyes. Look for

Finely embroidered textiles like this saddlebag are typically Kurdish.

UNITED ARAB EMIRATES
pop: 2,400,000

OMAN
pop: 2,500,000

QATAR
pop: 579,000

The Zagros Mountains lie in southwestern Iran.

OIL

The discovery of oil in the Persian Gulf region has brought enormous wealth to the Middle East. The region now supplies 30 percent of the world's oil; Saudi Arabia alone produces a tenth of the world's total. Pipelines cross the desert, and huge tankers pick up oil from the coastal terminals, making the gulf one of the world's busiest seaways. Look for

An oil pipeline snakes across the Arabian desert.

BAHRAIN
pop: 594,000

TURKEY
ARMENIA
AZERBAIJAN
CASPIAN SEA
TURKMENISTAN
AFGHANISTAN
PAKISTAN

Dahuk
Nineveh
Mosul
Arbil
Kirkuk
Tikrit
Samarra
Ar Ramadi
BAGHDAD
Babylon
Karbala
Al Hillah
An Najaf
Al Kut
Ad Diwaniyah
Al 'Amarah
An Nasiriyah
Ur
Basra
Az Zubayr
Abadan
KUWAIT
KUWAIT
Ash Shu'aybah

L. Urmia
Tabriz
Orumiyeh
Ardabil
Rasht
Zanjan
Qazvin
Amol
Sari
Gorgan
Karaj
TEHRAN
Semnan
Sabzevar
Neyshabur
Mashhad

Sanandaj
Khanaqin
Hamadan
Bakhtaran
Ilam
Borujerd
Arak
Qom
Kashan
Dezful
Isfahan
Shahr-e Kord
Yazd
Shiraz
Pasargadae
Persepolis
Bushire
Bandar-e Abbas
Kerman
Zahedan
Jask
Chabahar

Bartey
Wheat
Wheat
Wheat
Wheat
Wheat
Wheat
Wheat
Wheat
Wheat
Wheat
Wheat
Wheat
Wheat
Barley
Wheat

ELBURZ MTS
DASHT-E KAVIR
DASHT-E LUT
ZAGROS MTS
Hamun-e Jaz Murian
Qeshm I.
Strait of Hormuz
Hawr al Hammar
Buhayrat ath Tharthar
Tigris
Euphrates

Persian Gulf
Al Jubayl
Ad Damman
Dhahran
Al Hufuf
RIYADH (AR RIYAD)
Dukhan
Harad
MANAMA
BAHRAIN
QATAR
DOHA
Ras al Khaimah
Sharjah
Khasab (part of Oman)
Dubai
ABU DHABI
Fujairah
UNITED ARAB EMIRATES
Al Buraymi
Suhar
Al Khaburah
Ibri
Ar Rustaq
MUSCAT (MASQAT)
Nizwa
Sama'il
Sur

AD DAHNA
AD DAERAH
'AL KHALI (EMPTY QUARTER)
SAB'ATAYN
HADRAMAUT
OMAN
Gulf of Oman
Jasirat Masirah
Gulf of Masira
Kuria Muria Is.
ARABIAN SEA

Salalah
Raysut
Al Ghaydah
Al Mukalla
Millet
Millet
Wheat

N

0 100 200 300 400 500 KM
0 50 100 150 200 250 300 MILES

123

CENTRAL ASIA

THE CENTRAL ASIAN REPUBLICS lie on the ancient Silk Road between Asia and Europe, and their historic cities grew up along this route. Afghanistan controlled the route south into Pakistan and India, through the Khyber Pass in the Hindu Kush mountains. The hot, dry deserts of Central Asia and high, rugged mountain ranges of the Pamirs and Tien Shan were not suited to agriculture. For centuries people lived as nomads, herding sheep across the empty plains, or settled as merchants and traders in the Silk Road cities. When Central Asia became part of the communist Soviet Union everything changed: local languages and the Islamic religion (which had come to the region from the Middle East in the 8th century) were restricted; irrigation schemes made farming the arid land possible; oil, gas, and other minerals were exploited; industry was developed. Today, these newly independent republics are returning to the languages, religion, and traditions of their past. Afghanistan, independent since 1750, has recently suffered terrible conflict and economic collapse.

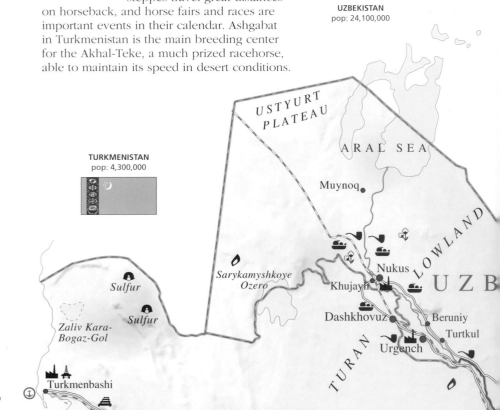

Akhal-Teke racehorse

HORSEMEN OF THE STEPPES

The nomadic peoples of the steppes travel great distances on horseback, and horse fairs and races are important events in their calendar. Ashgabat in Turkmenistan is the main breeding center for the Akhal-Teke, a much prized racehorse, able to maintain its speed in desert conditions.

UZBEKISTAN
pop: 24,100,000

TURKMENISTAN
pop: 4,300,000

AGRICULTURE

Farming in this dry region depends on irrigation. The Kara Kum Canal is 683 miles (1,100 km) long – the longest canal in the world. It carries water from the Amu Darya toward the Caspian Sea and waters vast areas of land. Draining the river, however, has reduced the size of the Aral Sea.

Opium poppies are grown all over the region. They provide illegal money for many farmers, who supply the international drug trade.

SULFUR

Turkmenistan's sulfur deposits are among the largest in the world. Sulfur is used in the manufacture of gunpowder, medicine, ointment, and drugs. Turkmenistan also has large reserves of oil and gas, but has yet to make money from its substantial resources.

MARKETS

Towns such as Samarqand have changed little since the days of the Silk Road, and are still full of merchants and traders. Bazaars and streetside stalls sell local fruit and vegetables, herbs, spices, silk, and cotton.

MAP FEATURES

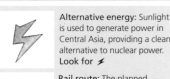

Alternative energy: Sunlight is used to generate power in Central Asia, providing a clean alternative to nuclear power. **Look for** ⚡

Rail route: The planned Trans-Asian Railroad will connect Beijing and Istanbul via Central Asia and the Caspian Sea. **Look for** 🚂

🐂	Cattle	⛰	Mining
🐑	Sheep	🛢	Oil
🍇	Mixed fruit	🔥	Natural gas
🚬	Tobacco	◆	Carpet weaving
🏭	Cotton	🏭	Industrial center

Carrots were first grown for food in Afghanistan.

CARPETS

Carpets from Uzbekistan, Turkmenistan, northern Afghanistan, and other parts of this region are world famous. They are made by hand-knotting and are woven from fine Karakul wool in a range of red, brown, and maroon colors. They follow distinctive geometric patterns. Carpets are used as saddle blankets, tent hangings, and prayer mats. **Look for** ◆

KARAKUL SHEEP

Karakul sheep are bred for their distinctive curly fleece. They are especially important in Afghanistan. Nomadic people have herded sheep in this region for many centuries. Each summer they take their flocks up to the lush mountain pastures, and in winter they are herded down onto the plains. **Look for** 🐑

Map labels

USTYURT PLATEAU
ARAL SEA
Muynoq
Sulfur
Sulfur
Sarykamyshkoye Ozero
Nukus
Khujayn
Dashkhovuz
Beruniy
Turtkul
Urgench
Zaliv Kara-Bogaz-Gol
CASPIAN SEA
Turkmenbashi
Cheleken
Nebitdag
TURKMENISTAN
TURAN LOWLAND
UZB
Gyzylarbat
Kizyl-Atrek
Byuzmeyin
ASHGABAT
IRAN
Bayramaly
Tedzhen
Mary
Gushgy
Herat
Namakzar
AFG
Hamun-e-Saberi
Dasht-e Gowd-e-Zereh

ARAL TRAGEDY

Water from the Amu Darya is being diverted to irrigate cotton fields. Since reduced amounts of water are now flowing into the Aral Sea, it is shrinking, and is now only 75 percent of its former size. Fishing villages that once stood on the sea coast are now stranded far inland, depriving villagers of their livelihood.

Sea level in year 2000
Sea level in 1989
Kokaral
Sea level in 1960
Exposed seabed becomes desert, 1960-89

ARAL SEA

The fishing village of Muynoq is now over 30 miles (48 km) from the sea

Amu Darya

KYRGYZSTAN
pop: 4,500,000

SAMARQAND

The Islamic religion reached this region in the 8th century AD. Today, after decades of suppression by the communists, Islam is once again widely followed. Most of the former Soviet Union's 60 million Muslims live in the Central Asian republics. New mosques are opened daily, and ancient religious buildings are being restored. The famous Registan Square at Samarqand is a magnificent monument to Islam, dating back to the 14th century.

N

| 0 | 100 | 200 | 300 | 400 KM |

| 0 | 100 | 200 | MILES |

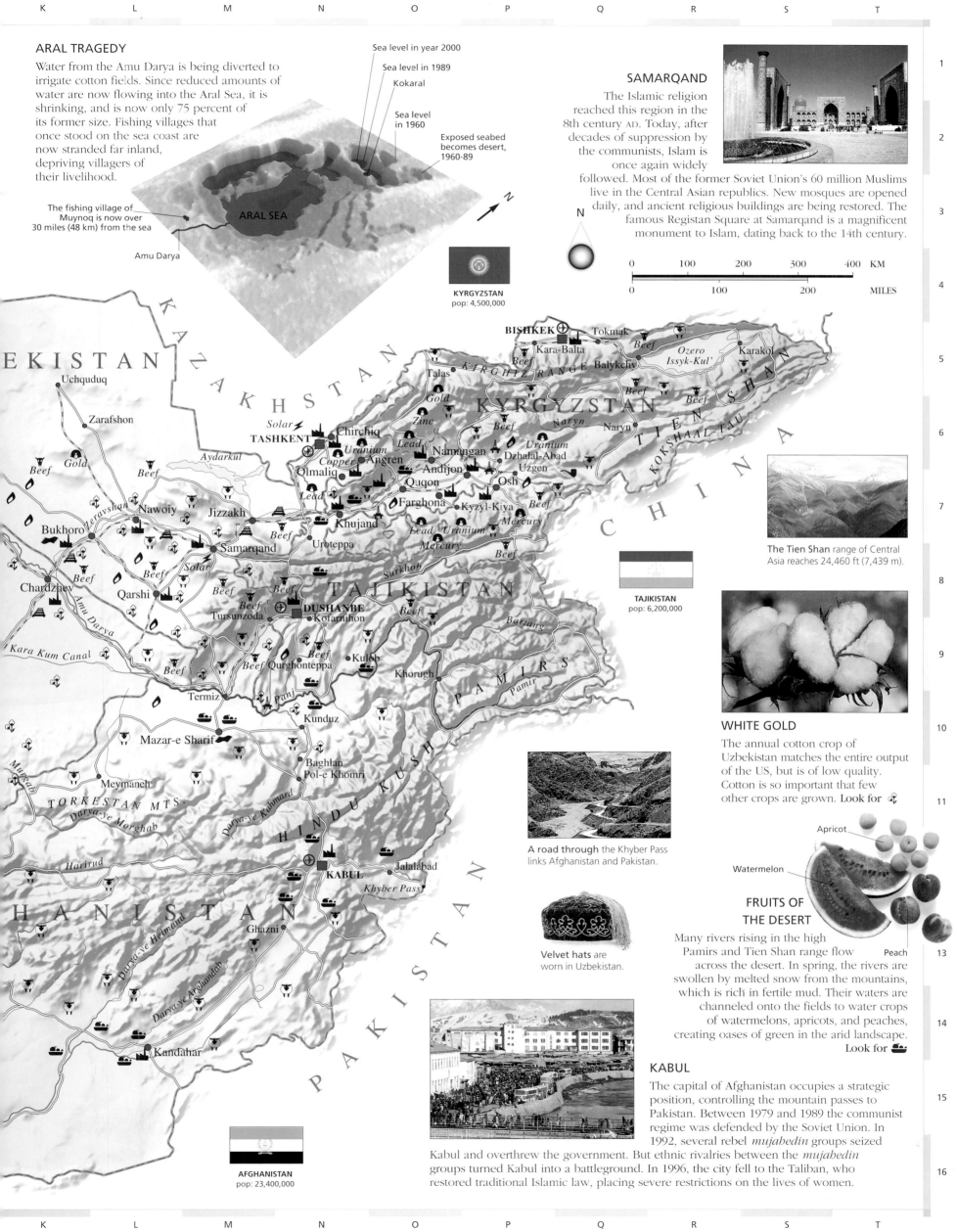

The **Tien Shan** range of Central Asia reaches 24,460 ft (7,439 m).

WHITE GOLD

The annual cotton crop of Uzbekistan matches the entire output of the US, but is of low quality. Cotton is so important that few other crops are grown. **Look for**

TAJIKISTAN
pop: 6,200,000

A **road through** the Khyber Pass links Afghanistan and Pakistan.

Apricot
Watermelon
Peach

FRUITS OF THE DESERT

Many rivers rising in the high Pamirs and Tien Shan range flow across the desert. In spring, the rivers are swollen by melted snow from the mountains, which is rich in fertile mud. Their waters are channeled onto the fields to water crops of watermelons, apricots, and peaches, creating oases of green in the arid landscape. **Look for**

Velvet hats are worn in Uzbekistan.

KABUL

The capital of Afghanistan occupies a strategic position, controlling the mountain passes to Pakistan. Between 1979 and 1989 the communist regime was defended by the Soviet Union. In 1992, several rebel *mujahedin* groups seized Kabul and overthrew the government. But ethnic rivalries between the *mujahedin* groups turned Kabul into a battleground. In 1996, the city fell to the Taliban, who restored traditional Islamic law, placing severe restrictions on the lives of women.

AFGHANISTAN
pop: 23,400,000

RUSSIA AND KAZAKHSTAN

THE URAL MOUNTAINS FORM a natural barrier between the European and the Asian parts of Russia. Although over 77 percent of the country lies in Asia, only 27 percent of the population live here. Siberia dominates Russia east of the Urals, stretching to the Pacific Ocean and northward into the Arctic. The climate is severe; parts of Siberia are colder in winter than the North Pole. Siberia has huge deposits of gold, coal, diamonds, gas, and oil, but workers had to be offered high wages and housing to work there. Today, both Russia and Kazakhstan have great economic potential, but are still coping with a legacy of severe industrial pollution.

HYDROELECTRIC POWER

Siberia's rivers provide 80 percent of Russia's hydroelectric power, fueling industry throughout eastern Russia. Massive dams, such as this one on the Angara River, provide the power for the aluminum industry.
Look for ⧯

Ear of wheat

VIRGIN LANDS

In the 1950s, the Soviet Union tried to increase grain production. The empty steppes of Kazakhstan, known as the "Virgin Lands," were ploughed up to grow crops. Today, much of this farmland is reverting to steppe.
Look for ⚭

MAP FEATURES

	Industrial center: This region produces one-third of the former USSR's iron and steel. Timber processing is also very important. Look for ⛏
	Pollution: Nearly 500 Soviet nuclear devices were detonated in Kazakhstan from 1949-1989. Many children in this area are malformed at birth. Look for ☢
	Military bases: Russia's far east is a highly militarized area. The Russian Pacific fleet is based at Vladivostok. Look for ⫴

⚭ Cereals		⛏ Coal	
⚓ Timber		⚓ Oil	
⚓ Fishing		◊ Natural gas	
⬤ Mining		⧯ Hydroelectric power	

A child's toy wooden sled from Siberia.

KAZAKH HORSEMEN

The first inhabitants of the steppe were a nomadic people who traveled on horseback, herding their sheep with them. They slept in felt tents like these, called *yurts*. Their descendants, the Kazakhs, still place great value on horses and riding skills, and horse racing is a popular sport. The Kazakh national drink is *kumiss* – fermented mare's milk. The traditional nomadic lifestyle of the steppe has gradually been replaced by large-scale agriculture and industry.

KAZAKHSTAN
pop: 16,900,000

SPACE CENTER

The Russian space program is based at Baykonur in Kazakhstan, where this Buran unmanned shuttle was launched in 1988. Russia's achievements in space technology started with the launch of the Sputnik satellite in 1957. Since then, Russia has been responsible for the first man in space, the first woman cosmonaut, and the first space walk. The Mir orbital station, in space since 1986, was manned by cosmonauts until 1999.

Map labels

NORWAY · FINLAND · ESTONIA · LATVIA · BELARUS · UKRAINE · GEORGIA · TURKMENISTAN · UZBEKISTAN · KYRGYZSTAN · CHINA

Franz Josef Land · Novaya Zemlya · KARA SEA · BARENTS SEA · Ostrov Kolguyev · Ostrov Belyy · Baydaratskaya Guba · POLUOSTROV YAMAL · GYDANSKIY POLUOSTROV · KOLA PENINSULA · WHITE SEA · SEA OF AZOV · BLACK SEA · CASPIAN SEA · ARAL SEA

Murmansk · Kem · Saint Petersburg (Sankt-Peterburg) · Pskov · Nevel · Novgorod · Petrozavodsk · Archangel · Smolensk · Bryansk · Kaluga · Orël · Tula · MOSCOW (MOSKVA) · Tver' · Yaroslavl' · Vologda · Kotlas · Syktyvkar · Vorkuta · Salekhard · Nakhodka · Cherepovets · Ivanovo · Vladimir · Kursk · Ryazan' · Lipetsk · Nizhniy Novgorod · Voronezh · Tambov · Saransk · Cheboksary · Kazan' · Kirov · Penza · Ul'yanovsk · Izhevsk · Perm' · Serov · Nizhniy Tagil · Yekaterinburg · Rostov-na-Donu · Saratov · Tol'yatti · Naberezhnyye Chelny · Ufa · Tyumen' · Nizhnevartovsk · Krasnodar · Balakovo · Samara · Chelyabinsk · Sochi · Stavropol' · Cherkessk · Elista · Volgograd · Ural'sk · Orenburg · Magnitogorsk · Kurgan · Kustanay · Petropavlovsk · Omsk · Tomsk · Vladikavkaz · Groznyy · Astrakhan' · Aktyubinsk · Kokshetau · Novosibirsk · Kemerovo · Makhachkala · Fort-Shevchenko · Aktau · Atyrau · Emba · KIRGHIZ STEPPE · ASTANA · Pavlodar · Barnaul · Novokuznetsk · Aleysk · Biysk · Baykonur · Zhezkazgan · Karaganda · Semipalatinsk · Ust'-Kamenogorsk · Kzyl-Orda · L. Balkhash · Balkhash · Ozero Zaysan · Shymkent · Zhambyl · Taldykorgan · Kapchagay · Alma-Ata (Almaty)

West Siberian Plain · Kirghiz Steppe · Kazakh Uplands · Ob' · Irtysh · Ural · Volga · Don · Kama · Pechora · Mezen · Syr Darya · Chu · Ili · Taz · Pur · Ket' · Vakh · Ishim · Tobol · Emba

L. Ladoga · L. Onega · Ozero Pyaozero · Ozero Tengiz

Iron · Aluminum · Uranium · Coal · Chromium · Platinum · Manganese · Nickel · Gold · Copper · Lead · Zinc · Sulfur · Oats · Wheat · Barley · Corn · Rye · Oats · Cereals

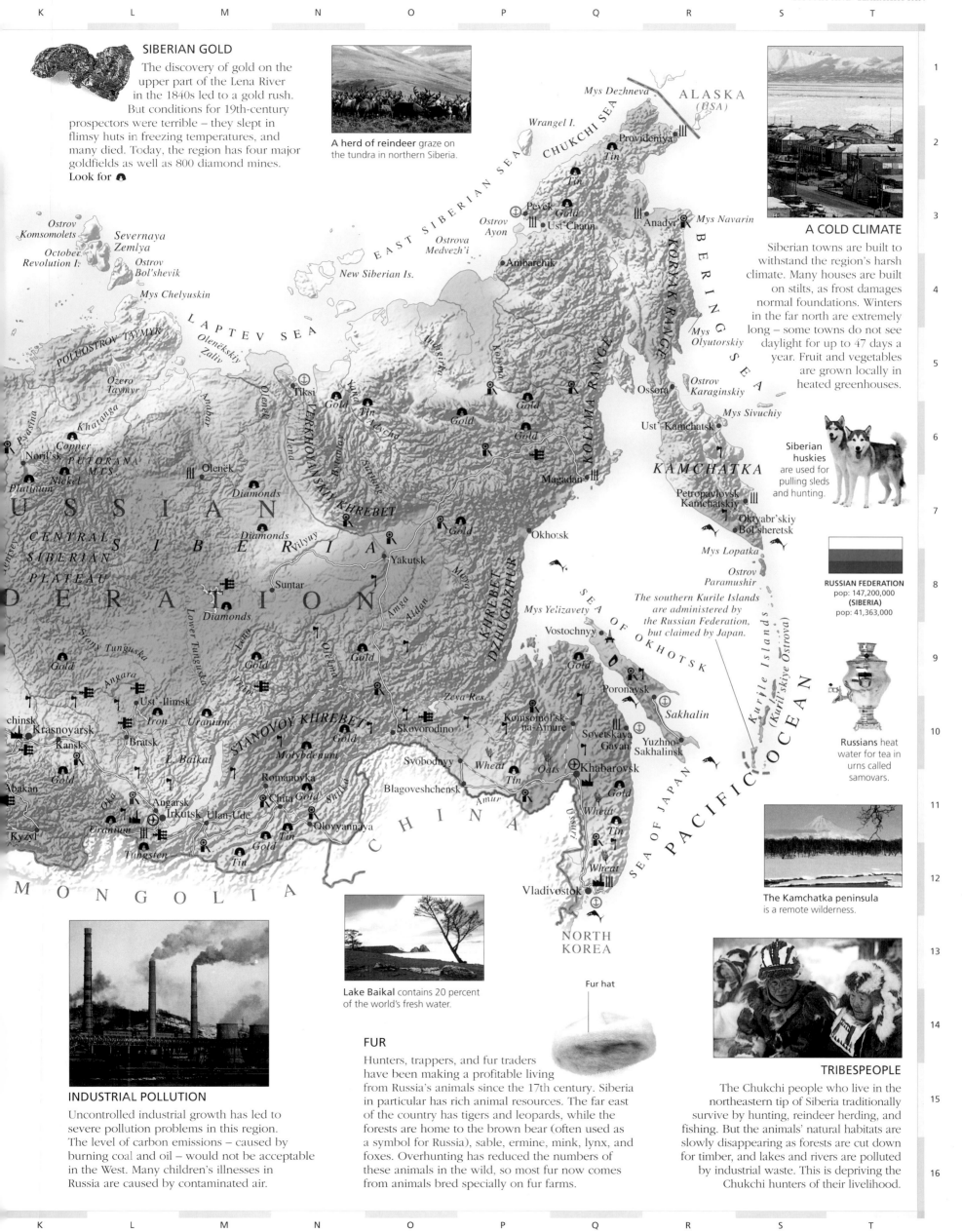

SIBERIAN GOLD

The discovery of gold on the upper part of the Lena River in the 1840s led to a gold rush. But conditions for 19th-century prospectors were terrible – they slept in flimsy huts in freezing temperatures, and many died. Today, the region has four major goldfields as well as 800 diamond mines.

Look for 🔨

A herd of reindeer graze on the tundra in northern Siberia.

A COLD CLIMATE

Siberian towns are built to withstand the region's harsh climate. Many houses are built on stilts, as frost damages normal foundations. Winters in the far north are extremely long – some towns do not see daylight for up to 47 days a year. Fruit and vegetables are grown locally in heated greenhouses.

Siberian huskies are used for pulling sleds and hunting.

RUSSIAN FEDERATION
pop: 147,200,000
(SIBERIA)
pop: 41,363,000

Russians heat water for tea in urns called samovars.

The Kamchatka peninsula is a remote wilderness.

TRIBESPEOPLE

The Chukchi people who live in the northeastern tip of Siberia traditionally survive by hunting, reindeer herding, and fishing. But the animals' natural habitats are slowly disappearing as forests are cut down for timber, and lakes and rivers are polluted by industrial waste. This is depriving the Chukchi hunters of their livelihood.

INDUSTRIAL POLLUTION

Uncontrolled industrial growth has led to severe pollution problems in this region. The level of carbon emissions – caused by burning coal and oil – would not be acceptable in the West. Many children's illnesses in Russia are caused by contaminated air.

Lake Baikal contains 20 percent of the world's fresh water.

Fur hat

FUR

Hunters, trappers, and fur traders have been making a profitable living from Russia's animals since the 17th century. Siberia in particular has rich animal resources. The far east of the country has tigers and leopards, while the forests are home to the brown bear (often used as a symbol for Russia), sable, ermine, mink, lynx, and foxes. Overhunting has reduced the numbers of these animals in the wild, so most fur now comes from animals bred specially on fur farms.

The southern Kurile Islands are administered by the Russian Federation, but claimed by Japan.

Golden pheasant
Chrysolophus pictus
Length: 3 ft (1 m)

King cobra
Ophiophagus hannah
Length: 18 ft (5.5 m)

Komodo dragon
Varanus komodoensis
Length:
10 ft (3 m)

SOUTH AND EAST ASIA

THE WORLD'S 10 HIGHEST PEAKS, including Mount Everest, are all found in the Himalayas and other mountain ranges in the center of this region. At these altitudes, monsoon rains fall as snow on mountain tops. The melted snow from the mountains feeds some of the largest rivers in the world, such as the Ganges and Irrawaddy, which have created huge deltas where they enter the sea. Fingers of land stretch into tropical seas and volcanic island chains border the continent. In tropical areas high rainfall and temperatures support vast areas of forest. Inland, a climate of extremes prevails, with baking hot summers and long harsh winters. Cold desert and grassy plains cover much of the interior.

■ ▲ VOLCANIC ROCK
This huge granite rock on Sri Lanka was formed in the mouth of a volcano. It is surrounded by forest.

Gingko
Gingko biloba
Height:
100 ft (30 m)

The tiger cowrie is found on coral reefs.

■ ▲ YOUNG MOUNTAINS
Himalaya is the Nepalese word for "home of the snows." The range began to form about 40 million years ago – recent in the Earth's history.

■ ▲ ISLAND VOLCANOES
Plants are growing again on the scorched slopes of Bromo in Java, one of a chain of active volcanoes around the southeast Pacific.

■ TROPICAL RAIN FOREST
Rain forests grow in layers: an understorey with creepers, and the main canopy through which the tallest trees protrude.

Giant panda
Ailuropoda melanoleuca
Length:
5 ft (1.5 m)

■ HIDDEN CAVES
This maze of limestone caves along the Gulf of Thailand has been carved out by rainwater.

The royal cloak scallop shell is found in the waters of the Pacific Ocean.

⊡ MANGROVES IN SILHOUETTE
Mangroves grow along many coastlines, giving some protection during tropical storms.

■ △ SACRED MOUNTAIN
Mount Fuji, Japan's highest peak, is surrounded by temperate broadleaf trees. Once an active volcano, Mount Fuji has not erupted for 300 years. The snow-capped summit is the rim of a volcanic crater.

Rafflesia
Rafflesia pricei
Width:
3 ft (1 m)

TROPICAL ISLAND
There are thousands of tiny coral islands in this region. Many are volcanic in origin, like this one in the South China Sea.

CROSS-SECTION THROUGH SOUTH AND EAST ASIA

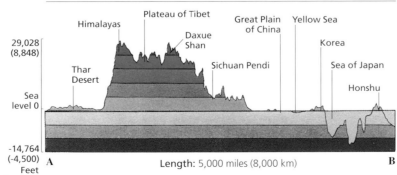

Himalayas
Plateau of Tibet
Daxue Shan
Great Plain of China
Yellow Sea
Korea
Sea of Japan
Sichuan Pendi
Honshu
Thar Desert
29,028 (8,848)
Sea level 0
-14,764 (-4,500)
Feet (meters)
A
B
Length: 5,000 miles (8,000 km)

■ COLD HIGH NEPAL
No trees are to be found above 10,000 ft (3,000 m) in the Himalayas, although dwarf shrubs and grasses can withstand the harsher conditions up to 15,000 ft (4,500 m). Higher still, the rock is bare, or covered in snow.

Wild yak
Bos grunniens
Length: 9 ft (3 m)

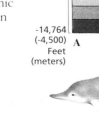

Chinese river dolphin
Lipotes vexillifer
Length: 8 ft (2.4 m)

Siberian tiger
Panthera tigris
Length: 8 ft (2.4 m)

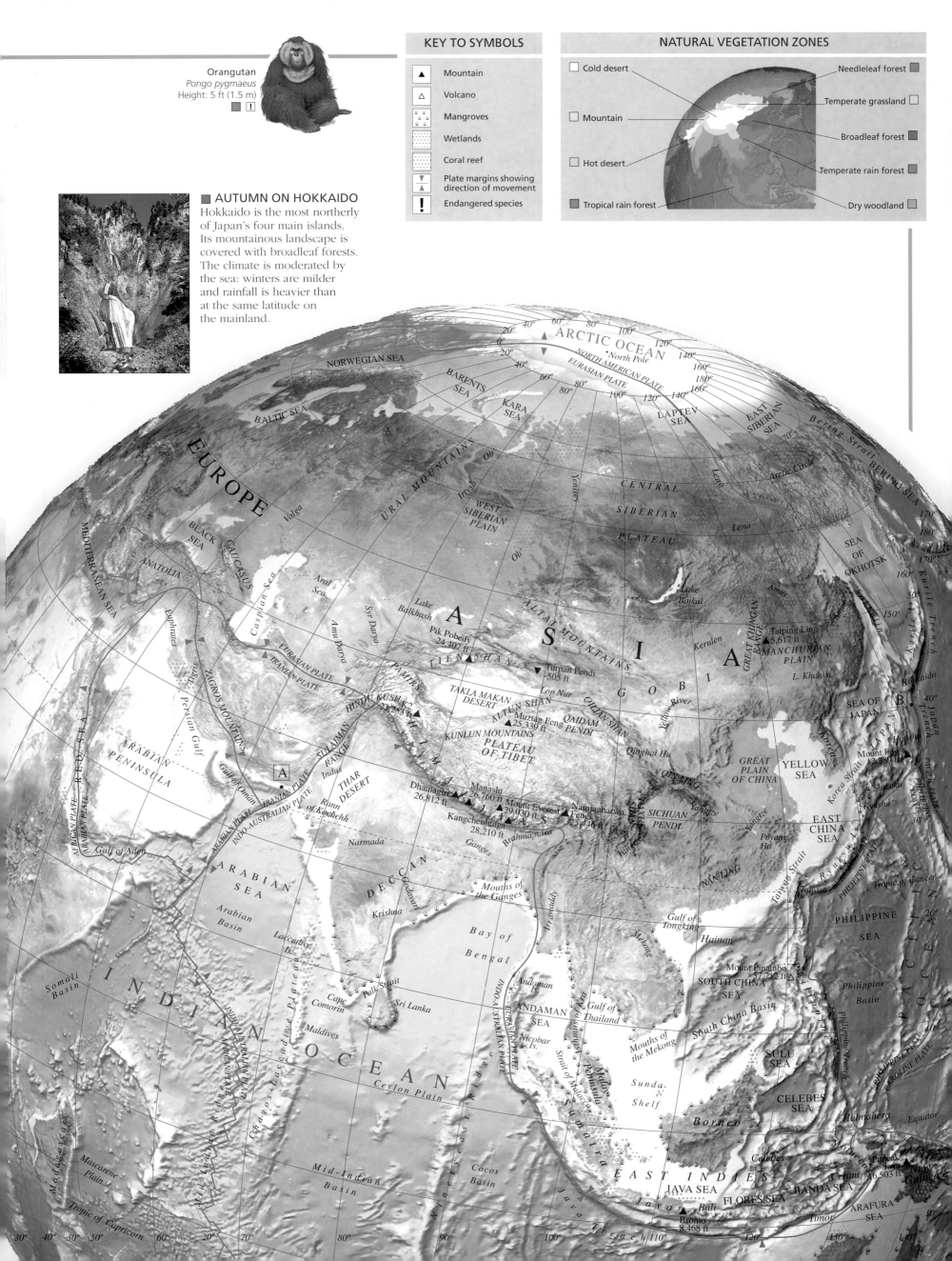

Orangutan
Pongo pygmaeus
Height: 5 ft (1.5 m)

KEY TO SYMBOLS

▲ Mountain
△ Volcano
Mangroves
Wetlands
Coral reef
▽ Plate margins showing
▲ direction of movement
! Endangered species

NATURAL VEGETATION ZONES

Cold desert
Mountain
Hot desert
Tropical rain forest

Needleleaf forest
Temperate grassland
Broadleaf forest
Temperate rain forest
Dry woodland

■ AUTUMN ON HOKKAIDO
Hokkaido is the most northerly
of Japan's four main islands.
Its mountainous landscape is
covered with broadleaf forests.
The climate is moderated by
the sea: winters are milder
and rainfall is heavier than
at the same latitude on
the mainland.

EUROPE

ASIA

ARCTIC OCEAN
North Pole

NORWEGIAN SEA

BARENTS SEA

KARA SEA

LAPTEV SEA

EAST SIBERIAN SEA

BERING SEA

Bering Strait

BALTIC SEA

MEDITERRANEAN SEA

BLACK SEA

CAUCASUS

ANATOLIA

Volga

URAL MOUNTAINS

Ob

Irtysh

WEST SIBERIAN PLAIN

Yenisey

Ob

CENTRAL SIBERIAN PLATEAU

Lena

Lena

Arctic Circle

Amur

SEA OF OKHOTSK

Kurile Trench

Caspian Sea

Aral Sea

Syr Darya

Amu Darya

Lake Balkhash

Pik Pobedy 24,407 ft

ALTAI MOUNTAINS

GOBI

Kerulen

GREAT KHINGAN RANGE

Taiping Ling 5,617 ft

MANCHURIAN PLAIN

L. Khanka

Amur

SEA OF JAPAN

Hokkaido

Euphrates

Tigris

ZAGROS MOUNTAINS

Persian Gulf

EURASIAN PLATE

IRANIAN PLATE

PAMIRS

TIEN SHAN

TAKLA MAKAN DESERT

Turpan Pendi -505 ft

Lop Nur

QILIAN SHAN

ALTUN SHAN

Muztag Feng 25,339 ft

QAIDAM PENDI

Yellow River

Qinghai Hu

QINLING

GREAT PLAIN OF CHINA

YELLOW SEA

Mount Fuji

Honshu

Shikoku

Kyushu

Korea Strait

Korea

HINDU KUSH

K2 28,253 ft

SULAIMAN RANGE

KUNLUN MOUNTAINS

PLATEAU OF TIBET

HIMALAYA

Manaslu 26,760 ft

Dhaulagiri 26,812 ft

Mount Everest 29,030 ft

Kangchenjunga 28,210 ft

Namjagbarwa Feng 25,446 ft

Brahmaputra

SICHUAN PENDI

Yangtze

Poyang Hu

EAST CHINA SEA

Ryukyu Is

Taiwan

Taiwan Strait

Tropic of Cancer

ARABIAN PENINSULA

Gulf of Oman

ARABIAN PLATE

IRANIAN PLATE

INDO-AUSTRALIAN PLATE

Indus

THAR DESERT

Rann of Kachchh

Narmada

Ganges

DECCAN

Godavari

Krishna

Mouths of the Ganges

NANLING

Yangtze

NANLING

RED SEA

AFRICAN PLATE

ARABIAN PLATE

Gulf of Aden

Gulf of Oman

ARABIAN SEA

Arabian Basin

Laccadive Is.

Cape Comorin

Palk Strait

Sri Lanka

Maldives

Laccadive Plateau

Bay of Bengal

Irrawaddy

Andaman Is.

ANDAMAN SEA

Nicobar Is.

Gulf of Thailand

Mekong

Gulf of Tongking

Hainan

SOUTH CHINA SEA

Mount Pinatubo 5,772 ft

PHILIPPINE SEA

Philippine Basin

Somali Basin

MADAGASCAR

Mascarene Plain

INDIAN OCEAN

INDO-AUSTRALIAN PLATE

AFRICAN PLATE

Mid-Indian Ridge

Chagos-Laccadive Plateau

Ceylon Plain

Mid-Indian Basin

Ninety East Ridge

Cocos Basin

Isthmus of Kra

Malay Peninsula

Strait of Malacca

Sunda Shelf

South China Basin

Mouths of the Mekong

SULU SEA

CELEBES SEA

Halmahera

Philippine Basin

PHILIPPINE PLATE

CAROLINE PLATE

Tropic of Capricorn

Java Trench

Sumatra

Java Sea

JAVA SEA

Java

Bali

Bromo 8,468 ft

FLORES SEA

EAST INDIES

Borneo

Celebes

Ceram 16,503 ft

BANDA SEA

Moluccas

New Guinea

Timor

ARAFURA SEA

PACIFIC OCEAN

Japan Trench

Philippine Trench

Equator

NORTH AMERICAN PLATE

EURASIAN PLATE

THE INDIAN SUBCONTINENT

SOUTH OF THE HIMALAYAS, the world's highest mountains, lies the Indian subcontinent. In the north of the region, the Buddhist kingdoms of Nepal and Bhutan cling to the slopes of the Himalayas. In the south, the island state of Sri Lanka hangs like a teardrop from the tip of India. The subcontinent has been invaded many times: the first invaders were Aryan tribes from the north, whose beliefs and customs form the basis of the Hindu religion. During the 16th century India was united and ruled by the Islamic Mughal emperors. Two centuries later it became a British colony. In 1947 India gained independence, but religious differences led to the creation of two countries – Hindu India and Muslim Pakistan. Today India is an industrial power, but most people still make their living from tiny farms. In spite of terrible poverty and a population of over 900 million people, India remains a relatively stable democracy. Since 1947, India and Pakistan, now both nuclear powers, have been locked in conflict over control of Kashmir.

PAKISTAN
pop: 137,400,000

The Thar Desert, a vast, arid region in India and Pakistan.

Sitar

MOOD MUSIC

Most traditional Indian music is improvised. Its purpose is to create a mood, such as joy or sorrow. One of the main instruments is the *sitar*, which is played by plucking seven of its strings. Other strings, which are not plucked, vibrate to give the distinctive sound of Indian music.

PAKISTAN

This bus illustrates a big problem in Pakistan: overpopulation. 95 percent of the people are Muslim, and traditional Islam rejects contraception, so the birthrate is high. The many refugees who fled the war in Afghanistan have stretched resources further.

A MARBLE MEMORIAL

The Taj Mahal at Agra in northern India was built in the 17th century by the Mughal Emperor, Shah Jahan, as a tomb for his beloved wife. She was the mother of 14 children. Built of the finest white marble, the Taj Mahal is a supreme example of Islamic architecture and one of the world's most beautiful buildings.

MAP FEATURES

 Aquaculture: This is a recent and highly successful industry in Bangladesh. Frog legs and shrimps are among the main products. Look for

 Hiking: Every year some 250,000 hikers visit Nepal, boosting its economy. But the extra visitors are damaging the environment. Look for

 **Dams:** Irrigation on a vast scale in the Indus Valley in Pakistan has sustained and increased the country's food production. Look for

	Cereals		Cotton
	Rice		Mining
	Sugarcane		Coal
	Tea		Industrial center

INDUSTRY

After independence, India started to modernize. It is now one of the most industrialized countries in Asia. Factories make a wide range of goods, from cement to cars. Recently, the manufacture of goods such as machine tools and electronic equipment has increased. Local cotton is processed in mills like these in Ahmadabad. Look for

INDIAN FILMS

More films are produced in India than anywhere else in the world – including Hollywood. Bombay is the center of the Indian film industry.

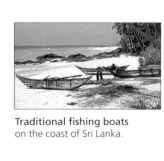

Traditional fishing boats on the coast of Sri Lanka.

N

0 100 200 300 400 500 KM
0   100   200   300 MILES

Map labels: Peshawar, Mardan, Tarbela Res, Tarbela Dam, ISLAMABAD, Srinagar, Jinnah Barrage, Rawalpindi, Mangla Res, Jhelum, AFGHANISTAN, Chashma Barrage, Chromium, Dera Ismail Khan, Sargodha, Chenab, Gujranwala, Gujrat, Wheat, Faisalabad, Lahore, Amritsar, Quetta, Trimmu Barrage, Emerson, Barrage, Kasur, Okara, TOBA KAKAR RANGE, CHAGAI HILLS, Dera Ghazi Khan, Multan, Islam Barrage, Panjnad Barrage, Bahawalpur, Guddu Barrage, Wheat, IRAN, PAKISTAN, CENTRAL MAKRAN RANGE, Shikarpur, Rahimyar Khan, THAR DESERT, Barley, Larkana, Sukkur, Wheat, Jaisalmer, Jodhpur, Ajmer, Jaipur, Ghulam Muhammad Barrage, Nawabshah, Wheat, Kota, Gandhi Res, Karachi, Hyderabad, Mirpur Khas, RANN OF KACHCHH, Wheat, Ahmadabad, Indore, Gulf of Kachchh, Kandla, Jamnagar, Rajkot, Vadodara, Narmada, Porbandar, Aluminum, Bhavnagar, Surat, Tapti, Dhule, Gulf of Khambhat, Daman, Nashik, Bombay (Mumbai), Thane, Pune, ARABIAN SEA, Solapur, Krishna, Aluminum, Belgaum, Dharwad, Panaji, Hubli, Davangere, Manganese, Iron, Chromium, Mangalore, Mysore, MALABAR COAST, WESTERN GHATS, Calicut, Coimbatore, Ernakulam, Cochin, Titanium, Trivandrum, Nagercoil

Kashmir: a "line of control" was established in 1972 by Simla (Shimla) Agreement between Pakistan and India.

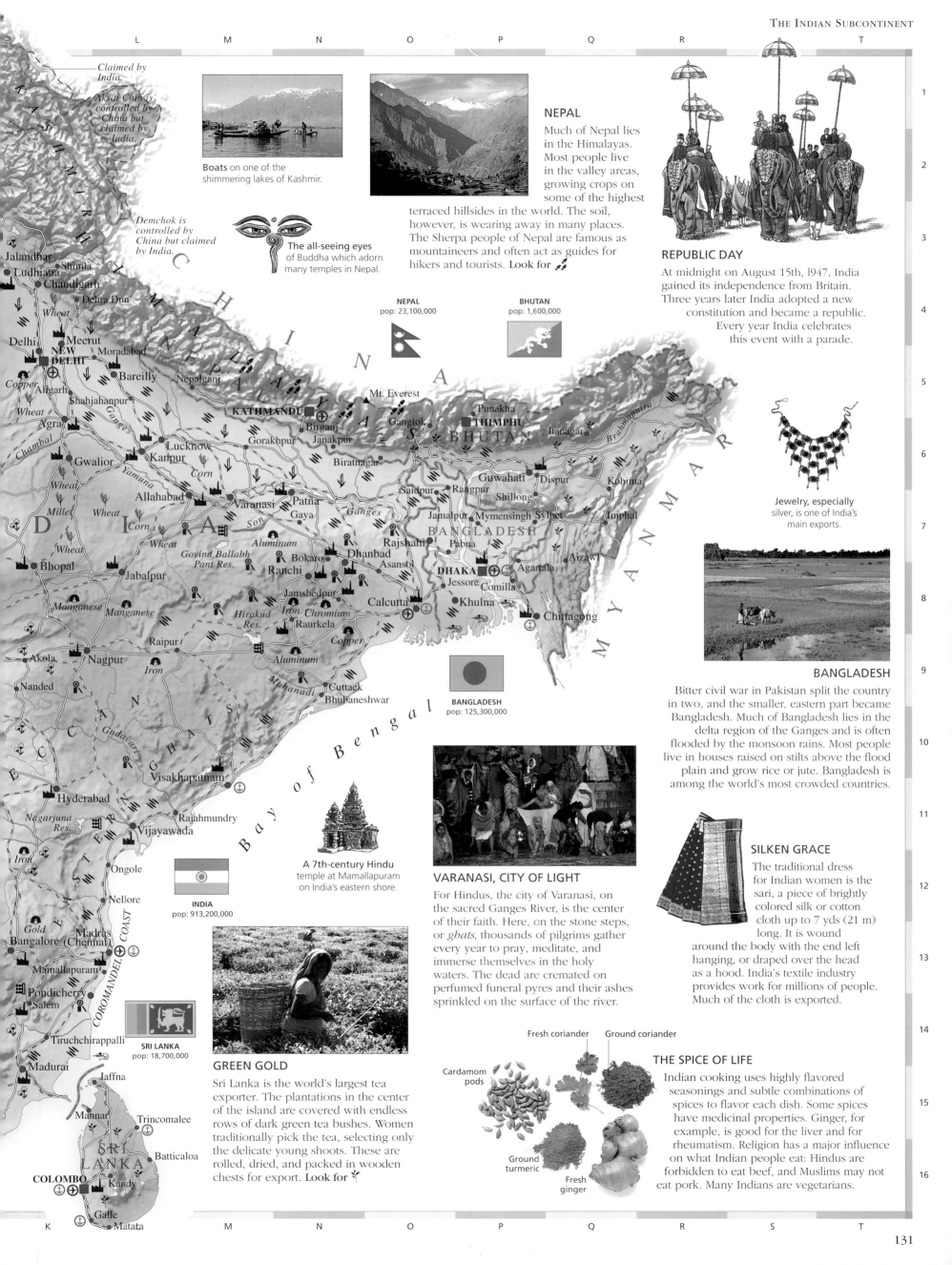

Claimed by India.

Aksai Chin is controlled by China but claimed by India.

Demchok is controlled by China but claimed by India.

Boats on one of the shimmering lakes of Kashmir.

The all-seeing eyes of Buddha which adorn many temples in Nepal.

NEPAL

Much of Nepal lies in the Himalayas. Most people live in the valley areas, growing crops on some of the highest terraced hillsides in the world. The soil, however, is wearing away in many places. The Sherpa people of Nepal are famous as mountaineers and often act as guides for hikers and tourists. **Look for**

NEPAL pop: 23,100,000

BHUTAN pop: 1,600,000

REPUBLIC DAY

At midnight on August 15th, 1947, India gained its independence from Britain. Three years later India adopted a new constitution and became a republic. Every year India celebrates this event with a parade.

Jewelry, especially silver, is one of India's main exports.

BANGLADESH

Bitter civil war in Pakistan split the country in two, and the smaller, eastern part became Bangladesh. Much of Bangladesh lies in the delta region of the Ganges and is often flooded by the monsoon rains. Most people live in houses raised on stilts above the flood plain and grow rice or jute. Bangladesh is among the world's most crowded countries.

BANGLADESH pop: 125,300,000

A 7th-century Hindu temple at Mamallapuram on India's eastern shore.

VARANASI, CITY OF LIGHT

For Hindus, the city of Varanasi, on the sacred Ganges River, is the center of their faith. Here, on the stone steps, or *ghats*, thousands of pilgrims gather every year to pray, meditate, and immerse themselves in the holy waters. The dead are cremated on perfumed funeral pyres and their ashes sprinkled on the surface of the river.

SILKEN GRACE

The traditional dress for Indian women is the sari, a piece of brightly colored silk or cotton cloth up to 7 yds (21 m) long. It is wound around the body with the end left hanging, or draped over the head as a hood. India's textile industry provides work for millions of people. Much of the cloth is exported.

INDIA pop: 913,200,000

SRI LANKA pop: 18,700,000

GREEN GOLD

Sri Lanka is the world's largest tea exporter. The plantations in the center of the island are covered with endless rows of dark green tea bushes. Women traditionally pick the tea, selecting only the delicate young shoots. These are rolled, dried, and packed in wooden chests for export. **Look for**

Fresh coriander   Ground coriander

Cardamom pods

Ground turmeric

Fresh ginger

THE SPICE OF LIFE

Indian cooking uses highly flavored seasonings and subtle combinations of spices to flavor each dish. Some spices have medicinal properties. Ginger, for example, is good for the liver and for rheumatism. Religion has a major influence on what Indian people eat: Hindus are forbidden to eat beef, and Muslims may not eat pork. Many Indians are vegetarians.

CHINA AND MONGOLIA

THE REMOTE MOUNTAINS, deserts, and steppes of Mongolia and the northwestern part of China are harsh landscapes; temperatures are extreme, the terrain is rugged, and distances between places are vast. Three large autonomous regions of China lie here – Inner Mongolia, Xinjiang Uygur, and Tibet. Remote Tibet, situated on a high plateau and ringed by mountains, was invaded by China in 1950. The Chinese have systematically destroyed Tibet's traditional agricultural society and Buddhist monasteries. Most of China's ethnic minorities and Muslims (a legacy of Silk Road trade with the Middle East) are located in Inner Mongolia and Xinjiang. Roads and railroads are being built to make these secluded areas accessible, and rich resources of coal are being exploited. Mongolia is a vast, isolated country. It became a communist republic in 1924 but has now reestablished democracy. Most people still live by herding animals, although new industries have begun to develop.

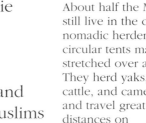

MONGOLIAN STEPPES

About half the Mongolian population still live in the countryside, many as nomadic herders. Nomads live in *gers* – circular tents made of felt and canvas stretched over a wooden frame. They herd yaks, sheep, goats, cattle, and camels and travel great distances on horseback.

Cylinder containing written prayer

In Tibet, written prayers are placed in prayer wheels. These small cylinders are rotated by hand.

The Tien Shan range in central Xinjiang Uygur.

KASHI MARKET

The city of Kashi is located in the far west of China. With its Muslim mosques, minarets, and lively bazaar, it is more like a city in the Middle East than China. Its Sunday market, the biggest in Asia, attracts up to 60,000 visitors. A vast array of goods are sold there: horses, camels, livestock, grains, spices, and cloth.

ADAPTABLE YAKS

Herders in Mongolia and Tibet keep yaks. They thrive at high altitudes, surviving extreme cold and even burrowing under snow for grass. Yaks provide milk, butter, meat, wool, and leather. In Tibet, yak butter is served with tea. Look for 🍶

MAP FEATURES

Timber: Forests in eastern Tibet have been cut down by the Chinese. Bare hillsides encourage flooding, landslides, and soil erosion. Look for 🌲

Coal: Mongolia is a major exporter of coal to the Russian Federation. There are also open-pit mines in Xinjiang Uygur and Inner Mongolia. Look for ⛏

Pollution: Nuclear tests in Xinjiang Uygur have caused radiation fallout, pollution, and many birth defects. Look for ☢

🐂	Cattle and yaks	🛢	Mining
🐑	Sheep	🛢	Oil
🌾	Cereals	🏭	Industrial center
🍓	Mixed fruit	🌴	Oases

Oases: winter and spring wheat, corn, rice, and cotton are grown

Takla Makan Desert

Tarim He

Lop Nur: saline lake

N

Passes through Tien Shan range

Boston Hu: fruit and cotton are grown on irrigated land

SILK ROAD OASES

The oases of Xinjiang Uygur lie on the edge of the Takla Makan Desert in the foothills of the Tien Shan range. They are watered by melted snow from the mountains and sheltered by warm winds coming down the mountain slopes. Towns grew up next to the oases, which lie along the ancient Silk Road.

The high plateau of Tibet, known as "the roof of the world."

KAZAKHSTAN
Uvs Nuur
Ulaangom
Hyargas Nuur
Beef
Wheat
Olgiy
Yaks
ALTAI MTS.
Irtysh
Altay
Wheat
Hovd
Charus Nuur
Beef
Beef
Karamay
XINJIANG UYGUR
Shihezi
Wheat
Kuytun
Beef
Yining
Wheat
Urumqi
AUTONOMOUS
KYRGYZSTAN
TIEN SHAN
Wheat
Turpan
Corn
Beef
Hami
Aksu
Korla
Iron
Wheat
Bosten Hu
Wheat
Tarim He
Corn
Lenghu
Kashi
Corn
Tarim Basin
REGION
CHI
Da Qaidam
Shache
TAKLA MAKAN
Wheat
DESERT
Lop Nur
TAJIKISTAN
Beef
Wheat
Golmud
AFGHANISTAN
Hotan
Wheat
ALTUN SHAN
Iron
Wheat
Beef
KUNLUN MTS.
PAKISTAN
Aksai Chin is controlled by China, but claimed by India
Yaks
Yaks
Tongtian He
KARAKORAM RANGE
Demchok is controlled by China, but claimed by India
Yaks
TANGGULA SHAN
Gar
Yaks
INDIA
Tangra Yumco
TIBET
Siling Co
Salween
GANGDISE SHAN
Nam Co
Naqqu
Yaks
Brahmaputra
HIMALAYAS
Wheat Wheat
Xigazê
Lhasa
Beef
Nyingchi
Mt. Everest
Yaks
Yamzho Yumco
Gyangze
Nyalam
NEPAL
BHUTAN
INDI

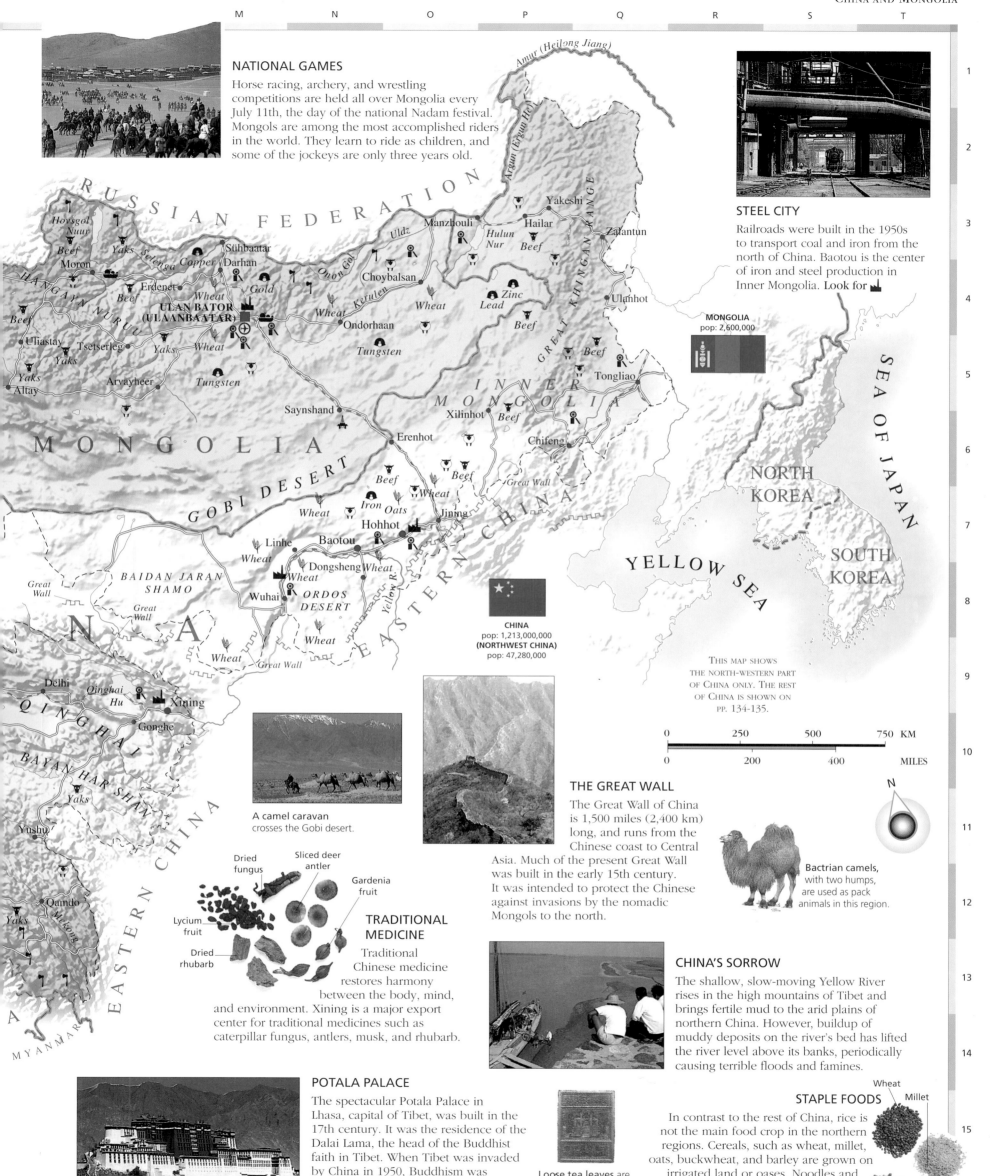

NATIONAL GAMES

Horse racing, archery, and wrestling competitions are held all over Mongolia every July 11th, the day of the national Nadam festival. Mongols are among the most accomplished riders in the world. They learn to ride as children, and some of the jockeys are only three years old.

STEEL CITY

Railroads were built in the 1950s to transport coal and iron from the north of China. Baotou is the center of iron and steel production in Inner Mongolia. Look for

MONGOLIA
pop: 2,600,000

CHINA
pop: 1,213,000,000
(NORTHWEST CHINA)
pop: 47,280,000

THIS MAP SHOWS THE NORTH-WESTERN PART OF CHINA ONLY. THE REST OF CHINA IS SHOWN ON PP. 134-135.

0   250   500   750 KM
0   200   400   MILES

A camel caravan crosses the Gobi desert.

THE GREAT WALL

The Great Wall of China is 1,500 miles (2,400 km) long, and runs from the Chinese coast to Central Asia. Much of the present Great Wall was built in the early 15th century. It was intended to protect the Chinese against invasions by the nomadic Mongols to the north.

Bactrian camels, with two humps, are used as pack animals in this region.

TRADITIONAL MEDICINE

Dried fungus
Sliced deer antler
Gardenia fruit
Lycium fruit
Dried rhubarb

Traditional Chinese medicine restores harmony between the body, mind, and environment. Xining is a major export center for traditional medicines such as caterpillar fungus, antlers, musk, and rhubarb.

CHINA'S SORROW

The shallow, slow-moving Yellow River rises in the high mountains of Tibet and brings fertile mud to the arid plains of northern China. However, buildup of muddy deposits on the river's bed has lifted the river level above its banks, periodically causing terrible floods and famines.

POTALA PALACE

The spectacular Potala Palace in Lhasa, capital of Tibet, was built in the 17th century. It was the residence of the Dalai Lama, the head of the Buddhist faith in Tibet. When Tibet was invaded by China in 1950, Buddhism was brutally repressed by the Chinese. In 1959 there were over 6,000 monasteries in Tibet – by 1979 only five remained.

Loose tea leaves are compressed into hard blocks, easily carried by Tibetan nomads.

STAPLE FOODS

In contrast to the rest of China, rice is not the main food crop in the northern regions. Cereals, such as wheat, millet, oats, buckwheat, and barley are grown on irrigated land or oases. Noodles and steamed buns (*mantou*) are the main bulk food of the north, served with spicy barbecued meat. Look for

Wheat
Millet
Barley

A   B   C   D   E   F   G   H   I   J

CHINA AND KOREA

THE LANDSCAPE OF SOUTHEASTERN CHINA ranges from mountains and plateaus to wide river valleys and plains. One-fifth of all the people on Earth live in China and most Chinese live in the eastern part of the country. For centuries, China was isolated from the rest of the world, ruled by powerful emperors and known to only a handful of traders. In the 19th century, the European powers and Japan forced China to open its borders to trade, starting a period of rapid change. In 1949, after a long struggle between nationalists and communists, the People's Republic of China was established as a communist state. Taiwan became a separate country. The communist government has encouraged foreign investment, technological innovation, and private enterprise, although calls for democracy have been suppressed. Korea was dominated by its powerful Chinese and Japanese neighbors for many years. After World War II, Korea was divided in two. North Korea became one of the most isolated and repressive communist regimes in the world. South Korea transformed itself into a highly industrialized nation.

BEIJING OPERA

Traditional Chinese opera dates back 2,000 years and combines many different elements – songs, dance, mime, and acrobatics. The stories are based on folktales. Makeup shows the characters' personalities – kind, loyal, or wicked, for example.

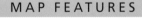

Sesame oil

Dried mushroom

FOOD

Chinese food varies widely from region to region. Its most famous cuisine comes from the area around Guangzhou and uses a huge range of ingredients – it is said that the people from this region will "eat anything with wings except airplanes and anything with legs except the table." Chinese food has become popular all over the world, transported to many countries by Chinese migrants.

Soy sauce

Dried prawn

INDUSTRY

Although China has extensive reserves of coal, iron ore, and oil, its heavy industry is state-run, old-fashioned, and inefficient. 70 percent of China's energy is provided by coal. About half of China's coal comes from large, well-equipped mines; the rest is extracted from small local pits. These mines are notorious for their high accident rates. Look for ⛏

The Great Wild

Goose pagoda at Xi'an was built in the 7th century AD. It formed part of a Buddhist monastery.

Tea, China's national drink, is grown on terraced hillsides in the south of the country.

BABY BOOM

China's population is now over a billion, stretching resources such as land, food, and education to the limit. Couples with only one child receive various benefits. If a second child is born, these benefits are withdrawn.

THIS MAP SHOWS THE SOUTH-EASTERN PART OF CHINA ONLY. THE REST OF CHINA IS SHOWN ON PP. 132-133.

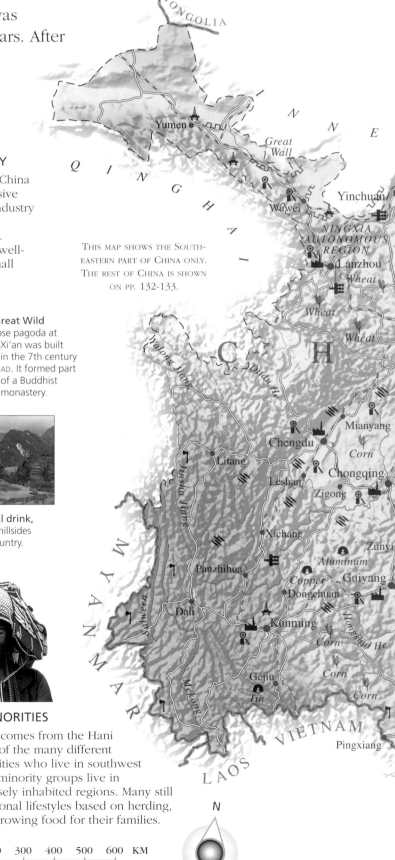

MAP FEATURES

Hydroelectric power: China's rivers have great potential; dams, lakes, and canals provide flood control and irrigation as well as electricity. Look for ⊞

Economic zones: The Chinese government has set up special industrial zones, encouraging foreign investment through tax incentives. Look for ⌂

Borders: The most militarized border in the world divides Korea into communist North and democratic South. Look for ⤴

🌾	Cereals	⛏	Mining
🌾	Rice	⛏	Coal
🌿	Tea	🛢	Oil
🌲	Timber	🏭	Industrial center
🎣	Fishing	🚢	Shipbuilding

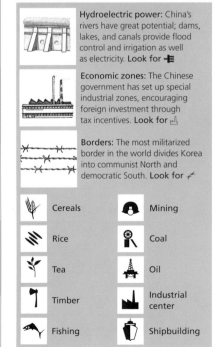

AGRICULTURE

China feeds its vast population from only 7 percent of the world's farmland. In the fertile southern part of the country, the fields can yield three harvests every year – two crops of rice and a third crop of vegetables or cereals. Look for 🌾

RACIAL MINORITIES

This woman comes from the Hani people, one of the many different ethnic minorities who live in southwest China. Most minority groups live in remote, sparsely inhabited regions. Many still follow traditional lifestyles based on herding, hunting, or growing food for their families.

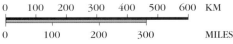

0   100   200   300   400   500   600 KM

0   100   200   300 MILES

N

A   B   C   D   E   F   G   H   I   J

THE DRAGON THRONE

The Hall of Supreme Harmony houses the Dragon Throne, seat of the former emperors of China. It is the largest building in Beijing's Forbidden City, and dates back to the 15th century. Ordinary citizens were banned from this area, which was reserved for the Emperor and his courtiers. Today, the Forbidden City has been restored and opened to the public; it attracts millions of tourists every year.

北京

The word *Beijing*, written in Chinese. Each symbol stands for a word or an idea.

A jade vase. Jade is China's most precious stone.

COMMUNISM

In the 1960s, China suffered a campaign of terror against artists, politicians, and intellectuals. Although the regime is now more liberal, political messages displayed on walls are often the only way of challenging the government.

NORTH KOREA
pop: 23,200,000

GINSENG

Korea exports this precious root, which is widely used in traditional Asian medicine. It is also popular in the West where it is thought to improve health and promote long life and vigor.

Ginseng roots are grown for 4-6 years, then steamed and dried

Rice fields in South Korea. Rice thrives in the mild south.

SOUTH KOREA
pop: 46,100,000

LAND OF MIRACLES

The Korean economy was devastated by World War II, but during the last 40 years South Korea has undergone an economic miracle. Today, it has a major shipbuilding industry and modern steelworks; textiles, cars, computers, and televisions pour off production lines. A quarter of all South Koreans live in the capital, Seoul, which has become one of the world's largest cities.

CHINA
pop: 1,213,000,000
(SOUTHEAST CHINA)
pop: 1,165,670,000

Playing Ping-Pong is a national passion in China.

SHANGHAI

The port of Shanghai is the largest city in China. In the 19th century, foreign countries who were involved in trade with China claimed sections of the city. They established commercial buildings and warehouses, giving central Shanghai the appearance of a European city. Today, Shanghai has become important as a center of heavy industry.

Carp fishing with cormorants, nets, and bamboo rafts in Guangxi Zhuangzu Autonomous Region.

TAIWAN
pop: 21,500,000

THE LITTLE DRAGON

Taiwan is one of Asia's wealthiest economies. The country produces about 10 percent of the world's computers and also specializes in textiles and shoe manufacturing.

The Taiwanese refer to their country as the Republic of China, but China does not recognize the country under this name.

HONG KONG

The rocky island of Hong Kong became a British Crown Colony in the 19th century. In 1997 it was returned to China, and became a "special administrative region." Hong Kong has the busiest container port in the world, and is a center of trade, finance, manufacturing, and tourism.

JAPAN

THE LAND OF THE RISING SUN, as Japan is sometimes called, was ruled for centuries by powerful warlords called *shoguns*, who discouraged any contact with the outside world. When traders from America and Europe arrived, Japan's isolation suddenly ended, the *shogun* was overthrown, and an emperor ruled the country. Over the next century, Japan transformed itself into one of the world's richest nations, a change in fortune all the more remarkable considering the country's geography. Japan consists of four main islands and 4,000 smaller islands. The majority of its 126 million people live closely packed together around the coast, since two-thirds of the land is mountainous and thickly forested. Japan has few natural resources and has to import most of its fuel and raw materials. The Japanese have concentrated on improving and adapting technology imported from abroad. Today, Japanese companies are world leaders in many areas of research and development, a success partly due to their management techniques, which ensure a well paid and loyal workforce.

RICE CULTIVATION

Rice is Japan's main food. Although only about 11 percent of the land is suitable for farming, Japan produces enough rice for its own needs. The crop is intensively cultivated on small plots of land using fertilizers and sophisticated machinery, like this rice planter. The warm, wet summers in southern Japan are ideal for growing rice. Look for ⧦

Silk *kimono*

FISHING

Fish is a very popular food in Japan. Huge quantities are caught each year by the country's fishing fleet – the world's largest. One million tons of fish and shellfish are also bred every year on fish farms. These tuna are on sale in Tokyo's fish market. Look for 🐟

TRADITIONAL DRESS

Until the 19th century Japanese traditional dress varied greatly between the social classes. In the royal courts, long-sleeved robes called *kimonos* were worn. Made of silk, these were wound round the body and tied with a sash. *Kimonos* are still worn on special occasions.

KABUKI THEATER

There are two forms of traditional Japanese theater: Noh and Kabuki. Noh is very old: the plays are based on myths of the gods and contain music and symbolic dancing. Kabuki theaters have plays based on stories of great heroes of the past. This photo shows a scene from a Kabuki play.

A miniature television produced in Japan.

The Japanese are skilled at *bonsai* – the art of producing miniature trees and shrubs.

The southern Kurile Islands are administered by the Russian Federation but claimed by Japan.

The Hidaka-sanmyaku mountains on the large island of Hokkaido.

FOOD

The Japanese eat a lot of fish because there is not enough farmland to keep cattle for meat or dairy produce.

Lacquer dish
Marinated raw fish
Seaweed
Rice

SHIPBUILDING

A large number of the ships sailing the world today were made in Japan. Countries such as South Korea can now build ships more cheaply, however, and Japan's industry is declining. To remain competitive, Japanese shipbuilders are building specialized ships such as cruise liners and developing new products like oil-drilling platforms. Look for 🚢

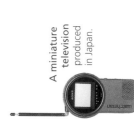

JAPAN
pop: 125,900,000

SEA OF OKHOTSK

Ostrov Iturup
Ostrov Shikotan
Ostrov Kunashir
Habomai Is.
Kurile Islands

Nemuro
Kushiro
Abashiri
Kitami
Obihiro
Wakkanai
La Perouse Strait
Rebun-to
Rishiri-to
Asahikawa
Ishikari-gawa
Sapporo
Otaru
Ishikari-wan
Tomakomai
HIDAKA-SANMYAKU
Hokkaido
Hakodate
Tsugaru-kaikyo
Uchiura-wan
Fukushima
Seikan Tunnel
Okushiri-to

Aomori
Hachinohe
Akita
Morioka
OU SANMYAKU
Yamagata
Sendai
Fukushima
Iwaki
Niigata
Koriyama
Utsunomiya
Nagano
Maebashi
Mito
Hitachi
Kasumiga-ura
Urawa
Honshu

Sado
Toyama-wan
Toyama
Kanazawa

SEA OF JAPAN

JAPAN'S CAPITAL CITY

During the 500 years of its existence, Tokyo has survived fire, flood, earthquakes, and destruction by war. Each disaster has required massive rebuilding. Earthquake-resistant materials and construction techniques, which enable a building to sway rather than fall, have allowed new skyscrapers to replace older buildings. But the danger of earthquakes remains, and there are plans to move the capital to a safer site farther north.

VEHICLE INDUSTRY

Japanese vehicle manufacturers became world leaders in the 1980s thanks to their stylish designs, new technology, and efficient production methods. Today, motor vehicles are the country's biggest export. Japanese vehicle manufacturers have also opened a number of factories overseas – in Europe, the USA and elsewhere. Countries in areas like eastern Europe can supply cheaper labor than in Japan. Look for 🚗

Japanese motorbike

MAP FEATURES

Financial center: Japan is a leading member of the world financial community. Its stock exchange ranks second in the world. Look for 📈

Skiing: The Hida-sanmyaku mountains in Honshu are excellent for skiing. In 1998, the Winter Olympics were held in Nagano. Look for ⛷

Rail routes: The Shinkansen, or bullet train, runs from Tokyo to Fukuoka at an average speed of 122 miles (195 km) per hour. Look for 🚄

Fishing ports
Industrial center
Vehicle manufacture
Shipbuilding
High-tech industry

Rice
Mixed fruit
Citrus fruits
Tea
Tobacco

Mount Fuji, Japan's sacred mountain, is crowned with snow.

RELIGION

There are two main religions in Japan – Buddhism and Shinto. People often follow both: it is common to be married with Shinto rituals, but buried with Buddhist ones. There are numerous Buddhist and Shinto shrines and temples in Japan. They are usually built of wood – and therefore vulnerable to fire – and temples like Ginkakuji in Kyoto have been rebuilt several times.

SITE OF TOKYO

Built around Tokyo Bay, and hemmed in by mountains, Tokyo is unable to spread farther inland or along the coast. The sprawling built-up region around Tokyo and Yokohama is the world's largest urban area and is sometimes called a megalopolis. It has a population of over 27 million people, and accounts for 25 percent of Japan's industrial production.

Rice and other crops grown in fertile volcanic soils and ideal climate
Industrial and urban areas
Intensively cultivated lowlands due to shortage of farmland
To relieve overcrowding, developers build upward, and into the sea on reclaimed land
Tokyo Bay
Yokohama
Tokyo
SAGAMI-NADA
Mt. Fuji

COMMUTING

Most Japanese people live in the cities, but few can afford to live in the city centers, so most have to commute to work. Trains are fast and efficient, but so overcrowded that special guards are employed to push commuters into the carriages.

COMPUTERS

The Japanese excel at producing miniature electronic goods, such as computers and televisions. They have set such high standards that few countries can match them. A silicon chip able to hold 1,000 pages of newsprint in its memory is being developed.

A bottle of rice wine, or sake, Japan's national drink.

The beautiful rocky coast of the Oki-shoto islands, which lie in the Sea of Japan.

Map labels

PACIFIC OCEAN
EAST CHINA SEA
Korea Strait
Tsushima

Dōgo, Dozen, Oki-shoto
Tottori
Matsue
Hamada
Hagi
Yamaguchi
Shimonoseki
Kitakyushu
Fukuoka
Saga
Sasebo
Nagasaki
Goto-retto
Shimo-jima
Kumamoto
Beppu
Oita
Nobeoka
Miyazaki
Kagoshima
Osumi-shoto
Osumi-kaikyo
Tanega-shima
Yaku-shima
AMAKUSA-NADA
Kyushu
CHUGOKU-SANCHI
Kurashiki
Okayama
Takamatsu
Tokushima
Kochi
Matsuyama
Uwajima
Nakamura
Shikoku
Inland Sea
Hiroshima
Kobe
Osaka
Kyoto
Wakayama
Biwa-ko
Wakasa-wan
Fukui
Gifu
Nagoya
HIDA-SAN
Okazaki
Shingu
Hamamatsu
Shizuoka
Mt. Fuji
Yokohama
Kawasaki
Yokosuka
Chiba
TOKYO
Hachiōji
Sagami-nada
Tzu-shoto

Ryukyu Is.
Amami-gunto
Amami o-shima
Tokuno-shima
Okinoerabu-jima
Okinawa
Okinawa-shoto
Naha
Tokara-retto

0 50 100 150 200 250 KM
0 50 100 150 MILES

MAINLAND SOUTHEAST ASIA

MUCH OF THIS REGION is mountainous and covered with forest. Most of the people live in the great river valleys, plateaus, or fertile plains. Farming is the main occupation, with rice the principal crop. Of the seven countries, only Thailand was not a British or French colony. Thais are deeply devoted to their royal family and the Buddhist faith. The Federation of Malaysia includes 11 states on the mainland, joined in 1963 by Sabah and Sarawak in Borneo. This union of east and west has produced one of the world's most successful developing countries. Singapore, at first part of Malaysia, became a republic in 1965. The island controls the busy shipping routes between the Indian and Pacific oceans. Cambodia, Laos, and Vietnam have all suffered from many years of warfare. Cambodia's future is still uncertain, but the other two countries show signs of economic recovery. Myanmar (Burma) has become increasingly isolated from the world by its repressive government.

MYANMAR (BURMA)
pop: 47,600,000

RUBIES
Several types of precious stones are mined in northeastern Myanmar. The glowing red rubies from this region are considered the finest in the world. Many people in the East believe that wearing a ruby protects you from harm. Today Myanmar has a virtual monopoly over the ruby trade. Look for ⚑

Ruby Calcite

FISHING
Fish is one of the main foods in this area. Thailand has a thriving fish canning industry. Fish farming in the inland lake of Tonle Sap, Cambodia, is also successful. Here, in Myanmar, fish are caught from small huts built over the water. Look for ⚑

BUDDHISM
Except for Malaysia, the main religion in this region is Buddhism. In Thailand and Myanmar, where almost all the people are Buddhists, every young man puts on the saffron robe, shaves his head, and enters a monastery for several months.

TIMBER
Thailand was once a major producer of teak, but so much of the country's forests have been cut down that commercial logging was banned in 1989 – until forests recover. Myanmar is now the world's principal teak exporter. Here, huge logs float down the Irrawaddy river. Look for ⚑

Making lacquer ware is a traditional craft in Thailand.

Lacquer tray

Boats on the Irrawaddy, the great river of Myanmar

OPIUM
For the poor hill tribes of the "Golden Triangle" – the remote area where Myanmar, Laos, and Thailand meet – growing opium poppies is one of the few sources of income. Useful painkillers can be made from the poppies, but so too are dangerous drugs such as heroin. Governments are encouraging people in this area to grow other crops, including flowers and tobacco.

Poppy seeds

Dried opium poppy

VIETNAM
Rice is the principal crop in this country. As Vietnam is so mountainous, most people live in the two main river deltas. Two-thirds of the farmed land is devoted to growing rice. The wetfield, or *paddy*, is planted by women. Look for ⚑

VIETNAM
pop: 77,900,000

Durian fruit is grown throughout the region.

LAOS
pop: 5,400,000

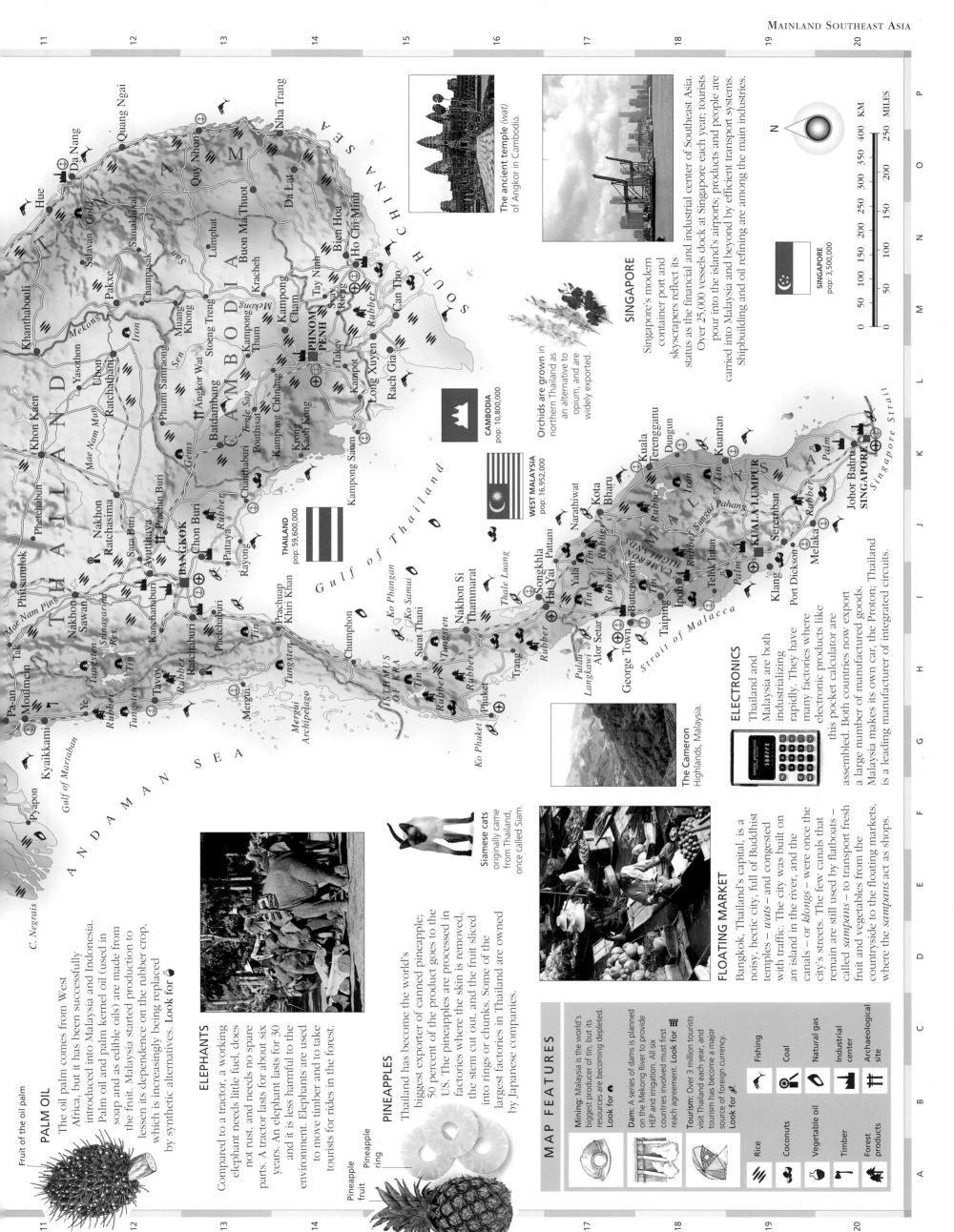

PALM OIL

Fruit of the oil palm

The oil palm comes from West Africa, but it has been successfully introduced into Malaysia and Indonesia. Palm oil and palm kernel oil (used in soap and as edible oils) are made from the fruit. Malaysia started production to lessen its dependence on the rubber crop, which is increasingly being replaced by synthetic alternatives. Look for 🌴

ELEPHANTS

Compared to a tractor, a working elephant needs little fuel, does not rust, and needs no spare parts. A tractor lasts for about six years. An elephant lasts for 30 and it is less harmful to the environment. Elephants are used to move timber and to take tourists for rides in the forest.

PINEAPPLES

Pineapple fruit

Pineapple ring

Thailand has become the world's biggest exporter of canned pineapple; 50 percent of the product goes to the US. The pineapples are processed in factories where the skin is removed, the stem cut out, and the fruit sliced into rings or chunks. Some of the largest factories in Thailand are owned by Japanese companies.

Siamese cats originally came from Thailand, once called Siam.

FLOATING MARKET

Bangkok, Thailand's capital, is a noisy, hectic city, full of Buddhist temples – *wats* – and congested with traffic. The city was built on an island in the river, and the canals – or *klongs* – were once the city's streets. The few canals that remain are still used by flatboats – called *sampans* – to transport fresh fruit and vegetables from the countryside to the floating markets, where the *sampans* act as shops.

MAP FEATURES

Mining: Malaysia is the world's biggest producer of tin, but its resources are becoming depleted. Look for 🛠

Dam: A series of dams is planned on the Mekong River to provide HEP and irrigation. All six countries involved must first reach agreement. Look for 🏛

Tourism: Over 3 million tourists visit Thailand each year, and tourism has become a major source of foreign currency. Look for 🏛

Rice	Fishing		
Coconuts	Coal		
Vegetable oil	Natural gas		
Timber	Industrial center		
Forest products	Archaeological site		

ELECTRONICS

Thailand and Malaysia are both industrializing rapidly. They have many factories where electronic products like this pocket calculator are assembled. Both countries now export a large number of manufactured goods. Malaysia makes its own car, the Proton; Thailand is a leading manufacturer of integrated circuits.

The Cameron Highlands, Malaysia.

SINGAPORE

Singapore's modern container port and skyscrapers reflect its status as the financial and industrial center of Southeast Asia. Over 25,000 vessels dock at Singapore each year; tourists pour into the island's airports; products and people are carried into Malaysia and beyond by efficient transport systems. Shipbuilding and oil refining are among the main industries.

Orchids are grown in northern Thailand as an alternative to opium, and are widely exported.

The ancient temple (*wat*) of Angkor in Cambodia.

CAMBODIA
pop: 10,800,000

THAILAND
pop: 59,600,000

WEST MALAYSIA
pop: 16,952,000

SINGAPORE
pop: 3,500,000

N

KM 0 50 100 150 200 250 300 350 400
MILES 0 50 100 150 200 250

MARITIME SOUTHEAST ASIA

SCATTERED between the Indian and Pacific oceans lies a huge crescent of mountainous tropical islands – the East Indies. The largest country in this region is Indonesia, which was ruled by the Dutch for nearly 350 years. Over half its 13,677 islands are still uninhabited. The island of Borneo is shared between Indonesia, the Malaysian states of Sabah and Sarawak, and the Sultanate of Brunei. Indonesia's national motto, "Unity in diversity," ideally suits a country made up of 362 different peoples speaking over 250 dialects and languages. Indonesia seized East Timor in 1975. In 1999, an overwhelming vote for independence led to violent clashes, and a UN peacekeeping force was sent to the island. The Philippines, ruled for three centuries by Spain, then for about 50 years by the US, consists of over 7,000 islands. It is the only mainly Christian country in Asia. Much of the region is covered by forests, which contain some of the finest timber in the world.

COCONUTS
Indonesia and the Philippines are the world's major coconut growers. Every part of the tree has its uses, even the leaves. The kernel is dried to make copra, from which a valuable oil is obtained. Look for 🥥

Kernel

STILT VILLAGES
Many of the villages in this region are built over water. The houses are made of local materials like wood and bamboo and built on stilts to protect them from vermin and flooding. For houses built on land, raised floors also provide shelter for the owner's animals which live underneath.

BRUNEI
The Sultanate of Brunei became rich when oil was discovered in 1929. This golden-domed mosque, built with the country's newfound wealth, towers above the capital, Bandar Seri Begawan. The small, predominantly Muslim population pays no taxes, and enjoys free education and health care.

BRUNEI
pop: 313,000

Helicopter

AIRCRAFT INDUSTRY
Indonesia has developed a thriving aircraft industry. About 12,000 workers assemble helicopters and aircraft at Bandung in Java. The factories are jointly owned by five international aircraft manufacturers. The first solely Indonesian-designed aircraft will soon be completed.

MALAYSIA
pop: 21,500,000
(EAST MALAYSIA: SABAH AND SARAWAK)
pop: 4,548,000

RELIGION
Although about 90 percent of Indonesians are Muslim, many of their religious ceremonies contain elements of other religions – like Hinduism and Buddhism – which blend with local traditions and beliefs. Recently, Islam has become more dominant. More girls now wear the Islamic headdress, like these pupils at a school in Sumatra.

Dense rain forest on Sumatra is home to elephants and tigers.

Borobudur, the great 8th-century Buddhist temple on Java.

MAP FEATURES

🍶	Vegetable oil: Indonesia is now one of the world's major producers of palm oil. It has many uses, from hydraulic brake fluids to cooking oil. Look for 🍶
🔬	Research center: Near Manila in the Philippines the Rice Research Institute has developed many of the world's modern high-yield types of rice. Look for 🔬
🏴‍☠️	Pirates: Pirate attacks on vessels in the area are increasing, especially at night and in the busy shipping lanes of the Singapore Strait. Look for 🏴‍☠️

〰️ Rice	⚓ Fishing
🥥 Coconuts	⛏️ Mining
🚩 Timber	🛢️ Oil
🌲 Forest products	🏭 Industrial center

JAKARTA
Situated on the island of Java, Indonesia's capital, Jakarta, has the largest population of any city in Southeast Asia – and is still growing rapidly. It was once the center of the region's Dutch trading empire, and many typical Dutch buildings still stand in the old part of the city. At night, skyscrapers glitter above the city's modern center.

Bandaaceh · Rubber · Belawan · Medan · Pematangsiantar · Danau Toba · Sibolga · Palm · Pulau Simeulue · Pulau Nias · Sumatra · Tanjungpinang · Pekanbaru · Pulau Batu · Pulau Pini · Padang · Batang Hari · Rubber · Jambi · Pulau Siberut · Pulau Sipura · Rubber · Pulau Pagai Utara · Pulau Pagai Selatan · PEGUNUNGAN BARISAN · Bengkulu · Rubber · Palm · Palembang · Bandarlampung · Pulau Enggano · Bogor · JAKARTA · Sukabumi · Bandung · Cirebon · Borobudur · Semarang · Yogyakarta · Kediri · Malang · Jember · Java · Denpasar Bali · Banyuwangi · Pulau Madura · Pulau Bawean · Pulau Kangean · Surabaya

SOUTH CHINA SEA · Kota Kinabalu · BANDAR SERI BEGAWAN · Miri · Kuala Belait · BRUNEI · MALAYSIA (EAST) · Pulau Natuna Besar · Kepulauan Natuna · Kepulauan Anambas · Sibu · Sarikei · SARAWAK · Kuching · Borneo · Pontianak · Sungai Kapuas · PEGUNUNGAN MULLER · PEGUNUNGAN SCHWANER · Sungai Barito · Rubber · Kualakapuas · Banjarmasin · Singapore Strait · Pulau Bintan · Pulau Lingga · Pulau Singkep · Kepulauan Karimata · Pulau Bangka · Pangkalpinang · Tin · Pulau Belitung · JAVA SEA · INDIAN OCEAN

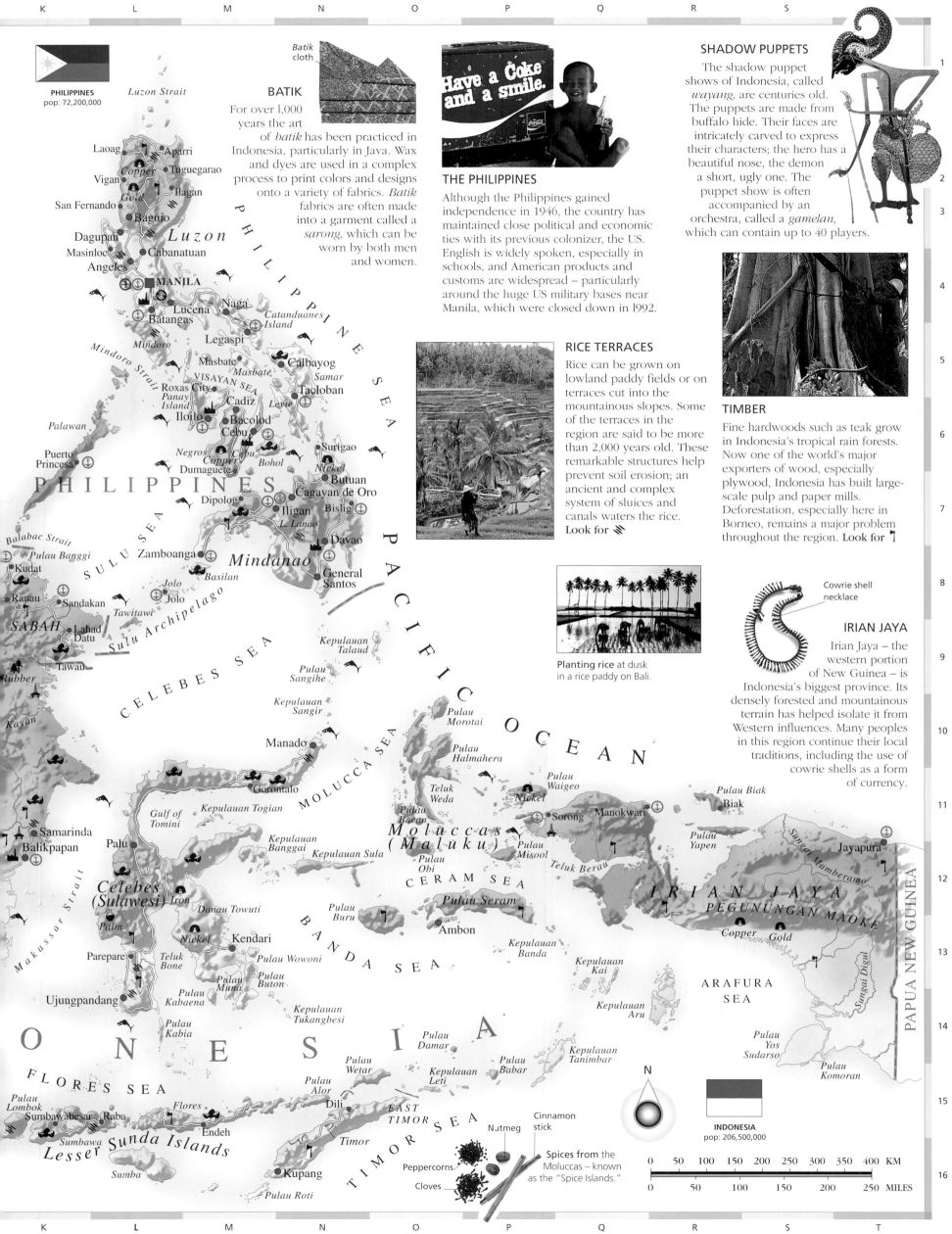

PHILIPPINES
pop: 72,200,000

BATIK

Batik cloth

For over 1,000 years the art of *batik* has been practiced in Indonesia, particularly in Java. Wax and dyes are used in a complex process to print colors and designs onto a variety of fabrics. *Batik* fabrics are often made into a garment called a *sarong*, which can be worn by both men and women.

THE PHILIPPINES

Have a Coke and a smile.

Although the Philippines gained independence in 1946, the country has maintained close political and economic ties with its previous colonizer, the US. English is widely spoken, especially in schools, and American products and customs are widespread – particularly around the huge US military bases near Manila, which were closed down in 1992.

SHADOW PUPPETS

The shadow puppet shows of Indonesia, called *wayang,* are centuries old. The puppets are made from buffalo hide. Their faces are intricately carved to express their characters; the hero has a beautiful nose, the demon a short, ugly one. The puppet show is often accompanied by an orchestra, called a *gamelan,* which can contain up to 40 players.

RICE TERRACES

Rice can be grown on lowland paddy fields or on terraces cut into the mountainous slopes. Some of the terraces in the region are said to be more than 2,000 years old. These remarkable structures help prevent soil erosion; an ancient and complex system of sluices and canals waters the rice. **Look for** ⧯

TIMBER

Fine hardwoods such as teak grow in Indonesia's tropical rain forests. Now one of the world's major exporters of wood, especially plywood, Indonesia has built large-scale pulp and paper mills. Deforestation, especially here in Borneo, remains a major problem throughout the region. **Look for** ⌐

Planting rice at dusk in a rice paddy on Bali.

IRIAN JAYA

Cowrie shell necklace

Irian Jaya – the western portion of New Guinea – is Indonesia's biggest province. Its densely forested and mountainous terrain has helped isolate it from Western influences. Many peoples in this region continue their local traditions, including the use of cowrie shells as a form of currency.

INDONESIA
pop: 206,500,000

Spices from the Moluccas – known as the "Spice Islands."
Nutmeg
Cinnamon stick
Peppercorns
Cloves

0 50 100 150 200 250 300 350 400 KM
0 50 100 150 200 250 MILES

Koala
Phascolarctos cinereus
Length:
31 in (80 cm)

Funnel-web spider
Atrax robustus
Length: 1 in (3 cm)

Raggiana's bird of paradise
Paradisaea raggiana
Length: 4 ft (1.4 m)

AUSTRALASIA AND OCEANIA

AUSTRALASIA AND OCEANIA includes Australia, New Zealand, and numerous island groups in the Pacific. Australia – the smallest, flattest, and driest continent – has been worn down by 3,000 million years of exposure to wind and rain. Away from Australia, along the edges of the continental plates, volcanic activity is common because the plates are still moving. These plate movements greatly affect New Guinea, many Pacific islands, and New Zealand. Elsewhere in the Pacific Ocean, thousands of tiny coral islands have grown on the tops of undersea volcanic mountains. Climates vary greatly across the region, from the wet tropical climates of the islands in the outer Pacific, to the hot, dry deserts of central Australia. Tropical rain forests can be found in northeastern Australia and much of New Guinea.

Cider gum tree
Eucalyptus gunnii
Height:
76 ft (25 m)

■ **SURF AND SAND**
Powerful waves from the Tasman Sea wash the southeast coast of Australia, creating long, sandy beaches.

■ **AUSTRALIA'S RAIN FOREST**
Over 600 different types of trees grow in the tropical rain forest on the Cape York Peninsula. Mists often hang over the forest.

□ **DESERT MOUNTAINS**
For millions of years, erosion has scoured the center of Australia. Rocky outcrops like Kata Tjuta have been reduced to sandstone domes.

Taipan
Oxyuranuus scutellatus
Length:
12 ft (3.6 m)

■ **TROPICAL GRASSLAND**
Deserts with arid shrubs and tussock grasses dominate the central third of Australia. Across northern Australia is a tropical grassland with scattered trees.

■ **DRY WOODLAND**
Eucalyptus – otherwise known as gum trees – abound in Australia. Most species are adapted to dry conditions, their tough, leathery leaves resisting the drying effects of the sun.

■ **TEMPERATE RAIN FOREST**
Far from other land and surrounded by ocean, much of New Zealand has high rainfall and is mild all year round. These conditions encourage the unique plants of the temperate rain forest.

△ **HOT NEW ZEALAND**
Steam rises from pools of sulfurous boiling water and mud, signs of volcanic activity along the plate margins. The heat comes from deep within the Earth.

Giant white buttercup
Ranunculus lyalii
Size: 3 ft (1 m)

■ **THE PINNACLES**
Western Australia's weird limestone pinnacles stand out in the sandy desert. Rain and plant roots have shaped the pillars over the last 25,000 years.

Black opal, a precious stone found in Australia.

CROSS-SECTION THROUGH AUSTRALASIA AND OCEANIA

Exmouth Plateau
Indian Ocean
Hamersley Range
Great Victoria Desert
Flinders Ranges
Australian Alps
New Zealand
Tasman Sea
Pacific Ocean

9,843 (3,000)
Sea level 0
-14,764 (-4,500)
Feet (meters)
A
Length: 4,500 miles (7,250 km)
B

△ **NEW ZEALAND'S ALPS**
Rising steeply from the west coast, the Southern Alps cover 80 percent of South Island. Glaciers moving down the mountains carved deep inlets – fjords – along the southwest coast.

Red kangaroo
Macropus rufus
Height: 6 ft (2 m)

Brown kiwi
Apteryx australis
Height: 14 in (35 cm)

Giant clam
Tridacna gigas
Shell: 5 ft (1.5 m)

Butterfly fish
Chaetodon auriga
Length: 8 in (20 cm)

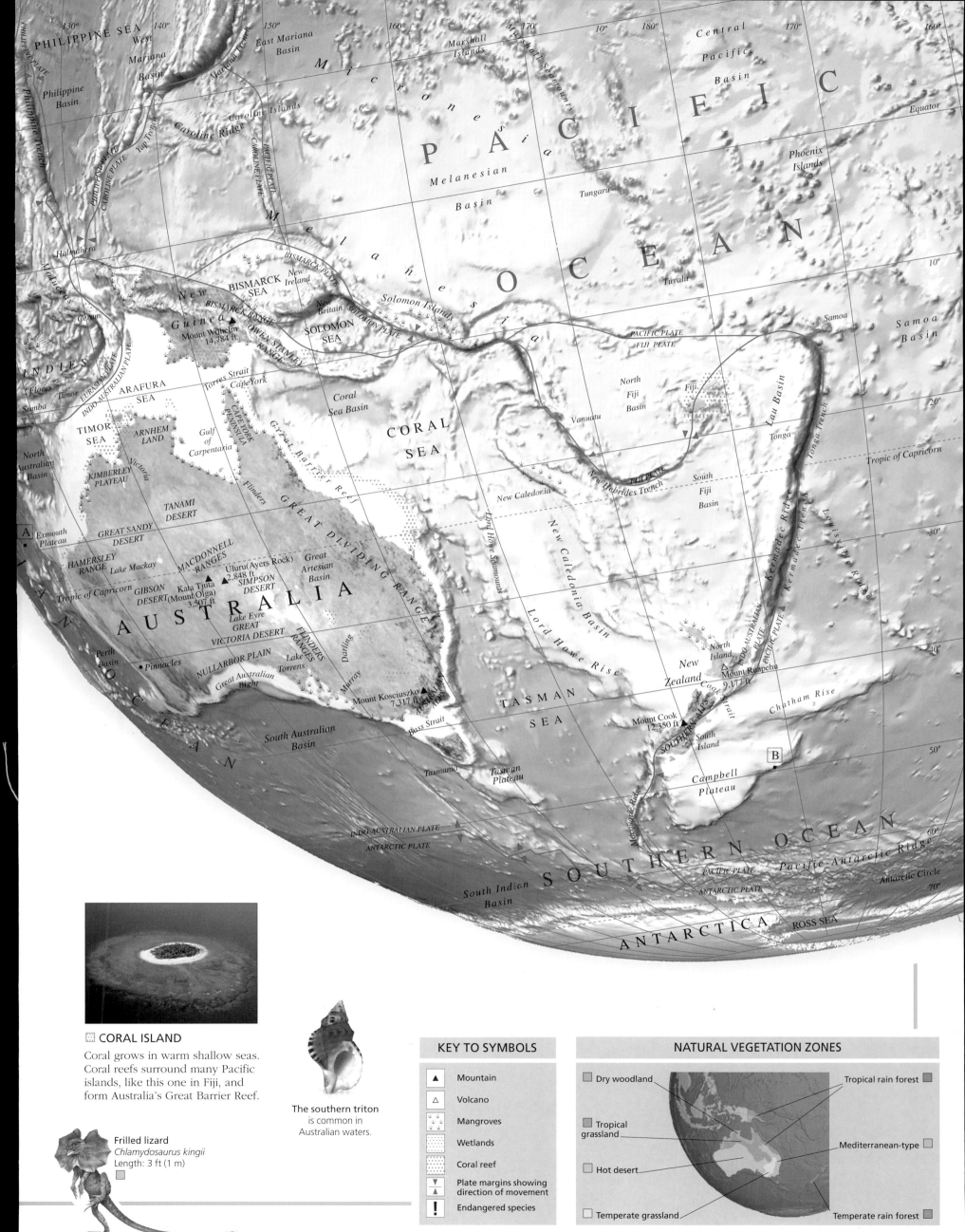

CORAL ISLAND

Coral grows in warm shallow seas. Coral reefs surround many Pacific islands, like this one in Fiji, and form Australia's Great Barrier Reef.

The southern triton is common in Australian waters.

Frilled lizard
Chlamydosaurus kingii
Length: 3 ft (1 m)

KEY TO SYMBOLS

▲	Mountain
△	Volcano
⁂	Mangroves
⠿	Wetlands
⠿	Coral reef
⊻	Plate margins showing direction of movement
!	Endangered species

NATURAL VEGETATION ZONES

- Dry woodland
- Tropical grassland
- Hot desert
- Temperate grassland
- Tropical rain forest
- Mediterranean-type
- Temperate rain forest

A B C D E F G H I J

THE PACIFIC OCEAN

THE PACIFIC IS THE LARGEST and deepest of the world's oceans. It covers a greater area of the Earth's surface than all the land areas combined. At its deepest point – 36,197 ft (11,033 m) down in the Mariana Trench – it is deep enough to cover Mount Everest. More than half the world's population lives around the shores of the Pacific. The ocean's northern and western edges, known as the outer Pacific, are fringed with chains of islands, such as the Aleutians. The inner Pacific islands fall into three main groups: Melanesia, Micronesia, and Polynesia. With the development of modern communications, trade and cooperation between countries surrounding the ocean – sometimes referred to as the "Pacific Rim" – is increasing. Countries such as Japan, Australia, and New Zealand want the south Pacific made into a nuclear-free zone, which would prevent all testing of nuclear weapons.

MICRONESIA
pop: 109,000

The Aleutians, a chain of volcanic islands in the Pacific.

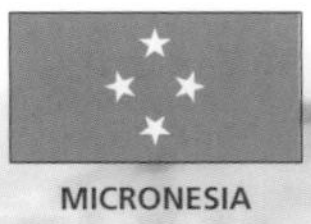

NAURU
pop: 11,000

PALAU
pop: 17,700

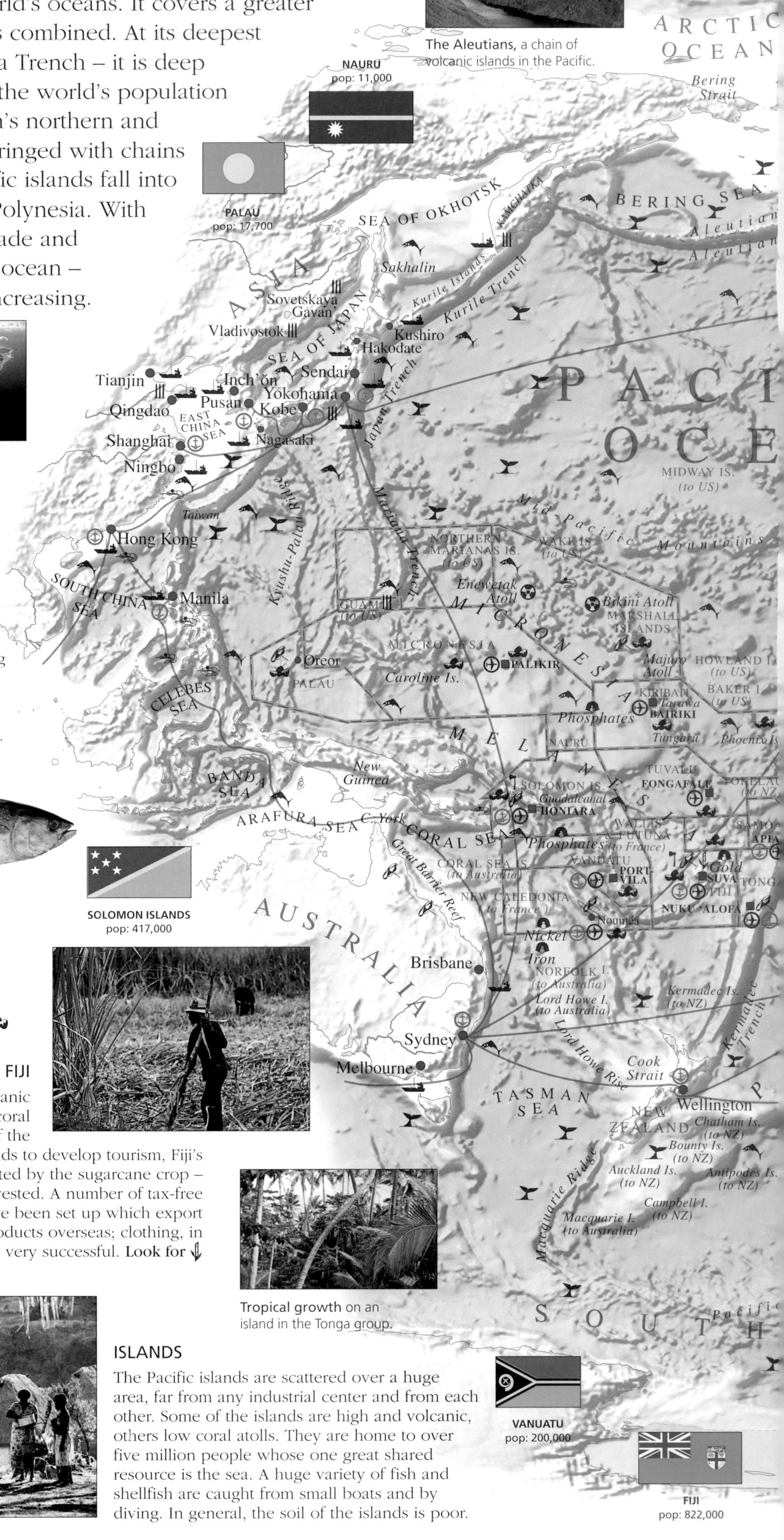

A coral atoll in French Polynesia.

FISHING

Pacific islanders fish mainly for food, although any surplus catch may be sold. Many fish are caught in the north Pacific by commercial fleets operating far from their home bases. The biggest catches are made by Japan, South Korea, Taiwan, and the US. The main fish caught is tuna. Look for 🐟

CONTAINER PORTS

Today, fruit, meat, and many other goods are moved round the world in huge metal containers. Here, a ship waits to be loaded at Kobe, one of Japan's main container ports.

Skipjack tuna

COCONUTS

The coconut palm is called "tree of life" by Pacific islanders because it provides so many of their daily needs, such as food and building materials. Here, the white "meat" of the coconut is dried to make copra, which yields oil. Look for 🥥

SOLOMON ISLANDS
pop: 417,000

MAP FEATURES

🐟	**Fishing:** Since the first salmon farms were set up in 1982 around Chiloé island, Chile, salmon farming has become a major industry. Look for 🐟
⛑️	**Mining:** The Pacific island of Nauru became prosperous through the export of phosphates, which are used to make fertilizers. Look for ⛏️
☢️	**Pollution:** Nuclear testing carried out by the US and France has polluted certain islands in the Pacific. Look for ☢️

⚓ Sugarcane	🚢 Fishing ports
🦐 Coconuts	🚣 Tourism
⚒️ Timber	🐋 Whales
🦞 Shellfishing	⛏️ Military bases

FIJI

Fiji is a group of volcanic islands surrounded by coral reefs. Although one of the few south Pacific islands to develop tourism, Fiji's economy is still dominated by the sugarcane crop – shown here being harvested. A number of tax-free factories have been set up which export a variety of products overseas; clothing, in particular, has proved very successful. Look for ⬇️

Tropical growth on an island in the Tonga group.

ISLANDS

The Pacific islands are scattered over a huge area, far from any industrial center and from each other. Some of the islands are high and volcanic, others low coral atolls. They are home to over five million people whose one great shared resource is the sea. A huge variety of fish and shellfish are caught from small boats and by diving. In general, the soil of the islands is poor.

VANUATU
pop: 200,000

FIJI
pop: 822,000

Map labels: ARCTIC OCEAN, Bering Strait, SEA OF OKHOTSK, BERING SEA, Aleutian, Kamchatka, Sakhalin, Kurile Islands, Kurile Trench, Sovetskaya Gavan, Vladivostok, Kushiro, Hakodate, SEA OF JAPAN, ASIA, Tianjin, Inch'on, Sendai, Qingdao, Pusan, Yokohama, Kobe, EAST CHINA SEA, Shanghai, Nagasaki, Japan Trench, Ningbo, PACIFIC OCEAN, Taiwan, MIDWAY IS. (to US), Mid Pacific Mountains, Hong Kong, Kyushu-Palau Ridge, NORTHERN MARIANAS IS. (to US), WAKE IS. (to US), SOUTH CHINA SEA, Mariana Trench, Enewetak Atoll, Bikini Atoll, Manila, GUAM (to US), MICRONESIA, MARSHALL ISLANDS, Majuro Atoll, HOWLAND I. (to US), Oreor, PALAU, Caroline Is., PALIKIR, KIRIBATI, Tarawa, BAKER I. (to US), CELEBES SEA, Phosphates, BAIRIKI, Tungaru, Phoenix Is., NAURU, TUVALU, New Guinea, MELANESIA, FONGAFALE, BANDA SEA, SOLOMON IS., TOKELAU (to NZ), Guadalcanal, HONIARA, WALLIS & FUTUNA (to France), SAMOA, APIA, ARAFURA SEA, C. York, CORAL SEA, Phosphates (to France), Gold, SUVA, TONGA, CORAL SEA IS. (to Australia), VANUATU, FIJI, Great Barrier Reef, PORT VILA, NUKU'ALOFA, NEW CALEDONIA (to France), Nickel, Noumea, Iron, AUSTRALIA, Brisbane, NORFOLK I. (to Australia), Kermadec Is. (to NZ), Lord Howe I. (to Australia), Sydney, Lord Howe Rise, Kermadec Trench, Cook Strait, Melbourne, TASMAN SEA, NEW ZEALAND, Wellington, Chatham Is. (to NZ), Bounty Is. (to NZ), Macquarie Ridge, Auckland Is. (to NZ), Antipodes Is. (to NZ), Campbell I. (to NZ), Macquarie I. (to Australia), SOUTH, Pacific

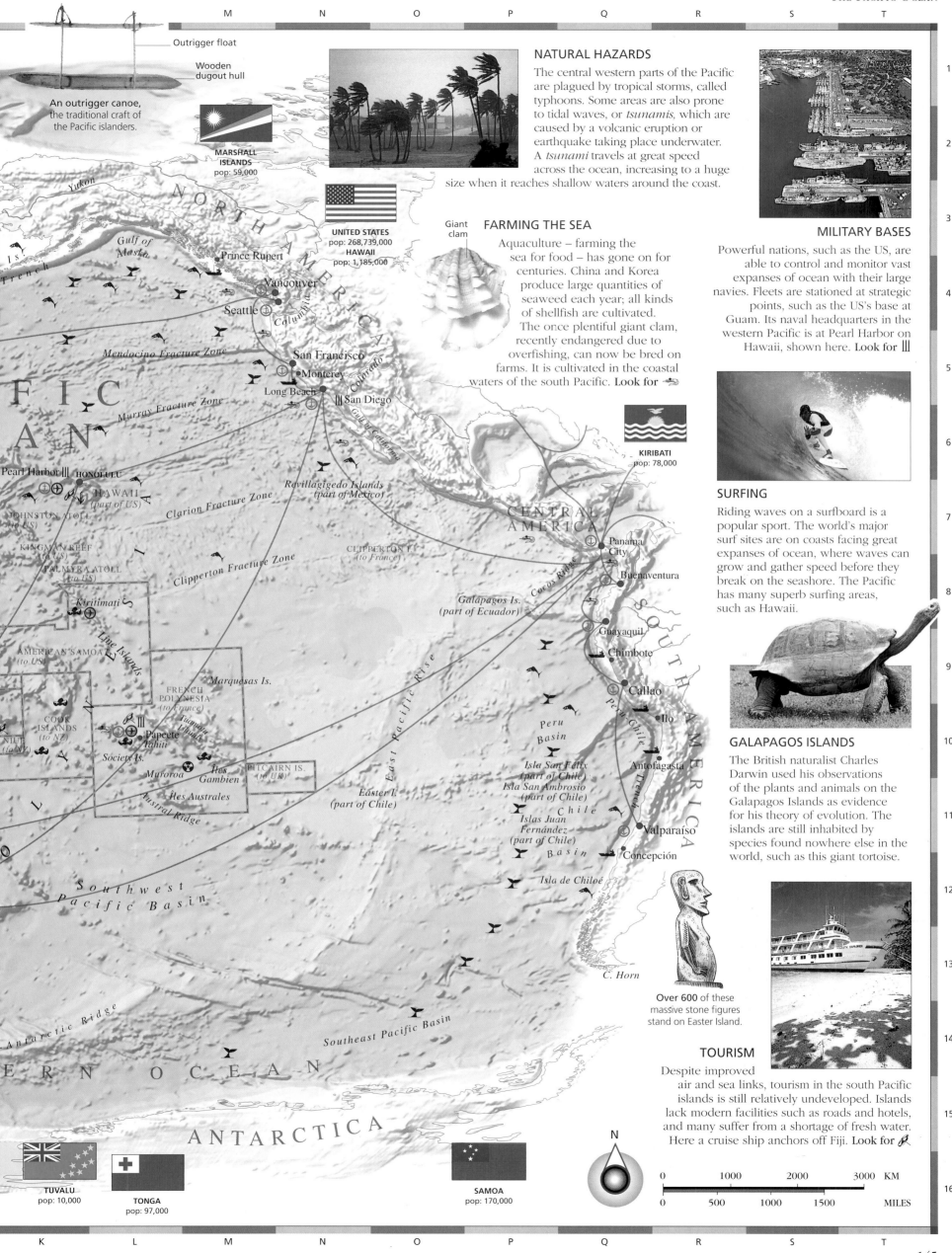

M N O P Q R S T

Outrigger float

Wooden dugout hull

An outrigger canoe, the traditional craft of the Pacific islanders.

MARSHALL ISLANDS
pop: 59,000

UNITED STATES
pop: 268,739,000
HAWAII
pop: 1,185,000

Giant clam

NATURAL HAZARDS

The central western parts of the Pacific are plagued by tropical storms, called typhoons. Some areas are also prone to tidal waves, or *tsunamis,* which are caused by a volcanic eruption or earthquake taking place underwater. A *tsunami* travels at great speed across the ocean, increasing to a huge size when it reaches shallow waters around the coast.

FARMING THE SEA

Aquaculture – farming the sea for food – has gone on for centuries. China and Korea produce large quantities of seaweed each year; all kinds of shellfish are cultivated. The once plentiful giant clam, recently endangered due to overfishing, can now be bred on farms. It is cultivated in the coastal waters of the south Pacific. **Look for**

MILITARY BASES

Powerful nations, such as the US, are able to control and monitor vast expanses of ocean with their large navies. Fleets are stationed at strategic points, such as the US's base at Guam. Its naval headquarters in the western Pacific is at Pearl Harbor on Hawaii, shown here. **Look for** |||

KIRIBATI
pop: 78,000

SURFING

Riding waves on a surfboard is a popular sport. The world's major surf sites are on coasts facing great expanses of ocean, where waves can grow and gather speed before they break on the seashore. The Pacific has many superb surfing areas, such as Hawaii.

GALAPAGOS ISLANDS

The British naturalist Charles Darwin used his observations of the plants and animals on the Galapagos Islands as evidence for his theory of evolution. The islands are still inhabited by species found nowhere else in the world, such as this giant tortoise.

Over 600 of these massive stone figures stand on Easter Island.

TOURISM

Despite improved air and sea links, tourism in the south Pacific islands is still relatively undeveloped. Islands lack modern facilities such as roads and hotels, and many suffer from a shortage of fresh water. Here a cruise ship anchors off Fiji. **Look for**

Map labels

Yukon

NORTH AMERICA

Gulf of Alaska

Trench

Prince Rupert

Vancouver

Seattle

Columbia

Mendocino Fracture Zone

San Francisco

Monterey

Colorado

Long Beach

San Diego

Gulf of California

Murray Fracture Zone

PACIFIC OCEAN

Pearl Harbor ||| HONOLULU

HAWAII (part of US)

JOHNSTON ATOLL (to US)

Clarion Fracture Zone

Revillagigedo Islands (part of Mexico)

CENTRAL AMERICA

Panama City

Buenaventura

KINGMAN REEF (to US)

PALMYRA ATOLL (to US)

Clipperton Fracture Zone

CLIPPERTON I. (to France)

Cocos Ridge

Kiritimati

Line Islands

Galapagos Is. (part of Ecuador)

Guayaquil

Chimbote

AMERICAN SAMOA (to US)

Marquesas Is.

SOUTH AMERICA

FRENCH POLYNESIA (to France)

Callao

Peru Basin

Ilo

NIUE (to NZ)

COOK ISLANDS (to NZ)

Tuamotu Islands

Papeete Tahiti

Society Is.

East Pacific Rise

Isla San Félix (part of Chile)

Isla San Ambrosio (part of Chile)

Antofagasta

Peru-Chile Trench

Muroroa

Îles Gambien

PITCAIRN IS. (to UK)

Easter I. (part of Chile)

Chile

Islas Juan Fernández (part of Chile)

Valparaíso

Îles Australes

Austral Ridge

Basin

Concepción

Isla de Chiloé

Southwest Pacific Basin

C. Horn

SOUTHERN OCEAN

Antarctic Ridge

Southeast Pacific Basin

ANTARCTICA

TUVALU
pop: 10,000

TONGA
pop: 97,000

SAMOA
pop: 170,000

N

0 1000 2000 3000 KM

0 500 1000 1500 MILES

K L M N O P Q R S T

AUSTRALIA AND PAPUA NEW GUINEA

AUSTRALIA IS A LAND OF EXTREMES. It is the world's smallest, flattest continent, with the lowest rainfall. The landscape ranges from scattered areas of rain forest along the northeast coast, to deserts, called the Outback, in the center, to snowfields in the southeast. It is also one of the most urbanized countries; 70 percent of the population live in towns and cities in the coastal regions, while much of the interior remains sparsely inhabited. Until two centuries ago this vast land was solely occupied by Aboriginal peoples, but in 1788 settlers from Britain established a colony on the southeast coast. Since then immigration, originally from Europe but now from Asia, has played a vital part in Australia's development. Australia is a wealthy and politically stable country with rich natural resources, steady population growth, and increasingly strong trade links in the Pacific area, especially with Japan and the US. Papua New Guinea, the eastern half of the mountainous island of New Guinea, was once an Australian colony, but became independent in 1975.

AUSTRALIA
pop: 18,966,800

FLYING DOCTORS

In the Australian Outback, the nearest neighbor can live vast distances away. For a doctor to cover such huge areas by road would be impossible. About 60 years ago, the Royal Flying Doctor Service was established. In an emergency, a caller can contact the service by radio, 24 hours a day, and receive medical treatment within hours.

Yam
Cassava

Cassava and yam are staple foods in Papua New Guinea.

THE GREAT OUTDOORS

Australia's climate is ideal for water-sports and other outdoor activities. But Australians are increasingly aware of the danger of skin cancer from the country's intense sunshine, and are learning to take precautions when in the sun.

MINING

Quartz
Gold

Australia has large deposits of minerals such as gold, uranium, coal, iron ore, aluminum and diamonds. The mining of these minerals played an important part in the early development of the continent. Improved mining techniques have led to a resurgence in gold mining in Western Australia. Look for 🪖

MAP FEATURES

🐄	**Cattle:** Australia has about 24 million cattle and exports beef and veal to over 100 countries, especially Japan and the US. Look for 🐂	
⛑️	**Mining:** Papua New Guinea has recently become a major producer of gold, which is mined on the mainland and on one of the outlying islands. Look for 🪖	
🦪	**Pearls:** Large South Sea pearls are cultivated in oysters in the waters along Australia's northwest coast. These are called "cultured" pearls. Look for 🦪	

🐑	Sheep	🚢	Fishing ports
🌾	Cereals	⛏️	Coal
🌾	Sugarcane	🏭	Industrial center
🌲	Timber	🚩	Major airstrips
🍷	Wine	🪃	Tourism

FIRST INHABITANTS

Aboriginal peoples believe they have occupied Australia since "before time began." Early Aboriginal societies survived by hunting and gathering. They had their own traditions of storytelling, ceremonies, and art. Today, 66 percent of Aboriginal peoples live in towns. Here, 200 years after the first European settlement, activists march through Sydney demanding land rights. The government has introduced programs to improve Aboriginal standards of living, education, and employment.

AUSTRALIA'S WATERSHED

The Great Dividing Range is a series of rugged hill-lands and plateaus extending along Australia's east coast from the Cape York Peninsula to Tasmania. When Europeans first crossed the barrier in 1813, they opened up the Outback to immigration and settlement. Today, the highlands include many major tourist centers, but farming, timber, and mining are also important.

Australian Alps: an important tourist and skiing center

Gentle western slopes, drained by Murray, Lachlan, Murrumbidgee, and Goulburn rivers

Grazing and fruit and vegetable farming on the well-watered eastern areas

Sydney

PACIFIC OCEAN

Coastal plain is the most densely populated region of Australia

N

Map labels

TIMOR SEA
INDIAN OCEAN

Melville I.
Croker I.
Bathurst I.
Clarence Strait
DARWIN
C. Londonderry
Joseph Bonaparte Gulf
ARNHEM LA
Beef
Wyndham
Victoria R.
Beef
Collier Bay
Diamonds
KIMBERLEY PLATEAU
KING LEOPOLD RANGES
Iron
Old R.
Beef
C. Leveque
Broome
Beef
Fitzroy R.
Halls Creek
Beef
Beef
NORTH
Monte Bello Is.
Port Hedland
GREAT SANDY DESERT
Copper
Barrow I.
Dampier
Iron
TERR
North West C.
HAMERSLEY RANGE
Manganese
L. Mackay
Ashburton R.
Iron
L. Disappointment
Iron
MACDONNELL
L. Macleod
Carnarvon
WESTERN
Gold
GIBSON DESERT
Uluru (Ayers Rock)
Shark Bay
AUSTRALIA
Dirk Hartog I.
Murchison R.
Gold
L. Carnegie
Meekatharra
Gold
L. Wells
GREAT VICTORIA DESERT
Mount Magnet
Nickel
Geraldton
AU
Oats
Nickel
Gold
Zinc
L. Barlee
Nickel
Dairy
L. Moore
Gold
Kalgoorlie
Wheat
Nickel
NULLARBOR PLAIN
PERTH
Fremantle
Gold
Dairy
Gold
Rockingham
Esperance
Great Australian Bight
C. Naturaliste
Bunbury
Gold
C. Pasley
Augusta
Barley
C. Leeuwin
Albany

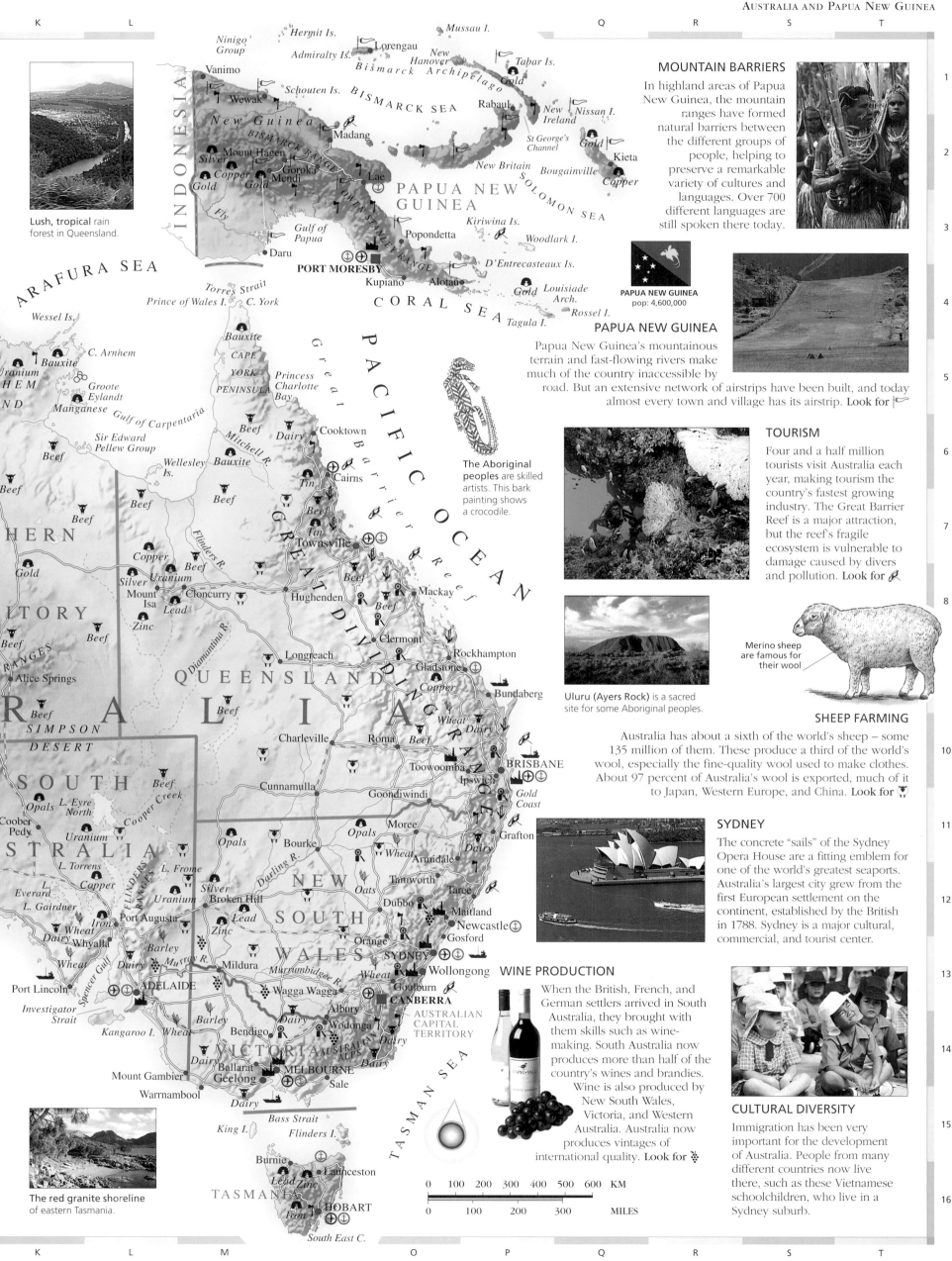

Lush, tropical rain forest in Queensland.

MOUNTAIN BARRIERS

In highland areas of Papua New Guinea, the mountain ranges have formed natural barriers between the different groups of people, helping to preserve a remarkable variety of cultures and languages. Over 700 different languages are still spoken there today.

PAPUA NEW GUINEA
pop: 4,600,000

PAPUA NEW GUINEA

Papua New Guinea's mountainous terrain and fast-flowing rivers make much of the country inaccessible by road. But an extensive network of airstrips have been built, and today almost every town and village has its airstrip. Look for

The Aboriginal peoples are skilled artists. This bark painting shows a crocodile.

TOURISM

Four and a half million tourists visit Australia each year, making tourism the country's fastest growing industry. The Great Barrier Reef is a major attraction, but the reef's fragile ecosystem is vulnerable to damage caused by divers and pollution. Look for

Uluru (Ayers Rock) is a sacred site for some Aboriginal peoples.

Merino sheep are famous for their wool

SHEEP FARMING

Australia has about a sixth of the world's sheep – some 135 million of them. These produce a third of the world's wool, especially the fine-quality wool used to make clothes. About 97 percent of Australia's wool is exported, much of it to Japan, Western Europe, and China. Look for

SYDNEY

The concrete "sails" of the Sydney Opera House are a fitting emblem for one of the world's greatest seaports. Australia's largest city grew from the first European settlement on the continent, established by the British in 1788. Sydney is a major cultural, commercial, and tourist center.

WINE PRODUCTION

When the British, French, and German settlers arrived in South Australia, they brought with them skills such as wine-making. South Australia now produces more than half of the country's wines and brandies. Wine is also produced by New South Wales, Victoria, and Western Australia. Australia now produces vintages of international quality. Look for

CULTURAL DIVERSITY

Immigration has been very important for the development of Australia. People from many different countries now live there, such as these Vietnamese schoolchildren, who live in a Sydney suburb.

The red granite shoreline of eastern Tasmania.

0 100 200 300 400 500 600 KM
0 100 200 300 MILES

NEW ZEALAND

NEW ZEALAND LIES deep in the southern Pacific, about halfway between the Equator and the South Pole, 932 miles (1,500 km) from Australia, its nearest large neighbor. New Zealand was one of the last places on Earth to be inhabited by people. The first settlers were Maoris from the Polynesian islands in the Pacific. They were followed by Europeans, who now make up about 86 percent of the population. From l840 to 1907 New Zealand was a British colony. Sheep farming was the main source of wealth. But since the l970s – when Britain joined the EU and cut its imports from New Zealand dramatically – new markets have had to be found in Southeast Asia.

Cheddar cheese

Butter

DAIRY PRODUCTS

Huge herds of dairy cattle are kept in New Zealand, mainly on North Island. Dairy produce is an important export. Large quantities of butter and cheese are sent overseas in chilled container ships. **Look for** ▼

TOURISM

Tourism is now New Zealand's largest source of foreign currency. The mild climate and spectacular scenery are ideal for hiking and the varied coastline is a sailor's paradise. National parks occupy 13 percent of the land area. **Look for** 👣

AUCKLAND

Most New Zealanders live in towns. About one-third of the population lives in the city of Auckland. It is the country's main port and industrial center, and has the world's largest Polynesian population.

GEOTHERMAL POWER

In the volcanic region of North Island, geothermal power stations like this one tap the vast underground supplies of hot water to generate electricity. **Look for** ⚡

Queen scallop

Oysters and queen scallops are bred on fish farms.

The Southern Alps in South Island.

NEW ZEALAND
pop: 3,700,000

RUGBY

Rugby was first played in New Zealand in 1870. Since then it has become the country's favorite sport. The national team, the "All Blacks," are world famous. They are named after their black shirts and shorts.

The volcanic peak of Mount Ngauruhoe in North Island.

Greenstone pendant, carved by a Maori artist.

MAORI

Maoris make up 13 percent of the population: the majority live in urban areas. Some, like those around Gisborne, continue their traditional way of life. Here a *haka*, or war dance, is performed.

Lemon

Apple

Kiwi fruit

FRUIT

New Zealand's mild climate is ideal for growing fruit. A lot of fruit is exported to countries in the Northern Hemisphere because the fruit season in New Zealand falls during the Northern Hemisphere's winter. **Look for** 🍱

SHEEP

In New Zealand sheep have right of way on the roads and outnumber people 20-1. Sheep were first bred for their wool. But when refrigerated ships were developed, frozen lamb could be exported to Europe. Now exports go to the Middle East, Asia, and the US. **Look for** 🐑

North Island

South Island

TASMAN SEA

PACIFIC OCEAN

SOUTHERN ALPS

NEW ZEALAND

Great Exhibition Bay
Waipapakauri
Dairy
Beef
Whangarei
Great Barrier I.
Kaipara Harbour
Coromandel
Auckland
Thames
Dairy
Bay of Plenty
Hamilton
Tauranga
Beef
Rotorua
Dairy
Beef
New Plymouth
L. Taupo
Taupo
Gisborne
Mt. Ngauruhoe
2291m
Hawke Bay
Dairy
Napier
Beef
Hastings
Wanganui
Dairy
Palmerston North
Cook Strait
Levin
Beef
Tasman Bay
Masterton
Beef
Nelson
Dairy
Picton
Blenheim
Westport
Wairau
Dairy
WELLINGTON

Beef
Greymouth
Hurunui
Kaikoura
Dairy
Pegasus Bay
Beef
Rakaia
Christchurch
Beef
Canterbury Bight
Beef
Timaru
Waitaki
Milford Sound
L. Te Anau
L. Wakatipu
Queenstown
Taieri
Dairy
Beef
Dunedin
Invercargill
Dairy
Foveaux Strait
Stewart I.

MAP FEATURES

Timber: New Zealand has recently developed its timber industry and now exports wood pulp, chipboard, and veneer. **Look for** 🌲

Fishing: Fish, especially hoki and orange roughy, have become a major export. Shellfish farming is also being developed. **Look for** 🐟

🐂	Cattle	⊞	Hydroelectric power
🐑	Sheep	⚡	Alternative power
🍱	Mixed fruit	🏭	Industrial center
🍇	Wine	👣	Hiking

N

0 50 100 150 200 250 300 KM

0 50 100 150 MILES

GLOSSARY

This list provides clear and simple meanings for certain geographical and technical terms used in this atlas.

Acid rain Rain which has been made poisonous by industrial pollution.

AIDS (Acquired Immune Deficiency Syndrome). A fatal condition spread by infected blood and certain body fluids.

Alliance A union of nations, which has been agreed by treaty for economic, political, or military purposes.

Alluvium Loose material, such as **silt**, sand, and gravel, carried by rivers.

Alternative energy Sources of energy which can be renewed – including solar or wind power. These forms of energy, unlike fossil fuel energy from coal and oil, do not produce pollution.

Apartheid The policy, developed in South Africa, of separating peoples by race. Non-whites did not have the same democratic rights, and many public institutions were restricted to one race only.

Aquaculture Cultivation of fish and shellfish in lakes, **estuaries**, rivers, or the sea.

Archipelago A group of islands.

Atoll A circular or horseshoe-shaped coral reef enclosing a shallow area of water.

Bilingual Speaking two languages.

Biotechnology The use of living organisms in the manufacture of food, drugs, and other products. Yeast, for example, is used to make beer and bread.

Buddhism A religion that began in India in about 500 BC. It is based on the teachings of Buddha, who believed that good or evil deeds can be rewarded or punished in this life, or in other lives that will follow. Buddhists aim to achieve inner peace by living their lives according to the example set by Buddha.

Cash crop Agricultural produce grown for sale, often for foreign export, rather than to be consumed by the country or locality where it was grown.

Christianity A religion that began in the 1st century BC. Christians believe in one God and follow the teachings of Jesus Christ, whom they believe was the Son of God.

Civil war A war between rival groups of people who live in the same country.

Classical Art, architecture, or literature which originated in the time of the ancient Greeks and Romans.

Colony A territory which belongs to another country. Also a group of people living separately within a country.

Communism An economic and political system of the 19th and 20th centuries in which farms, factories, and the goods they produce are owned by the state.

Coniferous Trees or shrubs, like pines and firs, which have needles instead of leaves. Most are evergreen.

Conquistador The word is Spanish for "conqueror," and was applied to the Spanish explorers and invaders of Mexico and parts of South America in the 16th century.

Consumer goods Objects such as food, clothing, furniture, cars, and televisions which are purchased by people for their personal and private use.

Continental plates The huge, interlocking plates which make up the Earth's surface. A plate margin is an area where two plates meet, and is the point at which **earthquakes** occur most frequently.

Continental shelf The edge of a landmass which forms a shallow, raised shelf in the sea.

Cosmopolitan Influenced by foreign cultures.

Cottage industry The manufacture of products – often traditional ones like textiles or pottery – by people in their own homes.

Crude oil Oil in its original state, before chemicals and other products have been removed by various processes in a refinery.

Crusades A series of wars from the 11th to 13th centuries when Christian European armies fought against non Christian, often Islamic, armies for possession of the Holy Land, or Palestine.

Cultural heritage Anything handed down from a country's past, such as its traditions, art, and architecture.

Currency The money of a particular country.

Deforestation The cutting of trees for timber or clearing of forest for farmland. The land is often left bare, leading to soil erosion and increasing the risk of flooding and landslides.

Democracy A political system in which everyone above a certain age has the right to vote for the election of his or her representative in the national and local governments.

Desertification The creation of deserts either by changes in climate or by overgrazing, overpopulation, **deforestation** or overcultivation.

Developing world Parts of the world which are still undergoing the process of industrialization.

Dictator A political leader who assumes absolute rule of a nation.

Earthquake A trembling or more violent movement of the ground caused by **seismic activity**. Earthquakes occur most frequently along **continental plate** margins.

Economy The organization of a country's finances, exports, imports, industry, agriculture, and services.

Ecosystem A community of plants and animals dependent on each other and on the habitat in which they live.

Electronics The use of electricity to produce signals that carry information and control devices such as telephones or computers.

Emigrant A person who has moved from one country or region to settle in another country or region.

Empire A large group of countries ruled by one person – an emperor.

Equator An imaginary East-West line that circles the middle of the Earth at equal distance from the **Poles**. The Equator also marks the nearest point on the Earth's surface to the Sun, so it has a consistently hot climate.

Estuary The mouth of a river, where the tide's salt water meets the fresh water of the river.

Ethnic diversity People of several different cultures living in the same region.

Ethnic minority A group of people who share a culture, and are outnumbered by others living in the same region.

European Union (EU) (or European Community, EC) A group of European countries linked together by treaty to promote trade, industry, and agriculture within a **free-market economy**.

Exports Goods produced in a country but sold abroad.

Fauna Animals of a region.

Flora Plants of a region.

Foreign debt The money owed by one country to the government, banks, or institutions of one or more other countries.

Foreign exchange Money brought into a country from abroad, usually by the sale of **exports**, by **service industries**, or by tourism.

Free-market economy An economy which is regulated by the price of goods bought and sold freely in national and international markets.

Geothermal energy Electricity produced from hot rocks under the Earth's surface. These heat water and produce steam, which can then be used to generate electricity.

Geyser A fountain of hot water or steam that erupts periodically as a result of underground streams coming into contact with hot rocks.

Greenhouse effect A rise in the global temperature caused as heat, reflected and radiated from the Earth's surface, is trapped in the atmosphere by a build up of "greenhouse" gases, such as carbon dioxide. Also called "global warming."

Habitat A place or region where a certain animal or plant usually lives.

Heavy industry Industry that uses large amounts of energy and raw materials to produce heavy goods, such as machinery, ships, or locomotives.

Hunter-gatherers People who do not grow their food, but obtain it by hunting it and gathering it from their environment. There are few hunter-gatherer groups left in the world today.

Hydroelectric power (HEP) Electricity produced by harnessing the force of falling water.

ICBM (Intercontinental Ballistic Missile) A missile, usually with a nuclear warhead, that can be fired from one continent to land in another.

Immigrant A person who has come to live in a country from another country or region.

Incentives Something that arouses or encourages people to greater efforts.

Inflation The rate at which a country's prices increase.

Informal economy An economy in which people buy and sell from each other, not through shops or markets.

Infrastructure The buildings, transportation, and communication links that enable goods to be produced and then moved around within a country.

Irrigation A system of watering dry areas. Water is carried or pumped to the area through pipes or ditches.

Islam A religion founded in the Middle East in the 7th century AD by the prophet Mohammed. Its followers, called Muslims (or Moslems), believe in one God – called Allah. The rules and beliefs of Islam are contained in its holy book, the *Koran.*

Islamic fundamentalist A person who strictly follows the rules and beliefs of Islam contained in the holy book, the *Koran.* See **Islam**.

Isthmus A narrow piece of land connecting two larger bodies of land, surrounded on two sides by water.

Labour intensive An activity which requires large amounts of work or large numbers of workers to accomplish it.

Lent A period of time lasting 40 days observed by Christians during which they fast and prepare for the festival of Easter.

Lignite Woody or brown coal.

Living standards The quality of life in a country, usually measured by income, material possessions, and levels of education and health care.

Malnutrition A prolonged lack of adequate food.

Market gardening Farms and **smallholdings** growing fruit and vegetables for sale.

Megalopolis A very large or continuous urban area in which several large towns or cities have joined as their urban areas have spread.

Metropolis A major city, often the capital.

Militarized zone An area occupied by armed military forces.

Multinational company A company which has branches, or factories, in several countries.

Nationalists Groups of people united in their wish for independence from a government or from foreign rule.

Neutral country A country which refrains from taking part in international conflicts.

Nomad A person who does not settle in one place for any length of time, but moves in search of hunting or grazing land.

Oil shale Flaky rock containing oil.

Pastoralist A person who makes a living from grazing livestock.

Peat Decomposed vegetation found in bogs. It can be dried and used as fuel.

Peninsula A strip of land surrounded on three sides by water.

Permafrost Permanently frozen ground. The surface thaws in summer, but water cannot drain away through the frozen subsurface. Typical of **subarctic** areas.

Pharmaceuticals The manufacture of medicinal drugs.

Plantation A large farm on which only one crop is usually grown.

Plate margin See **Continental plates**.

Polar regions The regions around the North and South Poles which are permanently frozen, and where the temperature only rises above the freezing point for a few months of the year.

Poles, the The term applied to the North and South Poles, the northernmost and southernmost points of the Earth's axis or rotation.

Prairie A Spanish/American term for a large area of grassland.

Privatization When state-owned activities and companies are taken over by private firms.

Protestant A member of one of the main Christian religions founded in the 16th century by those who did not agree with all aspects of the Roman Catholic Church. Protestantism became one of the main branches of **Christianity**.

Quota A maximum quantity imposed on the number of goods produced, imported, or exported by a country.

Rain forest Dense forest found in hot and humid equatorial regions; often called tropical rain forest.

Raw materials Substances in a natural or unrefined state used in the manufacture of goods, like cotton for textiles and bauxite for aluminum.

Refugees People who flee their own country or region because of political, religious, or racial persecution.

Republic The form of government in a country that has no monarch. The head of state is usually a president, like the President of the US.

Reservation An area of land set aside for occupation by specific people, plants, or animals.

Revenue Money paid to a government, like taxes.

Roman Catholic A Christian who accepts the Pope as his or her spiritual leader.

Rural In, or belonging to, the countryside.

Savannah Tropical grasslands where an annual dry season prevents the growth of most trees.

Seismic activity Tremors and shocks in the Earth's crust usually caused by the movement of plates along a fault.

Service industry An industry that supplies services, such as banking, rather than producing manufactured goods.

Shantytown An area in or around a city where people live in temporary shacks, usually without basic facilities such as running water.

Silt Small particles, finer than sand, often carried by water and deposited on riverbanks, at river mouths, and harbors. See also **alluvium**.

Smallholding A plot of agricultural land smaller than a farm.

Socialism Political system whereby the economy is owned and controlled by the state and not by private companies or individuals.

Soviet bloc All those countries which were ruled directly or indirectly by the communist government of the former USSR.

Staple crop The main crop grown in a region.

Staple food The basic part of a diet, such as rice or bread.

Steppes An extensive, grass-covered and virtually treeless plain, such as those found in Siberia.

Stock Exchange A place where people buy and sell government bonds, **currency**, stocks, and financial shares in large private companies.

Strategic Carefully planned or well placed from a military point of view.

Subarctic The climate in **polar** regions, characterized by extremely cold temperatures and long winters.

Technological The application of science through the use of machines.

Temperate The mild, variable climate found in areas between the **tropics** and cold **polar** regions.

Tropic of Cancer, Capricorn Two imaginary lines of latitude drawn on the Earth's surface above and below the **Equator**. The hottest parts of the world are between these two lines.

Tropics, the An area between the **Equator** and the **tropics of Cancer and Capricorn** that has heavy rainfall, high temperatures, and lacks any clear seasonal variation.

Tundra Vegetation found in areas within the Arctic Circle, such as dwarf bushes, very short grasses, mosses, and lichens.

United Nations (UN) An association of countries established to co-operate to prevent wars and to supply aid, advice, and research on an international basis.

Urban area Town, city, or extensive built-up area.

West, the Those countries in Europe and North America with **free-market economies** and **democratic** governments.

Western The economic, cultural, and political values shared by countries belonging to **the West**.

A Coruña – Angol

INDEX

Throughout the Atlas, population figures have been taken from the latest official estimates.

HOW TO USE THE GRID

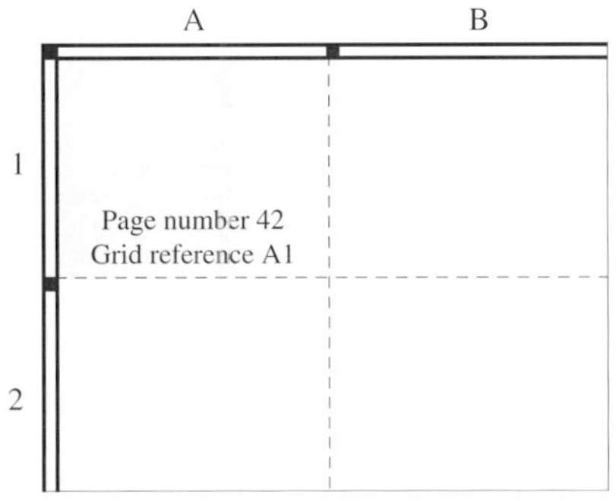

Grid references in the Index help you to find places on the map. For example, if you look up Nairobi in the Index, you will see the reference 111 O5. The first number, 111, is the page number of the map on which Nairobi appears. Find the letters and numbers which border the page and trace a line down from the letter and across from the number. This directs you to the exact grid square in which Nairobi is located.

The numbers that appear after the names are the page numbers, followed by the grid references.

In the country factboxes throughout the index, many statistics are not yet available for the new states of the world. When we have been unable to find the correct figure, N/A is given, which stands for not available.

Population density
This is the total population divided by the land area of a country.

Average life expectancy
This is the average life expectancy at birth, barring war or natural disasters.

Literacy
This is the percentage of people over the age of 15 years who can read and write a simple sentence. Where figures for male (m) and female (f) have not been available, we have used an average (av.).

Death penalty
The countries with 'Yes' use the death penalty regularly. Some of the states with 'No' still have a law permitting the death penalty but do not use it.

Percentage of urban population
This is the percentage of the total population who live in towns or cities.

Calories consumed daily
The recommended daily number for a healthy life is about 2500 calories; the inhabitants of some countries consume far more than others.

The following abbreviations have been used in the index:

anc. = ancient name
Arch. = Archipelago
C. = Cape
E. = East
Ft. = Fort
I. = Island
Is. = Islands
L. = Lake
Mt. = Mountain
Mts. = Mountains
N. = North
N.P. = National Park
Pen. = Peninsula
prev. = previously
Pt. = Point
Res. = Reservoir
R. = River
S. = South
St. = Saint
var. = variant name
W. = West

A

A Coruña (Eng. Corunna) Spain 66 J8 74 G3
Aachen Germany 81 C11
Aalst Belgium 79 F14
Aarau Switzerland 82 F9
Aare *River* Switzerland 82 F9
Aba Nigeria 107 O13
Abadan Iran 123 L7
Abajo Mountains *Mountain range* Utah, USA 49 K5
Abakan Russian Federation 127 K11
Abashiri Japan 136 M3
Abéché Chad 108 K7
Abengourou Ivory Coast 107 K13
Åbenrå Denmark 70 H15
Abeokuta Nigeria 107 N12
Aberdare Range *Mountain range* Kenya 111 O5
Aberdeen Scotland, United Kingdom 50 K7 56 J8
Aberdeen South Dakota, USA 31 N6
Aberdeen Washington, USA 34 G7
Aberystwyth Wales, United Kingdom 73 G14
Abha Saudi Arabia 122 H13
Abidjan Ivory Coast 107 K13
Abilene Kansas, USA 28 E10
Abilene Texas, USA 49 P10
Abitibi, Lake *Lake* Ontario, Canada 39 K11
Abomey Benin 107 M12
Abu Dhabi United Arab Emirates 107 N11
Abu Simbel *Ancient monument* Egypt 104 F10
Abuja Nigeria 107 O11
Abydos *Archaeological site* Egypt 104 F8
Acadia National Park *National park* USA 22 G11
Acapulco Mexico 20 D13 33 I18 52 M13
Accra Ghana 107 L13
Acheloos *River* Greece 92 H7
Achinsk Russian Federation 127 K10
Acklins Island *Island* Bahamas 57 M5
Acolhuacan *Historic site* Mexico 24 D8
Aconcagua, Cerro *Mountain* Argentina, 55
Acton *Battle site* USA 29 P2
Ad Dafrah *Desert* United Arab Emirates 123 M11
Ad Dahna' Saudi Arabia 123 K9
Ad Dakhla Western Sahara 102 E9
Ad Damman Saudi Arabia 123 M9
Ad Diwaniyah Iraq 123 K5
Adak Island *Island* Alaska, USA 36 A6
Adamawa Highlands *Mountain range* Cameroon, 101
Adana Turkey 119 M9
Adapazarı Turkey 118 J5
Adare, Cape *Cape* Antarctica 64 E12
Addis Ababa Ethiopia 105 J15
Adelaide South Australia, Australia 147 L13
Adelaide Island *Island* Antarctica 64 B8
Aden Yemen 122 I16
Aden Yemen 114 E7
Aden, Gulf of *Gulf* Indian Ocean 85 89 M14 98 E7 101 113
Adige *River* Italy 86 H7
Adiri Libya 103 O8
Adirondack Mountains *Mountain range* New York, USA 40 K8
Adıyaman Turkey 119 O8
Admiralty Islands *Island group* Papua New Guinea 147 N1
Adobe Walls *Battle site* USA 29 N4
Adrar Algeria 102 J8
Adrian Michigan, USA 45 O10
Adrianople *see* Edirne
Adriatic Sea *Sea* Mediterranean Sea 52 70 I8 72 F5
Adwa Ethiopia 105 J13
Adycha *River* Russian Federation 127 O6
Aegean Sea *Sea* Mediterranean Sea 52 77 L5
Aeolian Islands *Island group* Italy 87 K16
Afghanistan *Country* C Asia 108 I12

Afghanistan 124-125

1919 • a Persian and Pashtu • Afghani • 34 • 45 • 13 • 31.5 • N/A • 7358 • Yes • 20 • 1523

Africa *Continent* 100-101
Africa, Horn of *Physical region* Ethiopia/Somalia 105 N14
African Plate *Tectonic plate* 34 55 68 101 117 129
'Afrin Syria 121 N2
Afyon Turkey 118 J7
Agadez Niger 107 O7
Agadir Morocco 102 G6
Agartala India 131 P8
Agattu Island *Island* Alaska, USA 36 A4
Agen France 77 K13
Agios Efstratios *Island* Greece 93 M6
Agios Nikolaos Greece 93 N16
Agra India 131 K6
Ağrı Turkey 119 S6
Agri *River* Italy 87 M14
Agrigento Italy 87 J18
Aguarico, Río *River* Ecuador/Peru 58 D8
Aguascalientes Mexico 53 L10
Agulhas Basin *Undersea feature* Indian Ocean 101
Agulhas, Cape *Headland* South Africa 101 112 J16
Ahaggar *Plateau* Algeria 101 103 M10
Ahmadabad India 130 I7
Ahvaz Iran 123 M6
Aïr, Massif de l' *Mountain range* Niger 107 P7
Aix-en-Provence France 77 O13
Aizawl India 131 Q7
Ajaccio France 77 S16
Ajdabiya Libya 103 Q7
Ajmer India 130 J6
Akagera *National Park* Rwanda 111 L5
Akanthoú Cyprus, 119
Akhisar Turkey 118 H7
Akita Japan 136 K7
Aklavik Northwest Territories, Canada 20 D7
Akola India 131 K9
Akron Ohio, USA 45 Q10
Aksai Chin *Disputed region* China/India 130 L1 132 E10
Aksaray Turkey 119 L8
Akseki Turkey 118 J9
Aksu China 132 F7
Aksum Ethiopia 105 J13
Aktau Kazakhstan 126 D10
Aktyubinsk Kazakhstan 126 F9
Al 'Amarah Iraq 123 L6
Al 'Aqabah Jordan 121 L14
Al Azraq al Janubi Jordan 121 N10
Al Bahah Saudi Arabia 122 H12
Al Bayda' Libya 103 R6
Al Bayda' Yemen 122 I16
Al Buraymi Oman 123 O11
Al Ghaydah Yemen 123 M16
Al Hasakah Syria 121 R5
Al Hillah Iraq 123 K5
Al Hufuf Saudi Arabia 123 L10
Al Jaghbub Libya 103 S7
Al Jawf Saudi Arabia 122 I6
Al Jazirah *Physical region* Iraq/Syria 121 Q3
Al Jubayl Saudi Arabia 123 L9
Al Karak Jordan 121 M11
Al Khaburah Oman 123 O11
Al Khufrah Libya 103 R10
Al Khums Libya 103 O6
Al Kut Iraq 123 L5
Al Ladhiqiyah (Eng. Latakia) Syria 121 M4
Al Marj Libya 103 Q6
Al Matraq Jordan 121 N9
Al Mukalla Yemen 123 K16
Al Mukha (Eng Mocha) Yemen 122 H16
Al Qunaytirah Syria 121 M8
Al Qurnah Iraq 123 L6
Al-Hoceïma Morocco 102 J4
Alabama *State* USA 21 O6 23 Q13 29 P15 30 F13 33 K15 43 K7
Alabama River *River* Alabama, USA 23 Q7
Alajuela Costa Rica 56 E13
Alakol', Ozero *Lake* Kazakhstan, 117
Alamogordo New Mexico, USA 49 M10
Aland Islands *Island group* Finland 71 M11
Alanya Turkey 119 K10
Alaska *State* USA 19 D11 21 L2 23 L12 29 M11 30 B7 32 C8 36 G6 65 O6
Alaska, Gulf of *Gulf* Pacific Ocean 19 C12 22 C8 34 36 G9 145 L3
Alaska Peninsula *Peninsula* Alaska, USA, 34
Alaska Range *Mountain range* Alaska, USA 34 36 G7
Alassio Italy 86 C9
Alazani *River* Azerbaijan/Georgia 99 Q12
Alba Iulia Romania 90 I5
Albacete Spain 75 M10
Albania *Country* SE Europe 89 L13

Albania 89

1912 • a Albanian • Lek • 113 • 73 • 14 • 85 • 20 • 769 • Yes • 37 • 2605

Albany Western Australia, Australia 146 G13
Albany *River* Ontario, Canada 38 I9
Albany Oregon, USA 50 G9
Albany New York, USA 26 E10 27 R3 28 H9 33 M13, 41 M9
Albert Canal *Canal* Belgium 79 I14
Albert Lea Minnesota, USA 44 H8
Albert Nile *River* Uganda 111 M3
Albert, Lake *Lake* Congo (Zaire)/Uganda 101 109 P11 111 L3
Alberta *Province* Canada 21 M4 29 N13 30 C9 33 G11 37 K13
Albi France 77 L13
Albina Surname 58 O6
Ålborg Denmark 70 I14
Albuquerque New Mexico, USA 30 D13 33 G15 49 L8
Albury New South Wales, Australia 147 N13
Alcántara, Embalse de *Reservoir* Spain 74 H9
Aldabra Islands *Island Group* Seychelles 114 E9
Aldan *River* Russian Federation 127 O8
Aleg Mauritania 106 G7
Aleksinac Serbia, Yugoslavia 89 O7
Alençon France 76 J6
Aleppo Syria 121 O3
Alert Nunavut, Canada 65 O11
Alessandria Italy 86 D7
Ålesund Norway 66 K7 70 H8
Aleutian Basin *Undersea feature* Pacific Ocean 34 117
Aleutian Islands *Island group* Alaska, USA 19 B11 22 B8 32 A8 36 A6 144 J4
Aleutian Range *Mountain range* Alaska, USA 19 C12
Aleutian Trench *Undersea feature* Pacific Ocean 34, 144 J4
Alexander Archipelago *Island group* Alaska, USA 36 H11
Alexandretta *see* Iskernderun
Alexandria Egypt 104 F6
Alexandria Romania 91 L10
Alexandria Louisiana, USA 42 H8
Alexandroupoli Greece 93 N3
Aleysk Russian Federation 126 I11
Algeciras Spain 74 I15
Algeria *Country* NW Africa 102 I8

Algeria 102-103

1962 • a Arabic • Algerian dinar • 13 • 69 • 15 • 60.3 • 25 • 1250 • Yes • 56 • 2897

Alghero Italy 87 C13
Algiers Algeria 66 K9 103 L4
Aliakmonas *River* Greece 92 I4
Alicante Spain 75 N11
Alice Springs Northern Territory, Australia 147 K9
Alicudi *Island* Italy 87 K16
Aligarh India 131 K5
Alkmaar Netherlands 78 H9
Allahabad India 131 M7
Allentown Pennsylvania, USA 41 K13
Allier *River* France 77 M11
Alma-Ata (var. Almaty) Kazakhstan 126 H13
Almaty *see* Alma-Ata
Almelo Netherlands 78 M9
Almería Spain 75 L14
Alor, Pulau *Island* Indonesia 141 N15
Alor Setar Malaysia 139 I17
Alotau Papua New Guinea 147 O4
Alpena Michigan, USA 45 O6
Alphen aan den Rijn Netherlands 78 H10
Alps *Mountain range* C Europe 68 77 P11 82 G11 86 B7
Altai Mountains *Mountain range* C Asia 68 117 129, 132 I4
Altamura Italy 87 K16
Altar de Sacrificios *Historic site* Mexico 24 G10
Altay Mongolia 133 K5
Altay China 132 I4
Altdorf Switzerland 82 G10
Altınkaya Barajı *Reservoir* Turkey 119 M4
Alton Illinois, USA 44 J14
Altoona Pennsylvania, USA 40 H13
Altun Ha *Ruins* Belize 56 C6
Altun Shan *Mountain range* China 129 132 G9
Alturas California, USA 51 I12
Alytus Lithuania 94 I10
Am Timan Chad 108 K8
Amakusa-nada *Gulf* Japan 137 A14
Amami-gunto *Island group* Japan 137 A19
Amami-O-shima *Island* Japan 137 B18
Amarapura Myanmar 139 F7
Amarillo Texas, USA 49 O8
Amasya Turkey 119 M5
Amazon *River* Brazil/Peru, 55 58 G10 60 H7 67 F12
Amazon Basin *Basin* South America 55 60 D8
Ambarchik Russian Federation 127 P4
Ambato Ecuador 58 C9
Ambon Indonesia 141 O13
Amboseli *National Park* Kenya 111 P6
Ambriz Angola 112 G4
Ameland *Island* Netherlands 78 K6
American Samoa *Dependent territory* Pacific Ocean 145 K9
Amersfoort Netherlands 78 J10
Amery Ice Shelf *Ice shelf* Antarctica 64 G8
Ames Iowa, USA 47 Q9
Amfissa Greece 92 I8
Amga *River* Russian Federation 127 O8
Amiens France 77 L3
Amirante Islands *Island group* Seychelles 114 F9
Amistad Reservoir *Reservoir* Texas, Mexico/USA 49 O13
Amlia Island *Island* Alaska, USA 36 B7
Amman Jordan 121 M10
Ammersee *Lake* Germany 81 J16
Amol Iran 123 O4
Amorgos *Island* Greece 93 O12
Amritsar India 130 J3
Amstelveen Netherlands 78 I10
Amsterdam Netherlands 78 I9
Amsterdam New York, USA 41 L9
Amsterdam Island *Island* French Southern and Antarctic Territories 115 I13
Amstetten Austria 83 Q5
Amu Darya *River* C Asia 68 117 125 K8 129
Amundsen Gulf *Gulf* Arctic Ocean 37 K6
Amundsen-Scott *US research station* Antarctica 64 E9
Amundsen Sea *Sea* Antarctica 64 B10
Amur *River* China/Russian Federation 117 127 P11 129 133 P1 135 O1
An Nabk Syria 122 H5
An Nafud *Desert* Saudi Arabia 117 122 H6
An Najaf Iraq 123 K5
An Nasiriyah Iraq 123 L6
Anabar *River* Russian Federation 127 M5
Anaconda Montana, USA 46 G6
Anadyr' Russian Federation 127 R3
Anambas, Kepulauan *Island group* Indonesia 140 F10
Anamur Turkey 119 K11
Anatolia *Physical region* Turkey 68 117 129
Anatolian Plate *Tectonic plate* 68 117
Anchorage Alaska, USA 32 D8 36 G8
Ancona Italy 66 L8 86 J9
Andalucia *see* Andalusia
Andalusia (var. Andalucia) *Region* Spain 74 I13
Andaman Islands *Island group* India 114 K6 129
Andaman Sea *Sea* Indian Ocean 114 K6 117 129 139 E11
Anderson Indiana, USA 45 N12
Andes *Mountain range* South America 55 58 D8 62 H9
Andijon Uzbekistan 125 P7
Andorra *Country* W Europe 75 P4 77 L15

Andorra 77

1278 • a Catalan • French franc and Spanish peseta • 140 • 83 • 16 • 99 • N/A • 555 • No • 63 • 370

Andorra la Vella Andorra 77 K16
Andravida Greece 92 H9
Andros Greece 93 M9
Andros Island *Island* Bahamas 57 K3
Aneto *Mountain* Spain, 68
Angara *River* Russian Federation 117 127 L9
Angarsk Russian Federation 127 L11
Ángel de la Guarda, Isla *Island* Mexico 52 G4
Angel Falls *Waterfall* Venezuela, 55
Angeles Philippines 141 L4
Angermälven *River* Sweden 71 I8
Angers France 76 I7
Angkor Wat *Archaeological site* Cambodia 139 L13
Anglesey *Island* Wales, United Kingdom 73 G13
Angol Chile 63 G12

Date of independence • a Language (official or most commonly spoken) • Currency • Population density per square kilometre • Average life expectancy • School-leaving age • Literacy • Number of cars per 1,000 people • Number of people per doctor • Death penalty • Percentage of urban-based population • Average number of calories consumed daily per person

Angola – Barlee, Lake

Angola *Country* Southern Africa 112 H5

Angola 112

1975 • a Portuguese • kwanza • 10 • 47 • 15 • 45 • 18 • 14300 • No • 32 • 1839

Angola Basin *Undersea feature* Atlantic Ocean 67 K13 101
Angoulême France 76 J10
Angren Uzbekistan 125 N6
Anguilla *Dependent territory* West Indies 57 S9
Ankang China 135 K10
Ankara Turkey 119 K6
Ann Arbor Michigan, USA 45 O9
Annaba Algeria 103 M4
'Annah Iraq 122 J4
Annapolis Maryland, USA 28 H10 33 M14 43 S3
Annecy France 77 P9
Anshan China 135 O6
Antakya Turkey 119 N10
Antalya Turkey 118 J10
Antananarivo Madagascar 115 E11
Antarctic Circle *Line of latitude* Antarctica 55 143
Antarctic Plate *Tectonic plate* 55 101 143
Antarctica *Continent* Antarctica 55 G18 67 115 G17 145 143 M15
Anticosti, Île d' *Island* Quebec, Canada 39 Q9
Antigua *Island* Antigua and Barbuda 57 S11
Antigua and Barbuda *Country* West Indies 57 T10

Antigua and Barbuda 57

1981 • a English • Eastern Caribbean dollar • 156 • 75 • 16 • 95 • N/A • 1316 • Yes • 36 • 2458

Antipodes Islands *Island group* New Zealand 144 J13
Antofagasta Chile 62 G6 145 Q10
Antsirañana Madagascar 114 E10
Antwerp (var. Antwerpen) Belgium 79 G13
Antwerpen *see* Antwerp
Anzio Italy 87 I12
Aomori Japan 136 K6
Aosta Italy 86 B6
Aparri Philippines 141 L2
Apatin Serbia, Yugoslavia 89 L3
Apeldoorn Netherlands 78 L10
Apennines *Mountain range* Italy 68 86 E8
Aphrodisias *Archaeological site* Turkey 118 H9
Āpia Samoa 144 J9
Appalachian Mountains *Mountain range* Georgia/Maryland/NewHampshire/NewYork/ Pennsylvania/Tennessee/ Vermont/Virginia/, USA 19 K17 22 F12 23 R12 28 H11 29 R5 34 N5 40 H14
Appalachians *Physical region* USA 19 K17
Appenzell Switzerland 82 H9
Appleton Wisconsin, USA 45 K7
Apure, Río *River* Venezuela 58 H5
Aqaba, Gulf of *Gulf* Red Sea 104 H7 121 L15 122 F6
Ar Ramadi Iraq 123 K4
Ar Raqqah Syria 121 Q3
Ar Rub'al Khali (Eng. Empty Quarter) *Desert* Saudi Arabia 117 122 J13
Ar Rustaq Oman 123 O12
Arabian Basin *Undersea feature* Indian Ocean 117 129
Arabian Peninsula *Peninsula* SW Asia 101 114 E5 117 129
Arabian Plate *Tectonic plate* 68 101 117 129
Arabian Sea *Sea* Indian Ocean 114 117 123 M16 129 131 H9
Aracaju Brazil 60 O10
Arad Romania 90 G5
Arafura Sea *Sea* Pacific Ocean 129 141 R13 144 F9 143 147 K4
Araguaia, Río *River* Brazil 55 60 I10
Arak Iran 123 M5
Aral Sea *Lake* Kazakhstan/Uzbekistan 68 117 124 I3 126 F11 129
Arandelovac Serbia, Yugoslavia 89 N6
'Ar'ar Saudi Arabia 122 I5
Ararat, Mount *Mountain* Turkey, 68
Aras *River* SW Asia 99 R14
Arauca Colombia 58 G6
Arauca, Río *River* Colombia/Venezuela 58 F6
Arbil Iraq 123 K3
Arcachon France 76 I12
Archangel Russian Federation 96 J7 126 G5
Arches National Park *National park* USA 22 D12
Arctic Circle *Line of latitude* 34 68
Arctic Ocean *Ocean* 18 D6 22 E10 29 N11 34 36 F4 65 66 J2 68 71 N1 117 P9 129 G5 144
Arda *River* Bulgaria/Greece 91 K15
Ardabil Iran 123 M2
Ardennes *Physical region* Belgium/France 79 I18
Arendal Norway 70 I12
Arequipa Peru 59 G15
Arezzo Italy 86 H9
Argentina *Country* Argentina 63 I14

Argentina 62-63

1816 • a Spanish • Argentine peso • 13 • 73 • 14 • 96.5 • 127 • 370 • No • 88 • 2880

Argentine Basin *Undersea feature* Atlantic Ocean 55 67 G15
Argentino, Lago *Lake* Argentina 63 I18
Argeş *River* Romania 91 M9
Arghandab, Darya-ye *River* Afghanistan 125 L14
Argostoli Greece 92 F9
Argun (var. Ergun He) *River* China/Russian Federation 133 P2
Århus Denmark 70 I15
Arica Chile 62 F3
Arickara *Battle site* USA 29 O2
Arizona *State* USA 21 M6 23 O12 29 N15 30 C13 33 F15 48 H8
Arizona *State* USA 21 M6 23 O12 29 N15 30 C13 33 F15
Arkansas *State* USA 21 O6 23 Q12 29 P15 30 E13 33 J15
Arkansas City Kansas, USA 47 P13
Arkansas/Colorado/Kansas/Oklahoma, USA 19 I16 22 E12 23 P6 23 P12 33 J15 34 42 I5 46 N13 49 N5
Arlberg Tunnel *Tunnel* Austria 82 I9
Arles France 77 N13
Arlon Belgium 79 K19
Armenia Colombia 58 E6
Armenia *Country* SW Asia 99 Q14

Armenia 99

1991 • a Armenian • Dram • 117 • 71 • 17 • 98.8 • 0 • 298 • Yes • 69

Armidale New South Wales, Australia 147 O12
Arnhem Netherlands 79 K11
Arnhem Land *Physical region* Northern Territory, Australia 143 146 J5
Arnhem, Cape *Headland* Australia 147 L5
Arno *River* Italy 86 F9
Arran, Isle of *Island* Scotland, United Kingdom 72 G10
Arras France 77 N3
Arta Greece 92 G6
Artesia New Mexico, USA 49 M10
Artigas Uruguay 62 N10
Artvin Turkey 119 R4
Aru, Kepulauan *Island group* Indonesia 141 R14
Arua Uganda 111 L2
Aruba *Dependent territory* West Indies 57 N13
Arun *River* Nepal 131 O6
Arusha Tanzania 111 O7
Aruwimi *River* Dem. Rep. Congo (Zaire) 109 M12
Arvayheer Mongolia 133 L5
Arviat Nunavut, Canada 37 O10
Arvidsjaur Sweden 71 M6
As Salt Jordan 121 M9
As Sulaymaniyah Iraq 123 L3
As Suwayda' Syria 121 N8
Asahikawa Japan 136 L3
Asansol India 131 O8
Ascension Island *Dependent territory* Atlantic Ocean 67 J12
Aseb Eritrea 105 L13
Asela Ethiopia 105 J15
Ash Shu'aybah Kuwait 123 L8
Ashburton River *River* Western Australia, Australia 146 F9
Asheville North Carolina, USA 43 O5
Ashgabat Turkmenistan 124 H9
Ashland Oregon, USA 51 H11
Ashmore and Cartier Islands *Dependent territory* Indian Ocean 114 N10
Ashtabula Ohio, USA 45 Q9
Asia *Continent* 116-117 128-129,138-139
Asir *Mountain range* Saudi Arabia 122 H12
Asmara Eritrea 105 J12
Aspen Colorado, USA 49 L4
Assad, Lake *Reservoir* Syria 121 P3
Assen Netherlands 78 M7
Assisi Italy 86 I10
Astakos Greece 92 G8
Astana Kazakhstan 126 H10
Asti Italy 86 C7
Astoria Oregon, USA 50 G8
Astrakhan' Russian Federation 96 G15 126 D9
Astypalaia *Island* Greece 93 O13
Asunción Paraguay 62 N6
Asuncion Mita *Historic site* Mexico 24 H12
Aswan Egypt 104 G9
Aswan High Dam *Dam* Egypt 104 G9
Asyût Egypt 104 F8
At Ţafilah Jordan 121 M11
Atacama Desert *Desert* Chile 55 62 F4
Atakpamé Togo 107 M12
Atar Mauritania 106 H5
Atatürk Barajı *Reservoir* Turkey 119 O9
Atbara Sudan 105 H11
Atbara *River* Eritrea/Sudan 105 H12
Ath Belgium 79 F15
Athabasca Alberta, Canada 37 L13
Athabasca *River* Alberta, Canada 37 M12
Athabasca, Lake *Lake* Alberta/Saskatchewan, Canada 19 G13 33 B7 34 37 L11
Athens (Gr. Athina) Greece 93 K9
Athens Georgia, USA 43 N7
Athina *see* Athens
Athlone Republic of Ireland 73 D12
Ati Chad 108 J7
Atka Island *Island* Alaska, USA 36 A7
Atlan *Historic site* Mexico 24 D8
Atlanta Georgia, USA 20 F11 27 N13 28 G11 29 R5 33 L15 43 N7
Atlantic City New Jersey, USA 41 L15
Atlantic Ocean *Ocean* 19 L17 28 I12 29 Q16 29 S5 66-67
Atlantic-Indian Basin *Undersea feature* Indian Ocean 67 L16 115 D15
Atlantic-Indian Ridge *Undersea feature* Indian Ocean 67 L16
Atlas Mountains *Mountain range* NW Africa 68 101 102 H6
Atlixco Mexico 53 N12
Atotonilco *Historic site* Mexico 24 D8
Atotonilco *Historic site* Mexico 24 C8
Attawapiskat Ontario, Canada 38 I8
Attawapiskat *River* Ontario, Canada 38 H9
Attersee *Lake* Austria 83 O6
Attu Island *Island* Alaska, USA 36 A4
Atyrau Kazakhstan 126 E9
Auburn New York, USA 40 J9
Auch France 77 K14
Auckland New Zealand 148 H4
Auckland Islands *Island group* New Zealand 144 I13
Augrabies Falls *National Park* South Africa 112 J13
Augsburg Germany 81 I15
Augusta Italy 87 L18
Augusta Western Australia, Australia 146 F13
Augusta Georgia, USA 27 Q7 43 O7
Augusta Maine, USA 28 I8 29 T2 33 N12 41 P7
Aulavik National Park *National park* Canada 22 D7
Aurillac France 77 L11
Aurora Colorado, USA 49 M4
Aurora Illinois, USA 45 L10
Austin Minnesota, USA 44 H8
Austin Texas, USA 28 E13 29 O6 33 I16 49 Q12
Australasia *Geophysical region* 144-143
Australes, Îles *Island group* French Polynesia 145 L11
Australia *Country* 146 F9

Australia 146-147

1901 • a English • Australian dollar • 2 • 78 • 15 • 99 • 485 • 455 • No • 85 • 3179

Australian Alps *Mountain range* Australia 143 147 N14
Australian Capital Territory *Territory* Australia 147 O14
Austria *Country* C Europe 83 P6

Austria 82-83

1918 • a German • Schilling • 99 • 77 • 15 • 99 • 469 • 385 • No • 56 • 3497

Auxerre France 77 M7
Auyuittuq National Park *National park* Canada 22 G8
Aveiro Portugal 74 F7
Avignon France 77 N13
Ávila Spain 74 J8
Avilés Spain 74 I3
Awasa Ethiopia 105 J16
Awash Ethiopia 105 K15
Awash *River* Ethiopia 105 K14
Awbar Libya 103 O9
Axel Heiberg Island *Island* Northwest Territories, Canada 37 M3 65 O10
Axocopan *Historic site* Mexico 24 C8
Ayacucho Peru 59 E13
Aydarkul *Lake* Uzbekistan 125 M6
Aydın Turkey 118 H8
Ayers Rock *see* Uluru
Ayon, Ostrov *Island* Russian Federation 127 P3
Ayr Scotland, United Kingdom 72 G10
Ayutlá Guerrero, Mexico 24 C10
Ayutthaya Thailand 139 I12
Ayvalık Turkey 118 G7
Az Zarqa' Jordan 121 N9
Az Zubayr Iraq 123 L7
Azaouâd *Desert* Mali 107 K7
Azerbaijan *Country* SW Asia 99 R14

Azerbaijan 99

1991 • a Azerbaijani • Manat • 89 • 70 • 17 • 96.3 • 36 • 257 • No • 56

Azores *Island group* Portugal 34 66 I9
Azov, Sea of *Sea* Baltic Sea 68 96 C14 99 K9 126 C7
Aztec Ruins *Ancient site* USA 24 C13
Azul Argentina 63 M11

B

Baabda Lebanon 121 M7
Baalbek Lebanon 121 N6
Baarle-Hertog *Physical region* Belgium 79 I13
Bab el Mandeb *Strait* Gulf of Aden/Red Sea 122 H16
Babahoyo Ecuador 58 C9
Babar, Pulau *Island* Indonesia 141 P15
Babruysk Belarus 95 M13
Babylon *Site of ancient city* Iraq 123 K5
Bacan, Pulau *Island* Indonesia 141 O11
Bacău Romania 91 M4
Bačka Topola Serbia, Yugoslavia 89 M3
Bacolod Philippines 141 M6
Bad Ischl Austria 83 O7
Badajoz Spain 74 H10
Badalona Spain 75 Q6
Baden Austria 83 S5
Badgastein Austria 83 N8
Badlands *Physical region* North Dakota, USA 47 L6
Badlands *Physical region* North Dakota, USA 19 H14
Badlands National Park *National park* USA 22 E11
Bafatá Guinea-Bissau 106 G10
Baffin Bay *Bay* Atlantic Ocean 19 J11 22 F7 32 K7 34 37 O3 65 M13 66 F6
Baffin Island *Island* Nunavut, Canada 19 J11 22 F8 32 J8 34 37 P5 65 M12
Bafia Cameroon 108 F10
Bafoussam Cameroon 108 F10
Baghdad Iraq 123 K5
Baghlan Afghanistan 125 N10
Baguio Philippines 141 L3
Bahamas *Country* Bahamas 56 K3

Bahamas 57

1973 • a English • Bahamian dollar • 30 • 74 • 14 • 95.8 • 58 • 709 • Yes • 87 • 2624

Bahamas *Island group* Bahamas, 55
Bahawalpur Pakistan 130 I4
Bahía Blanca Argentina 63 L12 67 F14
Bahir Dar Ethiopia 105 I14
Bahrain *Country* SW Asia 123 M9

Bahrain 123

1971 • a Arabic • Bahrain dinar • 891 • 73 • 15 • 86.3 • 174 • 9090 • Yes • 91

Baia Mare Romania 90 I2
Baidan Jaran Shamo *Desert* China 133 L8
Baikal, Lake *Lake* Russian Federation 117 127 M10 129
Băile Herculane Romania 90 H8
Bairiki Kiribati 144 J8
Baja Hungary 85 L15
Baja California Sur *State* Mexico 21 M7
Baker Oregon, USA 50 L9
Baker Island *Island* Baker and Howland Islands 144 J8
Bakhtaran Iran 123 L4
Baku Azerbaijan 99 T13
Balabac Strait *Strait* South China Sea/Sulu Sea 141 K7
Balakovo Russian Federation 96 H13 126 E8
Balaton, Lake *Lake* Hungary 68 85 K14
Balbina, Represa *Reservoir* Brazil 60 F7
Baleares, Islas *see* Balearic Islands
Balearic Islands (Sp. Baleares, Islas) *Island group* Spain 68 75 P10
Baleine, Grande Rivière de la *River* Quebec, Canada 39 L6
Bali *Island* Indonesia 129 140 J15 143
Balıkesir Turkey 118 H6
Balikpapan Indonesia 141 K12
Balkan Mountains *Mountain range* Bulgaria/Yugoslavia 68 89 P10 90 I12
Balkhash Kazakhstan 126 H12
Balkhash, Lake (var. Ozero Balkhash) *Lake* Kazakhstan 68 117 126 H12 129
Balkhash, Ozero *see* Balkhash, Lake
Balkhash, Lake (var. Ozero Balkhash) *Lake* Kazakhstan 68 117 126 H12 129
Ballarat Victoria, Australia 147 M14
Balleny Islands *Island group* Antarctica 64 E12
Balsas, Río *River* Mexico 24 C9 53 M12
Bălţi Moldova 98 H7
Baltic Sea *Sea* Atlantic Ocean 66 68 71 M14 80 H5 84 I2 117 129 L8
Baltimore Maryland, USA 27 O10 29 S3 43 S2 66 D9
Baltiysk Russian Federation 94 E9
Balykchy Kyrgyzstan 125 Q5
Bamako Mali 106 I9
Bambari Central African Republic 108 K10
Bamberg Germany 81 I13
Bamenda Cameroon 108 E10
Bana, Wadi *Dry watercourse* Yemen 122 I16
Banda, Kepulauan *Island group* Indonesia 141 P13
Banda Sea *Sea* Pacific Ocean 129 141 N13 144 F9
Bandaaceh Indonesia 140 B9
Bandar Seri Begawan Brunei 140 J9
Bandar-e 'Abbas Iran 123 O9
Bandarlampung Indonesia 140 F14
Bandırma Turkey 118 H5
Bandon Oregon, USA 50 F10
Bandundu Dem. Rep. Congo (Zaire) 109 I14
Bandung Indonesia 140 G15
Banff National Park *National park* USA 22 D10
Bangalore India 131 K13
Bangassou Central African Republic 108 L10
Banggai, Kepulauan *Island group* Indonesia 141 M12
Banggi, Pulau *Island* Borneo, Malaysia 141 K8
Bangka, Pulau *Island* Indonesia 140 G12
Bangkok Thailand 139 I13
Bangladesh *Country* S Asia 131 O7

Bangladesh 131

1971 • a Bengali • Taka • 948 • 58 • 10 • 39.9 • 5000 • Yes • 18 • 2019

Bangor Northern Ireland, United Kingdom 73 F11
Bangor Maine, USA 41 Q6
Bangui Central African Republic 108 J10
Bangweulu, Lake *Lake* Zambia 111 L12
Banhine *National Park* Mozambique 113 N10
Banja Luka Bosnia and Herzegovina 88 J5
Banjarmasin Indonesia 140 J13
Banjul Gambia 106 F9
Banks Island *Island* Northwest Territories, Canada 34 37 K5 65 N8
Banks Lake *Reservoir* Washington, USA 50 K6
Banská-Bystrica Slovakia 85 L11
Bantry Bay *Bay* Atlantic Ocean 73 A14
Banyo Cameroon 108 F10
Banyuwangi Indonesia 140 J15
Baoji China 135 K9
Baotou China 133 N7
Bar Montenegro, Yugoslavia 89 L10
Bar-le-Duc France 77 N5
Barbados *Island* Barbados, 55
Barbados *Country* West Indies 57 T14

Barbados 57

1966 • a English • Barbados dollar • 626 • 76 • 16 • 97.6 • 44 • 885 • Yes • 48 • 3207

Barbuda *Island* Antigua and Barbuda 57 T10
Barcelona Spain 75 Q6
Barcelona Venezuela 58 J4
Bareilly India 131 L5
Barents Sea *Sea* Arctic Ocean 65 R12 68 96 K6 117 126 H4 129
Bari Italy 87 N13
Barinas Venezuela 58 G5
Barisan, Pegunungan *Mountain range* Indonesia 140 E12
Barito, Sungai *River* Indonesia 140 J11
Bârlad Romania 91 N5
Barlee, Lake *Lake* Western Australia, Australia 146 G11

Barnaul Russian Federation 126 J11
Barnstaple England, United Kingdom 73 G16
Barquisimeto Venezuela 58 H4
Barra *Island* Scotland, United Kingdom 72 E8
Barranca del Cobra National Park *National park* Mexico 22 D13
Barranquilla Colombia 58 E4
Barreiras Brazil 61 K11
Barreiro Portugal 74 F11
Barrie Ontario, Canada 39 K14
Barrow England, United Kingdom 65 O6
Barrow Alaska, USA 36 H4
Barrow *River* Republic of Ireland 73 D13
Barrow Island *Island* Western Australia, Australia 146 E8
Bartang *River* Tajikistan 125 P9
Bartica Guyana 58 M6
Barychavichy Belarus 94 J12
Barysaw Belarus 95 L10
Basel (Eng. Basle) Switzerland 82 F8
Basilan *Island* Philippines 141 M8
Basle *see* Basel
Basque Country, The *Region* Spain 75 L4
Basra Iraq 114 E4 123 L7
Bass Strait *Strait* Indian Ocean/Pacific Ocean 143 147 M15
Basse-Terre Guadeloupe 57 S12
Basse Terre *Island* Guadeloupe 57 T12
Bassein Myanmar 138 E10
Basseterre Saint Kitts and Nevis 57 S11
Bastia France 77 S14
Bastogne Belgium 79 K18
Bat Cave *Ancient site* Mexico 24 C14
Bata Equatorial Guinea 109 E12
Batangas Philippines 141 L4
Batavia New York, USA 40 I9
Batavia *see* Jakarta
Batdâmbâng Cambodia 139 K13
Bath England, United Kingdom 73 I16
Bathurst New Brunswick, Canada 39 P11
Bathurst Island *Island* Northern Territory, Australia 146 I4
Bathurst Island *Island* Nunavut, Canada 37 M4
Batman Turkey 119 Q8
Batna Algeria 102 M5
Baton Rouge Louisiana, USA 42 I9
Baton Rouge *Battle site* Louisiana, USA 27 L14
Baton Rouge Louisiana, USA 28 F12 29 P6 33 J16
Batticaloa Sri Lanka 131 L16
Battle Creek Michigan, USA 45 N9
Batu, Kepulauan *Island group* Indonesia 140 D11
Bat'umi Georgia 99 O13
Bauchi Nigeria 107 P11
Bautzen Germany 81 N11
Bavaria (Ger. Bayern) *Cultural region* Germany 81 I14
Bavarian Alps *Mountain range* Austria/Germany 81 J17
Bawean, Pulau *Island* Indonesia 140 I14
Bay City Michigan, USA 45 O8
Bayamo Cuba 57 K6
Bayan Har Shan *Mountain range* China 133 K10
Baydaratskaya Guba *Bay* Arctic Ocean 96 O6 126 I6
Baydhabo Somalia 105 M17
Bayern *see* Bavaria
Baykonur Kazakhstan 126 F11
Bayonne France 76 I14
Bayramaly Turkmenistan 124 J9
Bayreuth Germany 81 J13
Be'ér Sheva' Israel 121 L11
Beagle Channel *Channel* Atlantic Ocean 63 L20
Bear Lake *Lake* Idaho/Utah, USA 48 J1
Bear Paw Mountain *Battle site* USA 29 N1
Bear River *Battle site* USA 29 M3
Bear Valley California, USA 28 B10
Beaufort Sea *Sea* Arctic Ocean 18 G10 22 D7 32 F7 34 36 I5 65 N7
Beaufort West South Africa 112 J15
Beaumont Texas, USA 49 S12
Beauvais France 77 L4
Beaver Island *Island* Michigan, USA 45 M5
Becan *Historic site* Mexico 24 H9
Bečej Serbia, Yugoslavia 89 M3
Béchar Algeria 102 J6
Bedford Indiana, USA 45 M14
Bedford Virginia, USA 27 R5
Bei'an China 135 O3
Beijing (Eng. Peking) China 135 M6
Beira Mozambique 113 O9 115 D11
Beirut (var. Beyrouth) Lebanon 121 M6
Beja Portugal 74 G12
Béjaïa Algeria 103 L4
Belarus (var. Belorussia) *Country* E Europe 94 J12

Belarus 94

⚑1991 • a Belorussian • ≣ Belarusian rouble • ♟ 50 • ♥ 68 • 🎓15 • 📖 99 • 🚗 110 • ✚ 244 • ☠ Yes • ⌂ 71 •

Belawan Indonesia 140 D9
Beledweyne Somalia 105 M16
Belém Brazil 60 J7
Belfast Northern Ireland, United Kingdom 73 F11
Belfort France 77 P7
Belgaum India 130 I11
Belgium *Country* W Europe 79 E15

Belgium 79

⚑1966 • a English • ≣ Barbados dollar • ♟ 626 • ♥ 76 • 🎓16 • 📖 97.6 • 🚗 44 • ✚ 885 • ☠ Yes • ⌂ 48 • 🍴 3207

Belgorod Russian Federation 96 E12
Belgrade Yugoslavia 89 N5
Belgrano II *Argentinian research station* Antarctica 64 D7
Belice *River* Italy 87 I18
Belitung, Pulau *Island* Indonesia 140 G13
Belize *Country* C America 56 C7

Belize 56

⚑1981 • a English • ≣ Belizean dollar • ♟ 9 • ♥ 75 • 🎓14 • 📖 75 • 🚗 20 • ✚ 2128 • ☠ Yes • ⌂ 47 • 🍴 2662

Belize *River* Belize/Guatemala 56 C6
Belize City Belize 56 C6
Belle Fourche River *River* South Dakota/Wyoming, USA 47 K8
Belle Île *Island* France 76 G8
Belle Isle *Island* Newfoundland, Canada 39 R7
Belle Isle, Strait of *Strait* Atlantic Ocean 39 R8
Bellevue Washington, USA 50 H6
Bellingham Washington, USA 50 H5
Bellingshausen Plain *Undersea feature* Pacific Ocean 55
Bellingshausen Sea *Sea* Antarctica 64 B8
Bellinzona Switzerland 82 H12
Bello Colombia 58 E6
Belluno Italy 86 H6
Belmopan Belize 56 C6
Belo Horizonte Brazil 61 L13
Beloit Wisconsin, USA 45 K9
Belyy, Ostrov *Island* Russian Federation 126 J5
Bemidji Minnesota, USA 44 G3
Bemis Heights *Battle* New York, USA 27 R3
Ben Nevis *Mountain* Scotland, United Kingdom, 68
Bend Oregon, USA 50 I9
Bendigo Victoria, Australia 147 M14
Benevento Italy 87 K13
Bengal, Bay of *Bay* Indian Ocean 114 J6 117 129 131 M12 138 D9
Benghazi Libya 103 Q6
Bengkulu Indonesia 140 E13
Benguela Angola 112 G6
Beni, Río *River* Bolivia 59 I13
Beni Suef Egypt 104 F7
Beni-Mellal Morocco 102 I6
Benidorm Spain 75 O11
Benin *Country* W Africa 107 M11

Benin 107

⚑1960 • a French • ≣ Franc de la Communauté financière africaine • ♟ 53 • ♥ 53 • 🎓11 • 📖 33.9 • 🚗 7 • ✚ 10000 • ☠ Yes • ⌂ 31 • 🍴 2532

Benin City Nigeria 107 O13
Benin, Bight of *Gulf* Atlantic Ocean 107 M13
Bennington Vermont, USA 27 S3 41 M9
Benton Harbor Michigan, USA 45 M10
Benue *River* Cameroon/Nigeria 107 P12
Beppu Japan 137 D14
Berat Albania 89 M13
Berau, Teluk *Bay* Indonesia 141 Q12
Berbera Somalia 105 M14
Berbérati Central African Republic 109 H11
Berbice River *River* Guyana 58 M6
Berdyans'k Ukraine 99 L8
Berettyó *River* Hungary/Romania 85 N14
Bergamo Italy 86 E6
Bergen Norway 66 K7 70 H10
Bergen op Zoom Netherlands 79 G12
Bergisch Gladbach Germany 81 E11
Bering Sea *Sea* Pacific Ocean 19 B11 22 B7 32 B8 34 36 B6 117 I3 127 R3 129 144
Bering Strait *Strait* Arctic Ocean/Pacific Ocean 18 D10 32 C7 34 36 E4 117 129 J2 144
Berlin Germany 80 L9
Bermejo, Río *River* Argentina 62 K5
Bermuda *Dependent territory* Bermuda 66 E9
Bermuda Rise *Undersea feature* Atlantic Ocean 34
Bern Switzerland 82 E10
Berner Alpen (Eng. Bernese Oberland) *Mountain range* Switzerland 82 E12
Bernese Oberland *see* Berner Alpen
Berry Islands *Island group* Bahamas 57 K2
Bertoua Cameroon 108 G10
Beruniy Uzbekistan 124 J6
Besançon France 77 O7
Bethel Alaska, USA 36 E7
Bethlehem West Bank 121 M10
Beykoz Turkey 118 I5
Beyrouth *see* Beirut
Beysehir Turkey 118 J9
Beysehir Gölü *Lake* Turkey 118 J8
Bhamo Myanmar 138 G6
Bhavnagar India 130 I8
Bhopal India 131 K8
Bhubaneshwar India 131 N9
Bhutan *Country* S Asia 131 P6

Bhutan 131

⚑1656 • a Dzongkha • ≣ Ngultrum • ♟ 45 • ♥ 61 • 📖 44.2 • 🚗 10 • ✚ 5825 • ☠ No • ⌂ 6 • 🍴 2553

Biak Indonesia 141 R11
Biak, Pulau *Island* Indonesia 141 R11
Białystok Poland 85 O4
Bianco, Monte *see* Blanc, Mont
Bicuari *National Park* Angola 112 G7
Biddeford Maine, USA 41 O8
Biel Switzerland 82 E9
Bielefeld Germany 80 F9
Bieler See *Lake* Switzerland 82 E10
Bielsko-Biała Poland 85 L9
Biên Hoa Vietnam 139 N14
Big Bend National Park *National park* Texas, USA 22 D13
Big Cypress National Preserve *National park* USA 22 F13
Big Cypress Swamp *Battle site* USA 29 R7
Big Hole *Battle site* USA 29 M2
Big Meadows USA 29 K2
Big Mound *Battle site* USA 29 O1
Big Spring Texas, USA 49 O10
Bighorn Mountains *Mountain range* Wyoming, USA 46 J7
Bighorn River *River* Montana/Wyoming, USA 46 J7
Bihać Bosnia and Herzegovina 88 H5
Bijagos Archipelago *Island group* Guinea-Bissau 106 F10
Bijelo Polje Montenegro, Yugoslavia 89 M8
Bikini Atoll *Atoll* Marshall Islands 144 I7
Bila Tserkva Ukraine 98 I5
Bilbao Spain 75 L3
Bilecik Turkey 118 I6
Bilhorod-Dnistrovs'kyy Ukraine 98 I8
Billings Montana, USA 46 J6
Biloxi Mississippi, USA 42 J9
Biltine Chad 108 K6
Bindura Zimbabwe 113 M8
Binghamton New York, USA 41 K10
Bingöl Turkey 119 Q7
Bintan, Pulau *Island* Indonesia 140 F11
Bío Bío, Río *River* Chile 63 H12
Bioko *Island* Equatorial Guinea, 101
Birak Libya 103 O8
Birao Central African Republic 108 L8
Biratnagar Nepal 131 O6
Birch Creek *Battle site* USA 29 L2
Bird Creek *Battle site* USA 29 P4
Birganj Nepal 131 N6
Birkenhead England, United Kingdom 73 H13
Birmingham England, United Kingdom 73 I14
Birmingham Alabama, USA 33 K15 43 L7
Birnin Konni Niger 107 O9
Biscay Plain *Undersea feature* France/Spain, 68
Biscay, Bay of *Bay* Atlantic Ocean 68 75 L3
Biscayne National Park *National park* USA 22 G13
Bishkek Kyrgyzstan 125 Q5
Bisho South Africa 113 L15
Biskra Algeria 103 M5
Bislig Philippines 141 N7
Bismarck North Dakota, USA 28 E8 30 E11 33 I12, 47 M5
Bismarck Archipelago *Island group* Papua New Guinea 147 O1
Bismarck Plate *Tectonic plate* 143
Bismarck Range *Mountain range* Papua New Guinea 143 147 M2
Bismarck Sea *Sea* Papua New Guinea 143 147 O1
Bissau Guinea-Bissau 106 F10
Bitrita Romania 90 J3
Bitrita *River* Romania 91 L3
Bitlis Turkey 119 R7
Bitola FYR Macedonia 89 O12
Bitterroot Range *Mountain range* Idaho/Montana, USA 46 F5
Biwa-ko *Lake* Japan 137 H11
Biysk Russian Federation 126 J11
Bizerte Tunisia 103 N4
Bjelovar Croatia 88 I2
Black Forest (Ger. Schwarzwald) *Mountain range* Germany 81 F15
Black Hills *Mountain range* South Dakota/Wyoming, USA 47 L8
Black River *River* China/Vietnam 138 L8
Black River *River* Arkansas/Missouri, USA 42 I4
Black Rock Desert *Desert* Nevada, USA 48 F1
Black Sea *Sea* Asia/Europe 66 68 C15 90 O12 96 99 117 K10 119 L5 126 C8 129 N8
Black Volta *River* W Africa 101 107 K11
Blackpool England, United Kingdom 73 H12
Blackwater *River* Republic of Ireland 73 C14
Blagoveshchensk Russian Federation 127 P11
Blanc, Mont (It. Monte Bianco) *Mountain* France/Italy, 68
Blanca, Bahía *Bay* Atlantic Ocean 63 L13
Blanca, Costa *Physical region* Spain 75 N12
Blanco, Cape *Headland* Oregon, USA 50 F10
Blanice *River* Czech Republic 84 H10
Blantyre Malawi 111 O15
Blenheim New Zealand 148 G8
Blida Algeria 103 L4
Bloemfontein South Africa 113 K13
Blois France 77 K7
Bloomington Illinois, USA 45 K12
Bloomington Indiana, USA 45 M13
Bloomington Minnesota, USA 44 H7
Blue Mesa Dam *Dam* Colorado, USA 49 L5
Blue Mountains *Mountain range* Oregon/Washington, USA 50 K10
Blue Nile *River* Ethiopia/Sudan 101 105 H13
Bluefields Nicaragua 56 E11
Bo Sierra Leone 106 H12
Bo Hai *Gulf* Yellow Sea 135 N7
Boa Vista Brazil 60 E6
Boaco Nicaragua 56 D11
Bobaomby, Tanjona *Headland* Madagascar 114 E10
Bobo-Dioulasso Burkina 107 K10
Bóbr *River* Poland 84 I6
Bocas del Toro Panama 56 F14
Bochum Germany 80 E10
Bodø Norway 71 L4
Bodrum Turkey 118 G9
Boende Dem. Rep. Congo (Zaire) 109 K12
Bogor Indonesia 140 G15
Bogotá Colombia 58 E6
Bohemia *Region* Czech Republic 84 G10
Bohemian Forest *Mountain range* Austria/Czech Republic/Germany 81 L14
Bohol *Island* Philippines 141 M6
Boise Idaho, USA 20 D10 28 B9 29 M2 33 F13 46 F8
Bokaro India 131 N7
Boknafjorden *Fjord* Norway 70 G11
Bol Chad 108 H7
Bol'shevik, Ostrov *Island* Russian Federation 127 L4
Bolgatanga Ghana 107 L11
Bolivia *Country* C South America 59 H14

Bolivia 59

⚑1825 • a Spanish, Aymará and Quechua • ≣ Boliviano • ♟ 7 • ♥ 61 • 🎓14 • 📖 83.6 • 🚗 29 • ✚ 2500 • ☠ No • ⌂ 61 • 🍴 2094

Bologna Italy 86 G8
Bolsena, Lago di *Lake* Italy 86 H11
Bolton England, United Kingdom 73 I13
Bolu Turkey 118 J5
Bolvadin Turkey 118 J7
Bolzano Italy 86 G5
Boma Dem. Rep. Congo (Zaire) 109 G15
Bombay (var. Mumbai) India, 114 H6 130 I10
Bomu *River* Central African Republic/Congo (Zaire) 109 L10
Bonaire *Island* Netherlands Antilles 57 O14
Bonampak *Historic site* Mexico 24 G10
Bondo Dem. Rep. Congo (Zaire) 109 J11
Bone, Teluk *Bay* Indonesia 141 L13
Bonete, Cerro *Mountain* Argentina, 55
Bongor Chad 108 H8
Bonifacio France 77 S16
Bonifacio, Strait of *Strait* Mediterranean Sea 87 D12
Bonn Germany 81 D11
Boosaaso Somalia 105 O14
Boothia, Gulf of *Gulf* Arctic Ocean 37 N6
Borås Sweden 70 J13
Bordeaux France 76 I12
Borger Texas, USA 49 O8
Borlänge Sweden 71 L11
Borneo *Island* SE Asia 114 M8 129 140 I11 143
Bornholm *Island* Denmark 71 K16
Borobudur Indonesia 140 H15
Borujerd Iran 123 M5
Bosanska Gradiška Bosnia and Herzegovina 88 J4
Bosanska Krupa Bosnia and Herzegovina 88 I4
Bosna *River* Bosnia and Herzegovina 89 K6
Bosnia and Herzegovina *Country* SE Europe 88 I5

Bosnia and Herzegovina 88-89

⚑1992 • a Serbo-Croat • ≣ Marka • ♟ 74 • ♥ 63 • 🎓15 • 📖 92.7 • 🚗 43 • ✚ 1667 • ☠ No • ⌂ 49 •

Bosobolo Dem. Rep. Congo (Zaire) 109 J11
Bosporus *Strait* Turkey 118 I5
Bossangoa Central African Republic 108 I10
Bosten Hu *Lake* China 132 H7
Boston Massachusetts, USA 26 F10 27 S3 28 I9 29 S2 30 G11 33 N13 41 O10
Bothnia, Gulf of *Gulf* Baltic Sea 68 71 M9
Botoșani Romania 91 M2
Botswana *Country* Botswana 112 J10

Botswana 112-113

⚑1966 • a English • ≣ Pula • ♟ 3 • ♥ 47 • 📖 74.4 • 🚗 15 • ✚ 5000 • ☠ Yes • ⌂ 28 • 🍴 2266

Bouaké Ivory Coast 106 J12
Bouar Central African Republic 108 H10
Bougainville Island *Island* Papua New Guinea 147 P2
Bougouni Mali 106 I10
Boulder Colorado, USA 49 M4
Boulogne *see* Boulogne-sur-Mer
Boulogne-sur-Mer (var. Boulogne) France 66 K8 77 K2
Boumalne-Dad? ès Morocco 102 I6
Bountiful Utah, USA 48 J2
Bounty Islands *Island group* New Zealand 144 J12
Bourge-en-Bresse France 77 O9
Bourges France 77 L8
Bourgogne *see* Burgundy
Bourke New South Wales, Australia 147 N11
Bournemouth England, United Kingdom 73 I17
Bouvet Island *Dependent territory* Bouvet Island 67 K16
Bowling Green Kentucky, USA 43 M3
Boyoma Falls *Waterfall* Dem. Rep. Congo (Zaire) 109 M12
Bozeman Montana, USA 46 H6
Bozeman Pass *Pass* Montana, USA 28 C8
Brač *Island* Croatia 88 I7
Bracciano, Lago di *Lake* Italy 87 H11
Bradano *River* Italy 87 M13
Bradford England, United Kingdom 73 J13
Braga Portugal 74 F6
Bragança Portugal 75 H6
Brahmaputra *River* S Asia 129 131 Q6 132 G12
Brăila Romania 91 O7
Brainerd Minnesota, USA 44 G5
Branco, Rio *River* Brazil, 55
Brandenburg Germany 80 K9
Brandon Manitoba, Canada 37 O15
Brandywine *Battle* Pennsylvania, USA 27 R4
Brasília Brazil 61 K12
Brașov Romania 91 L6
Bratislava Slovakia 84 J12
Bratsk Russian Federation 127 L10
Brattleboro Vermont, USA 41 N9
Braunau am Inn Austria 83 N5
Braunschweig (Eng. Brunswick) Germany 80 I9
Brava, Costa *Coastal region* Spain 75 R6
Bravo Del Norte, Río *River* Mexico/USA 53 K3
Brawley California, USA 51 N19
Brazil *Country* Brazil 60-61

Brazil 60-61

⚑1822 • a Portuguese • ≣ Real • ♟ 20 • ♥ 67 • 🎓14 • 📖 84 • 🚗 128 • ✚ 714 • ☠ No • ⌂ 78 • 🍴 2824

Brazil Basin *Undersea feature* Atlantic Ocean 55 66 I12
Brazilian Highlands *Mountain range* Brazil 55 61 L12
Brazos River *River* Texas, USA 49 Q11
Brazzaville Congo 109 H14
Brecon Beacons *Mountain range* Wales, United Kingdom 73 G15
Breda Netherlands 79 H12
Bregalnica *River* FYR Macedonia 89 P10
Bregenz Austria 82 I8
Bremen Germany 80 G8
Bremerhaven Germany 66 L8 80 F7

⚑ Date of independence • a Language (official or most commonly spoken) • ≣ Currency • ♟ Population density per square kilometre • ♥ Average life expectancy • 🎓 School-leaving age • 📖 Literacy • 🚗 Number of cars per 1,000 people • ✚ Number of people per doctor • ☠ Death penalty • ⌂ Percentage of urban-based population • 🍴 Average number of calories consumed daily per person

Bremerton – Chatham Islands

Bremerton Washington, USA 50 I5
Brenner Pass *Pass* Austria/Italy 83 L9
Brescia Italy 86 F7
Breslau *see* Wrocπaw
Brest Belarus 94 H14
Brest France 76 F6
Bretagne *see* Brittany
Breton Sound *Sound* Louisiana, USA 42 I10
Bria Central African Republic 108 K10
Bridgeport Connecticut, USA 41 M12
Bridgetown Barbados 57 T14
Brienzer See *Lake* Switzerland 82 F11
Brig Switzerland 82 F12
Brigham City Utah, USA 48 J2
Bright Angel Point *Mountain* Arizona, USA 48 I7
Brighton England, United Kingdom 73 K17
Brindisi Italy 87 P13
Brisbane Queensland, Australia 144 H11 147 P10
Bristol England, United Kingdom 73 I16
Bristol Bay *Bay* Bering Sea 36 E8
Bristol Channel *Inlet* Wales, United Kingdom 73 G16
Britain (var. Great Britain) *Island* Wales, United Kingdom, 68
British Columbia *Province* Canada 21 M3 29 N13 30 C9 33 E10 36 I13
British Indian Ocean Territory *Dependent territory* Indian Ocean 114 I9
British Isles *Island group* NW Europe 68
British Virgin Islands (var. Virgin Islands) *Dependent territory* West Indies 57 R9
Brittany (Fr. Bretagne) *Region* France 76 G6
Brno Czech Republic 84 J10
Broken Arrow Oklahoma, USA 47 P14
Broken Hill New South Wales, Australia 147 M12
Broken Ridge *Undersea feature* Indian Ocean 115 J12
Brokopondo Suriname 58 O6
Brooks Range *Mountain range* Alaska, USA 19 E11 22 C7 32 D7 34 36 H5
Broome Western Australia, Australia 146 G7
Brownsville Texas, USA 49 Q16
Bruges (var. Brugge) Belgium 79 D13
Brugge *see* Bruges
Brunei *Country* SE Asia 140 J9

Brunei 140

1984 • Malay • Brunei dollar • 61 • 76 • 16 • 90.1 • 167 • 1133 • No • 70 • 2745

Brunswick Maine, USA 41 P7
Brunswick Georgia, USA 43 O10
Brunswick *see* Braunschweig
Brussel *see* Brussels
Brussels (var. Brussel, Bruxelles) Belgium 79 G15
Bruxelles *see* Brussels
Bryansk Russian Federation 96 E11 126 D6
Bryce Canyon *Canyon* Utah, USA 19 G16 48 G5
Bubiyan, Jazirat *Island* Kuwait 123 L7
Bucaramanga Colombia 58 F5
Buchanan Liberia 106 H13
Bucharest (Rom. Bucure@sti) Romania 91 L9
Bucuresti *see* Bucharest
Budapest Hungary 85 L13
Buenaventura Colombia 58 D7 145 Q8
Buenos Aires Argentina 62 M10 67 F14
Buenos Aires, Lago *Lake* Argentina/Chile 63 I16
Buffalo New York, USA 40 H9
Bug (Eng. Western Bug) *River* E Europe 68 85 O4 94 H15
Bujumbura Burundi 111 L7
Bukavu Dem. Rep. Congo (Zaire) 109 O13
Bukhoro Uzbekistan 125 K7
Bukoba Tanzania 111 M5
Bulawayo Zimbabwe 113 L9
Bulgaria *Country* SE Europe 90 J12

Bulgaria 90-91

1908 • Bulgarian • Lev • 75 • 71 • 16 • 98.2 • 208 • 303 • No • 71 • 2831

Bull Run *Battle site* USA 27 O10
Bumba Dem. Rep. Congo (Zaire) 109 L11
Bunbury Western Australia, Australia 146 F13
Bundaberg Queensland, Australia 147 P9
Bunia Dem. Rep. Congo (Zaire) 108 P12
Bunker Hill USA 27 S3
Buon Ma Thuot Vietnam 139 O13
Bûr Safâga Egypt 104 G8
Buraydah Saudi Arabia 122 J9
Burco Somalia 105 M14
Burdur Turkey 118 I9
Burgas Bulgaria 91 N13
Burgos Spain 75 K5
Burgundy (Fr. Bourgogne) *Cultural region* France 77 N8
Burkina *Country* W Africa 107 L9

Burkina 107

1960 • French • Franc de la Communauté financière africaine • 42 • 44 • 14 • 20.7 • 4 • 57300 • Yes • 27 • 2387

Burlington Iowa, USA 47 R10
Burlington Vermont, USA 41 M7
Burma *see* Myanmar
Burnie Tasmania, Australia 147 M15
Burns Oregon, USA 50 K10
Bursa Turkey 118 I6
Burt Corn Creek *Battle site* USA 29 Q5
Burtnieku Ezers *Lake* Latvia 94 I4
Buru, Pulau *Island* Indonesia 141 N12
Burundi *Country* C Africa 111 L7

Burundi 111

1962 • French and Kirundi • Burundi franc • 257 • 42 • 13 • 44.6 • 3 • 3326 • Yes • 8 • 1941

Bushire Iran 123 M8
Buta Dem. Rep. Congo (Zaire) 109 M11
Butare Rwanda 111 L6
Butembo Dem. Rep. Congo (Zaire) 109 O12
Butler Pennsylvania, USA 40 G12
Buton, Pulau *Island* Indonesia 141 M13
Butte Montana, USA 46 H6
Butterworth Malaysia 139 I17
Butuan Philippines 141 N7
Buyo, Lac de *Reservoir* Ivory Coast 106 J13
Buzau Romania 91 M7
Buzău *River* Romania 91 M7
Byaroza Belarus 94 I13
Bydgoszcz Poland 85 K4
Byerezino *River* Belarus 95 M11
Bykhaw Belarus 95 N12
Bytantay *River* Russian Federation 127 N6
Bytom Poland 85 L8
Byuzmeyin Turkmenistan 124 H9

C

Caazapá Paraguay 62 N6
Caballo Reservoir *Reservoir* New Mexico, USA 49 L10
Cabanatuan Philippines 141 L4
Cabimas Venezuela 58 G4
Cabinda Angola 109 F14 112 F3
Cabinda *Province* Angola 112 F3
Cabora Bassa, Lake *Reservoir* Mozambique 113 M7
Cabot Strait *Strait* Newfoundland/Nova Scotia, Canada 39 R11
Čačak Serbia, Yugoslavia 89 N7
Cáceres Spain 74 H9
Cadiz Philippines 141 M6
Cádiz Spain 74 H14
Cadiz, Gulf of *Gulf* Spain 74 G13
Caen France 76 I4
Caernarfon Wales, United Kingdom 73 G13
Cagayan de Oro Philippines 141 N7
Cagliari Italy 87 D15
Cagliari, Golfo di *Gulf* Italy 87 D16
Cahokia Illinois, USA 27 P5
Cahors France 77 K12
Caicos Islands *Island group* Turks and Caicos Islands 55 57 N6
Cairns Queensland, Australia 147 N6
Cairo Egypt 104 F6
Cajamarca Peru 59 C11
Čakovec Croatia 88 I2
Calabar Nigeria 107 P13
Calabria *Region* Italy 87 M16
Calais France 77 K1
Calais Maine, USA 41 R5
Calama Chile 62 G5
Călărași Romania 91 N9
Calbayog Philippines 141 N5
Calcutta India 114 J5 131 O8
Caldas da Rainha Portugal 74 F9
Caleta Olivia Argentina 63 J16
Calgary Alberta, Canada 30 C10 33 G12 37 L14
Cali Colombia 58 D7
Calicut India 130 J14
California *State* USA 21 M6 23 N11 29 N15 30 C12 33 E14 51 G13
California, Gulf of *Gulf* Pacific Ocean 19 F18 24 B15 33 G1634 52 H5 55 N6 145
Callao Peru 59 D13 145 Q9
Caltanissetta Italy 87 K18
Calvinia South Africa 112 I15
Camagüey Cuba 56 J5
Cambay, Gulf of *see* Khambhat, Gulf of
Cambodia *Country* Cambodia 139 K13

Cambodia 139

1953 • Khmer • Riel • 62 • 53 • 12 • 66 • 5 • 8120 • No • 21 • 2021

Cambrian Mountains *Mountain range* Wales, United Kingdom 73 G15
Cambridge England, United Kingdom 73 K15
Cambridge Massachusetts, USA 27 S2
Camden New Jersey, USA 41 K14
Camden South Carolina, USA 27 R6
Cameia *National Park* Angola 112 J5
Cameron Highlands *Region* Malaysia 139 I18
Cameroon *Country* C Africa 108 E10

Cameroon 108

1960 • English and French • Franc de la Coopération financière en Afrique central • 32 • 55 • 12 • 71.7 • 7 • 10000 • Yes • 45 • 1981

Campbell Island *Island* New Zealand 144 J13
Campbell Plateau *Undersea feature* Pacific Ocean 143
Campbell River British Columbia, Canada 36 I14
Campeche Mexico 53 S11
Campeche *State* Mexico 21 O8
Campeche, Bay of *Bay* Gulf of Mexico 24 F9 53 P12
Campina Grande Brazil 60 O9
Campinas Brazil 61 J14
Campo Grande Brazil 61 H13
Campobasso Italy 87 K12
Cân Thơ Vietnam 139 M15
Canada *Country* North America 21 M4 22 D9 28 D8, 36-39

Canada 36-39

1867 • English and French • Canadian dollar • 3 • 79 • 16 • 99 • 441 • 455 • No • 77 • 3094

Canada, Dominion of Canada 29 N1
Canadian River *River* USA 47 Q15 49 N8
Canadian Shield *Physical region* Canada 19 G12 34
Çanakkale Turkey 118 G6
Canary Islands *Island group* Spain 66 J10 101
Canberra Australian Capital Territory, Australia 147 O13
Cancer, Tropic of *Line of latitude* 34 55
Cancún Mexico 53 T10
Caniapiscau *River* Quebec, Canada 39 N6
Caniapiscau, Réservoir de *Reservoir* Quebec, Canada 39 M7
Çankırı Turkey 119 L5
Canna *Island* Scotland, United Kingdom 72 F8
Cannes France 77 Q13
Cantábrica, Cordillera *Mountain range* Spain 68 75 H4
Canterbury England, United Kingdom 73 L16
Canterbury Bight *Bight* Pacific Ocean 148 F10
Canton *see* Guangzhou
Canton Illinois, USA 44 J12
Canton Ohio, USA 45 Q11
Canton Georgia, USA 30 F13
Canyon de Chelly *Historic site* USA 29 M4 49 K7
Canyon Ferry Lake *Lake* Montana, USA 46 H5
Canyonlands National Park *National park* USA 22 D12
Cap-Haïtien Haiti 57 M7
Cape Basin *Undersea feature* Atlantic Ocean 67 K14 101
Cape Breton Highlands National Park *National park* Nova Scotia, Canada 22 H10
Cape Breton Island *Island* Nova Scotia, Canada 26 G9
Cape Canaveral Florida, USA 43 O12
Cape Coast Ghana 107 L13
Cape Girardeau Missouri, USA 47 T12
Cape Town South Africa 67 M14 112 I16 114 B12
Cape Verde *Country* Atlantic Ocean 66 I10

Cape Verde 66

1975 • Portuguese • Cape Verde escudo • 104 • 69 • 13 • 71 • 4 • 3448 • No • 56 • 2805

Cape Verde Basin *Undersea feature* Atlantic Ocean 67 H11
Cape Verde Islands *Island group* Cape Verde, 101
Cape York Peninsula *Peninsula* Queensland, Australia 143 147 M5
Capitán Pablo Lagerenza Paraguay 62 K3
Capitol Reef National Park *National park* USA 22 D12
Cappadocia *Physical region* Turkey 119 M7
Capri *Island* Italy 87 K14
Capricorn, Tropic of *Line of latitude* 55 129 143
Caquetá, Río *River* Brazil/Colombia 58 F8
Caracas Venezuela 58 I4
Caracol *Historic site* Mexico 24 H10
Caratasca, Laguna de *Lagoon* Honduras 56 F9
Carbondale Illinois, USA 45 K15
Carcassonne France 77 L14
Cardiff Wales, United Kingdom 73 H16
Cardigan Bay *Bay* United Kingdom 73 F14
Caribbean Plate *Tectonic plate* 34 55
Caribbean Sea *Sea* Atlantic Ocean 34 55 D10 56 58 I8 66 F3
Caribou Maine, USA 41 Q3
Carlisle England, United Kingdom 73 I11
Carlisle Pennsylvania, USA 40 I13
Carlsbad New Mexico, USA 49 M10
Carlsbad Caverns National Park *National park* USA 22 E13
Carlsberg Ridge *Undersea feature* Indian Ocean 114 G7
Carlyle Lake *Reservoir* Illinois, USA 45 K14
Carmen, Isla *Island* Mexico 52 H6
Carnarvon Western Australia, Australia 146 E10
Carnegie, Lake *Salt lake* Western Australia, Australia 146 G10
Carolina Brazil 60 K9
Caroline Islands *Island group* Micronesia 144 G8 143
Caroline Plate *Tectonic plate* Pacific Ocean 129 143
Caroline Ridge *Undersea feature* Pacific Ocean, 143
Carpathian Mountains *Mountain range* E Europe 68 85 L10 91 K2 98 E5
Carpentaria, Gulf of *Gulf* Australia 143 147 L5
Carson City Nevada, USA 28 B10 29 L3 33 E14 48 E3
Carson Pass *Pass* California, USA 28 A10
Cartagena Spain 75 N12
Cartagena Colombia 58 E4 67 D11
Cartago Costa Rica 56 E13
Cartwright Newfoundland, Canada 39 R6
Casa Grande Arizona, USA 48 I9
Casa Grande *Ancient site* Mexico 24 B14
Casablanca Morocco 66 K9 102 H5
Casas Grandes *Historic site* Mexico 24 C15
Cascade Range *Mountain range* Oregon/Washington, USA 19 E15 50 H10
Cascades *Battle site* USA 29 L1
Casey *Australian research station* Antarctica 64 G10
Casper Wyoming, USA 47 K9
Caspian Depression *Depression* Kazakhstan/Russian Federation, 68
Caspian Sea *Inland sea* Asia/Europe 68 96 99 117 F17 123 N2 124 E5 126 D10 129 S12
Castelló de la Plana Spain 75 O9
Castelo Branco Portugal 74 G9
Castries Saint Lucia 57 T13
Castro Chile 63 G15
Cat Island *Island* Bahamas 57 L3
Catalonia (Sp. Cataluña) Spain 75 P6
Cataluña *see* Catalonia
Catanduanes Island *Island* Philippines 141 M4
Catania Italy 87 L18
Catanzaro Italy 87 N16
Catskill Mountains *Mountain range* New York, USA 41 L10
Cauca, Río *River* Colombia 58 E5
Caucasus *Mountain range* Georgia/Russian Federation 68 96 I9 99 D15 117 O11 126 C9 129
Cauquenes Chile 63 G12
Cawnpore *see* Kanpur
Caxito Angola 112 G4
Cayenne French Guiana 58 P6 67 F11
Cayes Haiti 57 L8
Cayman Brac *Island* Cayman Islands 56 I6
Cayman Islands *Dependent territory* West Indies 56 H6
Ceará Plain *Undersea feature* Atlantic Ocean 55
Cebu Philippines 141 M6
Cebu *Island* Philippines 141 M6
Cedar Rapids Iowa, USA 47 R9
Cedar River *River* Iowa/Minnesota, USA 47 Q8
Cedros, Isla *Island* Mexico 52 F4
Cefalù Italy 87 K17
Celaya Mexico 53 M11
Celebes (var. Sulawesi) *Island* Indonesia 129 141 L12
Celebes Sea *Sea* SE Asia 129 141 L10 144 143 F8
Celje Slovenia 83 R10
Celle Germany 80 H9
Celtic Shelf *Undersea feature* 68
Central African Republic *Country* C Africa 108 J9

Central African Republic 108-109

1960 • French • Franc de la Coopération financière en Afrique centrale • 6 • 45 • 14 • 42.4 • 5000 • No • 39 • 1690

Central America *Region* 54-55
Central Arizona Project *Irrigated agriculture* USA 49 I9
Central Lowlands *Physical region* Canada/USA 19 F13
Central Makran Range *Mountain range* Pakistan 130 F5
Central Pacific Basin *Undersea feature* Pacific Ocean 143
Central Russian Upland *Mountain range* Russian Federation, 68
Central Siberian Plateau *Mountain range* Russian Federation 117 127 K7 129
Centralia Illinois, USA 45 K14
Ceram *Island* Indonesia 129 143
Ceram Sea *Sea* Indonesia 141 O12
Cerralvo, Isla *Island* Mexico 52 H8
Cerro de Pasco Peru 59 D12
Cervia Italy 86 H8
Cēsis Latvia 94 J5
České Budějovice Czech Republic 84 H11
Česma *River* Croatia 88 I3
Ceuta Spain 102 I4
Cévennes *Mountain range* France 77 M14
Ceyhan Turkey 119 N9
Ceylon Plain *Undersea feature* Indian Ocean 117 129
Ch'ŏngjin North Korea 135 Q5
Chabahar Iran 114 G5 123 Q11
Chaco Canyon *Ancient site* USA 24 C13
Chad *Country* C Africa 108 I6

Chad 108

1975 • Portuguese • Cape Verde escudo • 104 • 69 • 13 • 71 • 4 • 3448 • No • 56 • 2805

Chad, Lake *Lake* C Africa 101 107 R9 108 H7
Chagai Hills *Hill range* Pakistan 130 E4
Chagos-Laccadive Plateau *Undersea feature* Indian Ocean 114 H9 117 129
Chahbahar Iran,
Chalbi Desert *Desert* Kenya 111 P3
Chalco *Historic site* Mexico 24 D8
Chalkida Greece 93 K8
Châlons-en-Champagne France 77 N5
Chama *Historic site* Mexico 24 G11
Chambal *River* India 131 K6
Chambéry France 77 O10
Chambord France 77 K7
Champaign Illinois, USA 45 L12
Champasak Laos 139 M12
Champlain, Lake *Lake* Canada/USA 41 M6
Chañaral Chile 62 G7
Chancellorsville *Battle site* Virginia, USA 27 N10
Chandigarh India 131 K4
Changchun China 135 O4
Changsha China 135 L12
Changzhi China 135 L8
Chania Greece 93 L15
Channel Islands *Island group* W Europe 73 H18 76 H4
Channel Islands National Park *National park* USA 22 C12
Channel, The *see* English Channel
Channel Tunnel *Tunnel* France/United Kingdom 73 L16 77 K1
Channel-Port aux Basques Newfoundland, Canada 39 Q10
Chanthaburi Thailand 139 J13
Chapala, Lago de *Lake* Mexico 53 L11
Chardzhev Turkmenistan 125 K8
Charente *River* France 76 I10
Chari *River* Central African Republic/Chad 108 H8
Chariton River *River* Missouri, USA 47 R10
Charleroi Belgium 79 H16
Charleston South Carolina, USA 26 E12 27 R6 43 P8
Charleston West Virginia, USA 28 G10 33 L14 43 P3
Charleville Queensland, Australia 147 N10
Charleville-Mézières France 77 N3
Charlotte North Carolina, USA 27 R6 33 L15 43 P6
Charlotte Amalie Virgin Islands (US) 57 R9
Charlottesville Virginia, USA 43 Q3
Charlottesville Virginia, USA 27 R4
Charlottetown Prince Edward Island, Canada 33 O12 39 Q12
Chartres France 77 K6
Charus Nuur *Lake* Mongolia 133 N8
Chashma Barrage *Dam* Pakistan 130 I2
Châteaurox France 77 K8
Chatham Islands *Island group* New Zealand 144 J12

Chatham Rise *Undersea feature* Pacific Ocean 143
Chattanooga Tennessee, USA 43 M5
Chauk Myanmar 138 F8
Chaumont France 77 N6
Cheboksary Russian Federation 97 I11 126 F7
Cheboygan Michigan, USA 45 N5
Chechnya *Region* Russian Federation 96 E16
Cheju South Korea 135 P9
Chelan, Lake *Reservoir* Washington, USA 50 H6
Cheleken Turkmenistan 124 F7
Chelm Poland 85 P7
Chelyabinsk Russian Federation 126 G9
Chelyuskin, Mys *Cape* Russian Federation 127 L4
Chemnitz Germany 81 M11
Chenab *River* Pakistan 130 I3
Chengdu China 134 J10
Chennai *see* Madras
Cheraw South Carolina, USA 27 R6
Cherbourg France 76 H4
Cherepovets Russian Federation 96 G9 126 F5
Cherkasy Ukraine 98 J5
Cherkessk Russian Federation 97 D15 126 C9
Chernihiv Ukraine 98 I3
Chernivtsi Ukraine 98 F6
Chernobyl' Ukraine 98 I4
Chernyakhovsk Russian Federation 94 G10
Chesapeake Bay *Inlet* Virginia, USA 43 S3
Chester England, United Kingdom 73 H13
Chesterfield Inlet Canada 37 O9
Chesuncook Lake *Lake* Maine, USA 41 P4
Chetumal Mexico 53 T12
Chevaliers, Krak des *Castle* Syria 121 M5
Cheyenne Wyoming, USA 28 D10 33 H14 47 K10
Cheyenne River *River* South Dakota/Wyoming, USA 47 M7
Chiang Mai Thailand 138 H9
Chiang Rai Thailand 138 I9
Chiba Japan 137 L11
Chibougamau Québec, Canada 39 M10
Chicago Illinois, USA 23 P6 28 F9 29 Q3 30 F11, 33 K13 45 L10
Chichen Itza *Historic site* Mexico 24 H8
Chichén-Itzá *Ruins* Mexico 24 H8 53 T11
Chickamauga *Battle site* Alabama, USA 27 M13
Chiclayo Peru 59 C11
Chico California, USA 51 H13
Chicoutimi Quebec, Canada 39 N11
Chidley, Cape *Cape* Newfoundland, Canada 39 O3
Chiemsee *Lake* Germany 81 K16
Chifeng China 133 P6
Chihuahua Mexico 20 D12 33 G16 53 K5
Chihuahua *Chihuahua*, Mexico 20 D12 33 G16
Chile *Country* South America 62 G8

Chile 62-63

■1818 • **a** Spanish • 鬯 Chilean peso •
♦ 20 • ● 75 • ▮13 • ☞ 95.2 • ⇱ 71
• ✚ 909 • ☻ Yes • 🏠 84 • ⅱ 2582

Chile Basin *Undersea feature* Pacific Ocean 55 145 P11
Chile Chico Chile 63 I16
Chillán Chile 63 G12
Chillicothe Ohio, USA 45 P13
Chiloé, Isla de *Island* Chile 55 63 G14 145 P12
Chilpancingo Mexico 53 N13
Chilung Taiwan 135 O13
Chimborazo *Volcano* Ecuador, 55
Chimbote Peru 59 C12 145 Q9
Chimoio Mozambique 113 N9
Chin Hills *Mountain range* Myanmar 138 E7
China *Country* China 132-135

China 132-135

■1949 • **a** Mandarin • 鬯 Renminbi
(People's Bank dollar), usually called the yuan
• ♦ 136 • ● 70 • ▮15 • ☞ 83.9 • ⇱
3 • ✚ 629 • ☻ Yes • 🏠 30 • ⅱ 2727

China Lake Naval Weapons Center *Military base* California, USA 51 L17
Chinandega Nicaragua 56 C10
Chindwin *River* Myanmar 138 F6
Chingola Zambia 111 K13
Chinhoyi Zimbabwe 113 M8
Chinkultic *Historic site* Mexico 24 F11
Chioggia Italy 86 H7
Chios *Island* Greece 93 O8
Chios Greece 93 O8
Chipata Zambia 111 M14
Chippewa, Lake *Reservoir* Wisconsin, USA 44 J5
Chirchiq Uzbekistan 125 N7
Chiriquí Gulf *Gulf* Panama 56 E15
Chişinău Moldova 98 H8
Chita Russian Federation 127 N11
Chitré Panama 56 G15
Chittagong Bangladesh 131 P8
Chitungwiza Zimbabwe 113 M8
Chobe *National Park* Botswana 113 K8
Chobe *River* Botswana 113 K8
Chojnice Poland 85 K3
Cholula Mexico 53 N12
Choluteca Honduras 56 C10
Choma Zambia 110 J16
Chon Buri Thailand 139 J13
Ch'ŏngjin North Korea 135 Q5
Chongqing China 134 J11
Choybalsan Mongolia 133 O4
Christchurch New Zealand 148 F10
Christiansted Virgin Islands (US) 57 R10
Christmas Island *Dependent territory* Indian Ocean 114 M9
Christmas Island *see* Kiritimati
Chu *River* Kazakhstan/Kyrgyzstan 126 G12
Chubut, Río *River* Argentina 63 I14
Chugoku-sanchi *Mountain range* Japan 137 D12
Chukchi Sea *Sea* Arctic Ocean 65 P5 127 Q2
Chumphon Thailand 139 H14
Chuquicamata Chile 62 G5

Chur Switzerland 82 I10
Churchill Manitoba, Canada 20 E8 37 P11
Churchill *River* Manitoba/Saskatchewan, Canada 37 O11
Churchill Falls Newfoundland, Canada 39 P7
Chustenahlah *Battle site* USA 29 P4
Cienfuegos Cuba 56 I4
Cihuatlan *Historic site* Mexico 24 B9
Cincinnati Ohio, USA 27 M11 45 O13
Cincinnati Ohio, USA 27 M11
Čiovo *Island* Croatia 88 I7
Cirebon Indonesia 140 H15
Ciudad Bolívar Venezuela 58 J5
Ciudad del Este Paraguay 62 O6
Ciudad Guayana Venezuela 58 K5
Ciudad Juárez Mexico 52 J3
Ciudad Madero Mexico 53 O10
Ciudad Obregón Mexico 52 I5
Ciudad Real Spain 75 K10
Ciudad Victoria Mexico 53 N9
Civitavecchia Italy 87 G11
Clair Engle Lake *Reservoir* California, USA 51 G12
Claremont New Hampshire, USA 41 N8
Clarence Strait *Strait* Australia 146 I5
Clarenville Newfoundland, Canada 39 S9
Clarion Fracture Zone *Undersea feature* Pacific Ocean 34 145 L7
Clarksville Tennessee, USA 43 L4
Clearwater Florida, USA 43 N12
Clearwater *Battle site* Idaho, USA 29 M2
Clermont Queensland, Australia 147 O8
Clermont-Ferrand France 77 M10
Cleveland Ohio, USA 28 H9 29 R3 30 F11 33 L13, 45 P10
Clipperton Fracture Zone *Undersea feature* Pacific Ocean 34 145 L8
Clipperton Island *Dependent territory* Pacific Ocean 145 N7
Cloncurry Queensland, Australia 147 M8
Clovis New Mexico, USA 48 H9
Cluj-Napoca Romania 90 I4
Clyde *River* Scotland, United Kingdom 72 H10
Clyde, Firth of *Inlet* Scotland, United Kingdom 72 G10
Coast Mountains *Mountain range* British Columbia, Canada/USA 19 E12
Coast Ranges *Mountain range* California/Oregon/Washington, USA 19 E16 50 G10
Coats Island *Island* Nunavut, Canada 37 P9
Coatzacoalcos Mexico 53 P13
Coba *Historic site* Mexico 24 I8
Cobán Guatemala 56 B7
Cobija Bolivia 59 H13
Cochabamba Bolivia 59 I15
Cochin India 14 I7 130 J15
Cochrane Ontario, Canada 38 J11
Cochrane Chile 63 I17
Cockburn Sound *Sound* Australia 115 M12
Cockburn Town Turks and Caicos Islands 57 N6
Coco, Río *River* Honduras/Nicaragua 56 F9
Cocos Basin *Undersea feature* Indian Ocean 117 129
Cocos Islands *Island group* Indian Ocean 114 L10
Cocos Plate *Tectonic plate* 34 55
Cocos Ridge *Undersea feature* Indian Ocean 55 145 P8
Cod, Cape *Headland* Massachusetts, USA 19 M15 34 41 P10
Cody Wyoming, USA 30 D11 46 I7
Coeur d'Alene Idaho, USA 46 F4
Coiba, Isla de *Island* Panama 56 F15
Coihaique Chile 63 I16
Coimbatore India 130 J14
Coimbra Portugal 74 F8
Coixtlahuacan *Historic site* Mexico 24 E9
Colchester England, United Kingdom 73 L15
Colditz *Castle* Germany 81 K11
Colee Hammock *Battle site* USA 29 S6
Colhué Huapí, Lago *Lake* Argentina 63 I16
Colima Mexico 53 K12
Coll *Island* Scotland, United Kingdom 72 F8
Collier Bay *Bay* Western Australia, Australia 146 H6
Colmar France 77 P6
Cologne (Ger. Köln) Germany 81 D11
Colombia *Country* N South America 58 F9

Colombia 58

■1819 • **a** Spanish • 鬯 Colombian peso •
♦ 40 • ● 70 • ▮12 • ☞ 90.6 • ⇱ 19 •
✚ 1111 • ☻ No • 🏠 73 • ⅱ 2677

Colombian Basin *Undersea feature* Caribbean Sea 55
Colombo Sri Lanka 114 I7 131 K16
Colón Argentina 62 N9
Colón Panama 56 G14
Colonia del Sacramento Uruguay 62 N10
Colonsay *Island* Scotland, United Kingdom 72 F9
Colorado *State* USA 21 N6 23 P21 29 O15 30 D12 33 H14 34 49 L4
Colorado River *River* USA 21 N6 23 P21 29 O15 30 D12 33 H14
Colorado Plateau *Plateau* USA 19 G17 48 I7
Colorado Project *Irrigated agriculture* USA 49 H9
Colorado, Río *River* Argentina 55 63 K12
Colorado River *River* Mexico/USA 19 G16 22 D12 23 O12 24 C12 28 C11 29 M4 49 K5 51 O19 52 G1 145 N5
Colorado River *River* Texas, USA 33 G14 49 P11
Colorado Springs Colorado, USA 33 H14 49 M5
Columbia Missouri, USA 47 R11
Columbia *River* British Columbia/Oregon/Washington, Canada/USA 23 N5 34 37 K14 50 K6 145 N4
Columbia South Carolina, USA 28 H9 29 R5 33 L15
Columbia, District of *Federal district* District of Columbia, USA 29 Q15
Columbine, Cape *Headland* South Africa 112 I15
Columbus Georgia, USA 15 L13 43 M8 47 M4
Columbus Indiana, USA 45 N13
Columbus Ohio, USA 33 L14 45 P12
Colville River *River* Alaska, USA 36 H5
Comacchio, Valli di *Lagoon* Italy 86 H8
Comalcalco *Historic site* Mexico 24 F9
Comayagua Honduras 56 C9
Comilla Bangladesh 131 P8

Como, Lake *Lake* Italy 86 E6
Comodoro Rivadavia Argentina 63 J16
Comorin, Cape *Headland* India 114 I7 129
Comoro Islands *Island group* Comoros, 101
Comoros *Country* Indian Ocean 114 E10

Comoros 114

■1975 • **a** Arabic and French • 鬯
Comoros franc • ♦ 303 • ● 59 • ▮
16 • ☞ 55.4 • ⇱ 14 • ✚ 10000 •
☻ Yes • ⅱ 31 • 🏠 1897

Conakry Guinea 106 G11
Concepción Paraguay 62 M5
Concepción Chile 63 G12 145 Q12
Conchos *River* Mexico 52 J5
Concord California, USA 51 H15
Concord New Hampshire, USA 41 O9
Concord New Hampshire, USA 27 S2 28 I8 29 S2, 33 M13 41 O9
Concordia Argentina 62 N9
Congo *River* Angola/Congo/Congo (Zaire) 67 L12 101 109 J12 112 F3
Congo *Country* C Africa 109 H13

Congo 109

■1960 • **a** French • 鬯 Franc de la Coopération financière en Afrique • ♦ 8 • ●
49 • ▮16 • ☞ 76.9 • ⇱ 14 • ✚ 3333 •
☻ No • ⅱ 59 • 🏠 2296

Congo (Zaire), Democratic Republic of C Africa 109 K13

Congo (Zaire), Dem. Rep. of 108-109

■1960 • **a** French and English • 鬯
Congolese franc • ♦ 22 • ● 51 • ▮ 77 •
☞ 17 • ✚ 10000 • ☻ Yes • 🏠 29 • ⅱ
2060

Congo Basin *Drainage basin* Dem. Rep. C Africa 101
Connecticut *State* USA 21 P5 23 S11 29 Q14 30 G11 33 M13 41 M11
Connecticut *River* Canada/USA 40 N8
Connecticut *State* USA 21 P5 23 S11 29 Q14 30 G11 33 M13
Constance *see* Konstanz
Constance, Lake *Lake* C Europe 68 81 G17 82 H8
Constantine Algeria 103 M4
Constanța Romania 91 P9
Constantine *see* Konstanz
Contwoyto Lake *Lake* Nunavut, Canada 37 M8
Coober Pedy South Australia, Australia 147 K11
Cook Islands *Dependent territory* Pacific Ocean 145 K10
Cook Strait *Strait* New Zealand 144 I12 143 148 H7
Cook, Mount *Mountain* New Zealand, 143
Cooktown Queensland, Australia 147 N6
Cooper Creek *Seasonal river* Queensland/South Australia, Australia 147 L11
Coos Bay Oregon, USA 50 F10
Copan *Historic site* Mexico 24 H11
Copán Honduras 56 C8
Copenhagen Denmark 70 J15
Copiapó Chile 62 G7
Coppermine *River* Northwest Territories/Nunavut, Canada 37 L8
Coppermine Nunavut, Canada 20 D7 37 L8
Copşa Mică Romania 90 J5
Coquimbo Chile 62 G9
Corabia Romania 90 J10
Coral Sea *Sea* Pacific Ocean 144 H10 143 147 O4
Coral Sea Basin *Undersea feature* Pacific Ocean 143
Coral Sea Islands *Dependent territory* Pacific Ocean 144 H10
Córdoba (Eng. Cordova) Spain 74 J12
Córdoba Argentina 62 J9
Cordova *see* Córdoba
Cordova Alaska, USA 36 G9
Corfu (Gr. Kerkyra) *Island* Greece 92 F6
Corfu Greece 92 F5
Corinth (Gr. Korinthos) Greece 92 J10
Corinth Canal *Canal* Greece 92 J9
Corinth, Gulf of *Gulf* Greece 92 I9
Corinto Nicaragua 56 C10
Cork Republic of Ireland 73 C14
Corner Brook Newfoundland, Canada 39 R9
Corning New York, USA 40 J10
Corno Grande *Mountain* Italy, 68
Cornwall *County* England, United Kingdom 73 F17
Cornwallis Island *Island* Nunavut, Canada 37 N4
Coro Venezuela 58 H4
Coromandel New Zealand 148 H3
Coromandel Coast *Coast* India 131 L14
Coronel Chile 63 G12
Corpus Christi Texas, USA 33 S4 49 R14
Corrib, Lough *Lake* Republic of Ireland 73 B12
Corrientes Argentina 62 M7
Corsica *Island* France 68 77 S14
Cortland New York, USA 41 K9
Çorum Turkey 119 M5
Corumbá Brazil 61 G13
Corunna *see* A Coruña
Corvallis Oregon, USA 50 G9
Cosenza Italy 87 N15
Costa Rica *Country* Central America 56 D12

Costa Rica 56

■1838 • **a** Spanish • 鬯 Costa Rican colón
• ♦ 76 • ● 76 • ▮18 • ☞ 95.1 • ⇱ 85
• ✚ 1111 • ☻ No • 🏠 50 • ⅱ 2883

Côte d'Azur *Physical region* France 77 Q14
Cotonou Benin 107 M13
Cotopaxi *Volcano* Ecuador, 55
Cottbus Germany 80 M10

Council Bluffs Iowa, USA 47 P10
Courantyne River *River* Guyana/Suriname 58 N7
Courland Lagoon *Lagoon* Lithuania/Russian Federation 94 F9
Coventry England, United Kingdom 73 J14
Covilhã Portugal 74 G8
Coyolapan *Historic site* Mexico 24 E10
Cozumel, Isla *Island* Mexico 53 T11
Cracow *see* Kraków
Craiova Romania 90 J9
Crater Lake National Park *National park* USA 22 C11
Crawley England, United Kingdom 73 K16
Cree Lake *Lake* Saskatchewan, Canada 37 M12
Cremona Italy 86 E7
Cres *Island* Croatia 88 G4
Crescent City California, USA 51 F11
Crete *Island* Mediterranean Sea 68 93 L15
Crete, Sea of *Sea* Greece 93 L15
Crimea *Peninsula* Ukraine 68 98 J9
Crna Reka *River* FYR Macedonia 89 O12
Croatia *Country* SE Europe 88 I3

Croatia 88-89

■1991 • **a** Croatian • 鬯 Kuna • ♦ 80 •
● 73 • ▮15 • ☞ 97.7 • ⇱ 195 • ✚ 500
• ☻ No • 🏠 64 • ⅱ

Croker Island *Island* Northern Territory, Australia 146 J4
Crooked Creek *Battle site* USA 29 N4
Crooked Island *Island* Bahamas 57 M5
Crotone Italy 87 O15
Crown Point USA 27 R2
Crozet Basin *Undersea feature* 115 G13
Crozet Islands *Island group* French Southern and Antarctic Territories 64 I5 115 F14
Cruzeiro do Sul Brazil 60 A9
Cuahuacan *Historic site* Mexico 24 C8
Cuango *River* Angola/Congo (Zaire) 112 H3
Cuanza *River* Angola 112 G4
Cuauhtocho *Historic site* Mexico 24 E9
Cuba *Island* Cuba, 55
Cuba *Country* West Indies 56 I5

Cuba 56-57

■1902 • **a** Spanish • 鬯 Cuban peso • ♦
101 • ● 76 • ▮16 • ☞ 95.9 • ⇱ 16 •
✚ 278 • ☻ Yes • 🏠 76 • ⅱ 2833

Cubango *River* Southern Africa 112 H7
Cúcuta Colombia 58 F5
Cuenca Ecuador 58 C9
Cueno Italy 86 B8
Cuernavaca Mexico 53 N12
Cuiabá Brazil 61 G11
Cuito Cuanavale Angola 112 I7
Cuitzeo, Lago de *Lake* Mexico 53 M11
Culiacán Mexico 52 J4
Cumaná Venezuela 58 J4
Cumberland Plateau *Plateau* USA 43 M5
Cumberland Sound *Inlet* Nunavut, Canada 37 R6
Cunene *River* Angola/Namibia 112 G8
Cunnamulla Queensland, Australia 147 N10
Curaçao *Island* Netherlands Antilles 57 O14
Curicó Chile 63 G11
Curitiba Brazil 61 J15
Cusco Peru 59 F14
Cuttack India 131 N9
Cuxhaven Germany 80 G7
Cyclades (Gr. Kyklades) *Island group* Greece 93 M11
Cyprus *Country* SW Asia 119 L12

Cyprus 119

■1960 • **a** Greek and Turkish • 鬯 Cyprus
pound (Turkish lira in TRNC) • ♦ 84 • ● 78
• ▮15 • ☞ 95.9 • ⇱ 334 • ✚ 433 • ☻
No • 🏠 54 • ⅱ 3779

Cyprus *Island* SW Asia 68
Cyrenaica *Region* Libya 103 Q7
Cyrene Libya 103 R6
Czech Republic *Country* C Europe 84 G9

Czech Republic 84-85

■1993 • **a** Czech • 鬯 Czech koruna • ♦
131 • ● 74 • ▮15 • ☞ 99 • ⇱ 344 •
✚ 345 • ☻ No • 🏠 65 • ⅱ 3156

Częstochowa Poland 85 L8

D

Đa Lat Vietnam 139 O14
Da Nang Vietnam 139 O11
Da Qaidam China 132 J9
Dade's Battle *Battle site* USA 29 R6
Dadu He *River* China 134 I9
Dagupan Philippines 141 L3
Dahlak Archipelago *Island group* Eritrea 105 K12
Dahuk Iraq 123 K2
Dakar Senegal 106 F8
Dalaman Turkey 118 J7
Dali China 134 H13
Dalian China 135 O7
Dallas Texas, USA 30 E13 33 I15 49 R10
Dalmatia *Region* Croatia 88 H6
Daloa Ivory Coast 106 J12
Daman India 130 I9
Damar, Pulau *Island* Indonesia 141 O14
Damascus (var. Damashq) Syria 121 N7
Damashq *see* Damascus

■ Date of independence • **a** Language (official or most commonly spoken) • 鬯 Currency • ♦ Population density per square kilometre • ● Average life expectancy • ▮ School-leaving age • ☞ Literacy •
⇱ Number of cars per 1,000 people • ✚ Number of people per doctor • ☻ Death penalty • 🏠 Percentage of urban-based population • ⅱ Average number of calories consumed daily per person

155

Dampier – Erie, Lake

Dampier Western Australia, Australia 146 F8
Danbury Connecticut, USA 41 M11
Danmark Havn Greenland 65 P13
Danube (Ger. Donau, Hung. Duna, Rom. Dun˘area) *River* Europe 68 81 K14 83 Q5 85 L14 89 L4 90 I10
Danube-Black Sea Canal *Canal* Romania 91 O9
Danube Delta *Delta* Romania 91 P7
Danville Illinois, USA 45 L12
Danville Virginia, USA 43 Q5
Danzig, Gulf of (var. Gulf of Gda´nsk) *Gulf* Poland/Russian Federation 85 L1
Dapaong Togo 107 M10
Dar es Salaam Tanzania 111 Q9 114 D9
Dar'a Syria 121 N9
Darhan Mongolia 133 M4
Darien, Gulf of *Gulf* Colombia/Panama 55 56 I15 58 D5
Darling River *River* New South Wales, Australia 143 147 M12
Darmstadt Germany 81 F13
Darnah Libya 103 R6
Darnley, Cape *Cape* Antarctica 64 G8
Dartmoor *Moorland* England, United Kingdom 73 G17
Daru Papua New Guinea 147 M3
Darwin Northern Territory, Australia 146 J5
Dashkhovuz Turkmenistan 124 I5
Dasht-e Gowd-e-Zereh *Desert region* Afghanistan 124 J16
Dasht-e Lut *Desert* Iran 68 117 123 P7
Datong China 135 L6
Daugavpils Latvia 95 K7
Davangere India 130 J12
Davao Philippines 141 N7
Davenport Iowa, USA 47 S9
David Panama 56 F15
Davis Dam *Dam* USA 48 H7
Davis Mountains *Mountain range* Texas, USA 49 M12
Davis Sea *Sea* Antarctica 64 H9
Davis Strait *Strait* Atlantic Ocean 19 K11 22 G7 32 L8 34 37 R5 65 M13 66 F7
Dawson Yukon Territory, Canada 36 I8
Dawson Creek British Columbia, Canada 37 K12
Daxue Shan *Mountain range* China, 129
Dayr az Zawr Syria 121 R4
Dayton Ohio, USA 45 O12
Daytona Beach Florida, USA 43 O11
De Aar South Africa 113 K14
De Kalb Illinois, USA 45 K10
Dead Sea *Salt lake* Israel/Jordan 117 121 M10
Death Valley *Valley* California, USA 19 F16 34
Death Valley National Park *National park* California, USA 22 C12
Debre Birhan Ethiopia 105 J15
Debre Mark'os Ethiopia 105 J14
Debrecen Hungary 85 N13
Decatur Illinois, USA 45 K12
Deccan *Plateau* India 117 129 130 J11
Dee *River* Scotland, United Kingdom 72 I8
Dehra Dun India 131 K4
Del Rio Texas, USA 49 O13
Delaware *State* USA 21 P5 23 R11 29 Q15 30 G12 41 K16
Delaware River *River* Delaware/Pennsylvania/New Jersey/New York, USA 23 Q6 41 K12
Delémont Switzerland 82 E9
Delft Netherlands 79 G11
Delfzijl Netherlands 78 N6
Delhi India 131 K5
Delhi China 133 K9
Delicias Mexico 53 K5
Delphi Greece 92 I8
Demchok *Disputed region* China/India 130 L3 132 F11
Demerara Plain *Undersea feature* Atlantic Ocean 55
Demirkopru Baraji *Dam* Turkey 118 H7
Democratic Republic of Congo (Zaire) *Country* Dem. Rep. Congo (Zaire) 109 K13
Den Helder Netherlands 78 H7
Denali *see* McKinley, Mount
Denali National Park *National park* Alaska, USA 22 C8
Denizli Turkey 118 H8
Denmark *Country* N Europe 70 H13

Denmark 70-71

950 • Danish • Danish krone • 125 • 76 • 16 • 99 • 331 • 345 • No • 85 • 3664

Denmark Strait *Strait* Atlantic Ocean 34 65 O15 66 I7
Denpasar Indonesia 140 J15
D'Entrecasteaux Islands *Island group* Papua New Guinea 147 P3
Denver Colorado, USA 20 D11 23 O6 28 D10 29 N4 30 D12 33 H14 49 M4
Dera Ghazi Khan Pakistan 130 I4
Dera Ismail Khan Pakistan 130 I3
Derby England, United Kingdom 73 J14
Derg, Lough *Lake* Republic of Ireland 73 C13
Derry *see* Londonderry
Des Moines Iowa, USA 28 E10 29 P3 33 J14 47 Q9
Des Moines River *River* USA 47 Q9
Dese Ethiopia 105 J14
Deseado, Río *River* Argentina 63 J16
Desierto Central de Baja California National Park *National park* Mexico 22 C13
Desna *River* Russian Federation/Ukraine 98 J3
Dessau Germany 80 K10
Detroit Michigan, USA 26 D11 30 F11 33 L13 45 O9
Deva Romania 90 I6
Deventer Netherlands 78 L10
Devollit, Lumi i *River* Albania 89 M12
Devon Island *Island* Nunavut, Canada 34 37 N5 65 N11
Dezful Iran 123 M6
Dezhneva, Mys *Headland* Russian Federation 127 R1
Dhahran Saudi Arabia 123 M9
Dhaka Bangladesh 131 P8
Dhamar Yemen 122 I16
Dhanbad India 131 N7
Dharwad India 130 J11
Dhule India 130 J9
Diamantina River *River* Queensland/South Australia, Australia 147 M9
Dickinson North Dakota, USA 47 L5
Didyma *Archaeological site* Turkey 118 G9
Diego Garcia *Island* British Indian Ocean Territory 114 H9
Diekirch Luxembourg 79 L18
Dieppe France 77 K3
Diffa Niger 107 Q9
Digne France 77 P12
Digul, Sungai *River* Indonesia 141 T14
Dijon France 77 N7
Dikson Russian Federation 65 T11
Dili East Timor 141 N15
Dillon Montana, USA 46 H7
Dilolo Dem. Rep. Congo (Zaire) 109 L17
Dimbokro Ivory Coast 107 K13
Dinant Belgium 79 I17
Dinaric Alps *Mountain range* Bosnia and Herzegovina/Croatia 68 88 H5
Dingle Bay *Bay* Republic of Ireland 73 A14
Diourbel Senegal 106 F8
Dipkarpaz Cyprus 119 L11
Dipolog Philippines 141 M7
Dire Dawa Ethiopia 105 L15
Dirk Hartog Island *Island* Western Australia, Australia 146 E10
Disappointment, Lake *Salt lake* Western Australia, Australia 146 H9
Disney World *Theme park* Florida, USA 43 N12
Dispur India 131 P6
Divriği Turkey 119 O7
Diyarbakır Turkey 119 Q8
Djado, Plateau du *Mountain range* Niger 107 Q5
Djakarta *see* Jakarta
Djakovo Croatia 89 K4
Djambala Congo 109 H13
Djerba *Island* Tunisia 103 N5
Djibouti Djibouti 105 L14 114 E7
Djibouti *Country* E Africa 105 K14

Djibouti 105

1977 • Arabic and French • Djibouti franc • 27 • 50 • 12 • 48.6 • 11 • 5000 • No • 83 • 2338

Dnieper *River* Belorussia/Russian Federation/Ukraine 68 95 N15 96 E10 98 I5
Dniester *River* Moldava/Ukraine 68 98 F5
Dnipropetrovs'k Ukraine 99 K6
Dobele Latvia 94 H6
Doboj Bosnia and Herzegovina 89 K5
Dobrich Bulgaria 91 O11
Doctor Pedro P. Peña Paraguay 62 K5
Dodecanese *Island group* Greece 93 O11
Dodge City Kansas, USA 28 D11 47 N13
Dodoma Tanzania 111 O9
Dogo *Island* Japan 137 E11
Doha Qatar 123 M10
Dolisie Congo 109 G14
Dolomites *Mountain range* Italy 86 G6
Dolores Argentina 63 N11
Dominica *Country* West Indies 57 T12

Dominica 57

1978 • English • Eastern Caribbean dollar • 99 • 74 • 15 • 94 • 2174 • Yes • 69 • 2778

Dominican Republic *Country* West Indies 57 N8

Dominican Republic 57

1865 • Spanish • Dominican Republic peso • 174 • 71 • 14 • 82.6 • 28 • 909 • No • 65 • 2286

Don *River* Russian Federation 68 96 F13
Donau *see* Danube
Donawitz Austria 83 Q7
Donbass *Industrial region* Russian Federation/Ukraine 99 L6
Dondra Head *Headland* Sri Lanka 114 I7
Donegal Bay *Bay* Republic of Ireland 73 C11
Donets *River* Russian Federation/Ukraine 99 L5
Donets'k Ukraine 99 M7
Đông Hoi Vietnam 138 N10
Dongchuan China 134 I12
Dongguan China 135 M14
Dongsheng China 133 N8
Dongting Hu *Lake* China 135 L11
Dønna *Island* Norway 71 K5
Donner Pass *Pass* Nevada, USA 28 B10
Donostia-San Sebastián Spain 75 M3
Dordogne *River* France 76 J12
Dordrecht Netherlands 79 H11
Dornbirn Austria 82 I8
Dortmund Germany 80 E10
Dortmund-Ems-Canal *Canal* Germany 80 E9
Dosso Niger 107 N9
Dothan Alabama, USA 43 L9
Douala Cameroon 109 E11
Doubs *River* France/Switzerland 77 N8
Douglas Isle of Man 73 G12
Douglas Arizona, USA 48 J11
Douro *River* WA, Portugal/Spain 68 74 H7
Dove Creek *Battle site* 29 O6
Dover England, United Kingdom 73 M16
Dover New Hampshire, USA 41 O8
Dover Delaware, USA 28 I10 33 M14 41 K15
Dover, Strait of *Strait* France/United Kingdom 73 M17 77 K1
Dozen *Island* Japan 137 E11
Drachten Netherlands 78 L7
Drake Passage *Passage* Atlantic Ocean/Pacific Ocean 55 65 A6
Drakensberg *Mountain range* Lesotho/South Africa 101 113 K15
Drama Greece 93 L2
Drammen Norway 70 I11
Drau (Eng. Drave) *River* SE Europe *see also* Drava 83 Q9
Drava (Eng. Drave) *River* SE Europe 83 R9 89 K3 *see also* Drau
Drave *see* Drau and Drava
Drawa *River* Poland 84 I4
Dresden Germany 81 M11
Drin, Gulf of *Gulf* Albania 89 L11
Drina *River* Bosnia and Herzegovina/Yugoslavia, 68
Drinit, Lumi i *River* Albania 89 M10
Drobeta-Turnu Severin Romania 90 H8
Dronning Maud Land *Antarctica region* Dronning Maud Land 64 E6
Drumheller Alberta, Canada 37 L14
Drummondville Quebec, Canada 39 N13
Druskininkai Lithuania 94 H11
Dubai United Arab Emirates 123 O11
Dubăsari Moldova 98 H7
Dubawnt Lake *Lake* Nunavut, Canada 37 M9
Dubbo New South Wales, Australia 147 O12
Dublin Republic of Ireland 73 E13
Dubrovnik Croatia 89 K9
Dubuque Iowa, USA 47 R8
Duero *River* WA, Portugal/Spain 75 K6
Dugi Otok *Island* Croatia 88 G6
Duisburg Germany 80 D10
Dukhan Qatar 123 M10
Duluth Minnesota, USA 44 I4
Dumaguete Philippines 141 M6
Dumfries Scotland, United Kingdom 73 H11
Dumont d'Urville *French research station* Antarctica 64 F12
Dún Laoghaire Republic of Ireland 73 E13
Duna *see* Danube
Dunărea *see* Danube
Dundalk Republic of Ireland 73 E12
Dundee Scotland, United Kingdom 72 I9
Dunedin New Zealand 148 E12
Dungun Malaysia 139 K18
Dunkerque *see* Dunkirk
Dunkirk *see* Dunkerque77 L1
Dunkirk New York, USA 40 H10
Durance *River* France 77 P13
Durango Mexico 53 K8
Durango Colorado, USA 49 L6
Durazno Uruguay 62 N9
Durban South Africa 113 M14 115 C12
Durham North Carolina, USA 43 Q5
Durrës Albania 89 L11
Dushanbe Tajikistan 125 N8
Düsseldorf Germany 81 D11
Dutch Harbor Alaska, USA 36 C8
Dutch New Guinea *see* Irian Jaya
Dutch West Indies *see* Netherlands Antilles
Dzhalal-Abad Kyrgyzstan 125 P6
Dzhugdzhur, Khrebet *Mountain range* Russian Federation 127 P9
Dzibilchaltun *Historic site* Mexico 24 H8
Dzungaria *Physical region* China, 117

E

Eagle Lake *Lake* California, USA 51 I12
Eagle Lake *Lake* Maine, USA 41 P3
Eagle Mountain Lake *Reservoir* Texas, USA 49 Q10
Eagle Pass Texas, USA 49 P14
East Anglia *Physical region* England, United Kingdom 73 L14
East China Sea *Sea* Pacific Ocean 129 135 O12 137 A19 144 F5
East Frisian Islands *Island group* Germany 80 E7
East Indies *Island group* SE Asia 129 143
East Liverpool Ohio, USA 45 Q11
East London South Africa 113 L15
East Mariana Basin *Undersea feature* Pacific Ocean 143
East Pacific Rise *Undersea feature* Pacific Ocean 55 145 N10
East Saint Louis Illinois, USA 44 J14
East Siberian Sea *Sea* Arctic Ocean 65 R6 117 127 O3 129
East Timor *Disputed region* SE Asia 141 O15
Easter Island *Island* Chile 145 N11
Eastern Euphrates *see* Murat Nehri
Eastern Ghats *Mountain range* India 131 K12
Eastern Sierra Madre *see* Madre Oriental, Sierra
Eastmain *River* Quebec, Canada 39 M9
Eastmain Québec, Canada 26 E8
Eastport Maine, USA 41 R6
Eau Claire Wisconsin, USA 44 I7
Ebolowa Cameroon 109 F11
Ebro *River* Spain 68 75 M5
Ecuador *Country* W South America 58 D9

Ecuador 58

1830 • Spanish • Sucre • 45 • 70 • 15 • 90.7 • 40 • 667 • No • 58 • 2583

Ed Damazin Sudan 105 H14
Ed Damer Sudan 105 H11
Ed Dueim Sudan 105 G13
Ede Netherlands 79 K11
Edea Cameroon 109 F11
Eder *River* Germany 81 G11
Edessa Greece 92 I3
Edinburgh Scotland, United Kingdom 72 I10
Edirne (Eng. Adrianople) Turkey 118 G4
Edmonds Washington, USA 50 H6
Edmonton Alberta, Canada 30 D12 33 G11 37 L13
Edward, Lake *Lake* Congo (Zaire)/Uganda 109 O12 111 L5
Edwards Air Base *Military base* California, USA 51 L18
Edwards Plateau *Plain* Texas, USA 49 O12
Edzna *Historic site* Mexico 24 G9
Eforie-Nord Romania 91 P9
Egadi *Island group* Italy 87 H17
Eğridir Gölü *Lake* Turkey 118 J8
Egypt *Country* NE Africa 104 D7

Egypt 104

1936 • Arabic • Egyptian pound • 68 • 66 • 14 • 52.7 • 23 • 556 • Yes • 45 • 33

Eiger *Mountain* Switzerland 82 F11
Eigg *Island* Scotland, United Kingdom 72 F8
Eilat *see* Elat
Eindhoven Netherlands 79 J13
Eisenstadt Austria 83 S5
Eismitte Tunu, Greenland 20 F6
Eivissa *see* Ibiza
El Calafate Argentina 63 I18
El Faiyum Egypt 104 F7
El Fasher Sudan 105 C13
El Giza (Eng. Gîza) Egypt 104 F7
El Manşûra Egypt 105 F6
El Minya Egypt 104 F7
El Obeid Sudan 105 F13
El Oued Algeria 103 M6
El Paso Texas, USA 49 L11
El Paso Texas, USA 28 Q12 33 H15
El Salvador *Country* Central America 56 B9

El Salvador 56

1841 • Spanish • Salvadorean colón • 299 • 69 • 14 • 77 • 30 • 1429 • No • 45 • 2663

El'brus *Mountain* Russian Federation 68
Elat (var. Eilat) Israel 121 L14
Elâzığ Turkey 119 P7
Elba *Island* Italy 86 F10
Elbasan Albania 89 M12
Elbe *River* Czech Republic/Germany 68 80 I8 84 H8
Elbert, Mount *Mountain* Colorado, USA 19 H16 34
Elbląg Poland 85 L2
Elburz Mountains *Mountain range* Iran 123 M3
Elche (Sp. Elx) Spain 75 N11
Eldoret Kenya 111 O4
Elemi Triangle *Disputed region* Kenya/Sudan 105 H16 111 O1
Elephant Butte Reservoir *Reservoir* New Mexico, USA 49 L9
Elephant Island *Island* Antarctica 64 B6
Eleuthera Island *Island* Bahamas 57 L2
Elgin Scotland, United Kingdom 72 I7
Elista Russian Federation 96 F15 126 D9
Elk Poland 85 N3
Elko Nevada, USA 48 H2
Ellensburg Washington, USA 50 J7
Ellesmere Island *Island* Nunavut, Canada 32 J6 34 37 N1 65 O11
Ellsworth Land *Physical region* Antarctica 64 C9
Elmira New York, USA 40 J10
Eltz *Castle* Germay 81 E12
Elwell, Lake *Reservoir* Montana, USA 46 H4
Elx *see* Elche
Ely Nevada, USA 48 H4
Elyria Ohio, USA 45 P10
Emba *River* Kazakhstan 126 E10
Emden Germany 80 E7
Emerson Barrage *Dam* Pakistan 130 I3
Emi Koussi *Mountain* Chad, 101
Emmen Netherlands 78 N8
Emporia Kansas, USA 47 P12
Empty Quarter *see* Ar Rub 'al Khali
Ems *River* Germany 80 E8
Emuckfaw *Battle site* USA 29 Q5
En Nahud Sudan 105 E13
Encarnación Paraguay 62 O7
Endeh Indonesia 141 M15
Enderby Land *Physical region* Antarctica 64 F7
Enewetak Atoll *Atoll* Marshall Islands 144 H7
Enggano, Pulau *Island* Indonesia 140 E14
England *National region* United Kingdom 73 J15
English Channel (var. The Channel) *Channel* France/United Kingdom 68 73 I17 76 H3
Enguri *River* Georgia 99 O12
Enid Oklahoma, USA 47 O14
Enna Italy 87 K18
Enns *River* Austria 83 O7
Enotachopco Creek *Battle site* USA 29 R5
Enriquillo, Lago *Lake* Dominican Republic 57 N8
Enschede Netherlands 78 N10
Entebbe Uganda 111 M4
Enugu Nigeria 107 O13
Ephesus *Archaeological site* Turkey 118 G8
Epidaurus Greece 92 J10
Épinal France 77 P6
Equator *Line of latitude* 55 143
Equatorial Guinea *Country* C Africa 109 D11

Equatorial Guinea 109

1968 • Spanish • Franc de la Coopération financière en Afrique central • 16 • 50 • 11 • 79.9 • 2 • 4762 • Yes • 44 •

Er Roseires Dam *Dam* Sudan 105 H14
Er-Rachidia Morocco 102 I6
Erdenet Mongolia 133 L4
Ereğli Turkey 119 L9
Erenhot China 133 O6
Erfurt Germany 81 I11
Erg Chech *Desert Region* Mali 107 K4
Erguig, Bahr *River* Chad 108 H8
Ergun He *see* Argun
Erie Pennsylvania, USA 40 G10
Erie Canal *Canal* New York, USA 40 I8
Erie, Lake *Lake* New York/Ohio/Ontario/Pennsylvania, Canada/USA 19 K16 22 F11 23 R11 28 H9 29 R3 34 38 J15 45 P10

Eritrea *Country* E Africa 105 I12

Eritrea 105

⚑ 1993 • a Tigrinya • 🪙 Nakfa • 🧍 31 • ♥ 51 • 🎓 13 • 📖 25 • 🚗 2 • ✚ 5000 • ☠ Yes • ⌂ 17 • 🍴 1610

Erlangen Germany 81 I13
Ermoupoli Greece 93 M11
Ernakulam India 130 J14
Erzincan Turkey 119 P6
Erzurum Turkey 119 Q6
Esbjerg Denmark 66 L7 70 H15
Escanaba Michigan, USA 45 L5
Esch-sur-Alzette Luxembourg 79 L19
Escuintla Guatemala 56 A8
Eskisehir Turkey 118 G7
Esla, Embalse de *Reservoir* Spain 74 I6
Esmeraldas Ecuador 58 C8
Esperance Western Australia, Australia 146 H13
Espinho Portugal 74 F7
Espíritu Santo, Isla del *Island* Mexico 52 H7
Esquel Argentina 63 H15
Essaouira Morocco 102 H6
Essen Germany 80 D10
Essequibo River *River* Guyana 58 M6
Estelí Nicaragua 56 D10
Estevan Saskatchewan, Canada 37 N15
Estonia *Country* NE Europe 94 I3

Estonia 94-99

⚑ 1991 • a Estonian • 🪙 Kroon • 🧍 31 • ♥ 69 • 🎓 16 • 📖 99 • 🚗 293 • ✚ 323 • ☠ No • ⌂ 73 •

Ethiopia *Country* E Africa 105 I15

Ethiopia 105

⚑ 1896 • a Amharic • 🪙 Ethiopian birr • 🧍 67 • ♥ 42 • 🎓 13 • 📖 35.4 • 🚗 1 • ✚ 25000 • ☠ Yes • ⌂ 13 • 🍴 1610

Ethiopian Highlands *Plateau* Ethiopia 101 105 J14
Etna, Mount *Volcano* Italy, 68
Etosha *National Park* Namibia 112 G9
Etosha Pan *Salt lake* Namibia 113 H9
Etowah *Battle site* USA 29 Q5
Euboea (Gr. Evvoia) *Island* Greece 93 K7
Eugene Oregon, USA 33 E13 50 G9
Eupen Belgium 79 L15
Euphrates *River* SW Asia 68 114 D4 117 119 P8 121 R4 123 K5 129
Eurasian Plate *Tectonic plate* 34 68 101 117 129 143
Eureka California, USA 51 F12
Europe *Continent* 68-69
Europoort Netherlands 79 G11
Evanston Illinois, USA 45 L10
Evansville Indiana, USA 45 L15
Everard, Lake *Salt lake* South Australia, Australia 147 K12
Everest, Mount *Mountain* China/Nepal 129 131 O5 132 H13
Everett Washington, USA 50 H6
Everglades National Park *National park* Florida, USA 22 G14
Everglades, The *Wetland* Florida, USA 34 43 N14
Évora Portugal 74 G11
Évreux France 77 K5
Evvoia *see* Euboea
Exeter England, United Kingdom 73 G17
Exmoor *Moorland* England, United Kingdom 73 G16
Exmouth Plateau *Undersea feature* Pacific Ocean 143
Eyasi, Lake *Lake* Tanzania 111 O7
Eyre, Lake *Salt lake* South Australia, Australia 143 147 K11

F

Fada-Ngourma Burkina 107 M10
Faeroe Islands *Dependent territory* Atlantic Ocean 66 I7
Faeroe Islands *Island group* Atlantic Ocean 68
Faguibine, Lac *Lake* Mali 107 K8
Fairbanks Alaska, USA 20 C7 30 B7 36 H7
Fairmont Minnesota, USA 44 G8
Faisalabad Pakistan 130 J3
Falkland Escarpment *Undersea feature* Atlantic Ocean 55
Falkland Islands *Dependent territory* Atlantic Ocean 67 F15
Falkland Islands *Island group* Atlantic Ocean 55
Fall River Massachusetts, USA 41 O11
Fallen Timbers *Battle site* USA 29 Q3
Falmouth England, United Kingdom 73 F17
Falun Sweden 71 L11
Famagusta Cyprus 119 L12
Faraday *UK research station* Antarctica 64 B7
Faradje Dem. Rep. Congo (Zaire) 109 O11
Farafangana Madagascar 115 E11
Farghona Uzbekistan 125 O7
Fargo North Dakota, USA 47 O5
Faribault Minnesota, USA 44 H7
Farmington New Mexico, USA 49 K6
Faro Portugal 74 G13
Fårö Sweden 71 M13
Faro Yukon Territory, Canada 36 I9
Faya Chad 108 J5
Fayetteville Arkansas, USA 42 H3
Fayetteville North Carolina, USA 43 Q6
Fdérik Mauritania 106 H4
Fehmarn *Island* Germany 80 J6
Feira de Santana Brazil 61 M11
Felbertauern Tunnel *Tunnel* Austria 83 M8
Feldkirch Austria 82 I9
Felixstowe England, United Kingdom 73 M15
Femunden, Lake *Lake* Norway 70 J9
Fens, The *Wetland* England, United Kingdom 73 K14
Feodosiya Ukraine 99 K10
Fergus Falls Minnesota, USA 44 F5
Fernando de Noronha *Island* Brazil 67 H12
Ferrara Italy 86 G8
Ferrol Spain 74 G3
Fethiye Turkey 118 H10
Fetterman's Defeat *Battle site* USA 29 N2
Feuilles, Rivière aux *River* Quebec, Canada 39 L5
Fez Morocco 102 I5
Fezzan *Region* Libya 103 Q9
Fianarantsoa Madagascar 115 E11
Fier Albania 89 N13
Figueira da Foz Portugal 74 F8
Figuig Morocco 102 J6
Fiji *Country* Pacific Ocean 144 J10

Fiji 144

⚑ 1970 • a English • 🪙 Fiji dollar • 🧍 44 • ♥ 73 • 🎓 15 • 📖 91.8 • 🚗 59 • ✚ 1784 • ☠ No • ⌂ 41 • 🍴 3089

Fiji *Island group* Pacific Ocean 143
Fiji Plate *Tectonic plate* 143
Filadelfia Paraguay 62 L4
Filchner Ice Shelf *Ice shelf* Antarctica 64 D8
Filicudi *Island* Italy 87 K16
Fimbul Ice Shelf *Ice shelf* Antarctica 64 E6
Findlay Ohio, USA 45 O11
Finger Lakes *Lakes* New York, USA 40 J9
Finland *Country* NE Europe 71 O9

Finland 71

⚑ 1917 • a Finnish and Swedish • 🪙 Markka • 🧍 17 • ♥ 77 • 🎓 16 • 📖 99 • 🚗 379 • ✚ 370 • ☠ No • ⌂ 63 • 🍴 3018

Finland, Gulf of *Gulf* Baltic Sea 68 71 O12 96 E7
Firenze *see* Florence
Fishguard Wales, United Kingdom 73 F15
Fitzroy River *River* Western Australia, Australia 146 H7
Flagstaff Arizona, USA 48 I7
Flaming Gorge Dam *Dam* USA 49 K3
Flaming Gorge Reservoir *Reservoir* Utah/Wyoming, USA 46 I10
Flathead Lake *Lake* Montana, USA 46 G4
Flevoland *Province* Netherlands 78 J9
Flin Flon Manitoba, Canada 37 N13
Flinders *River* Queensland, Australia, 143
Flinders Island *Island* Tasmania, Australia 147 N15
Flinders Ranges *Mountain range* South Australia, Australia 143 147 L12
Flint Michigan, USA 45 O8
Florence South Carolina, USA 43 P7
Florence (It. Firenze) Italy 86 G9
Florence Alabama, USA 43 K5
Florencia Colombia 58 E8
Flores Guatemala 56 B6
Flores *Island* Indonesia 141 L15 143
Flores Sea *Sea* Indonesia 129 141 K15
Florianópolis Brazil 61 J15
Florida Uruguay 62 O10
Florida *State* USA 21 P7 23 R13 29 P16 30 F13 33 M16 43 N11
Florida Keys *Island group* Florida, USA 43 N16
Florida, Straits of *Strait* Atlantic Ocean 43 O15
Florina Greece 92 H3
Fly *River* Indonesia/Papua New Guinea 147 M3
Foča Bosnia and Herzegovina 89 L7
Focşani Romania 91 N6
Foggia Italy 87 M12
Föhr *Island* Germany 80 F5
Foix France 77 L15
Fond du Lac Wisconsin, USA 45 K8
Fongafale Tuvalu 144 J9
Forlì Italy 86 H8
Formentera *Island* Spain 75 P11
Formosa Argentina 62 M6
Formosa *see* Taiwan
Fort Albany Ontario, Canada 26 D8
Fort Bliss Military Reservation *Military base* New Mexico, USA 49 L10
Fort Chambly Canada 27 R2
Fort Churchill Canada 26 C7
Fort Collins Colorado, USA 49 M3
Fort Dearborn *Battle site* USA 29 Q3
Fort-de-France Martinique 57 T13
Fort Detroit USA 27 Q3
Fort Dodge Iowa, USA 47 Q9
Fort Douelson *Battle site* Kentucky, USA 27 M12
Fort Fisher *Fort* North Carolina, USA 27 N12
Fort Hatteras *Fort* USA 27 P12
Fort Henry USA 27 Q4
Fort Henry *Battle site* Missouri, USA 27 L12
Fort Jackson *Fort* USA 27 L15
Fort St.John British Columbia, Canada 20 C8 37 K12
Fort St John's USA 27 R2
Fort Kaministikwia Canada 26 C9
Fort Kearney *Battle site* USA 29 O3
Fort Lauderdale Florida, USA 43 O14
Fort Macon *Fort* North Carolina, USA 27 O12
Fort Malden USA 27 Q4
Fort McMurray Alberta, Canada 37 L12
Fort McPherson Northwest Territories, Canada 36 J7
Fort Mellon *Battle site* USA 29 S6
Fort Minas *Battle site* USA 29 Q6
Fort Monroe *Fort* USA 27 O11
Fort Myers Florida, USA 43 N14
Fort Nelson British Columbia, Canada 36 J11
Fort Niagara USA 27 R3
Fort Ninety Six South Carolina, USA 27 Q6
Fort Orange USA 26 E10
Fort Oswego USA 27 R3
Fort Peck Lake *Reservoir* Montana, USA 46 J5
Fort Pickens *Fort* Alabama, USA 27 M14
Fort Pitt USA 27 Q4
Fort Portal Uganda 111 L4
Fort Pulaski *Fort* USA 27 O13
Fort Resolution Northwest Territories, Canada 37 L10
Fort Sedgwick *Battle site* USA 29 N3
Fort-Shevchenko Kazakhstan 127 D10
Fort Simpson Northwest Territories, Canada 37 K10
Fort Smith Northwest Territories, Canada 37 L11
Fort Smith Arkansas, USA 42 H3
Fort St. Philip *Fort* USA 27 M15
Fort Stanwix USA 27 R3
Fort Sumter *Fort* USA 27 O13
Fort Vermilion Alberta, Canada 20 D8 37 L11
Fort Wayne Indiana, USA 45 N11
Fort William Scotland, United Kingdom 72 G8
Fort Worth Texas, USA 28 E12 49 Q10
Fortaleza Brazil 60 N8 67 H12
Forth *River* Scotland, United Kingdom 72 H9
Forth, Firth of *Estuary* Scotland, United Kingdom 72 I9
Foveaux Strait *Strait* New Zealand 148 C13
Fowltown *Battle site* USA 29 R5
Foxe Basin *Sea* Nunavut, Canada 19 J12 32 K9 37 P7
Foyle, Lough *Inlet* Northern Ireland, Ireland/United Kingdom 72 E10
France *Country* W Europe 76-77

France 62-63

⚑ 486 • a French • 🪙 French franc • 🧍 107 • ♥ 78 • 🎓 16 • 📖 99 • 🚗 442 • ✚ 357 • ☠ No • ⌂ 73 • 🍴 3633

Franceville Gabon 109 G13
Francis Case, Lake *Reservoir* South Dakota, USA 47 N8
Francistown Botswana 113 L10
Frankfort Indiana, USA 45 M12
Frankfort Kentucky, USA 28 G10 33 L14 43 N2
Frankfurt *see* Frankfurt am Main
Frankfurt am Main (var. Frankfurt) Germany 81 F12
Frankfurt an der Oder Germany 80 N9
Fränkische Alb *Mountain range* Germany 81 J14
Franz Josef Land *Island group* Russian Federation 65 R11 68 117 126 J3
Fraser *River* British Columbia, Canada 23 N4 36 J13
Fraserburgh Scotland, United Kingdom 72 J7
Frauenfeld Switzerland 82 H8
Fray Bentos Uruguay 62 N9
Fredericksburg *Battle site* USA 27 O11
Fredericton New Brunswick, Canada 33 N12 39 P12
Frederikshavn Denmark 70 I13
Fredrikstad Norway 70 J12
Freeport Bahamas 56 J1
Freeport Illinois, USA 45 K10
Freeport Texas, USA 49 S13
Freetown Sierra Leone 106 G12
Freiburg im Breisgau Germany 81 E16
Freistadt Austria 83 P4
Fremantle Western Australia, Australia 115 M12 146 F12
French Guiana *Dependent territory* N South America 58 O7
French Polynesia *Dependent territory* Pacific Ocean 145 L9
French Southern and Antarctic Territories *Dependent territory* Indian Ocean 115 G14
Fresno California, USA 51 J16
Fria, Cape *Headland* Namibia 101 112 F9
Fribourg Switzerland 82 E10
Friedrichshafen Germany 81 G16
Frobisher Bay *Inlet* Nunavut, Canada 37 R7
Frobisher Lake *Lake* Saskatchewan, Canada 37 M12
Frome, Lake *Salt lake* South Australia, Australia 147 L12
Frontera Mexico 53 Q12
Frosinone Italy 87 J12
Fuenlabrada Spain 75 K8
Fuerte Olimpo Paraguay 62 M4
Fujairah United Arab Emirates 123 O11
Fuji, Mount *Mountain* Japan 129 137 J11
Fukui Japan 137 H11
Fukuoka Japan 137 C13
Fukushima Japan 136 K5 136 K9
Fulda Germany 81 H12
Fulda *River* Germany 81 H11
Fundy, Bay of *Bay* Canada/USA 39 P13 66 F8
Furnas, Represa de *Reservoir* Brazil 61 K13
Fushun China 135 O5
Fuzhou China 135 N12
Fyn *Island* Denmark 70 I15

G

Gaalkacyo Somalia 105 N16
Gabcíkovo Slovakia 85 K13
Gabès Tunisia 103 N5
Gabon *Country* C Africa 109 E12

Gabon 109

⚑ 1960 • a French • 🪙 Franc de la Coopération financière en Afrique centrale • 🧍 5 • ♥ 52 • 🎓 16 • 📖 66.2 • 🚗 22 • ✚ 2000 • ☠ Yes • ⌂ 51 • 🍴 2500

Gaborone Botswana 113 K11
Gabrovo Bulgaria 91 L12
Gadsden Alabama, USA 43 L6
Gafsa Tunisia 103 N5
Gagnoa Ivory Coast 106 J13
Gagra Georgia 99 N11
Gaine's Battle *Battle site* USA 29 R6
Gairdner, Lake *Salt lake* South Australia, Australia 147 K12
Galapagos Islands *Island group* Ecuador 55 145 O8
Galaţi Romania 91 O7
Galesburg Illinois, USA 44 J11
Galicia *Cultural region* Spain 74 G3
Galilee, Sea of *see* Tiberias, Lake
Galle Sri Lanka 131 K16
Gallego Rise *Undersea feature* Pacific Ocean 55
Gallipoli Italy 87 P14
Gallipoli Turkey 118 G5
Gällivare Sweden 71 N4
Gallup New Mexico, USA 49 K7
Galveston Texas, USA 27 K15 49 S13
Galway Republic of Ireland 73 B12
Gambia *Country* W Africa 106 F9

Gambia 106

⚑ 1965 • a English • 🪙 Dalasi • 🧍 127 • ♥ 47 • 📖 33.1 • 🚗 8 • ✚ 5000 • ☠ Yes • ⌂ 30 • 🍴 2360

Gambier, Îles *Island group* French Polynesia 145 M10
Ganca Azerbaijan 99 R13
Gander Newfoundland, Canada 39 S9
Gandi Reservoir *Reservoir* India 130 J7
Gangdisê Shan *Mountain range* China 132 F12
Ganges *River* Bangladesh/India 114 J5 117 129 131 L5
Ganges, Mouths of the *Delta* Bangladesh/India 117 129
Gangtok India 131 O6
Ganzhou China 135 M13
Gao Mali 107 L8
Gap France 77 P12
Gar China 132 F11
Garda, Lake *Lake* Italy 86 F6
Garden City Kansas, USA 47 M13
Garissa Kenya 111 Q5
Garmisch-Partenkirchen Germany 81 J17
Garonne *River* France 68 76 J12
Garoowe Somalia 105 O15
Garoua Cameroon 108 G9
Garry Lake *Lake* Nunavut, Canada 37 N8
Gary Indiana, USA 45 L10
Gaspé Quebec, Canada 39 P10
Gastonia North Carolina, USA 43 P6
Gates of the Arctic National Park *National park* Alaska, USA 22 C7
Gatineau Quebec, Canada 39 L13
Gävle Sweden 71 L11
Gaya India 131 N7
Gaza Gaza Strip 121 L10
Gaza Strip *Disputed region* SW Asia 121 L10
Gaziantep Turkey 119 O9
Gbanga Liberia 106 I12
Gdańsk Poland 85 L2
Gdańsk, Gulf of *see* Danzig, Gulf of
Gdynia Poland 85 K2
Gedaref Sudan 105 H13
Geelong Victoria, Australia 147 M14
Gejiu China 134 I14
Gelsenkirchen Germany 80 D10
Gemena Dem. Rep. Congo (Zaire) 109 J11
Gemlik Turkey 118 I5
Gemsbok *National Park* Botswana 112 J12
Genale Wenz *River* Ethiopia 105 K16
General Eugenio A.Garay Paraguay 62 K4
General Santos Philippines 141 N8
Genesee River *River* New York/Pennsylvania, USA 40 I10
Geneva (Fr. Genève) Switzerland 82 C12
Geneva New York, USA 40 J9
Geneva, Lake *Lake* France/Switzerland 68 77 P9 82 D12
Genève *see* Geneva
Genk Belgium 79 K14
Genoa (It. Genova) Italy 86 D8
Genoa, Gulf of *Gulf* Mediterranean Sea 86 D8
Genova *see* Genoa
Gent *see* Ghent
Georg von Neumayer *German research station* Antarctica 64 D6
George Town Cayman Islands 56 H6
Georgetown Delaware, USA 41 K16
Georgetown Gambia 106 G9
Georgetown Guyana 58 M6 67 F11
George Town Malaysia 114 L8 139 I17
Georgia *Country* Georgia 99 O12

Georgia 99

⚑ 1991 • a Georgian • 🪙 Lari • 🧍 72 • ♥ 73 • 🎓 14 • 📖 99 • 🚗 79 • ✚ 238 • ☠ No • ⌂ 58 •

Georgia *State* USA 21 O6 23 R13 29 P15 30 F13 33 L15 43 N8
Gera Germany 81 K11
Geraldton Western Australia, Australia 146 E11
Germany *Country* W Europe 80-81

Germany 80-81

⚑ 1871 • a German • 🪙 Deutsche Mark • 🧍 235 • ♥ 77 • 🎓 18 • 📖 99 • 🚗 500 • ✚ 303 • ☠ No • ⌂ 87 • 🍴 3344

Getafe Spain 75 K8
Gettysburg Pennsylvania, USA 40 I14
Gettysburg *Battle site* Maryland, USA 27 O10
Getz Ice Shelf *Ice shelf* Antarctica 64 C10
Ghadaf, Wadi al *Seasonal watercourse* Iraq 122 J5
Ghadamis Libya 103 N7
Ghana *Country* W Africa 107 L12

Ghana 107

⚑ 1957 • a English • 🪙 Cedi • 🧍 86 • ♥ 60 • 🎓 14 • 📖 66.4 • 🚗 5 • ✚ 25000 • ☠ Yes • ⌂ 36 • 🍴 2199

Ghanzi Botswana 112 J10
Ghardaïa Algeria 103 L6
Gharyan Libya 103 O6
Ghat Libya 103 N10
Ghazni Afghanistan 125 N13
Ghent (var. Gent) Belgium 79 F14
Ghulam Muhammad Barrage *Dam* Pakistan 130 H6
Gibraltar *Dependent territory* S Europe 74 I15
Gibraltar Gibraltar 66 K9 74 I15

⚑ Date of independence • a Language (official or most commonly spoken) • 🪙 Currency • 🧍 Population density per square kilometre • ♥ Average life expectancy • 🎓 School-leaving age • 📖 Literacy • 🚗 Number of cars per 1,000 people • ✚ Number of people per doctor • ☠ Death penalty • ⌂ Percentage of urban-based population • 🍴 Average number of calories consumed daily per person

Gibraltar, Strait of – Hitachi

Gibraltar, Strait of *Strait* Atlantic Ocean/Mediterranean Sea 68 74 I15 101 102 I4
Gibson Desert *Desert* Western Australia, Australia 143 146 H9
Giessen Germany 81 F12
Gifu Japan 137 H11
Giganta, Sierra de la *Mountain range* Mexico 52 G6
Gijón Spain 74 I3
Gila River *River* Arizona, USA 49 K10
Gillette Wyoming, USA 47 K8
Giresun Turkey 119 O5
Girne Cyprus 119 L11
Girona Spain 75 Q5
Girre Cyprus 119 L11
Gisborne New Zealand 148 J5
Giurgiu Romania 91 L10
Giza *see* El Gîza
Gjøvik Norway 70 J10
Glacier Bay National Park *National park* Alaska, USA 22 C9
Glacier National Park *National park* Canada/USA 22 D11
Gladstone Queensland, Australia 147 O9
Glåma *River* Norway 70 J9
Glarus Switzerland 82 H10
Glasgow Montana, USA 47 K4
Glasgow Scotland, United Kingdom 72 H10
Glen Canyon Dam *Dam* Arizona, USA 48 J6
Glendale California, USA 51 K18
Glendale Arizona, USA 48 I9
Glendive Montana, USA 47 K5
Glens Falls New York, USA 41 M8
Gliwice Poland 85 L8
Gloucester England, United Kingdom 73 I15
Gloucester Massachusetts, USA 41 O9 66 E8
Gmünd Austria 83 P3
Gmunden Austria 83 O6
Gnjilane Serbia, Yugoslavia 89 O9
Goba Ethiopia 105 K16
Gobabis Namibia 112 I10
Gobi *Desert* China/Mongolia 117 129 133 M7
Godavari *River* India 129 131 L10 131 L10
Godoy Cruz Argentina 62 H10
Goiânia Brazil 61 J12
Golan Heights *Mountain range* Syria 121 M8
Gold Coast *Cultural region* Queensland, Australia 147 P11
Golmud China 132 J10
Goma Dem. Rep. Congo (Zaire) 109 O13
Gómez Palacio Mexico 53 L7
Gonaïves Haiti 57 M7
Gonâve, Île de la *Island* Haiti 57 M8
Gonder Ethiopia 105 I13
Gonghe China 133 L10
Good Hope, Cape of *Cape* South Africa 67 M14 101 112 I16 115 B12
Goondiwindi Queensland, Australia 147 N11
Goose Lake *Lake* California/Oregon, USA 51 I11
Gorakhpur India 131 M6
Gore Ethiopia 105 H15
Goré Chad 108 I9
Göreme Turkey 119 M7
Gorgan Iran 123 O3
Görlitz Germany 81 N11
Gorodets Russian Federation 96 H11
Goroka Papua New Guinea 147 N2
Gorongosa *National Park* Mozambique 113 N8
Gorontalo Indonesia 141 M11
Gorzów Wielkopolski Poland 84 I4
Gosford New South Wales, Australia 147 O13
Gospić Croatia 88 H5
Gosselies Belgium 79 H16
Gostivar FYR Macedonia 89 N11
Gotha Germany 81 I11
Gothenburg Sweden 70 J13
Gotland *Island* Sweden 71 L14
Goto-retto *Island group* Japan 137 A14
Göttingen Germany 81 H10
Gouda Netherlands 79 H11
Gough Island *Island* Tristan da Cunha 67 J15
Gouin, Réservoir *Reservoir* Quebec, Canada 39 L11
Goulburn New South Wales, Australia 147 O13
Govind Ballabh Pant Reservoir *Reservoir* India 131 M7
Gozo *Island* Malta 87 K20
Gračanica Bosnia and Herzegovina 89 K5
Grafton New South Wales, Australia 147 P11
Grahamstown South Africa 113 L15
Grampian Mountains *Mountain range* Scotland, United Kingdom 68 72 H8
Gran Chaco *Lowland plain* C South America 55 62 J7
Granada Spain 75 K13
Granada Nicaragua 56 D11
Grand Bahama Island *Island* Bahamas 57 K1
Grand Banks *Undersea feature* Atlantic Ocean 39 T10, 66 F8
Grand Canal *Canal* China 135 N9
Grand Canyon *Canyon* Arizona, USA 19 F17 24 B13 34 48 H7
Grand Canyon National Park *National park* USA 22 D12
Grand Cayman *Island* Cayman Islands 56 H6
Grand Erg Occidental *Desert* Algeria 103 K7
Grand Erg Oriental *Desert* Algeria/Tunisia 103 L7
Grand Falls New Brunswick, Canada 39 O12
Grand Falls Newfoundland, Canada 39 S9
Grand Forks North Dakota, USA 47 O4
Grand Island Nebraska, USA 47 O10
Grand Junction Colorado, USA 49 K4
Grand Prairie Texas, USA 30 E13
Grand Rapids Michigan, USA 45 M9
Grand Teton Mountains *Mountain range* Wyoming, USA 46 H8
Grand Teton National Park *National park* Wyoming, USA 22 D11
Grande Comore *Island* Comoros 114 E10
Grande de Matagalpa, Río *River* Nicaragua 56 E10
Grande de Santiago, Río *River* Mexico 53 K10
Grande Prairie Alberta, Canada 37 K13
Grande Terre *Island* Guadeloupe 57 T11
Grande, Bahía *Bay* Argentina 63 H17
Grande, Rio *River* Mexico/USA 19 H18 22 E13 23 P13 23 P8 24 D15 53 N6
Grandes, Salinas *Salt lake* Argentina, 55
Grangemouth Scotland, United Kingdom 72 H9
Grants Pass Oregon, USA 51 G11
Grasse France 77 Q13
Grattan's Defeat *Battle site* USA 29 N3
Grave Creek *Battle site* USA 29 K2
Graz Austria 83 R8
Great Abaco *Island* Bahamas 57 K1
Great Artesian Basin *Lowlands* Queensland, Australia, 143
Great Australian Bight *Bight* Indian Ocean 143 146 I13
Great Barrier Reef *Reef* Pacific Ocean 144 H10 143 147 N5 148 H3
Great Basin *Basin* Nevada, USA 19 F16 34 48 G2
Great Bear Lake *Lake* Northwest Territories, Canada 19 G12 22 D8 32 G9 34 37 K8
Great Bend Kansas, USA 47 O12
Great Britain *see* Britain and United Kingdom
Great Dividing Range *Mountain range* Australia 143 147 M7
Great Exhibition Bay *Inlet* New Zealand 148 G1
Great Exuma Island *Island* Bahamas 57 L4
Great Falls Montana, USA 46 H5
Great Hungarian Plain *Plain* C Europe 68 85 L15
Great Inagua *Island* Bahamas 57 M6
Great Khingan Range *Mountain range* China 129 133 P5
Great Lakes *Lakes* Canada/USA 19 J15 22 F11 23 Q10 23 P5 29 P14 34
Great Plain of China *Plain* China 117 129
Great Plains *Plains* Canada/USA 19 G15 28 D8 29 Q2 33 I13 34 46 J6
Great Rift Valley *Depression* Africa/Asia 101 111 O7
Great Ruaha *River* Tanzania 111 N10
Great Salt Desert *see* Kavir, Dasht-e
Great Salt Lake *Salt lake* Utah, USA 19 G16 22 D12 34 48 I2
Great Salt Lake Desert *Plain* Utah, USA 48 I3
Great Sandy Desert *Desert* Western Australia, Australia 143 146 G8
Great Slave Lake *Lake* Northwest Territories, Canada 19 H13 22 E9 26 A7 32 G10 34 37 L10
Great Smoky Mountains National Park *National park* USA 22 G12
Great St. Bernard Tunnel *Tunnel* Switzerland 82 E13
Great Victoria Desert *Desert* South Australia/Western Australia, Australia 143 146 H10
Great Wall of China *Ancient monument* China 133 P7 134 I7
Great Yarmouth England, United Kingdom 73 M14
Greater Antarctica *Physical region* Antarctica 64 F9
Greater Antilles *Island group* West Indies 34 55 56 H5
Gredos, Sierra de *Mountain range* Spain 74 I8
Greece *Country* SE Europe 92-93

Greece 92-93

1829 • Greek • Drachma • 81 • 78 • 15 • 96.6 • 223 • 250 • No • 65 • 3815

Greeley Colorado, USA 49 N3
Green Bay Wisconsin, USA 45 L7
Green River *River* Kentucky, USA 43 M3
Green River *River* USA 46 I9 49 K3
Greenfield Massachusetts, USA 41 N10
Greenland *Dependent territory* North America 22 F6 29 P10 34 65 N13
Greenland *Island* Atlantic Ocean 18 K9 32 K6 66 G6 117
Greenland Sea *Sea* Greenland/Jan Mayen/Svalbard 65 P14 66 J6 68
Greenock Scotland, United Kingdom 72 G9
Greensboro North Carolina, USA 43 P5
Greenville South Carolina, USA 43 O6
Greenville Liberia 106 I13
Greilswald Germany 80 L6
Grenada *Country* West Indies 57 S15

Grenada 57

1974 • English • Eastern Caribbean dollar • 290 • 72 • 16 • 96 • 2000 • Yes • 37 • 2402

Grenadines, The *Island group* Grenada/St Vincent and the Grenadines 57 S14
Grenoble France 77 O11
Grevena Greece 92 H4
Greymouth New Zealand 148 E9
Grijalva, Río *River* Chiapas/Tabasco, Guatemala/Mexico 24 F10
Grimsby England, United Kingdom 66 K8 73 K13
Groningen Netherlands 78 M7
Groote Eylandt *Island* Northern Territory, Australia 147 L5
Grootfontein Namibia 112 I9
Gros Morne National Park *National park* Canada 22 G10
Grosseto Italy 86 G10
Groznyy Russian Federation 97 F16 126 D9
Grudziądz Poland 85 L3
Gstaad Switzerland 82 E11
Guacanayabo, Golfo de *Gulf* Cuba 56 J6
Guadalajara Mexico 33 H17 53 L11
Guadalajara Spain 75 L8
Guadalcanal *Island* Solomon Islands 144 I9
Guadalquivir *River* Spain 68 74 I12
Guadalupe Mexico 53 L9
Guadalupe Mountains National Park *National park* USA 22 D13
Guadarrama, Sierra de *Mountain range* Spain 75 K7
Guadeloupe *Dependent territory* West Indies 57 S11
Guadiana *River* Portugal/Spain 74 G11
Gualeguaychú Argentina 62 M9
Guam *Dependent territory* Pacific Ocean 144 G7
Guanare Venezuela 58 H5
Guangxi Zhuangzu Zizhiqu *Region* China 135 K13
Guangzhou (Eng. Canton) China 135 L14
Guantánamo Cuba 57 L7
Guarda Portugal 74 H8
Guatemala *Country* Central America 56 A7

Guatemala 56

1838 • Spanish • Quetzal • 102 • 64 • 14 • 66.6 • 10 • 3333 • Yes • 41 • 2255

Guatemala Basin *Undersea feature* Pacific Ocean 55
Guatemala City Guatemala 56 B8
Guaviare, Río *River* Colombia 58 F7
Guayaquil Ecuador 58 C9 145 Q8
Guayaquil, Gulf of *Gulf* Pacific Ocean 58 B9
Guaymas Mexico, 20 D12 52 H5
Guddu Barrage *Dam* Pakistan 130 H4
Gulf, The *Gulf* 114 F5 123 M8
Guernsey *Dependent territory* NW Europe 73 H18
Guerrero *State* Mexico 21 O8
Guerrero National Park *National park* Mexico 22 D14
Guiana Highlands *Mountain range* N South America 34 55
Guider Cameroon 108 G8
Guilford North Carolina, USA 27 R5
Guilin China 135 K13
Guinea *Country* W Africa 106 G10

Guinea 106

1958 • French • Franc guinéen (Guinea franc) • 30 • 47 • 13 • 37.9 • 2 • 5000 • No • 30 • 2389

Guinea Basin *Undersea feature* Atlantic Ocean 67 K12 101
Guinea, Gulf of *Gulf* Atlantic Ocean 67 K11 101 109 D11
Guinea-Bissau *Country* W Africa 106 F10

Guinea-Bissau 106

1974 • Portuguese • Guinea peso • 43 • 45 • 13 • 33.6 • 6 • 5556 • No • 22 • 2556

Guiyang China 134 J12
Gujranwala Pakistan 130 J3
Gujrat Pakistan 130 J2
Gulf Atlantic Coastal Plain *Physical region* USA 19 I18
Gulfport Mississippi, USA 42 J9
Gulu Uganda 111 M3
Gümüshane Turkey 119 P5
Guri, Embalse de *Reservoir* Venezuela 58 K5
Gusau Nigeria 107 O10
Gusev Russian Federation 94 G10
Gushgy Turkmenistan 124 J11
Guwahati India 131 P6
Guyana *Country* N South America 58 L6

Guyana 58

1966 • English • Guyana dollar • 4 • 64 • 14 • 98.1 • 303 • Yes • 36 • 2384

Gwalior India 131 K6
Gweru Zimbabwe 113 M9
Gyangzê China 132 I13
Gydanskiy Poluostrov *Peninsula* Russian Federation 126 J6
Győr Hungary 85 K13
Gytheio Greece 92 I12
Gyumri Armenia 99 P13
Gyzylarbat Turkmenistan 124 G8
Gzhel' Russian Federation 96 G10

H

Ha Giang Vietnam 138 M7
Haapsalu Estonia 94 I2
Haarlem Netherlands 78 H9
Habomai Islands *Island group* Japan 136 O3
Hachinohe Japan 136 L6
Hachioji Japan 137 K11
Hadd, Ra's al *Headland* Oman 114 G5
Hadejia *River* Nigeria 107 P10
Hadhramaut *Mountain range* Yemen 122 J16
Haeju North Korea 135 P7
Hagen Germany 81 E11
Hagi Japan 137 D13
Hai Phong Vietnam 138 N8
Haifa Israel 121 L8
Haikou China 135 K15
Ha'il Saudi Arabia 122 I8
Hailar China 133 P3
Hainan *Province* China, 129
Hainan Dao *Island* China 135 K16
Hainburg Austria 83 T4
Haines Alaska, USA 36 I10
Haines Junction Yukon Territory, Canada 20 C8 36 H9
Haiti *Country* West Indies 57 M8

Haiti 57

1804 • French and French Creole • Gourde • 294 • 54 • 12 • 45.8 • 4 • 10000 • No • 32 • 1706

Hajir, Wadi *Dry watercourse* Yemen 123 J16
Hajjah Yemen 122 I15
Hakkâri Turkey 119 S8
Hakodate Japan 136 K5 144 G5
Halden Norway 70 J12
Halicarnassus Turkey 118 G9
Halifax Nova Scotia, Canada 26 G9 33 O12 39 P13 66 F8
Halle Germany 80 J10
Hallein Austria 83 N7
Halley *UK research station* Antarctica 64 D7
Halls Creek Western Australia, Australia 146 I7
Halmahera, Pulau *Island* Indonesia 129 141 O10
Halmstad Sweden 70 J14
Hamada Japan 137 D12
Hamadan Iran 123 M4
Hamah Syria 121 N4
Hamamatsu Japan 137 J12
Hamar Norway 70 J10
Hamburg Germany 80 H7
Hämeenlinna Finland 71 O10
Hamersley Range *Mountain range* Western Australia, Australia 143 146 F8
Hamhŭng North Korea 135 P6
Hami China 132 J7
Hamilton New Zealand 148 H4
Hamilton New York, USA 33 L13
Hamilton Ontario, Canada 23 Q5 39 K14
Hamm Germany 80 E10
Hammar, Hawr al *Lake* Iraq 123 L6
Hammerfest Norway 71 O1
Hamun-e-Saberi *Salt pan* Afghanistan 124 I14
Handan China 135 M8
Hangayn Nuruu *Mountain range* Mongolia 133 K4
Hangzhou China 135 O11
Hannover *see* Hanover
Hanoi Vietnam 138 M8
Hanover (Ger. Hannover) Germany 80 H9
Hanover New Hampshire, USA 30 G11
Happy Valley-Goose Bay Newfoundland, Canada 20 F8 39 Q7
Harad Saudi Arabia 123 L10
Harare Zimbabwe 113 M8
Harbin China 135 P4
Hardangerfjorden *Fjord* Norway 70 H10
Harderwijk Netherlands 78 K9
Harer Ethiopia 105 L15
Hargeysa Somalia 105 M15
Hari, Batang *River* Indonesia 140 E12
Harirud *River* Afghanistan 125 K12
Harlan County Lake *Reservoir* Nebraska, USA 47 N11
Harlingen Netherlands 78 J7
Harney Lake *Lake* Oregon, USA 50 K10
Härnösand Sweden 71 M9
Harper Liberia 106 I14
Harris *Physical region* Scotland, United Kingdom 72 F7
Harrisburg Pennsylvania, USA 28 H10 33 M13 40 J13
Harrodsburg Kentucky, USA 27 Q5
Harry S. Truman Reservoir *Reservoir* Missouri, USA 47 Q12
Harstad Norway 71 M3
Hartford Connecticut, USA 27 S3 28 I9 33 M13 41 M11
Hasselt Belgium 79 J14
Hastings New Zealand 148 I6
Hastings England, United Kingdom 73 L17
Hastings Nebraska, USA 47 O11
Hat Yai Thailand 139 I17
Hatteras Plain *Undersea feature* Atlantic Ocean 34
Hatteras, Cape *Headland* North Carolina, USA 20 G11 34 43 S6
Hattiesburg Mississippi, USA 42 J8
Haugesund Norway 66 K7 70 H11
Havana Cuba 56 H3
Havre Montana, USA 46 J6
Havre-St-Pierre Quebec, Canada 39 O9
Hawaii *State* USA 145 L7
Hawaii *Island* Hawaii, USA 23 M13
Hawaiian Islands *Island group* Hawaii, USA 23 M12
Hawke Bay *Bay* New Zealand 148 I6
Hawran, Wadi *Dry watercourse* Iraq 122 I4
Hay River Northwest Territories, Canada 37 K10
Hayes *River* Manitoba, Canada 37 P12
Hays Kansas, USA 47 H12
Hazleton Pennsylvania, USA 41 K12
Heard and McDonald Islands *Dependent territory* Indian Ocean 115 H15
Heard Island *Island* Heard and McDonald Islands 64 I7
Heathrow *International airport* England, United Kingdom 73 J16
Heber City Utah, USA 30 C12
Heerenveen Netherlands 78 K7
Heerlen Netherlands 79 L15
Hefei China 135 N10
Heidelberg Germany 81 F14
Heilbronn Germany 81 G14
Heilong Jiang *River* China/Russian Federation 135 O1
Hejaz *Physical region* Saudi Arabia 122 G7
Helena Montana, USA 28 C8 29 N2 33 G13 46 H5
Helgoland Bay *Bay* Germany 80 F6
Helmand, Darya-ye *River* Afghanistan 125 L13
Helmond Netherlands 79 K13
Helsingborg Sweden 70 J15
Helsingør Denmark 70 J15
Helsinki Finland 71 O11
Helwan Egypt 104 F7
Henderson Nevada, USA 48 H6
Hengelo Netherlands 79 N10
Henzada Myanmar 138 F10
Herat Afghanistan 124 J12
Herisau Switzerland 82 H9
Hermansverk Norway 70 H9
Hermit Islands *Island group* Papua New Guinea 147 N1
Hermosillo Mexico 52 H4
Herrenchiemsee *Castle* Germany 81 K16
Herstal Belgium 79 K15
Hialeah Florida, USA 43 O15
Hibbing Minnesota, USA 44 H3
Hida-sanmyaku *Mountain range* Japan 137 H11
Hidaka-sanmyaku *Mountain range* Japan 136 L4
Hidalgo *State* Mexico 21 N8
Hidalgo del Parral Mexico 53 K6
High Atlas *Mountain range* Morocco, 68
Hiiumaa *Island* Estonia 94 H2
Hildesheim Germany 80 H9
Hillsboro Oregon, USA 50 H8
Hilversum Netherlands 78 J10
Himalayas *Mountain range* S Asia 68 114 J5 117 129 131 K3 132 F12
Hims Syria 121 N5
Hindu Kush *Mountain range* Afghanistan/Pakistan 117 125 N11 129
Hinnøya *Island* Norway 71 L3
Hirakud Reservoir *Reservoir* India 131 M8
Hirfanlı Barajı *Reservoir* Turkey 119 L7
Hiroshima Japan 137 E13
Hispaniola *Island* Dominican Republic/Haiti 34 55
Hit Iraq 122 J4
Hitachi Japan 136 L10

Hitra *Island* Norway 70 I7
Hjørring Denmark 70 I13
Hlybokaye Belarus 95 L9
Hô Chi Minh (var. Ho Chi Minh City; prev. Saigon) Vietnam 139 N14
Ho Chi Minh City *see* Hô Chi Minh
Hobart Tasmania, Australia 147 N16
Hobbs New Mexico, USA 49 N10
Hodeida Yemen 122 H15
Hoek van Holland (Eng. Hook of Holland) Netherlands 79 G11
Hof Germany 81 K12
Hohe Tauern *Mountain range* Austria 83 N8
Hohenschwangau *Castle* Germany 81 I17
Hohhot China 133 O7
Hokkaido *Island* Japan 129 136 K3
Holguín Cuba 57 K6
Holland Michigan, USA 45 M9
Hollywood California, USA 51 K18
Hollywood Florida, USA 43 O15
Holon Israel 121 L10
Holstebro Denmark 70 H14
Holy Island *Island* Wales, United Kingdom 73 G13
Holyhead Wales, United Kingdom 73 G13
Homer Alaska, USA 36 F8
Homyel' Belarus 95 O14
Honduras *Country* Central America 56 C8

Honduras 56

⚑ 1838 • **a** Spanish • ⛁ Lempira • 👤 56 • ♥ 69 • 🎓 12 • 📖 70.7 • 🚗 13 • ✚ 2500 • ☠ No • 🏠 44 • 🍴 2305

Honduras, Gulf of *Gulf* Belize/Guatemala/Honduras 24 I10 56 C7
Hønefoss Norway 70 J11
Hông Gai Vietnam 138 N8
Hong Kong China 135 M14 144 E7
Hongshui He *River* China 134 J13
Hongze Hu *Lake* China 135 N9
Honiara Solomon Islands 144 I9
Honolulu Hawaii, USA 145 K6
Honshu *Island* Japan 129 136 J9
Hoogeveen Netherlands 78 M8
Hook of Holland *see* Hoek van Holland
Hoorn Netherlands 78 I8
Hoover Dam *Dam* Arizona/Nevada, USA 48 H7
Hopa Turkey 119 Q4
Hopedale Newfoundland, Canada 39 P6
Hopi Arizona, USA 30 D12
Hopkinsville Kentucky, USA 30 F12 43 L3
Horki Belarus 95 O11
Horlivka Ukraine 99 M6
Hormuz, Strait of *Strait* Gulf of Oman/The Gulf 123 O10
Horn, Cape *Headland* Chile 55 63 L20 66 E16 145 Q13
Horsens Denmark 70 I15
Horton Kansas, USA 30 E12
Hot Springs Arkansas, USA 42 H5
Hotan China 132 F9
Houayxay Laos 138 I9
Houlton Maine, USA 41 Q4
Houston Texas, USA 20 E12 23 P7 33 J16 49 S13
Hovd Mongolia 132 I4
Hovsgol Nuur *Lake* Mongolia 133 K3
Howland Island *Island* Baker and Howland Islands 144 J8
Hradec Králové Czech Republic 84 I9
Hrodna Belarus 94 H11
Hron *River* Slovakia 85 L12
Huainan China 135 N10
Huambo Angola 112 H6
Huancayo Peru 59 E13
Huánuco Peru 59 D12
Huascarán, Nevado *Mountain* Peru, 55
Hubli India 130 J12
Huddersfield England, United Kingdom 73 J13
Huddinge Sweden 71 L12
Hudiksvall Sweden 71 L10
Hudson Bay *Bay* Canada 19 J13 22 F9 29 P13 30 E9 32 J10 34 37 P10 38 I5 66 D7
Hudson River *River* New Jersey/New York, USA 23 Q5 41 M10
Hudson Strait *Strait* Nunavut/Québec, Canada 19 K12 32 K9 34 37 R8 39 L2
Hudson-Mohawk Gap *Gap* New York, USA 41 M9
Huê Vietnam 139 N11
Huehuetenango Guatemala 56 A7
Huelva Spain 74 H13
Huepochtlan *Historic site* Mexico 24 D7
Huesca Spain 75 N5
Hughenden Queensland, Australia 147 N8
Hull *see* Kingston upon Hull
Hulun Nur *Lake* China 133 P3
Humber *Estuary* England, United Kingdom 73 K13
Humboldt River *River* Nevada, USA 48 H2
Hun Libya 103 P8
Hungary *Country* C Europe 84 J13

Hungary 84-85

⚑ 1918 • **a** Hungarian • ⛁ Forint • 👤 109 • ♥ 71 • 🎓 16 • 📖 99 • 🚗 226 • ✚ 278 • ☠ No • 🏠 65 • 🍴 3503

Huntington West Virginia, USA 43 P3
Huntington Beach California, USA 51 L19
Huntsville Alabama, USA 43 L5
Huron South Dakota, USA 45 P10
Huron, Lake *Lake* Michigan/Ontario, Canada/USA 22 F11 23 R10 28 G9 29 R2 33 L13 34 38 I13 45 O5
Hurunui *River* New Zealand 148 F9
Husum Germany 80 G6
Hutchinson Kansas, USA 47 O13
Huy Belgium 79 J16
Hvar *Island* Croatia 88 I8
Hwange *National Park* Zimbabwe 113 L9
Hwange Zimbabwe 113 L8
Hyargas Nuur *Lake* Mongolia 133 J4
Hyderabad Pakistan 130 H6
Hyderabad India 131 K11
Hyères, Îles d' *Island group* France 77 P14
Hyvinkää Finland 71 O11

I

Ialomița *River* Romania 91 N9
Iași Romania 91 N3
Ibadan Nigeria 107 N12
Ibagué Colombia 58 E7
Ibar *River* Serbia, Yugoslavia 89 N8
Ibarra Ecuador 58 C8
Ibb Yemen 122 I16
Iberian Peninsula *Physical region* Portugal/Spain, 68
Ibiza (Sp. Eivissa) *Island* Spain 75 P10
Ibotirama Brazil 61 L11
Ibri Oman 123 O12
Ica Peru 59 E14
Iceland *Country* Atlantic Ocean 65 O16 66 I7

Iceland 66

⚑ 1944 • **a** Icelandic • ⛁ Icelandic króna • 👤 3 • ♥ 79 • 🎓 16 • 📖 99 • 🚗 142 • ✚ 333 • ☠ No • 🏠 92 • 🍴 3058

Iceland *Island* Iceland, 68
Iceland Plateau *Undersea feature* Atlantic Ocean 68
Idaho *State* USA 21 M5 23 O11 29 N14 30 C11 33 H13 46 F7
Idaho Falls Idaho, USA 46 H8
Idfu Egypt 104 G8
Ieper (Fr. Ypres) Belgium 79 C15
Ifôghas, Adrar des *Mountain range* Mali 107 M6
Iglesias Italy 87 C15
Igoumenitsa Greece 92 F6
Iguaçu Falls *Waterfall* Brazil 61 H14
Iguaçu, Rio *River* Argentina/Brazil 61 H15
Iisalmi Finland 71 P8
IJmuiden Netherlands 78 H9
IJssel *River* Netherlands 78 K9
IJsselmeer *Lake* Netherlands 78 J8
Ijzer *River* Belgium 79 C14
Ikaria *Island* Greece 93 O10
Iki *Island* Japan 137 B13
Ilagan Philippines 141 L3
Ilam Iran 123 L5
Ilebo Dem. Rep. Congo (Zaire) 109 K14
Ilgaz Dağları *Mountain range* Turkey 119 L5
Ili *River* Kazakhstan 117 126 H12
Iliamna Lake *Lake* Alaska, USA 36 F8
Iligan Philippines 141 N7
Illapel Chile 62 G10
Illinois *State* USA 21 O5 23 Q11 29 P15 30 F12 33 K14 44 J12
Illinois River *River* Illinois, USA 44 J13
Illizi Algeria 103 L11
Ilo Peru 145 R10
Iloilo Philippines 141 M6
Ilorin Nigeria 107 N12
Imandra, Ozero *Lake* Russian Federation 96 I5
Imatra Finland 71 Q10
Imperial Dam *Dam* California, USA 48 H9
Impfondo Congo 109 I12
Imphal India 131 Q7
Inarijärvi *Lake* Finland 71 P2
Inch'ŏn South Korea 135 P7 144 F5
Independence Missouri, USA 47 Q12
India *Country* S Asia 130 I7

India 130-131

⚑ 1947 • **a** Hindi and English • ⛁ Indian rupee • 👤 336 • ♥ 63 • 🎓 14 • 📖 53.5 • 🚗 4 • ✚ 2500 • ☠ Yes • 🏠 27 • 🍴 2395

Indian Ocean *Ocean* 114-115
Indiana Pennsylvania, USA 40 H12
Indiana *State* USA 21 O6 23 Q11 29 P15 30 F12 33 K14 45 L11
Indianapolis Indiana, USA 27 M11 28 G10 33 K14 45 M12
Indigirka *River* Russian Federation 127 O5
Indo-Australian Plate *Tectonic plate* 68 117 129 143
Indonesia *Country* E Asia 140 H13

Indonesia 140-141

⚑ 1949 • **a** Bahasa Indonesia • ⛁ Rupiah • 👤 116 • ♥ 65 • 🎓 15 • 📖 85 • 🚗 13 • ✚ 6423 • ☠ Yes • 🏠 35 • 🍴 2752

Indore India 130 J8
Indus *River* S Asia 114 H5 117 129 130 G5
Ingolstadt Germany 81 J15
Inhambane Mozambique 113 O11
Inland Sea *Sea* Japan 137 E13
Inle, Lake *Lake* Myanmar 138 G8
Inn *River* C Europe 81 L15 83 K8
Inner Mongolia *Region* China 133 P5
Innsbruck Austria 83 L8
Inongo Dem. Rep. Congo (Zaire) 109 J13
Insein Myanmar 138 F10
Interlaken Switzerland 82 F11
Inukjuak Quebec, Canada 39 K4
Inuvik Northwest Territories, Canada 36 J7
Invercargill New Zealand 148 C12
Inverness Scotland, United Kingdom 72 H7
Investigator Strait *Strait* South Australia, Australia 147 K13
Ioannina Greece 92 G5
Iona *National Park* Angola 112 F8
Ionian Islands *Island group* Greece 92 F9
Ionian Sea *Sea* Mediterranean Sea 68 87 N17 92 F7
Ios *Island* Greece 93 N12
Iowa *State* USA 21 O5 23 Q11 29 P14 30 E12 33 J14 47 P9
Iowa City Iowa, USA 47 R9
Ipel' *River* Hungary/Slovakia 85 L12
Ipoh Malaysia 139 I18
Ipswich Queensland, Australia 147 P10
Ipswich England, United Kingdom 73 L15
Iqaluit Nunavut, Canada 20 F7 37 R7
Iquique Chile 62 F4
Iquitos Peru 58 F10
Iracoubo French Guiana 58 P6
Irakleio Greece 93 M16
Iran *Country* SW Asia 123 M3

Iran 123

⚑ 1502 • **a** Farsi (Persian) • ⛁ Iranian rial • 👤 41 • ♥ 69 • 🎓 11 • 📖 73.3 • 🚗 30 • ✚ 3333 • ☠ Yes • 🏠 59 • 🍴 286

Iranian Plate *Tectonic plate* 68 101 117 129
Iranian Plateau *Plateau* Iran 68 117
Irapuato Mexico 53 M11
Iraq *Country* SW Asia 122 J5

Iraq 122-123

⚑ 1932 • **a** Arabic • ⛁ Iraqi dinar • 👤 51 • ♥ 62 • 🎓 12 • 📖 58 • 🚗 36 • ✚ 1667 • ☠ Yes • 🏠 75 • 🍴 2121

Irbid Jordan 121 M9
Ireland *Island* Republic of Ireland/United Kingdom, 68
Ireland, Republic of *Country* NW Europe 73 C12

Ireland 72-73

⚑ 1922 • **a** Irish and English • ⛁ Punt • 👤 54 • ♥ 76 • 🎓 15 • 📖 99 • 🚗 272 • ✚ 500 • ☠ No • 🏠 58 • 🍴 3847

Irian Jaya (prev. Dutch New Guinea) *Province* Indonesia 141 R12
Iringa Tanzania 111 O10
Irish Sea *Sea* Atlantic Ocean 73 F13
Irkutsk Russian Federation 127 L11
Irrawaddy *River* Myanmar 114 K6 117 129 138 G7
Irtysh *River* N Asia 68 117 126 H8 129 132 H4
Ischia, Isola d' *Island* Italy 87 J13
Iseo, L. d' *Lake* Italy 86 E6
Isfahan Iran 123 N6
Ishikari-gawa *River* Japan 136 K4
Ishikari-wan *Bay* Japan 136 K4
Ishim *River* Kazakhstan/Russian Federation 126 G10
Isiro Dem. Rep. Congo (Zaire) 109 N11
İskenderun (Eng. Alexandretta) Turkey 119 N10
Iskŭr *River* Bulgaria 90 J11
Iskŭr, Yazovir *Reservoir* Bulgaria 90 I13
Islam Barrage *Dam* 130 I4
Islamabad Pakistan 130 J2
Islay *Island* Scotland, United Kingdom 72 F10
Isle of Man *Dependent territory* NW Europe 73 G12
Isle Royale National Park *National park* Canada 22 E10
Isma'iliya Egypt 104 G6
Isparta Turkey 119 J9
Israel *Country* SW Asia 121 L9

Israel 121

⚑ 1948 • **a** Hebrew and Arabic • ⛁ New Israeli shekel • 👤 300 • ♥ 78 • 🎓 15 • 📖 95.4 • 🚗 213 • ✚ 350 • ☠ No • 🏠 91 • 🍴 3050

Issyk-Kul', Ozero *Lake* Kyrgyzstan 125 R5
Istanbul Turkey 118 H5
Itaipú Dam *Dam* Brazil/Paraguay 62 O6
Itaipú, Represa de *Reservoir* Brazil/Paraguay 55 61 H14
Italy *Country* S Europe 86-87

Italy 86-87

⚑ 1870 • **a** Italian • ⛁ Italian lira • 👤 195 • ♥ 78 • 🎓 14 • 📖 98.3 • 🚗 533 • ✚ 588 • ☠ No • 🏠 67 • 🍴 3561

Itanagar India 131 Q6
Itea Greece 92 I8
Ithaca New York, USA 40 J10
Ittoqqortoormiit (Eng. Scoresby Sound) Greenland 65 O15
Iturup, Ostrov *Island* Russian Federation 136 P1
Ivalo Finland 71 P3
Ivangrad Yugoslavia 89 M9
Ivano-Frankivs'k Ukraine 98 F5
Ivanovo Russian Federation 96 H10 126 F6
Ivory Coast *Country* W Africa 106 J12

Ivory Coast 106-107

⚑ 1960 • **a** French • ⛁ Franc de la Communauté financière africaine • 👤 46 • ♥ 47 • 🎓 13 • 📖 42.6 • 🚗 21 • ✚ 10000 • ☠ No • 🏠 44 • 🍴 2491

Iwaki Japan 136 L9
Izabal, Lago de *Lake* Guatemala 56 B8
Izamal *Historic site* Mexico 24 H8
Izhevsk Russian Federation 97 K11 126 F7
Izhma *River* Russian Federation 96 L8
İzmir Turkey 118 G8
İzmit Turkey 118 I5
İznik Turkey 118 I5
Iztaccíhuatl, Volcán *Volcano* Mexico 53 N12
Izu-shoto *Island group* Japan 136 K12

J

Jabalpur India 131 L8
Jackson Michigan, USA 45 N9
Jackson Mississippi, USA 28 F12 29 Q5 30 F13 33 K15 42 J7
Jackson Lake *Lake* Wyoming, USA 46 H8
Jacksonville Florida, USA 27 O14 33 L15 43 O10
Jacksonville Illinois, USA 44 J13
Jacmel Haiti 57 M8
Jaén Spain 75 K12
Jaffna Sri Lanka 131 L15
Jaipur India 130 J6
Jaisalmer India 130 I5
Jajce Bosnia and Herzegovina 88 J6
Jakarta (prev. Djakarta, Dut. Batavia) Indonesia 140 G14
Jakobstad Finland 71 N8
Jalalabad Afghanistan 125 O12
Jalandhar India 131 J3
Jalapa Mexico 53 O12
Jamaica *Country* West Indies 56 J8

Jamaica 56-57

⚑ 1962 • **a** English • ⛁ Jamaican dollar • 👤 240 • ♥ 75 • 🎓 12 • 📖 85.5 • 🚗 41 • ✚ 2000 • ☠ Yes • 🏠 54 • 🍴 2607

Jamaica *Island* Caribbean Sea 55
Jamalpur Bangladesh 131 P7
Jambi Indonesia 140 F12
James Bay *Bay* Ontario/Québec, Canada 38 J7
James River *River* North Dakota/South Dakota, USA 23 P5 47 O7
Jamestown New York, USA 26 E11 27 R5 40 H10
Jamestown North Dakota, USA 47 N5
Jamnagar India 130 H8
Jamshedpur India 131 N8
Jan Mayen *Dependent territory* Atlantic Ocean 65 P15
Jan Mayen *Island* Atlantic Ocean 68
Janakpur Nepal 131 N6
Janesville Wisconsin, USA 45 K9
Japan *Country* E Asia 136-137

Japan 136-137

⚑ 1600 • **a** Japanese • ⛁ Yen • 👤 336 • ♥ 80 • 🎓 15 • 📖 99 • 🚗 373 • ✚ 556 • ☠ Yes • 🏠 78 • 🍴 2903

Japan Trench *Undersea feature* Pacific Ocean 129 144 G6
Japan, Sea of *Sea* Japan/North Korea/Russ Fed/South Korea 127 Q12 129 G5 133 T5 136 H10 144
Jardines de la Reina, Archipiélago de los *Island group* Cuba 56 I5
Jari, Rio *River* Brazil 60 H6
Järvenpää Finland 71 O11
Jask Iran 123 P10
Jasper Alberta, Canada 37 K13
Jasper National Park *National park* Alberta/British Columbia, Canada 22 D10
Java *Island* SE Asia 114 M9 129 140 H15 143
Java Sea *Sea* SE Asia 114 M9 129 140 G13 143
Java Trench *Undersea feature* SE Asia 114 L9 129 143
Jaya, Puncak *Mountain* Indonesia, 129
Jayapura Indonesia 141 T12
Jaz Murian, Hamun-e *Lake* Iran 123 P10
Jazirat Masirah Oman 114 G6
Jebel Aulia Dam *Dam* Sudan 105 G13
Jedda Saudi Arabia 122 G11
Jefferson City Missouri, USA 28 F11 29 P4 47 R12
Jēkabpils Latvia 94 J7
Jelgava Latvia 94 I6
Jember Indonesia 140 J15
Jena Germany 81 J11
Jenbach Austria 83 L8
Jendouba Tunisia 103 N4
Jenny Lind California, USA 28 B10
Jérémie Haiti 57 L8
Jeréz de la Frontera Spain 74 I14
Jericho West Bank 121 M10
Jerid, Chott el *Salt lake* Tunisia 101 103 M5
Jersey *Dependent territory* NW Europe 73 I19
Jerusalem Israel 121 M10
Jesenice Slovenia 83 P10
Jessore Bangladesh 131 O8
Jeziorak, Jezioro *Lake* Poland 85 L3
Jhelum Pakistan 130 J2
Jiamusi China 135 Q3
Jihlava Czech Republic 84 I10
Jihlava *River* Czech Republic 84 I10
Jijiga Ethiopia 105 L15
Jilib Somalia 105 L18
Jilin China 135 P4
Jima Ethiopia 105 I15
Jinan China 135 M8
Jingdezhen China 135 N11
Jingmen China 135 L10
Jining China 133 O7
Jinja Uganda 111 N4
Jinnah Barrage *Dam* Pakistan 130 I2
Jinotega Nicaragua 56 D10
Jinsha Jiang *River* China 134 H11
Jiu *River* Romania 90 J10
Jixi China 135 Q4
Jizan Saudi Arabia 122 H14
Jizzakh Uzbekistan 125 M7
João Pessoa Brazil 60 P9
Jodhpur India 130 I6
Joensuu Finland 71 Q9
Johannesburg South Africa 113 L12
John Day River *River* Oregon, USA 50 J9
Johnson City Tennessee, USA 43 O5
Johnston Atoll *Dependent territory* Pacific Ocean 145 K7
Johnstown Pennsylvania, USA 40 H13
Johor Bahru Malaysia 139 K20
Joinville Brazil 61 J15

⚑ Date of independence • **a** Language (official or most commonly spoken) • ⛁ Currency • 👤 Population density per square kilometre • ♥ Average life expectancy • 🎓 School-leaving age • 📖 Literacy • 🚗 Number of cars per 1,000 people • ✚ Number of people per doctor • ☠ Death penalty • 🏠 Percentage of urban-based population • 🍴 Average number of calories consumed daily per person

Jokkmokk – Kosti

Jokkmokk Sweden 71 M5
Joliet Illinois, USA 45 L10
Jolo Philippines 141 L8
Jolo *Island* Philippines 141 L8
Jonglei Canal *Canal* Sudan 105 F16
Joniškis Lithuania 94 H7
Jönköping Sweden 71 K13
Jonquière Quebec, Canada 39 N11
Joplin Missouri, USA 47 Q13
Jordan *River* SW Asia 121 M9
Jordan *Country* SW Asia 121 N12

Jordan 121

1946 • a Arabic • Jordanian dinar • 73 • 70 • 15 • 87.2 • 50 • 625 • Yes • 71 • 3022

Jos Nigeria 107 P11
Jos Plateau *Plateau* Nigeria 107 P11
Joseph Bonaparte Gulf *Gulf* Australia 146 I5
Joshua Tree National Park *National park* USA 22 C12
Juan de Fuca Plate *Tectonic plate* 34
Juan de Fuca, Strait of *Strait* Pacific Ocean 50 F5
Juan Fernández, Islas *Island group* Chile 145 P11
Juazeiro Brazil 60 N10
Juba Sudan 105 F17
Juba *River* Ethiopia/Somalia 105 L18
Júcar *River* Spain 75 M10
Judenburg Austria 83 Q8
Juigalpa Nicaragua 56 D11
Juiz de Fora Brazil 61 L14
Juliaca Peru 59 G14
Junction City Kansas, USA 28 E10
Juneau Alaska, USA 20 C7 32 E10 36 H10
Jungfrau *Mountain* Switzerland 82 F11
Junín Argentina 62 O9
Jura *Island* Scotland, United Kingdom 72 F9
Jura (var. Jura Mountains) *Mountain range* France/Switzerland 77 O9 82 D10
Jura Mountains *see* Jura
Jurbarkas Lithuania 94 H9
Juruá, Rio *River* Brazil/Peru 55 60 B9
Juticalpa Honduras 56 D9
Jutland *Island* Denmark 70 H14
Jutland *see* Jylland
Juventud, Isla de la *Island* Cuba 56 G4
Jwaneng Botswana 113 K11
Jylland (Eng. Jutland) *Peninsula* Denmark, 68
Jyväskylä Finland 71 O9

K

K2 *Mountain* China/Pakistan, 129
Kabaena, Pulau *Island* Indonesia 141 M14
Kabah *Historic site* Mexico 24 H8
Kabalega Falls *Waterfall* Uganda 111 M3
Kabalo Dem. Rep. Congo (Zaire) 109 N15
Kabia, Palau *Island* Indonesia 141 L14
Kabul *River* Afghanistan/Pakistan 125 N12
Kabwe Zambia 111 K14
Kachchh, Gulf of *Gulf* India 130 G7
Kachchh, Rann of (var. Rann of Kutch) *Salt marsh* India/Pakistan 129 130 H7
Kadugli Sudan 105 F14
Kaduna Nigeria 107 O11
Kaédi Mauritania 106 G8
Kaesŏng North Korea 135 P7
Kafue Zambia 111 K15
Kafue *National park* Zambia 110 J14
Kafue *River* Zambia 110 J14
Kafue Flats *Plain* Zambia 110 J15
Kaga Bandoro Central African Republic 108 J10
Kagoshima Japan 137 C15
Kahmard, Darya-ye *River* Afghanistan 125 M11
Kahramanmaras Turkey 119 N9
Kai, Kepulauan *Island group* Indonesia 141 Q13
Kaikoura New Zealand 148 G9
Kainji Reservoir *Reservoir* Nigeria 107 N11
Kaipara Harbour *Harbour* New Zealand 148 G3
Kairouan Tunisia 103 N5
Kaiserslautern Germany 81 E14
Kajaani Finland 71 P7
Kakamega Kenya 111 N4
Kakhovka Reservoir *Reservoir* Ukraine 99 K7
Kalahari Desert *Desert* Southern Africa 101 112 J11
Kalahari Gemsbok *National Park* South Africa 112 J12
Kalamata Greece 92 I12
Kalamazoo Michigan, USA 45 M9
Kalamits'ka Zatoka *Gulf* Ukraine 98 J10
Kalemie Dem. Rep. Congo (Zaire) 109 O15
Kalgoorlie Western Australia, Australia 146 H12
Kaliningrad Russian Federation 94 F9
Kalispell Montana, USA 46 G4
Kalisz Poland 85 K6
Kalmar Sweden 71 L14
Kaluga Russian Federation 96 F10 126 E6
Kalyenkavichy Belarus 95 M15
Kama *River* Russian Federation 96 L10 126 G7
Kamaran *Island* Yemen 122 H15
Kamchatka *Peninsula* Russian Federation 117 127 R6 144 H4
Kamchatka *River* Russian Federation, 34
Kamchiya *River* Bulgaria 91 N12
Kamenjak, Rt *Headland* Croatia 88 F5
Kamina Dem. Rep. Congo (Zaire) 109 M16
Kamloops British Columbia, Canada 30 C10 37 K15
Kampala Uganda 111 M4
Kampong Cham Cambodia 139 M14
Kampong Chhnang Cambodia 139 L14
Kampong Saom Cambodia 139 K14
Kampong Thum Cambodia 139 L13
Kampot Cambodia 139 L14
Kamskoye Vodokhranilishche *Reservoir* Russian Federation 96 L11
Kamsyanets'-Podil's'kyy Ukraine 98 G6
Kananga Dem. Rep. Congo (Zaire) 109 L15
Kanazawa Japan 136 H10
Kanchanaburi Thailand 139 I12
Kandahar Afghanistan 125 L14
Kandi Benin 107 N10
Kandla India 130 H7
Kandy Sri Lanka 131 L16
Kangaroo Island *Island* South Australia, Australia 147 L14
Kangchenjunga *Mountain* India, 129
Kangean, Pulau *Island* Indonesia 140 J15
Kanggye North Korea 135 P6
Kangnŭng South Korea 135 Q7
Kanjiža Serbia, Yugoslavia 89 M2
Kankakee Illinois, USA 45 L11
Kankan Guinea 106 I11
Kano Nigeria 107 P10
Kanpur (Eng. Cawnpore) India 131 L6
Kansas *State* USA 21 N6 23 P12 29 O15 30 E12 33 I14 47 N12
Kansas City Kansas, USA 28 F10 33 J14 47 Q12
Kansk Russian Federation 127 K10
Kaohsiung Taiwan 135 O14
Kaolack Senegal 106 F9
Kapchagay Kazakhstan 126 H13
Kapfenberg Austria 83 Q7
Kapuas, Sungai *River* Indonesia 140 H11
Kara Togo 107 M11
Kara Kum *Desert* Turkmenistan 68 117
Kara Kum Canal *Canal* Turkmenistan 125 K9
Kara Sea (Rus. Karskoye More) *Sea* Arctic Ocean 65 68 96 N5 117 S11 126 I5 129
Kara-Balta Kyrgyzstan 125 P5
Kara-Bogaz-Gol, Zaliv *Bay* Turkmenistan 124 F6
Karabük Turkey 119 K5
Karachi Pakistan 114 H5 130 G6
Karaganda Kazakhstan 126 H11
Karaginskiy, Ostrov *Island* Russian Federation 127 R5
Karaj Iran 123 N4
Karakaya Barajı *Reservoir* Turkey 119 O7
Karakol Kyrgyzstan 125 S5
Karakoram Range *Mountain range* S Asia 132 E9
Karaman Turkey 119 L9
Karamay China 132 H5
Karasburg Namibia 112 I13
Karasjok Norway 71 O2
Karbala' Iraq 123 K5
Karditsa Greece 92 I6
Kärdla Estonia 94 H2
Kariba Dam *Dam* Zimbabwe 111 K15
Kariba, Lake *Reservoir* Zambia/Zimbabwe 101 111 K16 113 L8
Karimata, Kepulauan *Island group* Indonesia 140 H12
Karkinits'ka Zatoka *Gulf* Ukraine 98 J9
Karlovac Croatia 88 H3
Karlovy Vary Czech Republic 84 G8
Karlskrona Sweden 71 K15
Karlsruhe Germany 81 F14
Karlstad Sweden 71 K12
Karpathos *Island* Greece 93 Q15
Kars Turkey 119 R5
Karskoye More *see* Kara Sea
Karystos Greece 93 L9
Kasai *River* Angola/Congo (Zaire) 109 J14
Kasama Zambia 111 M11
Kasese Uganda 111 L4
Kashan Iran 123 N5
Kashi China 132 E8
Kashmir *Region* India 131 K1
Kaskaskia USA 27 P5
Kaskaskia River *River* Illinois, USA 45 K14
Kasongo Dem. Rep. Congo (Zaire) 109 N14
Kassala Sudan 105 I12
Kassandra, Gulf of *Gulf* Greece 93 K4
Kassel Germany 81 G11
Kastamonu Turkey 119 L4
Kastoria Greece 92 H3
Kastoria, Limni *Lake* Greece 92 H3
Kasumiga-ura *Lake* Japan 136 L10
Kasungu *National Park* Malawi 111 N13
Kasur Pakistan 130 J3
Kata Tjuta (var. Mount Olga) *Mountain* Northern Territory, Australia, 143
Katakolo Greece 92 H10
Katavi *National Park* Tanzania 111 L9
Katerini Greece 92 J4
Katha Myanmar 138 G6
Kathmandu Nepal 131 N5
Katmai National Park *National park* Alaska, USA 22 B8
Katowice Poland 85 L9
Katsberg Tunnel *Tunnel* Austria 83 O9
Katsina Nigeria 107 O9
Kattegat *Strait* Denmark 70 I14
Kauai *Island* Hawaii, USA 23 M12
Kaub *Castle* Germany 81 E12
Kaunas Lithuania 94 I9
Kavadarci FYR Macedonia 89 O11
Kavala Greece 93 L2
Kavir, Dasht-e (var. Great Salt Desert) *Salt pan* Iran 68 123 N5
Kawa *Archaeological site* Sudan 105 F11
Kawasaki Japan 137 K11
Kayan Myanmar 141 K10
Kayes Mali 106 H9
Kayseri Turkey 119 M7
Kazakh Uplands *Plateau* Kazakhstan 126 H11
Kazakhstan *Country* C Asia 126 E10

Kazakhstan 126

1991 • a Kazakh • Tenge • 6 • 68 • 17 • 99 • 62 • 265 • No • 60 •

Kazan' Russian Federation 96 I11 126 F7
Kazanlŭk Bulgaria 91 L13
Kea *Island* Greece 93 L10
Keban Barajı *Dam* Turkey 119 O7
Kebnekaise *Mountain* Sweden, 68
Kecskemét Hungary 85 M14
Kediri Indonesia 140 I15
Keetmanshoop Namibia 112 I12
Kefalonia *Island* Greece 92 G9
Kejimkujik National Park *National park* Canada 22 H11
Kelkit Çayı *River* Turkey 119 O6
Kelmė Lithuania 94 H8
Kem' Russian Federation 96 H7 126 G4
Kemerovo Russian Federation 126 J10
Kemi Finland 71 O6
Kemijärvi Finland 71 P5
Kemijoki *River* Finland 71 O5
Kenai Alaska, USA 36 G8
Kenai Fjords National Park *National park* Alaska, USA 22 B8
Kendari Indonesia 141 M13
Kenema Sierra Leone 106 H12
Kenge Dem. Rep. Congo (Zaire) 109 I14
Kénitra Morocco 102 I5
Kennebec River *River* Maine, USA 40 P5
Kennedy Space Center Florida, USA 43 O12
Kennesaw Mountain *Battle site* South Carolina, USA 27 N12
Kennewick Washington, USA 50 K8
Kenora Ontario, Canada 38 E9
Kenosha Wisconsin, USA 45 L9
Kentucky *State* USA 21 O6 23 Q12 29 P15 30 F12 33 K14 43 L3
Kenya *Country* E Africa 111 O4

Kenya 97

1963 • a Swahili and English • Kenya shilling • 52 • 52 • 14 • 79.3 • 10 • 6667 • Yes • 28 • 2075

Kenya, Mount *see* Kirinyaga
Kerch Ukraine 99 L9
Kerch Strait *Strait* Russian Federation/Ukraine 68 96 C14 99 L9
Kerguelen *Island* French Southern and Antarctic Territories 64 I7 115 H14
Kerguelen Plateau *Undersea feature* Indian Ocean 115 H14
Kerkyra *see* Corfu
Kermadec Islands *Island group* Pacific Ocean 144 J11
Kermadec Ridge *Undersea feature* Pacific Ocean 143
Kermadec Trench *Undersea feature* Pacific Ocean 144 J11 143
Kerman Iran 123 P8
Kerulen *River* China/Mongolia 117 129 133 N4
Keshena Wisconsin, USA 30 F11
Ket' *River* Russian Federation 126 J9
Ketchikan Alaska, USA 36 I12
Kewanee Illinois, USA 44 J11
Keweenaw Bay *Lake* Michigan, USA 45 K4
Key West Florida, USA 43 N16
Khabarovsk Russian Federation 127 Q11
Khambhat, Gulf of (Eng. Gulf of Cambay) *Gulf* India 130 I9
Khamis Mushayt Saudi Arabia 122 I13
Khan Yunis Gaza Strip 121 L11
Khanaqin Iraq 123 L4
Khanka, Lake *Lake* China/Russian Federation, 129
Khanthabouli Laos 139 L11
Kharkiv Ukraine 99 L5
Khartoum Sudan 105 G12
Khartoum North Sudan 105 G12
Khasab Oman 123 O10
Khashm el 'Girba Dam *Dam* Sudan 105 I12
Khaskovo Bulgaria 91 L14
Khatanga *River* Russian Federation 127 K6
Kherson Ukraine 98 J8
Khmel 'nyts'kyy Ukraine 98 G5
Khon Kaen Thailand 139 K11
Khorramshahr Iran 123 L7
Khorugh Tajikistan 125 O9
Khouribga Morocco 102 I5
Khujand Tajikistan 125 N7
Khujayli Uzbekistan 124 I5
Khulna Bangladesh 131 O8
Khyber Pass *Pass* Afghanistan/Pakistan 125 O12
Kičevo FYR Macedonia 89 N11
Kidepo *National Park* Uganda 111 N2
Kiel Germany 80 H6
Kiel Canal *Canal* Germany 80 H6
Kielce Poland 85 M8
Kiet Siel *Ancient site* USA 24 B13
Kieta Papua New Guinea 147 Q2
Kiev (Ukr. Kyyiv) Ukraine 98 I4
Kiev Reservoir *Reservoir* Ukraine 98 I4
Kiffa Mauritania 106 H7
Kigali Rwanda 111 L6
Kigoma Tanzania 111 L8
Kikwit Dem. Rep. Congo (Zaire) 109 J14
Kilimanjaro *Volcano* Tanzania 101 111 P6
Kilis Turkey 119 N10
Kilkis Greece 92 J2
Killarney Republic of Ireland 73 B14
Kilwa Masoko Tanzania 111 Q10
Kimberley South Africa 113 K13
Kimberley Plateau *Plateau* Western Australia, Australia 143 146 H6
Kimito *Island* Finland 71 N11
Kindia Guinea 106 G11
Kindu Dem. Rep. Congo (Zaire) 109 M13
King Island *Island* Tasmania, Australia 147 M15
King Leopold Ranges *Mountain range* Western Australia, Australia 146 H6
King William Island *Island* Nunavut, Canada 37 N7
Kingman Reef *Dependent territory* Pacific Ocean 145 K8
Kings Canyon National Park *National park* USA 22 C12
King's Lynn England, United Kingdom 73 L14
Kingston Jamaica 57 K8
Kingston Ontario, Canada 39 L14
Kingston New York, USA 41 L11
Kingston upon Hull (var. Hull) England, United Kingdom 73 K13
Kingstown Saint Vincent and the Grenadines 57 S14
Kinishba *Ancient site* Mexico 24 B14
Kinshasa Dem. Rep. Congo (Zaire) 109 H14
Kintyre *Peninsula* Scotland, United Kingdom 72 F10
Kirghiz Range *Mountain range* Kazakhstan/Kyrgyzstan 125 P5
Kirghiz Steppe *Grassland* Kazakhstan 68 117 126 F10
Kiribati *Country* Kiribati 144 J8

Kiribati 144

1979 • a English • Australian dollar • 110 • 60 • 15 • 98 • 1939 • No • 36 • 2651

Kırıkkale Turkey 119 L6
Kirinyaga (var. Mount Kenya) *Volcano* Kenya 101 111 P5
Kiritimati (prev. Christmas Island) *Atoll* Kiribati 145 K8
Kiriwina Islands *Island group* Papua New Guinea 147 P3
Kirkenes Norway 71 P2
Kırklareli Turkey 118 G4
Kirksville Missouri, USA 47 R10
Kirkuk Iraq 123 K3
Kirkwall Scotland, United Kingdom 72 J6
Kirov Russian Federation 96 J10 126 F7
Kirovohrad Ukraine 98 J6
Kirsehir Turkey 119 L7
Kiruna Sweden 71 N4
Kisangani Dem. Rep. Congo (Zaire) 109 M12
Kiska Island *Island* Alaska, USA 36 A5
Kismaayo Somalia 105 L18
Kisumu Kenya 111 N4
Kitakyushu Japan 137 C13
Kitale Kenya 111 O4
Kitami Japan 136 M3
Kitchener Ontario, Canada 38 J14
Kitimat British Columbia, Canada 36 I12
Kitwe Zambia 111 K13
Kitzbühel Austria 83 M8
Kiunga Marine Reserve *National Park* Tanzania/Kenya 111 R6
Kivu, Lake *Lake* Congo (Zaire)/Rwanda, 109 O13 111 K6
Kızıl Irmak *River* Turkey 119 L5
Kizyl-Atrek Turkmenistan 124 F9
Klagenfurt Austria 83 P10
Klaipėda Lithuania 94 G8
Klamath Falls Oregon, USA 51 H11
Klang Malaysia 139 I19
Klerksdorp South Africa 113 L12
Ključ Bosnia and Herzegovina 88 I5
Klosterneuburg Austria 83 S4
Kluane Lake *Lake* Yukon Territory, Canada 36 H9
Kluane National Park *National park* Canada 22 C8
Klyuchevskaya Sopka, Vulkan *Volcano* Russian Federation, 117
Knin Croatia 88 I6
Knittelfeld Austria 83 Q8
Knossos *Prehistoric site* Greece 93 M16
Knoxville Tennessee, USA 27 N12 43 N5
Knud Rasmussen Land *Physical region* Greenland 65 O12
Kobe Japan 137 G12 144 F5
Koblenz Germany 81 E12
Kobryn Belarus 94 I14
Kobuk Valley National Park *National park* Alaska, USA 22 C7
Kočani FYR Macedonia 89 P11
Kočevje Slovenia 83 Q12
Kochi Japan 137 F13
Kodiak Alaska, USA 36 F9
Kodiak Island *Island* Alaska, USA 36 F9
Kofarnihon Tajikistan 125 N9
Kohima India 131 Q6
Kohtla-Järve Estonia 95 K1
Kokkola Finland 71 N8
Kokomo Indiana, USA 45 M12
Kokshaal-Tau *Mountain range* China/Kyrgyzstan 125 R6
Kokshetau Kazakhstan 126 H10
Kola Peninsula *Peninsula* Russian Federation 68 96 J6 126 G4
Kolda Senegal 106 G9
Kölen *Mountain range* Norway/Sweden, 68
Kolguyev, Ostrov *Island* Russian Federation 90 H5
Kolka Latvia 94 H4
Köln *see* Cologne
Kolubara *River* Serbia, Yugoslavia 89 M6
Kolwezi Dem. Rep. Congo (Zaire) 109 M17
Kolyma *River* Russian Federation 127 P5
Kolyma Range *Mountain range* Russian Federation 127 Q6
Kôm Ombo Egypt 104 G9
Komoé *River* Ivory Coast 107 K11
Komoran, Pulau *Island* Indonesia 141 S14
Komotini Greece 93 N2
Komsomolets, Ostrov *Island* Russian Federation 127 K3
Komsomol'sk-na-Amure Russian Federation 127 Q10
Kongolo Dem. Rep. Congo (Zaire) 109 N14
Kongsberg Norway 70 I11
Konjic Bosnia and Herzegovina 89 K7
Konstanz (Eng. Constance) Germany 81 G16
Konya Turkey 119 K8
Kopaonik *Mountain range* Serbia, Yugoslavia 89 N8
Koper Slovenia 83 P13
Koprivnica Croatia 88 I2
Korçë Albania 89 N13
Korčula *Island* Croatia 88 I8
Korčulanski Kanal *Channel* Croatia 88 I8
Korea Bay *Bay* China/North Korea 135 O7
Korea Strait *Channel* Japan/South Korea 129 135 P9 137 A13
Korhogo Ivory Coast 106 J11
Korinthos *see* Corinth
Koriyama Japan 136 K9
Korla China 132 H7
Kornat *Island* Croatia 88 H6
Körös *River* Hungary 85 M14
Kortrijk Belgium 79 D15
Koryak Range *Mountain range* Russian Federation 127 R3
Kos Greece 92 Q12
Kos *Island* Greece 93 Q12
Kosciusko, Mount *Mountain* New South Wales, Australia 143
Koscice Poland 85 N11
Kosovo *Cultural region* Serbia, Yugoslavia 89 N10
Kosovska Mitrovica Serbia, Yugoslavia 89 N8
Kossou, Lac de *Lake* Ivory Coast 106 J12
Kosti Sudan 105 G13

Kostroma – Lomond. Loch

Kostroma Russian Federation 96 H10
Koszalin Poland 84 J2
Kota India 130 J6
Kota Bharu Malaysia 139 J17
Kota Kinabalu Borneo, Malaysia 140 J8
Kotka Finland 71 P11
Kotlas Russian Federation 96 J9 126 G6
Kotto *River* Central African Republic/Congo (Zaire) 109 L10
Kotzebue Alaska, USA 36 G5
Kotzebue Sound *Inlet* Alaska, USA 36 F4
Koudougou Burkina 107 K10
Kourou French Guiana 58 P6
Kouvola Finland 71 P10
Kozani Greece 92 H4
Kozina Slovenia 83 P12
Kra, Isthmus of *Isthmus* Malaysia/Thailand 129 139 H15
Kracheh Cambodia 139 M13
Kragujevac Serbia, Yugoslavia 89 N7
Kraków (Eng. Cracow) Poland 85 M9
Kralendijk Netherlands Antilles 57 O14
Kraljevo Serbia, Yugoslavia 89 N7
Kramators'k Ukraine 99 L6
Kranj Slovenia 83 P11
Krāslava Latvia 95 K8
Krasnodar Russian Federation 96 D14 126 C8
Krasnoyarsk Russian Federation 127 K10
Krefeld Germany 81 D11
Kremenchuk Ukraine 98 J6
Kremenchuk Reservoir *Reservoir* Ukraine 98 J5
Krems an der Donau Austria 83 R4
Kretinga Lithuania 94 G7
Kribi Cameroon 109 E11
Krishna *River* India 129 130 J11
Kristiansand Norway 70 H12
Kristianstad Sweden 71 K15
Kristiansund Norway 66 L7
Krk *Island* Croatia 88 G4
Krka *River* Slovenia 88 H6
Krong Kaoh Kong Cambodia 139 K14
Krško Slovenia 83 R11
Kruger National Park *National Park* South Africa 113 M11
Kruševac Serbia, Yugoslavia 89 O7
Krychaw Belarus 95 O11
Kryvyy Rih Ukraine 98 J7
Kuala Belait Brunei 140 J9
Kuala Lumpur Malaysia 139 J19
Kuala Terengganu Malaysia 139 K18
Kualakapuas Indonesia 140 J13
Kuantan Malaysia 139 K19
Kuban' *River* Russian Federation 96 D15
Kuching Borneo, Malaysia 140 H10
Kudat Borneo, Malaysia 141 K8
Kufstein Austria 83 M7
Kuito Angola 112 H6
Kujawy Poland 85 K4
Kuldīga Latvia 94 G5
Kulob Tajikistan 125 N9
Kuma *River* Russian Federation 96 F15
Kumamoto Japan 137 C14
Kumanovo FYR Macedonia 89 O10
Kumasi Ghana 107 L13
Kumon Range *Mountain range* Myanmar 138 G5
Kunashir, Ostrov *Island* Russian Federation 136 O2
Kunduz Afghanistan 125 N10
Kunlun Mountains *Mountain range* China 129 132 F10
Kunming China 134 I13
Kuopio Finland 71 P8
Kupa *River* Croatia/Slovenia 88 I3
Kupang Indonesia 141 N16
Kupiano Papua New Guinea 147 N4
Kura *River* SW Asia 99 P13
Kurashiki Japan 137 F12
Kuressaare Estonia 94 H3
Kurgan Russian Federation 126 H9
Kuria Muria Islands *see* =Hal'ān īy'āt, Juzur al 123 N15
Kurile Islands *Island Group* Japan 127 129 H4 136 O2 144 S10
Kurile Trench *Undersea feature* Alaska, USA 129 144 H4
Kursk Russian Federation 96 E11 126 D6
Kusadası Turkey 119 G8
Kushiro Japan 136 N4 144 G5
Kustanay Kazakhstan 126 G9
Kütahya Turkey 119 I7
K'ut'aisi Georgia 99 P12
Kutch, Rann of *see* Kachchh, Rann of
Kuujjuaq Quebec, Canada 39 M4
Kuujjuarapik Quebec, Canada 39 K7
Kuusamo Finland 71 P5
Kuusankoski Finland 71 P10
Kuwait *Country* SW Asia 123 L7

Kuwait 123

1961 • Arabic • Kuwaiti dinar • 107 • 76 • 14 • 80.4 • 317 • 5000 • Yes • 97 • 2523

Kuwait Kuwait 114 E5 123 L7
Kuytun China 132 H6
Kvarner *Gulf* Croatia 88 F4
Kvarnerićka Vrata *Channel* Croatia 88 G4
Kwa *River* Dem. Rep. Congo (Zaire) 109 I13
Kwangju South Korea 135 P8
Kwango *River* Angola/Congo (Zaire) 109 I15
Kwilu *River* Dem. Rep. Congo (Zaire) 109 I15
Kyaikkami Myanmar 139 G11
Kyklades *see* Cyclades
Kyllini Greece 92 G9
Kymi Greece 93 L8
Kyoga, Lake *Lake* Uganda 111 M4
Kyoto Japan 137 H12
Kyrgyzstan *Country* Kyrgyzstan 125 P6

Kyrgyzstan 125

1991 • Kyrgyz and Russian • Som • 24 • 68 • 16 • 97 • 32 • 291 • No • 39 • N/A

Kythira *Island* Greece 92 J13
Kythnos *Island* Greece 93 L11
Kyūshū *Island* Japan 129 137 C14
Kyushu *Island* Japan 137 C14
Kyushu-Palau Ridge *Undersea feature* Japan 144 G7
Kyyiv *see* Kiev
Kyzyl Russian Federation 127 K11
Kyzyl Kum *Desert* Kazakhstan/Uzbekistan, 117
Kyzyl-Kiya Kyrgyzstan 125 O7
Kzyl-Orda Kazakhstan 126 F11

L

La Asunción Venezuela 58 J4
La Ceiba Honduras 56 D8
La Chaux-de-Fonds Switzerland 82 D10
La Crosse Wisconsin, USA 44 J8
La Esperanza Honduras 56 C9
La Grande Oregon, USA 50 K8
La Grande Rivière *River* Quebec, Canada 39 K7
La Grande Rivière HEP Project *Dam* Canada 39 L8
La Guaira Venezuela 58 I4 67 E11
La Honradez *Historic site* Mexico 24 H10
La Libertad El Salvador 56 B9
La Ligua Chile 62 G10
La Louvière Belgium 79 G16
La Martre, Lac *Lake* Northwest Territories, Canada 37 K9
La Oroya Peru 59 E13
La Palma Panama 56 H15
La Paz Bolivia 59 H15
La Perouse Strait *Strait* Japan/Russian Federation 136 K1
La Plata Argentina 62 N10
La Rance *Power station* France 66 K8
La Rioja Argentina 62 I8
la Roche-sur-Yon France 76 I9
la Rochelle France 76 I10
La Romana Dominican Republic 57 O9
La Salle Illinois, USA 45 K11
La Serena Chile 62 G9
La Spezia Italy 86 E9
La Tuque Quebec, Canada 39 M12
Laâyoune Western Sahara 102 F7
Labé Guinea 106 H10
Labna *Historic site* Mexico 24 H8
Laborec *River* Slovakia 85 N10
Labrador *Cultural region* Newfoundland, Canada 19 L1, 29 Q13 34 39 O7
Labrador City Newfoundland, Canada 39 N8
Labrador Sea *Sea* Atlantic Ocean 19 L12 22 G9 32 L9 34 39 O3 66 F7
Laccadive Islands *Island group* India 114 H7 129
Laconia New Hampshire, USA 41 O8
Ladoga, Lake *Lake* Russian Federation 68 96 G7 126 F4
Lae Papua New Guinea 147 N2
Lafayette Louisiana, USA 42 H9
Lagdo, Lac de *Lake* Cameroon 108 G9
Lågen *River* Norway 70 J9
Laghouat Algeria 103 M5
Lagos Nigeria 67 L11 107 N13
Lagos Portugal 74 F13
Lagos de Moreno Mexico 53 L10
Lagouira Western Sahara 102 D10
Laguna de Chacahua National Park *National park* Mexico 22 E15
Lahad Datu Borneo, Malaysia 141 K9
Lahij Yemen 122 I16
Lahore Pakistan 130 J3
Laï Chad 108 I9
Lake Clark National Park *National park* Alaska, USA, 22 B8
Lake District *Physical region* England, United Kingdom, 73 I11
Traun, Lake *Lake* Austria 83 O6
Lakewood Colorado, USA 49 M4
Lakonikos Kolpos *Gulf* Greece 92 J13
Lambaréné Gabon 109 F13
Lambert Glacier *Glacier* Antarctica 64 G8
Lamia Greece 92 I7
Lampang Thailand 138 I10
Lampedusa *Island* Italy 87 I20
Lanao, Lake *Lake* Philippines 141 N7
Lancaster England, United Kingdom 73 I2
Lancaster New Hampshire, USA 41 N6
Lancaster Ohio, USA 45 P12
Lancaster Pennsylvania, USA 40 J13
Lancaster Sound *Sound* Nunavut, Canada 37 O4
Land's End *Headland* England, United Kingdom 73 E17
Landeck Austria 82 J9
Landshut Germany 81 K15
Lang Son Vietnam 138 N8
Langkawi, Pulau *Island* Malaysia 139 H17
Länkäran Azerbaijan 99 S15
Lansing Michigan, USA 28 G9 33 K13 45 N9
Lanzhou China 134 J8
Laoag Philippines 141 L2
Laon France 77 M4
Laos *Country* SE Asia 138 J8

Laos 138-139

1953 • Laotian • New kip • 23 • 53 • 15 • 58.6 • 3 • 5000 • No • 22 • 2259

Lapland *Cultural region* N Europe 71 M4
Lappeenranta Finland 71 P10
Laptev Sea *Sea* Arctic Ocean 65 S7 68 117 127 M4 129
L'Aquila Italy 87 J11
Laramie Wyoming, USA 47 K10
Laramie River *River* Wyoming, USA 47 K10
Laredo Texas, USA 49 P15
Larisa Greece 92 I5
Larkana Pakistan 130 H5
Larnaca Cyprus 119 L12
Larsen Ice Shelf *Ice shelf* Antarctica 64 B7
Las Cruces New Mexico, USA 49 L10
Las Tablas Panama 56 G16
Las Tunas Cuba 57 K6
Las Vegas Nevada, USA 20 D11 33 F14 48 G6
Lashio Myanmar 138 H7
Lassen Volcanic National Park *National park* USA 22 C11
Lastovo *Island* Croatia 88 I9
Lastovski Kanal *Channel* Croatia 88 I8
Latacunga Ecuador 58 C9
Latvia *Country* NE Europe 94 G6

Latvia 94-95

1991 • Latvian • Lat • 37 • 68 • 15 • 99 • 175 • 333 • No • 73 •

Lau Basin *Undersea feature* Pacific Ocean 143
Launceston Tasmania, Australia 147 N16
Laurentian Mountains *Plateau* Canada/USA 19 L13 34
Lausanne Switzerland 82 D11
Laval France 76 I6
Laval Quebec, Canada 39 M13
Lavon, Lake *Lake* USA 49 R10
Lavrio Greece 93 L10
Lawrence Massachusetts, USA 41 O9
Lawrence Kansas, USA 30 E12
Lawton Oklahoma, USA 47 O16
Lázaro Cárdenas Mexico 53 L13
le Havre France 76 J4
le Mans France 76 J6
Le Port Réunion 115 F11
le Puy France 77 N11
Lebanon New Hampshire, USA 41 N8
Lebanon *Country* SW Asia 121 M7

Lebanon 121

1944 • Arabic • Lebanese pound • 313 • 70 • 84.4 • 299 • 526 • Yes • 87 • 3317

Lebu Chile 63 G12
Lecce Italy 87 P14
Leduc Alberta, Canada 37 L13
Leech Lake *Lake* Minnesota, USA 44 G4
Leeds England, United Kingdom 73 J13
Leeuwarden Netherlands 78 K7
Leeuwin, Cape *Headland* Western Australia, Australia, 115 M12 146 F13
Leeward Islands *Island group* West Indies 55 57 R9
Lefkada Greece 92 G7
Lefkada *Island* Greece 92 G7
Legaspi Philippines 141 M5
Leghorn *see* Livorno
Legnica Poland 84 J7
Leicester England, United Kingdom 73 J14
Leiden Netherlands 78 H10
Leipzig Germany 81 K11
Leiria Portugal 74 F9
Leizhou Peninsula *Peninsula* China 135 K15
Lek *River* Netherlands 79 I11
Lelystad Netherlands 78 J9
Lena *River* Russian Federation 117 127 N6 129
Lenghu China 132 J9
Lenin Peak *Mountain* Kyrgyzstan/Tajikistan, 117
Leningradskaya *Russian research station* Antarctica, 64 F12
Leoben Austria 83 Q7
León Mexico 53 L10
León Nicaragua 56 C10
León Spain 74 I4
León Guanajuato, Mexico 33 H17
Leonido Greece 92 J11
Lepontine Alps *Mountain range* Italy/Switzerland 82 G11
Leptis Magna Libya 103 O6
Lérida *see* Lleida
Lerwick Scotland, United Kingdom 72 K4
les Sables-d'Olonne France 76 H9
Lesbos *Island* Greece 93 O7
Leshan China 134 I11
Leskovac Serbia, Yugoslavia 89 O8
Lesotho *Country* Southern Africa 113 L13

Lesotho 113

1966 • English and Sesotho • Loti • 69 • 56 • 13 • 82.3 • 6 • 20000 • Yes • 23 • 2201

Lesse *River* Belgium 79 J17
Lesser Antarctica *Physical region* Antarctica 64 D9
Lesser Antilles *Island group* West Indies 34 55 57 Q10
Lesser Slave Lake *Lake* Alberta, Canada 37 L12
Lesser Sunda Islands *Island group* Indonesia 141 K16
Leszno Poland 84 J6
Lethbridge Alberta, Canada 37 L15
Lethem Guyana 58 L7
Leti, Kepulauan *Island group* Indonesia 141 O15
Leticia Peru 58 G10
Leuven Belgium 79 H15
Lévêque, Cape *Cape* Western Australia, Australia 146 G6
Leverkusen Germany 81 D11
Levin New Zealand 148 H7
Levittown Pennsylvania, USA 41 L13
Lewis, Isle of *Island* Scotland, United Kingdom 72 F6
Lewiston Idaho, USA 46 F5
Lewiston Maine, USA 41 O7
Lewistown Pennsylvania, USA 40 I13
Lexington Georgia, USA 27 S2
Lexington Kentucky, USA 43 N3
Lexington Missouri, USA 27 K11
Leyte *Island* Philippines 141 N6
Lhasa China 132 I13
Lianyungang China 135 N9
Liaoyuan China 135 O5
Liberal Kansas, USA 47 M14
Liberec Czech Republic 84 I8
Liberia Costa Rica 56 D12
Liberia *Country* W Africa 106 H13

Liberia 106

1847 • English • Liberian dollar • 30 • 47 • 16 • 38.3 • 41 • 9350 • Yes • 45 • 1640

Libreville Gabon 67 L12 109 E12
Libya *Country* N Africa 103 O8

Libya 103

1951 • Arabic • Libyan dinar • 3 • 70 • 15 • 76.5 • 159 • 909 • Yes • 86 • 3308

Libyan Desert *Desert* N Africa, 101
Lida Belarus 94 J11
Liechtenstein *Country* W Europe 82 I9

Liechtenstein 82

1719 • German • Swiss franc • 196 • 78 • 16 • 99 • 948 • No • 21 •

Liège Belgium 79 K15
Lienz Austria 83 N9
Liepāja Latvia 66 M7 94 F6
Liestal Switzerland 82 F8
Liezen Austria 83 P7
Liffey *River* Republic of Ireland 73 E13
Ligurian Sea *Sea* Mediterranean Sea 86 D9
Likasi Dem. Rep. Congo (Zaire) 109 N17
Lille France 77 L2
Lillehammer Norway 70 J10
Lilongwe Malawi 111 N14
Lima Peru 59 D13
Lima Ohio, USA 45 O11
Limassol Cyprus 119 K12
Limbe Cameroon 109 E11
Limerick Republic of Ireland 73 C13
Limnos *Island* Greece 93 M5
Limoges France 77 K10
Limón Costa Rica 56 E13
Limpopo *River* Southern Africa 101 113 L11 115 C11
Linares Chile 63 G11
Lincoln England, United Kingdom 73 K13
Lincoln Nebraska, USA 28 E10 33 I14 47 O10
Linderhof *Castle* Germany 81 I17
Lindi Tanzania 111 Q11
Line Islands *Island group* Kiribati 145 K8
Lingga, Pulau *Island* Indonesia 140 F11
Linhe China 133 N7
Linköping Sweden 71 K13
Linosa *Island* Italy 87 I20
Linth Walensee *Lake* Switzerland 82 H9
Linz Austria 83 P5
Lion, Gulf of *Gulf* France, 68
Lipari *Island* Italy 87 L16
Lipetsk Russian Federation 96 F12 126 E7
Lisboa *see* Lisbon
Lisbon (Port. Lisboa) Portugal 74 F10
Litang China 134 H11
Lithuania *Country* NE Europe 94 G8

Lithuania 94-94

1991 • Lithuanian • Litas • 57 • 70 • 15 • 99 • 238 • 250 • No • 72

Little Abaco *Island* Bahamas 57 K1
Little Bighorn *Battle site* USA 29 N2
Little Cayman *Island* Cayman Islands 56 I6
Little Minch, The *Strait* Scotland, United Kingdom 72 E8
Little Missouri River *River* USA 47 L6
Little Rock Arkansas, USA 20 E11 28 F12 29 P5 33 J15 42 I4
Liuwa Plain *Plain* Zambia 110 H14
Liuzhou China 135 K13
Liverpool Nova Scotia, Canada 39 P13
Liverpool England, United Kingdom 73 H13
Livingston, Lake *Reservoir* Texas, USA 49 S12
Livingstone Zambia 110 J16
Livno Bosnia and Herzegovina 88 J7
Livorno (Eng. Leghorn) Italy 66 L8 86 F9
Liwonde *National Park* Malawi 111 O14
Lixouri Greece 92 F9
Ljubljana Slovenia 83 Q11
Ljusnan *River* Sweden 71 L9
Llanos *Physical region* Colombia/Venezuela, 55
Lleida (Sp. Lérida) Spain 75 O6
Lloydminster Alberta/Saskatchewan, Canada 30 D10, 37 M13
Lobatse Botswana 113 K12
Lobito Angola 112 G6
Locarno Switzerland 82 H12
Lockport New York, USA 40 H8
Lodja Dem. Rep. Congo (Zaire) 109 L14
Łódź Poland 85 L6
Loei Thailand 138 J10
Lofoten *Island group* Norway 71 L3
Logan Utah, USA 48 J2
Logansport Indiana, USA 45 M11
Logroño Spain 75 L5
Loire *River* France 68 76 J8
Loja Ecuador 58 C10
Lokichokio Kenya 111 N2
Lokoja Nigeria 107 O12
Loksa Estonia 94 J1
Lomami *River* Dem. Rep. Congo (Zaire) 109 M13
Lombardy *Cultural region* Italy 86 E7
Lombok, Pulau *Island* Indonesia 141 K15
Lomé Togo 107 M13
Lomond, Loch *Lake* Scotland, United Kingdom 72 G9

Date of independence • Language (official or most commonly spoken) • Currency • Population density per square kilometre • Average life expectancy • School-leaving age • Literacy • Number of cars per 1,000 people • Number of people per doctor • Death penalty • Percentage of urban-based population • Average number of calories consumed daily per person

London Ontario, Canada 38 J15
London England, United Kingdom 73 K16
Londonderry (var. Derry) Northern Ireland, United Kingdom 72 E10
Londonderry, Cape *Cape* Western Australia, Australia 146 H5
Londrina Brazil 61 I14
Long Beach California, USA 51 K19 145 M5
Long Branch New Jersey, USA 41 L13
Long Island *Island* Bahamas 57 L4
Long Island *Island* New York, USA 41 N12
Long Xuyên Vietnam 139 M15
Longmont Colorado, USA 49 M3
Longreach Queensland, Australia 147 N9
Longview Washington, USA 50 H8
Longyearbyen Svalbard 65 R13
Lop Nur *Seasonal lake* China 129 132 I8
Lopatka, Mys *Headland* Russian Federation 127 S8
Lord Howe Island *Island* Australia 144 I11
Lord Howe Rise *Undersea feature* Pacific Ocean 144 I11 143
Lord Howe Seamounts *Undersea feature* Pacific Ocean 143
Lorengau Papua New Guinea 147 O1
Lorient France 66 K8 76 G7
Los Alamos New Mexico, USA 49 L7
Los Ángeles Chile 63 G12
Los Angeles California, USA 20 C11 23 N7 28 A11, 29 L5 30 C12 33 E15 51 K18
Los Mochis Mexico 52 I7
Lošinj *Island* Croatia 88 G5
Lot *River* France 77 K12
Lötschbergtunnel *Tunnel* Switzerland 82 F11
Louangnamtha Laos 138 J8
Louangphabang Laos 138 K9
Louga Senegal 106 F8
Louisiade Archipelago *Island group* Papua New Guinea 147 Q4
Louisiana *State* USA 21 O6 23 Q13 29 P16 30 E13 33 J16 42 G7
Louisville Kentucky, USA 33 K14 43 M2
Louisville Ridge *Undersea feature* Pacific Ocean 143
Loutra Aidipsou Greece 92 J7
Lovech Bulgaria 91 K12
Lowell Massachusetts, USA 41 O9
Lower California *Peninsula* Mexico 19 F17 33 F16 34, 52 P3
Lower Lough Erne *Lake* Northern Ireland, United Kingdom 73 D11
Lower Red Lake *Lake* Minnesota, USA 44 G3
Lower Tunguska *River* Russian Federation 127 M8
Lower Zambezi *National Park* Zambia 111 L15
Lowry *Ancient site* USA 24 C13
Loznica Serbia, Yugoslavia 89 L5
Lucenec Poland 85 M12
Luznice *River* Czech Republic 84 H10
Lualaba *River* Dem. Rep. Congo (Zaire) 109 M13
Luanda Angola 112 G4
Luang, Thale *Lagoon* Thailand 139 I16
Luangwa *River* Mozambique/Zambia 111 M12
Luanshya Zambia 111 K13
Lubaantun *Historic site* Mexico 24 H10
Lubango Angola 112 G7
Lubāns *Lake* Latvia 95 K6
Lubbock Texas, USA 49 O9
Lübeck Germany 80 I7
Lubin Poland 85 O7
Lubumbashi Dem. Rep. Congo (Zaire) 109 N17
Lucapa Angola 112 J4
Lucca Italy 86 F9
Lucena Philippines 141 L4
Lucknow India 131 L6
Lüderitz Namibia 66 M14 112 H12
Ludhiana India 131 K3
Ludza Latvia 95 L6
Luena Angola 112 I5
Lugano Switzerland 82 H12
Lugano, Lago di *Lake* Switzerland 82 H13
Lugenda, Rio *River* Mozambique 113 O6
Lugo Spain 74 G4
Luhans'k Ukraine 99 M6
Luke Air Force Range *Military base* USA 48 H10
Lukusuzi *National Park* Zambia 111 M13
Luleå Sweden 71 N6
Luleälven *River* Sweden 71 M4
Lulua *River* Dem. Rep. Congo (Zaire) 109 L16
Lumbala N'Guimbo Angola 112 J6
Lumberton North Carolina, USA 30 G12
Lumphat Cambodia 139 N13
Lundazi Zambia 111 N13
Lundy *Island* England, United Kingdom 73 F16
Lüneburg Germany 80 I8
Luninyets Belarus 95 K14
Luoyang China 135 L9
Lusaka Zambia 111 K15
Lusambo Dem. Rep. Congo (Zaire) 109 L14
Luton England, United Kingdom 73 K15
Luts'k Ukraine 98 F4
Lutzow-Holm Bay *Bay* Antarctica 64 F6
Luxembourg Luxembourg 79 L19
Luxembourg *Country* W Europe 79 K18

Luxembourg 77

⚑1867 • a French, German and Letzebuergeisch • ⛁ Luxembourg franc. The Belgian franc is also legal tender • ♟ 165 • ☻ 77 • 👤15 • 📖 99 • 🚗 248 • ✚ 476 • ☠ No • ⌂ 90 • 🍴 3681

Luxor Egypt 104 G8
Luzern Switzerland 82 G10
Lužnice *River* Czech Republic 84 H10
Luzon *Island* Philippines 141 L3
Luzon Strait *Strait* Philippines/Taiwan 141 L1
L'viv Ukraine 98 F4
Lyepyel' Belarus 95 M9
Lyme Bay *Bay* England, United Kingdom 73 H17
Lynn Massachusetts, USA 41 O10
Lynn Lake Manitoba, Canada 37 N12
Lyon (Eng. Lyons) France 77 N10
Lyons *see* Lyon

M

Ma'an Jordan 121 M13
Maas *River* W Europe 79 L12
Maastricht Netherlands 79 H14
Macao China 135 M14
Macapá Brazil 60 J7
Macdonnell Ranges *Mountain range* Northern Territory, Australia 143 146 I9
Macedonia *Country* SE Europe 89 N11

Macedonia 89

⚑1991 • a Macedonian • ⛁ Macedonian denar • ♟ 78 • ☻ 73 • 👤15 • 📖 94 • 🚗 141 • ✚ 435 • ☠ No • ⌂ 6

Maceió Brazil 60 O10
Machakos Kenya 111 P6
Machala Ecuador 58 C10
Machaquila *Historic site* Mexico 24 G11
Machupicchu Peru 59 F13
Mackay Queensland, Australia 147 O8
Mackay, Lake *Salt lake* Northern Territory/Western Australia, Australia 143 146 J8
Mackenzie *River* Northwest Territories, Canada 19 F12, 22 D8 37 K9
Mackenzie Bay *Bay* Antarctica 64 G8
Mackenzie Bay *Bay* Yukon Territory, Canada 36 J6
Mackenzie Delta *Delta* Northwest Territories, Canada, 19 F11
Mackenzie Mountains *Mountain range* Northwest Territories, Canada 19 F11 32 F8 36 J8
Mackinac, Straits of *Lake* Michigan, USA 45 M5
Macleod, Lake *Lake* Western Australia, Australia 146 E9
Macomb Illinois, USA 44 J12
Mâcon France 77 N9
Macon Georgia, USA 43 N8
Macquarie Island *Island* New Zealand 144 I13
Macquarie Ridge *Undersea feature* Pacific Ocean 144 I13 143
Madagascar *Country* Indian Ocean 114 F10

Madagascar 114

⚑1960 • a French and Malagasy • ⛁ Franc malagache (Malagasy franc) • ♟ 27 • ☻ 58 • 👤13 • 📖 47 • 🚗 5 • ✚ 10000 • ☠ No • ⌂ 27 • 🍴 2135

Madagascar *Island* Indian Ocean 101 129
Madagascar Basin *Undersea feature* Indian Ocean 101, 115 F11
Madagascar Plateau *Undersea feature* Indian Ocean 115 E12
Madang Papua New Guinea 147 N2
Madeira *Island* Portugal 66 J9 101
Madeira Ridge *Undersea feature* Atlantic Ocean, 101
Madeira, Rio *River* Bolivia/Brazil 55 60 F8
Madeleine, Îles de la *Island group* Quebec, Canada 39 Q11
Madison Wisconsin, USA 28 F9 29 P3 33 J13 45 K9
Madona Latvia 95 K6
Madras (var. Chennai) India 114 I7 131 L13
Madre de Dios, Río *River* Bolivia/Peru 59 H13
Madre del Sur, Sierra *Mountain range* Mexico 19 H20, 22 E15 24 C9 53 M13
Madre Occidental, Sierra (var. Western Sierra Madre) *Mountain range* Mexico 19 G18 22 D13 24 C16 34 52 I5
Madre Oriental, Sierra (var. Eastern Sierra Madre) *Mountain range* Mexico 19 H18 22 E13 34 53 M7
Madre, Sierra *Mountain range* Guatemala/Mexico 55, 24 F10
Madrid Spain 75 K8
Madura, Pulau *Island* Indonesia 140 I15
Madurai India 131 K15
Mae Nam Mun *River* Thailand 139 K12
Mae Nam Ping *River* Thailand 139 I11
Maebashi Japan 136 J10
Mafeteng Lesotho 113 L14
Mafia *Island* Tanzania 111 Q10
Magadan Russian Federation 127 Q7
Magdalena, Río *River* Colombia 55 58 E5
Magdeburg Germany 80 J9
Magellan, Strait of *Strait* Argentina/Chile 55 63 J19
Magerøya *Island* Norway 71 O1
Maggiore, Lake *Lake* Italy/Switzerland 82 G12 86 D6
Magnitogorsk Russian Federation 126 G9
Mahajanga Madagascar 114 E10
Mahalapye Botswana 113 L11
Mahanadi *River* India 131 N9
Mahé *Island* Seychelles 114 F9
Mahilyow Belarus 95 N11
Mahón Spain 75 S8
Mai-Ndombe, Lake *Lake* Dem. Rep. Congo (Zaire) 109 J13
Maiduguri Nigeria 107 R10
Main *River* Germany 81 G13
Maine *State* USA 21 P4 23 S10 29 Q14 30 G10 33 N12 41 P4
Mainz Germany 81 F13
Maitland New South Wales, Australia 147 O12
Majorca (Sp. Mallorca) *Island* Spain 75 R9
Majuro Atoll *Atoll* Marshall Islands 144 J8
Makassar Strait *Strait* Indonesia 141 K13
Makeni Sierra Leone 106 H11
Makhachkala Russian Federation 96 F17 127 D10
Makiyivka Ukraine 99 M7
Makkovik Newfoundland, Canada 39 Q6
Makokou Gabon 109 G12
Makurdi Nigeria 107 P12
Malabar Coast *Coast* India 130 I13
Malabo Equatorial Guinea 109 F11
Malacca *see* Melaka
Malacca, Strait of *Strait* Indonesia/Malaysia 114 K7 129 139 H18
Maladzyechna Belarus 95 K10
Málaga Spain 74 J14
Malakal Sudan 105 G15
Malang Indonesia 140 I15
Malanje Angola 112 H4
Malatya Turkey 119 O8
Malawi *Country* Southern Africa 111 N13

Malawi 111

⚑1964 • a English • ⛁ Malawi kwacha • ♟ 113 • ☻ 39 • 👤14 • 📖 57.7 • 🚗 3 • ✚ 50000 • ☠ No • ⌂ 14 • 🍴 1825

Malay Peninsula *Peninsula* Malaysia/Thailand, 129
Malaysia *Country* SE Asia 139 J18 140 H10

Malaysia 139

⚑1963 • a English and Bahara Malay • ⛁ Ringgit (Malaysian dollar) • ♟ 66 • ☻ 72 • 👤16 • 📖 85.7 • 🚗 154 • ✚ 2076 • ☠ Yes • ⌂ 54 • 🍴 2888

Maldives *Country* Indian Ocean 114 H8

Maldives 114

⚑1965 • a Dhivehi (Maldivian) • ⛁ Rufiyaa (Maldivian rupee) • ♟ 927 • ☻ 65 • 📖 95.7 • 🚗 2 • ✚ 1955 • ☠ No • ⌂ 27 • 🍴 2580

Male Maldives 114 H8
Malheur Lake *Lake* Oregon, USA 50 K10
Mali *Country* W Africa 106 K7

Mali 106-107

⚑1960 • a French • ⛁ Franc de la Communauté financière africaine • ♟ 9 • ☻ 53 • 👤16 • 📖 35.5 • 🚗 3 • ✚ 10000 • ☠ Yes • ⌂ 27 • 🍴 2278

Malinalco *Historic site* Mexico 24 C8
Malindi Kenya 111 Q7
Mallaig Scotland, United Kingdom 72 G8
Mallorca *see* Majorca
Malmédy Belgium 79 L16
Malmö Sweden 70 J15
Małopolska *Plateau* Poland 85 M9
Malta *Country* S Europe 87 K20

Malta 87

⚑1964 • a English and Maltese • ⛁ Maltese lira • ♟ 1206 • ☻ 77 • 👤16 • 📖 91.1 • ✚ 406 • ☠ No • ⌂ 89 • 🍴 3486

Maltahöhe Namibia 112 H11
Mamallapuram India 131 L13
Mamberamo, Sungai *River* Indonesia 141 S11
Mammoth Cave National Park *National park* USA 22 F12
Mamoré, Rio *River* Bolivia/Brazil 59 J13
Mamry, Jezioro *Lake* Poland 85 N2
Man Ivory Coast 106 I12
Mana Pools *National Park* Zimbabwe 113 M7
Manado Indonesia 141 N10
Managua Nicaragua 56 D11
Managua, Lake *Lake* Nicaragua 56 D11
Manama Bahrain 114 F5 123 M10
Manaslu *Mountain* Nepal, 129
Manaus Brazil 60 F8
Manchester England, United Kingdom 73 I13
Manchester New Hampshire, USA 41 O9
Manchuria *Cultural region* China 135 O4
Manchurian Plain *Plain* China 117 129
Mandalay Myanmar 138 G7
Mandera Kenya 111 R2
Manfredonia Italy 87 M12
Mangalia Romania 91 O10
Mangalore India 130 J13
Mangla Reservoir *Reservoir* Pakistan 130 J2
Mangueni, Plateau du *Mountain range* Niger 107 Q4
Manhattan Kansas, USA 47 P12
Manicouagan, Réservoir *Lake* Quebec, Canada 39 N9
Manila Philippines 141 L4 144 F7
Manisa Turkey 118 G7
Manistee Michigan, USA 45 M7
Manistee River *River* Michigan, USA 45 M7
Manitoba *Province* Canada 21 N4 29 O13, 30 E9 33 I11 37 N12
Manitoba, Lake *Lake* Manitoba, Canada 19 H15 34
Manitowoc Wisconsin, USA 45 L7
Manizales Colombia 58 E6
Mankato Minnesota, USA 44 H7
Mannar Sri Lanka 131 K15
Mannheim Germany 81 F14
Mannu *River* Italy 87 D15
Manokwari Indonesia 141 Q11
Manono Dem. Rep. Congo (Zaire) 109 N15
Mansa Zambia 111 K12
Mansfield Ohio, USA 45 P11
Manta Ecuador 58 B9
Mantova Italy 86 F7
Manyara, Lake *Lake* Tanzania 111 O7
Manzanillo Mexico 53 K12
Manzhouli China 133 O3
Manzini Swaziland 113 M12
Mao Chad 108 H7
Maoke, Pegunungan *Mountain range* Indonesia 141 R12
Maputo Mozambique 113 N13
Mar Chiquita, Laguna *Lake* Argentina 62 K8
Mar del Plata Argentina 63 N12 67 F14
Mar'ib Yemen 122 I15
Maracaibo Venezuela 58 G4
Maracaibo, Lake *Inlet* Venezuela 55 58 G5
Maracay Venezuela 58 I4
Maradi Niger 107 I9
Marambio *Argentinian research station* Antarctica 64 B7
Maranhão, Barragem do *Reservoir* Portugal 74 G10
Marañón, Río *River* Peru 55 58 D10
Marathon Greece 93 L9
Marbella Spain 74 J14
Marche-en-Famenne Belgium 79 J17
Mardan Pakistan 130 I2
Mardin Turkey 119 Q9
Margarita, Isla de *Island* Venezuela 58 J4
Margherita, Lake *Lake* Ethiopia 105 I16
Mariana Trench *Undersea feature* Pacific Ocean 144 G6 143
Maribor Slovenia 83 R9
Marie Byrd Land *Physical region* Antarctica 64 C9
Marie-Galante *Island* Guadeloupe 57 T12
Mariehamn Finland 71 M11
Mariental Namibia 112 I11
Mariestad Sweden 71 K12
Marijampolė Lithuania 94 H10
Marinette Wisconsin, USA 45 L6
Marion Indiana, USA 45 N11
Marion Ohio, USA 45 O11
Maritsa *River* Bulgaria/Greece/Turkey 91 L14
Mariupol' Ukraine 99 L8
Marka Somalia 105 M18
Marmara, Sea of *Sea* Turkey 118 H5
Marmaris Turkey 118 H10
Marne *River* France 77 M4
Maroni River *River* French Guiana/Suriname 58 O7
Maroua Cameroon 108 H8
Marquesas Islands *Island group* French Polynesia 145 M9
Marquette Michigan, USA 45 L4
Marrakech (Eng. Marrakesh) Morocco 102 H6
Marrakesh *see* Marrakech
Marsá al Burayqah Libya 103 Q7
Marsabit *National Park* Kenya 111 P3
Marseille (Eng. Marseilles) France 66 L8 77 O14
Marseilles *see* Marseille
Marsh Island *Island* Louisiana, USA 42 H9
Marshall Islands *Country* Pacific Ocean 144 I7

Marshall Islands 144

⚑1986 • a Marshallese and English • ⛁ United States dollar • ♟ 327 • ☻ 64 • 👤14 • 📖 91 • ✚ 3294 • ☠ No • ⌂ 69 •

Marshall Islands *Island group* Pacific Ocean, 143
Marshall Seamounts *Undersea feature* Pacific Ocean 143
Marshfield Wisconsin, USA 44 J7
Martaban, Gulf of *Gulf* Indian Ocean 139 F11
Martha's Vineyard *Island* Massachusetts, USA 41 O11
Martigny Switzerland 82 E12
Martin Slovakia 85 L11
Martinique *Dependent territory* W Indies 57 T13
Mary Turkmenistan 124 J9
Maryland *State* USA 21 P6 23 R11 29 Q15 30 G12, 33 M14 43 R3
Maryville Missouri, USA 47 P10
Masai Mara *National Park* Kenya 111 N5
Masai Steppe *Grassland* Tanzania 111 O8
Masaka Uganda 111 M5
Masbate Philippines 141 M5
Masbate *Island* Philippines 141 M5
Mascarene Plain *Undersea feature* Indian Ocean 129
Mascarene Plateau *Undersea feature* Indian Ocean 114 G9
Maseru Lesotho 113 L14
Mashhad Iran 123 Q4
Masinloc Philippines 141 L3
Masira, Gulf of *Gulf* Indian Ocean 123 P14
Masirah, Jasirat *Island Group* Oman 123 P14
Masqat *see* Muscat
Massachusetts *State* USA 21 Q5 23 S11 29 Q14 30 G11 33 N13 41 N10
Massacre Canyon *Battle site* USA 29 O3
Massada Israel 121 L11
Massawa Eritrea 105 J12
Massena New York, USA 41 L6
Massif Central *Plateau* France 68 77 L10
Massillon Ohio, USA 45 Q11
Masterton New Zealand 148 H7
Masvingo Zimbabwe 113 M9
Matadi Dem. Rep. Congo (Zaire) 109 G15
Matagalpa Nicaragua 56 D10
Matam Senegal 106 G8
Matamoros Mexico 53 O7
Matanzas Cuba 56 H3
Matara Sri Lanka 131 L16
Mato Grosso, Planalto de *Plateau* Brazil 60 G10
Matruh Egypt 104 D6
Matsue Japan 137 E11
Matsuyama Japan 137 E13
Matterhorn *Mountain* Italy/Switzerland 82 F13
Mattoon Illinois, USA 45 L13
Maturín Venezuela 58 K4
Maumee River *River* Indiana/Ohio, USA 45 N11
Maun Botswana 113 K9
Mauritania *Country* W Africa 106 G6

Mauritania 106

⚑1960 • a Arabic and French • ⛁ Ouguiya • ♟ 3 • ☻ 54 • 👤12 • 📖 38.4 • 🚗 8 • ✚ 10000 • ☠ Yes • ⌂ 54 • 🍴 2685

Mauritius *Country* Indian Ocean 115 F11

Mauritius 115

⚑1968 • a English • ⛁ Mauritian rupee • ♟ 645 • ☻ 71 • 👤12 • 📖 83 • 🚗 64 • ✚ 1250 • ☠ No • ⌂ 41 • 🍴 2690

Mawson *Australian research station* Antarctica 64 G7

Maya – Nafplio

Maya *River* Russian Federation 127 O8
Mayaguana *Island* Bahamas 57 M5
Mayagüez Puerto Rico 57 P9
Mayotte *Dependent territory* Indian Ocean 114 E10
Mazar-e Sharif Afghanistan 125 M10
Mazaruni River *River* Guyana 58 L6
Mazatenango Guatemala 56 A8
Mazatlán Mexico 52 J4
Mažeikiai Lithuania 94 G7
Mazyr Belarus 95 M15
Mbabane Swaziland 113 M12
Mbaïki Central African Republic 109 I11
Mbala Zambia 111 M10
Mbale Uganda 111 N4
Mbalmayo Cameroon 109 F11
Mbandaka Dem. Rep. Congo (Zaire) 109 J12
Mbarara Uganda 111 L5
Mbeya Tanzania 111 N10
Mbuji-Mayi Dem. Rep. Congo (Zaire) 109 L15
McAllen Texas, USA 49 Q16
McClellan Air Base *Military base* California, USA 51 I14
McClellan Creek *Battle site* USA 29 N5
McClintock Channel *Channel* Nunavut, Canada 37 M6
McClure Strait *Strait* Northwest Territories, Canada 37 K5
McKinley, Mount (var. Denali) *Mountain* Alaska, USA 19 E11 34
McMillan, Lake *Reservoir* New Mexico, USA 49 M10
Mead, Lake *Reservoir* Arizona/Nevada, USA 48 H6
Meadville Pennsylvania, USA 40 G11
Mecca Saudi Arabia 122 H11
Mechelen Belgium 79 H14
Mecklenburger Bucht *Bay* Germany 80 J6
Medan Indonesia 140 D10
Medellín Colombia 58 E6
Médenine Tunisia 103 N6
Medford Oregon, USA 51 H11
Medicine Hat Alberta, Canada 20 D9 37 L15
Medina Saudi Arabia 122 H9
Medina Lake *Lake* USA 49 P13
Mediterranean Sea *Sea* Africa/Asia/Europe 66 68 75 N13 77 M15 93 K16 101 102 J4 117 121 L6 129 K9
Medvezh'i, Ostrova *Island group* Russian Federation, 127 P4
Meekatharra Western Australia, Australia 146 F10
Meeker Agency *Battle site* USA 29 N3
Meerut India 131 K4
Mek'ele Ethiopia 105 J13
Meknès Morocco 102 I5
Mekong *River* SE Asia 114 L5 117 129 133 K12, 134 H14 138 I8
Mekong, Mouths of the *Delta* Vietnam, 129
Melaka (var. Malacca) Malaysia 114 L8 139 J20
Melanesia *Island group* Pacific Ocean 144 H8 143
Melanesian Basin *Undersea feature* Pacific Ocean 143
Melbourne Victoria, Australia 144 G12 147 N14
Melbourne Florida, USA 43 O12
Melghir, Chott *Salt lake* Algeria 103 M5
Melilla *Spanish enclave* NW Africa 102 J4
Melitopol' Ukraine 99 K8
Melk Austria 83 Q5
Melo Uruguay 62 P9
Melun France 77 L5
Melville Saskatchewan, Canada 37 N14
Melville Island *Island* Northern Territory, Australia 146 J4
Melville Island *Island* Northwest Territories/Nunavut, Canada 37 L4 65 N9
Memphis Tennessee, USA 27 L12 33 K15 42 J4
Mendawai, Sungai *River* Indonesia 140 I12
Mende France 77 M12
Mendi Papua New Guinea 147 M2
Mendocino Fracture Zone *Undersea feature* Pacific Ocean 34 145 L5
Mendoza Argentina 62 H10
Menongue Angola 112 H7
Menorca *see* Minorca
Meppel Netherlands 78 L8
Mequinenza, Embalse de *Reservoir* Spain 75 O6
Merced California, USA 51 I15
Mercedes Argentina 62 J10
Mercedes Uruguay 62 N9
Mergui Myanmar 139 H13
Mergui Archipelago *Island group* Myanmar 139 G14
Mérida Mexico 20 E13 26 D15 53 S11
Mérida Spain 74 H10
Mérida Venezuela 58 G5
Meridian Mississippi, USA 42 J7
Meroe *Archaeological site* Sudan 105 G11
Mersin Turkey 119 M10
Merthyr Tydfil Wales, United Kingdom 73 H15
Meru Kenya 111 P4
Mesa Arizona, USA 48 I9
Mesa Verde *Ancient site* USA 24 C13
Mesolongi Greece 92 H8
Messenia, Gulf of *Gulf* Greece 92 I12
Messina Italy 87 M17
Messina, Strait of *Strait* Italy 68 87 M17
Mestre Italy 86 H7
Meta, Río *River* Colombia/Venezuela 58 G6
Metković Croatia 88 J8
Metz France 77 O4
Meuse *River* W Europe 68 77 N4 79 I16
Mexico *Country* C America 21 N7 22 E14 28 C12, 29 N16 29 N6 33 H17 52-53

Mexico 52-53

1836 • a Spanish • Mexican peso • 51 • 72 • 14 • 90.1 • 93 • 769 • No • 75 • 3146

Mexico Basin *Undersea feature* Gulf of Mexico 34 55
Mexico City Mexico 23 O8 33 I18 53 N12
Mexico, Gulf of *Gulf* Atlantic Ocean 19 J18 20 E12 21 O7 22 F14 23 P8 28 F13 29 P16 29 Q7 34 43 K10 49 R15 55 66 C10
Meymaneh Afghanistan 125 L11
Mezen' *River* Russian Federation 96 K7 126 G5
Miami Florida, USA 20 F12 33 M16 43 O15
Mianyang China 134 J10
Michigan *State* USA 21 O5 23 Q11 29 P14 30 F11, 33 K13 45 K5
Michigan City Indiana, USA 45 M10
Michigan, Lake *Lake* USA 19 J16 22 F11 23 Q11 28 F9 29 Q2 33 K13 34 45 L7
Michilimackinac USA 26 D10
Micronesia *Country* Pacific Ocean 144 H7

Micronesia 144

1986 • a English • United States dollar • 156 • 67 • 14 • 89 • 2311 • No • 28 •

Micronesia *Island group* Pacific Ocean 144 G8 143
Mid-Atlantic Ridge *Undersea feature* Atlantic Ocean 34 55 66 G10 101
Mid-Indian Basin *Undersea feature* Indian Ocean 129
Mid-Indian Ridge *Undersea feature* Indian Ocean 114 G8 129
Mid-Pacific Mountains *Undersea feature* Pacific Ocean 144 I6
Middelburg Netherlands 79 E12
Middle America Trench *Undersea feature* Pacific Ocean, 55
Middle Atlas *Mountain range* Morocco, 68
Middle Loup River *River* Nebraska, USA 47 M9
Middlesbrough England, United Kingdom 73 J12
Middletown New York, USA 41 L11
Midland Michigan, USA 45 N8
Midland Texas, USA 49 O11
Midway Islands *Dependent territory* Pacific Ocean 144 J6
Mikkeli Finland 71 P10
Mikumi *National Park* Tanzania 111 P9
Milagro Ecuador 58 C9
Milan (It. Milano) Italy 86 D7
Milano *see* Milan
Milas Turkey 118 G9
Mildura Victoria, Australia 147 M13
Miles City Montana, USA 47 K6
Miletus *Archaeological site* Turkey 118 G9
Milford Delaware, USA 41 K15
Milford Haven Wales, United Kingdom 73 F15
Milford Sound New Zealand 148 C11
Mille Lacs Lake *Lake* Minnesota, USA 44 H5
Millstätter See *Lake* Austria 83 O9
Mílos *Island* Greece 93 L12
Milwaukee Wisconsin, USA 30 F11 33 K13 45 L9
Minatitlán Mexico 53 P13
Minbu Myanmar 138 F8
Minch, The *Strait* Scotland, United Kingdom 72 G7
Mindanao *Island* Philippines 141 N8
Minden Germany 80 G9
Mindoro *Island* Philippines 141 L5
Mindoro Strait *Strait* Philippines 141 L5
Mingäçevir Su Anbarı *Reservoir* Azerbaijan 99 R13
Minna Nigeria 107 O11
Minneapolis Minnesota, USA 30 E11 33 J13 44 H6
Minnesota *State* USA 21 N5 23 P10 29 O14 30 E10, 33 J12 44 F3
Miño Spain 74 G4
Minorca (Sp. Menorca) *Island* Spain 75 S8
Minot North Dakota, USA 47 M4
Minsk Belarus 95 L11
Miri Borneo, Malaysia 140 J9
Mirim Lagoon *Lagoon* Brazil/Uruguay 55 61 I17 62 P9
Mirimar Naval Air Station *Military base* California, USA 51 L19
Mirny *Russian research station* Antarctica 64 G9
Mirpur Khas Pakistan 130 H6
Miskolc Hungary 85 M12
Misool, Pulau *Island* Indonesia 141 P12
Misratah Libya 103 P6
Mississippi *State* USA 21 O6 23 Q12 29 P15 30 F13, 33 K15 42 I8
Mississippi Delta *Delta* Louisiana, USA 19 J18 33 K16 34 42 I10
Mississippi River *River* USA 19 J17 22 F13 23 P7, 23 Q13 28 F11 29 Q5 33 J15 34 42 H8 45 K15 47 R10 66 C9
Missoula Montana, USA 46 G5
Missouri *State* USA 21 O6 23 Q12 29 P15 30 E12, 33 J14 34 47
Missouri River *River* USA 19 H15 22 E12 23 P6 23 P11 28 E9 29 O3 33 I14 46 I4
Mistassini, Lac *Lake* Quebec, Canada 39 L9
Mitchell South Dakota, USA 47 O8
Mitchell River *River* Queensland, Australia 147 M6
Mito Japan 136 L10
Mittelland Canal *Canal* Germany 80 J9
Mittersill Austria 83 M8
Mitú Colombia 58 G8
Mitumba Range *Mountain range* Dem. Rep. Congo (Zaire) 109 O15
Mixtlan *Historic site* Mexico 24 E9
Miyazaki Japan 137 D15
Mjøsa *Lake* Norway 70 J10
Mljet *Island* Croatia 88 J9
Mmabatho South Africa 113 K12
Mo i Rana Norway 71 L5
Mobile Alabama, USA 29 Q6 33 K16 43 K9
Mobile *Battle site* Alabama, USA 27 M14
Mobile Bay *Battle site* USA 27 M14
Moçambique Mozambique 113 Q7
Mocha *see* Al Mukha
Mocímboa da Praia Mozambique 113 Q5
Mocoa Colombia 58 D8
Modena Italy 86 F8
Modesto California, USA 51 I15
Mödling Austria 83 S5
Modriča Bosnia and Herzegovina 89 K4
Mogadishu (var. Muqdisho) Somalia 105 M15
Mogollon *Ancient site* Mexico 24 C14
Mohawk River *River* New York, USA 41 L9
Mojave California, USA 51 K17
Mojave Desert *Plain* California, USA 19 F17 24 A13 34 51 L18
Molde Norway 70 I8
Moldova *Country* SE Europe 98 G7

Moldova 98

1991 • a Romanian • Leu • 131 • 68 • 17 • 98.3 • 39 • 278 • No • 52 •

Mollendo Peru 59 F15
Molodezhnaya *Russian research station* Antarctica 64 G7
Molokai Fracture Zone *Undersea feature* Pacific Ocean 34
Molucca Sea *Sea* Pacific Ocean 141 N11
Moluccas *Island group* Indonesia 129 141 O11 143
Mombasa Kenya 111 Q7 114 D9
Mona Passage *Channel* Dominican Republic/Puerto Rico 57 O9
Monaco Monaco 77 Q13
Monaco *Country* W Europe 77 Q13

Monaco 77

1861 • a French • French franc • 16410 • 78 • 16 • 99 • 373 • No • 100 •

Monastir Tunisia 103 N5
Mönchengladbach Germany 81 D11
Monclova Mexico 53 M6
Moncton New Brunswick, Canada 39 P12
Monessen Pennsylvania, USA 40 G13
Mongo Chad 108 J7
Mongolia *Country* E Asia 133 K6

Mongolia 133

1924 • a Khalka Mongol • Tugrik (tögrög) • 2 • 66 • 16 • 84 • 14 • 370 • Yes • 61 • 1899

Mongu Zambia 110 H15
Monmouth New Jersey, USA 27 S4
Mono Lake *Lake* California, USA 51 K15
Monolithos Greece 93 Q14
Monroe Louisiana, USA 42 H7
Monroe Michigan, USA 45 O10
Monrovia Liberia 106 H13
Mons Belgium 79 F16
Mont-de-Marsan France 76 I13
Montana Bulgaria 90 I11
Montana *State* USA 21 N5 23 O10 29 N14 30 D11, 33 G12 46 H5
Montauban France 77 K13
Monte Albán *Ruins* Mexico 24 E10 53 O13
Monte Bello Islands *Island group* Australia 146 E8
Monte Cristi Dominican Republic 57 N7
Montego Bay Jamaica 56 J7
Montenegro *Region* Yugoslavia 89 L8
Monterey California, USA 51 H16 145 N5
Montería Colombia 58 D5
Monterrey Mexico 33 I17 53 M7
Montevideo Uruguay 62 O10
Montgomery Alabama, USA 27 M13 28 G12 29 R5, 33 L15 43 L8
Montpelier Vermont, USA 28 H8 33 M13 41 N7
Montpellier France 77 N13
Montréal (Eng. Montreal) Quebec, Canada 20 G10 23 Q5 26 E10 27 R2 33 M12 39 M13
Montreux Switzerland 82 E11
Montserrat *Dependent territory* W Indies 57 S11
Monument Valley *Valley* Arizona/Utah, USA 48 J6
Monywa Myanmar 138 F7
Monza Italy 86 D6
Moore, Lake *Lake* Western Australia, Australia 146 F11
Moorhead Minnesota, USA 44 F4
Moose Factory Ontario, Canada 26 D9
Moose Jaw Saskatchewan, Canada 37 N15
Moosehead Lake *Lake* Maine, USA 41 P4
Moosonee Ontario, Canada 38 J9
Mopti Mali 107 K9
Mora Sweden 71 K10
Moradabad India 131 L5
Morava *River* C Europe 85 K11
Moravia *Cultural region* Czech Republic 84 J11
Moray Firth *Inlet* Scotland, United Kingdom 72 H7
Moreau River *River* South Dakota, USA 47 L7
Morecambe Bay *Inlet* England, United Kingdom 73 H12
Moree New South Wales, Australia 147 O11
Morehead City North Carolina, USA 43 R7
Morelia Mexico 53 M11
Morena, Sierra *Mountain range* Spain 74 H12
Morghab, Darya-ye *River* Afghanistan 125 K11
Morioka Japan 136 L7
Mornington Abyssal Plain *Undersea feature* Pacific Ocean 55
Morocco *Country* NW Africa 102 H5

Morocco 102-103

1956 • a Arabic • Moroccan dirham • 63 • 67 • 16 • 45.9 • 38 • 2500 • Yes • 48 • 2984

Morogoro Tanzania 111 P9
Mörön Mongolia 133 K4
Moroni Comoros 114 E10
Morotai, Pulau *Island* Indonesia 141 O10
Moroto Uganda 111 N3
Moscow (Rus. Moskva) Russian Federation 96 F10 126 E6
Moscow-Volga Canal *Canal* Russian Federation 96 G10
Mosel (Fr. Moselle) *River* W Europe 81 E13 *see also* Moselle
Moselle (Ger. Mosel) *River* W Europe 77 O5 79 M19 *see also* Mosel
Moses Lake *Lake* Washington, USA 50 K7
Moshi Tanzania 111 P7
Moskva *see* Moscow
Mosquito Gulf *Gulf* Caribbean Sea 56 F14
Moss Norway 70 J11
Mossendjo Congo 109 G13
Mossoró Brazil 60 O9
Mostaganem Algeria 103 K4
Mostar Bosnia and Herzegovina 89 K8
Móstoles Spain 75 K8
Mosul Iraq 123 K3
Motagua, Río *River* Chiquimula/El Progreso/Izabal/Zacapa, Guatemala/Honduras 24 H11
Motala Sweden 71 K12
Motril Spain 75 K14
Mouila Gabon 109 F13
Mould Bay Northwest Territories, Canada 65 O9
Moulins France 77 M9
Moulmein Myanmar 139 G11
Moundou Chad 108 H9
Mount Gambier South Australia, Australia 147 L14
Mount Hagen Papua New Guinea 147 M2
Mount Magnet Western Australia, Australia 146 F11
Mount Pleasant Michigan, USA 45 N8
Mount Rainer National Park *National park* USA 22 C11
Mount Vernon Illinois, USA 45 K14
Mouscron Belgium 79 D15
Moyale Ethiopia 105 J17
Mozambique *Country* Southern Africa 113 N11

Mozambique 113

1975 • a Portuguese • Metical • 25 • 45 • 14 • 40.5 • 0 • 50000 • No • 34 • 1680

Mozambique Channel *Strait* Indian Ocean 113 Q8
Mpika Zambia 111 M12
Mtwara Tanzania 111 Q11
Muang Khong Laos 139 M12
Muchinga Escarpment *Escarpment* Zambia 111 L14
Muck *Island* Scotland, United Kingdom 72 F8
Mufulira Zambia 111 K13
Muğla Turkey 118 H9
Mühlhausen Germany 81 I11
Mulhouse France 77 P6
Mull *Island* Scotland, United Kingdom 72 F8
Muller, Pegunungan *Mountain range* Indonesia 140 I11
Multan Pakistan 130 I4
Mumbai *see* Bombay
Mumbres Valley *Ancient site* Mexico 24 C14
Muna, Pulau *Island* Indonesia 141 M13
München *see* Munich
Muncie Indiana, USA 30 F12 45 N12
Munich (Ger. München) Germany 81 J16
Münster Germany 81 E10
Muonioälv *River* Finland/Sweden 71 N3
Mupa *National Park* Angola 112 H7
Muqdisho *see* Mogadishu
Mur *River* C Europe 83 P8 *see also* Mura
Mura *River* C Europe 83 S9 *see also* Mur
Murat Nehri (var. Eastern Euphrates) *River* Turkey 119 Q7
Murchison River *River* Western Australia, Australia 146 F10
Murcia Spain 75 N12
Mureş *River* Hungary/Romania 90 H6
Murfreesboro Tennessee, USA 43 L4
Murfreesboro *Battle site* Tennessee, USA 27 M12
Murgab *River* Afghanistan/Turkmenistan 125 K11
Müritz *Lake* Germany 80 K7
Murmansk Russian Federation 66 M7 96 I5 126 G3
Murmansk Rise *Undersea feature* Arctic Ocean, 68
Murray Fracture Zone *Undersea feature* Pacific Ocean34 145 L5
Murray River *River* New South Wales/South Australia/Victoria, Australia 143 147 L13
Murrumbidgee River *River* New South Wales, Australia 147 M13
Murska Sobota Slovenia 83 S9
Murzuq Libya 103 O9
Mus Turkey 119 R7
Muscat (var. Masqat) Oman 123 P12
Muskegon Michigan, USA 45 M8
Muskegon River *River* Michigan, USA 45 M7
Muskogee Oklahoma, USA 47 Q14
Musoma Tanzania 111 N6
Mussau Island *Island* Papua New Guinea 147 O1
Mutare Zimbabwe 113 N9
Muynoq Uzbekistan 124 I4
Muztag Feng *Mountain* China, 129
Mwanza Tanzania 111 M6
Mwene-Ditu Dem. Rep. Congo (Zaire) 109 L15
Mweru Wantipa *National Park* Zambia 111 K10
Mweru, Lake *Lake* Dem. Rep. Congo (Zaire)/Zambia 101 109 O16 111 K10
Myanmar (var. Myanmar) *Country* SE Asia 138 D8

Myanmar 138-139

1948 • a Burmese • Kyat • 69 • 60 • 10 • 83.6 • 2.6 • 10000 • Yes • 26 • 2598

Mycenae Greece 92 J10
Myingyan Myanmar 138 F8
Myitkyina Myanmar 138 H5
Mykolayiv Ukraine 98 J8
Mykonos *Island* Greece 93 N11
Mymensingh Bangladesh 131 P7
Mysore India 130 J13
Mytilini Greece 93 O7
Mzuzu Malawi 111 N12

N

Naberezhnyye Chelny Russian Federation 97 J12 126 F8
Nacala Mozambique 113 Q7
Naestved Denmark 70 I16
Nafplio Greece 92 J10

Date of independence • a Language (official or most commonly spoken) • Currency • Population density per square kilometre • Average life expectancy • School-leaving age • Literacy • Number of cars per 1,000 people • Number of people per doctor • Death penalty • Percentage of urban-based population • Average number of calories consumed daily per person

163

Naga – Nzérékoré

Naga Philippines 141 M4
Nagano Japan 136 J10
Nagarjuna Reservoir *Reservoir* India 131 K11
Nagasaki Japan 137 B14 144 F6
Nagercoil India 130 J15
Nagornyy Karabakh *Region* Azerbaijan 99 R14
Nagoya Japan 137 I11
Nagpur India 131 K9
Nagqu China 132 I12
Nagykanizsa Hungary 84 J15
Naha Japan 137 A20
Nahanni National Park *National park* Canada 22 D9
Nahuel Huapí, Lago *Lake* Argentina 63 H14
Nain Newfoundland, Canada 39 O5
Nairobi Kenya 111 P5
Naissaar *Island* Estonia 94 I1
Najran Saudi Arabia 122 I14
Nakamura Japan 137 E14
Nakhodka Russian Federation 126 J6
Nakhon Ratchasima Thailand 139 J12
Nakhon Sawan Thailand 139 I11
Nakhon Si Thammarat Thailand 139 I16
Nakskov Denmark 70 I16
Nakum *Historic site* Mexico 24 H10
Nakuru Kenya 111 O5
Nam Co *Lake* China 132 I12
Nam Định Vietnam 139 M9
Nam Ngum Dam *Dam* Laos 138 K10
Nam Ou *River* Laos 138 K8
Nam Theun *River* Laos 138 L10
Namakzar *Marsh* Afghanistan/Iran 124 I12
Namangan Uzbekistan 125 O6
Namib Desert *Desert* Namibia 101 112 G9
Namib Naukuuft *National Park* Namibia 112 H12
Namibe Angola 112 F7
Namibia *Country* Southern Africa 112 H10

Namibia 112

1990 • a English • Namibian dollar • 2 • 52 • 16 • 79.8 • 47 • 5000 • No • 37 • 2134

Namjagbarwa Feng *Mountain* China, 129
Nampa Idaho, USA 46 F8
Namp'o North Korea 135 P7
Nampula Mozambique 113 P7
Namur Belgium 79 I16
Nan Thailand 138 J9
Nan Ling *Mountain range* China, 129
Nanchang China 135 M11
Nancy France 77 O5
Nanded India 131 K9
Nanjing China 135 N10
Nanning China 135 K14
Nanping China 135 N12
Nantes France 76 H8
Nantucket Massachusetts, USA 41 P12
Napa Valley *Valley* California, USA 51 H15
Napier New Zealand 148 I6
Naples (It. Napoli) Italy 66 L9 87 K13
Naples, Gulf of *Gulf* Italy 87 K13
Napo, Río *River* Ecuador/Peru 58 E9
Napoli *see* Naples
Narach, Vozyera *Lake* Belarus 95 K10
Naranjo *Historic site* Mexico 24 H10
Narathiwat Thailand 139 J17
Nares Plain *Undersea feature* Atlantic Ocean 34 55
Nares Strait *Strait* Canada/Greenland 37 N1
Narew *River* Poland 85 N4
Narmada *River* India 129 130 I8
Narodnaya, Gora *Mountain* Russian Federation 68 117
Narsarsuaq Greenland 65 M15
Narva Estonia 95 L1
Narva *River* Estonia/Russian Federation 95 L2
Narvik Norway 71 M3
Naryn Kyrgyzstan 125 Q6
Naryn *River* Kyrgyzstan/Uzbekistan 125 Q6
Nashik India 130 I9
Nashua New Hampshire, USA 41 O9
Nashville Tennessee, USA 27 M12 28 G11 29 Q4 33 K15 43 L4
Nassau Bahamas 57 K2
Nasser, Lake *Lake* Egypt/Sudan 101 104 G9
Natal Brazil 60 P9
Natal Basin *Undersea feature* Atlantic Ocean 101
Natitingou Benin 107 M11
Natuna Besar, Pulau *Island* Indonesia 140 G9
Natuna, Kepulauan *Island group* Indonesia 140 G9
Naturaliste, Cape *Headland* Australia 146 F13
Nauru *Country* Pacific Ocean 144 I9

Nauru 144

1968 • a Nauruan • Australian dollar • 514 • 67 • 16 • 99 • 700 • No • 100 •

Navajo Dam *Dam* New Mexico, USA 49 L6
Navajo Indian Reservation *Reservation* New Mexico, USA 49 K7
Navapolatsk Belarus 95 L8
Navarin, Mys *Cape* Russian Federation 127 R3
Nawabshah Pakistan 130 H6
Nawoiy Uzbekistan 125 L7
Naxçıvan Azerbaijan 99 Q15
Naxos *Island* Greece 93 N12
Nazareth Israel 121 M8
Nazca Peru 59 E14
Nazca Plate *Tectonic plate* 55
Nazca Ridge *Undersea feature* Pacific Ocean 55
Nazilli Turkey 118 H8
N'Dalatando Angola 112 G4
Ndélé Central African Republic 108 K9
Ndjamena Chad 108 H7
Ndola Zambia 111 K13
Neagh, Lough *Lake* Northern Ireland, United Kingdom, 73 E11
Neapoli Greece 92 J13
Nebas *Historic site* Mexico 24 G11
Nebitdag Turkmenistan 124 F7
Nebraska *State* USA 21 N5 23 P11 29 O15 30 D12, 47 L10
Nechako *River* British Columbia, Canada 36 I13
Neches River *River* Texas, USA 49 S11
Neckar *River* Germany 81 G15
Necochea Argentina 63 N12
Negev *Desert* Israel 121 L12
Negrais, Cape *Headland* Myanmar 139 E11
Negro, Rio *River* South America 55 60 D7
Negro, Río *River* Brazil/Uruguay 62 O9
Negro, Río *River* Argentina 63 K13
Negro, Río *see* Chixoy, Río 55
Negros *Island* Philippines 141 M6
Neiva Colombia 58 E7
Nejd *Cultural region* Saudi Arabia 122 I9
Nek'emte Ethiopia 105 I15
Nellis Air Force Range *Military base* Nevada, USA 48 G5
Nellore India 131 L12
Nelson *River* Manitoba, Canada 37 O12
Nelson New Zealand 148 G7
Néma Mauritania 106 J8
Neman *River* E Europe 94 I12
Nemuro Japan 136 O3
Neosho River *River* Kansas/Oklahoma, USA 47 P12
Nepal *Country* S Asia 131 L4

Nepal 131

1769 • a Nepali • Nepalese rupee • 171 • 57 • 11 • 38.1 • 1 • 12500 • No • 14 • 1957

Nepalganj Nepal 131 M5
Neretva *River* Bosnia and Herzegovina/Croatia 89 K7
Neris *River* Belarus/Lithuania 94 I9
Nesebŭr Bulgaria 91 O12
Ness, Loch *Lake* Scotland, United Kingdom 72 H8
Netherlands *Country* NW Europe 79 G12

Netherlands 78-79

1815 • a Dutch • Netherlands gulden (guilder) or florin • 463 • 78 • 18 • 99 • 372 • 400 • No • 89 • 3222

Netherlands Antilles (prev. Dutch West Indies) *Dependent territory* Netherlands Antilles 57 N14
Neubrandenburg Germany 80 L7
Neuchâtel Switzerland 82 E10
Neuchâtel, Lac de *Lake* Switzerland 82 D10
Neufchâteau Belgium 79 J18
Neukirchen Austria 83 S6
Neumünster Germany 80 H6
Neuquén Argentina 63 I13
Neuschwanstein *Castle* Germany 81 I16
Neusiedler See *Lake* Austria/Hungary 83 S5
Nevada *State* USA 21 M5 23 N11 29 N15 30 C12, 33 E13 48 F3
Nevada Test Site *Military base* Nevada, USA 48 G6
Nevada, Sierra *Mountain range* California, USA 19 E15 34 51 I13
Nevada, Sierra *Mountain range* Spain 75 K14
Nevel' Russian Federation 96 E9 126 E5
Nevers France 77 M8
Nevşehir Turkey 119 M8
New Albany Indiana, USA 45 N14
New Amsterdam Guyana 58 M6
New Bedford Massachusetts, USA 41 O11
New Britain *Island* Papua New Guinea 143 147 P2
New Brunswick New Jersey, USA 41 L13
New Brunswick *Province* Canada 21 P4 29 Q13 33 N12 39 P11
New Caledonia *Dependent territory* Pacific Ocean 144 H10
New Caledonia *Island* Pacific Ocean, 143
New Caledonia Basin *Undersea feature* Pacific Ocean, 143
New Castle Pennsylvania, USA 40 G12
New Delhi India 131 K5
New England *Cultural region* USA 41 N8
New France *Region* Canada 26 E10
New Guinea *Island* Indonesia/Papua New Guinea 129, 144 G9 143 147 M2
New Hampshire *State* USA 21 P5 23 R10 29 Q14, 30 G11 33 M12 41 N9
New Hanover *Island* Papua New Guinea 147 O1
New Haven Connecticut, USA 27 S3 41 M12
New Hebrides Trench *Undersea feature* Pacific Ocean 143
New Ireland *Island* Papua New Guinea 143 147 P1
New Jersey *State* USA 21 P5 23 R11 29 Q15 30 G11, 33 M13 41 L14
New London Connecticut, USA 27 S3 41 N12
New Mexico *State* USA 21 N6 23 O12 29 O15 30 D13, 33 H15 49 K8
New Orleans Louisiana, USA 20 E12 26 D13 27 L14, 28 F13 29 P6 30 F13 33 K16 43 I9 66 C9
New Plymouth New Zealand 148 G5
New Providence *Island* Bahamas 57 K2
New River *River* West Virginia, USA 43 P3
New Siberian Islands *Island group* Russian Federation, 65 R7 117 127 N4
New South Wales *State* Australia 147 N12
New Ulm Minnesota, USA 44 G7
New Ulm *Battle site* Minnesota, USA 29 P3
New York New York, USA 20 G10 23 R6 27 S3 28 I9 29 S3 30 G11 33 M13 41 L12 66 E9
New York *State* USA 21 P5 23 R11 29 Q14 30 G11 33 M13 40 I10
New Zealand *Country* Pacific Ocean 148

New Zealand 148

1926 • a English and Maori • New Zealand dollar • 14 • 77 • 16 • 99 • 451 • 476 • No • 86 • 3669

New Zealand *Island group* Pacific Ocean, 143
Newark Delaware, USA 41 K14
Newark New Jersey, USA 41 L13
Newark Ohio, USA 45 P12
Newburgh New York, USA 41 L11
Newcastle New South Wales, Australia 147 O12
Newcastle *see* Newcastle upon Tyne
Newcastle upon Tyne (var. Newcastle) England, United Kingdom 73 J11
Newfoundland *Province* Canada 21 P3 29 Q13 32 G9, 33 N10 39 P6
Newfoundland *Island* Newfoundland, Canada 19 M14, 22 H10 33 O11 34 39 R9 66 F8
Newfoundland Basin *Undersea feature* Atlantic Ocean 66 G9
Newport England, United Kingdom 73 J17
Newport Wales, United Kingdom 73 H15
Newport Oregon, USA 50 G9
Newport Rhode Island, USA 41 O11
Newport News Virginia, USA 43 S5
Newry Northern Ireland, United Kingdom 73 E12
Neyshabur Iran 123 Q4
Ngaoundéré Cameroon 108 G9
Ngauruhoe, Mount *Mountain* New Zealand 148 H5
N'Giva Angola 112 H8
Ngorongoro Crater *Crater* Tanzania, 101
Nguigmi Niger 107 R9
Nguru Nigeria 107 P9
Nha Trang Vietnam 139 O14
Niagara Wisconsin, USA 26 E10
Niagara Falls Ontario, Canada 39 K15
Niagara Falls New York, USA 30 F11 40 H9
Niagara Falls *Waterfall* Canada/USA, 34
Niagara Peninsula *Peninsula* Ontario, Canada 39 K15
Niamey Niger 107 M9
Niangay, Lac *Lake* Mali 107 K8
Nias, Pulau *Island* Indonesia 140 C11
Nicaragua *Country* C America 56 D10

Nicaragua 56

1838 • a Spanish • Córdoba oro • 41 • 68 • 12 • 63.4 • 16 • 1429 • No • 63 • 2293

Nicaragua, Lake *Lake* Nicaragua 55 56 D11
Nice France 77 Q14
Nicobar Islands *Island group* India 114 K7 129
Nicosia Cyprus 119 L12
Nicoya, Golfo de *Gulf* Costa Rica 56 D13
Niedere Tauern *Mountain range* Austria 83 O8
Nifa Italy 87 I12
Niğde Turkey 119 M8
Niger *River* W Africa 67 K11 101 107 L7
Niger *Country* W Africa 107 O8

Niger 107

1960 • a French • Franc de la Communauté financière africaine • 8 • 49 • 15 • 14.3 • 4 • 33333 • No • 17 • 2257

Niger Delta *Delta* Nigeria, 101
Niger, Mouths of the *Delta* Nigeria 107 O14
Nigeria *Country* W africa 107 N10

Nigeria 107

1960 • a English • Naira • 120 • 50 • 12 • 59.5 • 7 • 5000 • Yes • 39 • 2124

Niigata Japan 136 J9
Nijmegen Netherlands 79 K11
Nikopol' Ukraine 99 K7
Nikšić Montenegro, Yugoslavia 89 L9
Nile *River* NE Africa 66 N10 101 104 F8 114 C5
Nile Delta *Delta* Egypt, 101
Niles Michigan, USA 45 M10
Nîmes France 77 N13
Ninetyeast Ridge *Undersea feature* Indian Ocean 114 J10 117 129
Nineveh Iraq 123 K2
Ningbo China 135 O11 144 F6
Ningxia *Region* China 134 J8
Ninigo Group *Island group* Papua New Guinea 147 M1
Niobrara River *River* Nebraska/Wyoming, USA 47 L9
Nioro Mali 106 I8
Nipigon, Lake *Lake* Ontario, Canada 38 G10
Niš Serbia, Yugoslavia 89 O8
Nissan Island *Island* Papua New Guinea 147 Q2
Nitra Slovakia 85 K12
Niue *Dependent territory* Pacific Ocean 145 K10
Nivelles Belgium 79 G16
Nixon Nevada, USA 30 C12
Nizhnevartovsk Russian Federation 126 I8
Nizhniy Novgorod Russian Federation 97 H11 126 F7
Nizhniy Tagil Russian Federation 126 G8
Nizwa Oman 123 O12
Njombe Tanzania 111 N11
Nkhotakota Malawi 111 N13
Nkongsamba Cameroon 108 E10
Nobeoka Japan 137 D14
Nogales Mexico 52 H3
Nome Alaska, USA 20 C6 36 F5
Nonacho Lake *Lake* Northwest Territories, Canada 37 M10
Nord Greenland 65 P12
Nordfjord *Fjord* Norway 70 H8
Nordhausen Germany 80 I10
Nordstrand *Island* Germany 80 G6
Norfolk Massachusetts, USA 27 O11
Norfolk Nebraska, USA 47 O9
Norfolk Virginia, USA 27 S5 43 S5
Norfolk Island *Dependent territory* Pacific Ocean 144 H11
Noril'sk Russian Federation 127 K6
Norman Oklahoma, USA 47 O15
Norman Wells Northwest Territories, Canada 36 J8
Normandie *see* Normandy
Normandy (Fr. Normandie) *Cultural region* France 76 I5
Norrköping Sweden 71 L12
Norrtälje Sweden 71 M12
North America *Continent* 34-35
North American Plate *Tectonic plate* 19 E12 55 68 117 129
North Australian Basin *Undersea feature* Indian Ocean 143
North Battleford Saskatchewan, Canada 37 M14
North Bay Ontario, Canada 39 K13
North Cape *Headland* Norway 70 O1
North Carolina *State* USA 21 P6 23 R12 29 Q15 30 G12 33 M14 43 Q6
North Cascades *National park* USA 22 C10
North Dakota *State* USA 21 N5 23 P10 29 O14 30 D11 33 I12 47 L5
North European Plain *Plain* N Europe, 68
North Fiji Basin *Undersea feature* Pacific Ocean 143
North Frisian Islands *Island group* Germany 80 F5
North Island *Island* New Zealand 143 148 G4
North Korea *Country* E Asia 135 P6

North Korea 135

1948 • a Korean • North Korean won • 197 • 63 • 15 • 95 • 370 • Yes • 61 • 2833

North Las Vegas Nevada, USA 48 H6
North Luangwa *National Park* Zambia 111 M12
North Platte Nebraska, USA 47 M10
North Pole *Pole* 34 65 Q10 68 117 129
North Sea *Sea* Atlantic Ocean 66 K7 68 72 J9 79 D12, 80 D7
North Uist *Island* Scotland, United Kingdom 72 E7
North West Cape *Cape* Western Australia, Australia, 115 M11 146 E8
Northampton England, United Kingdom 73 J15
Northampton Massachusetts, USA 41 M10
Northern Dvina *River* Russian Federation 68 96 J8
Northern Ireland *Political division* United Kingdom, 73 E11
Northern Mariana Islands *Dependent territory* Pacific Ocean 144 H7
Northern Sporades *Island group* Greece 93 L7
Northern Territory *Territory* Australia 146 J7
Northwest Territories *Territory* Canada 21 M3 29 N12 30 C8 32 F9 37 K9
Norton Sound *Inlet* Alaska, USA 36 F6
Norway *Country* N Europe 70 I9

Norway 70-71

1905 • a Norwegian • Norwegian krone • 14 • 78 • 15 • 99 • 399 • 303 • No • 73 • 3244

Norwegian Basin *Undersea feature* Atlantic Ocean, 68
Norwegian Sea *Sea* Atlantic Ocean 34 68 71 K5 117 129
Norwich England, United Kingdom 73 M14
Noteć *River* Poland 85 K4
Nottingham England, United Kingdom 73 J14
Nouâdhibou Mauritania 106 F5
Nouâdhibou, Râs *Headland* Mauritania 106 F5
Nouakchott Mauritania 106 F7
Nouméa New Caledonia 144 I10
Nova Gorica Slovenia 83 O12
Nova Gradiška Croatia 88 J4
Nova Kakhovka Ukraine 98 J8
Nova Scotia *Province* Canada 21 Q4 29 Q14 30 H10, 33 N12 39 P12
Nova Scotia *Physical region* Canada, 19 M15 34
Novara Italy 86 D7
Novato California, USA 51 G15
Novaya Zemlya *Island group* Russian Federation 68, 96 M5 117 126 I4
Novgorod Russian Federation 96 F8 126 E5
Novi Pazar Serbia, Yugoslavia 89 N8
Novi Sad Serbia, Yugoslavia 89 M4
Novo Mesto Slovenia 83 R12
Novokuznetsk Russian Federation 126 J11
Novolazarevskaya *Russian research station* Antarctica, 64 E6
Novosibirsk Russian Federation 126 J10
Nsanje Malawi 111 O16
Ntomba, Lake *Lake* Dem. Rep. Congo (Zaire) 109 I13
Nubian Desert *Desert* Sudan 101 105 G10
Nuevo Laredo Mexico 53 N6
Nuevo León *State* Mexico 21 N7
Nuku'alofa Tonga 144 J10
Nukus Uzbekistan 124 I5
Nullarbor Plain *Plain* South Australia/Western Australia, Australia 143 146 H12
Nunap Isua *Headland* Greenland 65 M16
Nunavut *Territory* Canada 21 N3 29 O12 30 E8 32 I9, 37 N7
Nunivak Island *Island* Alaska, USA 36 D6
Nuoro Italy 87 D14
Nuremberg (Ger. Nürnberg) Germany 81 I14
Nuri *Archaeological site* Sudan 105 G11
Nürnberg *see* Nuremberg
Nuuk Greenland 65 M14
Nxai Pan *National Park* Botswana 113 K9
Nyala Sudan 105 C14
Nyalam China 132 G13
Nyasa, Lake *Lake* Malawi/Mozambique/Tanzania/Zambia 101 111 N13 113 O6
Nyeri Kenya 111 P5
Nyika *National Park* Malawi 111 N11
Nyingchi China 132 J13
Nyíregyháza Hungary 85 N12
Nykøbing Denmark 70 I16
Nyköping Sweden 71 L12
Nzérékoré Guinea 106 I12

Oakland – Philippeville

O

Oakland California, USA 30 B12 50 H15
Oakley Kansas, USA 47 M12
Oaxaca Mexico 53 O13
Ob' *River* Russian Federation 68 117 126 129 I7
Ob', Gulf of *Gulf* Arctic Ocean 126 I7
Oban Scotland, United Kingdom 72 G9
Obertshausen Germany 80 D10
Obi, Pulau *Island* Indonesia 141 O12
Obihiro Japan 136 M4
Obo Central African Republic 108 N10
Oceanside California, USA 51 L19
Och'amch'ire Georgia 99 O12
Ocotlán Mexico 53 L11
October Revolution Island *Island* Russian Federation, 127 K4
Ocuilan *Historic site* Mexico 24 C9
Odense Denmark 70 I15
Oder *River* C Europe 68 80 M8 84 H4
Odesa Ukraine 98 I8
Odessa Texas, USA 49 O11
Odienné Ivory Coast 106 I11
Ofanto *River* Italy 87 M13
Offenbach Germany 81 G13
Ogallala Nebraska, USA 28 E10 47 M10
Ogbomosho Nigeria 107 N12
Ogden Utah, USA 48 J2
Ogdensburg New York, USA 41 K6
Ogooué *River* Congo/Gabon 109 E13
Ogre Latvia 94 I6
Ogulin Croatia 88 H4
Ohio *State* USA 21 P5 23 R11 29 P15 30 F12 33 L14 45 O11
Ohio River *River* USA 19 K16 22 F12 23 Q6 23 Q12 28 H10 29 R3 43 O5 45 O13
Ohre *River* Czech Republic/Germany 84 G8
Ohrid FYR Macedonia 89 N12
Ohrid, Lake *Lake* Albania/FYR Macedonia 89 N12
Oil City Pennsylvania, USA 40 G11
Oita Japan 137 D14
Ojos del Salado, Cerro *Mountain* Argentina, 55
Oka *River* Russian Federation 127 L11
Okahandja Namibia 112 H10
Okara Pakistan 130 J3
Okavango *River* Southern Africa, 101
Okavango Delta *Wetland* Botswana 101 112 J9
Okayama Japan 137 F12
Okazaki Japan 137 I12
Okeechobee, Lake *Lake* Florida, USA 34 43 O1
Okefenokee Swamp *Wetland* Georgia, USA 34 43 N10
Okhotsk Russian Federation 127 P7
Okhotsk, Sea of *Sea* Pacific Ocean 34 117 127 Q8, 129 G4 136 M2 144
Oki-shoto *Island group* Japan 137 E11
Okinawa *Island* Japan 137 A20
Okinawa-shoto *Island group* Japan 137 A20
Okinoerabu-jima *Island* Japan 137 A19
Oklahoma *State* USA 21 N6 23 P12 29 O15 30 E13 33 I15 47 N14
Oklahoma City Oklahoma, USA 33 I15 47 O15
Oktyabr'skiy Bol'sheretsk Russian Federation 127 R7
Okushiri-to *Island* Japan 136 J5
Öland *Island* Sweden 71 L14
Olavarría Argentina 63 M11
Olbia Italy 87 E13
Old Crow Yukon Territory, Canada 36 I7
Oldenburg Germany 81 F8
Olean New York, USA 40 I10
Olëkma *River* Russian Federation 127 N9
Olenëk Russian Federation 127 M7
Olenëk *River* Russian Federation 127 M5
Olenëkskiy Zaliv *Bay* Russian Federation 127 M5
Olga, Mount *see* Kata Tjuta
Olgiy Mongolia 132 I4
Ollantaytambo *Archaeological site* Peru 59 G13
Olmaliq Uzbekistan 125 N7
Olomouc Czech Republic 84 J10
Olovyannaya Russian Federation 127 N11
Olsztyn Poland 85 M3
Olt *River* Romania 91 K10
Olten Switzerland 82 F9
Ölüdeniz Turkey 118 H10
Olustee *Battle site* Florida, USA 27 N14
Olympia Greece 92 H10
Olympia Washington, USA 28 A8 29 L1 33 E12 50 H7
Olympic National Park *National Park* Washington, USA 22 C10 50 G6
Olympus, Mount *Mountain* Greece 309
Olyutorskiy, Mys *Headland* Russian Federation 127 R4
Omaha Nebraska, USA 33 I14 47 P10
Oman *Country* SW Asia 123 N14

Oman 123

1951 • Arabic • Omani rial • 12 • 71 • 67.1 • 97 • 1111 • Yes • 13 • 3013

Oman, Gulf of *Gulf* Indian Ocean 114 G5 117 123 P11 129
Omdurman Sudan 105 G12
Omo *River* Ethiopia/Kenya 105 I16
Omsk Russian Federation 126 H10
Ondangwa Namibia 112 H8
Ondava *River* Slovakia 85 N10
Ondorhaan Mongolia 133 N4
Onega *River* Russian Federation 96 I8
Onega, Lake *Lake* Russian Federation 68 96 H8 126 F5
Ongole India 131 L12
Onitsha Nigeria 107 O13
Onon Gol *River* Mongolia 133 N4
Ontario *Province* Canada 21 O4 29 P13 33 J12 38 F9
Ontario, Lake *Lake* Canada/USA 22 G11 23 R10 28 H9 29 R2 33 L13 34 39 L14
Oostende *see* Ostend
Oosterschelde *Inlet* Netherlands 79 D12
Opole Poland 85 K8
Oporto (Port. Porto) Portugal 66 J9
Oradea Romania 90 G3
Oran Algeria 103 K4
Orange New South Wales, Australia 147 N12
Orange Park Florida, USA 30 F13
Orange River *River* Southern Africa 101 112 I13
Oranjestad Aruba 57 N13
Orapa Botswana 113 K10
Ord River *River* Australia 146 I6
Ordos Desert *Desert* China 133 N8
Ordu Turkey 119 O5
Ore Mountains *Mountain range* Czech Republic/Germany 81 K12
Örebro Sweden 71 K12
Oregon *State* USA 21 M5 23 N10 29 N14 30 C11 33 E13 50 G9
Orël Russian Federation 96 E11 126 D6
Orellana, Embalse de *Reservoir* Spain 74 I10
Orem Utah, USA 48 J3
Orenburg Russian Federation 96 K14 126 F9
Oreor Palau 144 G8
Orinoco, Río *River* Colombia/Venezuela 34 55 58 K5
Oristano Italy 87 C14
Orivesi, Lake *Lake* Finland 71 Q9
Orizaba Mexico 53 O12
Orizaba, Volcán Pico de *Mountain* Mexico, 19 I19 34
Orkney Islands *Island group* Scotland, United Kingdom, 68 72 J6
Orlando Florida, USA 33 M16 43 O12
Orléans France 77 K6
Örnsköldsvik Sweden 71 M8
Orontes *River* SW Asia 121 N4
Orsha Belarus 95 N10
Orsk Russian Federation 96 L14
Orumiyeh Iran 123 L2
Oruro Bolivia 59 I15
Osaka Japan 137 G12
Osceola's Capture *Battle site* USA 29 S6
Osh Kyrgyzstan 125 P7
Oshkosh Wisconsin, USA 45 K7
Oshogbo Nigeria 107 N12
Osijek Croatia 89 L3
Oskarshamn Sweden 71 L14
Oslo (prev. Christiania, Kristiania) Norway 70 J11
Oslofjorden *Fjord* Norway 70 I12
Osmaniye Turkey 119 N9
Osnabrück Germany 80 F9
Osorno Chile 63 G14
Oss Netherlands 79 J12
Ossora Russian Federation 127 R5
Ostend (var. Oostende) Belgium 79 C13
Östersund Sweden 71 L8
Ostia Italy 87 H12
Ostrava Czech Republic 85 K9
Ostrołęka Poland 85 N4
Osumi-kaikyo *Strait* Japan 137 C16
Osumi-shoto *Island group* Japan 137 C16
Osumit, Lumi i *River* Albania 89 M13
Oswego New York, USA 40 J8
Otaru Japan 136 K4
Otjiwarongo Namibia 112 H9
Otra *River* Norway 70 H12
Otranto Italy 87 P14
Otranto, Strait of *Strait* Mediterranean Sea 68 89 L13
Ottawa Ontario, Canada 33 M12 39 L13
Ottawa Illinois, USA 45 K11
Ottawa Kansas, USA 47 P12
Ottawa *River* Ontario/Quebec, Canada 39 K12
Ötztaler Alpen *Mountain range* Austria 83 K10
Ou-sanmyaku *Mountain range* Japan 136 K7
Ouachita River *River* Arkansas/Louisiana, USA 42 H5
Ouagadougou Burkina 107 L10
Ouahigouya Burkina 107 L9
Ouargla Algeria 103 L6
Oudtshoorn South Africa 112 J15
Ouémé *River* Benin 107 M11
Ouessant, Île d' *Island* France 76 E6
Ouésso Congo 109 H12
Oujda Morocco 102 J5
Oulu *River* Finland 71 P7
Oulu Finland 71 M6
Oulujärvi *Lake* Finland 71 P7
Ounasjoki *River* Finland 71 O3
Ourense Spain 74 G5
Ouro Preto Brazil 61 L13
Ourthe *River* Belgium 79 J16
Ouse *River* England, United Kingdom 73 L14
Outer Hebrides (var. Western Isles) *Island group* Scotland, United Kingdom 68 72 E7
Ovalle Chile 62 G9
Overflakkee *Island* Netherlands 79 G12
Oviedo Spain 74 I3
Owando Congo 109 H12
Owatonna Minnesota, USA 44 H7
Owen Sound Ontario, Canada 38 J13
Owen Stanley Range *Mountain range* Papua New Guinea 143 147 N3
Owerri Nigeria 107 O13
Owosso Michigan, USA 45 N8
Owyhee Nevada, USA 30 C11
Owyhee Forks *Battle site* USA 29 M2
Owyhee River *River* Idaho/Oregon, USA 50 L10
Oxford England, United Kingdom 73 J15
Oxitipan *Historic site* Mexico 24 D7
Oxnard California, USA 51 J18
Oyem Gabon 109 F12
Ozark Plateau *Plain* Arkansas/Missouri, USA 47 R13
Ozarks, Lake of the *Reservoir* Missouri, USA 47 R12

P

Paamiut Greenland 65 M15
Pa-an Myanmar 139 G11
Pabna Bangladesh 131 O7
Pachuca Mexico 53 N11
Pacific Ocean *Ocean* 19 E14 28 A8 29 K1 29 M12 144-145
Pacific Plate *Tectonic plate* 19 E13 34 55 129 143
Pacific-Antarctic Ridge *Undersea feature* Pacific Ocean 144 J14 143
Padang Indonesia 140 D12
Paderborn Germany 80 G10
Padova *see* Padua
Padua (It. Padova) Italy 86 H7
Paducah Kentucky, USA 43 K3
Páfos Cyprus 119 K12
Pag *Island* Croatia 88 G5
Pagai Selatan, Pulau *Island* Indonesia 140 D13
Pagai Utara, Pulau *Island* Indonesia 140 D13
Pagan *Archaeological site* Myanmar 138 F8
Pahang, Sungai *River* Malaysia 139 J18
Paide Estonia 94 J2
Painted Desert *Desert* Arizona, USA 48 J6
Pakistan *Country* S Asia 130 F4

Pakistan 130

1947 • Urdu • Pakistani rupee • 198 • 64 • 40.9 • 5 • 1915 • Yes • 35 • 2315

Pakokku Myanmar 138 F8
Pakwach Uganda 111 M3
Pakxan Laos 138 L10
Pakxe Laos 139 M12
Palau *Country* Pacific Ocean 144 G8

Palau 144

1994 • Palauan and English • United States dollar • 36 • 71 • 14 • 92 • 83 • No • 29 •

Palawan *Island* Philippines 141 K6
Paldiski Estonia 94 I1
Palembang Indonesia 140 F13
Palencia Spain 74 J5
Palenque *Ruins* Mexico 24 F10 53 R13
Palermo Italy 87 J17
Palikir Micronesia 144 H8
Palk Strait *Strait* India/Sri Lanka, 129
Palm Springs California, USA 51 M19
Palma de Mallorca Spain 75 R9
Palmas do Tocantins Brazil 60 K10
Palmer Alaska, USA 36 G8
Palmer Land *Physical region* Antarctica 64 C8
Palmerston North New Zealand 148 H7
Palmira Colombia 58 D7
Palmyra Atoll *Dependent territory* Pacific Ocean 145 K8
Palo Duro Canyon *Battle site* USA 29 N5
Palu Indonesia 141 L12
Pamir *River* Afghanistan/Tajikistan 125 P10
Pamirs *Mountain range* C Asia 117 125 O10 129
Pampa Texas, USA 49 O8
Pampas *Plain* Argentina 55 63 J12
Pamplona Spain 75 M4
Pamukkale Turkey 118 H8
Pan-American Highway *Road* Chile 62 G8
Panaji India 130 I11
Panama *Country* C America 56 F15

Panama 56

1903 • Spanish • Balboa • 37 • 74 • 15 • 91.1 • 76 • 556 • No • 53 • 2242

Panama Canal *Canal* Panama 56 G14
Panama City Panama 56 G15 67 D11 145 Q7
Panama City Florida, USA 43 L10
Panama, Gulf of *Gulf* Panama 55 56 G15
Panama, Isthmus of *Isthmus* Panama, 55
Panay Island *Island* Philippines 141 M5
Pančevo Serbia, Yugoslavia 89 N5
Panevėžys Lithuania 94 I8
Pangani Tanzania 111 Q8
Pangani *River* Tanzania 111 P7
Pangkalpinang Indonesia 140 G12
Pangnirtung Nunavut, Canada 37 R6 65 M13
Panj *River* Afghanistan/Tajikistan 125 N10
Pantanal *Swamp* Brazil 61 G12
Pantelleria Italy 87 H19
Pánuco, Río *River* Mexico 24 D7 53 N10
Panzhihua China 134 I12
Papaloapan, Río *River* Mexico 24 E9
Papeete French Polynesia 145 L10
Papua New Guinea *Country* Pacific Ocean 147 O2

Papua New Guinea 147

1975 • English • Kina • 10 • 58 • 73.7 • 7 • 10000 • No • 16 • 2613

Papua, Gulf of *Gulf* Papua New Guinea 147 N3
Paraguarí Paraguay 62 N6
Paraguay *Country* C South America 62 K5

Paraguay 62

1811 • Spanish • Guaraní • 14 • 70 • 12 • 92.4 • 14 • 3333 • No • 53 • 2670

Paraguay *River* C South America 55 61 G13 62 M5
Parakou Benin 107 N11
Paramaribo Suriname 58 O6
Paramushir, Ostrov *Island* Russian Federation 127 S8
Paraná Argentina 62 L9
Paraná *River* South America 55 61 H14 62 N7
Paranaíba, Rio *River* Brazil 60 K9
Pardubice Czech Republic 84 I9
Parecis, Chapada dos *Mountain range* Brazil 60 E10
Parepare Indonesia 141 L13
Paris France 77 L5
Parker Dam *Dam* USA 48 H8
Parma Italy 86 F8
Parnaíba Brazil 60 M8
Parnaíba, Rio *River* Brazil, 55
Pärnu Estonia 94 I3
Pärnu *River* Estonia 94 J3
Paros *Island* Greece 93 M12
Parry Islands *Island group* Nunavut, Canada 37 M4
Pasadena California, USA 51 L18
Pasadena Texas, USA 49 S13
Pasargadae *Site of ancient city* Iran 123 N7
Pasley, Cape *Headland* Australia 146 H13
Passau Germany 81 M15
Passo Fundo Brazil 61 H15
Pasto Colombia 58 D8
Patagonia *Semi arid region* Argentina/Chile 55 63 J18
Paterson New Jersey, USA 41 L12
Pathfinder Reservoir *Reservoir* Wyoming, USA 46 J9
Patna India 131 N7
Patos, Lagoa dos *Lagoon* Brazil 61 I16
Patra Greece 92 H9
Patra, Gulf of *Gulf* Greece 92 G9
Pattani Thailand 139 J17
Pattaya Thailand 139 J13
Patuca, Río *River* Honduras 56 E9
Pátzcuaro, Lago de *Lake* Mexico 53 L12
Pau France 76 J14
Pavlodar Kazakhstan 126 I11
Pays d'en Haut *Region* Canada 26 D10
Paysandú Uruguay 62 N9
Pazardzhik Bulgaria 90 J14
Pearl Harbor *Inlet* Hawaii, USA 145 K7
Pearl River *River* Louisiana/Mississippi, USA 42 J8
Peć Serbia, Yugoslavia 89 M9
Pechora *River* Russian Federation 68 96 L8 126 H6
Pecos Texas, USA 49 N11
Pecos River *River* New Mexico/Texas, USA 24 D15 49 M9
Pécs Hungary 85 K15
Pedro Juan Caballero Paraguay 62 N4
Pegasus Bay *Bay* New Zealand 148 F9
Pegu Myanmar 138 F10
Peipus, Lake *Lake* Estonia/Russian Federation 95 L2
Pekanbaru Indonesia 140 E11
Peking *see* Beijing
Pelagie, Isole *Island group* Italy 87 I20
Pelée, Montagne *Mountain* Martinique, 55
Pelješac *Peninsula* Croatia 88 J8
Peloponnese *Region* Greece 92 H9
Pelotas Brazil 61 I16
Pematangsiantar Indonesia 140 D10
Pemba Mozambique 113 Q6
Pemba *Island* Tanzania 111 Q8
Pendleton Oregon, USA 50 K8
Pennine Alps *Mountain range* Italy/Switzerland 82 E13
Pennines *Mountain range* England, United Kingdom 68, 73 I11
Pennsylvania *State* USA 21 P5 23 R11 29 P14 30 G11 33 L13 40 H12
Penobscot River *River* Maine, USA 41 Q5
Penonomé Panama 56 G15
Pensacola Florida, USA 27 M14 29 Q6 43 K9
Penticton British Columbia, Canada 37 K15
Penza Russian Federation 96 H12 126 E7
Penzance England, United Kingdom 73 E17
Peoria Illinois, USA 45 K11
Pereira Colombia 58 E6
Pergamon *Archaeological site* Turkey 118 G7
Perge *Archaeological site* Turkey 118 J9
Périgueux France 77 K11
Perito Moreno Argentina 63 I16
Perm' Russian Federation 96 L11 126 G8
Pernik Bulgaria 90 I13
Perpignan France 77 M15
Perryville *Battle site* Kentucky, USA 27 N11
Persepolis *Site of ancient city* Iran 123 N7
Persian Gulf *Gulf* Indian Ocean 68 101 114 F5 117 123 M8 129
Perth Western Australia, Australia 146 F12
Perth Scotland, United Kingdom 72 I9
Perth Basin *Undersea feature* Indian Ocean 143
Peru *Country* South America 59 E11

Peru 58-59

1824 • Spanish and Quechua • Nuevo sol (new sol) • 20 • 68 • 12 • 88.7 • 59 • 1000 • No • 72 •

Peru Basin *Undersea feature* Pacific Ocean 55
Peru-Chile Trench *Undersea feature* Pacific Ocean 55, 145 Q9
Perućko Jezero *Lake* Croatia 88 I6
Perugia Italy 86 H10
Pesaro Italy 86 I9
Pescara Italy 87 K11
Peshawar Pakistan 130 I2
Petah Tiqwa Israel 121 L9
Petaluma California, USA 51 G15
Peter I Island *Dependent territory* Antarctica 64 B9
Peterborough Ontario, Canada 39 K14
Peterborough England, United Kingdom 73 K14
Peterhead Scotland, United Kingdom 72 J8
Petersburg Alaska, USA 36 I11
Petersburg *Battle site* Virginia, USA 27 R5 27 O11
Petra *Archaeological site* Jordan 121 M12
Petroglyph Canyons *Ancient site* USA 24 A13
Petropavlovsk Kazakhstan 127 H9
Petropavlovsk-Kamchatskiy Russian Federation 127 S7
Petrozavodsk Russian Federation 96 G8 126 F5
Pevek Russian Federation 65 Q5 127 P3
Pforzheim Germany 81 F14
Phangan, Ko *Island* Thailand 139 I15
Phetchabun Thailand 139 J11
Phetchaburi Thailand 139 I13
Philadelphia Pennsylvania, USA 26 E11 27 O10 27 S4 28 I10 29 S3 33 M13 41 K14
Philae *Archaeological site* Egypt 104 G9
Philippeville Belgium 79 H17

Date of independence • Language (official or most commonly spoken) • Currency • Population density per square kilometre • Average life expectancy • School-leaving age • Literacy • Number of cars per 1,000 people • Number of people per doctor • Death penalty • Percentage of urban-based population • Average number of calories consumed daily per person

Philippine Basin – Rhaetian Alps

Philippine Basin *Undersea feature* Pacific Ocean 129 143
Philippine Plate *Tectonic plate* 129 143
Philippine Sea *Sea* Pacific Ocean 129 141 M3 143
Philippine Trench *Undersea feature* Pacific Ocean129 143
Philippines *Country* SE Asia 141 K7

Philippines 141

1946 • English and Filipino • Philippine peso • 250 • 68 • 12 • 94.6 • 10 • 10000 • Yes • 54 • 2257

Philippines *Island group* SE Asia 129 143
Phitsanulok Thailand 139 I11
Phnom Penh Cambodia 139 L14
Phoenix Arizona, USA 20 D11 23 O7 28 28 29 M5, 33 F15 48 I9
Phoenix Islands *Island group* Kiribati 144 J8 143
Phofung *Mountain* Lesotho, 101
Phôngsali Laos 138 K8
Phuket Thailand 139 G16
Phuket, Ko *Island* Thailand 139 G16
Phumĭ Sâmraông Cambodia 139 K12
Piacenza Italy 86 E7
Piţra-Neamt Romania 91 M3
Piave *River* Italy 86 H6
Pichilemu Chile 63 G11
Picos Brazil 60 M9
Picton New Zealand 148 G7
Piedras Negras Mexico 53 M5
Piedras Negras *Historic site* Mexico 24 F10
Pielinen *Lake* Finland 71 P8
Pierre South Dakota, USA 28 E9 33 I13 47 N7
Pietermaritzburg South Africa 113 M14
Pietersburg South Africa 113 M11
Pilar Paraguay 62 M6
Pilcomayo *River* C South America 62 M5
Pinar del Río Cuba 56 G3
Pinatubo, Mount *Volcano* Philippines, 129
Pindus Mountains *Mountain range* Greece 68 92 G5
Pine Bluff Arkansas, USA 42 I5
Pine Ridge South Dakota, USA 30 D11
Pinega *River* Russian Federation 96 J8
Pineios *River* Greece 92 I5
Pingxiang China 134 J14
Pingxiang China 134 M12
Pini, Pulau *Island* Indonesia 140 D11
Pinsk Belarus 94 J15
Pioneer Fracture Zone *Undersea feature* Pacific Ocean 34
Piotrków Trybunalski Poland 85 L7
Piqua Ohio, USA 45 O12
Piraeus Greece 93 K9
Pisa Italy 86 F9
Pisac Peru 59 G13
Pistoia Italy 86 F9
Pit River *Battle site* USA 29 L3
Pita Guinea 84 J4
Pitcairn Islands *Dependent territory* Pacific Ocean 145 N10
Piteå Sweden 71 N6
Piteälven *River* Sweden 71 M5
Pitești Romania 91 K8
Pittsburg Kansas, USA 47 Q13
Pittsburgh Pennsylvania, USA 33 L14 40 G13
Pittsfield Massachusetts, USA 41 M10
Piura Peru 58 B10
Pivdennyy Buh *River* Ukraine 98 I6
Placentia Bay *Inlet* Newfoundland, Canada 39 S10
Plainview Texas, USA 49 O9
Plata, Río de la *Estuary* Argentina/Uruguay, 55
Plate *River* Argentina/Uruguay 63 N10
Plate Bridge *Battle site* USA 29 N3
Platte River *River* Nebraska, USA 23 P6 34 47 N10
Plattsburgh New York, USA 41 M6
Plauen Germany 81 K12
Plenty, Bay of *Bay* New Zealand 148 I4
Pleven Bulgaria 91 K11
Plock Poland 85 L5
Ploiești Romania 91 L8
Płońsk Poland 85 M5
Plovdiv Bulgaria 91 K14
Plungė Lithuania 94 G7
Plymouth Montserrat 57 S11
Plymouth England, United Kingdom 73 G17
Plzeň Czech Republic 84 G9
Po *River* Italy 68 86 C7
Pobedy, Pik *Mountain* China/Kyrgyzstan 117 129
Pocatello Idaho, USA 46 H9
Podgorica Montenegro, Yugoslavia 89 L9
Podlasie Poland 85 O5
Poinsett, Cape *Cape* Antarctica 64 G10
Pointe-à-Pitre Guadeloupe 57 T12
Pointe-Noire Congo 109 F14
Points of Pines *Ancient site* Mexico 24 C14
Poitiers France 76 J9
Pol-e Khomri Afghanistan 125 N11
Poland *Country* C Europe 84 J5

Poland 84-85

1918 • Polish • Zloty • 127 • 73 • 15 • 99 • 221 • 435 • No • 65 • 3301

Polatsk Belarus 95 M8
Pólis Cyprus 119 K12
Poltava Ukraine 99 K5
Polygyros Greece 93 K4
Polynesia *Island group* Pacific Ocean 144 J12
Pomerania *Cultural region* Germany/Poland 84 H3
Pomeranian Bay *Bay* Baltic Sea 84 H2
Pompei Italy 87 K13
Ponca City Oklahoma, USA 47 P14
Ponce Puerto Rico 57 Q9
Pondicherry India 131 K14
Pontchartrain, Lake *Lake* Louisiana, USA 42 I5
Pontevedra Spain 74 F4
Pontiac Michigan, USA 45 O9
Pontianak Indonesia 140 H11
Ponziane *Island* Italy 87 I13
Poopó, Lago *Lake* Bolivia 59 I15
Popayán Colombia 58 D7
Poplar Bluff Missouri, USA 47 S13
Popocatépetl *Volcano* Mexico 34 53 N12
Popondetta Papua New Guinea 147 O3
Poprad Slovakia 85 M10
Porbandar India 130 H8
Porcupine River *River* Canada/USA 36 H6
Pori Finland 71 N10
Poronaysk Russian Federation 127 R10
Porpoise Bay *Bay* Antarctica 64 G11
Porsangen *Fjord* Norway 71 O1
Porsgrunn Norway 70 I12
Port Angeles Washington, USA 50 G6
Port Antonio Jamaica 57 K8
Port Arthur Texas, USA 49 T13
Port Augusta South Australia, Australia 147 L12
Port-au-Prince Haiti 57 M8
Port-de-Paix Haiti 57 M7
Port Dickson Malaysia 139 J19
Port Elizabeth South Africa 113 K16
Port-Gentil Gabon 109 E13
Port Harcourt Nigeria 107 O13
Port Hardy British Columbia, Canada 36 I14
Port Hedland Western Australia, Australia 146 G8
Port Hope Simpson Newfoundland, Canada 39 R7
Port Hudson *Fort* Louisiana, USA 27 L14
Port Huron Michigan, USA 45 P8
Port Lincoln South Australia, Australia 147 K13
Port Louis Mauritius 115 F11
Port Moresby Papua New Guinea 147 N3
Port Nolloth South Africa 67 M14
Port-of-Spain Trinidad and Tobago 57 S16
Port Said Egypt 66 N9 104 G6 114 D4
Port Sudan Sudan 105 I11
Port-Vila Vanuatu 144 I10
Portalegre Portugal 74 G10
Portales New Mexico, USA 49 N9
Portimão Portugal 74 F13
Portland Maine, USA 41 O8 66 E8
Portland Oregon, USA 30 C11 33 E12 50 H8
Portland *International airport* Oregon, USA 28 A8
Porto *see* Oporto
Porto Alegre Brazil 61 I16
Porto Velho Brazil 60 E9
Porto-Novo Benin 107 M13
Portoviejo Ecuador 58 B9
Portsmouth England, United Kingdom 73 J17
Portsmouth New Hampshire, USA 41 O9
Portsmouth Ohio, USA 45 P13
Portugal *Country* SW Europe 74 G12

Portugal 74

1640 • Portuguese • Portuguese escudo • 108 • 75 • 15 • 90.8 • 288 • 345 • No • 36 • 3634

Porvenir Chile 63 J19
Posadas Argentina 62 O7
Postojna Slovenia 83 P12
Potenza Italy 87 M13
Potenza *River* Italy 86 I10
P'ot'i Georgia 99 O12
Potosí Bolivia 59 I16
Potsdam Germany 80 L9
Poughkeepsie New York, USA 41 L11
Poŭthĭsăt Cambodia 139 L13
Powder River *Battle site* USA 29 N2
Powder River *River* Montana/Wyoming, USA 47 K7
Powell, Lake *Lake* Utah, USA 48 J5
Poyang Hu *Lake* China 129 135 M11
Poza Rica Mexico 53 O11
Požarevac Serbia, Yugoslavia 89 N5
Poznań Poland 84 J5
Pozo Colorado Paraguay 62 M5
Prachin Buri Thailand 139 J12
Prachuap Khiri Khan Thailand 139 I14
Prague Czech Republic 84 H9
Praia Cape Verde 66 I10
Prato Italy 86 G9
Pratt Kansas, USA 47 O13
Pravets Bulgaria 90 J12
Presov Slovakia 85 N11
Prescott Arizona, USA 48 I8
Prespa, Limni *Lake* SE Europe 89 N12 92 G
Presque Isle Maine, USA 41 Q3
Preston England, United Kingdom 73 I13
Pretoria South Africa 112 L12
Preveza Greece 92 G7
Priboj Serbia, Yugoslavia 89 M7
Priene *Archaeological site* Turkey 118 G8
Prijedor Bosnia and Herzegovina 88 I4
Prilep FYR Macedonia 89 O12
Prince Albert Saskatchewan, Canada 37 N14
Prince Albert National Park *National park* Canada 22 E10
Prince Charles Island *Island* Northwest Territories, Canada 37 Q6
Prince Edward Island *Province* Canada 21 Q4 39 Q11
Prince Edward Island *Island* Canada 33 N12
Prince Edward Island National Park *National park* Prince Edward Island, Canada 22 G10
Prince Edward Islands *Island group* South Africa 115 E14
Prince George British Columbia, Canada 36 J13
Prince of Wales Island *Island* Queensland, Australia, 147 L4
Prince of Wales Island *Island* Nunavut, Canada 37 M6
Prince Patrick Island *Island* Northwest Territories/Nunavut, Canada 37 L4 65 O9
Prince Rupert British Columbia, Canada 36 I12 145 M3
Prince William Sound *Inlet* Alaska, USA 23 N4
Princess Charlotte Bay *Bay* Queensland, Australia 147 N5
Princeton New Jersey, USA 27 S3 41 L13
Príncipe *Island* Sao Tome and Principe 67 L12 101, 109 D12
Pripet *River* Belarus/Ukraine 95 L14
Priština Serbia, Yugoslavia 89 N9
Prizren Serbia, Yugoslavia 89 N10
Progreso Mexico 53 S10
Prome Myanmar 138 F9
Prosna *River* Poland 85 K6
Provence *Cultural region* France 77 O13
Providence Rhode Island, USA 27 S3 28 I9 33 N13, 41 O11
Provideniya Russian Federation 127 R2
Provo Utah, USA 48 J3
Prudhoe Bay Alaska, USA 36 I5
Prudhoe Bay *Bay* Alaska, USA 65 O6
Prut *River* SE Europe 91 O5
Pruzhany Belarus 94 I13
Prydz Bay *Bay* Antarctica 64 G8
Pskov Russian Federation 96 E8 126 E4
Ptsich *River* Belarus 95 M13
Ptuj Slovenia 83 S10
Pucallpa Peru 59 E12
Puebla Mexico 33 I18 53 N12
Pueblo Colorado, USA 49 N5
Pueblo Grande *Ancient site* Mexico 24 B14
Puerto Aisén Chile 63 H16
Puerto Ayacucho Venezuela 58 I6
Puerto Barrios Guatemala 56 C8
Puerto Cabello Venezuela 58 H4
Puerto Cabezas Nicaragua 56 F10
Puerto Carreño Colombia 58 I6
Puerto Cortés Honduras 56 C8
Puerto Deseado Argentina 63 K17
Puerto Inírida Colombia 58 H7
Puerto Madryn Argentina 63 K14
Puerto Montt Chile 63 H14
Puerto Natales Chile 63 I19
Puerto Plata Dominican Republic 57 N7
Puerto Princesa Philippines 141 K6
Puerto Rico *Dependent territory* W Indies 57 Q10
Puerto Rico Trench *Undersea feature* Atlantic Ocean 55
Puerto Santa Cruz Argentina 63 J18
Puerto Vallarta Mexico 53 K11
Pukaskwa National Park *National park* Canada 22 F10
Pula Croatia 88 F4
Punakha Bhutan 131 P5
Pune India 130 I10
Puno Peru 59 G14
Punta Arenas Chile 63 J19
Puntarenas Costa Rica 56 D13
Pur *River* Russian Federation 126 J7
Purgatoire River *River* Colorado, USA 49 N6
Purmerend Netherlands 78 I9
Purus, Rio *River* Brazil/Peru 55 60 D9
Pusan South Korea 135 Q8 144 F5
Pusilha *Historic site* Mexico 24 H11
Putorana Mountains *Mountain range* Russian Federation 127 K6
Putumayo, Río *River* South America 55 58 F9
Puyo South Korea 135 P8
Pyaozero, Ozero *Lake* Russian Federation 96 H6 126 G4
Pyapon Myanmar 139 F11
Pyasina *River* Russian Federation 127 K6
Pyinmana Myanmar 138 F9
Pylos Greece 92 H12
Pyongyang North Korea 135 P7
Pyramid Lake *Battle site* Nevada, USA 29 L3
Pyramid Lake *Lake* Nevada, USA 48 F2
Pyrenees *Mountain range* SW Europe 68 75 M4 76 I14
Pyrgos Greece 92 H10

Q

Qaanaaq Greenland 65 O11
Qaidam Pendi *Basin* China, 129
Qamdo China 133 K12
Qaqortoq Greenland 65 M15
Qarshi Uzbekistan 125 L8
Qatar *Country* Qatar 123 M10

Qatar 123

1971 • Arabic • Qatar riyal • 54 • 72 • 80 • 190 • 699 • No • 92 •

Qattara Depression *Desert* Egypt, 101 104 E6
Qazvin Iran 123 N3
Qena Egypt 104 G8
Qeqertarsuaq Greenland 65 N13
Qeshm Island *Island* Iran 123 O10
Qilian Shan *Mountain range* China, 129
Qin Ling *Mountain range* China 129 135 K9
Qingdao China 135 N8 144 E6
Qinghai *Province* China 133 K9
Qinghai Hu *Lake* China 129 133 L9
Qinhuangdao China 135 N6
Qiqihar China 135 O3
Qom Iran 123 N4
Quang Ngai Vietnam 139 O12
Quba Azerbaijan 99 S12
Québec (var. Quebec) Quebec, Canada 26 F9 27 S1, 30 G10 33 M12 39 M12
Quebec *Province* Canada 21 P4 30 F9 29 P13 33 L11, 39 L10
Queen Charlotte Islands *Island group* British Columbia, Canada 33 D11 36 H12
Queen Charlotte Sound *Sound* Pacific Ocean 36 H13
Queen Elizabeth Islands *Island group* Northwest Territories/Nunavut, Canada 37 L3 65 N10
Queensland *State* Australia 147 L9
Queenstown New Zealand 148 D11
Quelimane Mozambique 113 O8
Querétaro Mexico 33 I17 53 M11
Quetta Pakistan 130 G3
Quetzaltepec *Historic site* Mexico 24 E10
Quezaltenango Guatemala 56 A8
Quiauhteopan *Historic site* Mexico 24 D9
Quibdó Colombia 58 D6
Quicama *National Park* Angola 112 G5
Quillota Chile 62 G10
Quimper France 76 F6
Quincy Illinois, USA 44 I12
Quintana Roo *State* Mexico 21 P8
Quirigua *Historic site* Mexico 24 H11
Quito Ecuador 58 C8
Quqon Uzbekistan 125 O7
Qurghonteppa Tajikistan 125 N9
Quy Nhơn Vietnam 139 O13

R

Raba Indonesia 141 L15
Rába *River* Austria/Hungary 84 J14
Rabat Morocco 102 I5
Rabaul Papua New Guinea 147 P2
Race, Cape *Cape* Newfoundland, Canada 34 39 T10
Rach Gia Vietnam 139 L15
Racine Wisconsin, USA 45 L9
Radom Poland 85 N7
Radstadt Austria 83 O8
Rafah Gaza Strip 121 L11
Ragusa Italy 87 L19
Rahimyar Khan Pakistan 130 H5
Rainier, Mount *Volcano* Washington, USA 34 50 I7
Rainier, Mount *Volcano* Washington, USA 19 F15
Raipur India 131 L9
Rajahmundry India 131 L11
Rajang, Batang *River* Borneo, Malaysia 140 I10
Rajkot India 130 H8
Rajshahi Bangladesh 131 O7
Rakaia *River* New Zealand 148 E10
Rakvere Estonia 95 K1
Raleigh North Carolina, USA 43 Q5
Raleigh North Carolina, USA 28 H11 33 M14
Ramla Israel 121 L10
Râmnicu Vâlcea Romania 90 J7
Ramree Island *Island* Myanmar 138 E9
Ranau Borneo, Malaysia 141 K8
Rancagua Chile 63 H11
Ranchi India 131 N8
Randers Denmark 70 I14
Rangoon Myanmar 114 K6 138 F10
Rangoon Myanmar,
Rangpur Bangladesh 131 O6
Rankin Inlet Northwest Territories, Canada 37 O9
Rantoul Illinois, USA 45 L12
Rapid City South Dakota, USA 47 L8
Ras al Khaymah United Arab Emirates 123 O10
Râs Ghârib Egypt 104 G7
Rasht Iran 123 N3
Ratchaburi Thailand 139 I13
Rathburn Lake *Lake* Iowa, USA 47 Q10
Ratisbon *see* Regensburg
Rauma Finland 71 N10
Raurkela India 131 N8
Ravenna Italy 86 H8
Rawalpindi Pakistan 130 J2
Rawlins Wyoming, USA 46 J10
Rawson Argentina 63 K14
Rayong Thailand 139 J13
Raysut Oman 123 M15
Razgrad Bulgaria 91 M11
Razim, Lacul *Lagoon* Romania 91 P8
Reading England, United Kingdom 73 J16
Reading Pennsylvania, USA 41 K13
Rebun-to *Island* Japan 136 K2
Rechytsa Belarus 95 N14
Recife Brazil 60 P9 67 H12
Recklinghausen Germany 80 E10
Red Bluff Lake *Lake* USA 49 M11
Red Deer Alberta, Canada 37 K14
Red Lake River *River* Minnesota, USA 44 F3
Red River *River* China/Vietnam 138 L7
Red River *River* USA 34 47 O16 49 R9
Red River *River* Louisiana, USA 42 G6
Red River *Cession* 29 O14
Red River *River* Arkansas/Louisiana/Oklahoma/Texas, USA 23 P7 28 E12 29 P5
Red Sea *Sea* Indian Ocean 101 104 H8 114 D5 117 122 G10 129
Red Volta *River* Burkina/Ghana 107 L10
Red Wing Minnesota, USA 44 I7
Redding California, USA 51 H13
Redstone Fort USA 27 Q4
Redwood National Park *National park* USA 22 C11
Ree, Lough *Lake* Republic of Ireland 73 D12
Rega *River* Poland 84 I3
Regensburg (Eng. Ratisbon) Germany 81 K14
Reggio di Calabria Italy 87 M17
Reggio nell' Emilia Italy 86 F8
Regina Saskatchewan, Canada 37 N15
Regina Saskatchewan, Canada 33 H12
Rehoboth Namibia 112 H11
Reims (Eng. Rheims) France 77 M4
Reindeer Lake *Lake* Manitoba/Saskatchewan, Canada 34 37 M12
Reindeer Lake *Lake* Manitoba/Saskatchewan, Canada 19 H14
Remscheid Germany 81 E11
Rend Lake *Reservoir* Illinois, USA 45 K15
Reni Ukraine 98 H9
Rennes France 76 H6
Reno *River* Italy 86 G8
Reno Nevada, USA 48 E3
Reno Nevada, USA 33 E14
Republican River *River* Kansas/Nebraska, USA 47 N11
Resistencia Argentina 62 M7
Reșița Romania 90 G7
Resolute Northwest Territories/Nunavut, Canada 37 N5 65 N10
Resolute Northwest Territories/Nunavut, Canada 20 E7
Rethymno Greece 93 L16
Réunion *Dependent territory* Indian Ocean 115 F11
Reus Spain 75 P7
Revillagigedo Islands *Island group* Mexico 145 N7
Rey, Isla del *Island* Panama 56 H15
Reykjavík Iceland 66 I7
Reynosa Mexico 53 N7
Rhaetian Alps *Mountain range* Austria/Itlay/Switzerland 82 I12

Rheims *see* Reims
Rhein *see* Rhine
Rheinfels *Castle* Germany 81 E12
Rhine (var. Rhein) *River* W Europe 68 77 Q4 79 L11 81 E15 82 H10
Rhode Island *State* USA 21 P5 23 S11 29 Q14 30 G11 33 N13 41 N11
Rhodes *see* Rodos
Rhodope Mountains *Mountain range* Bulgaria/Greece 68 90 I14
Rhône *River* France/Switzerland 68 77 N12 82 E12
Rhum *Island* Scotland, United Kingdom 72 F8
Ribe Denmark 70 H15
Ribeirão Preto Brazil 61 J13
Riccione Italy 86 I9
Richland Washington, USA 50 K8
Richmond Indiana, USA 45 N12
Richmond Virginia, USA 26 E11 27 O11 27 R5 28 H10 29 S4 33 M14
Ricobayo, Embalse de *Reservoir* Spain 74 I6
Riding Mountain National Park *National park* Canada 22 E10
Riesa Germany 81 L11
Riffe Lake *Lake* Washington, USA 50 H7
Riga Latvia 94 I6
Riga, Gulf of *Gulf* Estonia/Latvia 94 I4
Riihimäki Finland 71 O11
Riiser-Larsen Ice Shelf *Ice shelf* Antarctica 64 D6
Rijeka Croatia 88 G4
Rila *Mountain range* Bulgaria 90 I14
Rimini Italy 86 H8
Ringkøbing Denmark 70 H14
Ringvassøy *Island* Norway 71 M2
Rio Bec *Historic site* Mexico 24 H9
Rio Branco Brazil 60 B10
Rio Bravo National Park *National park* Mexico 22 E13
Río Cuarto Argentina 62 K10
Rio de Janeiro Brazil 61 L14 66 G13
Río Gallegos Argentina 63 J19
Río Grande Argentina 63 K19
Rio Grande Brazil 61 I17
Rio Grande *River* Texas, USA 34 49 M6
Rio Grande *River* Texas, USA 28 E13 29 O6 33 I16
Rio Grande Rise *Undersea feature* Atlantic Ocean 55
Riobamba Ecuador 58 C9
Riohacha Colombia 58 F4
Rishiri-to *Island* Japan 136 K2
Rivas Nicaragua 56 D11
Rivera Uruguay 62 O8
Riverside California, USA 51 L18
Rivne Ukraine 98 G4
Riyadh Saudi Arabia 123 K10
Rize Turkey 119 Q5
Rizhao China 135 N8
Rkîz, Lac *Lake* Mauritania 106 G7
Road Town British Virgin Islands 57 R9
Roanoke Virginia, USA 43 Q4
Roanoke River *River* North Carolina/Virginia, USA 23 Q6 43 R5
Robertsport Liberia 106 H12
Rocha Uruguay 62 P10
Rochester Minnesota, USA 44 I8
Rochester New Hampshire, USA 41 O8
Rochester New York, USA 40 I9
Rock Island Illinois, USA 44 J11
Rock Springs Wyoming, USA 46 I10
Rockall *Island* United Kingdom 66 J7
Rockford Illinois, USA 45 K10
Rockhampton Queensland, Australia 147 P9
Rockies *see* Rocky Mountains
Rockingham Western Australia, Australia 146 F13
Rockwood Maine, USA 41 P5
Rocky Mountains *Mountain range* Canada/USA 19 F12 22 D9 23 O10 28 C8 29 M1 33 E10 34 36 I10 46 G4 49 L3
Rodez France 77 L12
Rodos (Eng. Rhodes) Greece 93 R13
Rodos (Eng. Rhodes) *Island* Greece 93 R14
Roermond Netherlands 79 L14
Roeselare Belgium 79 D14
Roggeveen Basin *Undersea feature* Pacific Ocean 55
Rogue River *Battle site* USA 29 L2
Roma Queensland, Australia 147 N10
Roma *see* Rome
Romania *Country* SE Asia 90 H5

Romania 90-91

⚑ 1878 • a Romanian • 🪙 Leu • 👤 97 • ♥ 70 • 🎓 15 • 📖 97.8 • 🚗 107 • ✚ 556 • ☠ No • 🏠 55 • 🍴 3051

Romanovka Russian Federation 127 M11
Rome (It. Roma) Italy 87 H12
Rome Georgia, USA 43 M6
Rome New York, USA 41 K9
Roncador, Serra do *Mountain range* Brazil 61 I11
Rønne Denmark 71 K16
Ronne Ice Shelf *Ice shelf* Antarctica 64 C8
Ronse Belgium 79 E15
Roosendaal Netherlands 79 H12
Roraima, Mount *Mountain* South America 55
Røros Norway 70 J8
Rosario Argentina 62 L9
Roseau Dominica 57 T12
Roseburg Oregon, USA 50 G10
Rosenheim Germany 81 K16
Roses Spain 75 R5
Ross Ice Shelf *Ice shelf* Antarctica 64 D10
Ross Lake *Lake* Washington, USA 50 I5
Ross Sea *Sea* Antarctica 64 D11 143
Rossel Island *Island* Papua New Guinea 147 Q4
Rössing Namibia 112 H10
Rosso Mauritania 106 F7
Rostock Germany 80 K6
Rostov-na-Donu (Eng. Rostov-on-Don) Russian Federation 96 D14 126 D8
Rostov-on-Don *see* Rostov-na-Donu
Roswell New Mexico, USA 49 M9
Roti, Pulau *Island* Indonesia 141 M16
Rotorua New Zealand 148 I5
Rotterdam Netherlands 66 K8 79 H11
Rouen France 77 K4
Rovaniemi Finland 71 O5
Rovuma *River* Mozambique 113 O5
Roxas City Philippines 141 M5
Royale, Isle *Island* Michigan, USA 45 K3
Ruaha *National Park* Tanzania 111 N9
Ruapehu, Mount *Volcano* New Zealand, 143
Rudolf, Lake *Lake* Kenya 101 105 I17 110 O2
Rufiji *River* Tanzania 111 P10
Rügen *Cape* Germany 80 L6
Ruhr *River* Germany 81 F11
Rukwa, Lake *Lake* Tanzania 101 111 M10
Rum Cay *Island* Bahamas 57 L4
Rum, Wadi *Seasonal watercourse* Jordan 121 M13
Rumbek Sudan 105 F16
Rumford Maine, USA 41 O6
Rundu Namibia 112 I8
Rupert House Canada 26 E9
Rupert's Land *Region* Canada 26 D8
Rupert, Rivière de *River* Quebec, Canada 39 K9
Ruse Bulgaria 91 L10
Rush Creek *Battle site* USA 29 N3
Rushmore, Mount *Mountain* South Dakota, USA 47 L8
Russian Federation *Country* Asia/Europe 94 96-97 126-127

Russian Federation 94, 96-97, 126-127

⚑ 1991 • a Russian • 🪙 Rouble; official; market • 👤 9 • ♥ 67 • 🎓 15 • 📖 99 • 🚗 120 • ✚ 219 • ☠ No • 🏠 76

Rust'avi Georgia 99 Q13
Rutland Vermont, USA 41 M8
Ruvuma *River* Mozambique/Tanzania 111 P12
Ruwenzori *Mountain range* Congo (Zaire)/Uganda 111 L4
Ruwenzori *National Park* Uganda 111 L5
Rwanda *Country* E Africa 111 L6

Rwanda 111

⚑ 1962 • a French and Rwandan • 🪙 Franc Rwandais (Rwanda franc) • 👤 289 • ♥ 41 • 🎓 13 • 📖 63 • 🚗 2 • ✚ 40600 • ☠ Yes • 🏠 6 • 🍴 1821

Ryazan' Russian Federation 96 G11 126 E6
Rybnik Poland 85 K9
Rye Patch Reservoir *Reservoir* Nevada, USA 48 F2
Ryukyu Islands *Island group* Japan 129 137 B20
Rzeszów Poland 85 N9

S

Saale *River* Germany 80 J10
Saarbrücken Germany 81 D14
Saaremaa *Island* Estonia 94 H2
Šabac Serbia, Yugoslavia 89 M5
Sabadell Spain 75 Q6
Sabah *Region* Malaysia 141 K9
Sabaki *River* Kenya 111 Q7
Sab'atayn, Ramlat as *Desert* Yemen 122 J15
Sabha Libya 103 O9
Sabine River *River* Louisiana/Texas, USA 49 S10
Sable, Cape *Cape* Newfoundland, Canada 39 P14
Sabzevar Iran 123 Q4
Sachsen *see* Saxony
Sacramento California, USA 28 A10 29 K3 33 E14 51 I14
Sacramento River *River* California, USA 23 N6
Sa'dah Yemen 122 I14
Sado *Island* Japan 136 I9
Safi Morocco 66 J9 102 H5
Saga Japan 137 C14
Sagaing Myanmar 138 F7
Sagami-nada *Inlet* Japan 137 K11
Saginaw Michigan, USA 45 O8
Saginaw Bay *Lake bay* Michigan, USA 45 O7
Sahara *Desert* N Africa 101 102 J10 106 H6
Saharan Atlas *Mountain range* Algeria/Morocco, 68
Sahel *Physical region* W Africa 101 106 I9
Saïda Lebanon 121 M7
Saidpur Bangladesh 131 O7
Saigon *see* Hô Chi Minh
Saimaa *Lake* Finland 71 P10
St Anton Austria 82 J9
Saint Augustine Florida, USA 26 E13 27 O14
St-Brieuc France 76 G6
Saint Charles Missouri, USA 47 S11
St. Clair's Defeat *Battle site* USA 29 R3
Saint Clair Shores Michigan, USA 45 O9
Saint Cloud Minnesota, USA 44 G6
St Croix *Island* Virgin Islands (US) 57 R10
St-Étienne France 77 N10
Saint Eustatius *Island* Netherlands Antilles 57 S10
St.George's Grenada 57 S15
Saint George's Channel *Channel* Ireland/United Kingdom 73 E14 147 P2
St.Gotthard Tunnel *Tunnel* Switzerland 82 G11
Saint Helena *Dependent territory* Atlantic Ocean 67 K13
Saint Helens, Mount *Volcano* Washington, USA, 19 F15 34
St Helier Jersey 73 I19
St-Jean, Lac *Lake* Quebec, Canada 39 M11
St.John New Brunswick, Canada 39 O13 66 E8
St.John's Antigua and Barbuda 57 S11
St.John's Newfoundland, Canada 39 S9 66 G8
St John's Isle of Man 33 P11
Saint Joseph Missouri, USA 47 Q11
Saint Kitts and Nevis *Country* West Indies 57 S11

St Kitts and Nevis 57

⚑ 1983 • a English • 🪙 Eastern Caribbean dollar • 👤 114 • ♥ 70 • 🎓 17 • 📖 90 • ✚ 1124 • ☠ Yes • 🏠 34 • 🍴 2419

St-Laurent-du-Maroni French Guiana 58 O6
St.Lawrence, Gulf of *Gulf* Canada 39 P10
Saint Lawrence Island *Island* Alaska, USA 36 E5
Saint Lawrence River *River* Canada/USA 19 L15 34 66 E8
St.Lawrence Seaway *River* Canada 22 G11 39 N10
St-Lô France 76 I5
Saint Louis Senegal 106 F8
Saint Louis Missouri, USA 23 P6 27 L11 27 O5 28 F10 30 E12 33 K14 47 S11
Saint Lucia *Country* West Indies 57 T13

St. Lucia 57

⚑ 1979 • a English • 🪙 Eastern Caribbean dollar • 👤 249 • ♥ 70 • 🎓 15 • 📖 82 • 🚗 16 • ✚ 2857 • ☠ Yes • 🏠 38 • 🍴 2588

St-Malo France 76 H5
St. Marks *Battle site* USA 29 R6
St. Martin *Island* Guadeloupe/Netherlands Antilles 57 S10
Saint Matthew Island *Island* Alaska, USA 36 D5
St.Moritz Switzerland 82 I11
St-Nazaire France 76 H8
Saint Paul Minnesota, USA 28 F9 29 P2 33 J13 44 H6
St. Paul Island *Island* French Southern and Antarctic Territories 115 I13
St Peter Port Guernsey 73 H18
Saint Petersburg (Rus. Sankt-Petersburg) Russian Federation 96 F8 126 E4
Saint Petersburg Florida, USA 43 N13
Saint Petersburg Florida, USA 33 L16 43 N13
Saint-Pierre Saint Pierre and Miquelon 39 R10
Saint Pierre and Miquelon *Dependent territory* North America 39 R10
St-Quentin France 77 M3
Saint Vincent *Island* Saint Vincent and the Grenadines 57 S14
Saint Vincent and the Grenadines *Country* West Indies 57 T14

St Vincent and the Grenadines 57

⚑ 1979 • a English • 🪙 Eastern Caribbean dollar • 👤 327 • ♥ 73 • 🎓 15 • 📖 82 • ✚ 2174 • ☠ Yes • 🏠 50 • 🍴 2347

Saintes France 76 I10
Sajama, Nevado *Mountain* Bolivia, 55
Sakakah Saudi Arabia 122 I6
Sakakawea, Lake *Reservoir* North Dakota, USA 47 M5
Sakarya *River* Turkey 118 I6
Sakhalin *Island* Russian Federation 117 127 R10 129 144 G4
Sala y Gomez Ridge *Undersea feature* Pacific Ocean 55
Salado, Río *River* Argentina 55 62 K7
Salalah Oman 114 F6 123 N15
Salamanca Spain 74 I7
Salamat, Bahr *River* Chad 108 J8
Salamis *Archaeological site* Cyprus 119 L11
Salavan Laos 139 N11
Saldanha South Africa 112 I15
Saldus Latvia 94 G6
Sale Victoria, Australia 147 N14
Salekhard Russian Federation 126 I6
Salem Oregon, USA 29 L2 33 E13 28 A8 50 H9
Salem India 131 K14
Salerno Italy 87 K13
Salerno, Gulf of *Gulf* Italy 87 K14
Salihorsk Belarus 95 L13
Salima Malawi 111 N14
Salina Kansas, USA 47 O12
Salina Utah, USA 48 J4
Salina *Island* Italy 87 L16
Salinas Mexico 53 P12
Salinas California, USA 51 H16
Salisbury England, United Kingdom 73 I16
Salmon River *River* Idaho, USA 46 F6
Salo Finland 71 O11
Salonica (Gr. Thessaloniki) Greece 92 J3
Salso *River* Italy 87 J18
Salt Lake City Utah, USA 20 C10 28 C10 29 M3 33 G14 48 J3
Salt River *River* Arizona, USA 48 J9
Salta Argentina 62 I6
Saltillo Mexico 53 M7
Salto Argentina 62 N9
Salto del Guairá Paraguay 62 O5
Salton Sea *Lake* California, USA 51 M19
Salvador Brazil 61 N11 67 H13
Salween *River* SE Asia 132 J12 134 H13 138 H9
Salzburg Austria 83 N7
Salzgitter Germany 80 H9
Sama'il Oman 123 P12
Samakhixai Laos 139 N12
Samaná Dominican Republic 57 O8
Samar *Island* Philippines 141 N5
Samara Russian Federation 96 I13 126 F8
Samarinda Indonesia 141 K11
Samarqand Uzbekistan 125 M8
Samarra' Iraq 123 K4
Sambre *River* Belgium/France 79 G17
Samoa *Country* Pacific Ocean 144 J9

Samoa 144

⚑ 1962 • a English and Samoan • 🪙 Tala • 👤 63 • ♥ 71 • 📖 98 • ✚ 2632 • ☠ No • 🏠 22 • 🍴 2828

Samoa Basin *Undersea feature* Pacific Ocean 143
Samobor Croatia 88 H2
Samos Greece 93 P10
Samos *Island* Greece 93 P10
Samothraki *Island* Greece 93 N3
Samsun Turkey 119 N4
Samui, Ko *Island* Thailand 139 I15
San *River* Cambodia 139 N13
San *River* Poland 85 O8
San Ambrosio, Isla *Island* Chile 145 P11
San Andreas Fault *Fault* USA 19 E17 34
San Andrés Colombia 58 F6
San Andres Mountains *Mountain range* New Mexico, USA 49 L10
San Angelo Texas, USA 49 P11
San Antioco, Isola di *Island* Italy 87 C16
San Antonio Chile 62 G10
San Antonio Florida, USA 28 H13
San Antonio *International airport* Texas, USA 33 I16
San Antonio Texas, USA 28 E13 49 Q13
San Antonio Oeste Argentina 63 K13
San Antonio River *River* Texas, USA 49 Q13
San Benedetto del Tronto Italy 86 J10
San Bernardino California, USA 51 L18
San Bernardino Tunnel *Tunnel* Switzerland 82 H11
San Bernardo Chile 62 H10
San Carlos Nicaragua 56 E12
San Carlos Venezuela 58 H4
San Carlos de Bariloche Argentina 63 H14
San Clemente California, USA 51 L19
San Cristóbal Venezuela 58 F5
San Diego California, USA 23 N7 28 B12 29 L5 30 C13 33 E15 51 L20 145 N5
San Felipe Chile 62 G10
San Felipe Venezuela 58 H4
San Félix, Isla *Island* Chile 145 P10
San Fernando Philippines 141 L3
San Fernando Spain 74 H14
San Fernando Trinidad and Tobago 57 S16
San Fernando Venezuela 58 I5
San Fernando del Valle de Catamarca Argentina 62 I8
San Francisco California, USA 20 C10 28 A10 29 K3 30 B12 33 E14 51 H15 145 N5
San Francisco de Macorís Dominican Republic 57 O8
San Gorgonio Pass *Pass* California, USA 51 L18
San Ignacio Belize 56 C6
San Joaquin River *River* California, USA 23 N6 51 I15
San Jorge, Gulf of *Gulf* Argentina 63 K16
San José Costa Rica 20 F14 56 E13
San Jose California, USA 30 B12 33 E14 51 H15
San José del Guaviare Colombia 58 F7
San José, Isla *Island* Mexico 52 H7
San José, Isla *Island* Panama 56 H15
San Juan Argentina 62 H9
San Juan Peru 59 E14
San Juan Puerto Rico 57 Q9
San Juan Mountains *Mountain range* Colorado, USA 49 L5
San Juan Bautista Paraguay 62 N6
San Juan de los Morros Venezuela 58 H4
San Juan Islands *Island group* Washington, USA 50 H5
San Juan River *River* Colorado/Utah, USA 49 K6
San Juan, Río *River* Costa Rica/Nicaragua 56 E12
San Lorenzo Honduras 56 C10
San Luis Argentina 62 J10
San Luis Obispo California, USA 51 I17
San Luis Potosí Mexico 53 M10
San Luis Potosí *State* Mexico 21 O8
San Marino *Country* S Europe 86 H9

San Marino 86

⚑ 301 • a Italian • 🪙 Lira (the Italian lira is also legal) • 👤 431 • ♥ 81 • 🎓 14 • 📖 96.1 • ✚ 375 • ☠ No • 🏠 94 • 🍴 3561

San Marino San Marino 86 H9
San Martín Argentina 64 B8
San Martín, Lago *Lake* Argentina 63 I18
San Matías, Gulf of *Gulf* Argentina 63 K14
San Miguel El Salvador 56 C9
San Miguel de Tucumán Argentina 62 J7
San Miguel, Río *River* Bolivia 59 K14
San Nicolás de los Arroyos Argentina 62 M10
San Pedro Paraguay 62 N5
San Pedro Sula Honduras 56 C8
San Pietro, Isola di *Island* Italy 87 C15
San Rafael Argentina 63 I11
San Remo Italy 86 B9
San Salvador El Salvador 20 E14 56 B9
San Salvador *Island* Bahamas 57 M3
San Salvador de Jujuy Argentina 62 I6
Sana Yemen 123 I15
Sanaga *River* Cameroon 108 F10
Sanandaj Iran 123 L4
Sand Creek *Battle site* USA 29 N4
Sandakan Borneo, Malaysia 141 K8
Sandanski Bulgaria 90 I15
Sandnes Norway 70 H11
Sandoway Myanmar 138 E9
Sandviken Sweden 71 L11
Sanford Maine, USA 41 O8
Sângeorz-Băi Romania 90 J3
Sangha *River* Central African Republic/Congo 109 I12
Sangihe, Pulau *Island* Indonesia 141 N9
Sangir, Kepulauan *Island group* Indonesia 141 N10
Sangre de Cristo Mountains *Mountain range* Colorado/New Mexico, USA 49 M7
Sangro *River* Italy 87 K12
Sankt Gallen Switzerland 82 H8
Sankt Pölten Austria 83 R5
Sankt Veit an der Glan Austria 83 P9
Sankt-Peterburg *see* Saint Petersburg
Sankt-Vith Belgium 79 L17
Şanlıurfa Turkey 119 P9
Sant Jordi, Golf de *Gulf* Spain 75 P7
Santa Ana El Salvador 56 B9
Santa Ana California, USA 51 L19
Santa Barbara California, USA 51 J18
Santa Catalina, Isla *Island* Mexico 52 H7
Santa Clara Cuba 56 I4
Santa Clara Valley *Valley* California, USA 51 H15
Santa Cruz Bolivia 59 K15
Santa Cruz California, USA 51 H16
Santa Cruz River *River* Arizona, USA 48 I11
Santa Elena de Uairén Venezuela 58 L6
Santa Fe Argentina 62 L9
Santa Fe New Mexico, USA 26 B12 28 D11 29 N5 33 H15 49 M7

⚑ Date of independence • a Language (official or most commonly spoken) • 🪙 Currency • 👤 Population density per square kilometre • ♥ Average life expectancy • 🎓 School-leaving age • 📖 Literacy • 🚗 Number of cars per 1,000 people • ✚ Number of people per doctor • ☠ Death penalty • 🏠 Percentage of urban-based population • 🍴 Average number of calories consumed daily per person

South Dakota *State* USA 21 N5 23 P11 29 O14 30 D11 33 I14 47 L7
South East Cape *Headland* Tasmania, Australia 147 N16
South Fiji Basin *Undersea feature* Pacific Ocean 143
South Georgia *Island* South Georgia and the South Sandwich Islands 55 66 H16
South Indian Basin *Undersea feature* 115 K15 143
South Island *Island* New Zealand 143 148 B12
South Korea *Country* E Asia 135 P8

South Korea 135

⚑ 1948 • a Korean • ¤ South Korean won • ♟ 471 • ♥ 72 • 🎓 15 • 📖 97.2 • 🚗 165 • ✚ 784 • ☠ Yes • 🏛 81 • 🍴 3285

South Luangwa *National Park* Zambia 111 M13
South Orkney Islands *Island group* Antarctica 64 B6 67 G16
South Pass *Pass* Wyoming, USA 28 D9
South Platte River *River* Colorado/Nebraska, USA 49 N3
South Pole *Pole* Antarctica 64 E9
South Sandwich Islands *Island group* South Georgia and the South Sandwich Islands 67 I16
South Sandwich Trench *Undersea feature* Atlantic Ocean 55
South Shetland Islands *Island group* Antarctica 64 B7 67 F16
South Uist *Island* Scotland, United Kingdom 72 E7
Southampton England, United Kingdom 73 J16
Southampton Island *Island* Nunavut Canada 34 37 P8
Southeast Indian Ridge *Undersea feature* Indian Ocean 115 K14
Southeast Pacific Basin *Undersea feature* Pacific Ocean 145 N14
Southend-on-Sea England, United Kingdom 73 L16
Southern Alps *Mountain range* New Zealand 143 148 D11
Southern Ocean *Ocean* 144 I14 143
Southern Uplands *Mountain range* Scotland, United Kingdom 72 H10
Southwest Indian Ridge *Undersea feature* Indian Ocean 101 115 D14
Southwest Pacific Basin *Undersea feature* Pacific Ocean 145 K12
Sovetsk Russian Federation 94 G9
Sovetskaya Gavan' Russian Federation 127 Q10 144 G4
Soweto South Africa 113 L12
Sozopol Bulgaria 91 O13
Spain *Country* SW Europe 74J7

Spain 74-75

⚑ 1492 • a Spanish, Galician, Basque and Catalan • ¤ Spanish peseta • ♟ 79 • ♥ 78 • 🎓 16 • 📖 97.2 • 🚗 389 • ✚ 244 • ☠ No • 🏛 76 • 🍴 3708

Spanish Town Jamaica 56 J8
Sparks Nevada, USA 48 E3
Spartanburg South Carolina, USA 43 O6
Sparti Greece 92 I12
Spartivento, Capo *Headland* Italy 87 D16
Spencer Iowa, USA 47 P8
Spencer Gulf *Gulf* South Australia, Australia 147 K13
Spey *River* Scotland, United Kingdom 72 I8
Spitsbergen *Island* Svalbard 65 R13 68
Spittal Austria 83 O9
Split Croatia 88 I7
Spokane Washington, USA 50 L6
Spokane Plain *Battle site* USA 29 M1
Springfield Illinois, USA 28 F10 29 P3 33 J14 45 K13
Springfield Ohio, USA 45 O12
Springfield Oregon, USA 50 H9
Springfield Massachusetts, USA 41 N10
Springfield Missouri, USA 27 K12 33 J14 47 R13
Squamish British Columbia, Canada 36 J15
Squillace, Golfo di *Gulf* Italy 87 N16
Srebrenica Bosnia and Herzegovina 89 L6
Sri Lanka *Country* S Asia 131 L15

Sri Lanka 131

⚑ 1948 • a Sinhala, Tamil and English • ¤ Sri Lanka rupee • ♟ 287 • ♥ 73 • 🎓 15 • 📖 90.7 • 🚗 6 • ✚ 10000 • ☠ Yes • 🏛 22 • 🍴 2273

Sri Lanka *Island* S Asia 114 I7 117 129
Srinagar Pakistan 130 J2
Srinagarind Reservoir *Lake* Thailand 139 H12
Stalingrad *see* Volgograd
Stanovoy Khrebet *Mountain range* Russian Federation 117 127 M10
Stans Switzerland 82 G10
Stara Zagora Bulgaria 91 L13
Starnberger See *Lake* Germany 81 J16
State College Pennsylvania, USA 40 I12
Staunton *Battle site* West Virginia, USA 27 N11
Stavanger Norway 66 K7 70 H11
Stavropol' Russian Federation 96 E15 126 D8
Steen Mountains *Battle site* USA 29 L3
Steinkjer Norway 70 J7
Stendal Germany 80 J9
Steptoe Butte *Battle site* USA 29 M1
Sterling Colorado, USA 49 N3
Sterling Illinois, USA 45 K10
Sterling Heights Michigan, USA 45 O9
Steubenville Ohio, USA 45 Q11
Stevens Point Wisconsin, USA 45 K7
Stewart Island *Island* New Zealand 148 C13
Steyr Austria 83 P6
Stillman's Defeat *Battle site* USA 29 P3
Stillwater Minnesota, USA 44 H6
Štip FYR Macedonia 89 O11
Stirling Scotland, United Kingdom 72 H9
Stockerau Austria 83 R4
Stockholm Sweden 71 L12
Stockton California, USA 51 I15
Stŏeng Trêng Cambodia 139 M13
Stoke *see* Stoke-on-Trent
Stoke-on-Trent (var. Stoke) England, United Kingdom 73 I14
Stonehenge *Ancient monument* England, United Kingdom 73 I16
Stony Lake *Battle site* USA 29 O2
Stony Tunguska *River* Russian Federation 127 K9
Stornoway Scotland, United Kingdom 72 F6
Storsjön *Lake* Sweden 71 K8
Storuman Sweden 71 M6
Stralsund Germany 80 L6
Stranraer Scotland, United Kingdom 73 G11
Strasbourg France 77 Q5
Stratford *see* Stratford-upon-Avon
Stratford-upon-Avon (var. Stratford) England, United Kingdom 73 J15
Stromboli *Volcano* Italy 87 L16
Stromness Scotland, United Kingdom 72 I6
Struma *River* Bulgaria/Greece 90 H13
Strumica FYR Macedonia 89 P12
Strymonas *River* Bulgaria/Greece 93 K2
Stupia *River* Poland 85 K2
Stuttgart Germany 81 G15
Stylida Greece 92 J7
Styr *River* Belorussia/Ukraine 98 G3
Suakin Sudan 105 I11
Subotica Serbia, Yugoslavia 89 M2
Sucre Bolivia 59 J16
Sudan *Country* NE Africa 105 D11

Sudan 104-105

⚑ 1956 • a Arabic • ¤ Sudanese pound or dinar • ♟ 12 • ♥ 55 • 🎓 13 • 📖 53.3 • 🚗 10 • ✚ 10000 • ☠ Yes • 🏛 25 • 🍴 2202

Sudbury Ontario, Canada 23 Q5 38 J12
Sudd *Swamp region* Sudan 101 105 E15
Sudeten *Mountain range* Czech Republic/Poland 84 I8
Suez Egypt 114 D4
Suez Canal *Canal* Egypt 104 G6 114 D4
Suez, Gulf of *Gulf* Red Sea 104 G7 120 I13
Suhar Oman 123 O11
Sühbaatar Mongolia 133 M3
Suhl Germany 81 I12
Sukabumi Indonesia 140 G15
Sukkur Pakistan 130 H5
Sula *River* Ukraine 98 J5
Sula, Kepulauan *Island group* Indonesia 141 N12
Sulaimān Range *Mountain range* Pakistan, 129
Sulawesi *see* Celebes
Sulb Temple *Archaeological site* Sudan 104 F10
Sullana Peru 58 B10
Sulu Archipelago *Island group* Philippines 141 L9
Sulu Sea *Sea* Pacific Ocean 129 141 K8
Sumatra *Island* Indonesia 114 L8 129 140 D11 143
Sumba *Island* Indonesia 141 L16
Sumbawa *Island* Indonesia 141 K16
Sumbawabesar Indonesia 141 K15
Sumbawanga Tanzania 111 M10
Sumbe Angola 112 G5
Sumbu *National Park* Zambia 111 L10
Summer Lake *Lake* Oregon, USA 50 I10
Sumqayıt Azerbaijan 99 T13
Sumy Ukraine 99 K4
Sun City South Africa 113 L12
Sunbury Pennsylvania, USA 40 J12
Sunda Shelf *Undersea feature* Indian Ocean/Pacific Ocean 129 143
Sunderland England, United Kingdom 73 J11
Sundsvall Sweden 71 L9
Suntar Russian Federation 127 M8
Sunyani Ghana 107 L12
Superior Wisconsin, USA 44 I4
Superior, Lake *Lake* Canada/USA 34 38 G11 45 K3
Superior, Lake *Lake* Canada/USA 19 J15 22 F11 23 Q10 28 F8 29 Q1 33 K12 34 38 G11 45 K3
Sur Oman 123 P12
Surabaya Indonesia 140 I15
Surat India 130 I8
Surat Thani Thailand 139 H15
Sûre *River* NW Europe 79 L18
Surigao Philippines 141 N6
Suriname *Country* N South America 58 N7

Suriname 58

⚑ 1975 • a Dutch • ¤ Surinam gulden (guilder) or florin • ♟ 3 • ♥ 70 • 🎓 12 • 📖 93.5 • 🚗 59 • ✚ 2500 • ☠ No • 🏛 50 • 🍴 2547

Surkhob *River* Tajikistan 125 O8
Surt Libya 103 P7
Susquehanna River *River* New York/Pennsylvania, USA 40 J10
Suva Fiji 144 J10
Suwałki Poland 85 O2
Svalbard *Dependent territory* Arctic Ocean 65 R12
Svay Riĕng Cambodia 139 M14
Svobodnyy Russian Federation 127 O10
Svyetlahorsk Belarus 95 M13
Swakopmund Namibia 112 G11
Swansea Wales, United Kingdom 73 G15
Swaziland *Country* Southern Africa 113 M12

Swaziland 113

⚑ 1968 • a English and Swazi • ¤ Lilangeni • ♟ 57 • ♥ 60 • 🎓 13 • 📖 77.5 • 🚗 61 • ✚ 18800 • ☠ Yes • 🏛 32 • 🍴 2706

Sweden *Country* N Europe 71 K11

Sweden 70-71

⚑ 1809 • a Swedish • ¤ Swedish krona • ♟ 22 • ♥ 79 • 🎓 15 • 📖 99 • 🚗 418 • ✚ 333 • ☠ No • 🏛 83 • 🍴 2972

Sweetwater Texas, USA 49 P10
Swift Current Saskatchewan, Canada 37 M14
Swindon England, United Kingdom 73 I15
Switzerland *Country* W Europe 82 E10

Switzerland 82

⚑ 1291 • a French, German and Italian • ¤ Swiss franc • ♟ 184 • ♥ 79 • 🎓 16 • 📖 99 • 🚗 469 • ✚ 323 • ☠ No • 🏛 61 • 🍴 3379

Sydney New South Wales, Australia 144 H12 147 O13
Sydney Nova Scotia, Canada 39 R11
Syktyvkar Russian Federation 96 K9 126 G6
Sylhet Bangladesh 131 P7
Sylt *Island* Germany 80 F5
Syowa *Japanese research station* Antarctica 64 F6
Syr Darya *River* C Asia 68 117 126 F13 129
Syracuse New York, USA 41 K9
Syracuse *see* Siracusa
Syria *Country* SW Asia 121 N5

Syria 121

⚑ 1946 • a Arabic • ¤ Syrian pound • ♟ 85 • ♥ 69 • 🎓 12 • 📖 71.6 • 🚗 10 • ✚ 1250 • ☠ Yes • 🏛 52 • 🍴 3175

Syrian Desert *Desert* SW Asia 68 117 121 O9 122 I5
Syros *Island* Greece 93 M11
Szczecin Poland 84 H3
Szeged Hungary 85 M15
Székesfehérvár Hungary 85 K14
Szekszárd Hungary 85 M15
Szolnok Hungary 85 M14
Szombathely Hungary 84 J14

T

Ta'if Saudi Arabia 122 H11
Ta'izz Yemen 122 I16
Tabar Islands *Island group* Papua New Guinea 147 P1
Tabasco Mexico 53 L10
Table Bay *Bay* South Africa 112 I16
Table Mountain *Mountain* South Africa 112 I16
Tábor Czech Republic 84 H10
Tabora Tanzania 111 M8
Tabriz Iran 123 L2
Tabuk Philippines 122 G6
Tacloban Philippines 141 N5
Tacna Peru 59 G15
Tacoma Washington, USA 50 H7
Tacuarembó Uruguay 62 O9
Taegu South Korea 135 Q8
Taejŏn South Korea 135 P8
Tagula Island *Island* Papua New Guinea 147 P4
Tagus *River* WA, Portugal/Spain 68 74 G9
Tahat *Mountain* Algeria, 101
Tahiti *Island* French Polynesia 145 L10
Tahoe, Lake *Lake* California/Nevada, USA 48 E3 51 J14
Tahoua Niger 107 N8
Tai'an China 135 N8
Taieri *River* New Zealand 148 D11
Taipei Taiwan 135 O13
Taiping Malaysia 139 I18
Taiping Ling *Mountain* China, 129
Taiwan *Country* E Asia 135 O13

Taiwan 135

⚑ 1949 • a Mandarin Chinese • ¤ Taiwan dollar • ♟ 673 • ♥ 77 • 🎓 15 • 📖 94 • 🚗 203 • ✚ 894 • ☠ Yes • 🏛 69 •

Taiwan (var. Formosa) *Island* Taiwan, 129
Taiwan Strait *Strait* China/Taiwan 129 135 N14
Taiyuan China 135 L7
Tajikistan *Country* C Asia 125 N8

Tajikistan 125

⚑ 1991 • a Tajik • ¤ Tajik rouble • ♟ 43 • ♥ 67 • 🎓 17 • 📖 98.9 • 🚗 0 • ✚ 476 • ☠ Yes • 🏛 32 •

Tak Thailand 139 H11
Takamatsu Japan 137 F12
Takev Cambodia 139 L14
Takla Makan Desert *Desert* China 117 129 132 F8
Talak *Desert Region* Niger 107 N7
Talas Kyrgyzstan 125 O5
Talaud, Kepulauan *Island group* Indonesia 141 O9
Talca Chile 63 G11
Talcahuano Chile 63 G12
Taldykorgan Kazakhstan 126 H13
Tallahassee Florida, USA 27 N14 28 H12 29 R6 33 L16 43 M10
Tallasahatchee *Battle site* USA 29 Q5
Tallinn Estonia 66 M7 94 J1
Talsi Latvia 94 H5
Tamabo, Banjaran *Mountain range* Borneo, Malaysia 140 J10
Tamale Ghana 107 L11
Tamanrasset Algeria 103 L11
Tamaulipas *State* Mexico 21 N7
Tambacounda Senegal 106 G9
Tambov Russian Federation 96 G12 126 E7
Tampa Florida, USA 33 L16 43 N12
Tampere Finland 71 O10
Tampico Mexico 26 C15 53 O10
Tamworth New South Wales, Australia 147 O12
Tan-Tan Morocco 102 G7
Tana Norway 71 O3
Tana, Lake *Lake* Ethiopia 101 105 I14
Tanami Desert *Desert* Northern Territory, Australia, 143
Tanana River *River* Alaska, USA 36 H7
Tanega-shima *Island* Japan 137 D16
Tanga Tanzania 111 Q8
Tanganyika, Lake *Lake* E Africa 101 109 O14 111 L9
Tanggula Shan *Mountain range* China 132 I11
Tangier Morocco 102 I4
Tangra Yumco *Lake* China 132 I13
Tangshan China 135 N7
Tanimbar, Kepulauan *Island group* Indonesia 141 Q14
Tanjungpinang Indonesia 140 F11
Tanta Egypt 104 F6
Tanzam Railway *Railway* Tanzania 111 N10
Tanzania *Country* E Africa 111 L8

Tanzania 111

⚑ 1961 • a English and Swahili • ¤ Tanzanian shilling • ♟ 37 • ♥ 48 • 🎓 14 • 📖 71.6 • 🚗 1 • ✚ 25000 • ☠ Yes • 🏛 24 • 🍴 2018

Taormina Italy 87 L17
Taos New Mexico, USA 26 B12 30 D12 49 M7
Tapachula Mexico 53 R15
Tapajós, Rio *River* Brazil 55 60 G8
Tapti *River* India 130 J8
Taranto Italy 87 O14
Taranto, Golfo di (Eng. Gulf of Taranto) *Gulf* Italy 87 N14
Taranto, Gulf of *see* Taranto, Golfo di
Tarawa *Atoll* Kiribati 144 J8
Tarbela Dam *Dam* Pakistan 130 J2
Tarbela Reservoir *Reservoir* Pakistan 130 J1
Tarbes France 76 J14
Taree New South Wales, Australia 147 O12
Târgovişte Romania 91 L8
Târgu Jiu Romania 90 I8
Târgu Mureş Romania 91 K4
Tarija Bolivia 59 J17
Tarim Basin *Basin* China 132 F8
Tarim He *River* China 132 G7
Tarn *River* France 77 L13
Tarnów Poland 85 N9
Tarragona Spain 75 P7
Tarsus Turkey 119 M10
Tartu Estonia 95 K3
Tartus Syria 121 M5
Tashkent Uzbekistan 125 N6
Tasiilaq Greenland 65 N15
Tasman Bay *Inlet* New Zealand 148 G7
Tasman Plateau *Undersea feature* Pacific Ocean 143
Tasman Sea *Sea* Pacific Ocean 144 H12 143 147 O15 148 C10
Tasmania *State* Australia 147 M16
Tasmania *Island* Australia, 143
Tassili-n-Ajjer *Plateau* Algeria 101 103 M9
Tatlısu Cyprus 119 L11
Tatvan Turkey 119 R7
Tauern Tunnel *Tunnel* Austria 83 N9
Taunggyi Myanmar 138 G8
Taunton England, United Kingdom 73 H16
Taupo New Zealand 148 I5
Taupo, Lake *Lake* New Zealand 148 H5
Taurage Lithuania 94 G8
Tauranga New Zealand 148 I4
Taurus Mountains *Mountain range* Turkey, 68
Tavoy Myanmar 139 H12
Tawakoni, Lake *Reservoir* Texas, USA 49 R10
Tawau Borneo, Malaysia 141 K9
Tawitawi *Island* Philippines 141 L8
Taxco Mexico 53 N12
Tây Ninh Vietnam 139 M14
Taylor's Battle *Battle site* USA 29 S6
Taymyr, Ozero *Lake* Russian Federation 127 L5
Taymyr, Poluostrov *Peninsula* Russian Federation 65 T9 117 127 K5
Taz *River* Russian Federation 126 J7
Tazumal *Historic site* Mexico 24 H12
Tbilisi Georgia 99 Q12
Tchibanga Gabon 109 F13
Te Anau, Lake *Lake* New Zealand 148 C11
Tébessa Algeria 103 M5
Tedzhen Turkmenistan 124 I9
Tedzhen *River* Afghanistan/Iran 124 J10
Tees *River* England, United Kingdom 73 J12
Tegucigalpa Honduras 56 D9
Tehran Iran 123 N4
Tehuantepec Mexico 53 P14
Tehuantepec, Gulf of *Gulf* Caribbean Sea 24 E11 53 P15
Tehuantepec, Isthmus of *Coastal feature* Mexico 24 E10
Tekirdağ Turkey 118 G5
Tel Aviv-Yafo Israel 121 L9
Telluride Colorado, USA 49 L5
Teloapan *Historic site* Mexico 24 C9
Teluk Intan Malaysia 139 I18
Temuco Chile 63 G13
Ténéré *Physical region* Niger 107 Q6
Tengiz, Ozero *Salt lake* Kazakhstan 126 G10
Tennessee *State* USA 21 O6 23 Q12 29 P15 30 F12 33 K15 34 43 K5
Tennessee River *River* USA 28 G11 29 Q4 43 K4
Tenochtitlan *Historic site* Mexico 24 C8
Teotihuacán *Ruins* Mexico 53 N11
Tepecuacuilco *Historic site* Mexico 24 D9
Tepic Mexico 53 K10
Tequila Mexico 53 K10
Teresina Brazil 60 L8
Termiz Uzbekistan 125 M10
Terneuzen Netherlands 79 F13

⚑ Date of independence • a Language (official or most commonly spoken) • ¤ Currency • ♟ Population density per square kilometre • ♥ Average life expectancy • 🎓 School-leaving age • 📖 Literacy • 🚗 Number of cars per 1,000 people • ✚ Number of people per doctor • ☠ Death penalty • 🏛 Percentage of urban-based population • 🍴 Average number of calories consumed daily per person

Terni Italy 87 I11
Ternopil' Ukraine 98 F5
Terrassa Spain 75 Q6
Terre Haute Indiana, USA 45 L13
Terschelling *Island* Netherlands 78 J6
Teruel Spain 75 N8
Tete Mozambique 113 N7
Tétouan Morocco 102 I4
Tetovo FYR Macedonia 89 N10
Tevere *see* Tiber
Texas *State* USA 21 N6 23 P13 29 O16 30 E13 33 I16
    49 O11
Texas City Texas, USA 49 S13
Texcoco *Historic site* Mexico 24 D8
Texcoco, Lake *Lake* Mexico 24 D8
Texel *Island* Netherlands 78 H7
Thac Ba, Lake *Lake* Vietnam 138 M8
Thai Nguyên Vietnam 138 M8
Thailand *Country* SE Asia 139 I11

Thailand 138-139

🏴1782 • **a** Thai • 💰 Baht • ♦ 119 • ●
69 • 🚹 15 • 💧 94.7 • 🚗 28 • ✚ 4180 •
☠ Yes • 🏠 20 • 🍴 2432

Thailand, Gulf of *Gulf* South China Sea 114 L7 117 129
    139 I14
Thakhèk Laos 138 L10
Thames New Zealand 148 H4
Thames *River* England, United Kingdom 68 73 I15
Thane India 130 I9
Thanh Hoa Vietnam 138 M9
Thar Desert *Desert* India/Pakistan 68 117 129 130 H5
Tharthar, Buhayrat ath *Lake* Iraq 123 K4
Thasos *Island* Greece 93 M3
Thaton Myanmar 138 G10
Thayetmyo Myanmar 138 F9
The Dalles Oregon, USA 50 I8
The Hague (Dut. 's-Gravenhage) Netherlands 78 G10
The Pas Manitoba, Canada 37 N13
The Valley Anguilla 57 S10
The Wilderness *Battle site* Virginia, USA 27 N11
Thebes *Archaeological site* Egypt 104 G8
Theodore Roosevelt Lake *Reservoir* Arizona, USA 48 J9
Theodore Roosevelt National Park *National park* USA
    22 D11
Thermaic Gulf *Gulf* Greece 92 J4
Thessaloniki *see* Salonica
Thienen Belgium 79 I15
Thika Kenya 111 P5
Thimphu Bhutan 131 P6
Thionville France 77 O4
Thira *Island* Greece 93 N13
Thohoyandou South Africa 113 M11
Thompson Manitoba, Canada 37 O12
Thrace Greece 93 N2
Thun Switzerland 82 F10
Thunder Bay Ontario, Canada 33 J12 38 G11
Thuner See *Lake* Switzerland 82 F11
Thuringia *Cultural region* Germany 81 I12
Thuringian Forest *Mountain range* Germany 81 I11
Thurso Scotland, United Kingdom 72 I6
Tianjin China 135 M7 144 E5
Tiaret Algeria 103 K5
Tiber (It. Tevere) *River* Italy 68 87 H11
Tiberias, Lake (var. Sea of Galilee) *Lake* Israel 121 M8
Tibesti *Mountain range* N Africa 101 109 I4
Tibet *Cultural region* China 132 H12
Tibet, Plateau of *Plateau* E Asia 117 129
Tiburón, Isla *Island* Mexico 52 G4
Tidjikja Mauritania 106 H6
Tien Shan *Mountain range* C Asia 68 117 125 Q6 129 132 F7
Tierra del Fuego *Island* Argentina/Chile 55 63 J20
Tighina Moldova 98 H8
Tigris *River* Iraq/Turkey 68 114 E4 117 119 Q8 121 T1 123
    K3 129
Tikal *Archaeological site* Guatemala 56 C6
Tikal *Historic site* Mexico 24 H10
Tikrit Iraq 123 K4
Tiksi Russian Federation 65 T7 127 N5
Tilburg Netherlands 79 I12
Tillabéri Niger 107 M9
Timaru New Zealand 148 E11
Timbuktu Mali 107 K8
Timgad Algeria 103 M5
Timirist, Râs *Headland* Mauritania 106 F6
Timiş *River* Romania 90 N6
Timişoara Romania 90 G6
Timmins Ontario, Canada 38 J11
Timor *Island* Indonesia 129 141 N16 143
Timor Sea *Sea* Indian Ocean 141 N16 143 146 H5
Tindouf Algeria 102 H8
Tinos *Island* Greece 93 M10
Tippecanoe *Battle site* USA 29 Q3
Tirana Albania 89 M12
Tiraspol Moldova 98 H8
Tiree *Island* Scotland, United Kingdom 72 E9
Tirso *River* Italy 87 D14
Tiruchchirappalli India 131 K14
Tisza *River* C Europe 68 85 N12
Titicaca, Lake *Lake* Bolivia/Peru 55 59 H14
Tiznit Morocco 102 G7
Tlachco *Historic site* Mexico 24 C9
Tlachquiauhco *Historic site* Mexico 24 D9
Tlacopan *Historic site* Mexico 24 D8
Tlalcozauhtitlan *Historic site* Mexico 24 D9
Tlapan *Historic site* Mexico 24 D9
Tlatauhquitepec *Historic site* Mexico 24 E8
Tlaxcala Mexico 53 N12
Tlaxcala *Historic site* Mexico 24 D8
Tlemcen Algeria 102 J5
Toamasina Madagascar 114 E10
Toba Kakar Range *Mountain range* Pakistan 130 G3
Toba, Danau *Lake* Indonesia 140 D10
Tobago *Island* Trinidad and Tobago 34 55 57 T16
Tobruk Libya 103 R6
Tocantins, Rio *River* Brazil 55 60 J10
Tochpan *Historic site* Mexico 24 E7

Tochtepec *Historic site* Mexico 24 E9
Tocopilla Chile 62 F5
Togian, Kepulauan *Island group* Indonesia 141 M11
Togo *Country* W Africa 107 M12

Togo 107

🏴1960 • **a** French • 💰 Franc de la
Communauté financière africaine • ♦ 83 • ●
49 • 🚹 12 • 💧 53.2 • 🚗 19 • ✚ 10000
• ☠ No • 🏠 31 • 🍴 2242

Tokara-retto *Island Group* Japan 137 B17
Tokat Turkey 119 N6
Tokelau *Dependent territory* Tokelau 144 J9
Tokmak Kyrgyzstan 125 Q5
Tokuno-shima *Island* Japan 137 B19
Tokushima Japan 137 G13
Tokyo Japan 137 K11
Tol'yatti Russian Federation 97 I12 126 F8
Toledo Spain 75 K9
Toledo Ohio, USA 45 O10
Toledo Bend Reservoir *Reservoir* Louisiana/Texas,
    USA 49 T11
Toliara Madagascar 115 E11
Tolmin Slovenia 83 O11
Toluca Mexico 33 I17
Tomakomai Japan 136 L4
Tomé Chile 63 G12
Tomini, Gulf of *Bay* Indonesia 141 L11
Tomsk Russian Federation 126 J10
Tonga *Country* Pacific Ocean 144 J10

Tonga 144

🏴1970 • **a** English and Tongan • 💰
Pa'anga (Tongan dollar) • ♦ 135 • ● 70 •
🚹 14 • 💧 99 • 🚗 2 • ✚ 2176 • ☠
No • 🏠 42 • 🍴 2946

Tonga *Island group* Pacific Ocean 143
Tonga Trench *Undersea feature* Pacific Ocean 143
Tongking, Gulf of *Gulf* South China Sea 129 135 K15 138 N9
Tongliao China 133 Q5
Tongtian He *River* China 132 J11
Tonle Sap *Lake* Cambodia 139 L13
Tooele Utah, USA 48 J3
Toowoomba Queensland, Australia 147 O10
Topeka Kansas, USA 28 F10 29 P4 33 I14 47 P12
Torbay Newfoundland and Labrador, Canada 20 H9
Torhout Belgium 79 D14
Torino *see* Turin
Torkestan Mountains *Mountain range* Afghanistan
    125 K11
Torneälven *River* Finland/Sweden 71 N4
Torneträsk *Lake* Sweden 71 N3
Tornio Finland 71 O6
Toronto Ontario, Canada 20 F10 33 L13 39 K14
Torremolinos Spain 74 J14
Torrens, Lake *Salt lake* South Australia, Australia
    143 147 K11
Torreón Mexico 53 L7
Torres del Paine *National Park* Chile 63 I19
Torres Strait *Strait*
    Australia/Papua New Guinea 143 147 M4
Torrington Wyoming, USA 47 P9
Toruń Poland 85 L4
Toscano, Arcipelago (Eng. Tuscan Archipelago) *Island
    group* Italy 87 E11
Tottori Japan 137 F11
Toubkal, Jbel *Mountain* Morocco, 101
Touggourt Algeria 103 M6
Toulon France 77 P14
Toulouse France 77 K14
Toungoo Myanmar 138 G9
Tournai Belgium 79 E16
Tours France 76 J7
Townsville Queensland, Australia 147 N7
Towuti, Danau *Lake* Indonesia 141 M12
Toyama Japan 136 I10
Toyama-wan *Bay* Japan 136 I10
Tozeur Tunisia 103 M5
Tpalacoyan *Historic site* Mexico 24 D8
Trabzon (Eng. Trebizond) Turkey 119 P5
Tralee Republic of Ireland 73 A14
Trang Thailand 139 H16
Trans-Canada Highway *Road* Canada 36 I15
Transantarctic Mountains *Mountain range* Antarctica
    64 D8
Transylvania *Cultural region* Romania 90 H5
Transylvanian Alps *Mountain range* Romania
    68 90 H7
Trapani Italy 87 I17
Trasimeno, Lago *Lake* Italy 86 H10
Traun Austria 83 P5
Traverse City Michigan, USA 45 M6
Travis, Lake *Reservoir* Texas, USA 49 Q12
Trbovlje Slovenia 83 R11
Trebinje Bosnia and Herzegovina 89 K9
Trebizond *see* Trabzon
Treinta y Tres Uruguay 62 P9
Trelew Argentina 63 K14
Tremiti, Isole *Island group* Italy 87 L11
Trenčín Slovakia 85 K11
Trento Italy 86 G6
Trenton New Jersey, USA 27 S4 28 I9 33 M13
    41 L13
Tres Arroyos Argentina 63 M12
Tres Marías, Islas *Island group* Mexico 52 J10
Treviso Italy 86 H6
Trichonis, Limni *Lake* Greece 92 H8
Trier Germany 81 D13
Trieste Italy 86 J6
Trikala Greece 92 H6
Trincomalee Sri Lanka 114 I7 131 L15
Trindade, Ilha da *Island* Brazil 67 I13
Trinidad Bolivia 59 J14

Trinidad *Island* Trinidad and Tobago 34 55 57 S16
Trinidad and Tobago *Country* West Indies 57 S16

Trinidad and Tobago 57

🏴1962 • **a** English • 💰 Trinidad and
Tobago dollar • ♦ 253 • ● 74 • 🚹 12 •
💧 97.8 • 🚗 94 • ✚ 1429 • ☠ Yes •
🏠 72 • 🍴 2585

Trinity River *River* Texas, USA 49 R11
Tripoli Greece 92 I10
Tripoli Lebanon 121 M6
Tripoli Libya 103 O6
Tripolitania Libya 103 N7
Tristan da Cunha *Dependent territory* Atlantic Ocean
    67 J14
Trivandrum India 130 J15
Trnava Slovakia 85 K12
Trois-Rivières Quebec, Canada 39 M12
Trollhättan Sweden 70 J13
Tromsø Norway 71 M2
Trondheim Norway 70 J8
Troy *Archaeological site* Turkey 118 G6
Troyes France 77 M6
Truckee *Battle site* USA 29 L3
Trujillo Honduras 26 E16 56 E8
Trujillo Peru 59 C11
Trujillo Venezuela 58 G5
Truro Nova Scotia, Canada 39 Q12
Tsaritsyn *see* Volgograd
Tsavo Kenya 111 P6
Tsetserleg Mongolia 133 L5
Tshikapa Dem. Rep. Congo (Zaire) 109 K15
Tshuapa *River* Dem. Rep. Congo (Zaire) 109 K12
Tsimlyanskoye Vodokhranilishche *Reservoir* Russian
    Federation 96 F14
Tsugaru-kaikyo *Strait* Japan 136 K5
Tsumeb Namibia 112 H9
Tsushima *Island* Japan 137 B13
Tuamotu Islands *Island group* French Polynesia
    145 M10
Tübingen Germany 81 G15
Tucson Arizona, USA 33 G15 48 J10
Tucupita Venezuela 58 C8
Tucuruí, Represa de *Reservoir* Brazil 60 J8
Tudmur Syria 121 N5
Tugela *River* South Africa 113 M13
Tuguegarao Philippines 141 L2
Tuiucan *Historic site* Mexico 24 C8
Tukangbesi, Kepulauan *Island group* Indonesia
    141 N14
Tuktoyaktuk Northwest Territories, Canada 36 J6
Tuktut Nogait National Park *National park* Canada
    22 D8
Tula Russian Federation 96 F11 126 E6
Tulcea Romania 91 P7
Tulsa Oklahoma, USA 33 I15 47 P14
Tunceli Turkey 119 P7
Tundzha *River* Bulgaria/Turkey 91 M14
Tungaru *Island group* Kiribati 144 J9 143
Tunis Tunisia 103 N4
Tunisia *Country* N Africa 103 N6

Tunisia 103

🏴1956 • **a** Arabic • 💰 Tunisian dinar • ♦
61 • ● 70 • 🚹 16 • 💧 67 • 🚗 30 • ✚
1667 • ☠ Yes • 🏠 57 • 🍴 3330

Tunja Colombia 58 F6
Tupungato, Volcán *Volcano* Argentina, 55
Turan Lowland *Plain* C Asia 124 I6
Turin (It. Torino) Italy, B6 B7
Turkey *Country* SW Asia 118 I7

Turkey 118-119

🏴1923 • **a** Turkish • 💰 Turkish lira •
85 • ● 69 • 🚹 14 • 💧 83.2 • 🚗 59 • ✚
909 • ☠ Yes • 🏠 69 • 🍴 3429

Turkmenbashi Turkmenistan 124 F6
Turkmenistan *Country* C Asia 124 G7

Turkmenistan 124-125

🏴1991 • **a** Turkmen • 💰 Manat •
♦ 9 • ● 65 • 🚹 17 • 💧 98 • ✚ 313
• ☠ Yes • 🏠 45 •

Turks and Caicos Islands *Dependent territory* West Indies
    57 N6
Turks Islands *Island group* Turks and Caicos Islands
    55 57 N6
Turku Finland 71 N11
Turnhout Belgium 79 I13
Turpan China 132 I7
Turpan Pendi *Depression* China, 129
Tursunzoda Tajikistan 125 M9
Turtkul Uzbekistan 124 I6
Tuscan Archipelago *see* Toscana, Arcipelago
Tuscany *Cultural region* Italy 86 F9
Tuvalu *Country* Pacific Ocean 144 J9

Tuvalu 144

🏴1978 • **a** English • 💰 Australian dollar
and Tuvaluan dollar • ♦ 377 • ● 64 • 🚹 14
• 💧 95 • ✚ 2767 • ☠ No • 🏠 40 •

Tuxpán Mexico 53 O11
Tuxtla Mexico 53 Q14
Tuz, Lake *Lake* Turkey 68 119 L7
Tuzla Bosnia and Herzegovina 89 L5

Tver' Russian Federation 96 F10 126 E6
Tweed *River* Scotland, United Kingdom 72 I10
Twin Falls Idaho, USA 46 G9
Tyler Texas, USA 49 S10
Tyne *River* England, United Kingdom 73 I11
Tyrrhenian Sea *Sea* Mediterranean Sea 68 87 F13
Tyumen' Russian Federation 126 H9
Tziccoac *Historic site* Mexico 24 D7
Tzintuntzan *Historic site* Mexico 24 B8

U

Uaxactun *Historic site* Mexico 24 G10
Ubangi *River* C Africa 101 109 J10
Uberlândia Brazil 61 K13
Ubon Ratchathani Thailand 139 L12
Ucayali, Río *River* Peru 55 59 E11
Uchiura-wan *Bay* Japan 136 K5
Uchquduq Uzbekistan 125 K5
Uddevalla Sweden 70 J13
Uddjaur *Lake* Sweden 71 M5
Udine Italy 86 I6
Udon Thani Thailand 138 K10
Uele *River* Dem. Rep. Congo (Zaire) 109 M11
Ufa Russian Federation 96 K13 126 G8
Uganda *Country* E Africa 111 M4

Uganda 111

🏴1962 • **a** English and Swahili • 💰
New Uganda shilling • ♦ 106 • ● 40
• 🚹 64 • 🚗 2 • ✚ 25000 • ☠ Yes
• 🏠 13 • 🍴 2159

Úhlava *River* Czech Republic 84 G10
Uíge Angola 112 G3
Ujungpandang Indonesia 141 L14
Ukmergė Lithuania 84 I9
Ukraine *Country* E Europe 98 H6

Ukraine 98-99

🏴1991 • **a** Ukrainian • 💰 Hryvnia • ♦
84 • ● 69 • 🚹 15 • 💧 99 • 🚗 96 • ✚
227 • ☠ Yes • 🏠 70 •

Ulaangom Mongolia 132 J4
Ulan Bator Mongolia 133 M4
Ulan-Ude Russian Federation 127 M11
Ulanhot China 133 Q4
Uldz *River* Mongolia 133 O3
Uliastay Mongolia 133 K5
Ullapool Scotland, United Kingdom 72 G7
Ulm Germany 81 H15
Ulster *Province* Northern Ireland, United Kingdom/Ireland
    73 D11
Uluru (var. Ayers Rock) *Rocky outcrop* Northern Territory,
    Australia 143 146 J10
Ul'yanovsk Russian Federation 97 I12 126 F7
Umeå Sweden 71 M8
Umeälven *River* Sweden 71 M7
Umnak Island *Island* Alaska, USA 36 B8
Umtata South Africa 113 L15
Una *River* Bosnia and Herzegovina/Croatia 88 H4
Unalaska Island *Island* Alaska, USA 36 C8
Ungava Bay *Bay* Quebec, Canada 39 N4
Unimak Island *Island* Alaska, USA 36 C8
Uniontown Pennsylvania, USA 40 I14
United Arab Emirates *Country* SW Asia 123 M11

United Arab Emirates 123

🏴1971 • **a** Arabic • 💰 UAE dirham • ♦
29 • ● 75 • 🚹 12 • 💧 74.8 • 🚗 82 • ✚
1250 • ☠ Yes • 🏠 84 • 🍴 3384

United Kingdom *Country* NW Europe 72 E10

United Kingdom 72-73

🏴1707 • **a** English, Welsh (in Wales)
• 💰 Pound sterling • ♦ 243 • ● 77 •
🚹 16 • 💧 99 • 🚗 371 • ✚ 667 • ☠
No • 🏠 89 • 🍴 3317

United States of America *Country* North America 21 N6 22
    D12 28 E10 29 O3 40-51

United States of America 24-35

🏴1776 • **a** English • 💰 United States
dollar • ♦ 30 • ● 77 • 🚹 16 • 💧
99 • 🚗 489 • ✚ 400 • ☠ Yes •
🏠 76 • 🍴 3732

Ünye Turkey 119 N5
Upernavik Greenland 65 N13
Upington South Africa 112 J13
Upper Klamath Lake *Lake* Oregon, USA 51 H11
Upper Red Lake *Lake* Minnesota, USA 44 G3
Uppsala Sweden 71 L11
Ur *Site of ancient city* Iraq 123 K6
Ural *River* Kazakhstan/Russian Federation 68 126 F9
Ural Mountains *Mountain range* Kazakhstan/Russian
    Federation 68 96 L13 117 126 F9 129
Ural'sk Kazakhstan 126 F9
Uranium City Saskatchewan, Canada 37 M11
Urawa Japan 137 K11
Urmia, Lake *Lake* Iran 68 123 L2
Urgench Uzbekistan 124 J6
Uroševac Serbia, Yugoslavia 89 N10
Uroteppa Tajikistan 125 N7
Uruapan Mexico 53 L12

🗺 Date of independence • **a** Language (official or most commonly spoken) • 🖳 Currency • ♦ Population density per square kilometre • ● Average life expectancy • 👤 School-leaving age • ♛ Literacy •
🚗 Number of cars per 1,000 people • ✚ Number of people per doctor • 🐍 Death penalty • 🏠 Percentage of urban-based population • ⑪ Average number of calories consumed daily per person

171

X

Y

Yemen 122-123

 1990 • **a** Arabic • Rial North Yemen and dinar (South Yemen) are both legal tender throughout Yemen • 33 • 58 • 15 • 42.5 • 15 • 10000 • Yes • 34 • 2203

Yugoslavia 89

 1992 • **a** Serbo-croat • Yugoslav dinar • 104 • 72 • 15 • 93.3 • 173 • 500 • Yes • 57 •

Z

Zambia 110-111

1964 • **a** English • Zambian kwacha • 12 • 40 • 14 • 75.1 • 17 • 10000 • Yes • 43 • 1931

Zimbabwe 113

1980 • **a** English • Zimbabwe dollar • 30 • 44 • 15 • 90.9 • 29 • 10000 • Yes • 32 • 1985